D0152880

REGIS COLLEGE LIBRARIES
U18990 1371819

Colorado Flora: Eastern Slope

Colorado Flora: Eastern Slope

William A. Weber
Fellow of the Linnean Society of London
University of Colorado Museum

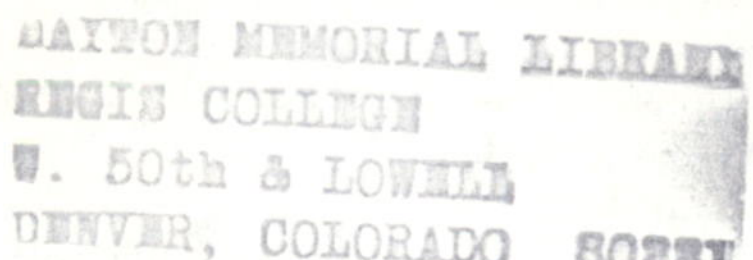

UNIVERSITY PRESS OF COLORADO

Published by University Press of Colorado
Niwot, Colorado 80544

ISBN: 0-87081-213-0 (cloth) and 0-87081-214-9 (kivar)

Library of Congress Cataloging-in-Publication Data

Weber, William A. (William Alfred), 1918–
Colorado flora: eastern slope / William A. Weber.
p. cm.
"Companion volume to Colorado flora: western slope" — Introd.
Includes indexes.
ISBN 0-87081-213-0. — ISBN 0-87081-214-9 (pbk.)
1. Botany — Colorado. 2. Plants — Identification. I. Title.
QK150.W38 1990
581.9788—dc20 90-12603
CIP

This book is dedicated

to

Alice Eastwood
first resident botanist on the Eastern Slope
and first writer of a local flora of the Denver region

CONTENTS

PREFACE

The previous volume in this pair, *Colorado Flora: Western Slope*, contains acknowledgements that apply in some measure to this one as well. The success of the Western Slope flora enables us to publish the sequel without further subsidy. I wish to acknowledge the fine jobs of copy editing done for this volume by Harold Dahnke, my volunteer *privat docent* in the herbarium, and Tom Schwab, of Colorado Springs, and the final proof reading by Alice Colwell. The format and typography was accomplished with the expertise and professional help of my close colleague Ronald Wittmann, who, besides being a fine amateur botanist, knows word processors and computers far beyond my capabilities. It is becoming clear that, over the past forty years, an avid and informed readership, as well as a camaraderie of amateur botanists, has grown out of our efforts at producing these field manuals.

I should like to describe here, in detail, the history of the present volume, *Colorado Flora: Eastern Slope.* When I arrived in Colorado in 1946, I came with the intention of continuing the work for which I received the Ph.D. degree at Washington State College, namely, studies in the cytotaxonomy of the Helianthoid composites, including *Wyethia, Balsamorhiza*, and their immediate relatives. The prospect was dim. The University of Colorado had no research microscopes; the university frowned on the use of any of its land for experimental research gardens; there were no granting agencies (this was long before Sputnik). On the other hand, I had a new flora to learn and a responsibility to teach. The small herbarium, about 20,000 specimens mostly accumulated as ecological material by Professor Ramaley in the Biology Department, had been poorly mounted and curated, and needed revision and adequate housing. It did not even belong to the University Museum and was being held by the Biology Department as a trust in Dr. Ramaley's memory. The herbarium, moreover, while not the property of the Museum, was housed in the attic of the Henderson Building, where it shared a room with the collections of the Anthropology Section and the Zoology Section. The space also contained the private herbarium of the former curator (at that time the curatorship was a purely honorary, not a salaried, position) who removed it to another institution during my first year. Otherwise, there would not have been any room to expand the collections, much less to reorganize them.

My position was an Instructorship in the Department of Biology. From 1946 to 1962, I worked full time in the department, and donated my services to the Museum. Fortunately, I was able to have a part-time undergraduate assistant in the herbarium who went through the collection, accessioning each specimen and mending those that were in disrepair. This assistant was Margaret Mattoon, a student from Loveland. In time, Margaret developed not only a strong interest in plant taxonomy, but showed that she had an extraordinarily keen eye for rare plants. She later married John Douglass, and for a number of years following graduation, she and John were associated in the National Park Service in several parks on the Southwest. Particularly valuable to us, Peg made very important collections in Rocky Mountain National Park, including several species new to the Colorado Flora.

Continuation of my chosen research being impossible under the circumstances, the reorganization of the herbarium claimed first priority. My obligation to teach a course in the local flora encouraged me to learn the plants of the area, and to find a text for the students to use. Coulter & Nelson, *Manual of Rocky*

Mountain Botany, was out of print. Dr. H. D. Harrington was working on a manual of the Colorado Flora, but it would not be published until 1954. So I began to assemble the pieces of a catalog of the plants of Boulder County, and prepared keys to the families, genera, and species.

The Arts and Science College, at that time, had one typist whom the faculty could use. Mrs. Suma Service. As I completed treatments, I typed them on stencils and, as she found spare time, Mrs. Service made a hundred mimeographed copies of each. Dr. Gordon Alexander provided the funds for the paper from a very limited departmental budget. In 1949, the *Flora of Boulder County*, comprising 300 pages, was ready, and the hundred copies were distributed and became the text for the Field Botany course. The *Boulder County Flora* contained citations of the specimens documenting the work, and has become the base line for a current check list of the county flora.

George Kelly, beloved gardener of the Denver region and writer of many popular books on Rocky Mountain Horticulture, Katherine Kalmbach, and I, among others, worked together in the Colorado Forestry and Horticulture Association, building a small herbarium that eventually became the nucleus of the herbarium of the Denver Botanical Garden. I taught a number of volunteer women to mount plants, and together we worked toward the establishment of a State Parks system, which, at the time, was only a remote "pie-in-the-sky" concept that begrudgingly limited itself to roadside rest stops. George was very enthusiastic about the *Flora of Boulder County*, and talked me into expanding it into a book of keys, and increasing the coverage to include a larger area.

Fortunately, the University of Colorado Press undertook, in 1953, to publish the book, revised in 1961, entitled *Handbook of Plants of the Colorado Front Range*. It purported to cover the area from Pike's Peak to Rocky Mountain National Park, and from the Continental Divide to the plains. There were no illustrations, save for some line sketches contributed by Dr. Sam Shushan, to illustrate the glossary. It was a "bare bones" production, but it was all the Press could afford. Nevertheless, it was successful enough to justify a more pretentious edition published in 1967. This time the Press made more of a textbook style production, called it *Rocky Mountain Flora*, and I was fortunate in being able to add line drawings. Dr. Charles Yocom, with whom I attended college in Pullman and Ames, had become a wildlife specialist with a hobby of drawing plants. He had a large selection, including many species occurring in this region, and invited me to use them. Unfortunately, many of them were drawn to specifications incompatible with our format, with the result that, while we did use them, many of them lost a great deal in reduction. But beggars can't be choosers, and thus the book began slowly to improve.

The University of Colorado Press was replaced by a consortium, the Colorado Associated University Press. Under the editorship of John Schwartz, a thoroughly professional hand was brought to bear on subsequent editions, many of the Yocom illustrations were replaced by better ones contributed by Ann Pappageorge, thanks to financial help from friends of the Flora. Thirty-two color plates were added, and a more attractive format, featuring a soft cover, with a colored cover plate, and rounded corners, assured the popularity of the book.

During all this time, there was no subsidization of the research by any governmental or private agency. All of the clerical work was done by the author. The entire project was a labor of love, accomplished on the proverbial shoestring. Thanks to the understanding nature of the leaders of the Press, the price of the various editions has remained well within the ability of the user to pay.

INTRODUCTION

Scope of the Book

This companion volume to *Colorado Flora: Western Slope* covers all of Colorado east of the Continental Divide and across the plains to the borders of Wyoming, Nebraska, Kansas, Oklahoma, and New Mexico (Fig. 1). With *Colorado Flora: Eastern Slope*, I complete this pair of field guides to the flora of Colorado. My earlier volume, *Rocky Mountain Flora*, has been in print continuously since 1952, and its coverage included only the Front Range and the adjacent piedmont valleys, from Rocky Mountain National Park to Pikes Peak. This coverage was expedient because in previous years the population centers in the Eastern Slope (the potential market for the book) were localized along the Front Range, but I have always felt that the people in the Arkansas Valley and San Luis Valley were short-changed. In the thirty-seven years that have elapsed since the first edition, we have seen a great development of interest in the plants of Colorado on the part of the present population, through the development of concerns about threatened and endangered species, botany as recreation, and a general enhancement of the general educational level of our citizens. I feel fortunate to have been given the opportunity to devote forty-three years to a study of the flora and to be able to complete this long-term educational goal.

The Eastern Slope

The Eastern Slope of Colorado comprises the High Plains, which includes the drainages of the South Platte and the Arkansas Rivers, each of which tends to have a distinctive flora. The South Platte drainage contains characteristic species of the northern Great Plains, while the Arkansas drainage is a highway of migration northward of the Chihuahuan floristic elements. Separating these drainages is a relatively low forested divide that is referred to as the Black Forest, an area of pine forests and outcrops of sedimentary rocks. The Black Forest is being developed rather rapidly as the Front Range Urban Corridor and its critical habitats are disappearing. In many respects the flora of the Black Forest resembles that of the Black Hills of South Dakota, inasmuch as the region harbors small relictual colonies of eastern American prairie and woodland species otherwise unknown in Colorado except for some protected canyons of the outer Front Range.

The High Plains, North and South

The northern High Plains, or the Platte River drainage contains several special habitats worth the attention of botanists. The Pawnee Buttes National Grassland contains outcroppings of rock that stand as islands in a sea of short-grass plains. Its most unusual feature is a stand of limber pine, *Pinus flexilis*, isolated at a much lower altitude than expected. This species evidently extended onto the high plains during the Pleistocene and has been stranded on the Pawnee Buttes following the change in climate that produced the modern High Plains and eliminated the populations in the middle altitudes. Its numerous rimrock bluffs support a number of cushion plants and dryland species unable to compete in grasslands. Among these are *Leptodactylon caespitosum, Oreocarya celosioides, Musineon tenuifolium*, and *Astragalus sericoleucus*.

The northern High Plains also contains areas of unstable sand dunes that have a distinctive flora. Some of the special plants to be found here are the bush

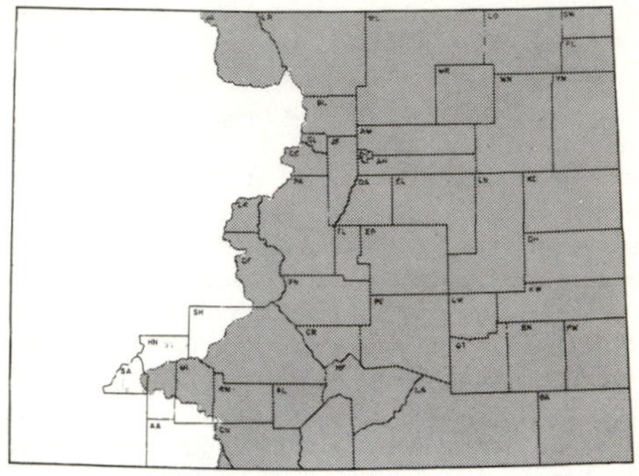

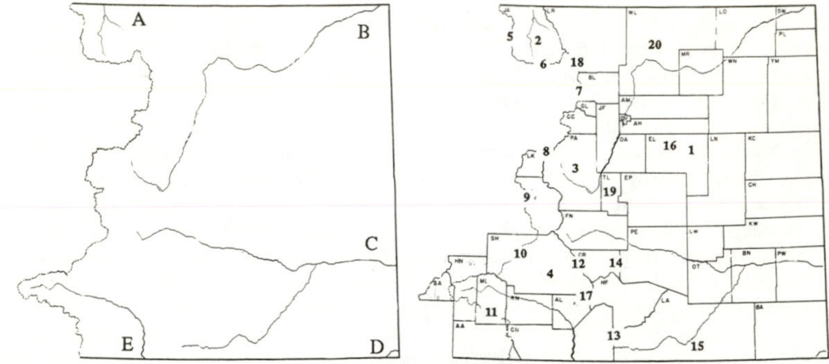

Figure 1. The Eastern Slope of Colorado

Top: Area covered by this book (shaded area); refer to text for county abbreviations.

Lower left: River systems: **A**, North Platte; **B**, South Platte; **C**, Arkansas; **D**, Cimarron; **E**, Rio Grande.

Lower right: Major topographic features: **1**, Arkansas Divide; **2**, North Park; **3**, South Park; **4**, San Luis Valley; **5**, Park Range; **6**, Rabbit-ears Range; **7**, Front Range; **8**, Mosquito Range; **9**, Saguache Range; **10**, Cochetopa Range; **11**, San Juan Range; **12**, Sangre de Cristo Range; **13**, Culebra Range; **14**, Wet Mountains; **15**, Mesa de Maya; **16**, Black Forest; **17**, Great Sand Dunes National Monument; **18**, Rocky Mountain National Park; **19**, Florissant National Monument; **20**, Pawnee Buttes National Grassland.

morning-glory, *Ipomoea leptophylla*, which has a root as thick as a fence-post. A white phlox covers the ground in season, and roadsides support stands of ring muhly grasses, *Muhlenbergia torreyi*, whose circular patches look like targets. In the summer and early fall, these sandy areas are glorious with displays of the sand penstemon, *Penstemon ambiguus*, *Palafoxia* and the common sunflower, *Helianthus annuus*.

The southern High Plains, dominated by the Arkansas River Valley, has as its hallmark the candelabra cactus, *Cylindropuntia imbricata*, which marches up the valley as far north as Colorado Springs, along with the One-seed Juniper, *Sabina monosperma*. The southeast corner of Colorado, where the Cimarron River cuts a small triangle of sand across it, supports a number of species that barely enter our state. The Arkansas valley has extensive outcrops of limestone that support a number of local, often rare, and sometimes endemic species, especially in the area between Pueblo and Cañon City. This is a dry valley, and only in exceptional years does it display its best botanical dress.

Large areas of the High Plains have been modified by agriculture and no longer support native vegetation. However, wherever there are bluffs, badlands, and bottomlands, the native flora can still be found. Bonny Reservoir State Park is such an area, and the north-facing bluffs at Wray are good places to visit. Colorado botanists have tended to ignore the eastern plains because of the thunderstorms and tornadoes, the biting midges, and the heat, and have turned most of their attention to the mountains. Eastern Colorado, therefore, has been investigated more by botanists from Kansas, resulting in the 1986 publication, *Flora of the Great Plains*. But the easternmost tier of counties still will yield new additions to the Colorado Flora of plants of the neighboring plains states.

The Mountain Front

The Mountain Front includes foothills and mesas bordering the High Plains on the west and south. The southern margin of the Eastern Slope is occupied by the Mesa de Maya, which extends from Trinidad to Baca County and the westernmost part of the Oklahoma Panhandle. This long mesa is forested and farmed on top, and its slopes are covered by dense oak brush. There are deep canyons such as the Purgatoire feeding the Arkansas River system. The Mesa de Maya also has canyons running to the south into New Mexico, in which plants of the New Mexico flora barely enter Colorado. The area is very rugged and difficult of access, and it has never been thoroughly explored for plants. Here is where Colorado's only stands of beargrass, *Nolina texana*, and mesquite, *Prosopis glandulosa*, occur. One problem with this area is that good flowering years are few and far between. The Mesa de Maya will continue to be a prime area for the discovery of new Colorado plants.

The Spanish Peaks, the Cucharas Valley, and the Culebra Range have a floristic individuality. A number of species either are endemic here or reach their northern limits here: *Valeriana arizonica, Castilleja haydenii, Rydbergia brandegei*, and *Townsendia eximia*.

North of the Arkansas Valley the mountain front is occupied by the Wet Mountains (Sierra Mojada). This range has a relatively undistinguished flora but it is interesting for its small, isolated patch of tundra at the south end. The east face of the range was ravaged by fire some years ago.

The mountainous southern anchor of the Front Range, Pikes Peak, differs from the northern portion by having a bedrock of a very coarse, friable granite that does not hold moisture well. Pikes Peak has several very special species. It is a very good place to see the dwarf blue columbine, *Aquilegia saximontana*, two endemics: the alpine bluebell, *Mertensia alpina*, *Oreoxis humilis*, and the finest stands of boykinia, *Telesonix jamesii*, the latter best seen at Windy Point on the Cog Railroad. The Rampart Range runs north from Pikes Peak to the Platte Canyon, and contains many unexplored canyons, especially in the vicinity of the Air Force Academy and Palmer Lake. The Devil's Head area is noted for the occurrence of isolated stands of rare species, such as *Viola biflora* on the forest floor, *Viola selkirkii*, and the sensitive fern, *Onoclea sensibilis*, which is probably extinct at the only site at which it occurred, west of Sedalia.

The Front Range, strictly speaking, is the great mountain mass anchored by Mount Evans on the south and Long's Peak on the north. Here the Continental Divide reaches its easternmost approach on the North American Continent, as well as its steepest gradient to the Great Plains. It is an area of extreme diversity, beginning in the Boulder area with a narrow strip we call the piedmont valleys, interspersed by low hogbacks and cliffs of shale and sandstone, followed on the west by sedimentary rocks of the Dakota Ridge and the Flatiron formations that overlie the Pre-Cambrian granite. Hard granite intrusive batholiths form spectacular "narrows" for the local canyons, providing cool and shaded north slopes and cliffs. The canyon of Clear Creek is composed in part of extensive calcareous schists, on which we have found the moss, *Leptodon smithii*, at its only known station in North America.

Mount Evans is the botanical jewel of the Front Range. To enjoy a vicarious visit to the Arctic, nothing is easier or more rewarding to the botanist than a drive to Summit Lake, 13,000 feet above sea level. Summit Lake lies above timberline in a shoulder of the mountain where sunlight only briefly bathes the lake and its inlet and shores. Standing at the inlet, one cannot see out over the tundra to the plains or the surrounding mountains, and it is as if one is in the true Arctic. This fragile wet-tundra site has become an object of botanical pilgrimages by botanists from all over the world because of the exciting alpine species that occur here and often no other place in Colorado, recurring again only in the Arctic or in the Eurasian mountains.

Summit Lake became so renowned for its botanical treasures that it was designated in 1965 as Colorado's first Registered Natural Landmark. To ensure its preservation, a plaque has been anchored to a lakeside boulder, fishing and stocking of trout has been discontinued, and huge boulders have been placed across the former vehicle access to the shore. For several years, each visit to the lake turned up some new and exciting botanical find. The list includes rare and disjunct mosses, lichens, and liverworts. Among the vascular plants, one can see *Phippsia algida, Kobresia sibirica, Spathularia foliolosa, Ranunculus pygmaeus,* and many other rare wet-tundra species.

From Echo Lake to the summit, the drive up Mount Evans traverses subalpine forests, a renowned stand of gnarled bristlecone pine, *Pinus aristata*, dry, rocky tundra, massive talus block slopes and a summit area of dwarf cushion plants including *Claytonia megarhiza, Draba species, Taraxacum scopulorum, Mertensia,* and *Eritrichum*. From the summit, one has a panoramic view of the Front Range, the Plains, Gray's and Torrey's Peaks, and the expanse of South Park.

The crest of the Front Range from Mount Evans to Rocky Mountain National Park is accessible and botanically very interesting. In Boulder County alone there are over 1,500 species of flowering plants. I believe that considering all groups of plants, including the lichens and mosses, this is the richest area of Colorado, and would repay an interested amateur or professional botanist an entire summer's stay.

North and south of the Front Range the Continental Divide recedes to the west. This is very apparent especially to the north of Fort Collins, where the foothills take on a decidedly desert-steppe aspect. At Owl Canyon, north of Fort Collins, is an isolated stand of piñon pine far from its northernmost outpost at Colorado Springs. Confined to a surface outcrop of limestone that has been quarried for many years, a large part of the population was destroyed, but this stand is now a preserve. However, it is not a natural occurrence, but dates back, based on archeological evidence, to an accidental planting of seeds evidently taken by squirrels or cached by native American traders bringing seed from the south. Finding no competition on this bare outcrop, the trees thrived. The oldest trees, about 350 years old, consist of a small handful in a ravine near the north end.

North of Fort Collins to the Wyoming border is a large arid highland grassland with eroded pinnacles of sedimentary rock on the east, and granite domes on the west. This area is not very well explored for plants, and it is here we can expect to find some species of the Laramie Plains of Wyoming dropping over the Colorado line. One of these is *Besseya wyomingensis*. Serious study of this area is suggested.

The "Parks"

A unique feature of the Southern Rockies is the chain of intermountain "parks" that divide the mountain ranges. From north to south, the principal ones are North Park, Middle Park (on the western slope), South Park, and the San Luis Valley. These are essentially grasslands, with dry and wet facies supporting steppe plants and fen plants, respectively. They tend to be cold-air drainage basins, hemmed around with high mountains on three sides, and draining into one of the major river systems. Each park has a personality of its own.

North Park

North Park is a combination of dry sage plains, willow and sedge meadows, lakes, and clay or sandy river benches. A shifting dune area lies on the east side against the confining Rawah Range. The Continental Divide forms the southern (Fairview Mountain) and the western (Park Range) boundary. Tributaries of the North Platte River drain the park to the north into Wyoming. While the basin of North Park looks rather uninteresting botanically, it supports a rich flora of sedges and willows, and aquatic plants of both fresh and alkaline requirements. The Park Range is easily accessible by trails along the base and up almost every valley.

Here is where many plants characteristically found only on the western slope drop down on the east side of the Park Range. We have just begun to find them, and for this reason, a number of plants thus far not yet reported are listed as likely to be found in North Park. The Big Creek Lake area is particularly rich in these. *Trillium ovatum*, *Piperia unalascensis*, *Mimulus lewisii*, *M. moschatus* and *Azaleastrum albiflorum* occur along the flanks of the Park Range. North Park has its own endangered species, *Phacelia formosula*, known from a half-dozen small populations near Walden. One of the most spectacular displays of wild flowers may be seen on a tour of Independence Mountain, where whole hillsides are covered by golden colonies of *Helianthella uniflora* and purple lupines.

South Park

South Park and its surrounding unglaciated mountain ranges, some granitic and calcareous, comprise the crown jewels of the Southern Rocky Mountains. Here are concentrated more rare and disjunct alpine, subalpine, and wetland species than anywhere else.

South Park is a large grassland and wetland park bounded on the north and west by probably the richest alpine botanical area in Colorado. Hoosier Ridge, between Fairplay and Breckenridge, has many botanical treasures, but one must walk up the tundra to see them. The east side of Hoosier Pass is granitic, and the west (Mosquito Range) calcareous, so a different flora awaits one in each direction. On Hoosier Ridge one can see *Armeria scabra*, *Ipomopsis globularis*, *Eutrema penlandii*, *Oxytropis podocarpa* and *O. viscida*; on the calcareous slopes of Mount Bross and Mt. Lincoln, *Braya humilis*, *Trifolium attenuatum*, *Parnassia kotzebuei*, and *Physaria alpina*. And penetrating the Mosquito Range to Mt. Sherman and Horseshoe Cirque, more aristocrats may be found: *Salix lanata*, *Saussurea weberi*, *Eriophorum altaicum*, and *Trichophorum pumilum*.

South Park is bounded on the east by the Tarryall Range, a rugged but relatively low range most famous for its mountain sheep, and on the west by the Mosquito Range and the volcanic Buffalo Peaks (to which, because of their inaccessibility, we have never mounted a botanical excursion). On the south, the Park empties west into the Arkansas drainage through the low Trout Creek Pass, and eastward out to the main South Platte.

The northern basin of South Park, until very recently, was a great expanse of wet meadows that were harvested for wild hay. Through the season these meadows were changing carpets of color formed by dense stands of elephantella, *Pedicularis groenlandica* and *P. crenulata*, bistort, *Bistorta bistortoides*, marsh-marigold, *Psychrophila leptosepala*, and fringed gentians, *Gentianopsis thermalis*. But recent drainage and ditching of these meadows to supply more water to Denver suburbs has dried them out and replaced many of them, temporarily we hope, with an uninteresting flora of silver sage, *Artemisia frigida*.

In the middle of the Park is an area of grassland punctuated by scattered small stands of *Picea pungens*. These trees grow with their feet in the water, in the midst of quaking fens fed by streams flowing out of the calcareous Mosquito Range. The water is also quite sulphurous. Shallow pools occur within the extensive sedge and willow fens. Here we have a remarkably rich assemblage of rare boreal disjunctive species: the rare willows, *Salix candida* and *S. myrtillifolia*; rare sedges, *Carex scirpoidea*, *C. viridula*, and *Trichophorum pumilum*; and the primroses, *Primula incana* and *P. egaliksensis*. Another rich, but not calcareous, fen area in East Lost Park, in the adjacent Tarryall Range, displays extensive quaking fens dominated by the rare cotton-grass, *Eriophorum gracile*, up until recently thought to have become extinct in Colorado. With it occur two very rare sedges, *Carex livida* and *C. tenuiflora*, widely disjunct from their nearest localities in boreal North America. And on the fringes of the wetland, in cool, north-facing forest edges, the remarkable lichen, *Cladina stellaris,* occurs in small patches, at its only station in the western contiguous United States. This beautiful little plant is a dominant understory in the subarctic muskeg, and most people recognize it as the little rubberized dyed-green "trees" that are used in miniaturizations of three-dimensional realtors' plans.

At the south end of South Park lies shallow Lake Antero, whose shores are vast alkaline flats. However, even these relatively unattractive places have their botany. Here we have a small annual mustard, *Thellungiella salsuginosa*, that is known from only about four localities, all of them alkaline flats, in North America, while its main area is in eastern Siberia! Also, on hummocks of grass in these flats there is a rare occurrence of the alkali-tolerant *Phlox kelseyi* ssp *salina*, known elsewhere in Nevada. A recent visit to the site, showed, however, that the highway maintenance people have leveled the hummocks and poured gravel in its place, destroying the colony. Perhaps another might be discovered elsewhere on the vast expanse of alkaline flats around the reservoir.

The San Luis Valley

The San Luis Valley is the largest of the parks, bounded on the east by the Sangre de Cristo Range and the Great Sand Dunes in the north and the Culebra Range in the south; across its north edge by Poncha Pass; and on the west by the La Garita and Cochetopa Hills in the north, and the San Juan Mountains in the south. The Rio Grande arises in the San Juans and flows out of the valley southward into New Mexico. The valley has a rich supply of artesian water, and the basin is very sandy and alkaline, full of introduced weeds. Interestingly enough, one of the weed genera, *Descurainia*, produces a bushy-branched type in the valley bottom that was recently described as a completely new species, *D. ramosissima*.

A very few endemic species are known in the San Luis Valley. *Astragalus ripleyi* occurs in the southern end, in Conejos County. Otherwise it ranges south to Tres Piedras, New Mexico. When first discovered here, it was abundant along roadsides, but has recently been disappearing because it appears to be selectively grazed by cattle. Recent studies of the flora of the western side of the Valley at the base of the San Juans show that, floristically, those foothills are somewhat of an extension of the Front Range.

The Sawatch Range and Upper Arkansas Valley

The desert-steppe vegetation of the lower Arkansas Valley follows the river almost to Leadville, and it is most surprising to see that the piñon pine climbs up on the south-facing slopes as high as 9,000 feet along the road to Monarch Pass! The Sawatch Range includes the Collegiate Peaks, Mount Elbert and Mount Massive. We have few or no collections from these high peaks, but recently a great deal of interest has been generated by the limestone and dolomite exposures in the tundra around Cottonwood Pass and Mineral Basin, where new discoveries of *Braya glabella*, and *Antennaria aromatica* were recently made. It seems obvious that more attention needs to be paid to limestone areas at high altitudes.

The Wet Mountain Valley

The Wet Mountain Valley is a small park surrounded by the Sangre de Cristo Mountains on the west and the Wet Mountains on the east. It is a beautiful relatively unspoiled grass- and wetland, draining, by way of Texas Creek, into the canyon of the Arkansas River. This is a fine area for botanical exploration because one can headquarter at the old village of Westcliffe and reach rich areas easily. The tundra is accessible by several roads. The valley is not noted for endemics, but it is an excellent place to see *Coriflora scottii*, in openings in the oak brush. *Draba smithii*, an endemic of these southern mountains, occurs on alpine ledges.

Native or Introduced?

I am often asked, "How do you know if a plant is native or not?" This is a question that is very difficult to answer in general, but not very difficult on a case-by-case basis. For example, we have ways of knowing whether a genus has ever been native in North America; we have case histories of weeds that first appeared on ballast dumps along the east or west coast, and know that they followed the railroads westward. Very recent introductions are fairly easy to explain.

After all of the easy questions are answered, several difficult ones remain, especially along the Front Range. Several species, native in eastern North America, occur sporadically near the cities of the Front Range, particularly Boulder. We know that Darwin M. Andrews had a nursery at the south edge of Boulder and that he specialized in native plants. We feel fairly sure that the occurrence of *Sambucus canadensis*, *Aster novae-angliae*, *Scirpus lineatus* and possibly *Impatiens capensis* spread from his garden along the irrigation ditches. However, plants that were really native, but just hanging on in a few mesic pockets may have gotten a new lease on life by the white man's development of irrigation ditches, because now they seem to exist only thanks to these ditches. A few possibilities are *Thalictrum dasycarpum* and *Eupatorium maculatum*.

The mining days brought in several introductions. The Clear Creek Valley is now full of the yellow oriental clematis, originally grown alongside some house in Idaho Springs for its ornamental value. Butter-and-eggs, *Linaria vulgaris,* and Bouncing Bet, *Saponaria vulgaris*, were common garden flowers. Look at them now!

I also believe that the early settlers in the Boulder Valley, lacking irrigation, planted some of their ornamental plants in the creeks, such as Bluebell Gulch, near their homes, where they would get Nature's water. How else can we explain the ornamental iris, Oriental poppies, *Viburnum lantana*, *Viburnum lentago*, and *Berberis vulgaris*, that persist there today?

More species are being introduced in the urban corridors at the present time than ever before. Significant alterations are being made in the Colorado landscape. The bulldozer and its mass movement of soil tend to transport seeds and roots far from where they originate. Revegetation of burned areas and scattering of wild flower packets and instant "meadows-in-a-can" bring in new plants that are not native to the area. Many of them are undesirable; most do not survive, but some, unfortunately, compete too successfully with the native vegetation that might return naturally if given a chance.

Jays and magpies carry seeds of ornamental plants from the cities out into the foothills, where some sprout and persist or actually thrive. Boulder is a case in point. Many years ago Mr. Ernest Greenman planted oaks on Green Mountain to see if they would survive north of their normal geographic limit. They certainly do, and more and more of them are appearing, probably started by acorns carried by the birds. In Long Canyon we recently found a large *Cotoneaster* bush, a species commonly cultivated in Boulder, and a fairly large red oak. On the foot of one of the Flatirons, a scarlet oak has established itself, and the cultivated rose with purple foliage now occurs nearby.

The Families Treated In This Book

The following alphabetical list of plant families is grouped in four categories: ferns, gymnosperms, monocots, and dicots. In three columns are the scientific names, common names, and international three-letter acronyms. Because the International Rules of Botanical Nomenclature recommends that all family names end in *-aceae*, several of the large old families have unfamiliar new names. The old name is placed in square brackets, and a reference is made to the new name by citing both of the pertinent acronyms. I do not applaud this recommendation because, while it makes things neat, we still will need to know the old names in order to use the literature. Wasn't it Emerson who said, "Consistency is the hobgoblin of small minds"?

One hundred fifty-five families are recognized here. A number of those usually recognized in American floras have been broken up into two or more. To aid readers in finding these segregates, the acronyms of the families concerned (published by the author in *Taxon* 31:74-88. 1982) of the families concerned are given in a second line, e.g., "was UMB" or "see also ASN." The number of species recorded for our area in each family is given in parentheses after the name.

Common names of families vary from place to place and often embody the name of a genus common to the area. Pea Family is not more correct than Legume Family. In this sense common names of families, genera, and species are variable, and no useful purpose is served by trying to standardize them, since they differ among different language groups as well as between local areas.

Fern Families

ADIANTACEAE (1)	MAIDENHAIR	ADI
ASPIDIACEAE (3)	SHIELDFERN (was PLP)	ASD
ASPLENIACEAE (5)	SPLEENWORT (was PLP)	ASL
ATHYRIACEAE (8)	ATHYRIUM (was PLP)	ATY
CRYPTOGRAMMACEAE (1)	ROCK BRAKE (was PLP)	CRG
EQUISETACEAE (5)	HORSETAIL	EQU
HYPOLEPIDACEAE (1)	BRACKEN (was PLP)	HPL
ISOETACEAE (3)	QUILLWORT	ISO
LYCOPODIACEAE (3)	CLUB-MOSS	LYC
MARSILEACEAE (1)	PEPPERWORT	MSL
OPHIOGLOSSACEAE (9)	ADDER'S TONGUE	OPH
POLYPODIACEAE (1)	POLYPODY	PLP
(See also ADI, ASD, ASL, ATY, CRG, HPL, SIN, WDS)		
SALVINIACEAE (1)	WATERFERN	SVN
SELAGINELLACEAE (5)	LITTLE CLUB-MOSS	SEL
SINOPTERIDACEAE (9)	LIPFERN (was PLP)	SIN
WOODSIACEAE (4)	WOODSIA (was PLP)	WDS

total: 14 families, 57 species

Gymnosperm Families

CUPRESSACEAE (3)	CYPRESS FAMILY	CUP
PINACEAE (11)	PINE	PIN

total: two families, 14 species

Monocot Families

ACORACEAE (1)	SWEETFLAG	ACO
AGAVACEAE (2)	AGAVE (was LIL)	AGA
ALISMATACEAE (5)	WATER-PLANTAIN	ALI
ALLIACEAE (8)	ONION (was LIL)	ALL
ASPARAGACEAE (1)	ASPARAGUS (was LIL)	ASG
CALOCHORTACEAE (1)	MARIPOSA (was LIL)	CCT
COMMELINACEAE (3)	SPIDERWORT	CMM
CONVALLARIACEAE (2)	MAYFLOWER (was LIL)	CVL
CYPERACEAE (155)	SEDGE	CYP
CYPRIPEDIACEAE (2)	LADY'S SLIPPER	CPD
[GRAMINEAE]	GRASS	GRM/POA

HYDROCHARITACEAE (3)	FROGBIT	HDC
HYPOXIDACEAE (1)	YELLOW STARGRASS	HPX
IRIDACEAE (5)	IRIS	IRI
JUNCACEAE (37)	RUSH	JUN
JUNCAGINACEAE (3)	ARROWGRASS	JCG
LEMNACEAE (7)	DUCKWEED	LMN
LILIACEAE (5)	LILY	LIL
(see also AGA, ALL, ASG, CCT, CVL, MLN, TRI, UVU)		
MELANTHIACEAE (3)	FALSE HELLEBORE (was LIL)	MLN
NAJADACEAE (1)	WATERNYMPH	NAJ
NOLINACEAE (1)	SOTOL	NLN
ORCHIDACEAE (21)	ORCHID	ORC
POACEAE (261)	GRASS	POA/GRM
PONTEDERIACEAE (2)	PICKERELWEED	PON
POTAMOGETONACEAE (16)	PONDWEED	POT
RUPPIACEAE (1)	DITCHGRASS	RUP
SMILACACEAE (1)	SMILAX	SML
SPARGANIACEAE (4)	BURREED	SPG
TRILLIACEAE (1)	TRILLIUM (was LIL)	TRL
TYPHACEAE (3)	CATTAIL	TYP
UVULARIACEAE (2)	BELLWORT (was LIL)	UVU
ZANNICHELLIACEAE (1)	HORNED PONDWEED	ZAN

total: 31 families, 557 species

Dicot Families

ACERACEAE (2)	MAPLE	ACE
ADOXACEAE (1)	ADOXA	ADX
AIZOACEAE (1)	FIG-MARIGOLD	AIZ
ALSINACEAE (34)	CHICKWEED (was CRY)	ASN
AMARANTHACEAE (10)	AMARANTH	AMA
ANACARDIACEAE (3)	SUMAC	ANA
APIACEAE (41)	PARSLEY	UMB/API
APOCYNACEAE (2)	DOGBANE	APO
ARALIACEAE (2)	GINSENG	ARL
ASCLEPIADACEAE (16)	MILKWEED	ASC
ASTERACEAE (371)	SUNFLOWER	CMP/AST
BALSAMINACEAE (1)	JEWELWEED	BLS
BERBERIDACEAE (4)	BARBERRY	BER
BETULACEAE (5)	BIRCH	BET
BIGNONIACEAE (1)	CATALPA	BIG
BORAGINACEAE (38)	BORAGE	BOR
BRASSICACEAE (109)	MUSTARD	CRU/BRA
CACTACEAE (11)	CACTUS	CAC
CALLITRICHACEAE (2)	WATER STARWORT	CLL
CAMPANULACEAE (9)	BELLFLOWER	CAM
CANNABACEAE (2)	HOPS	CAN
CAPPARACEAE (5)	CAPER	CPP
CAPRIFOLIACEAE (13)	HONEYSUCKLE	CPR
CARYOPHYLLACEAE (19)	PINK	CRY
(See also ASN)		
CELASTRACEAE (1)	STAFFTREE	CEL
CERATOPHYLLACEAE (1)	HORNWORT	CTP
CHENOPODIACEAE (43)	GOOSEFOOT	CHN
CISTACEAE (1)	ROCKROSE	CIS
[COMPOSITAE]	SUNFLOWER	CMP/AST
CONVOLVULACEAE (5)	MORNINGGLORY	CNV
COPTACEAE (4)	MEADOWRUE	COP
CORNACEAE (2)	DOGWOOD	COR
CRASSULACEAE (4)	STONECROP	CRS
CROSSOSOMATACEAE (1)	CROSSOSOMA	CRO
[CRUCIFERAE]	MUSTARD	CRU/BRA
CUCURBITACEAE (3)	GOURD	CUC

CUSCUTACEAE (4)	DODDER	CUS
DIPSACACEAE (2)	TEASEL	DPS
DROSERACEAE (1)	SUNDEW	DRS
ELAEAGNACEAE (4)	OLEASTER	ELE
ELATINACEAE (2)	WATERWORT	ELT
ERICACEAE (8) (see also MNT, PYR)	HEATH	ERI
EUPHORBIACEAE (24)	SPURGE	EUP
FABACEAE (140)	PEA	LEG/FAB
FAGACEAE (4)	OAK	FAG
FRANKENIACEAE (1)	FRANKENIA	FNK
FUMARIACEAE (4)	FUMITORY	FUM
GENTIANACEAE (16)	GENTIAN	GEN
GERANIACEAE (4)	GERANIUM	GER
GROSSULARIACEAE (13)	GOOSEBERRY (was SAX)	GRS
HALORAGACEAE (1)	WATER MILFOIL	HAL
HELLEBORACEAE (15)	HELLEBORE (was RAN)	HEL
HIPPURIDACEAE (1)	MARE'S TAIL	HPU
HYDRANGEACEAE (2)	HYDRANGEA (was SAX)	HDR
HYDROPHYLLACEAE (11)	WATERLEAF	HYD
HYPERICACEAE (3)	ST. JOHNSWORT	HYP
KRAMERIACEAE (1)	RATANY	KRM
[LABIATAE]	MINT	LAB/LAM
LAMIACEAE (31)	MINT	LAM
[LEGUMINOSAE]	PEA	LEG/FAB
LENTIBULARIACEAE (3)	BLADDERWORT	LNT
LIMNANTHACEAE (1)	MEADOWFOAM	LIM
LIMONIACEAE (1)	THRIFT (was Plumbaginaceae)	LMO
LINACEAE (6)	FLAX	LIN
LOASACEAE (11)	LOASA	LOA
LYTHRACEAE (4)	LOOSESTRIFE	LYT
MALVACEAE (18)	MALLOW	MLV
MARTYNIACEAE (1)	UNICORN PLANT	MAR
MENYANTHACEAE (1)	BUCKBEAN	MNY
MOLLUGINACEAE (1)	CARPETWEED	MOL
MONOTROPACEAE (2)	PINESAP (was ERI)	MNT
MORACEAE (2)	MULBERRY	MOR
NYCTAGINACEAE (13)	FOUR-O'CLOCK	NYC
NYMPHAEACEAE (1)	WATERLILY	NYM
OLEACEAE (2)	OLIVE	OLE
ONAGRACEAE (40)	EVENING-PRIMROSE	ONA
OROBANCHACEAE (5)	BROOMRAPE	ORO
OXALIDACEAE (3)	WOODSORREL	OXL
PAPAVERACEAE (8)	POPPY	PAP
PARNASSIACEAE (3)	GRASS-OF-PARNASSUS	PAR
PLANTAGINACEAE (6)	PLANTAIN	PTG
POLEMONIACEAE (33)	PHLOX	PLM
POLYGALACEAE (1)	MILKWORT	PGL
POLYGONACEAE (55)	KNOTWEED	PLG
PORTULACACEAE (11)	PURSLANE	POR
PRIMULACEAE (15)	PRIMROSE	PRM
PYROLACEAE (7)	WINTERGREEN (was ERI)	PYR
RANUNCULACEAE (40) (see also HEL)	BUTTERCUP	RAN
RESEDACEAE (2)	MIGNONETTE	RES
RHAMNACEAE (5)	BUCKTHORN	RHM
ROSACEAE (69)	ROSE	ROS
RUBIACEAE (9)	MADDER	RUB
RUTACEAE (2)	CITRUS	RUT
SALICACEAE (34)	WILLOW	SAL
SANTALACEAE (1)	SANDALWOOD	SAN
SAPINDACEAE (1)	SOAPBERRY	SAP
SAURURACEAE (1)	LIZARDTAIL	SAU
SAXIFRAGACEAE (28)	SAXIFRAGE	SAX

(see also PAR, HDG, GRS)		
SCROPHULARIACEAE (88)	FIGWORT	SCR
SIMAROUBACEAE (1)	QUASSIA	SMR
SOLANACEAE (24)	NIGHTSHADE	SOL
TAMARICACEAE (2)	TAMARISK	TAM
ULMACEAE (2)	ELM	ULM
[UMBELLIFERAE]	PARSLEY	UMB/API
URTICACEAE (2)	NETTLE	URT
VALERIANACEAE (4)	VALERIAN	VAL
VERBENACEAE (7)	VERVAIN	VRB
VIOLACEAE (16)	VIOLET	VIO
VISCACEAE (5)	MISTLETOE	VIS
VITACEAE (3)	GRAPE	VIT
ZYGOPHYLLACEAE (2)	CALTROP	ZYG

total: 106 families, 1,632 species

Some Floristic Statistics

The total number of species recognized here is approximately 2,260. The larger (twenty-two) families and their numbers are AST (370), POA (261), CYP (155), FAB (140), BRA (109), SCR (88), ROS (66), PLG (54), CHN (43), API (41), ONA (40), RAN (40), BOR (38), JUN (37), ASN (34), PLM (33), SAL (34), LAM (31), SAX (28), EUP (24), SOL (23), ORC (21). The rest of the families have fewer than 20 taxa. Thirty-nine families have only one taxon. Twenty-two have only two. Seven families have only three. This means that, while we have 153 families to reckon with, 1,700, or about 70 percent of the taxa fall into the "big 22" families! If you can learn to recognize these families, you can avoid using the family key that much of the time. Success in using a field guide comes when one knows the large families without using the key. But the sobering fact is that you eventually have to learn to recognize all of those families with one or two species!

How to Learn to Recognize the "Big Twenty-two"

Here are some hints about recognizing the largest families. Warning: there are exceptions to almost all of these statements!

Asteraceae (371): flowers in dense heads subtended by an involucre of bracts. Ray-flowers are good field marks but they may not be present. Heads need not be showy, but can be green and very small, as in the ragweeds and sagebrushes. Other families that mimic Asteraceae are Valerianaceae and Dipsacaceae.

Poaceae (261): grasses have leaves 2-ranked, with a sheath, blade, and a ligule where the blade meets the sheath. The unit of inflorescence is the spikelet, which consists of a pair of glumes subtending 1 or more florets, consisting of a lemma, palea, 3 stamens, and an ovary with 2 feathery styles. Compare with Cyperaceae, Juncaceae, Juncaginaceae.

Cyperaceae (155): sedges usually have 3-angled stems, but some have terete ones, and 3-, hardly ever 2-ranked, leaves. The unit of inflorescence is usually a spike, each flower consisting of three stamens, an ovary with 2 or 3 styles, a subtending bract (never a lemma and palea) below each flower.

Fabaceae (140): Possess a type of fruit common to all, a legume, exemplified by the pea or bean. Most of ours have papilionaceous flowers (like sweet-pea) with banner, wings, and keel, and 10 stamens of which 9 are united and 1 free (there are exceptions), but some have flowers lacking petals, or with many stamens. Leaves are usually, but not necessarily, compound.

Brassicaceae (109): Mustards have cross-shaped corolla, with 4 sepals, 4 petals, 4 long and 2 short stamens. Ovary superior (inferior in Onagraceae, another 4-merous family) with 2 compartments separated by a thin membrane (replum) to which the seeds are attached. Most mustards lack bracts beneath the individual flowers.

Scrophulariaceae (88): Flowers are, with few exceptions, bilaterally symmetrical, leaves opposite, stem terete, ovary not lobed, with 2 internal compartments (compare Lamiaceae). *Scrophularia* has square stems!

Rosaceae (69): Radially symmetrical flowers, with 5 petals and sepals, many stamens, a hypanthium and superior ovaries (akenes or follicles). When in doubt, Rosaceae generally have stipules, Ranunculaceae do not.

Polygonaceae (55): Except for *Eriogonum*, the presence of an ochrea (sheathing stipule, is characteristic. No differentiation between petals and sepals, fruit a 3-sided akene.

Chenopodiaceae (43): Flowers greenish, radially symmetric, petals none, ovary 1-seeded; leaves often with a mealy coating.

Apiaceae (41): Flowers in umbels, ovary inferior with 2 1-seeded mericarps separating at maturity. Leaves usually compound, aromatic (soap, anise, carrot).

Ranunculaceae (40): Herbaceous, flowers with often undifferentiated colored petals and sepals, numerous stamens and carpels (akenes).

Onagraceae (40): Flowers 4-merous, as in Brassicaceae, but stamens usually 8, and ovary inferior.

Boraginaceae (38): Flowers radially symmetric, short- or long-tubular, 5-merous, ovary with 4 distinct nutlets; foliage, except for Mertensia, with stiff hairs.

Juncaceae (34): Grasslike, but leaves often terete or like *Iris*. Flowers have all the parts of those of a lily, but they are small and brown or green.

Alsinaceae (34): Herbaceous, leaves opposite, simple, nodes swollen, flowers 5-merous, calyx of separate sepals, petals usually white, ovary with free-central placentation.

Salicaceae (34): Shrubs or trees, leaves alternate; catkins formed in spring. Willows have a single scale covering the bud, cottonwoods several.

Polemoniaceae (33): Herbaceous, flowers 5-merous, styles 3. A family not easy to characterize. Think of *Phlox*.

Lamiaceae (31): Leaves opposite, stem square (but see also *Scrophularia*), plants usually aromatic; flowers zygomorphic, ovary formed of 4 nutlets.

Saxifragaceae (28): Herbaceous; flowers 5-merous, radially symmetrical, but occasionally a few petals longer than the others, ovary with 2 united carpels, tending to be half-inferior. A difficult family to characterize, best understood by learning first one, then another, until you get a feel for it.

Euphorbiaceae (23): Plants mostly with milky juice; inflorescence usually a cyathium (see glossary), with the 3-carpellate ovary exserted from the cup on a curved stalk.

Solanaceae (23): Herbs and shrubs with radially symmetric 5-merous flowers, ovary superior, with 2 carpels and 1 style. Flowers and fruit are very diverse. The family is best learned one by one. Think of *Petunia*, sweet or chili peppers, tobacco, tomato, potato.

Orchidaceae (21): A monocot with bilaterally symmetrical flowers, inferior ovary, and essential organs that are extremely difficult to interpret! But orchids are not hard to recognize as such.

Unfortunately for beginners, the large families are also the most diverse. An understanding of them comes from learning first some species, then seeing that they are related as a genus, and gradually getting a feeling for the family by association rather than by memorization of a group of characters common to the family. A family or a genus cannot be narrowly defined. Just as a species is a group of closely related individuals, a genus is a group of closely related species, and a family is a group of closely related genera. Of course, we like to measure relationship roughly by morphological similarity, but other important things are involved. Davis and Gilmartin point out (*Systematic Botany* 10:417. 1985), "Species concepts have evolved to the point that morphology is now considered one of the weaker criteria of 'true' speciation. In adhering to a biological species concept the significance of morphological change in the speciation process can be trivialized on definitional grounds." The same may be said of generic concepts.

Generic Concepts

To some criticisms that have been leveled at my adoption of generic names unfamiliar to some readers, I can only quote from a review (1821) by Caleb Cushing, of Nuttall's *Genera of North American Plants*. "He has proposed above sixty new genera . . . chiefly by the subdivision of old genera. And we think here lies the greatest defect of the work; namely, in a disposition to innovate upon the established genera, not always on the safest grounds. Thus to make a new genus *Comandra* of *Thesium umbellatum* and a genus *Epifagus* of *Orobanche virginiana*, in separating the genus *Juglans* and *Carya*, in adopting Desfontaines' dismemberment of the genus *Convallaria* into *Convallaria*, *Smilacina*, and *Polygonatum*, in confirming Michaux's and Pursh's division of the genus *Pyrola* into *Pyrola* and *Chimaphila*, in these and in other instances that could be pointed out, Nuttall appears to us to have ventured upon or assented to changes, which the generic differences he has indicated do not warrant, and which materially injure the science of botany by embarrassing its nomenclature and impairing the symmetry of its arrangements." A hundred years later, all of the genera mentioned have been universally accepted. Graustein, in her biography of Nuttall, after making this quotation, comments further: "That objection should ever have been made to such improvements as these exemplifies the pronouncement that "scientists . . . create not what is acceptable but what will become acceptable" (letter from Boott to Hooker, 1819).

Miscellaneous Notes

Generic names: I have presented generic names together with their authors and dates of publication. I have also tried to present a derivation of each name for its educational value.

Specific names: A specific name consists of a generic name and a specific epithet, followed by the name of the author of the name. Botanical nomenclature differs from zoological in the way authors of the names are cited. The name of an author in parentheses means that this author first published the species. The second author is the person responsible for the name in its present form, usually under another genus.

Author citations: In order to save space, I have deliberately omitted the initials of authors, as A. Gray and A. Nelson. I have also omitted the second author when his name follows *ex*. The citation, Nuttall *ex* Torrey & Gray means that Torrey and Gray described the plant but gave credit to Nuttall for recognizing it, informally naming it and perhaps furnishing the description. There is a tendency now to omit the first author, e.g., Nuttall, to save space, but the whole point of authorship in such instances is to give credit where credit is due. I prefer to honor Nuttall and Douglas; this was the intent of the authors who picked up their unpublished names. The name of Carl Linné (Linnaeus) is always abbreviated "L." Full citations of all names for Colorado plants are given in Wittmann & Weber, *Natural History Inventory of Colorado, 1. Vascular Plants, Lichens and Bryophytes* (1989).

Counties: Abbreviations for the Colorado counties are taken from the Smithsonian Institution River Basin Surveys, as follows:

ARAPAHOE (AH)	ADAMS (AM)	ALAMOSA (AL)
BACA (BA)	BENT (BN)	BOULDER (BL)
CHAFFEE (CF)	CHEYENNE (CH)	CLEAR CREEK (CC)
CONEJOS (CN)	COSTILLA (CT)	CROWLEY (CW)
CUSTER (CR)	DENVER (DV)	DOUGLAS (DA)
ELBERT (EL)	EL PASO (EP)	FREMONT (FN)
GILPIN (GL)	HINDALE (HN)	HUERFANO (HF)
JACKSON (JA)	JEFFERSON (JF)	KIOWA (KW)
KIT CARSON (KC)	LAKE (LK)	LARIMER (LR)
LAS ANIMAS (LA)	LINCOLN (LN)	LOGAN (LO)
MINERAL (ML)	MORGAN (MR)	OTERO (OT)
PARK (PA)	PHILLIPS (PL)	PROWERS (PW)
PUEBLO (PE)	RIO GRANDE (RG)	SAGUACHE (SH)
SEDGWICK (SW)	TELLER (TL)	WASHINGTON (WN)
WELD (WL)	YUMA (YM)	

Family acronyms: Collectors should indicate on their labels the family to which a species belongs. This makes for ease in filing and retrieval from collections. Because family names are usually very long, I have developed a standard 3-letter acronym for each family, which should serve a useful purpose as a shorthand reference. These names are given at the head of each family treatment and are utilized in the running heads.

Family arrangement: Except for the gymnosperms and ferns, the families are listed alphabetically irrespective of whether they are monocots or dicots. A list of the families, with their alternative names and acronyms, under each group, is provided.

How to Collect and Preserve Botanical Specimens

An herbarium, or collection of dried and pressed plants, is very useful as an aid to remembering the plants you have already named, and as a reference whereby you can check your "unknowns" against the plants you already know. A collection of carefully named and preserved plants is better for these purposes than the best description or picture you might find.

Collecting specimens for personal pleasure and aids to the memory is very different from collecting them professionally. In the first instance all one needs is an old book that you don't mind ruining (please don't use this one), a Sears-Roebuck catalog, a telephone directory, or just newspapers. You can make a small press, using plywood, and cut corrugated cardboard for ventilation as the plants are drying. You can put these in manila folders (but don't use Scotch tape). My recommendation for making a file of them is to simply place the dried specimens in a folded sheet of paper, and pin the label on the right-hand corner. I would strongly recommend against mounting the specimens if you ever plan to give your collection to a school or other institution. It is extremely expensive, and in time you may wind up with a white elephant on your hands. If you ever decide to give the collection to an herbarium, its staff will prefer to receive them unmounted because each institution has its own ideas of proper mounting and supplies. For most casual collectors only snippets of specimens are needed as reminders, and these can be kept in notebooks or in the way I suggested above.

Collecting plants need not be an environmentally detrimental pursuit. Common sense should be your guide. A tree or a shrub is not destroyed or damaged by collecting a small branch. A perennial plant or vine is not harmed by taking part of the aerial growth. Reasonable restraints should be put upon collecting entire plants, especially if the population is small. It is important to make notes on those parts of the plants that are not collected: height, flower color, branching mode, nature of the underground parts (rhizomes, bulbs, fibrous roots, massive underground roots, etc.). Color photographs, including one of the entire plant, and a closeup of the flower, are very useful; in fact, I suggest that with plants of special environmental concern, like orchids, these can be used for the record, even in an herbarium. In the future, sight records of plants are going to have to be accepted just as they are in ornithology.

However, if you intend to collect specimens ultimately destined for an herbarium, or if you plan to send specimens to an herbarium for identification, you will want to operate on a higher level of sophistication. An excellent guide for this is D.B.O. Savile, *Collection and Care of Botanical Specimens*, available from Queens Printer and Controller of Stationery, Ottawa, Canada. My own suggestions are as follows:

In order to make a plant collection, there are a few things that everyone should have.

1. Some sort of digging tool (a trowel, prospector's pick, hunting knife, or weed digger, and a good sharp pen-knife for cutting twigs.

2. A stock of old newspapers; tabloids are best, but full-size papers torn along the main fold so as to make single sheets folded once into 12 x 18 inch (30 x 40 cm) folders. For the more affluent, blank newsprint is more elegant and can be written upon more effectively.

3. At least 100 felt blotters, 12 x 18 inches, and twice as many corrugated cardboard (ventilators).

4. A plant press (two flat frames of wood, either solid or a lattice of slats, 12 x 18 inches).

5. Two lengths of rope, parachute cord, or trunk straps to tie the press together.

6. A field press (12 x 18 inch satchel of lightweight waterproof fabric) for pressing along the trail. I can't overemphasize the importance of this. Do not use plastic bags; they sweat, flowers come off, the stems bend into odd shapes, species get mixed together, and putting the specimens in the plant press at the end of the day is wearisome and disappointing in terms of quality. Specimens pressed immediately in a field press can be kept for several days before being transferred to the standard press.

7. A small field notebook for recording the collection data, flower colors, plant height, and character of the underground parts if not collected.

My favorite supplier is Herbarium Supply Co., 955 West Catching Inlet, Coos Bay, OR 97420.

The quality of specimens varies with the good sense of the collector. The specimen is cut, pulled, or dug, and placed in the newsprint folder, with care used to clean off adhering soil and to arrange the specimen neatly. If the specimen does not have sufficient flowers or fruits, collect some extra and press them separately. Plants that are too large to fit in the folder should be folded. This especially applies to grasses. Here, simple folding is not enough (it can still produce hay; Aven Nelson once commented, on receiving a mess of folded grasses, "probably was good hay, too!"); at each fold, slip a piece of light card stock that has been slit in the middle, over the fold to hold it in place. Such specimens won't get out of hand later on. Remember that a standard sheet of herbarium paper is 12 x 16 inches, and that a label will occupy about 3 x 5 inches at the lower right hand corner. Your specimen should fit without lopping over the edges of the paper.

If you anticipate having to examine flowers or fruits in detail after they are dry, be sure that you press enough extra of them that this examination will not destroy the only flowers on a specimen. Take notes on flower color, height of plant, nature of the root system, and anything else that you leave in the field but might be needed later.

The quality of your specimens will depend on care of preparation for the press: selecting the specimen that best exemplifies the population, cleaning off any adhering mud or soil, and collecting enough material. You can be as fastidious as you like in arranging the leaves and spreading the petals, but this must be done at the moment you first place the plant in the folder; afterwards it will be too late. Beyond this, ample pressure in the press is needed, as well as frequent changing of the blotters to carry off the accumulated moisture. When the leaves crack when manipulated, and when the stem feels dry, the specimen is ready to remove from the press.

A field notebook is essential. Number your specimens. I suggest that a simple consecutive number system be used. (I abhor systems that combine year, month, day, and specimen number!) Numbers are cheap; they can be used or deleted, and your ego will swell after your numbered list gets to a thousand or more. Place the number in big, bold black characters in the middle of the newspaper sheet (edges of sheets tend to get gnawed by use or rodents). For each collecting foray, start a new heading: state, county, locality, altitude (rounded out to the nearest 500 feet or 100 meters is good enough), and date. Follow this with your numbers; ecological situation and supplemental information can be added after the number. Sticking to a standard routine will make it easier to produce labels, either by hand, or on a computer program.

It seems that there are as many formats of specimen labels as there are curators. Some labels seem to be more interested in trumpeting ownership or advertising an herbarium (HERBARIUM OF Y. Y. FLERTCH, PEORIA, ILLINOIS, for instance, spread in block letters across the top) than giving specimen information. I have tried, by precept and example, to minimize the advertising on specimen labels. The identification of the herbarium can be relegated to an unobtrusive line at the bottom. One important feature I would like to see on more labels is the family name, or, alternatively, its acronym. Labels can be printed in two columns on standard 8-1/2 x 11 inch acid-free 100 percent rag paper (other stocks are unstable over time). I prefer to use unperforated stock because some labels will be more detailed than others; a paper cutter does not add too much time. A sample label is given here:

COLORADO, U.S.A.

Eriophorum gracile W.D.J. Koch CYP

PARK COUNTY: East Lost Park, ca. 1.5 mi downstream from Lost Park Campground, T9S R72W S18, Pike National Forest, ca. 3000 msm. Dominant in rich fens. With *Carex limosa.*

16 August 1989 Weber & Cooper 18035

Herbarium COLO

Plant Identification

No single book is enough to help you learn the art of analysis and identification of plants. For beginners, some elementary book in plant analysis is essential. There are many and they go back over a hundred years. Asa Gray's *Lessons in Botany*, written in the 1850s, is still extremely useful and editions of it still can be found in used book stores. For general vocabulary and descriptions and illustrations of families, V. H. Heywood (ed.), *Flowering Plants of the World* (1978) is ideal. H. D. Harrington & L. W. Durrell's *How to Identify Plants* (1957), P. H. Davis & J. Cullen, *The Identification of Flowering Plant Families* (1979), J. P. Baumgardt, *How to Identify Flowering Plant Families* (1982), J. P. Smith, *Vascular Plant Families* (1977), and S. B. Jones & A. E. Luchsinger, *Plant Systematics* (1986) are all useful. The two biggest hurdles in becoming adept at plant identification are mastering the terminology, and learning to recognize the bigger plant families so as to avoid having to use the family key. Family keys are extremely difficult to write because there are so many exceptions to the stereotype. Small families are usually much easier to learn because they are more cleanly circumscribed.

How to Use the Keys

The dichotomous key has become the standard method for the identification of organisms and should need little introduction. It involves the presentation of successive pairs of choices, from which the reader arrives at a decision and then proceeds to the next choice (as indicated by the parenthetical number on the right) and the next, until arriving at the name of the organism. Keys are simply means by which one arrives at a tentative decision, which should be followed up by a careful reading of a detailed description and examination of authentically named specimens and illustrations. This is why we have herbaria for reference, and great multivolume editions of regional and state floras. In a field guide (the so called *Excursion-flora* of the European), the need for conciseness makes an extensive treatment impossible. As a compromise, the keys are somewhat more detailed, and notes are added concerning the habitat, altitudinal range, and special characteristics that help to confirm the final decision.

There are several kinds of keys. The first is a key that is relatively infallible because it uses all the critical features of the plants regardless of whether they are easily visible or require elaborate techniques of dissection. It might require observation of features, such as flower buds, seeds, or winter buds that are not always present. It also tends to place related species or genera close to each other. This kind of key is written for the person who makes it rather than for the user in the field. The second kind of key is designed for the user, and its intention is to make possible identification of plants under almost any field conditions. This is an impossible task, at best, but is a goal that writers of field handbooks aim for. Such a key may also deliberately make mistakes, that is, it will assume the reader's observation may be incorrect but will bring him to the correct conclusion anyway. Key-writing is a fine art, and the use of keys has to be developed in somewhat the same spirit.

One key-writer of note has pointed out that "if the presence of various small features is useful as a means of identifying some kinds of plants, then the absence of the same features must be equally useful in distinguishing other kinds. Persons using a key for identification seldom have any difficulty in recognizing the presence of a structural feature but often find it difficult to convince themselves of its absence. This is purely a matter of mental attitude and has nothing to do with the size and conspicuousness of the feature in question. Those who use this or any similar work should guard against this tendency" (Gleason, *New Britton & Brown Illustrated Flora*, 1952, page *xxx*).

The limitations of the author's experience and the fact that ecological compensation places plants of higher altitudes lower down on a north-facing slope than plants of lower altitudes should be a warning to the reader that alpine species might be expected occasionally to occur at lower altitudes and vice versa. In such matters the reader is requested to bear with the author, for a definite statement subject to modification is often preferable to silence. Plants with blue flowers will throw white-flowered mutants. Low plants growing on a well-manured site may assume giant proportions. And the beginner will always find a flower with six petals when there should be only five. One of my old bird-watching mentors always used to mumble under his breath: "Birds don't read books." Neither do plants.

Some Basic Terminology

There is a comprehensive glossary at the end of the book, and users are urged to seek other source books for basic botanical information. What follows are merely answers to a few of the most commonly asked questions that require interpretation.

Growth Forms

In order to use the keys intelligently, we must become familiar with some of the characteristic growth forms of plants. This takes some practice in keen observation. Take, for instance, the differences between annuals and perennials. It is easy to find a book that defines an annual as a plant that lives for one season, blossoms and then dies, and a perennial as one that lives for an indefinite number of years. It is not so easy to look at a plant and say, "This is a perennial." Gardeners learn to do this with experience, because the growth forms of plants have much to do with their performance in the garden. Here are a few definitions and hints.

Trees, Shrubs, and Herbs

Trees. Woody plants, usually over 5 meters tall, with a single main stem.

Shrubs. Woody plants, usually less than 7 meters tall, with several more or less equal main stems.

Subshrubs. Herbaceous plants that do not die back completely to the ground, but whose main annual growth is herbaceous.

Herbs. Nonwoody plants. Another term for herbs, which I dislike very much, *forbs*, was coined by F. E. Clements to apply to nongrasslike herbs. The word is composed of the first two letters of the word *forest* and the last two letters of *herbs*.

Annuals, Biennials, and Perennials

Annual. Never woody, reproducing by seed each year, developing to maturity within a few weeks' or months' time. Annuals usually have rather shallow root systems and are easily pulled out of the ground intact. Some perennials with deep-seated rhizomes are mistaken for annuals, but look for the broken end of the "root" that indicates that the rhizome was left in the ground. Annuals never have rhizomes, bulbs, or corms.

Biennial. This term has been replaced recently by *monocarpic*, indicating a plant that is of more than one season duration and flowers only once before dying. Monocarpic plants commonly begin with a basal rosette of leaves crowning a taproot. Some flower the second year and die, thus are true biennials. However, *Swertia*, the Green Gentian or Monument Plant, is monocarpic, and shows the rosette stage for from 20 to 50 years before it finally flowers. In the last year, the rosette is used up and disappears as the flowering shoot arises.

Perennial. Either woody or herbaceous, having a well-developed root system or some means (corms, bulbs, winter buds [turions] at the base of the stem, or rhizomes) of carrying the plant through the winter. Usually hard to pull out of the ground without breaking off some of the roots. With experience, perennials may be recognized by the remnants of last years' leaves withered at the base of the plant.

Ferns, Gymnosperms, and Angiosperms

Many times, members of the carrot and sunflower families are mistaken for ferns because of their finely cut leaves. Since the first choices in the key call for distinguishing between the three great groups of vascular plants, a few hints may be in order concerning these misleading individuals.

Ferns. Ferns never have flowers. Thus, any plant that has a flower must never be mistaken for a fern. The flowering plants that are most commonly mistaken for ferns are almost all in the Carrot Family (Apiaceae). Most of these have leaves that give off a strong odor when crushed. Ferns sometimes smell faintly like hay but never smell like anise, carrot, soap or parsley. Most fern leaves (fronds) arise directly from a horizontal rhizome just below the surface of the ground. Most flowering plants that have fernlike leaves have them arising from an erect stem or from a fleshy taproot.

Gymnosperms and *Angiosperms.* The seed plants are divided into two main groups, called *gymnosperms* (meaning "naked-seed") and *angiosperms* (meaning "covered seed"). The gymnosperms include our common needle-leaved evergreen trees such as pines, spruces, firs and junipers. Only one species in our area, the common juniper, is shrubby. Mormon Tea (*Ephedra*) is also shrubby, but it does not occur on the Eastern Slope. Gymnosperms produce their seeds on the open faces of scales that make up the cone, and the seeds are shed simply by the separating of the cone scales when the cone becomes mature (everybody who has eaten piñon nuts should know this). In the angiosperms, or flowering plants, the seeds are always confined within an ovary, as in apples, peas, peanuts, and squash.

Flowers

A simple chart and diagram (Fig. 2) of flower parts is shown below. It presents the minimum knowledge needed in the use of the keys. The other terms used in this book are explained in the Glossary, page 000, or at appropriate places in the text.

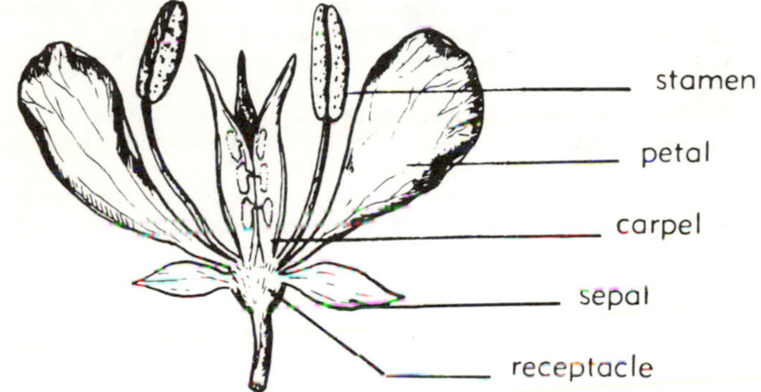

Figure 2. Parts of a flower

Class of organs	*Individual name*	*Collective name*
Floral envelope (perianth, or accessory organs)	sepal (tepal) petal	calyx corolla
Essential organs	stamen	androecium
	carpel	gynoecium
Floral axis	receptacle	————

Here are some simple answers to a few of the questions that come up most often in using the keys.

How many carpels are there?

When the gynoecium consists of more than one separate unit (carpel; notice, I never use the word *pistil* because it is misleading), all we have to do is count the units. Thus, in buttercups (Fig. 3), there are a great many carpels; in larkspur (Fig. 4) there are usually three. However, when the carpels are fused into a single unit,

Figure 3　　　　Figure 4

it is more difficult to decide. Here are a few rules of thumb, none of them a hundred percent reliable, but they should help in most instances:

1. There are usually as many carpels as there are stigmas or branches of the style (Fig. 5).

2. There are usually as many carpels as there are locules ("cells", or compartments, of the ovary). To see this, make a cross-section with a pocket knife or razor blade. Try to find a large ovary for this (Fig. 6).

3. There are usually as many carpels as there are *parietal* placentae (if the plant has this type of placentation). Plants with parietal placentation have the ovules attached to the side walls of the ovary (Fig. 7)

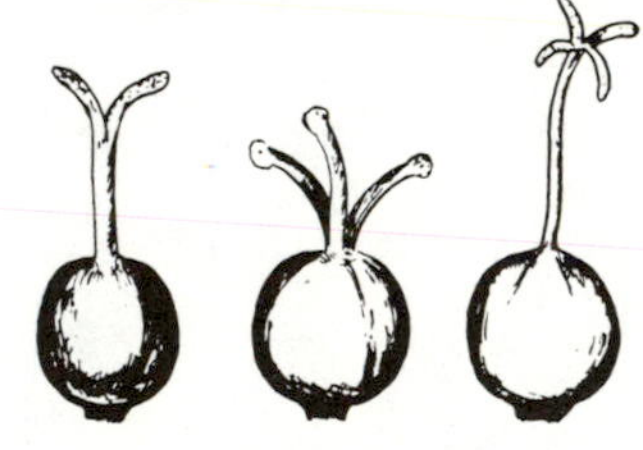

Figure 5

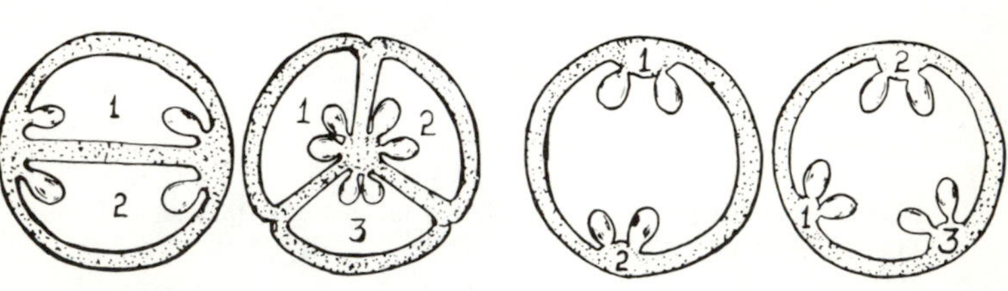

Figure 6　　　　Figure 7

Is the ovary superior or inferior? Is there a hypanthium?

A plant with a superior ovary has the petals, sepals, and stamens attached below the ovary or at the base of it, and not fused to the side of it. The floral parts may surround the ovary in any way, but as long as they are not fused to it, the ovary is superior (Fig. 8).

If the ovary is inferior, the floral parts are fused to it, or the ovary itself is imbedded in the floral axis so that the floral parts appear to be attached to the top of the ovary. The ovary cannot be removed in one piece without tearing away the tissues in which it is imbedded (Fig. 9). Examples: apple is inferior; rose is superior, even though the ovaries are inside the hip; they are completely free from the surrounding parts. In some saxifrages the ovary may have its lower half imbedded and fused to the floral parts, and the upper half free; this condition may be called "half-inferior."

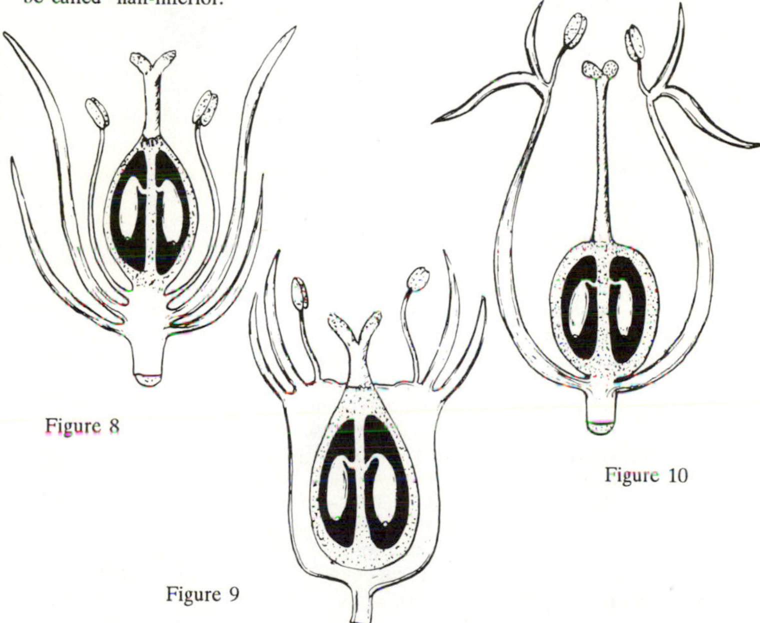

Figure 8

Figure 10

Figure 9

A *hypanthium* (Fig. 10) is a structure that forms a cup around the gynoecium. It may consist of the fused bases of the stamens, petals, and sepals, but usually looks like a green calyx-cup, with the petals and stamens mounted on the rim. A tubular corolla, with the stamens attached to it, should not be confused with an hypanthium. Examples of hypanthiums: rose, evening primrose.

When is a leaf simple and when is it compound?

A compound leaf is one that is divided into a few or several separate leaflets. Since the leaflets themselves resemble leaves, students sometimes have trouble deciding where a leaf ends and a leaflet begins. Here are some rules of thumb:

1. In most plants a bud is always present where the leaf joins the stem (Fig. 11). There are no buds where the leaflets join the common leaf-stalk (rachis).

2. In woody plants, and in many non-woody plants, the petiole (leaf-stalk) has a different color or texture than that of the stem to which it is attached; there is usually hardly any difference or demarcation between the stalks of leaflets and the main leaf rachis.

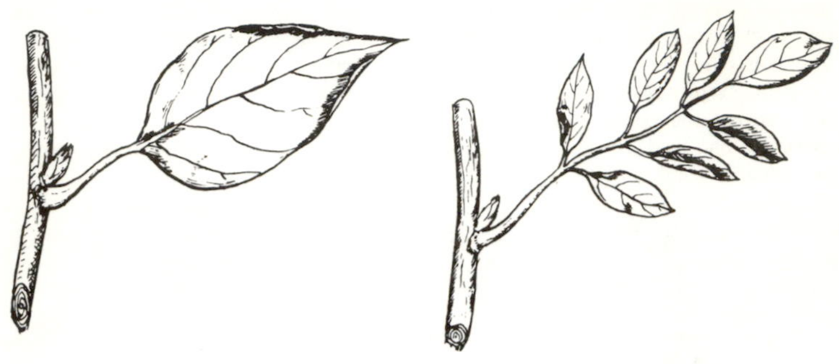

Figure 11

Eponymy. Botanists honored in Colorado Plant Names

To identify all the people who have been honored in the names of Rocky Mountain plants would fill this book. Most of them are mentioned briefly in the text. The ones listed here are those who, again and again, appear in the specific epithets or in generic names. Most of these were collectors in Colorado or worked intensively on Rocky Mountain plants. For additional names and details, see Joseph and Nesta Dunn Ewan, 1981. *Biographical Dictionary of Rocky Mountain Naturalists: a guide to the writings and collections of botanists, zoölogists, geologists, artists and photographers, 1682-1932*. The best index to biographical and bibliographic information on botanists will be found in the three-volume reference work, *Bibliographic Notes on Botanists*, produced from a card file accumulated over many years by the later George Hendley Barnhart, of the New York Botanical Garden. This man entered briefly into my career, for in the first half of the first decade of my life, Mr. Barnhart lived in the apartment above ours on Valentine Avenue in the North Bronx, and my mother often invited him down for tea by knocking on the ceiling with her broomstick.

Baker, Charles F., 1872-1927, collected extensively in Montrose and Gunnison counties. His collections were described by Greene in a series of papers called *Plantae Bakerianae*.

Brandegee, Townshend Stith, 1843-1925, botanist with the Hayden Surveys, also surveyor of Fremont County, made important collections in the Mesa Verde area.

Clements, Frederick E., 1874-1945, ecologist, originator of plant succession concept, had experimental gardens on Pikes Peak.

Coulter, John Merle, 1851-1928, botanist with the Hayden Surveys and author of *Manual of Botany of the Rocky Mountain Region*, (1885).

Crandall, Charles Spencer, 1852-1929, horticulturist, professor at Colorado Agricultural College, collected extensively in Colorado.

Douglas, David, 1799-1834, Scottish botanist and explorer of the West, never visited Colorado but described and collected many plants native to the State.

Eastwood, Alice, 1859-1953, high school teacher in Denver, collected around Grand Junction in 1890, later became curator at the California Academy of Sciences where she gained lasting fame by segregating the type specimens and eventually saving them during the great earthquake.

Engelmann, George, 1809-1884, St. Louis physician-botanist and a founder of the Missouri Botanical Garden. Collected with Hall & Harbour in South Park, and had a cabin under Gray's Peak. Major contributions were made in the cacti and conifers.

Fendler, Augustus, 1813-1883, collector for Engelmann and Gray, mostly in New Mexico.

Frémont, John Charles, 1813-1890, explored widely in the West and collected plants and animals. Unfortunately, many of his plant specimens were lost in accidents along the way.

Gray, Asa, 1810-1888, student of Torrey and developer of the Harvard Herbarium, the dominant taxonomist of his era. Visited Colorado twice, in 1872 for the dedication of Gray's and Torrey's Peak, and for a few days in 1877, with Sir Joseph Dalton Hooker.

Greene, Edward Lee, 1843-1915, field botanist and clergyman in Colorado and New Mexico, later botanist at the University of California, Berkeley, one of the most knowledgeable persons of his time as to the Colorado flora.

Hall, Elihu, 1820 (or 22?)-1882, Illinois botanist, collected in South Park with J. P. Harbour in 1862.

Harbour, J. P., dates unknown, thought to be an acquaintance of C. C. Parry, and collected in South Park in 1862 with Elihu Hall.

Harrington, Harold D., 1903-1981, professor at Colorado State University, Fort Collins, author of *Manual of the Plants of Colorado* (1954), still the only complete flora of the state with keys and descriptions, indispensable to present and future floristic work.

Hayden, Ferdinand Vandiveer, 1829-1887, leader of the U.S. Geological and Geographical Survey of the Territories, 1867-1879, in which many botanists participated.

Holm, Herman Theodor, 1854-1932, Danish botanist, collected in Colorado in 1896 and 1899, published a classic paper on the plant geography of the Rocky Mountains.

Hooker, Sir Joseph Dalton, 1817-1911, director of the Royal Botanic Gardens, Kew, an early leader in plant geography, visited Colorado with Asa Gray in 1877 and was the first to note the strong Asiatic element in our flora.

Hooker, Sir William Jackson, 1785-1865, British botanist, described many western North American plants from the historic voyages of exploration and from Geyer's trip across Wyoming, director of the Royal Botanic Gardens, Kew. Most species commemorating Hooker in our flora refer to W. J., rather than to his son, Sir Joseph Dalton Hooker.

James, Edwin, 1797-1861, surgeon-naturalist with the Long expedition, collected plants in 1820 from Pikes Peak to the Platte River.

Jones, Marcus Eugene, 1852-1934, exceptional field botanist, probably the greatest collector the West has known, mining engineer, contemporary and great competitor of Greene.

Letterman, George Washington, 1841-1913, a reclusive Missouri schoolteacher, collected on Long's Peak.

Löve, Áskell, 1916-, Icelandic cytotaxonomist, professor at the University of Colorado and prolific botanical writer; *Flora of Iceland*, *Cytotaxonomical Atlas of the Arctic Flora*.

Nelson, Aven, 1859-1952, Wyoming botanist and founder of the Rocky Mountain Herbarium at Laramie, first life-long resident botanist of this region. Great teacher and developer of botanists, such as L. N. Goodding, Elias Nelson, J. F. Macbride, Marion Ownbey, and George J. Goodman.

Nuttall, Thomas, 1786-1859, English botanist, explorer of the West with the Second Wyeth Expedition, Harvard professor, and a perceptive taxonomist, especially in Asteraceae.

Osterhout, George E., 1858-1937, amateur naturalist and resident collector in Colorado and southern Wyoming.

Parry, Charles Christopher, 1823-1890, physician-botanist of Davenport, Iowa, collected extensively on the east slope.

Patterson, Harry Norton, 1853-1919, botanist-printer of Oquawka, Ill., collected in the Gray's Peak area.

Payson, Edwin Blake, 1893-1927, promising student of Cockerell and Nelson, collected extensively from his father's cattle ranch at Naturita. A brilliant botanist, specialized in Brassicaceae and Boraginaceae.

Penland, C. William T., 1899-1982, professor at Colorado College, avid alpine botanist, discovered many rare alpine species on Hoosier Pass, specialized in *Penstemon*.

Pennell, Francis W., 1886-1952, Pennsylvania botanist, specialized in the Scrophulariaceae of the Rocky Mountain region.

Porter, Thomas C., 1822-1901, professor at Lafayette College, Pennsylvania, collected with the Hayden Survey and published the first Colorado Flora in 1874.

Pursh, Frederick, 1774-1820, German botanist, author of *Flora Americae Septentrionalis*, which described the collections of the Lewis & Clark Expedition.

Rothrock, J. T., 1839-1922, student of Asa Gray, botanist with the Wheeler Expeditions, 1869-1879.

Rydberg, Per Axel, 1860-1931, Swedish immigrant, curator at New York Botanical Garden, with Greene and Nelson, one of the most important figures in Rocky Mountain botany, published *Flora of the Rocky Mountains and Adjacent Plains*, 1917, ed. 2, 1923, and collected extensively in Colorado.

Schmoll, Hazel M., 1891-1990, University of Chicago student, wrote thesis on Chimney Rock area, Pagosa-Piedra region, was curator of botany at the Colorado State Museum, 1919-1923, collected at Mesa Verde National Park, had been mayor and "majordomo" of the town of Ward for many years, after giving up botany completely.

Vasey, George, 1822-1893, curator in the U.S. National Herbarium, collected extensively in eastern Colorado.

Watson, Sereno, 1826-1892, botanist on the U.S. Exploring expeditions, later assistant to Asa Gray at Harvard and then curator.

Colorado Flora: Eastern Slope

KEY TO THE FAMILIES

Note: In the longer keys reference is made, in square brackets, to the number of the couplet from which you last came; page references are not given, since the families are in alphabetic order. Starting pages for major groups are as follows:

Ferns and Fern Allies, p. 19.
Gymnosperms, p. 31.
Angiosperms, Flowering Plants, p. 35.

1a. Plants not producing seeds or true flowers, but reproducing by spores; fernlike, mosslike, rushlike plants. **Ferns and Fern Allies**
1b. Plants producing seeds, either by means of flowers or cones; plants of various aspects (seed plants) . . . . (2)

2a. Leaves needlelike or scalelike; evergreen trees and shrubs, never with flowers; ovules and seeds on the open face of a scale or bract (rarely the cone becomes a fleshy "berry" in *Juniperus* and *Sabina*). **Gymnosperms**
2b. Leaves various, seldom needlelike or scalelike (if so, flowers are present), rarely evergreen; ovules and seeds borne in a closed cavity (carpel; ovary). **Angiosperms**, FLOWERING PLANTS . . . . (3)

3a. Parasitic or saprophytic, often highly colored but not green (mistletoe, in this category, has some chlorophyll but is yellowish and epiphytic) . . . . **Key A**
3b. Not parasitic, or at least having green leaves . . . . (4)

4a. Stems thick and succulent, spiny; true leaves absent or greatly reduced and early deciduous. **Cactaceae**, CACTUS FAMILY
4b. Not as above . . . . (5)

5a. Leaves all basal, with circular blades covered with stalked, glistening red glands; flowers in a raceme. **Droseraceae**, SUNDEW FAMILY
5b. Not as above, not insectivorous plants . . . . (6)

6a. Submerged plants, with or without floating leaves . . . . **Key B**
6b. Terrestrial or semiaquatic, not submerged nor with floating leaves . . . (7)

7a. Vines, climbing or twining among other plants, often possessing suckers or tendrils, not merely creeping on the ground . . . . **Key C**
7b. Herbaceous or woody plants, not vines (the Smilacaceae have tendrils) (8)

8a. Leaves usually parallel-veined; flower parts in 3s; stem hollow or with scattered vascular bundles; herbaceous (except Agavaceae and Nolinaceae); seeds with 1 cotyledon (but see also Limnanthaceae, which has floral parts in 3s, otherwise a typical dicot) . . . . **Key D**
8b. Leaves usually netted-veined; flower parts in 5s, 4s, or 2s; stems with vascular bundles arranged in a ring around the pith; herbaceous or woody; seeds usually with 2 cotyledons . . . . (9)

9a. Trees or shrubs . . . . **Key E**
9b. Herbaceous, sometimes woody at the very base . . . . **Key F**

KEY A. PARASITES / SAPROPHYTES

1a. Attached to the bark of trees, or by suckers to the aerial stems of herbs . . . . (2)
1b. Without obvious attachments to the aerial parts of their hosts . . . . . (3)

2a. Attached to the trunks of branches of evergreen trees. **Viscaceae,** MISTLETOE FAMILY
2b. Threadlike orange or yellow plants attached by suckers to aerial parts of herbs. **Cuscutaceae,** DODDER FAMILY

3a. Flowers actinomorphic, in a spikelike erect or nodding raceme. **Monotropaceae,** PINESAP FAMILY
3b. Flowers zygomorphic . . . . (4)

4a. Flowers tubular, the petals united; ovary superior. **Orobanchaceae,** BROOM-RAPE FAMILY
4b. Flowers with separate petals; ovary inferior. **Orchidaceae,** ORCHID FAMILY

KEY B. AQUATICS

1a. Plants usually not more than 1 cm long, free-floating or submerged, with no attachment whatever . . . . (2)
1b. Plants not free-floating, or much larger if appearing so . . . . (3)

2a. [1] Plants disklike or thalluslike, without true stems and leaves, free-floating or submerged. **Lemnaceae,** DUCKWEED FAMILY
2b. Plants with obvious leaves arranged in 2 ranks along a short stem, free-floating. **Salviniaceae,** WATERFERN FAMILY, in Ferns and Fern Allies

3a. [2] Stems short and lacking, the leaves attached to the bottom, linear-elongate, the tips floating on the surface. **Sparganiaceae,** BURREED FAMILY
3b. Plants with definite stems . . . . (4)

4a. [3] Leaves simple, entire or slightly toothed . . . . (5)
4b. Leaves distinctly lobed, compound, or finely dissected . . . . (17)

5a. [4] Leaves linear or oblong, arranged in whorls . . . . (6)
5b. Leaves variously shaped, not whorled . . . . (7)

6a. [5] Leaves translucent, lax, 2 cell-layers thick; flowers, if present, sessile (carpellate) or long-pedicelled (staminate). **Hydrocharitaceae,** FROGBIT FAMILY
6b. Leaves opaque, rather rigid unless submerged, more than 2 cell-layers thick; flowers sessile in the leaf axils. **Hippuridaceae,** MARE'S TAIL FAMILY

7a. [5] Leaves almost orbicular, deeply cordate, very thick and leathery; flowers large, yellow, solitary. **Nymphaeaceae,** WATERLILY FAMILY
7b. Leaves narrower, not cordate; flowers not as above . . . . (8)

8a. [7] Flowers blue or yellow, with 6 tepals and 3 stamens. **Pontederiaceae,** MUD-PLANTAIN FAMILY
8b. Flowers greenish or colored, but not blue or yellow . . . . (9)

9a. [8] Leaves linear or filiform . . . . (10)
9b. Leaves with distinctly broadened blades . . . . (14)

10a. [9] Flowers in spikes. **Potamogetonaceae,** PONDWEED FAMILY
10b. Flowers sessile in the leaf axils or on slender, often coiled peduncles. (11)

11a. [10] Fruit minute, blackish, on an elongate, often coiled peduncle; leaves filiform, over 3 cm long. **Ruppiaceae,** DITCHGRASS FAMILY
11b. Flowers and fruits sessile in the leaf axils; leaves shorter . . . . (12)

12a. [11] Fruit rounded or emarginate, oblong or wider, not beaked. **Callitrichaceae**, WATER STARWORT FAMILY
12b. Fruit narrowly cylindric, tapered to a beak . . . . (13)

13a. [12] Fruit flattened, slightly curved, with a stout beak; leaves filiform. **Zannichelliaceae**, HORNED PONDWEED FAMILY
13b. Fruit terete, straight, the beak whitish, not rigid; leaves linear, flat, the margins very finely toothed (under high magnification). **Najadaceae**, WATERNYMPH FAMILY

14a. [9] Leaves alternate, at least 1 cm long; flowers not sessile in the leaf axils . . . . (15)
14b. Leaves opposite, less than 1 cm long; flowers inconspicuous, sessile in the leaf axils . . . . (16)

15a. [14] Floating leaves pinnately veined; flowers pink, with showy pink perianth parts. *Persicaria*, in **Polygonaceae**, BUCKWHEAT FAMILY
15b. Floating leaves with parallel veins, or floating leaves absent; flowers greenish, not showy. **Potamogetonaceae**, PONDWEED FAMILY

16a. [14] Stipules lacking; calyx and corolla absent; ovary 4-locular; floating and submerged leaves often strikingly different. **Callitrichaceae**, WATER STARWORT FAMILY
16b. Stipules present; calyx and corolla often present; ovary 3- or 5-locular; leaves not dimorphic. **Elatinaceae**, WATERWORT FAMILY

17a. [4] Leaves 3-foliolate; flowers white, petals fringed. **Menyanthaceae**, BUCKBEAN FAMILY
17b. Leaves not 3-foliolate . . . . (18)

18a. [17] Leaves bearing small balloonlike traps; flowers showy, yellow, spurred, on racemes projecting above water level. **Lentibulariaceae**, BLADDERWORT FAMILY
18b. Leaves not bearing bladders; flowers not spurred . . . . (19)

19a. [18] Leaves alternate; flowers with white or yellow petals. **Ranunculaceae**, BUTTERCUP FAMILY
19b. Leaves whorled; flowers greenish, inconspicuous . . . . (20)

20a. [19] Leaf divisions dichotomous, finely serrate; flowers sessile in the axils of normal leaves. **Ceratophyllaceae**, HORNWORT FAMILY
20b. Leaf divisions pinnate, entire; flowers in an interrupted spike resembling a knotted cord. **Haloragaceae**, WATER MILFOIL FAMILY

KEY C. VINES

1a. Leaves simple . . . . (2)
1b. Leaves compound (Caution! Poison ivy in this category) . . . . (7)

2a. Leaves palmately lobed, sometimes only slightly so . . . . (3)
2b. Leaves not lobed . . . . (5)

3a. Plants with tendrils . . . . (4)
3b. Tendrils absent. *Humulus*, in **Cannabaceae**, HOPS FAMILY

4a. Herbaceous; fruit a papery, spiny balloon or a gourd. **Cucurbitaceae**, CUCUMBER FAMILY
4b. Woody; fruit a fleshy "grape." **Vitaceae**, GRAPE FAMILY

5a. Venation parallel; flowers and fruits in umbels. **Smilacaceae**, SMILAX FAMILY
5b. Venation netted; flowers and fruits not umbellate . . . . (6)

6a. Flowers 1 cm long or more; petals united, pleated. **Convolvulaceae**, MORNINGGLORY FAMILY
6b. Flowers smaller; perianth parts (tepals) separate. **Polygonaceae**, BUCKWHEAT FAMILY

7a. Leaves pinnately compound . . . . (8)
7b. Leaves trifoliolate, palmately 5-7-foliolate, or ternately compound . . . (9)

8a. Leaflets entire; flowers with banner, wings, and keel (sweetpea type). **Fabaceae**, PEA FAMILY
8b. Leaflets serrate; flowers tubular. **Bignoniaceae**, CATALPA FAMILY

9a. Leaves palmately 5-7-foliolate. **Vitaceae**, GRAPE FAMILY
9b. Leaves not as above . . . . (10)

10a. Leaves with 3 shiny leaflets; flowers greenish; plant short (scarcely viny in this area), commonly bearing clusters of greenish-white berries. *Toxicodendron*, poison ivy, in **Anacardiaceae**, SUMAC FAMILY
10b. Leaves twice ternately compound or, if 3-foliolate, the flowers blue or yellow, with long feathery styles in fruit. **Ranunculaceae**, BUTTERCUP FAMILY

KEY D. MONOCOTS

1a. Woody plants with narrow evergreen leaves . . . . (2)
1b. Herbs; leaves otherwise . . . . (3)

2a. [1] Leaves stiff and erect; flowers perfect, more than 3 cm long, pendent, white. **Agavaceae**, AGAVE FAMILY
2b. Leaves supple, long, and arching; flowers unisexual, less than 1 cm long, not pendent, cream-colored. **Nolinaceae**, SOTOL FAMILY

3a. [1] Tall, fernlike plants, the true leaves minute, triangular, papery, subtending clusters of filiform green cladodes; flowers small, yellowish; fruit a red berry. **Asparagaceae**, ASPARAGUS FAMILY
3b. Not as above . . . . (4)

4a. Leaves cordate-ovate; stem with stipular tendrils. **Smilacaceae**, SMILAX FAMILY
4b. Not as above . . . . (5)

5a. Cattaillike plants with a tight spike of minute flowers protruding from the side of the stem; foliage very fragrant when fresh. **Acoraceae**, SWEETFLAG FAMILY
5b. Not as above . . . . (6)

6a. [5] Flowers minute, enclosed in chaffy bracts; 3- or 6-parted perianth lacking; flowers arranged in spikes or spikelets (grasses and sedges) . . . . (7)
6b. Flowers not enclosed in chaffy bracts or scales; perianth usually present, with 3 or 6 parts that may themselves appear papery or chaffy . . . . (8)

7a. [6] Leaves 2-ranked (in 2 rows on the stem), the sheaths usually open, the margins not fused (few exceptions); stems cylindric or flattened and almost always hollow; anthers attached to filaments at their middles. **Poaceae**, GRASS FAMILY

7b. Leaves 3-ranked, sometimes absent; sheaths usually closed, the margins fused; stems almost always triangular and solid (a few cylindric and hollow); anthers attached at one end. **Cyperaceae**, SEDGE FAMILY

8a. [6] Flowers with a rudimentary perianth consisting of bristles or scales, or none . . . . (9)
8b. Flowers with sepals and petals (sometimes the two are similar in shape and texture: tepals) . . . . (10)

9a. [8] Flowers in elongate terminal spikes, the looser staminate flowers in a separate group above the dense brown carpellate ones. **Typhaceae**, CATTAIL FAMILY
9b. Flowers in spherical clusters, staminate ones above the carpellate ones. **Sparganiaceae**, BURREED FAMILY

10a. [8] Carpels numerous (over 6), separate and distinct, in a whorl or ball. **Alismataceae**, WATER-PLANTAIN FAMILY
10b. Carpels 3 or 6 . . . . (11)

11a. [10] Ovary wholly inferior, the floral parts attached to the top of the ovary . . . . (12)
11b. Ovary superior or only partly inferior . . . . (15)

12a. [11] Flowers radially symmetrical . . . . (13)
12b. Flowers bilaterally symmetrical . . . . (14)

13a. [12] Flowers blue; leaves gladiate. **Iridaceae**, IRIS FAMILY
13b. Flowers yellow; leaves grasslike. **Hypoxidaceae**, YELLOW STARGRASS FAMILY

14a. [12] Flowers slipper-shaped with a rounded toe; leaves more than 1; functional stamens 2. **Cypripediaceae**, LADY'S SLIPPER FAMILY
14b. Flowers, if slipper-shaped, the toe pointed and leaf solitary; functional stamens 1. **Orchidaceae**, ORCHID FAMILY

15a. [11] Perianth of 6 chaffy or scalelike similar segments, hardly petallike, but arranged in 2 alternating groups of 3; grasslike plants. **Juncaceae**, RUSH FAMILY
15b. Perianth segments petal- or sepallike, not chaffy or scalelike . . . . . . (16)

16a. [15] Tepals minute, greenish; stamens sessile; carpels separating as units at maturity; annual, or perennial from a rhizome; grasslike plants of alkaline flats and mountain fens. **Juncaginaceae**, ARROWGRASS FAMILY
16b. Not as above . . . . (17)

17a. [16] Outer and inner perianth segments strongly differentiated in color or size . . . . (18)
17b. Outer and inner perianth segments similar (tepals) . . . . (20)

18a. [17] Petals less than 2 cm long, all purple or 2 blue, 1 white. **Commelinaceae**, SPIDERWORT FAMILY
18b. Petals over 2 cm long, white or rose-colored . . . . (19)

19a. [18] Leaves broadly ovate, in a whorl of 3; flowers white, with green sepals. **Trilliaceae**, TRILLIUM FAMILY
19b. Leaves linear, alternate; flowers white or rose, with a prominent gland of colored hairs. **Calochortaceae**, MARIPOSA FAMILY

20a. [17] Flowers in umbels subtended by a group of papery bracts; stem arising from a bulb. **Alliaceae**, ONION FAMILY

20b. Flowers not in umbels; stems from fibrous roots, rhizomes, or bulbs. (21)

21a. [20] Low, weak plants rooted in mud; flowers blue or yellow; stamens 3; leaves linear or narrowly oval. **Pontederiaceae**, PICKERELWEED FAMILY

21b. Not as above . . . . (22)

22a. [21] Inner tepals with a prominent gland at the base; ovary with prominent styles; carpels separate part way down. **Melanthiaceae**, FALSE HELLEBORE FAMILY

22b. Tepals without glands, or the gland small and indistinct; ovary usually without styles (don't confuse these with separate stigmas); carpels united . . . (23)

23a. [22] Leaves basal; if not, then the flowers large and showy. **Liliaceae**, LILY FAMILY

23b. Leaves alternate, cauline; flowers small, 2 cm or less . . . . (24)

24a. [23] Inflorescence a terminal raceme or panicle; tepals white, wide spreading. **Convallariaceae**, MAYFLOWER FAMILY

24b. Inflorescence axillary or terminal, flowers solitary or a few; flowers bell-shaped, tepals yellowish. **Uvulariaceae**, BELLWORT FAMILY

KEY E. WOODY DICOTS

(See Key C for woody vines)

1a. Leaves minute (less than 5 mm long), scalelike, overlapping, and appressed to the stem. **Tamaricaceae**, TAMARISK FAMILY

1b. Leaves larger and otherwise not as above . . . . (2)

2a. [1] Leaves covered by silvery or brownish peltate scales. **Elaeagnaceae**, OLEASTER FAMILY

2b. Leaves not covered by peltate scales . . . . (3)

3a. [2] Leaves and branches opposite . . . . (4)

3b. Leaves and branches alternate or scattered . . . . (16)

4a. [3] Fruit a samara . . . . (5)

4b. Fruit otherwise (or fruits not present) . . . . (6)

5a. [4] Leaves pinnately veined and pinnately compound, with a leathery texture. *Fraxinus*, in **Oleaceae**, OLIVE FAMILY

5b. Leaves palmately veined, simple or compound (*Negundo* sometimes has 5 leaflets, thus pinnately compound); leaves not leathery. **Aceraceae**, MAPLE FAMILY

6a. [4] Leaves palmately lobed or compound . . . . (7)

6b. Leaves neither palmately lobed nor palmately compound . . . . (9)

7a. [6] Terminal bud long-pointed, not protected by overlapping scales; fruit a berry. *Viburnum*, in **Caprifoliaceae**, HONEYSUCKLE FAMILY

7b. Terminal bud blunt or merely acute, covered by overlapping scales . . (8)

8a. [7] Leaves pinnately compound. *Fraxinus*, in **Oleaceae**, OLIVE FAMILY

8b. Leaves never simple nor leathery. **Aceraceae**, MAPLE FAMILY

9a. [6] Leaves evergreen . . . . (10)

9b. Leaves deciduous . . . . (12)

10a. [9] Leaves entire, paler beneath; plants of subalpine fens and pond margins. *Kalmia*, in **Ericaceae**, HEATH FAMILY

10b. Leaves serrulate or crenate, not pale beneath . . . . (11)

11a. [10] Leaves elliptic; low, spreading shrubs, leaves spreading in one plane; flowers small, axillary, reddish. **Celastraceae**, STAFFTREE FAMILY

11b. Leaves broadly oval; creeping plant with only slightly woody stems; flowers in pairs, pendent from an erect stalk. *Linnaea*, in **Caprifoliaceae**, HONEYSUCKLE FAMILY

12a. [9] Leaves linear, with smaller leaves fascicled in the axils; leaves glabrous, appearing terete, the margins tightly revolute; flowers white; restricted to gypsum soils. **Frankeniaceae**, FRANKENIA FAMILY

12b. Leaves broader, not in axillary fascicles . . . . (13)

13a. [12] Leaves pinnately compound. *Sambucus*, in **Caprifoliaceae**, HONEYSUCKLE FAMILY

13b. Leaves simple . . . . (14)

14a. [13] Twigs red; buds not covered by scales; leaves oval, ± parallel-veined; flowers in compound cymes. **Cornaceae**, DOGWOOD FAMILY

14b. Twigs not red; buds scaly; leaves and flowers not as above . . . . (15)

15a. [14] Bark exfoliating; leaves oblong or oval, commonly distinctly hairy; flowers white, waxy; fruit a dry capsule. **Hydrangeaceae**, HYDRANGEA FAMILY

15b. Bark not exfoliating; leaves ovate; if oblong, then glabrous or very minutely hairy, sometimes slightly lobed. **Caprifoliaceae**, HONEYSUCKLE FAMILY

16a. [3] Leaves compound . . . . (17)

16b. Leaves simple . . . . (25)

17a. [16] Leaves spine-margined, evergreen (resembling holly); inner bark yellow. **Berberidaceae**, BARBERRY FAMILY

17b. Leaves not as above . . . . (18)

18a. [17] Leaves with 3 leaflets; stems never prickly (Caution! Poison ivy is in this category) . . . . (19)

18b. At least some leaves not trifoliolate, usually pinnately compound (stems may be prickly) . . . . (20)

19a. [18] Low shrub less than 1 m tall; fruit an ivory-white, hard berry. **Anacardiaceae**, SUMAC FAMILY

19b. Small tree; fruit a disk-shaped samara. *Ptelea*, in **Rutaceae**, RUE FAMILY

20a. [18] Leaves even-pinnately compound (lacking a terminal leaflet) . . (21)

20b. Leaves odd-pinnately compound . . . . (22)

21a. Trees, never with thorns. **Sapindaceae**, SOAPBERRY FAMILY

21b. Shrubs, sometimes with thorns. **Fabaceae**, PEA FAMILY

22a. [20] Fruit a legume; leaflets more than 9, entire. **Fabaceae**, PEA FAMILY

22b. Fruit not a legume; leaflets various, but if numerous, then serrate or with shallow lobes or auricles at the base of the leaflets . . . . (23)

23a. [22] Leaflets 11 or fewer; if more, then the pith not occupying a major portion of the stem section. **Rosaceae**, ROSE FAMILY

23b. Leaflets more than 11; branches stout, the pith occupying a major portion of the cross-section . . . . (24)

24a. [23] Leaflets serrate; fruits red, round, with a velvety surface. **Anacardiaceae**, SUMAC FAMILY

24b. Leaflets entire except for basal auricles; fruit an elongate samara with a central seed. **Simaroubaceae**, QUASSIA FAMILY

25a. [16] Stems with thorns or spines . . . . (26)

25b. Stems spineless . . . . (34)

26a. [25] Thorns often more than 1 cm long, formed by modification of whole branchlets . . . . (27)

26b. Thorns shorter, formed at the nodes (modified leaves or stipules) . . (32)

27a. [26] Leaves linear, often somewhat thick and succulent . . . . (28)

27b. Leaves not succulent, broader . . . . (29)

28a. [27] Rigid, short-branched, dense, low shrub less than 1 m tall, with narrowly oblong pale green leaves, the older branches rigid, thornlike; flowers small, white, with petals and sepals. **Crossosomataceae**, CROSSOSOMA FAMILY

28b. Shrubs either over 1 m tall, or not rigidly branched, with succulent or gray-farinose leaves; flowers lacking petals, subtended by characteristic bracts. **Chenopodiaceae**, GOOSEFOOT FAMILY

29a. [27] Thorns smooth, sharp, reddish, over 2 cm long, derived from branchlets but along the normal branches. *Crataegus*, in **Rosaceae**, ROSE FAMILY

29b. Thorns either terminating short branchlets, or representing stipules, at the leaf bases, less than 2 cm long . . . . (30)

30a. [29] Fruit a berry; petals united; leaves usually with indistinct lateral veins. **Lycium**, MATRIMONY-VINE; WOLFBERRY, in **Solanaceae**, NIGHTSHADE FAMILY

30b. Fruit not a berry; petals separate; leaves usually with distinct lateral veins. . . . . (31)

31a. [30] Leaves with 3 prominent veins; thorn a modified branchlet; low shrub. *Ceanothus*, in **Rhamnaceae**, BUCKTHORN FAMILY

31b. Leaves with pinnate venation; thorn replacing a stipule; introduced tree. *Maclura*, in **Moraceae**, MULBERRY FAMILY

32a. [26] Leaves linear; young twigs woolly tomentose. *Tetradymia*, in **Asteraceae**, SUNFLOWER FAMILY

32b. Leaves broader; young twigs not tomentose . . . . (33)

33a. [32] Leaves elliptic, entire, toothed, or spine-toothed; fruit elliptical. **Berberidaceae**, BARBERRY FAMILY

33b. Leaves ovate, lobed and toothed; fruit globose. **Grossulariaceae**, GOOSEBERRY FAMILY

34a. [25] Leaves pinnately lobed or spine-toothed, leathery; fruit an acorn. **Fagaceae**, OAK FAMILY

34b. Leaves not as above; fruit not an acorn . . . . (35)

35a. [34] Leaf blades unequal at the base (one side attached lower than the other). **Ulmaceae**, ELM FAMILY

35b. Leaf blades not unequal at the base . . . . (36)

36a. [35] Leaves broadly ovate-cordate or deeply 5-7-lobed, crenate; fruits juicy, blackberrylike (a fleshy catkin); introduced. **Moraceae**, MULBERRY FAMILY

36b. Not as above . . . . (37)

37a. [36] Leaves palmately lobed (sometimes shallowly) . . . . (38)
37b. Leaves not palmately lobed . . . . (40)

38a. [37] Foliage aromatic (sagebrush odor). **Asteraceae**, SUNFLOWER FAMILY
38b. Foliage not aromatic . . . . (39)

39a. [38] Stamens numerous; carpels few to numerous, separate; fruit dry; flowers never tubular. **Rosaceae**, ROSE FAMILY
39b. Stamens 5 or fewer; carpels 2, united, forming a fleshy berry; flowers often tubular. **Grossulariaceae**, GOOSEBERRY FAMILY

40a. [37] Leaf buds (in the leaf axils) with a single covering scale; leaves from narrowly linear to broadly lanceolate or elliptic. *Salix*, in **Salicaceae**, WILLOW FAMILY
40b. Not as above . . . . (41)

41a. [40] Petiole flattened perpendicular to the leaf face; leaves deltoid-serrate, evenly serrate, or crenulate. *Populus*, in **Salicaceae**, WILLOW FAMILY
41b. Petiole not flattened . . . . (42)

42a. [41] Either staminate or carpellate catkins present through most of the year (in *Alnus* the carpellate catkin is persistent and woody); leaves irregularly serrate; horizontal lenticels present on the trunk. **Betulaceae**, BIRCH FAMILY
42b. Catkins not present . . . . (43)

43a. [42] Flowers in heads, each flower cluster surrounded by an involucre; mostly low desert shrubs. **Asteraceae**, SUNFLOWER FAMILY
43b. Flowers not as above . . . . (44)

44a. [43] Desert shrubs with farinose pubescence. **Chenopodiaceae**, GOOSEFOOT FAMILY
44b. Not as above . . . . (45)

45a. [44] Leaves never with 3 prominent veins; flowers usually vase-shaped (but wide open in *Azaleastrum* and campanulate in *Gaultheria*); petals united, waxy. **Ericaceae**, HEATH FAMILY
45b. Not as above . . . . (46)

46a. [45] Leaves with 3 prominent veins (or, in *Rhamnus* and *Frangula*, with many parallel lateral veins), elliptic or ovate; stamens opposite the petals. **Rhamnaceae**, BUCKTHORN FAMILY
46b. Leaves variously toothed or lobed; stamens numerous or not opposite the petals (when in doubt, it is usually this choice; it is just difficult to write a key separating these families without flowers). **Rosaceae**, ROSE FAMILY

KEY F. HERBACEOUS DICOTS

1a. Cauline leaves in whorls . . . . (2)
1b. Cauline leaves not in whorls . . . . (6)

2a. Leaves in a single whorl of broad leaf blades at the top of the stem. **Cornaceae**, DOGWOOD FAMILY
2b. Leaves in several whorls along the stem . . . . (3)

3a. Stems square, usually with recurved hooks. **Rubiaceae**, MADDER FAMILY
3b. Stems not square, not armed . . . . (4)

4a. Plant prostrate; petals lacking. **Molluginaceae,** CARPETWEED FAMILY
4b. Plant erect; petals present . . . . (5)

5a. Plants tall, stout; leaves oblanceolate; flowers 4-merous, greenish. *Frasera,* in **Gentianaceae,** GENTIAN FAMILY
5b. Plants low, slender; leaves linear; flowers 5-merous, white. *Spergula,* in **Alsinaceae,** CHICKWEED FAMILY

6a. Flowers several to many, sessile in heads, each flower cluster surrounded or subtended by an involucre . . . . **Key F-1**
6b. Flowers not as above . . . . (7)

7a. Perianth none or of a single set of parts (tepals or sepals), these all much alike in color and texture . . . . **Key F-2**
7b. Perianth present, evidently double, the outer segments (sepals) and inner segments (petals) usually conspicuously different in texture, color, or both. . . . . (8)

8a. Petals separate . . . . **Key F-3**
8b. Petals united (at least at the base) . . . . (9)

9a. Corolla radially symmetrical . . . . **Key F-4**
9b. Corolla bilaterally symmetrical . . . . **Key F-5**

KEY F-1. (Flowers in heads with involucre)

1a. Leaves linear, all basal; head single, scapose; flowers pink, the head papery-textured; ovary superior. **Limoniaceae,** THRIFT FAMILY
1b. Not as above; ovary inferior . . . . (2)

2a. [1] Involucre papery or umbrellalike, consisting of a single, undivided cup; flowers obviously separate and not tightly confined by the involucre. **Nyctaginaceae,** FOUR-O'CLOCK FAMILY
2b. Involucre not papery or umbrellalike, the flower cluster confined in a dense head . . . . (3)

3a. Inflorescence a spike of inconspicuous flowers, below which is a circle of large white or pink petallike bracts, producing the effect of a single flower; leaves basal, fleshy; plant stoloniferous, pepper-scented. **Saururaceae,** LIZARD-TAIL FAMILY
3b. Plants not as above . . . . (4)

4a. [3] Corolla 4-lobed; stamens separate. **Dipsacaceae,** TEASEL FAMILY
4b. Corolla 5-lobed or strap-shaped or of both types; stamens with united anthers. **Asteraceae,** SUNFLOWER FAMILY

KEY F-2. (Perianth absent or of tepals)

1a. Plants dioecious . . . . (2)
1b. Plants not dioecious . . . . (4)

2a. Leaves simple, not lobed or compound. **Amaranthaceae,** AMARANTH FAMILY
2b. Leaves lobed or compound . . . . (3)

3a. [2] Staminate flowers in racemes, carpellate in clusters; fruit nutlike; leaves digitately compound with narrow serrate leaflets. *Cannabis,* in **Cannabaceae,** HOPS FAMILY

3b. All flowers in open panicles; achenes ribbed, in clusters; leaves ternately compound with small palmately lobed leaflets. **Coptaceae**, MEADOWRUE FAMILY

4a. [1] Ovary inferior . . . . (5)
4b. Ovary superior . . . . (9)

5a. [4] Ovary with 2 locules, 1 ovule in each; fruit 2-seeded . . . . (6)
5b. Ovary with 1 locule, this with 1-2 ovules (or ovary with 1-3 locules but only 1 locule containing an ovule); fruit 1-seeded . . . . (7)

6a. [5] Petals united at the base; leaves opposite or whorled; flowers in cymes, never umbels. **Rubiaceae**, MADDER FAMILY
6b. Petals separate; leaves alternate or basal; flowers in umbels. **Apiaceae/Umbelliferae**, PARSLEY FAMILY

7a. [5] Leaves alternate, glaucous; flowers greenish-white; fruit a drupe. **Santalaceae**, SANDALWOOD FAMILY
7b. Leaves opposite; flowers white or pink; fruit an achene . . . . (8)

8a. [7] Leaves simple, entire; flowers pinkish or flesh-colored; fruits hard and bony or with papery wings. **Nyctaginaceae**, FOUR-O'CLOCK FAMILY
8b. Leaves pinnately lobed or divided; flowers white; fruits provided with a delicate parachute of feathery bristles. **Valerianaceae**, VALERIAN FAMILY

9a. [4] Carpels separate, 2-many in each flower (if 1, the fruit a fleshy several-seeded berry); stamens usually numerous . . . . (10)
9b. Carpels solitary or several united; stamens 1-many (usually not over 10 in most families) . . . . (12)

10a. Carpels enclosed in a 4-angled calyx cup; leaves with stipules; flowers in a dense head. **Sanguisorba**, BURNET, in **Rosaceae**, ROSE FAMILY
10b. Carpels not enclosed in the calyx; leaves lacking stipules; flowers not in a dense head . . . . (11)

11a. [10] Carpels consisting of dehiscent, several-seeded follicles (in *Actaea* a berry). **Helleboraceae**, HELLEBORE FAMILY
11b. Carpels consisting of 1-seeded indehiscent achenes. **Ranunculaceae**, BUTTERCUP FAMILY

12a. [10] Ovary with 2 or more locules . . . . (13)
12b. Ovary with 1 locule . . . . (18)

13a. [12] Plants with milky juice. **Euphorbiaceae**, SPURGE FAMILY
13b. Plants without milky juice . . . . (14)

14a. [13] Flowers unisexual; ovary on a stalk (in this group the flowers are reduced to single stamens on single gynoecia, but the stamens and gynoecium are surrounded by a cuplike involucre that resembles a perianth). **Euphorbiaceae**, SPURGE FAMILY
14b. Flowers perfect . . . . (15)

15a. [14] Leaves opposite or whorled, entire; stamens 1-many (rarely 2); flowers axillary, solitary, or in small clusters . . . . (16)
15b. Leaves alternate or crowded at the base of the stem, usually toothed; stamens 2; flowers in terminal spikes or racemes . . . . (17)

16a. [15] Calyx lobes hooded, with a subapical, prolonged appendage; capsule circumscissile; plants perennial, prostrate, succulent. **Aizoaceae**, FIG-MARIGOLD FAMILY

16b. Calyx lobes not as above; capsule not circumscissile. **Alsinaceae**, CHICKWEED FAMILY

17a. [15] Perennials; flowers in spikes; fruit several-seeded. *Besseya*, in **Scrophulariaceae**, FIGWORT FAMILY

17b. Annuals; flowers in racemes; fruit 2-seeded (1 seed in each locule. *Lepidium*, in **Brassicaceae/Cruciferae**, MUSTARD FAMILY

18a. [12] Ovary with several-many ovules; fruit a capsule, several- to many-seeded . . . . (19)

18b. Ovary with 1 ovule; fruit a 1-seeded achene or utricle . . . . (20)

19a. [18] Perianth of united tepals, pink; leaves oblong, glaucous. *Glaux*, in **Primulaceae**, PRIMROSE FAMILY

19b. Perianth of separate tepals; leaves otherwise. **Alsinaceae**, CHICKWEED FAMILY

20a. [18] Leaves with stipules either papery or sheathing the stem . . . . . (21)

20b. Stipules none or not sheathing the stem . . . . (22)

21a. [20] Leaves opposite; stipules papery. *Paronychia*, in **Alsinaceae**, CHICKWEED FAMILY

21b. Leaves alternate; stipules united around the stem in a sheath just above the nodes. **Polygonaceae**, BUCKWHEAT FAMILY

22a. [20] Conspicuous, persistent stipules present; leaves opposite . . . . . (23)

22b. Stipules lacking; leaves usually alternate (except in a few Amaranthaceae). . . . . (24)

23a. [22] Plants small, with spreading, prostrate, or densely caespitose stems rarely over 30 cm tall; stinging hairs not present. **Alsinaceae**, CHICKWEED FAMILY

23b. Plants with erect stems usually over 30 cm tall; stinging hairs present. **Urticaceae**, NETTLE FAMILY

24a. [22] Flowers perfect, the flower clusters subtended by a cuplike involucre; stamens 6-9; fruit an achene. **Polygonaceae**, BUCKWHEAT FAMILY

24b. Flowers perfect or unisexual but not subtended by a cuplike involucre; stamens 1-5; fruit an achene or utricle . . . . (25)

25a. [24] Bracts and perianth ± papery or membranaceous. **Amaranthaceae**, AMARANTH FAMILY

25b. Bracts and perianth herbaceous to fleshy . . . . (26)

26a. [25] Style and stigma 1; leaves alternate and entire; fruit an achene; annuals. *Parietaria*, in **Urticaceae**, NETTLE FAMILY

26b. Styles and stigmas 1-3 (but, if 1, the leaves toothed); fruit a utricle; annuals or perennials; weedy species, often coarse and scurfy-pubescent. **Chenopodiaceae**, GOOSEFOOT FAMILY

KEY F-3. (Petals present, separate)

1a. Stamens alternating with branched staminodia with terminal yellow antherlike glands. **Parnassiaceae**, GRASS-OF-PARNASSUS FAMILY

1b. Stamens lacking alternating branched staminodia . . . . (2)

2a. Sepals and petals 3, petals shorter than sepals; ovary superior, fruit a schizocarp of 3 nutlets; delicate wetland plants with pinnatifid leaves. **Limnanthaceae**, MEADOWFOAM FAMILY

2b. Floral parts not in 3s; otherwise not as above . . . . (3)

3a. [2] Ovary inferior, at least part of the lower half fused to the hypanthium or calyx tube . . . . (4)

3b. Ovary superior (if hypanthium is present, the ovary may seem to be inferior, but upon dissection it is seen not to be imbedded in the hypanthium tissues, cf. rose hip) . . . . (9)

4a. [3] Prostrate succulent herbs with rounded oblanceolate, thick leaves; stamens variable in number; petals yellow. *Portulaca*, in **Portulacaceae**, PURSLANE FAMILY

4b. Not prostrate, succulent herbs; otherwise not as above. . . . . (5)

5a. [4] 2 or more styles present. **Saxifragaceae**, SAXIFRAGE FAMILY

5b. Only 1 style present (stigmas may be lobed) . . . . (6)

6a. [5] Foliage sand-papery, with minutely barbed hairs. **Loasaceae**, LOASA FAMILY

6b. Plants lacking barbed hairs . . . . (7)

7a. [6] Stamens 2, 4, or 8; petals 2 or 4; style 1, locules usually 4 (2 in *Circaea*). **Onagraceae**, EVENING-PRIMROSE FAMILY

7b. Stamens 5, rarely 4; petals usually 5; styles 2 or more; locules 2-6. . . (8)

8a. [7] Locules 4-6; fruit a several-seeded berry; leaves basal, ternately compound. **Araliaceae**, GINSENG FAMILY

8b. Locules 2; fruit dry, separating into 2, 1-seeded mericarps. **Apiaceae/Umbelliferae**, PARSLEY FAMILY

9a. [2] Flowers asymmetrical; petals 4-7, toothed or cleft; stamens numerous, inserted on one side of the flower; leaves pinnatifid. **Resedaceae**, MIGNONETTE FAMILY

9b. Not as above . . . . (10)

10a. [9] Corolla bilaterally symmetrical . . . . (11)

10b. Corolla radially symmetrical . . . . (17)

11a. [10] Leaves pinnately or palmately compound . . . . (12)

11b. Leaves simple, entire, to deeply lobed or pinnatifid, but never truly compound . . . . (14)

12a. [11] Sepals 2, very minute and scalelike; corolla spurred; leaves greatly dissected. **Fumariaceae**, FUMITORY FAMILY

12b. Sepals 4 or 5; corolla not or very inconspicuously spurred; leaves once or twice compound . . . . (13)

13a. [12] Ovary with 1 placenta; petals 5 (a banner, 2 wings, and a keel that consists of 2 partly united petals enclosing the stamens and style); flowers usually shaped like those of sweet-pea. **Fabaceae/Leguminosae**, PEA FAMILY

13b. Ovary with 2 placentae on opposite sides of the ovary; petals 4; stamens exserted. **Capparaceae**, CAPER FAMILY

14a. [11] Stamens many; carpels more than 1; capsule dehiscing along 1 suture (thus a follicle). **Helleboraceae**, HELLEBORE FAMILY

14b. Stamens 10 or fewer; ovary of a single or several united carpels; fruit a dehiscent capsule . . . . (15)

15a. [14] Flowers not spurred, but with a larger upper petal (the banner). **Polygalaceae**, MILKWORT FAMILY

15b. Flowers spurred . . . . (16)

16a. [15] 1 sepal spurred, petaloid (only 3 present); ovary with 5 locules; flower shaped like a gnome's slipper. **Balsaminaceae**, JEWELWEED FAMILY

16b. Sepals not spurred (5 sepals present), but a petal prominently spurred; ovary with 1 locule and 3 parietal placentae. **Violaceae**, VIOLET FAMILY

17a. [10] Stamens of the same number as the petals and opposite them . (18)

17b. Stamens fewer or more numerous than the petals, or, if the same number, then alternate with them . . . . (20)

18a. [17] Sepals, petals, and stamens each 6 in number, 3 of the sepals petallike; leaf margins spiny. **Berberidaceae**, BARBERRY FAMILY

18b. Sepals, petals, and stamens 2-5 (sepals rarely 6); branches and leaves spineless . . . . (19)

19a. [18] Styles and stigmas 1; sepals usually 5. **Primulaceae**, PRIMROSE FAMILY

19b. Styles and stigmas 2 or more; sepals usually 2. **Portulacaceae**, PURSLANE FAMILY

20a. [17] Ovary deeply lobed; plants with glandular dots, very strongly scented; floral parts in 4s. *Thamnosma*, in **Rutaceae**, RUE FAMILY

20b. Plants not as above . . . . (21)

21a. [20] Ovary 1 (a single unit) with 1 locule . . . . (22)

21b. Ovaries more than 1 (several separate units), or, if 1, then with 2 or more locules . . . . (36)

22a. [21] Stamens 13 or more . . . . (23)

22b. Stamens 12 or fewer . . . . (29)

23a. [22] Ovary simple (of a single carpel having 1 placenta, 1 style, 1 stigma; many such ovaries may be present in a single flower) . . . . (24)

23b. Ovary compound (2 or more placentae, styles, or stigmas) . . . . (25)

24a. [23] Fruit a 1-seeded achene. **Ranunculaceae**, BUTTERCUP FAMILY

24b. Fruit a several-seeded, dehiscent follicle or a fleshy berry. **Helleboraceae**, HELLEBORE FAMILY

25a. [23] Placenta free-central or basal. **Portulacaceae**, PURSLANE FAMILY

25b. Placentae parietal . . . . (26)

26a. [25] Ovary with 2 parietal placentae; plants usually viscid and ill-smelling. **Capparaceae**, CAPER FAMILY

26b. Ovary with 3 or more placentae; plant not viscid nor ill-smelling . . . (27)

27a. [26] Leaves simple, alternate, entire; flowers of 2 kinds, conspicuous ones with large yellow petals and many stamens, and inconspicuous, cleistogamous, axillary ones lacking petals. **Cistaceae**, ROCKROSE FAMILY

27b. Plants not as above . . . . (28)

28a. [27] Leaves opposite, entire, with minute translucent dots (hold up to the light); juice not milky; leaves and petals often with black marginal dots. **Hypericaceae**, ST. JOHNSWORT FAMILY

28b. Leaves alternate, toothed or lobed, without translucent dots; juice milky; calyx forced off intact as a cone by the swelling petals; flowers white or cream-colored, rarely yellow or orange. **Papaveraceae**, POPPY FAMILY

29a. [22] Gynoecium a single carpel with 1 placenta, style, and stigma . . (30)
29b. Gynoecium compound (more than 1 placenta, style, or stigma) . . . . (31)

30a. [29] Stamens and petals attached to the rim of the calyx tube (hypanthium). **Rosaceae**, ROSE FAMILY
30b. Stamens and petals not attached to the calyx tube. **Fabaceae/Leguminosae**, PEA FAMILY

31a. [29] Petals inserted on the throat of a bell-shaped or tubular calyx. **Lythraceae**, LOOSESTRIFE FAMILY
31b. Petals inserted on the receptacle; calyx of separate or united sepals . (32)

32a. [31] Ovules attached to base of ovary or to a free-central placenta (never parietal) . . . . (33)
32b. Ovules attached to 2 or more parietal placentae . . . . (35)

33a. [32] Calyx of united sepals; petals with claws. **Caryophyllaceae**, PINK FAMILY
33b. Calyx of separate sepals; petals not stalked . . . . (34)

34a. Sepals 2 or numerous; stamens commonly opposite the petals, sometimes fewer than the petals, sometimes numerous; leaves commonly basal and succulent. **Portulacaceae**, PURSLANE FAMILY
34b. Sepals usually 5; stamens not opposite the petals, usually 5 or 10 (rarely 3); leaves usually opposite, not especially succulent. **Alsinaceae**, CHICKWEED FAMILY

35a. [32] Ovary with 2 parietal placentae; sepals and petals 4 each. **Capparaceae**, CAPER FAMILY
35b. Ovary with 3-5 parietal placentae; sepals and petals 5. **Hypericaceae**, ST. JOHNSWORT FAMILY

36a. [21] Plants with milky juice or stinging hairs; ovary stipitate, exserted from the cyathium. **Euphorbiaceae**, SPURGE FAMILY
36b. Plants without milky juice or stinging hairs . . . . (37)

37a. [36] Flower parts in 2s or 4s. **Brassicaceae/Cruciferae**, MUSTARD FAMILY
37b. Flower parts in 5s or numerous . . . . (38)

38a. [37] Leaves trifoliolate, acrid tasting. **Oxalidaceae**, WOOD SORREL FAMILY
38b. Leaves not trifoliolate nor acrid tasting . . . . (39)

39a. [38] Stamens united in a column around the styles. **Malvaceae**, MALLOW FAMILY
39b. Stamens not united in a column around the styles . . . . (40)

40a. [39] Leaves linear or oblong, succulent. **Crassulaceae**, STONECROP FAMILY
40b. Leaves not as above . . . . (41)

41a. [40] Stamens numerous . . . . (42)
41b. Stamens not more than 10 . . . . (44)

42a. [41] Leaves elliptic, with translucent dots and often minute, black, marginal dots on leaves and petals; stamens tending to be in 5 groups; fruit a capsule. **Hypericaceae**, ST. JOHNSWORT FAMILY

42b. Leaves and stamens not as above; fruit an achene . . . . (43)

43a. [42] Stipules lacking; hypanthium not developed. **Ranunculaceae**, BUTTERCUP FAMILY

43b. Stipules present; hypanthium always developed. **Rosaceae**, ROSE FAMILY

44a. [41] Petals waxy; anthers opening by terminal pores; leaves often leathery. **Pyrolaceae**, WINTERGREEN FAMILY

44b. Petals not waxy; anthers opening by slits . . . . (45)

45a. [44] Fruit 5-carpellate, separating at maturity into 5, 1-seeded segments (mericarps) . . . . (46)

45b. Fruit not 5-carpellate, or, if so, not separating into mericarps . . . . . (47)

46a. [45] Flowers pink or white; mericarps not spiny. **Geraniaceae**, GERANIUM FAMILY

46b. Flowers yellow; pericarps stoutly spiny. **Zygophyllaceae**, CALTROP FAMILY

47a. [45] Petals yellow, copper, or blue, falling within a few hours; capsule 10-locular (5 locules each with an additional septum). **Linaceae**, FLAX FAMILY

47b. Petals white, yellow, or pink-purple, not fugacious; capsule not as above (48)

48a. [47] All leaves opposite, with scarious stipules; stem glandular-hairy; low, prostrate-spreading plants of mud flats in the piedmont valleys. *Bergia*, in **Elatinaceae**, WATERWORT FAMILY

48b. Plants not as above . . . . (49)

49a. [48] Calyx completely free from the ovary but tightly surrounding it; petals mounted on the calyx tube. **Lythraceae**, LOOSESTRIFE FAMILY

49b. Calyx fused to the lower part of the ovary only; petals on the margin of a hypanthium. **Saxifragaceae**, SAXIFRAGE FAMILY

KEY G-4. (Petals united; radially symmetrical)

1a. Plants with milky juice . . . . (2)

1b. Plants without milky juice . . . . (3)

2a. [1] Corolla bell-shaped, without special hornlike structures. **Apocynaceae**, DOGBANE FAMILY

2b. Corolla rotate, with a central body consisting of the fused stigmas and stamens; corona present, enclosing hornlike structures. **Asclepiadaceae**, MILKWEED FAMILY

3a. [1] Ovary superior . . . . (4)

3b. Ovary inferior or half-inferior . . . . (17)

4a. [3] Ovary deeply 2-lobed, circumscissile; corolla yellow, 7-12 mm long, the lobes longer than the tube. *Menodora*, in **Oleaceae**, OLIVE FAMILY

4b. Ovary not 2-lobed nor circumscissile . . . . (5)

5a. [4] Stamens more numerous than the corolla lobes, 6-many . . . . (6)

5b. Stamens as many as the corolla lobes or fewer . . . . (7)

6a. [5] Stamens many, united into a tube around the style. **Malvaceae**, MALLOW FAMILY

6b. Stamens 6-10, separate and distinct; anthers opening by pores at the basal end; petals waxy. **Pyrolaceae**, WINTERGREEN FAMILY

7a. [5] Stamens 5, opposite the petals; ovary with 1 locule; placenta basal or free-central. **Primulaceae**, PRIMROSE FAMILY
7b. Stamens alternate to the petals or fewer; ovary more than 1-loculed, or, if 1-loculed, then the placenta rarely basal or free-central . . . . (8)

8a. [7] Ovary 4-lobed, developing into 4 (or by abortion fewer), 1-seeded nutlets . . . . (9)
8b. Ovary not 4-lobed; fruit a capsule or berry, usually several-seeded. . . (10)

9a. Leaves alternate; stem not square in cross-section; not aromatic. **Boraginaceae**, BORAGE FAMILY
9b. Leaves opposite; stems square in cross-section. **Lamiaceae**, MINT FAMILY

10a. [8] Ovary with 1 locule . . . . (11)
10b. Ovary with 2 or more locules . . . . (13)

11a. [10] Leaves basal; flowers solitary, scapose; stoloniferous plants rooted in mud. *Limosella*, in **Scrophulariaceae**, FIGWORT FAMILY
11b. Not as above . . . . (12)

12a. [11] Leaves opposite or whorled, entire; style 1 or none; plants mostly glabrous; inflorescence not curled in the bud. **Gentianaceae**, GENTIAN FAMILY
12b. Leaves usually alternate (if opposite, then not entire); styles 2, or single and 2-cleft above; plants mostly hairy; inflorescence commonly curled in the bud. **Hydrophyllaceae**, WATERLEAF FAMILY

13a. [10] Stigma 3-lobed or style 3-branched; ovary with 3 locules. **Polemoniaceae**, PHLOX FAMILY
13b. Stigma entire or 2-lobed, or style 2-cleft; ovary usually with 2 locules (14)

14a. [13] Flowers yellow, in dense terminal spikes or racemes over 20 cm long; filaments hairy. *Verbascum*, in **Scrophulariaceae**, FIGWORT FAMILY
14b. Flowers variously colored, never in spikes or elongate racemes . . . . (15)

15a. [14] Styles 2, distinct, each one again 2-cleft; ovules 2 in each locule; flowers axillary, the corolla lavender, with darker pleats; foliage silky-hairy. **Convolvulaceae**, MORNINGGLORY FAMILY
15b. Style 1, or if 2, rarely separate to the base, never again 2-cleft; ovules usually more than 2 per locule; inflorescence various . . . . (16)

16a. [15] Style 1, the stigma entire or 2-lobed; fruit a capsule or berry. **Solanaceae**, NIGHTSHADE FAMILY
16b. Styles 2 or definitely 2-branched below the stigmas; fruit a capsule. **Hydrophyllaceae**, WATERLEAF FAMILY

17a. [3] Leaves ternately compound, basal; flowers in a few-flowered, tight umbellike cyme; delicate herbs. **Adoxaceae**, ADOXA FAMILY
17b. Not as above . . . . (18)

18a. [17] Leaves alternate or basal. **Campanulaceae**, BELLFLOWER FAMILY
18b. Leaves opposite or whorled . . . . (19)

19a. [18] Stem creeping, slightly woody; leaves opposite, crenate; flowers 2, pink, pendent from an erect stalk. *Linnaea*, in **Caprifoliaceae**, HONEYSUCKLE FAMILY
19b. Stem erect or sprawling, herbaceous; leaves opposite or whorled, entire; flowers white, minute, in cymes. **Rubiaceae**, MADDER FAMILY

KEY F-5. (Petals united; bilaterally symmetrical)

1a. Corolla with 3 petals united at the base by their narrowed claws, the other 2 minute, glandlike; fruit globose, spiny. **Krameriaceae**, RATANY FAMILY

1b. Not as above . . . . (2)

2a. Ovary superior . . . . (3)

2b. Ovary inferior . . . . (7)

3a. [2] Stem 4-angled; leaves opposite . . . . (4)

3b. Stem not 4-angled; leaves opposite, alternate, or basal . . . . (5)

4a. [3] Corolla usually strongly 2-lipped; style arising from the base of the gynoecium between the nutlets; foliage usually with a minty odor. **Lamiaceae**, MINT FAMILY

4b. Corolla open, flat, from a narrow tube; style terminal; foliage never with a minty odor. **Verbenaceae**, VERVAIN FAMILY

5a. [3] Corolla papery; leaves basal; inflorescence a spike; fruit a circumscissile capsule (dehiscent as one would open a soft-boiled egg). **Plantaginaceae**, PLANTAIN FAMILY

5b. Corolla not papery; otherwise not as above . . . . (6)

6a. [5] Calyx split to the base along the lower side; corolla 3-5 cm long and nearly as wide; fruit woody, with 2 long curved claws. **Martyniaceae**, UNICORN PLANT FAMILY

6b. Calyx not split to the base on the lower side; corolla various; fruit not as above. **Scrophulariaceae**, FIGWORT FAMILY

7a. [2] Flowers not spurred or gibbous-based but highly colored, red, or blue-and-white striped. *Lobelia*, in **Campanulaceae**, BELLFLOWER FAMILY

7b. Flowers gibbous-based, white or cream-colored. **Valerianaceae**, VALERIAN FAMILY

FERNS AND FERN ALLIES

1a. Plants floating on the water, about 1 cm long, with minute, sessile, 2-lobed leaves arranged on 2 sides of the stems, giving a braided appearance. **Salviniaceae**, WATERFERN FAMILY

1b. Plants not as above . . . . (2)

2a. Stems jointed, hollow, green (except the fertile stems of *Equisetum arvense*, which are yellowish-brown), the nodes circled by sheaths. **Equisetaceae**, HORSETAIL FAMILY

2b. Stems not jointed, seldom green; sheaths absent . . . . (3)

3a. Plants aquatic, inhabiting lakeshores or actually submerged in ponds and lakes . . . . (4)

3b. Plants terrestrial, growing on soil or rocks . . . . (5)

4a. Leaves grasslike, their bases swollen, each bearing a pair of sporangia, the whole forming an onionlike bulb; plants submerged in shallow water of mountain lakes and ponds for the greater part of the growing season. **Isoëtaceae**, QUILLWORT FAMILY

4b. Leaves with distinct petioles and blades, the blades 4-parted, resembling a four-leaf clover; spores borne at the base of the plant in round, nutlike "sporocarps"; borders of ponds and sandy streamsides at lower altitudes. **Marsileaceae**, PEPPERWORT FAMILY

5a. Leaves very numerous, lanceolate or linear, often bractlike, sessile, spirally or oppositely arranged in 4-many ranks upon branched perennial stems (6)

5b. Leaves relatively few, broad or ± dissected (except in *Asplenium septentrionale*, the GRASSFERN, which has linear leaves), arising from an underground stem . . . . (7)

6a. Leaves minute (less than 3 mm long). **Selaginellaceae**, LITTLE CLUB-MOSS FAMILY

6b. Leaves larger (5 mm-1 cm or more long). **Lycopodiaceae**, CLUB-MOSS FAMILY

7a. Fronds (the "leaves" of ferns) linear, undivided except for a few narrow forks at the tip. *Asplenium septentrionale*, in **Aspleniaceae**, SPLEENWORT FAMILY

7b. Fronds broader, ± dissected (fernlike) . . . . (8)

8a. Not all fronds alike; entire fronds or branches modified for spore production . . . . (9)

8b. All fronds essentially alike, whether fertile or sterile . . . . (10)

9a. One entire branch of each frond completely altered in appearance, modified for spore production, the remainder of the frond green and not producing spores. **Ophioglossaceae**, ADDER'S TONGUE FAMILY

9b. Fronds of two kinds, the sterile ones short, yellow-green, with much-divided pinnae, their ultimate divisions blunt-tipped; fertile fronds taller, with pod-shaped pinnules. **Cryptogrammaceae**, ROCK BRAKE FAMILY

10a. Fronds with the lower pair of branches ± equalling the central branch or facing forward, creating the illusion of a 3-branched frond . . . . (11)

10b. Fronds distinctly pinnate, with 1 main axis from which the pinnae arise along the sides . . . . (12)

11a. Fronds tall and coarse, forming thicketlike stands; sporangia, when present, borne on the infolded edges of the pinnules. **Hypolepidaceae**, BRACKEN FAMILY

11b. Fronds small, delicate; sporangia, when present, borne on the flat undersides of the pinnules. *Gymnocarpium*, in **Athyriaceae**, LADYFERN FAMILY

12a. Fronds with submarginal sori, the indusium formed by the rolled or folded edge of the pinnule . . . . (13)

12b. Fronds with the sori on the face of the pinnule . . . . (14)

13a. Pinnules large, thin, smooth, green, fan-shaped or reniform. **Adiantaceae**, MAIDENHAIR FAMILY

13b. Pinnules small, often thickish, hairy or scaly or wax-coated below. **Sinopteridaceae**, LIPFERN FAMILY

14a. Frond merely deeply pinnatifid, the pinnae not separated from the stipe. **Polypodiaceae**, POLYPODY FAMILY

14b. Frond distinctly pinnate . . . . (15)

15a. Sori linear-elliptic, indusium curved, crescentic, or absent. **Athyriaceae**, LADYFERN FAMILY

15b. Sori round; indusia not crescent-shaped . . . . (16)

16a. Plants large, stout; indusium forming a somewhat circular shield, attached at the sinus. **Aspidiaceae**, SHIELDFERN FAMILY

16b. Plants small, delicate; indusia not as above . . . . (17)

17a. Indusium cuplike, attached centrally under sporangia, deeply cleft at maturity; pinnae thickish, widest above the middle. **Woodsiaceae**, WOODSIA FAMILY

17b. Indusium hoodlike, attached by its side at the base, not cleft at maturity; pinnae thin, broadest below the middle or at the base. *Cystopteris*, in **Athyriaceae**, LADYFERN FAMILY

ADIANTACEAE MAIDENHAIR FAMILY (ADI)

Maidenhairs are the most delicate and rarest of our ferns. The fronds are sometimes branched once dichotomously, with the pinnae radiating from one side of each branch like the comb of a Spanish mantilla. In our species the frond has one main branch, from which the pinnae arise on each side in a pyramidal form. The sori are arranged in a row underneath the folded margin of the pinnule. Most species are found in the tropical highlands.

ADIANTUM L. 1753 [the ancient name, meaning unwetted, shedding raindrops]

One species, **A. capillus-veneris** L., VENUS' HAIR FERN. Rare or infrequent, on dripping sandstone cliffs, Mesa de Maya.

ASPIDIACEAE SHIELDFERN FAMILY (ASD)

The term shieldfern alludes to the shape of the indusium, which covers the cluster of sori like a circular shield, attached by the middle. This family is very well represented in eastern North America but only a few species occur in the Rocky Mountain states. *Polystichum munitum*, a common species in the redwood forests of the Pacific Northwest, is imported to our area for use in floral arrangements. One's first examination of the sporangia of ferns under the microscope is an exciting experience. Each sporangium is shaped like a swollen coin, with easily ruptured faces and a rim of cells with differentially thickened walls, with the outer wall thin and the side and bottom ones thick. The interaction of wetting and drying causes the rim to fly open and reverse itself, scattering the spores far and wide.

1a. Frond simply pinnate, the pinnae spine-toothed, with an auricle at the upper base. **Polystichum**, CHRISTMASFERN

1b. Frond more than once-pinnate. **Dryopteris**, SHIELDFERN

DRYOPTERIS Adanson 1763 [Greek, *drys*, oak, + *pteris*, fern]. SHIELDFERN

1a. Frond bipinnatifid, the ultimate divisions blunt; indusium very prominent. **D. filix-mas** (L.) Schott, MALEFERN, **13A**. Infrequent, shaded canyons, foothills of Front Range. Formerly gathered for the oil in the rhizomes, from which a worm medicine was prepared; no longer gathered commercially, but could be exterminated easily and should be protected.

1b. Frond bipinnate, the ultimate divisions sharp-pointed; indusium not so prominent. **D. expansa** (C. Presl) Fraser-Jenkins & Jermy (*D. assimilis*). Rare, in rich subalpine forests, known only from Rocky Mountain National Park.

POLYSTICHUM Roth 1799 [Greek, *polys*, many, + *stichos*, row, referring to the sori]. CHRISTMASFERN

One species, **P. lonchitis** (L.) Roth [a name used by Pliny for some plant with a tongue-shaped leaf], HOLLYFERN, **13B**. Infrequent among rocks, alpine and subalpine.

ASPLENIACEAE SPLEENWORT FAMILY (ASL)

One of the crown jewels of the Colorado flora belongs to this family. D. M. Andrews, a Boulder nurseryman, discovered an *Asplenium* at the turn of this century, in horizontal crevices on the south-facing cliffs of Boulder Creek at the White Rocks, in the valley east of Boulder. It was described by Aven Nelson in 1904 as a new species, but its relationship is so close to the widely world-disjunctive *A. adiantum-nigrum* that controversy has surrounded it ever since. We know now that this species, or race, occurs in one other place in the United States (Zion Canyon, Utah) and in the Sierra Madre Occidental near Creel, in Chihuahua, Mexico. If recognized as a species in its own right, it would be on the federally endangered list because of its rarity. If united with *A. adiantum-nigrum* there would be no way to afford it this recognition. This fact illustrates a fallacy in the Endangered Species Act, which appears to pay no attention to the preservation of differing genotypes of widespread species, especially on the edges of their ranges.

ASPLENIUM L. 1753 [Greek, *asplenon*, a name used by Dioscorides for some fern supposed to cure spleen diseases]. SPLEENWORT

1a. Fronds linear, simple or only forked at the tips, in dense clumps in rock crevices, resembling dark green grass. **A. septentrionale** (L.) Hoffmann [northern], GRASSFERN, **18A**. Fairly common on arkosic rocks in the outer foothills. A species widely scattered in the mountains of the Northern Hemisphere, including the Altai, Alps, Pyrenees, the Caucasus, and in Scandinavia.

1b. Fronds with distinct pinnae, not grasslike . . . . (2)

2a. Fronds broadly triangular in outline, with branches bearing pinnae. **A. andrewsii** Nelson [for Darwin Maxon Andrews, 1869-1938, Boulder nurseryman], **14A**. Restricted to sandstone cliffs, White Rocks, BL. Protected.

2b. Fronds unbranched, with lateral oblong pinnae . . . . (3)

3a. Pinnae opposite. **A. resiliens** Kunze [resilient]. Sandstone cliffs, Mesa de Maya region.
3b. Pinnae alternate . . . . (4)

4a. Pinnae with a basal auricle (shallow lobe), at least on the leading edge. **A. platyneuron** Britton, Sterns & Poggenburg [flat vein]. EBONY SPLEENWORT. Sandstone cliffs and rimrock, BA, LA.
4b. Pinnae lacking any auricles. **A. trichomanes** L., MAIDENHAIR SPLEENWORT, **13C**. Infrequent, cliff crevices, canyons of Front Range foothills.

ATHYRIACEAE LADYFERN FAMILY (ATY)

The earmark of the ladyferns is in the shape of the indusium, which, instead of being round as in the shieldferns, is crescent- or comma-shaped. But the indusium varies from genus to genus in the family. In the Aspleniaceae the indusium is linear. These are indications of how important it is for students to learn the fine details of the sporangia, sori, indusium, and, in fact, the venation of ferns, since the sori are positioned at different points on the fronds vis-à-vis the veins of the pinnules.

1a. Fronds large, over 3 dm long, up to 15 cm or more wide. **Athyrium**, LADYFERN
1b. Fronds less than 3 dm long, up to about 10 cm wide . . . . (2)

2a. Fronds broadly triangular, with three main branches . . . . (3)
2b. Fronds pinnate. **Cystopteris**, BRITTLEFERN

3a. Pinnules oblong, not deeply toothed. **Gymnocarpium**, OAKFERN
3b. Pinnules tapered, deeply toothed or lobed. **Cystopteris**, BRITTLEFERN

ATHYRIUM Roth 1799 [Greek, *athyros*, doorless, the sporangia only tardily forcing back the margin of the indusium]. LADYFERN
1a. Indusium crescentic, usually plainly visible; frond well expanded, the pinnae not appearing crowded or directed sharply toward the apex of the frond; fronds few to a clump . . . . (2)
1b. Indusium rarely seen, minute, withering early; frond narrow, the pinnae rather crowded or directed sharply toward the frond apex. **A. distentifolium** Tausch. Subalpine screes (*A. alpestre* subsp. *americanum*).

2a. Indusium short, strongly recurved, sometimes almost circular, bearing marginal hairs as long as or longer than the indusium width. **A. filix-femina** (L.) Roth subsp. **cyclosorum** (Ruprecht) C. Christensen. Frequent in moist forests of lower altitudes, never at or above timberline.
2b. Indusium long, slightly curved, with marginal hairs shorter than the indusium width. **A. filix-femina** subsp. **angustum** (Willdenow) Clausen. Evidently rare, known from a single small colony near Sedalia.

CYSTOPTERIS Bernhardi 1805 [Greek, *cystis*, bladder, + *pteris*, fern]. BRITTLEFERN. (Key adapted from Lellinger, *Field Manual of Ferns*. 1985)
1a. Fronds broadly triangular, with three main branches. **C. montana** (Lamarck) Bernhardi. Rare and local in moist, rich spruce forests, on the Eastern Slope known from a collection near Mount Antero in the Collegiate Range.
1b. Fronds pinnate . . . . (2)

2a. Fronds compact, narrow, mostly (2.5)3-4 times longer than wide; basal pinnules sessile, truncate to obtuse at the base; indusia lanceolate . . . (3)
2b. Fronds lax, broad, mostly 2-2.5(3) times longer than wide; basal pinnules short-stalked to sessile, obtuse to cuneate at the base; indusia round to ovate . . . . (4)

3a. Spores echinate, appearing slightly spiny at 60x magnification. **C. fragilis** (L.) Bernhardi, **14D**. Our most common fern, from low to high altitudes. The stipes are produced in clusters and are very brittle. The following species have only recently been recognized as occurring in Colorado, and their distributions are not known. One other species may be expected here, since it occurs in northern New Mexico: *C. bulbifera* (L.) Bernhardi, BULBLET BLADDER-FERN, **14E**, in which the fronds are long-attenuate at the apex and sometimes bear small bulblets on the underside.
3b. Spores rugose-verrucose, appearing smooth at 60x magnification. **C. dickieana** Sim [for George Dickie, 1812-1892, Scottish algologist].

4a. Pinnules with a broad, uncut center; segments mostly rounded at the apex; frond pinnate-pinnatifid to 2(3)-pinnate-pinnatifid; basal pinnules cuneate in less divided forms, obtuse in more divided ones; usually on rock. **C. tenuis** (Michaux) Desvaux.
4b. Pinnules lacking a broad, uncut center; segments mostly acute at the apex; fronds 2-3-pinnate-pinnatifid; basal pinnules mostly cuneate at the base; plants usually on soil. **C. reevesiana** Lellinger.

GYMNOCARPIUM Newman 1851 [Greek, *gymno*, naked, + *carpos*, fruit]. OAKFERN

One species, **G. dryopteris** (L.) Newman subsp. **disjunctum** (Ruprecht) Sarvela, **14B**. Shaded woods and thickets, montane, subalpine.

CRYPTOGRAMMACEAE ROCK BRAKE FAMILY (CRG)

Our single genus, *Cryptogramma*, contains two species, one of them extremely common and the other extremely rare. These plants are known by their development of a special fertile frond in which the pinnules are converted to podlike sporangial units, with the pinnule margins rolled over the sori. The rare species, *C. stelleri*, instead of being densely tufted, is slender and rhizomatous, forming very few fronds and growing in the crevices of limestone cliffs. A prime area for one to discover this might be in the limestone areas of the Collegiate and Sangre de Cristo ranges.

CRYPTOGRAMMA R. Brown 1823 [Greek, *cryptos*, hidden, + *gramme*, a line, alluding to the lines of sporangia]. ROCK BRAKE

One species, fronds robust, crowded on a short rhizome; lower parts of the stipes persistent. **C. acrostichoides** R. Brown [like the genus *Acrostichum*]. Rocky places, montane to alpine [*C. crispa* subsp.].

EQUISETACEAE HORSETAIL FAMILY (EQU)

The horsetails belong to one of the most ancient lineages of land plants, abundantly found fossilized in the Coal Measures of the Paleozoic era. Their basic structures have changed relatively little over time. The deposition of mineral silica on the surface of the stems gives them the name of scouring rushes, and they served very nicely in scouring out pots and pans in colonial times, as they do now at modern-day campgrounds. What we see is the sporophyte only. The gametophytes are almost never encountered, since they are small, rarely produced, and are strictly underground.

1a. Green stems bearing numerous branches in whorls at the nodes (fertile, simple brown stems also belong here). **Equisetum**, HORSETAIL

1b. Green stems stout, simple or occasionally with a few short branches scattered irregularly on the main stem. **Hippochaete**, SCOURING-RUSH

EQUISETUM L. 1753 [Greek, *equus*, horse, + Latin, *seta*, bristle]. HORSETAIL

1a. Sterile stems with ascending branches, 4-angled; central cavity a fourth the diameter of the stem; rhizome with scattered, blackish tubers; fertile stems brown, abruptly wilting; stem smoothly tuberculate, the teeth in whorls of 3-5(6). **E. arvense** L., FIELD HORSETAIL, **16C**. Wet ditches and floodplains. The stems are of two kinds, branched and sterile, or brown, unbranched, and bearing a sporangiate cone at the apex. The latter are produced in early spring and soon wither.

1b. Stems with horizontal or gently down-curving branches, 3-angled; central cavity about half the stem diameter; rhizome without tubers; cone produced at the apex of the green, branched stem; stem sharply papillate, with whorls of 8-15 teeth. **E. pratense** Ehrhardt, MEADOW HORSETAIL. Wet spruce-fir forests, less common than the last.

HIPPOCHAETE Milde 1865 [Greek, *hippos*, horse, + *chaite*, mane] (formerly included in *Equisetum*). SCOURING-RUSH

1a. Stems slender, 5-12-angled and -grooved; sheaths loose, with fine-pointed persistent teeth; central cavity of stem usually half its diameter. **H. variegata** (Schleicher) Bruhin. Sand bars of streams.

1b. Stems stout, 16-48-angled and -grooved; sheaths loose or tight, the teeth persistent or deciduous; central cavity of the stem more than half its diameter . . . . (2)

2a. Stem dying after one season; sheaths lacking a dark band at base; cone rounded at apex. **H. laevigata** (A. Braun) Farwell [smooth], **16A**. Wet ground of ditches and streamsides.

2b. Stem enduring several years; sheaths commonly with a dark band at the base; cone pointed at the apex. **H. hyemalis** (L.) Bruhin subsp. **affinis** (A. Braun) Weber [of winter; related], **16B**. Similar habitats.

HYPOLEPIDACEAE BRACKEN FAMILY (HPL)

Bracken is a fern found almost everywhere in the world, in the tropics as well as the northern and southern temperate zones. Bracken forms an almost impenetrable brushland on the highlands of the Galápagos Islands. It is easily recognized as a large fern with three obvious main branches, and the sori are marginal on the pinnules and protected by their folded edges. Fiddleheads of bracken are said to be edible, but the enzyme thiaminase in bracken is very poisonous to livestock if much is ingested, either green or dry.

PTERIDIUM Gleditsch 1760 [diminutive of *Pteris*, another genus]. BRACKEN

One species, **P. aquilinum** (L.) Kuhn subsp. **lanuginosum** (Bongard) Hultén [of an eagle, from the wing-shaped fronds; woolly]. Dry, open woodlands. Our largest native fern.

ISOËTACEAE QUILLWORT FAMILY (ISO)

Identification of the quillworts is a technical task requiring examination of the megaspores with a high-powered dissecting microscope and comparison material of correctly named specimens. Mature plants are needed, which means collecting in late summer or fall, when the spores in the leaf bases are ripe, and the plants then tend to fall apart. Young culms of grasses, sedges, and burreeds may easily be mistaken for quillworts if they are submerged by seasonal high water at the margins of ponds.

ISOËTES L. 1753 [name used by Pliny for a species of *Sedum*]. QUILLWORT

1a. Megaspores with scattered low tubercles becoming joined to form low ridges. **I. bolanderi** Engelmann [for H. N. Bolander, 1831-1897, California botanist], **17D**. Small lakes and ponds, upper montane and subalpine.
1b. Megaspores with high, sharp spines and jagged ridges . . . . (2)

2a. Leaves strictly erect, rather stiff; megaspores 0.5-0.6 mm diameter, with long low ridges and micro-ornamentation of short spines joined at bases. **I. lacustris** L. Deep water of larger lakes. The plants are often washed ashore by wave action.
2b. Leaves somewhat recurved, rather flexible; megaspores 0.2-0.5 mm diameter, spiny with spines of two distinct sizes. **I. setacea** Lamarck subsp. **muricata** (Durieu) Holub. Known from an old collection from Pikes Peak, and more recently from Grand Lake in Rocky Mountain National Park.

LYCOPODIACEAE CLUB-MOSS FAMILY (LYC)

The spores of *Lycopodium* were once used as a fine baby powder and an inflammable powder for flash photography. In Scandinavia, where they are abundant ground cover in forests, lycopods are gathered in enormous quantities for ornamental Christmas greens. In Colorado they are so infrequent as to be considered in need of protection.

1a. Stem not creeping, the erect branches tightly bunched; sporangia in the axils of unmodified leaves, not in discrete cones. **Huperzia**, FIR CLUB-MOSS
1b. Stem creeping extensively, the erect branches not tightly bunched; spores produced in an elongate cone. **Lycopodium**, CLUB-MOSS

HUPERZIA Bernhardi 1801 [for Johann Peter Huperz, died 1816]. FIR CLUB-MOSS
One species, **H. selago** (L.) Bernhardi [the ancient generic name], **17B**. Local in rocky cirque-basins and cliffs near or above timberline (*Lycopodium*). A separate family, Huperziaceae, may be used for this species and its relatives.

LYCOPODIUM L. 1753 [Greek, *lycos*, wolf, + *pous*, paw]. CLUB-MOSS

1a. Leaves widely spreading or somewhat reflexed, rich green, 5-10 mm long, acute, regularly toothed; branches 10-15 mm wide. **L. annotinum** L. [a year old, from the marked separation of annual branches], STIFF CLUB-MOSS, **17A**. Infrequent in subalpine spruce forests and under willow thickets.
1b. Leaves ascending, yellowish-green, 3-7 mm long, sparingly toothed or entire; branches 3-7 mm wide. **L. dubium** Zoëga. Rare, upper subalpine and alpine.

MARSILEACEAE PEPPERWORT FAMILY (MSL)

Plants of *Marsilea* are very unfernlike and might be passed off as four-leaf clovers, but the venation is dichotomous-parallel. In late summer the sporocarps, hard, nutlike organs at the base of the plants, are conspicuous. The sporocarps of Nardoo, *M. drummondii*, of Australia, are edible and gathered by the aborigines, who taught the early explorers to use this wild food as a last resort against starvation in the outback.

MARSILEA L. 1753 [for Luigi Marsigli, 1658-1730, Italian naturalist]. PEPPERWORT

One species, **M. mucronata** A. Braun, HAIRY PEPPERWORT, **17C**. Edges of muddy streams and ponds at low altitudes on the plains and piedmont valleys. The plants become conspicuous in August and September when ponds dry up.

OPHIOGLOSSACEAE ADDER'S TONGUE FAMILY (OPH)

Most of the members of this family are rare subalpine and alpine species and should not be collected with their roots. Fortunately for them, they are exceedingly difficult to see in the field; one either stumbles on them or finds them only after much diligent searching. Populations are usually very small.

1a. Several dm tall, the green, sterile portion ± less triangular in gross outline, very delicately and finely dissected; fertile branch narrow, consisting of a spike of brown, spore-bearing branches. **Botrypus**, RATTLESNAKEFERN

1b. Small (15 cm or less tall), the green sterile portion unbranched or only pinnatifid; fertile branch short, yellowish-brown, sporangia in a grapelike cluster. **Botrychium**, GRAPEFERN

BOTRYCHIUM Swartz 1801 [Greek, *botrys*, cluster of grapes]. GRAPEFERN

(Key adapted from Wagner & Wagner, *Amer. Fern J.* 76:33-47. 1986)

1a. Usually over 5 cm high, with leathery, much-divided fronds. **B. multifidum** (Gmelin) Ruprecht subsp. **coulteri** (Underwood) Clausen [for J. M. Coulter, collector on the Hayden Surveys, 1872-1873], **15E**. Mountain meadows, long known from RT and recently discovered on the Western Slope in Rocky Mountain National Park. To be expected on the east base of the Park Range in North Park.

1b. Plants less than 5 cm tall; fronds merely pinnate or with the lower lobes ternate . . . . (2)

2a. Lower pinnae linear, lanceolate, or ovate, with a central or at least a basal midrib . . . . (3)

2b. Lower pinnae or pinnules lunulate, fan-shaped, wedge-shaped, or square, with flabellate venation, a central midrib lacking . . . . (6)

3a. Trophophore (sterile segment) broadly deltate, usually subsessile; pinnae linear; sporophore (fertile segment) divided near base into 2 or more major axes. **B. lanceolatum** (Gmelin) Ångström, **15C**. This and the remainder of the species are subalpine and alpine, infrequent, inconspicuous, and rarely collected except by those such as Peter Root, our Colorado field specialist with a "*Botrychium*-eye."

3b. Trophophore mostly oblong to ovate, subsessile to long-stalked; segments linear to oblong to spatulate; sporophores with only 1 major axis, or if more, the laterals arising well above the base . . . . (4)

4a. Pinnae usually well separated, linear to oblanceolate with pointed tips; basal pinnae mostly cleft into a smaller lower segment and larger upper segment; frond shiny green in life. **B. echo** W. Wagner [for Echo Lake].

4b. Pinnae usually approximate, oblong to ovate with rounded or blunt tips; basal pinnae not cleft in 2; luster various . . . . (5)

5a. Pinnae with few lobes, these mainly on the basal side; lowest pinnae mostly exaggerated, ascending and commonly subclasping; pinnae broadly adnate, strongly asymmetrical; frond dull gray in life. **B. hesperium** (Maxon & Clausen) Wagner & Lellinger [western].

5b. Pinnae with numerous lobes, these roughly equal in number on upper and basal sides; lowest pinnae symmetrical, mostly equal in length to those above; frond bright shiny green in life. **B. pinnatum** St. John.

6a. Apex of trophophore usually not deeply divided, commonly concave (in life); upper pinnae or lobes tending to be somewhat irregularly fused; sporophore arising at various positions, from ground level to near the apex; trophophore sessile to long-stalked. **B. simplex** E. Hitchcock, **15D**.

6b. Apex of trophophore usually deeply divided, mostly flat (in life); upper lateral pinnae and lobes regularly separated; sporophore attachment high on the common stalk; trophophore sessile to short-stalked . . . . (7)

7a. Pinnae lunate to broadly cuneate, the sides of the lower pinnae at a 90°-180° angle, remote to overlapping. **B. lunaria** (L.) Swartz, MOONWORT, **15B**. This is the most common species of the group.

7b. Pinnae cuneate to oblong, the sides of the pinnae at a 0°-90° angle, usually remote. **B. minganense** Victorin [of the Mingan Islands, Quebec].

BOTRYPUS Michaux 1803 [name derived from *Botrychium*]. RATTLESNAKEFERN

One species, **B. virginianus** (L.) Holub, **15A**. Infrequent and local, in cool, moist ravines of the foothills canyons (*Botrychium*). Collections should be avoided, since this is in danger of extinction.

POLYPODIACEAE POLYPODY FAMILY (PLP)

Until very recently, most of the true ferns were placed in this large "wastebasket" family, partly because of convenience, and partly because very important morphological and genetic information had not yet become available. This simplistic classification has now been abandoned and a large number of families are recognized. As a rule of thumb, the polypodies may be recognized by their disk-shaped sori that lack indusia.

POLYPODIUM L. 1753 [Greek, *polys*, many, + *pous*, foot]. POLYPODY

One species, **P. amorphum** Suksdorf [formless]. Boulders and cliff faces in the outer foothills.

SALVINIACEAE WATERFERN FAMILY (SVN)

Once one has seen a waterfern, there is no mistaking it a second time. However, these little floating plants do not look much like ferns. The entire plant is not much more than a centimeter long and has closely overlapping leaves in two ranks, appearing as if braided. Simple roots extend into the water. The leaves have a very small upper and a much larger lower lobe. The color is usually deep purplish in life, and more bluish when dried. Symbiotic colonies of blue-green algae live air spaces inside the leaves.

AZOLLA Lamarck 1783 [derivation unknown]. WATERFERN

One species, **A. mexicana** K. Presl. Floating on slow streams and oxbows along the lower South Platte River in the northeastern corner of Colorado.

SELAGINELLACEAE LITTLE CLUB-MOSS FAMILY (SEL)

This family contains the strange resurrection-plants of Texas and Mexico, that roll into balls when dry and revive spectacularly under humid conditions. As in the Isoëtaceae, the spores are of two sizes (micro- and megaspores). This difference is evident even with the hand-lens or naked eye. The orange-yellow sporangia are in the upper leaf-axils, the megasporangia containing no more than four spores and bulging irregularly by their contours. Microsporangia contain hundreds of very minute spores. The different spores produce male and female gametophytes, respectively.

Selaginella weatherbiana is a conspicuous plant, forming large mats on north-facing cliffs of the foothills canyons. It is endemic in the foothills from Larimer County to near Santa Fe, New Mexico. Probably it is an ancient relict from the Tertiary age, and it appears to have its closest relative in the mountains of north Africa. *S. selaginoides* is one for which we have a sight record only. Dr. Dieter Wilken collected some mosses from a canyon in the eastern Park Range of North Park a few years ago, and, having placed them in a terrarium for class use, he discovered that he had found the *Selaginella* for the first time in Colorado. However, by some strange accident, a specimen was not preserved, and we have never been able to locate it in the field again. Here is a challenge for someone.

SELAGINELLA P. Beauvois 1805 [diminutive of *selago*, ancient name for a club-moss]. LITTLE CLUB-MOSS

1a. Plants forming dense, erect tufts, not rooting along a creeping stem. **S. weatherbiana** Tryon [for C. A. Weatherby, 1875-1949, American fern specialist]. Endemic. Abundant on north-facing cliffs of the Front Range, and near the Great Sand Dunes.

1b. Plants creeping, rooting at intervals along the stem . . . . (2)

2a. Leaves thin and soft, without a dorsal groove; cone not 4-sided; sporophylls lax. **S. selaginoides** (L.) Link [like *Selaginella*; Linnaeus included this species in *Lycopodium*], **18C**. Marshy places by beaver ponds and wet spruce forests, east side Park Range.

2b. Leaves thick and firm, with a dorsal groove; cone 4-sided; sporophylls appressed . . . . (3)

3a. Leaves blunt, ciliate-margined but lacking a white hair-point. **S. mutica** D. C. Eaton [blunt], **18E**. Rocky, arid canyonsides.

3b. Leaves narrowed to a slender white hair-point . . . . (4)

4a. Creeping stems very short, the leaves curved upward, gray-green; fruiting branches erect, elongate, 4-angled. **S. densa** Rydberg [clumpy], **18B**. Common on rocks and soil, from the outer foothills to the tundra. By the inexperienced, this plant will be mistaken for the common hair-cap moss, *Polytrichum piliferum*, which has similar leaves but lacks the creeping branches.

4b. Stems elongate, the leaves not strongly upcurved, bright green; fruiting branches inconspicuous. **S. underwoodii** Hieronymus [for L. M. Underwood, 1853-1907, American fern specialist], **18D**. Moist, protected canyonsides.

SINOPTERIDACEAE LIPFERN FAMILY (SIN)

The name lipfern alludes to the fact that the margins of the pinnules curve over the sori, not in itself a really diagnostic character, since it is shared by other families. The family is essentially one of the dry tropics, only a few of them reaching Colorado in rocky steppe-desert and foothill sites. A variety of growth forms occur, some pinnate, others dichotomous or even triangular. The species often are distinguished by deposits of white or yellow wax, or various combinations of hairs and scales, on the stypes and pinnules.

1a. Fronds green and glabrous. **Pellaea**, CLIFF BRAKE
1b. Fronds either hairy or scaly, or with a white or yellow wax on the underside . . . . (2)

2a. Fronds with hairs or scales, not waxy beneath. **Cheilanthes**, LIPFERN
2b. Fronds waxy beneath . . . . (3)

3a. Fronds triangular, with a yellow wax beneath. **Cheilanthes**, LIPFERN
3b. Fronds widely branched, with very small ternate pinnules, white waxy beneath. **Argyrochosma**, LIPFERN

ARGYROCHOSMA Windham 1987 [Greek, *argyros*, silver, + *chosma*, flow, alluding to the white waxy coat on the pinnules]. LIPFERN

One species, **A. fendleri** (Kunze) Windham (*C. cancellata, Notholaena fendleri*), **14C**. Talus and cliff crevices of arid canyonsides. Windham, (*Amer. Fern J.* 7:37-41. 1987) has shown conclusively that this is not a *Cheilanthes*.

CHEILANTHES Swartz 1806 [Greek, *cheilos*, margin, + *anthos*, flower]. LIPFERN

1a. Frond triangular, yellow waxy beneath. **C. standleyi** Maxon [for P. C. Standley, 1884-1963, botanist of Chicago Field Museum, author of *Flora of New Mexico*]. Sandstone cliffs of the Mesa de Maya (*Notholaena*). This species obviously is not a *Cheilanthes*, but the group to which it belongs does not as yet have a generic name.
1b. Fronds simply pinnate . . . . (2)

2a. Fronds densely tomentose, at least below, the pinnules hairy above; rhizomes erect or decumbent but not long-creeping . . . . (3)
2b. Fronds glabrous except for scales; pinnules glabrous above; rhizomes slender, creeping . . . . (4)

3a. Scales present on rachises of pinnae; stipes usually scaly. **C. eatonii** Baker [for D. C. Eaton, 1834-1895, American fern specialist]. Cliffs of the Mesa de Maya, and Front Range canyons to CC.
3b. Fronds reddish-hairy beneath, lacking scales. **C. feei** Moore [for Antoine L. A. Fée, French pteridologist, 1789-1874]. Sandstone cliffs and overhangs, the most common species.

4a. Scales of frond rachises ciliate; rhizome scales persisting. **C. wootonii** Maxon [for E. O. Wooton, 1865-1945, New Mexican botanist, author, with Standley, of *Flora of New Mexico*]. Cliffs of Mesa de Maya.

4b. Scales not ciliate; rhizome scales deciduous. **C. fendleri** Hooker. On granitic rocks, foothills of Front Range, and Great Sand Dunes.

PELLAEA Link 1841 [Greek, *pellos*, dusky, from the dark stipes]. CLIFF BRAKE

1a. Stipes and rachises sparsely pilose, dull; pinnae long-stalked, the basal ones stalked 5-15 mm; fronds dimorphic, the fertile exceeding the sterile ones, which are often simple and cordate. **P. x atropurpurea** (L.) Link. An apogamous triploid derived from interspecific hybridization. In rock crevices of sedimentary formations from LR to BA and LA. Reports of the closely related *P. occidentalis* (E. Nelson) Rydberg, and *P. x suksdorfiana* Butters, in which the fronds are apparently monomorphic, need to be verified.

1b. Stipes and rachises glabrous or nearly so; pinnae sessile to short-stalked, the basal ones stalked 0-4 mm; fronds monomorphic . . . . (2)

2a. Fronds lanceolate, usually widest near the base; pinnae pinnate or bipinnate with more than 4 pairs of pinnules. **P. truncata** Goodding. Cliffs of canyons, known from Royal Gorge and Phantom Canyon near Cañon City.

2b. Fronds oblong or narrowly elliptic, widest near the middle; pinnae simple or ternate, rarely pinnate with up to 4 pairs of pinnules. **P. wrightiana** Hooker [for Charles Wright, 1811-1855, plant collector). Cliffs, Mesa de Maya.

WOODSIACEAE WOODSIA FAMILY (WDS)

This small family is characterized by having the indusium arising at the base of the sorus and arching over the sporangia. It splits down from the top into several narrow lobes that spread out in a stellate pattern around the sorus. *Woodsia* can be confused with *Cystopteris*, which, however, has an indusium attached at one side to form a hood. Our species are always associated with rock crevices.

WOODSIA R. Brown 1810 [for Joseph Woods, 1776-1864, English architect and botanist]

1a. Stems and fronds with stiffly spreading, multicellular hairs. **W. scopulina** D. C. Eaton [of rocks]. Rock crevices in cool canyons of the foothills.

1b. Stems and fronds lacking multicellular hairs . . . . (2)

2a. Indusium strongly ciliate; pinnules with broadly and shallowly incised lobes, appearing toothed . . . . (3)

2b. Indusium not ciliate, entire, fragmenting into several broad segments; pinnules with narrowly and usually deeply incised lobes, appearing somewhat lacerate; copiously glandular throughout, even on the indusium. **W. plummerae** Lemmon [for Lemmon's wife, Sarah A. Plummer]. Cliffs, Mesa de Maya.

3a. Stipes pale almost to the brown or dark brown base; margins of pinnules thickened. **W. mexicana** Fée. Rock crevices in cool canyons at lower altitudes than the next and in the southern counties.

3b. Stipes dark brown or dark reddish-brown at and above the base; pinnule margins thin. **W. oregana** D. C. Eaton. More common than the last.

GYMNOSPERMS

The gymnosperms are woody vascular plants that do not produce true flowers, but instead bear mega- and microsporangia on the open faces of sporophylls that are often grouped together in cones. In eastern Colorado these fall into two families, separated by the following key.

1a. Fruit a gray, berrylike cone, the scales fused together and only detectable by their protruding tips; shrubs or small trees with decussately arranged, scalelike leaves or flat sharp needles. **Cupressaceae**, CYPRESS FAMILY

1b. Fruit a woody cone with spirally arranged scales; small or large trees with needle leaves. **Pinaceae**, PINE FAMILY

CUPRESSACEAE CYPRESS FAMILY (CUP)

This is a very ancient family, with relictual species and genera scattered over the world. *Cupressus*, the true Cypress, has centers of diversity in California and around the Mediterranean. *Juniperus* is also essentially a Mediterranean genus, with a single outlier, *J. communis*, in the mountains of the Northern Hemisphere. *Sabina* is well represented by a number of species in the mountains and steppes of North America and Eurasia. The common names cedar and juniper are very loosely used for various genera of this family. In fact, the true cedars (*Cedrus*) belong to the pine family.

1a. Low, sprawling shrub with strongly bicolored needle-leaves, white above, green below; cones almost sessile (on extremely short shoots with a few scale-leaves), in the axils of the large vegetative needles; needles 3 at a node. **Juniperus**, JUNIPER

1b. Erect small tree with decussate, triangular scale-leaves appressed to the branches (a few injured or juvenile branches may revert to the *Juniperus* type); cones terminating short shoots not differentiated in any way from the vegetative branches; leaves 2 at a node. **Sabina**, RED CEDAR, SAVIN, JUNIPER

JUNIPERUS L. 1753 [old Latin name used by Virgil and Pliny]. JUNIPER

One species, **J. communis** L. subsp. **alpina** (Smith) Celakovsky, **19A.** Common undershrub throughout the coniferous forest area (*J. sibirica*).

SABINA Miller 1754 [the ancient Latin name]. RED CEDAR, SAVIN, JUNIPER

Note: The *Atlas of the Flora of the Great Plains* reports *Juniperus (Sabina) horizontalis* in southeastern Colorado. These records represent misidentifications of *S. monosperma*.

1a. All branchlets stout, not tapering; berries more than 5 mm diameter. **S. monosperma** (Engelmann) Rydberg, ONESEED JUNIPER. Piñon-juniper zone from Colorado Springs southward. The trees usually taper to the top, not irregularly branching as in the Western Slope *S. osteosperma*. The species are easily distinguished by their cones: In *S. osteosperma* the cones are dry and mealy when crushed, while in *S. monosperma* they are full of liquid resin. *S. monosperma* has more of a groomed, upward-tapering growth form, while *S. osteosperma*, except for young plants, has a very irregular one.

1b. Ultimate branchlets slender and elongate; berries less than 7 mm diameter. **S. scopulorum** (Sargent) Rydberg, ROCKY MOUNTAIN JUNIPER, **19B.** Abundant at higher altitudes, requiring more moisture.

PINACEAE PINE FAMILY (PIN)

The pine family is another ancient family. Our bristlecone pine is known from fossils in the Creede Oligocene formation of Colorado. The Californian *P. longaeva* has been claimed to be the oldest living plant, with a trunk about 4,600 years old, although there are some competitors, including the creosote bush, *Larrea tridentata*, and some lichens belonging to the genus *Rhizocarpon*. The geography and taxonomy of the bristlecone pines was worked out by Dana K. Bailey, a research associate of the University of Colorado Museum. His collections of this and other pines have built one of the finest pine collections in any American herbarium.

1a. Leaves sheathed at the base, at least when young, usually in clusters of 2 or more; cone scales thick and woody, with swollen tips; bracts minute, much shorter than the scales; fruit maturing the second year. **Pinus**, PINE
1b. Leaves not sheathed at the base, nor in clusters; cone scales not thick and woody nor swollen at the tip; bracts relatively large; fruit maturing in one season . . . . (2)

2a. Older twigs studded with the persistent stumps of fallen needles. **Picea**, SPRUCE
2b. Older twigs smooth . . . . (3)

3a. Leaf scars elliptical; needles stalked; cones hanging down, the scales persistent at maturity and the cone falling in one piece; bracts of the cone-scales longer than the scales, 3-cleft. **Pseudotsuga**, DOUGLAS-FIR
3b. Leaf scars round; needles sessile; cones erect, the scales falling away from the axis at maturity; cone scales not much exceeded by the bracts. **Abies**, FIR

ABIES Miller 1754 [ancient Latin name of an Old World species]. FIR

1a. Cones grayish-green; bracts of the cone scales with a short triangular tip; cones 7-12 cm long; resin ducts of the leaves (in cross-section) near the lower epidermis. **A. concolor** (Gordon) Lindley, WHITE FIR. Montane canyonsides, southern counties. A handsome fir, usually easily recognized by its long needles, but needle-length alone can be misleading.
1b. Cones dark brown-purple; bracts of the cone scales with long, subulate tips; cones 5-10 cm long; resin ducts of the needles equidistant from each epidermis. **A. lasiocarpa** (Hooker) Nuttall, SUBALPINE FIR, **19E**. Characteristic associate of Engelmann spruce at high altitudes. It has been suggested, on biochemical grounds, that our plant should be called *A. bifolia* Murray and the name *A. lasiocarpa* must be applied to a northwest coast species, but the evidence is still somewhat inconclusive.

PICEA A. Dietrich 1824 [Latin name of some pine, from *pix*, pitch]. SPRUCE

1a. Young branches and leaf bases minutely pubescent; needles acute or acutish at apex, not rigid; cones about 5 cm long, the scales ± rounded and distinctly thinner at apex. **P. engelmannii** (Parry) Engelmann, ENGELMANN SPRUCE, **19F**. Dominant forest tree of the subalpine, not necessarily near streamsides.
1b. Young branches glabrous; needles rigid, almost spine-tipped; cones commonly 8 cm long, the scales truncate and not distinctly thinner at the apex. **P. pungens** Engelmann, COLORADO BLUE SPRUCE, **19G**. Always very close to streamsides in the canyons and in the wetlands of South Park.

PINUS L. [the classical Latin name]. PINE, **19I**

1a. Fascicles (leaf clusters) containing 5 needles . . . . (2)
1b. Fascicles containing 2 or 3 needles . . . . (4)

2a. Needles commonly less than 5 cm long, usually strongly curved, with a few white resin drops on the surface; cone scales bristle-tipped. **P. aristata** Engelmann, BRISTLECONE PINE. Upper montane and subalpine.
2b. Needles usually longer than 5 cm, straight or only slightly curved, not sticky; cone lacking bristles . . . . (3)

3a. Small tree with irregular trunk and branching pattern; needles not minutely toothed near the apex; mature, open cones ovoid. **P. flexilis** James, LIMBER PINE. Common on rocky tors and gravelly knolls, upper montane and subalpine, usually in open sites. An isolated relictual stand occurs at low altitudes at Pawnee Buttes. Presumably it reached the area during the Pleistocene as a result of a climatic depression of timberline and has persisted in a relatively small favorable site.
3b. Tall tree with straight, unbranched trunk; needles with a few very minute teeth near the apex; mature, open cones cylindric. **P. strobiformis** Engelmann [resembling *P. strobus*, another 5-needled pine], MEXICAN WHITE PINE. Frequent along the eastern base of the San Juan Mountains, on river benches in spruce forests, not forming dominant stands. The cones average longer and narrower than those of the last.

4a. Needles 10-18 mm long, in 3s or 2s; cones 7-12 cm long; fascicles crowded at ends of branches, at least in older trees. **P. ponderosa** Douglas subsp. **scopulorum** (Watson) Weber, PONDEROSA PINE. Common from the outer foothills to the lower subalpine (on south-facing slopes) and on the Arkansas Divide, reaching as far east as Kim, on the north base of the Mesa de Maya.
4b. Needles 3-7 cm long, usually in pairs; cones 5 cm long or less; fascicles scattered along the branches . . . . (4)

5a. Tall, slender tree, cone scales bristle-tipped; cones persistent for several years after maturity; needle, in cross-section, with 2 vascular bundles. **P. contorta** Douglas subsp. **latifolia** (Engelmann) Critchfield [contorted, alluding to the dwarfed populations on the Oregon coast], LODGEPOLE PINE. Forming uniform forests with little underbrush, following fires, montane and subalpine.
5b. Low, bushy tree; cone scales not bristle-tipped; cones falling soon after maturity; needle, in cross-section, with one vascular bundle. **P. edulis** Engelmann, PIÑON PINE. Abundant at lower elevations of the plateaus and mesas. At the base of Poncha Pass it reaches to about 9,000 feet (2,750 m) on south slopes. A stand at Owl Canyon north of Fort Collins is not native but derived from an accidental cache of nuts from an aboriginal trading party. This was verified recently from packrat midden evidence, which dates the stand as being no older than 400 years. Scattered single juvenile trees now occur, bird-dispersed, in the foothill canyons nearby.

PSEUDOTSUGA Carrière 1867 [false (differing from) *Tsuga*]. DOUGLAS-FIR

One species, **P. menziesii** (Mirbel) Franco, **19H**. Moist canyon walls and slopes, montane. The 3-pronged bracts are diagnostic. The trees of our area are puny copies of the giants that inhabit the forests of the Pacific Northwest, and they generally occur on steep slopes of north-facing canyons.

ANGIOSPERMS

(MONOCOTS AND DICOTS)

ACERACEAE MAPLE FAMILY (ACE)

Maples of our area can always be recognized by the combination of three characters: palmately lobed (rarely pinnately compound) leaves; opposite arrangement; and two-winged fruits (samaras). Several genera of the Rosaceae as well as the genus *Ribes* have "maple leaves" but lack the other features. In Japan there are maples with elmlike leaves, so really the only reliable features, if flowers are lacking, are the opposite leaf-arrangement and the samara.

1a. Leaves simple and 3-5-lobed, or sometimes palmately 3-parted; twigs slender, reddish, with a narrow pith. **Acer**, MAPLE
1b. Leaves pinnately compound, with 3-5 leaflets; twigs stout, green or gray, with a thick pith. **Negundo**, BOX-ELDER

ACER L. 1753 [the ancient Latin name]. MAPLE

One species, **A. glabrum** Torrey, MOUNTAIN MAPLE, **20A**. 3-parted leaves (forma **trisectum** Sargent) are more common in the southern counties. In midsummer the leaves develop large, bright red blotches. These are galls containing Eriophyid mites.

NEGUNDO Boehmer 1760 [a Malayan name for *Vitex negundo*, according to E. L. Little]. BOX-ELDER

One species, **N. aceroides** Moench subsp. **interius** (Britton & Shafer) Löve & Löve **20B**. Gulches and streamsides at low elevations. This, the native western race, has the branchlets covered with short hairs, while subsp. **violaceus**, introduced from the east as a shade tree, has smooth, pale, glaucous twigs (*Acer negundo*).

ACORACEAE SWEETFLAG FAMILY (ACO)

A small family consisting of the single genus, *Acorus*. The plants somewhat resemble cattails but the leaves are ensiform, as in *Iris*. The flowering stem produces a single, densely flowered, fingerlike spadix, sessile and at almost right angles to it. The crushed foliage and rhizomes have a very pleasant, sweet fragrance. Until recently the genus was included in the Araceae (aroids).

ACORUS L. 1753 [Latin name of some aromatic plant]. SWEETFLAG

One species, **Acorus calamus** L. [old name for a reed]. Formerly frequent along the meadows of the piedmont valleys but disappearing as wetlands are drained for development. Extinct at Boulder, but still persisting near Fort Collins where it has been protected.

ADOXACEAE ADOXA FAMILY (ADX)

A monotypic family, that is, one consisting of a single genus and species. *Adoxa* occurs in mountains throughout the Northern Hemisphere. The inflorescence is unique. The terminal flower has a 2-lobed calyx (bracts?) and a 4-lobed greenish corolla, and 4 stamens alternating with the lobes. The filaments are deeply divided, giving the impression of 8 stamens. The lateral flowers (close to the terminal one) have a 3-lobed calyx and a 5-lobed greenish corolla and 5 (looking like 10) stamens. The ovary is half-inferior, of 3-4 united carpels.

ADOXA L. 1753 [from Greek, *adoxos*, without glory]. MOSCHATEL

One species, **A. moschatellina** L., **20D**. Moist, often shaded sites, upper montane, subalpine, and alpine. Inconspicuous and growing in such diverse sites as forested streambanks and alpine rockslides. The pale green flowers have a musky odor. With its ternate leaves and umbellike flower cluster, the plant suggests a small umbellifer.

AGAVACEAE AGAVE FAMILY (AGA)

Plants of the agave family, along with the cacti, create much of the exotic living landscapes of the American Southwest. These plants also have been some of the most useful plants for native Americans, giving fiber for sandals and baskets, food from the seeds, and fermented drinks such as pulque and tequila from the sap. Our only genus, *Yucca*, is of consuming biological interest because it illustrates the phenomenon of symbiosis. *Yucca* is visited by a night-flying pronuba moth, *Tegeticula yuccasella*. Alighting on the flower, the moth first stabs the ovary and lays an egg inside. Then it mounts a stamen and collects a mass of pollen from the anther. It is not possible to pollinate *Yucca* by merely brushing the stigma with pollen accidentally, for the stigmatic surface is deeply seated in the bottom of the funnel-shaped style. As if understanding the problem, the moth proceeds to stuff the wad of pollen deep in the funnel, thus assuring pollination and, consequently, ample food for the developing larva inside. Pollination results in the production of hundreds of seeds, so that neither actor in the drama loses anything and each achieves posterity. The hole bored in the ovary is easily visible on mature fruits.

YUCCA L. [from *yuca*, the Carib name for the manihot, erroneously used]. SPANISH BAYONET

1a. Plants with thick, rigid, broad, curved leaves; fruit indehiscent, fleshy; flowers pendent in dense panicles. **Y. baccata** Torrey, BANANA YUCCA. Rocky piñon-juniper stands south of the Arkansas River valley in western LA. It is becoming rare as a result of exploitation by collectors for landscaping new homes.

1b. Plants with slender, flexible, narrow, straight leaves; fruit dehiscent, dry; flowers erect or spreading, only drooping in age, in narrow panicles. **Y. glauca** Nuttall. Abundant in rocky areas on the plains. In southeastern Colorado the inflorescences, which are usually simple, become branched. This seems to be a feature gained by introgression with the New Mexican *Yucca elata*, which actually becomes treelike.

AIZOACEAE FIG-MARIGOLD FAMILY (AIZ)

A small family of succulent plants with opposite leaves, often placed in the Alsinaceae. The flowers, however, are perigynous or almost epigynous (with inferior ovary).

SESUVIUM L. 1753 [an unexplained name]. SEA-PURSLANE

One species, **S. verrucosum** Rafinesque [warty]. Alkaline flats in the San Luis Valley and lower Arkansas Valley. A prostrate, branched, succulent perennial with opposite, entire leaves lacking stipules. Flowers are perfect, the calyx of 3-5 purple tepals, united below; petals lacking, stamens numerous.

ALISMATACEAE WATER-PLANTAIN FAMILY (ALI)

The English family name alludes to the resemblance of the leaves of *Alisma*, with its numerous parallel veins, to those of *Plantago major*. These plants always grow with their "feet in the water." Their petioles and stems are spongy, filled with air spaces, permitting oxygenation of the tissues. The rhizomes of arrowheads were the *wappata* eaten by native Americans, and some species are cultivated by the Chinese for food. The numerous achenes are eaten by waterfowl.

1a. Leaves sagittate; flowers in whorls of 3 along a central axis; achenes in a tight ball. **Sagittaria**, ARROWHEAD

1b. Leaves oval or almost linear; flowers in a diffusely branched panicle; flowers in umbels; achenes in a ring. **Alisma**, WATER-PLANTAIN

ALISMA L. 1753 [ancient name for a water plant]. WATER-PLANTAIN

1a. Leaves usually elliptic to ovate-elliptic, 2-20 cm wide, rarely narrower; pedicels ascending to erect; petals 3.5-6 mm long; inflorescence surpassing the leaves; achenes centrally grooved at the tip, the style straight. **A. triviale** Pursh, **21B**. Muddy ditches and ponds (*A. plantago-aquatica* of manuals).

1b. Leaves linear to narrowly elliptic, less than 2 cm wide; pedicels widely spreading and curved; petals 2-4 mm long; inflorescence about as long as the leaves; achenes centrally ridged, with two grooves near the tip, the style curled. **A. gramineum** Lejeune [grasslike], **21A**. San Luis Valley (*A. brevipes*).

SAGITTARIA L. 1753 [Latin, *sagitta*, arrow]. ARROWHEAD

1a. Petiole terete; inflorescence becoming procumbent in age; sepals appressed to the fruiting head; most or all flowers perfect, their pedicels thick. **S. montevidensis** Chamisso & Schlechtendahl subsp. **calycina** (Engelmann) Bogin [of Montevideo; with a developed calyx]. South Park. The plants are very low and spreading, quite unlike the other species.

1b. Petiole angular; inflorescence erect or inclined in fruit but not procumbent; few or no flowers perfect, their pedicels not thick . . . . (2)

2a. Beak of achene horizontal or nearly so (at right angles to the long axis). **S. latifolia** Willdenow, **21D**. Muddy ditches, pondshores.

2b. Beak of achene erect or nearly so (parallel to the long axis). **S. cuneata** Sheldon, **21C**. Similar habitats.

ALLIACEAE ONION FAMILY (ALL)

Usually included in the lily family, the onions, for reasons other than their distinctive odors, stand alone because of their umbellate flower clusters and papery spathelike bract, as well as numerous other technical features. In the family we find the culinary leek *(Allium porrum)*, garlic *(Allium sativum)*, commercial onion (strains of *Allium cepa*), and chives *(Allium schoenoprasum)*. *Allium* is a particularly diversified genus in the arid West and in southwest Asia and contributes many showy species to rock garden culture.

ALLIUM L. 1753 [ancient Latin name of garlic]. ONION

1a. Leaves hollow, terete. **A. schoenoprasum** L. [rush-leek], WILD CHIVES. Wet meadows in the mountain parks.

1b. Leaves not hollow (but may be flat or terete) . . . . (2)

2a. Most flowers replaced by fleshy, reddish bulblets. **A. rubrum** Osterhout. Springs and marshy places. Considered by some to be a race of *A. geyeri* (var. *tenerum* Jones).
2b. Bulblets absent . . . . (3)

3a. Umbel nodding. **A. cernuum** Roth. Grassy slopes and dry meadows. Flowers pink, the petals rounded, concave, the tips not spreading.
3b. Umbel erect . . . . (4)

4a. Bulb coats persisting as a network of coarsely woven fibers . . . . (5)
4b. Bulb coats either nonfibrous or with parallel, not woven, fibers . . . . . (6)

5a. Leaves 3 or more per scape; tepals pink. **A. geyeri** Watson [for Carl A. Geyer, 1809-1853, collector with the Nicollet expedition on the Oregon Trail]. Moist meadows, montane and subalpine.
5b. Leaves usually only 2 per scape; tepals white or slightly pinkish. **A. textile** Nelson & Macbride [referring to the "woven" bulb coat]. Plains and outer foothill mesas.

6a. Bulb elongate, terminating a stout short *Iris*like rhizome; outer bulb coats with elongate cells in vertical rows. **A. brevistylum** Watson. Meadows and dry wooded slopes, North Park and LR.
6b. Bulb ovoid to globose; outer bulb coats patterned but not with vertical rows of elongate cells . . . . (7)

7a. Flowers red-purple, tepals acuminate with flaring tips. **A. acuminatum** Hooker. Sagebrush zone. Not reported, but to be expected in North Park.
7b. Flowers pale pink or white; tepals merely acute. **A. brandegei** Watson [for T. S. Brandegee]. Mountain sagebrush and oak, not reported east of RT but to be expected on the east base of Park Range in North Park.

ALSINACEAE CHICKWEED FAMILY (ASN)

This family is usually placed as a subfamily of Caryophyllaceae, but differs obviously in having its flowers constructed differently, with separate instead of united sepals and petals without narrow basal claws. The family is founded upon *Alsine media*, the common garden weed. To beginners, the chickweeds and sandworts seem to be an exasperating group, so many of them looking alike, but careful study shows a number of discrete genera with clear-cut characters.

Alert observers will note that the petals of *Lidia obtusiloba*, *Alsinanthe*, and several other alsinoids will vary a great deal in length and showiness from plant to plant in the same population. Closer examination will reveal differences in the size and development of the stamens and carpels. Plants with small petals, often hardly longer than the sepals, will tend to have abortive and nonfunctional anthers but well-developed ovaries, while plants with showy petals often have well-developed anthers and poorly developed ovaries. In other words, different plants will show different degrees of "maleness" and "femaleness" and in fact may be quite dioecious. The phenomenon, floral or sexual dimorphism, is very common in certain families and is especially well developed in the Alsinaceae and Apiaceae, where the variation in floral structure may occur on the same plant.

1a. Leaves with colorless, papery stipules (extremely minute in the very rare *Drymaria*) . . . . (2)
1b. Leaves lacking stipules . . . . (5)

2a. Annual . . . . (3)
2b. Perennial, somewhat woody at the base; variously pubescent or glabrous but seldom glandular. **Paronychia**, NAILWORT

3a. Erect herb with whorls of linear leaves. **Spergula**, SPURREY
3b. Spreading or depressed herbs with opposite leaves . . . . (4)

4a. Sprawling, glandular-pubescent herb with entire petals. **Spergularia**, SAND SPURREY
4b. Very condensed glabrous herb with minute bifid white petals. **Drymaria**

5a. Annual; stem rough-pubescent, diffusely branched; leaves ciliate, ovate to lanceolate, scabrous, sessile; sepals scabrous, strongly 3-nerved; seeds rugose, 0.4-0.6 mm long. **Arenaria**, SANDWORT
5b. Perennial or, if appearing annual, otherwise not as above . . . . (6)

6a. Minute (2 cm or less high) from a slender taproot; leaves mostly basal, linear; stems 1-flowered; muddy or moist sites, subalpine to alpine. **Sagina**, PEARLWORT
6b. Larger, rarely less than 5 cm high or, if low, then perennial or leaves otherwise . . . . (7)

7a. Styles 5; capsule cylindric, often curved, dehiscent by 10 apical teeth. **Cerastium**, MOUSE-EAR
7b. Styles 3; capsule short, ovoid or oblong, splitting into 3 or 6 segments (8)

8a. Petals deeply 2-lobed . . . . (9)
8b. Petals entire or only shallowly notched . . . . (11)

9a. Leaves ovate, or at least the lower ones petiolate; number of flower parts variable; stem with 2 lines of hairs. **Alsine**, CHICKWEED
9b. Leaves elliptic or lanceolate to linear, never petiolate . . . . (10)

10a. Plant arising from fleshy tubers (easily detached in collecting), glandular-pubescent; petals 6-8 mm long, cleft not more than halfway to the base; leaves lanceolate. **Pseudostellaria**, TUBER STARWORT
10b. Plant not glandular-pubescent; petals not over 5 mm long; leaves various. **Stellaria**, CHICKWEED

11a. Leaves elliptic, 5 pairs or more . . . . (12)
11b. Leaves linear, mostly basal; flowers solitary or in many-flowered cymes or clusters . . . . (13)

12a. Stems usually elongate, branched and sprawling; stems and leaves densely and minutely short-pubescent; nodes and leaf pairs numerous; the leaves acute. **Spergulastrum**
12b. Stems simple or branched only from the base, erect; stems and leaves sparsely and inconspicuously pubescent; nodes about 5; the leaves obtuse or rounded at the apex. **Moehringia**

13a. Leaves narrowly linear or filiform, grasslike, over 1 cm long; ovary splitting at maturity into 3 valves that are again partly split to form 6 teeth. **Eremogone**, DESERT SANDWORT
13b. Leaves linear but very short and thickish, less than 1 cm long; ovary splitting at maturity into 3 valves . . . . (14)

14a. Sepals cucullate at the tip; stems short, 1-flowered, and plants usually tightly matted at ground level. **Lidia**, ALPINE SANDWORT

14b. Sepals acute or acuminate; stems with simple or compound cymes; plants loosely caespitose . . . . (15)

15a. Plants delicate, from a slender taproot, with numerous unbranched stems bearing simple cymes at the apex; calyx and pedicels glandular-pubescent. **Tryphane**

15b. Plants well developed, with a strong taproot supporting numerous leafy, branched stems with more developed cymes; plant totally glabrous. **Alsinanthe**

ALSINANTHE Reichenbach 1841 [from a resemblance to *Alsine*]

1a. Petals short, inconspicuous; plants only a few cm diameter, resembling *Sagina*. **A. stricta** (Swartz) Reichenbach. Rare, only known from bare, saturated frost scars, Mount Evans (*Minuartia*).

1b. Petals exceeding the sepals (but see below), broad and conspicuous; plants much-branched, forming loose, rounded clumps. **A. macrantha** (Rydberg) Weber [large-flowered]. Common on well-developed tundra (*Arenaria*, *Minuartia*). Two markedly different petal sizes occur within the same population (see notes on floral dimorphism).

ALSINE L. 1753 [ancient name for chickweeds, possibly Greek *alysson* of Dioscorides]. CHICKWEED

One species, **A. media** L., **26B**. Adventive weed of poorly drained, shaded lawns (*Stellaria*). Flower parts are variable in number. The ovate leaves, abruptly narrowed to the petiole, are diagnostic.

ARENARIA L. 1753 [Latin, *arena*, sand]. SANDWORT

One species, **A. serpyllifolia** L. Adventive weed, definitely recorded only once in Colorado, occurring in sandy soil in ruderal sites, CC.

CERASTIUM L. 1753 [Greek, *cerastes*, horned, alluding to the curved capsule]. MOUSE-EAR

1a. Petals at least half again as long as the sepals; capsule not much longer than the sepals; native perennials . . . . (2)

1b. Petals about as long as the sepals or slightly exceeding them; capsule about twice as long as sepals; annual or weedy biennial or perennial . . . . . (3)

2a. Bracts of the inflorescence not at all scarious; flowering stems usually without leafy tufts in their axils; calyx glandular with long multicellular hairs; low, loosely matted plants. **C. beeringianum** Chamisso & Schlechtendal subsp. **earlei** (Rydberg) Hultén [for Graf von Beering; for F. S. Earle, collector with C. F. Baker], **26E**. Tundra and alpine rockslides. In areas of compensating environment the next (lowland) species may come into contact with and presumably hybridize with *C. beeringianum,* in which case there is no sure way to distinguish them.

2b. Bracts of the inflorescence scarious-margined; floral stems with tufts of sterile shoots in the leaf axils; plants with tall, erect floral stems. **Cerastium strictum** L. *emend.* Haenke [straight], **26D**. Abundant in meadows and openings of pine forests, from medium to high altitudes (*C. arvense* of manuals). *C. arvense* is a northern European tetraploid occurring in America at low altitudes only as a weed. Our plants are diploid and are related to, if not identical, to the diploid *C. strictum* of the high mountains of Eurasia.

3a. Annual, blooming in early spring; stem ascending or erect, not matted or rooting at the nodes; petals usually equalling or slightly exceeding the sepals.

C. nutans Rafinesque var. **brachypodum** Engelmann [nodding; short-stalked]. Frequent in moist gulches on the outwash mesas of the Front Range.

3b. Perennial weed of gardens and disturbed shady sites; stem weak and trailing, often matted and rooting at the nodes; petals about equalling the sepals. **C. fontanum** Baumgartner [of springs], COMMON MOUSE-EAR.

DRYMARIA Willdenow 1819 [Greek, *drymos*, forest]

One species, **Drymaria effusa** Gray var. **depressa** (Greene) Duke. A diminutive annual (to 2 cm high), the internodes condensed. Extremely minute stipules distinguish this from other genera. One occurrence known in Colorado, on rocky mudflats by a small reservoir in Rocky Mountain National Park.

EREMOGONE Fenzl 1833 [Greek, *eremos*, desert] (formerly included in *Arenaria*). DESERT SANDWORT

1a. Flowers in dense clusters or heads; inflorescence not glandular . . . . . (2)

1b. Flowers in open cymes; inflorescence glandular. **E. fendleri** (Gray) Ikonnikov, **25A**. Common in forested and high mountain areas. In the alpine it tends to become reduced in size and very glandular.

2a. Sepals about 3 mm long; flowers in a tight head; flowering stems usually over 15 cm tall. **E. congesta** (Nuttall) Ikonnikov, **25C**. Gravelly soil, upper montane and subalpine, Independence Pass and Mount Elbert; to be expected on the east base of Park Range in North Park.

2b. Sepals about 6 mm long; flowers in a condensed cyme but not a tight head; flowering stems rarely over 10 cm tall. **E. hookeri** (Nuttall) Weber [for Sir Joseph Hooker], **25B**. Sandstone outcrops on the northern plains and piñon-juniper belt in Arkansas River drainage.

LIDIA Löve & Löve 1976 [for Johannes Lid, 1886-1971, Norwegian botanist]. ALPINE SANDWORT

One species, **L. obtusiloba** (Rydberg) Löve & Löve, **27D**. Abundant mat-former on dry tundra (*Minuartia*). Very closely related to the Eurasian *L. biflora* but, in contrast, forming very dense mats. Two distinct petal sizes occur (see notes on floral dimorphism). We used to think that small-petaled, juvenile, loosely matted plants occurring on pioneer, open unstable sites were distinct (*L. biflora*) from the tightly matted, large-flowered plants on stable sites (*L. obtusiloba*), but they are not clearly separated.

MOEHRINGIA L. 1753 [for Paul H. G. Moehring, 1710-1792, German botanist]

One species, **M. lateriflora** (L) Fenzl. Sepals rounded at the apex, leaves about as long as the internodes, narrowly oval, rounded at the apex. Stems delicate and slender, finely pubescent with recurved hairs. Moist or swampy forest, montane and subalpine.

PARONYCHIA Miller 1754 [Greek name for whitlow, a disease of the nails, and for plants with whitish or scaly parts, thought to cure it]. NAILWORT

1a. Densely matted alpine; leaves elliptic, obtuse; flowers sessile; aerial branches absent. **P. pulvinata** Gray, **27A**. Gravelly tundra, the most extreme of dwarf mat plants.

1b. Plants freely branching or with foreshortened aerial branches, not alpine; leaves linear, sharp-pointed . . . . (2)

2a. Flowers solitary or in pairs; leaves and bracts of equal length; leaves and stipules 4-6 mm long. **P. sessiliflora** Nuttall. Sagebrush on the plains and in the intermountain basins.

2b. Flowers numerous, in branched cymes; leaves 6-20 mm long, longer than the bracts and stipules. **P. jamesii** Torrey & Gray, **27B**. Very common in the ponderosa pine belt.

PSEUDOSTELLARIA Pax 1934 [false *Stellaria*]. TUBER STARWORT

One species, **P. jamesiana** (Torrey) Weber & Hartman, **26A**. Forest openings, middle altitudes (*Stellaria*). Most of the showy (functionally staminate) white flowers do not produce seeds. The few fertile ones point to the ground, and their capsule valves roll outward, forming a flat, shiny disk. The genus is Eurasian, this being the only American species. Rhizomes are rarely collected because the stem is so brittle.

SAGINA L. 1753 [Latin, *sagina*, fattening, applied earlier to *Spergula*, a European forage plant]. PEARLWORT

One species, **S. saginoides** (L.) Karstens. Subalpine, alpine; common but overlooked because of its small size; among rocks or in muddy depressions.

SPERGULA L. 1753 [Latin, *spargere*, to scatter or sow]. SPURREY

One species, **S. arvensis** L. Adventive in cultivated ground, LR.

SPERGULARIA Presl & Presl 1819 [derived from *Spergula*]. SAND SPURREY

1a. Stamens 2-5. **S. marina** (L.) Grisebach [of the seacoast]. Muddy pastures and pond shores, WL, AM.
1b. Stamens 6-10 . . . . (2)

2a. Seeds smooth, not papillose, usually (but not always) surrounded by a wing; capsule large, 5-7 mm long; large, robust plants with fleshy leaves. **S. media** (L.) K. Presl. Alkaline flats in the piedmont valleys.
2b. Seeds roughened or sculptured, always papillose; capsule smaller; plants prostrate, more delicate, with less fleshy leaves. **S. rubra** (L.) K. Presl. Adventive, a prostrate, pink-flowered weed coming in, especially along logging trails, the only species occurring in the mountains.

SPERGULASTRUM Michaux 1803 [*Spergula*, + Latin, *astrum*, related]

One species, **S. lanuginosum** Michaux subsp. **saxosum** (Gray) Weber. Rocky open sites of forested zones, southern counties (*Arenaria*). Variable in size and branching.

STELLARIA L. 1753 [Latin, *stella*, star]. CHICKWEED

1a. Flowers subtended by scarious bracts (in *S. irrigua* and *S. umbellata* the inflorescence is condensed and the bracts may be somewhat hidden). (2)
1b. Flowers subtended by green leaves . . . . (5)

2a. Leaves elliptic-oblong; inflorescence subumbellate and condensed or cymose and open, pedicels tending to be reflexed . . . . (3)
2b. Leaves lanceolate or lance-linear; inflorescence cymose, pedicels ascending or divaricate, rarely actually reflexed . . . . (4)

3a. Petals absent; plants green, extremely variable (in shaded places with long internodes and very open cymes; in sunny alpine sites dwarfed, fleshy, with short internodes and condensed cymes). **S. umbellata** Turczaninow, **26C**. Subalpine, lower alpine (*S. weberi* Boivin is a dwarfed, fleshy, alpine ecotype).
3b. Petals present, filiform, 2-divided to the base; plants strongly purplish-tinged in all parts; pedicels short, inflorescence always congested and somewhat

hidden in the upper leaves; internodes about as long as the leaves, the lower ones longer; leaves fleshy, rather blunt, shriveling when pressed. **S. irrigua** Bunge, ALTAI STITCHWORT. Locally common on alpine screes, San Juans. First discovered in the Altai Mountains of Siberia, where it evidently is extremely rare.

4a. Calyx 2-3 mm long, broadly acute or obtuse, sepals almost nerveless; cymes commonly axillary as well as terminal; leaves very minutely tuberculate on the margins, dull. **S. longifolia** Mühlenberg, STITCHWORT. Common in moist meadows in the mountains.

4b. Calyx 4-8 mm long, sharply acute or acuminate, strongly 3-nerved; cymes terminal; leaves with smooth margins, shiny, sometimes slightly ciliate at the base. **S. longipes** Goldie subsp. **stricta** (Rydberg) Weber, STITCHWORT. Wet ground, montane and subalpine.

5a. Low, decumbent and creeping; leaves less than 1 cm long, almost round, pointed, subpetiolate; flowers solitary, axillary or terminal, on short pedicels less than 1 cm long. **S. obtusa** Engelmann. Gravelly streamsides, RT, but to be expected in western North Park.

5b. Erect; leaves usually over 1 cm long, elliptic-lanceolate, lanceolate, or lance-linear; flowers solitary or cymose, on longer pedicels . . . . (6)

6a. Stem pilose with multicellular hairs; leaves strongly ciliate, elliptic-oblong, acute; petals vestigial (1 mm long), with narrowly oblong divisions, or absent. **S. calycantha** (Ledebour) Bongard [cupped flower] (a sporadic variant that has been recognized by some as *S. simcoei* [Howell] C. L. Hitchcock). Subalpine meadows and willow carrs.

6b. Stem glabrous or very nearly so; leaves smooth or somewhat ciliate at the base, lanceolate to lance-linear; petals well developed (about as long as or longer than the sepals) . . . . (7)

7a. Leaves lustrous, firm, thick and keeled, green or glaucous; plant usually with a single terminal flower, sometimes irregularly cymose; sepals smooth, rarely ciliate; petals about twice as long as the sepals. **S. longipes** Goldie. Subalpine, alpine (including *S. laeta*, *S. monantha*).

7b. Leaves not lustrous, flat, not keeled; flowers solitary or in cymes; petals equalling or shorter than the sepals . . . . (8)

8a. Leaf margins completely smooth and the surfaces glabrous. **S. crassifolia** Ehrhart. Wet mountain meadows.

8b. Leaf margins ciliate, at least lower half. **S. calycantha** (Ledebour) Bongard. Wet forests, meadows, and willow swamps.

TRYPHANE Reichenbach 1841 [Greek, *trypheros*, delicate]

One species, **T. rubella** (Wahlenberg) Reichenbach [reddish]. Moraines, gravel bars, and unstable tundra slopes, subalpine and lower alpine (*Arenaria*, *Minuartia*).

AMARANTHACEAE AMARANTH FAMILY (AMA)

The family name comes from a Greek word meaning unfading, alluding to the "everlasting" quality of the papery perianth parts. Many amaranths are cultivated for this quality: the prince's feather, *Amaranthus hypochondriacus*, with red, nodding, "melancholy" spikes, and the cockscomb, *Celosia argentea*. Our local amaranths are weeds of late summer, growing in waste or fallow ground, but in tropical America and Asia grain amaranths are important food crops at high elevations. The seeds are popped and made into balls with a syrup binder, or ground to meal and baked into cakes or drunk in a slurry.

1a. Leaves alternate; plants glabrous or pubescent but not tomentose or stellate-pubescent. **Amaranthus**, AMARANTH
1b. Leaves opposite; plants stellate-pubescent or tomentose . . . . (2)

2a. Leaves covered by a dense mat of minute white stellate hairs; plants prostrate, dichotomously branched, the flowers clustered in rosettes of leaves at the branch tips. **Cladothrix**, ESPANTA VAQUERO
2b. Leaves tomentose; plants erect, not dichotomous, the flowers in cottony spikes. **Froelichia**, COTTONWEED.

AMARANTHUS L. 1753 [Greek, *amarantos*, unfading]. AMARANTH

1a. Plants monoecious with staminate and carpellate flowers intermingled or in nearly separate inflorescences . . . . (2)
1b. Plants dioecious . . . . (5)

2a. Flowers in bracteate clusters in the leaf axils; leaves seldom more than 5 cm long, oblong or obovate, with whitish margins and veins . . . . (3)
2b. Flowers in dense, spikelike panicles at the ends of the branches . . . . (8)

3a. Plant densely viscid-pubescent; leaf blades undulate-crisped. **A. pubescens** (Uline & Bray) Rydberg. Adventive, an old collection from Colorado Springs.
3b. Plant glabrous or sparingly pubescent; leaves flat or nearly so . . . . . . (4)

4a. Prostrate, branching in all directions; seeds over 1 mm broad. **A. blitoides** Watson [like the genus *Blitum*], **22C**. Ruderal weed, but evidently native in America (*A. graecizans* of some manuals).
4b. Erect with widely open or ascending branches; seeds less than 1 mm broad. **A. albus** L., **22B**. Less common, adventive.

5a. Staminate plants . . . . (6)
5b. Carpellate plants . . . . (7)

6a. Bracts with midveins scarcely excurrent. **A. arenicola** I. M. Johnston [of sandy places], **22D**. Common in sandy areas on the plains.
6b. Bracts with midveins clearly excurrent. **A. palmeri** Watson [for Edward Palmer, 1831-1911, American ethnobotanist]. Adventive, occasional weed on the eastern plains.

7a. All sepals obtuse or retuse, midveins scarcely excurrent; bract and outer sepals scarcely longer than inner ones. **A. arenicola** I. M. Johnston, **22D**.
7b. Outer sepals acute or acuminate with excurrent spinose midvein; bract and outer sepals much longer than the inner ones. **A. palmeri** Watson.

8a. Inflorescence usually tipped with red; carpellate tepals 1.5-2 mm long; plants nearly glabrous. **A. wrightii** Watson [for Charles Wright, 1811-1885, Texas botanist]. Infrequent or rarely collected, lower Arkansas River Valley.
8b. Inflorescence pale green; carpellate tepals 3 mm long. **A. retroflexus** L., **22A**. Adventive ruderal weed of late summer, very common.

CLADOTHRIX Watson 1880 [Greek, *klados*, twig, + *trichos*, hair]. ESPANTA VAQUERO

One species, **C. lanuginosa** Nuttall. Sand dunes along the Arkansas drainage, BA (*Tidestromia*).

FROELICHIA Moench 1794 [for J. A. Froelich, 1766-1841, German botanist]. COTTONWOOL

1a. Stem usually divergently branched from the base; lateral spikes sessile; mature calyx tube with lateral rows of distinct, rather sharp spines. **F. gracilis** (Hooker) Moquin, **23A**. Common in the piedmont valleys, lower foothills canyons and Arkansas Valley.

1b. Stem simple or with few erect branches; some lateral spikes usually pedunculate; mature calyx tube with lateral dentate crests or wings. **F. floridana** (Nuttall) Moquin. Infrequently collected on the plains, SW, PL.

ANACARDIACEAE SUMAC FAMILY (ANA)

It is easier to learn by rote to recognize our genera and species than to get a feeling for the family. This is usually the case with large, essentially tropical families of which we have only some few outliers. In general we can say that the leaves are usually alternate and usually pinnately compound. Stipules are absent. The flowers are radially symmetrical with united sepals, 5 free petals and 5-10 or more stamens. A prominent fleshy disk is found between the stamens and the ovary.

Many anacards have poisonous or irritating parts. While a bout with poison ivy will instill certain knowledge of this family, it is nice to know that the anacards contain some of our most delicious fruits and nuts. *Anacardium occidentale* is the cashew, *Pistacia vera* the pistachio, and *Mangifera indica* the mango, which has to be picked dead ripe from the tree to be appreciated. Under cultivation as an ornamental in city parks is *Cotinus coggygria*, the smoke tree, so named for the exceedingly slender, plumose sterile branches of the inflorescence that create an illusion of mist. The ubiquitous cultivated pepper tree, *Schinus molle* of southern California, also belongs to this family.

1a. Leaflets 3, shiny; terminal leaflet petiolate; fruits white, smooth. **Toxicodendron**, POISON IVY

1b. Leaflets 3 or more, dull and pubescent (if leaflets 3, terminal leaflet sessile); fruit red, hairy. **Rhus**, SUMAC

RHUS L. 1753 [the ancient name]. SUMAC

1a. Leaflets 9 or more, regularly serrate; tall shrub with thick twigs and much pith; fruits in pyramidal clusters. **R. glabra** L., SMOOTH SUMAC, **24A**. Infrequent on canyonsides. The staghorn sumac, *R. typhina* L., is occasionally found as an escape from cultivation. It differs by having velvety-hairy twigs. *Ailanthus*, in the Simaroubaceae, looks like a sumac but has entire leaves with a few shallow lobes at the bases of the leaflets and produces papery samaras.

1b. Leaflets 3 or sometimes 1, coarsely crenate; fruits in dense, small clusters. **R. aromatica** Aiton subsp. **trilobata** (Nuttall) Weber, SKUNKBRUSH, LEMONADEBUSH (*R. trilobata*), **24B**. Canyonsides and rimrock. In the southern counties a very pubescent race, subsp. **pilosissima** (Engelmann) Weber, occurs.

TOXICODENDRON Miller 1754. POISON IVY, POISON-OAK

One species, **T. rydbergii** (Small) Greene, **24C, Pl. 16**. Common in the outer foothills at the bases of cliffs and increasing with trampling of the ground. Never climbs high into trees like its eastern counterpart.

APIACEAE/UMBELLIFERAE PARSLEY FAMILY (API/UMB)

The so called umbels are recognized by the usually ternately (sometimes pinnately) compound leaves with a sheathing petiole (the edible part of celery), the umbellate flower clusters, the fruits that separate at maturity into 2 1-seeded nutlets (think of caraway seeds), and a generally pungent, specific odor or taste. The flowers are basically very uniform, with 4 minute sepals, 4 petals, 4 stamens and an inferior ovary of 2 united carpels, each one with a single seed. The carpel walls, in cross-section, show oil ducts, often in distinct numbers and arrangements.

In order to use the key successfully, knowledge of the type of root system, presence or absence of caudices, leaves on the flowering stem, flower color, characteristics of the mature fruit, and type of odor of the foliage may all be helpful. Also, the flowers are not always alike in the same umbel, often showing a division of labor, some being functionally male, female, or neuter.

Many important culinary herbs belong here: dill (*Anethum graveolens*), carrot (*Daucus carota*), coriander or cilantro (*Coriandrum sativum*), cumin (*Cuminum cyminum*), fennel (*Foeniculum vulgare*), celery (*Apium graveolens*), parsley (*Petroselinum hortense*), anise (*Pimpinella anisum*), parsnip (*Pastinaca sativa*), caraway (*Carum carvi*), and myrrh (*Myrrhis odorata*). But beware of chewing the leaves, stalks, roots, or seeds of any umbel whose identity is the slightest bit doubtful! Two of the most poisonous plants in our region are *Conium*, poison Hemlock, and *Cicuta*, water hemlock. Cases of fatal or near-fatal poisoning are reported every season. Learn to recognize these species before using wild umbels for food.

1a. Leaves palmately cleft into 5-9 simple, toothed segments; flowers yellow; fruit covered with hooked bristles. **Sanicula**, SNAKEROOT

1b. Leaves various; fruits not covered by bristles or, if so (as in *Daucus*), flowers white . . . . (2)

2a. [1] Basal leaves simple, cordate, crenate; stem leaves usually with only 3 leaflets. **Zizia**

2b. Basal leaves, when present, never simple . . . . (3)

3a. [2] Leaves basically pinnately compound, only the lowermost pair of leaflets occasionally incised or lobed . . . . (4)

3b. Leaves basically ternate or, if pinnate, the leaflets commonly further subdivided. . . . . (9)

4a. [3] Flowers yellow . . . . (5)

4b. Flowers white . . . . (6)

5a. [4] Tall, leafy herb; leaves simply pinnate, leaflets large and coarsely toothed; weed of cultivated ground. **Pastinaca**, PARSNIP

5b. Low stemless (or apparently stemless) early spring herbs with a basal rosette of leaves. **Musineon**

6a. [4] Leaflets linear, entire; plant very slender, arising from a globose or fusiform corm. Yampa drainage only. **Perideridia**, YAMPA

6b. Leaflets broader, toothed or lobed; plant not arising from a corm; widely distributed . . . . (7)

7a. [6] Leaflets elongate, broadly linear, finely toothed; tall marsh plant. **Sium**, WATER PARSNIP

7b. Leaflets broader, coarsely toothed or incised . . . . (8)

8a. [7] Leaflets broadly elliptic-ovate, crenate; plants of mountain streamsides. **Oxypolis**, COWBANE

8b. Leaflets narrowly elliptic-oblong, deeply toothed, the lowest pair usually with a large lobe; plants of irrigation ditches. **Berula**, WATER PARSNIP

9a. [3] Low plants of tundra, sagebrush, or arid clay-shale areas . . . . . . (10)

9b. Tall or coarsely weedy plants of mountain forests or roadsides . . . . (19)

10a. [8] Very slender and weak, arising singly from a globose or fusiform corm; leaves ternate with usually linear (only rarely wider) leaflets. **Orogenia**, TURKEYPEA

10b. Stout, the stems never arising singly from a corm; leaves various . . . (11)

11a. [10] Plants of subalpine meadows and alpine tundra . . . . (12)

11b. Plants of desert-steppe, foothill rock ledges, or sagebrush . . . . (14)

12a. [11] Leaves ternately pinnate, the leaflets long and narrow. **Pseudocymopterus** (dwarfed forms of high altitudes)

12b. Leaves pinnately divided or, if somewhat ternate, the leaflets very short and crowded . . . . (13)

13a. [12] Leaflets digitately incised, the group distinctly fan-shaped; floral stems erect, the umbel very conspicuous; flowers bright yellow; plants of subalpine meadows. **Podistera**

13b. Leaflets incised but not distinctly fan-shaped; floral stems spreading; flowers pale yellow, rarely purplish, inconspicuous; tundra plants. **Oreoxis**, ALPINE PARSLEY

14a. [11] Stemless; leaves all basal, none on the flowering stem . . . . (15)

14b. Stem present; leaves on the flowering stem or on a pseudoscape . . . (16)

15a. [14] Over 10 cm tall, with numerous stout caudices; arid, rocky ledges or clay-shale slopes. **Aletes**

15b. Less than 10 cm tall, with few caudices; sagebrush communities in the intermountain basins. **Oreoxis**, ALPINE PARSLEY

16a. [14] Leaf divisions narrowly linear (showing hardly any widening in the middle); basal leaves numerous, stiff and broomlike. **Harbouria**, WHISKBROOM PARSLEY

16b. Leaf divisions broader, the leaflets wider at base or middle; basal leaves few; not stiff and broomlike . . . . (17)

17a. [16] Fruits strongly dorsiventrally flattened, laterally thin-margined and winged. **Lomatium**

17b. Fruits not strongly flattened dorsiventrally, the dorsal ribs conspicuous and often winged . . . . (18)

18a. [17] Fruits strongly corky-winged; arid desert-steppe, piñon-juniper, and sagebrush; flowers white, yellow, or dull red. **Cymopterus**

18b. Fruits with conspicuous dorsal ribs but with poorly developed wings; pine, aspen forests and subalpine meadows. **Pseudocymopterus**, MOUNTAIN PARSLEY

19a. [9] Flowers yellow . . . . (20)

19b. Flowers white . . . . (21)

20a. [19] Fruits strongly dorsiventrally flattened, laterally thin-margined and winged. **Lomatium dissectum**

20b. Fruits with conspicuous dorsal ribs but with poorly developed wings; pine, aspen forests and subalpine meadows. **Pseudocymopterus**

21a. [19] Fruits 4-5 times longer than wide; fruits and roots with an anise odor when crushed. **Osmorhiza**, SWEET CICELY

21b. Fruits short, about as wide as long; fruit and roots lacking anise odor. (22)

22a. [21] Tall, coarse plants, the ultimate leaf segments 1 cm or more broad; leaves generally not more than twice pinnately compound . . . . (23)

22b. Slender plants, or, if tall and coarse, the ultimate leaf segments less than 0.5 cm wide; leaves generally very finely dissected, fernlike . . . . (25)

23a. [22] Principal leaves divided into 3 or 5 huge, maple-shaped leaflets, the leaf sheath over 2 cm wide; stems up to 3-4 cm thick. **Heracleum**, COW PARSNIP

23b. Principal leaves not as above . . . . (24)

24a. [23] Leaf segments lanceolate; ribs of fruit prominent but not forming wings; roots tuberous, clustered; sloughs and ditches in the valleys. **Cicuta**, WATER HEMLOCK

24b. Leaf segments ovate; ribs of fruit forming wings; plant with a taproot; mountain streamsides and screes. **Angelica**

25a. [22] Fruits covered with hooked bristles; umbels subtended by a conspicuous ring of leaflike bracts, sometimes equalling the umbel rays. **Daucus**, WILD CARROT

25b. Fruits not bristly; umbels subtended by very inconspicuous small bracts or none . . . . (26)

26a. [25] Adventive weeds of irrigation ditches and roadsides . . . . (27)

26b. Natives of forests and subalpine streamsides . . . . (28)

27a. [26] Stem spotted with purple; tall plants with hollow stems over 1 m tall and huge fernlike basal leaves; fruit (do not chew!) with a soapy or celery odor. **Conium**, POISON HEMLOCK

27b. Stem not spotted; plants not over 1 m tall, smaller in all details; fruit with caraway odor, edible. **Carum**, CARAWAY

28a. [26] Leaflets linear, 1-3 mm wide. **Ligusticum**, LOVAGE

28b. Leaflets ovate, oblong, or lanceolate, 5-40 mm broad . . . . (29)

29a. [28] Less than 1 m tall, unbranched, with 1-2 stem leaves; ultimate leaf lobes with 1 principal vein, the lateral veins, if present, inconspicuous; fruits oval, flattened dorsally. **Conioselinum**, HEMLOCK PARSLEY

29b. Over 1 m tall, branched, with numerous large leaves; ultimate leaf lobes with many lateral veins as conspicuous as the midvein; fruits oblong, not flattened dorsally. **Ligusticum**, LOVAGE

ALETES Coulter & Rose 1888 [Greek, Aletes, a wanderer, from the fact that *A. acaulis* was known under at least six generic names prior to *Aletes*, including *Lomatium*]

1a. Crushed leaves with a strong anise or citronella odor; leaflets not differentiated well from the rachises, sharp-pointed. **A. anisatus** (Gray) Theobald & Tseng. Common on canyonsides from the Platte River southward through the Tarryalls and South Park to the west side of the San Luis Valley.

1b. Crushed leaves with a celery or soapy odor; leaflets either distinct from the rachis by a constriction, or not . . . . (3)

2a. Lateral leaf lobes linear . . . . (3)
2b. Lateral leaf lobes broad, incised, with flaring tips . . . . (4)

3a. Most lateral leaf lobes entire. **A. lithophilus** (Mathias) Weber [rock-loving]. Endemic. Huerfano Creek drainage, on volcanic dikes; upper San Luis Valley (*Neoparrya*).
3b. Most lateral leaf lobes pinnatifid. **A. nuttallii** (Gray) Weber. Known on the Eastern Slope only on clay soils at Chalk Bluffs, WL (*Neoparrya megarrhiza*).

4a. Peduncles shorter than the leaves; ribs of the fruit obscure; plants forming very low, tight mats on rock ledges. **A. humilis** Coulter & Rose. Endemic in the outer foothills, BL, LR. Phantom Canyon has been made a reserve by Nature Conservancy to protect this rare species.
4b. Peduncles longer than the leaves; ribs of the fruit conspicuous, corky-thickened; plants forming loose clumps rather than mats. **A. acaulis** (Torrey) Coulter & Rose [stemless], **Pl. 42**. Very common on cliffs in the foothill canyons.

ANGELICA L. 1753 [named *angelic* from cordial and medicinal properties of some species]
1a. Coarse, stout herbs of streambanks, middle altitudes; over 2 m tall with very large umbels. **A. ampla** Nelson, **Pl. 55**.
1b. Lower herbs less than 2 m tall; aspen zone to alpine screes . . . . (2)

2a. Involucel (bract of the smallest umbel) lacking. **A. pinnata** Watson. Aspen groves and streamsides, known on the Eastern Slope only from Cameron Pass, but probably in North Park.
2b. Involucel present; fruit glabrous; involucel of lanceolate bracts often longer than the flowers; alpine screes. **A. grayi** (Coulter & Rose) Coulter & Rose. The similar *A. roseana* Henderson was reported from "Cassell's Canyon," possibly near Mount Harvard, but the identification may have been incorrect and the species has not been found again.

BERULA Besser 1826 [Latin name of some aquatic plant]. WATER PARSNIP

One species, **B. erecta** (Hudson) Coville. Weak herb of sloughs and irrigation ditches in the lower valleys.

CARUM L. 1753 [modification of old Latin name, *Careum*]. CARAWAY

One species, **C. carvi** L. Adventive. A locally common weed, in mountain town sites and hay meadows. Source of the commercial caraway seed.

CICUTA L. 1753 [ancient Latin name of poison hemlock]. WATER HEMLOCK

One species, **C. douglasii** (de Candolle) Coulter & Rose, **30B**. Swamps and roadside ditches in the lower valleys. Extremely poisonous. Certain identification can be made by making a longitudinal section of the thick root; it has cross-partitions separating air spaces.

CONIOSELINUM G. Hoffmann 1814 [merger of two generic names of umbels, *Conium* and *Selinum*]. HEMLOCK PARSLEY

One species, **C. scopulorum** (Gray) Coulter & Rose. Wet meadows and roadside ditches in the mountains. A low herb with usually 1 or 2 stem leaves, little-branched, never tall and rank like its close relative, *Ligusticum porteri*.

CONIUM L. 1753 [Greek, *coneion*, the hemlock, by which Socrates and various criminals were put to death]. POISON HEMLOCK

One species, **C. maculatum** L. [spotted], **30A**. An abundant tall, rank, adventive weed in towns, especially near irrigation ditches and wet ground. The plant produces a rosette of fernlike leaves the first year and can be hoed out easily at that stage. Children have been poisoned by using the hollow stems for whistles. Every effort should be made to eliminate this from our area because of the potential danger of poisoning.

CYMOPTERUS Rafinesque 1819 [Greek, *cyma*, wave + *pteron*, wing, alluding to the fruit wings]

1a. Flowers pink; leaves glaucous-bluish; bracts with papery margins. **C. montanus** Nuttall. Common early spring flower on dry shale outcrops, plains, and outwash mesas of the Front Range.

1b. Flowers white; leaves glossy green; bracts lacking papery margins. **C. acaulis** (Pursh) Rafinesque [stemless]. Common in early spring, on sandstone or sandy substrates on the plains and mesas.

DAUCUS L. 1753 [the ancient Greek name]. CARROT, QUEEN ANNE'S LACE

One species, **D. carota** L. Adventive weed or garden escape, established along roadsides in the mountain valleys. The first blooming flower (center of umbel) is often deep purple.

HARBOURIA Coulter & Rose 1888 [for J. P. Harbour, who collected plants in South Park in 1861-1862]

One species, **H. trachypleura** (Gray) Coulter & Rose [rough-ribbed], **Pl. 1**. Endemic. On open slopes of the outwash mesas of the Front Range up to warm south slopes in the montane. This is a monotypic genus, retirtcted to a narrow band on the Eastern Slope.

HERACLEUM L. 1753 [dedicated to Hercules, Pliny having thought our species to be of great medicinal value]. COW PARSNIP

One species, **H. sphondylium** L. subsp. **montanum** (Schleicher) Briquet [*Sphondylium*, a pre-Linnaean genus name for this], **Pl. 46**. A plant of giant proportions, in swampy thickets and streamsides in the middle mountains. The outer petals of the outer flowers of the umbel are usually enlarged and 2-cleft, creating the impression of a single large flower, not an umbel of small ones.

LIGUSTICUM L. 1753 [Latin, *ligusticus*, of the country Liguria, where the garden lovage abounded]. LOVAGE

1a. Leaflets linear, 1-3 mm broad; low, slender plant less than 0.5 m tall. **L. tenuifolium** Watson. Wet mountain meadows, grassy slopes, subalpine (*L. filicinum* var.).

1b. Leaflets ovate, oblong, or lanceolate, 5-40 mm wide; tall, rank plants over 1 m tall. **L. porteri** Coulter & Rose [for T. C. Porter], OSHÁ. Forested ravines and aspen groves. This is currently regarded as a medicinal plant of miraculous qualities. If exploited by digging roots, the species could well become endangered.

LOMATIUM Rafinesque 1819 [Greek, *lomation*, a little border, alluding to the winged fruit]

1a. Flowers clearly white, with red anthers. **L. orientale** Coulter & Rose. Blooming in very early spring on the plains and outwash mesas of the Front Range.

1b. Flowers distinctly yellow, anthers concolorous . . . . (2)

2a. Well over 2 dm tall, with large ternate leaves, usually more than 1 elongate internode, and large umbels (more resembling *Ligusticum* than *Lomatium*). **L. dissectum** (Nuttall) Mathias & Constance. Frequent in North Park. Easily confused with *Ligusticum porteri* but not so tall, and the ultimate leaf lobes have only a single midvein, while in *Ligusticum* the venation is pinnate.

2b. Low or slender, less than 2 dm tall, the internodes few and short; umbels small; leaves densely pubescent with very short, stiff hairs. **L. foeniculaceum** (Nuttall) Coulter & Rose [resembling the genus *Foeniculum*]. Local, arid sites, Mesa de Maya.

MUSINEON Rafinesque 1820 [derivation?]

1a. Plants caulescent, with a usually buried, erect pseudoscape, dichotomously branched when well developed. **M. divaricatum** (Pursh) Nuttall. Abundant early spring flower on the eastern plains and outwash mesas, the leaves spreading out on the surface of the ground; flowers yellow.

1b. Plants stemless. **M. tenuifolium** Nuttall. Locally common at Pawnee Buttes National Grassland.

OREOXIS Rafinesque 1830 [Greek, *oros*, mountain]. ALPINE PARSLEY

1a. Bractlets broad, toothed at the apex, often purplish. **O. bakeri** Coulter & Rose [for C. F. Baker]. Tundra, Sangre de Cristo Mountains and upper Rio Grande Valley.

1b. Bractlets linear, entire, green . . . . (2)

2a. Entire plant totally glabrous; oil tubes several in the intervals (cross-section of the mericarp should show these) between the ribs. **O. humilis** Rafinesque. Endemic on Pikes Peak, where, evidently, the next does not occur. The distinctions between these two species are not clearly stated in any descriptions, and one is tempted to consider the more widespread *O. alpina* a trivial race.

2b. At least the fruits slightly puberulent; oil tubes usually solitary in the intervals . . . . (3)

3a. Foliage and stems glabrous and glossy. **O. alpina** (Gray) Coulter & Rose. Common dwarf alpine on granitic central mountains.

3b. Distinctly puberulent. **O. alpina** subsp. **puberulenta** Weber. Sagebrush, high interior basins.

OROGENIA Watson 1871 [Greek, *oros*, mountain, + *genia*, alluding to a resemblance to the genus *Erigenia*]. TURKEYPEA

One species, **O. linearifolia** Watson. Sagebrush meadows, east side of Rabbit Ears Pass, Cameron Pass, and Cherokee Park, LR. Very inconspicuous and easily overlooked, blooming in May. This and *Perideridia* are our only umbels arising from a globose or fusiform corm.

OSMORHIZA Rafinesque 1819 [Greek, *osmo*, scent, + *rhiza*, root]. SWEET CICELY [corruption of a genus name, *Seseli*]

1a. Leaves distinctly pinnate-ternate with several pairs of lateral ternate leaflets, the lobes shallow and also finely toothed; fruit glabrous or sparsely bristly at base, obtuse at apex, not caudate; fruits and umbel rays stiffly ascending. **O. occidentalis** (Nuttall) Torrey. Oak-aspen and mountain meadows, Rabbit Ears Pass.

1b. Leaves clearly ternate, with one pair of lateral ternate leaflets, the lobes deep and simple; fruits bristly hispid, caudate at the base with conspicuous tails; fruits and umbel rays spreading-ascending or divaricate . . . . (2)

2a. Bracts present at base of umbels well-developed, green, hairy; styles 2-3 mm long. **O. longistylis** (Torrey) de Candolle. Rare in cool canyons in the outer Front Range foothills.

2b. Bracts lacking at base of umbels or very inconspicuous; styles 0.5 mm long or less . . . . (3)

3a. Rays and pedicels spreading-ascending; fruit linear-oblong, cylindric. **O. chilensis** Hooker & Arnott. Not as common as the next, shaded forests along streams.

3b. Rays and pedicels divaricate; fruit clavate, widest near the apex. **O. depauperata** Philippi. Very common, foothills and montane.

OXYPOLIS Rafinesque 1825 [Greek, *oxys*, sharp, + *polios*, white, from the slender involucels and white petals]. COWBANE

One species, **O. fendleri** (Gray) Heller. Along rivulets in subalpine forests. Easily recognized by the simple stem with pinnately compound leaves with broad ovate leaflets.

PASTINACA L. 1753 [Latin, *pastino*, to prepare the ground for planting of the vine]. PARSNIP

One species, **P. sativa** L. Commonly escaped from cultivation and adventive, becoming established in neglected agricultural land.

PERIDERIDIA Reichenbach 1837 [Greek, *peri*, around, + *derris*, a leather coat]. YAMPA

One species, **P. gairdneri** (Hooker & Arnott) Mathias subsp. **borealis** Chuang & Constance. Wet meadows, North Park. Corms of this plant were gathered for food by the Indians.

PODISTERA Watson 1887 [alluding to the entanglement of the pedicels and involucels in the original species]

One species, **P. eastwoodiae** (Coulter & Rose) Mathias & Constance. Endemic, subalpine meadows, Independence Pass.

PSEUDOCYMOPTERUS Coulter & Rose 1888 [Greek, *pseudo*, false, + *Cymopterus*]. MOUNTAIN PARSLEY

One species, **P. montanus** (Gray) Coulter & Rose. Probably the most abundant yellow umbel in the mountains, from the pine-oak to subalpine, extremely variable in height and leaf-cutting (*Cymopterus lemmonii*).

SANICULA L. 1753 [Latin, *sanare*, to heal]. SNAKEROOT

One species, **S. marilandica** L. A relictual eastern woodland species locally frequent along streamlets in cool canyons in the eastern foothills.

SIUM L. 1753 [Greek, *sion*, the name of a water plant]. WATER PARSNIP

One species, **S. suave** Walter. Swales and wet meadows, San Luis Valley, North Park. Leaves typically simply pinnate with serrulate margins, but in "drowned" situations some may develop more dissection. The stem base is partitioned internally as in *Cicuta*.

ZIZIA W.D.J. Koch 1825 [for Johannes Baptist Ziz, 1779-1829, a Rhenish botanist]

One species, **Z. aptera** (Gray) Fernald [wingless]. Localized in wet meadows of the Wet Mountain Valley and North Park. A characteristic plant with simple, crenate basal leaves, merely ternate or 5-parted stem leaves and yellow flowers.

APOCYNACEAE DOGBANE FAMILY (APO)

On the Eastern Slope, the dogbanes are easily recognized by their opposite leaves, milky juice, and small, pink or white, bell-shaped corollas. They are close relatives of the milkweeds, producing 2 long, narrow pods from each flower. The carpels are free except at the apex! Dogbanes lack the complicated flower structure of the milkweeds.

The dogbane family is diversified in the tropics, where members are used as fiber plants, sources of india rubber, and arrow poisons. In recent years, *Rauwolfia*, a tropical tree, was found to yield a wonder drug for high blood pressure. Most of the well-known genera are ornamentals. In our gardens, *Vinca minor*, periwinkle, is a standard ground cover in shaded corners, and the extremely poisonous oleander, *Nerium oleander*, separates lanes of divided highways in California and Arizona. *Plumeria* provides the lovely frangipani flowers of the Hawaiian lei.

APOCYNUM L. 1753 [Greek, *apo*, away, + *cyno*, dog]. DOGBANE

1a. Corolla pink, 3 times the length of the calyx; branching mostly dichotomous; leaves usually drooping. **A. androsaemifolium** L., SPREADING DOGBANE. This and the next species hybridize freely in the wild. Intermediates are called *Apocynum x medium*. Gravelly soil, open pine woods.

1b. Corolla greenish-white, 1.5-2 times the length of the calyx; branching opposite; leaves erect or spreading, not drooping. **A. cannabinum** L., INDIAN HEMP. Roadside ditches and floodplains. Plants with sessile, clasping lower leaves (*A. sibiricum*), while possibly once distinct, merge with *A. cannabinum*. The lower leaves soon fall away.

ARALIACEAE GINSENG FAMILY (ARL)

Aralias resemble the Apiaceae except for the fact that their flowers are 5-merous and, in our species, the fruit is a berry. *Aralia racemosa* is a relictual eastern species known from a few localities from the Black Hills to Texas. It was first seen in Colorado by Edwin James in the rugged mountains near the mouth of the South Platte, on a memorable day when the party climbed the first foothills to see the junction of the North and South forks. They got lost and had a difficult time returning to camp. On the way, they saw this species, but no specimens were collected. It should be expected in the bottoms of canyons along small streamlets, in deep shade. Searches should be made for this species throughout the area scheduled to be impounded by the Two Forks Dam.

Rice paper is not made from rice at all but from an aralia, *Tetrapanax papyrifera*. The English ivy, symbolic of the "ivory tower" of academia, is an aralia, *Hedera helix*. The spiny devil's club of the rain forests of the Pacific Northwest is an aralia, *Oplopanax horrida*. And ginseng, one of the most ancient of medicines, is an aralia, *Panax ginseng*.

ARALIA L. 1753 [origin of name unknown]

1a. Umbels numerous in a large compound panicle or raceme; cauline leaves present. **A. racemosa** L., SPIKENARD. Shaded streamsides. First seen by Edwin James in foothills above the mouth of the Platte, but not collected again. An eastern woodland relictual species occurring sporadically in New Mexico and Texas and in western Colorado, always infrequent or rare.

1b. Umbels several in a corymb; leaf solitary, basal, long-petioled. **A. nudicaulis** L. [naked-stemmed], WILD SARSAPARILLA, **23B**. Infrequent in cool ravines, foothills and montane. A plant of the northeastern American forests, disjunct in our eastern foothills. Formerly used as a substitute for sarsaparilla (see also Smilacaceae).

ASCLEPIADACEAE MILKWEED FAMILY (ASC)

To understand the milkweed flower some explanation is needed. The milkweed flower contains 5 sepals, 5 petals, which are usually reflexed, 5 stamens, which, as such, cannot easily be recognized, and a gynoecium composed of 2 carpels that are free for most of their length, but united at the apex. Each carpel (follicle) splits down one side at maturity, liberating the seeds, which are equipped with a tuft of silky hairs (coma) at one end, serving as a parachute.

Milkweed flowers are unique in their possession of what would appear to be a whorl of floral organs between the petals and the stamens. This whorl of 5 petallike parts is called a corona, and each segment is a hood. On its inner surface, the hood may or may not have a protruding hornlike structure. The base of the hood may be expanded into flaplike structures called auricles.

The stamens themselves are united to the style, the two structures together forming a unit in the central part of the flower. The pollen grains formed within the anther sacs are sticky and hang together in masses called pollinia. The pollinia of adjacent anthers are united by a threadlike structure called a translator. The pollinia and connecting translator are hidden in the style column except for a black center piece protruding from a vertical slit. Insects, during visits to the flowers, accidentally catch the spines of their feet on the translators, yanking the pollinia free (or sometimes losing a leg) and carry the pollen to other flowers, where it must be deposited on the stigmatic surface. This is no easy chance, which explains why this overspecialization of pollination mechanism results in very few fertilizations. However, one fertilization can compensate for this, because the enormous number of pollen grains in a pollinium can fertilize an enormous number of ovules in a single follicle!

1a. Plants erect or prostrate, but not a twining vine. **Asclepias**, MILKWEED
1b. Plant a twining vine with linear, opposite leaves. **Sarcostemma**, TWINEVINE

ASCLEPIAS L. 1753 [Greek, Aesculapius, god of medicine]. MILKWEED

1a. Corolla lobes erect or only spreading at anthesis. **A. asperula** (Decaisne) Woodson. [rough], CREEPING MILKWEED, **31G**. Frequent on the outwash mesas of the outer foothills. The long purple hoods curve out and up, contrasting with the large, spreading, greenish petals.

1b. Corolla lobes reflexed . . . . (2)

2a. Entire plant usually not much more than 10 cm high. **A. uncialis** Greene [an inch long, alluding to the small size]. Leaves linear, marginally ciliate with incurved hairs; corolla greenish to rose. Rare or inconspicuous on outwash mesas of the Front Range and plains.

2b. Plant larger, usually at least 2 dm high . . . . (3)

3a. Flowers orange, petals usually darker than the hoods. **A. tuberosa** L. subsp. **terminalis** Woodson, ORANGE MILKWEED, BUTTERFLYWEED, **30E**. Foothills near Colorado Springs; a few records from northeastern Colorado.

3b. Flowers not orange . . . . (4)

4a. Hoods of the corona each bearing an incurved horn; flower clusters terminal and/or in the axils of only the uppermost leaves . . . . (5)

4b. Hoods of the corona lacking horns; flower clusters axillary . . . . (14)

5a. Leaves lanceolate or broader; flowers variously colored . . . . (6)

5b. Leaves narrowly linear; flowers white or greenish . . . . (10)

6a. Flowers large, the lobes 7-13 mm long; leaves ovate to orbicular, not more than twice as long as wide . . . . (7)

6b. Flowers smaller, the lobes 3-6 mm long; leaves usually narrower . . . (12)

7a. Hoods narrow at the base and broadest at the apex. **A. oenotheroides** Chamisso & Schlechtendal [from a fancied resemblance to *Oenothera*]. Known in Colorado from a single collection near Troy, Mesa de Maya.

7b. Hoods broadest at the base and tapering upwards . . . . (8)

8a. Flowers pink to purple; fruits white-tomentose, knobby; leaves oblong to lance-ovate, almost twice as long as broad. **A. speciosa** Torrey [showy] **31D**. Our most abundant milkweed, on roadsides, fencerows, and fields everywhere, occasionally in the mountain parks.

8b. Flowers greenish-white; fruits not tomentose, not knobby; leaves ovate-orbicular, not tapering to apex . . . . (9)

9a. Stems and leaves canescent-tomentose; petioles usually over 8 mm long in some leaves. **A. arenaria** Torrey [of sandy places]. Sandhills on the plains.

9b. Stems and leaves nearly or quite glabrous; petioles shorter. **A. latifolia** (Torrey) Rafinesque. Arkansas River drainage, on clay soils.

10a. Leaves opposite; stems bushy-branched; follicles erect from a reflexed pedicel. **A. macrotis** Torrey [for the slenderly acuminate horns]. A unique species, bushy-branched from the base, with rigid stems and filiform revolute leaves. The flowers, with their elongate slender horns, are greenish to pale purple, in loose, few-flowered umbels. East end of Mesa de Maya, BA.

10b. Leaves scattered-alternate to whorled; stems never bushy-branched; follicles erect on erect pedicels . . . . (11)

11a. Plants low, usually not more than 2 dm high, the leaves crowded, not very obviously whorled. **A. pumila** (Gray) Vail [dwarf]. Common on the mesas and plains, often forming large stands.

11b. Plants 3 dm or more high, the leaves whorled, internodes several cm long. **A. subverticillata** (Gray) Vail, **31F**. Mesas and plains, southern counties.

12a. Corolla and hoods bright red or purple; lateral veins directed forward, curving to parallel the midrib. **A. incarnata** L. [flesh-colored, a misnomer]. Wet meadows, ditches, and sloughs in the piedmont valleys.

12b. Corolla and hoods varying from pink to dull purplish to white . . . . (13)

13a. Inflorescence sessile, subtended closely by several leaves; plant low, to 2.5 dm high; petals greenish to pale pink; hoods erect, not tapering. **A. involucrata** Engelmann. Known from a single collection, Mesa de Maya.

13b. Inflorescence peduncled, not subtended closely by leaves; plant tall, erect; petals dull purple; hoods spreading widely, tapering to the top. **A. hallii** Gray [for Elihu Hall], **31C**. Common in the intermontane parks and San Luis Valley, southern counties.

14a. Auricles at the base of the hoods concealed; leaves oval to broadly linear. **A. viridiflora** Rafinesque [green-flowered]. Common on dry slopes of mesas and plains, a sprawling species.

14b. Auricles at the base of the hoods conspicuously spreading; leaves narrowly linear . . . . (15)

15a. Hoods 3-lobed at the apex; corolla greenish-white. **A. stenophylla** Gray [narrow-leaved]. Infrequent on the outwash mesas.

15b. Hoods entire or merely notched in the middle; corolla white. **A. engelmanniana** Woodson, **31B**. Habitats of the preceding.

SARCOSTEMMA R. Brown, 1810 [Greek, *sarco*, fleshy, + *stemma*, wreath, alluding to the inflated vesicles around the anther head]. TWINEVINE

One species, **S. crispum** Bentham [crinkled, alluding to the leaf margins]. Known from a few collections in extreme southeastern Colorado.

ASPARAGACEAE ASPARAGUS FAMILY (ASG)

This family consists of one genus, most species of which occur around the Mediterranean region and most of Africa and Asia. A few, like our vegetable, and some ornamental greenhouse species, are rather delicate plants, but many of the others are horribly spiny shrubs that make impenetrable thickets. The potted asparagus fern is *Asparagus sprengeri*, a broad-"leaved" type; the the one used by florists in bouquets is *A. plumosus*.

ASPARAGUS L. 1753 [the name given it by Theophrastus]

One species, **A. officinalis** L., **29A**. Escaped and adventive along irrigation ditches. The young shoots that we eat are extraordinarily different in appearance from the older, mature ones. The succulent shoots possess triangular scale leaves that are lost when the shoot elongates, shrinks in diameter, and branches to form an intricate, fernlike growth. The filiform green "leaves" are modified shoots and not true leaves at all. The plants bear small, yellowish, lilylike flowers and bright red berries.

ASTERACEAE/COMPOSITAE SUNFLOWER FAMILY (AST/CMP)

Except for the cockleburs and ragweeds, which may be better regarded as a separate family, this family is easily recognized if one can think of a dandelion and a sunflower as being representative of the group. Here are a few guidelines for analysis. The **flower head** usually consists of a number of flowers surrounded by an involucre of bracts called phyllaries. The **phyllaries** may all be equal in size and texture; they may be progressively reduced in size from the inside to the outside of the head; they may be in two distinct series, one outer and another inner. The **receptacle** is the flat or conical disk to which the flowers are attached. This usually is best seen after the flowers fall away; it may be naked or provided with erect hairs, bristles, or scales. The **flowers** are of two possible forms; tubular ones (usually called disk-flowers) are radially symmetrical with a tube, limb, and lobes; and strap-shaped, also called ligulate (ray-flowers), like the daisy "petals" that tell you whether he or she loves you or not. Where the corolla is attached to the inferior ovary (**achene**) there may or may not be a ring of scales or simple or plumose bristles (the **pappus**). The **stamens** have free filaments, but their anthers are fused in a ring around the style. In some genera the anthers are caudate, with a tail at the base. There are two **stigmas**, with the stigmatic (receptive) surface on the inner side.

One of the great sources of variability in this family is the differentiation of the flowers within a head. In the dandelion, for instance, all of the flowers are alike and strap-shaped, but with both stamens and styles. In some other genera, all the flowers are tubular, with no rays. The flowers themselves may vary in their possession of essential organs. Most ray-flowers have only styles; if these are functional, the flower is **fertile**, but if there is no stigmatic surface the ovary does not produce a seed and these flowers are **sterile**. Disk flowers may be perfect (with stamens and styles) or sterile (with only stamens). The achenes are also important to observe, for they can be quadrangular, terete, or flattened either laterally or dorsiventrally. In analyzing members of this family, it is important to examine the head thoroughly for these features, including the pappus, before proceeding with the key.

The family illustrates a very interesting evolutionary tendency: When the number of flowers in an inflorescence is enormously increased at the same time as the flower size is decreased, the visibility of the flowers to pollinating insects probably is decreased as well. This disadvantage is often compensated for in some plant families by massing the flowers into tight clusters and setting up a division of labor among the flowers. This is usually accomplished by enlarging and changing the shape of the marginal flowers of the cluster in such a way as to cause the entire flower cluster to resemble a single flower and thus restore the visibility of the inflorescence. The composites achieve this in a variety of ways, making them a very complex and diverse family.

1a. Flowers all strap-shaped (ligulate) and perfect; juice milky, white or brownish . . . . **Key A**
1b. Flowers not all ligulate; ray-(ligulate) flowers, when present, marginal, either with stigmas only or with no stigmas or stamens; juice usually watery. (2)

2a. Heads with flattened and opened ray-flowers . . . . (3)
2b. Heads with only disk-flowers (sometimes as large as ray-flowers but then distinctly radially symmetrical) . . . . (5)

3a. Rays yellow or orange (sometimes marked with purple or reddish-brown at the base) . . . . (4)
3b. Rays white, pink, purple, red, or blue . . . . **Key B**

4a. Pappus chaffy or of firm awns, or absent; receptacle chaffy, bristly, or naked . . . . **Key C**
4b. Pappus partly or wholly of capillary, sometimes plumose, bristles . . **Key D**

5a. Involucre either a spiny bur or with phyllaries that are either fringed or spiny or in one genus very broadly rounded with a broad papery margin **Key E**
5b. Involucre not as above . . . . (6)

6a. Pappus partly or wholly of numerous capillary, sometimes plumose, bristles (sometimes with an outer row of broader bristles or scales) . . . . . **Key F**

6b. Pappus absent or of scales or awns or very short, chaffy bristles or of a few low teeth, never plumose . . . . **Key G**

KEY A

1a. Flowers blue, pink, purple, or white . . . . (2)
1b. Flowers yellow or orange (sometimes drying pinkish) . . . . (9)

2a. [1] Flowers sky blue (rare mutants white), sessile on nearly leafless, stiffly branched stems; pappus a crown of blunt scales. **Cichorium**, CHICORY
2b. Flowers a shade of pink, lavender, or purple, rarely white; pappus of capillary bristles . . . . (3)

3a. [2] Pappus bristles plumose . . . . (4)
3b. Pappus bristles simple . . . . (5)

4a. [3] Leaves elongate, grasslike; tall, relatively unbranched; heads large, with swollen peduncle. **Tragopogon**, SALSIFY
4b. Leaves short, inconspicuous; richly branched, wiry; heads small; peduncles not swollen. **Stephanomeria**, WIRELETTUCE

5a. [3] Stems low, branched; leaves narrowly linear or bractlike . . . . (6)
5b. Stems tall, simple; leaves well developed, often large . . . . (7)

6a. [5] Annual; fruit with a beak; pappus snow white. **Shinnersoseris**, BEAKED SKELETONWEED
6b. Perennial; fruit beakless; pappus tawny. **Lygodesmia**, SKELETONWEED

7a. [5] Leaves lanceolate, tapered to a point, entire or variously toothed or lobed; fruits flattened. **Lactuca**, LETTUCE
7b. Leaves oblanceolate, rounded, very shallowly if at all toothed. . . . . (8)

8a. [7] Leaves glabrous and glaucous; heads nodding, in a raceme. **Prenanthes**
8b. Leaves hirsute; heads few, erect in an open panicle. **Chlorocrepis**, HAWKWEED

9a. [1] Leaves primarily basal, the stem leaves, when present, near the base of the plant and greatly reduced upwards . . . . (10)
9b. Leaves not primarily basal; stem-leaves well developed . . . . (19)

10a. [9] Pappus of plumose bristles . . . . (11)
10b. Pappus of simple bristles . . . . (12)

11a. [10] Fruits truncate at the apex, not beaked; leaves glabrous; native plant of the mountains. **Microseris**
11b. Fruits with long beaks; leaves hirsute; weed of lawns. **Hypochaeris**

12a. [10] Plants glaucous, with a rosette of oblanceolate entire or denticulate basal leaves; heads about 3, subtended by a leaflike bract; pappus composed of 10-15 small, oblong scales and an inner group of long capillary bristles. **Krigia**
12b. Plants without the above combination of characteristics . . . . (13)

13a. [12] Heads solitary on a leafless scape . . . . (14)
13b. Heads (or buds) few to numerous, rarely solitary; stem usually with 1 or more well-developed leaves . . . . (16)

14a. [13] Leaves with ± wavy margins bordered with crinkly white hairs; early spring plant of the outwash mesas. **Nothocalais**
14b. Leaf margins neither wavy nor crinkly hairy . . . . (15)

15a. [14] Fruit 10-ribbed or 10-nerved, without minute spines on the surface; outer phyllaries erect. **Agoseris**, FALSE DANDELION
15b. Fruits 4-5-ribbed, with minute spines at least near the apex; phyllaries reflexed (except in a few tundra species). **Taraxacum**, DANDELION

16a. [13] Ray-flowers deep orange; stems with short, gland-tipped hairs and stiffly spreading hirsute pubescence. **Hieracium**, HAWKWEED
16b. Ray-flowers yellow; stems variously pubescent or glabrous .... (17)

17a. [16] Pappus white; fruits tapering upwards; phyllaries ± thickened at base and on the midrib .... (18)
17b. Pappus brownish or reddish; fruits not tapering upwards; phyllaries not thickened. **Chlorocrepis**, HAWKWEED

18a. [17] Dwarf alpine rosette-plants with succulent, simple, glabrous, entire leaves and inflorescence no longer than the leaves. **Askellia**, ALPINE HAWKSBEARD
18b. Tall plants with basal, usually hairy, often deeply pinnatifid leaves and elongate flowering stem; never alpine. **Psilochenia**, AMERICAN HAWKSBEARD

19a. [9] Leaves simple, grasslike, not toothed or divided. **Tragopogon**, SALSIFY
19b. Leaves toothed, lobed, or pinnatifid .... (20)

20a. [19] Leaves ovate, petiolate, shallowly dentate, rounded at the apex and never lobed; pappus none. **Lapsana**, NIPPLEWORT
20b. Leaves various, often lobed, but not ovate and petiolate or rounded at the apex; pappus of bristles .... (21)

21a. [20] Pappus plumose; plants resembling *Tragopogon* but with pinnatifid leaves. **Podospermum**, FALSE SALSIFY
21b. Pappus simple .... (22)

22a. [21] Fruits beaked; involucre cylindric or ovoid-cylindric. **Lactuca**, LETTUCE
22b. Fruits not beaked .... (23)

23a. [22] Heads over 1 cm long; involucre turbinate or hemispheric. **Sonchus**, SOWTHISTLE
23b. Heads less than 1 cm long; involucre narrow at the base. **Crepis**, HAWKSBEARD

KEY B

1a. Plants stemless, the extremely short-rayed heads almost hidden in clusters of oblanceolate basal leaves crowning several stout caudices; gypsophile. **Bolophyta**
1b. Plants with distinct stems, or otherwise not as above .... (2)

2a. [1] Leaves (at least the lower) opposite .... (3)
2b. Leaves alternate or basal .... (5)

3a. [2] Ray-flowers pink. **Palafoxia**
3b. Ray-flowers white .... (4)

4a. [3] Perennial; leaves linear-oblong, sessile or gradually narrowed to the base. **Melampodium**, BLACKFOOT DAISY
4b. Annual; leaves ovate, distinctly petiolate. **Galinsoga**

5a. [2] Receptacle conical; rays purple. **Echinacea**, PURPLE CONEFLOWER
5b. Receptacle flat .... (6)

6a. [5] Receptacle chaffy, at least in the middle; rays white, rarely pinkish. (7)
6b. Receptacle not chaffy . . . . (9)

7a. [6] Rays few, commonly 3-5, short and broad, less than 5 mm long; perennial. **Achillea**, YARROW
7b. Rays numerous, mostly 5-10 mm long or more . . . . (8)

8a. [7] Native perennial with prominent rosettes and tall, few-leaved floral stems. **Hymenopappus**
8b. Introduced annual weeds with leafy stems. **Anthemis**

9a. [6] Pappus lacking . . . . (10)
9b. Pappus present, of capillary or stouter bristles . . . . (11)

10a. [9] Leaves simple, toothed or the basal somewhat pinnatifid; perennial. **Leucanthemum**, OX-EYE DAISY
10b. Leaves finely pinnatisect; annual. **Matricaria**

11a. [9] Leaves cordate-triangular, sagittate, white beneath; stem leaves reduced to bracts. **Petasites**, SWEET COLTSFOOT
11b. Leaves not as above . . . . (12)

12a. [11] Pappus (at least in the disk flowers) of several to many rigid bristles; achenes pubescent with 2-forked or glochidiate hairs; usually low, often stemless plants. **Townsendia**, EASTER DAISY
12b. Pappus of many long capillary bristles; achenes glabrous or pubescent with simple hairs . . . . (13)

13a. [12] Phyllaries subequal or ± imbricate, often green in part but neither definitely leaflike nor with chartaceous base and herbaceous green tip; style branches lanceolate or broader, acute to obtuse, 0.5 mm long or less (14)
13b. Phyllaries either subequal and the outer leaflike, or more commonly imbricate, with chartaceous base and evident green tip, sometimes chartaceous throughout; style branches lanceolate or narrower, acute or acuminate, usually over 5 mm long . . . . (18)

14a. [13] Carpellate (ray) flowers very numerous, filiform, with very narrow, short, erect ligules, these sometimes not exceeding the disk, or the inner carpellate flowers tubular and without ligules . . . . (15)
14b. Carpellate flowers few to numerous, the tube generally cylindrical, the ligules well-developed and spreading, or occasionally reduced and absent but not short, narrow and erect . . . . (16)

15a. [14] Ligule of ray florets minute, rarely exceeding the involucre; involucre 3-4(5) mm high. **Conyza**, HORSEWEED
15b. Ligules conspicuous or, if reduced, the involucre larger. **Erigeron**, DAISY

16a. [14] True perennials, often with deep-seated rhizomes or well-developed, woody caudices. **Erigeron**, DAISY
16b. Annuals, biennials, or short-lived perennials, without deep-seated rhizomes or well-developed, woody caudices . . . . (17)

17a. [16] Pappus of the ray and disk flowers alike, of bristles, sometimes also with outer short setae or scales. **Erigeron** (*divergens* group)
17b. Pappus of the the disk flowers composed of bristles and short outer setae, that of the ray-flowers lacking the bristles. **Stenactis**

18a. [13] Annual; involucre 5-10 mm high; pappus longer than the flowers, very conspicuous in fruit (like a powderpuff). **Brachyactis**
18b. Perennial, otherwise not as above . . . . (19)

19a. [18] Leaves linear; ray-flowers white, rarely pink . . . . (20)
19b. Leaves broader; rays white or colored; plants not as above . . . . (21)

20a. [19] Leaves less than 1 cm long; plants much branched, forming low, rounded clumps; arid grasslands. **Leucelene**, SAND ASTER
20b. Leaves over 3 cm long; plants unbranched, with a few-headed, flat-topped inflorescence; pine forests and adjacent meadows. **Unamia**

21a. [19] Leaves toothed or divided; rays either lavender or yellow . . . . . (22)
21b. Leaves entire; rays never yellow . . . . (24)

22a. [21] Low, alpine mat-plants from woody branched caudices. **Machaeranthera coloradoënsis**
22b. Taller plants, of lower altitudes, mostly from taproots . . . . (23)

23a. [22] Phyllaries recurved; common roadside plants. **Machaeranthera**, TANSY ASTER
23b. Phyllaries erect; very rare plant of Raton Pass area. **Herrickia**

24a. [22] Inner phyllaries dry and chartaceous, strongly keeled, in 4-5 very distinct imbricate rows; pappus often brownish. **Eucephalus**
24b. Inner phyllaries at least with green tips, commonly chartaceous on the sides and base; pappus white . . . . (25)

25a. [24] Phyllaries glandular-puberulent. **Virgulus campestris**
25b. Phyllaries not glandular . . . . (26)

26a. [25] Involucre 3-4 mm high; leaves linear or oblong, short; leaves and stems generally stiff-hairy; heads very numerous. **Virgulus**
26b. Involucre 5-15 mm high; leaves broader, elongate; leaves usually glabrate except above; heads relatively few . . . . (27)

27a. [26] Stems from a woody, thickened, cormlike base, with 3-nerved basal leaves; achenes fusiform, strigose; phyllaries glandular or stipitate-glandular. **Virgulus**
27b. Plants not as above. **Aster**

KEY C

1a. Deep-seated perennials with massive taproots and caudices, very large basal leaves and large heads . . . . (2)
1b. Annuals or perennials, but not as above . . . . (3)

2a. [1] Leaves lanceolate or lance-oblong, glutinous or hirsute. **Wyethia**, MULES EARS
2b. Leaves cordate or pinnatifid, appressed hairy or hirsute-scabrous. **Balsamorhiza**, BALSAMROOT

3a. [1] Phyllaries covered with a sticky-gummy exudate . . . . (4)
3b. Phyllaries not sticky-gummy, sometimes with glandular hairs or spots . (6)

4a. [3] Leaves opposite; exudate confined to very narrow lines. **Flaveria**
4b. Leaves alternate; exudate generally covering the phyllaries . . . . (5)

5a. [4] Leaves lanceolate or oblong, commonly toothed; heads large, over 10 mm diameter. **Grindelia**, GUMWEED
5b. Leaves narrowly linear, entire; heads small, less than 5 mm diameter. **Gutierrezia**, SNAKEWEED

6a. [3] Receptacle chaffy or bristly . . . . (7)
6b. Receptacle naked (rarely with a few chaffy scales between the ray and disk flowers) . . . . (23)

7a. [6] Receptacle bristly; rays usually bicolored, yellow and orange-red. **Gaillardia**, BLANKETFLOWER
7b. Receptacle chaffy . . . . (8)

8a. [7] Phyllaries very broad and rounded, not at all acute . . . . (9)
8b. Phyllaries acute, not broad and rounded; leaves not velvety-hairy . . . (10)

9a. [8] Low herbs, much branched from a woody base; leaves linear; ray-flowers much broader than the phyllaries, persistent. **Zinnia**
9b. Tall, little-branched herbs; leaves lyrate-pinnatifid; ray-flowers much narrower and less conspicuous than the phyllaries. **Berlandiera**, GREEN EYES

10a. [8] Achenes flattened at right angles to the radius of the head . . . . (11)
10b. Achenes either not flattened or flattened parallel to the radius . . . . (16)

11a. [10] Foliage harshly hispid or scabrous . . . . (12)
11b. Foliage glabrous or nearly so . . . . (14)

12a. [11] Leaves simple, ovate, sessile. **Silphium**, ROSINWEED
12b. Leaves pinnatifid, petiolate . . . . (13)

13a. [12] Plant low; leaves hispid, up to 30 cm long. **Engelmannia**
13b. Plant 1-3 m tall; leaves up to 4 dm long and over 1 dm wide, scabrous. **Silphium**

14a. [11] Pappus of 2-4 firm, retrorsely barbed awns; leaves entire, pinnatifid or pinnately compound. **Bidens**, BEGGAR'S TICK
14b. Pappus of 2 minute teeth, or lacking; leaves pinnately divided, mostly basal . . . . (15)

15a. [14] Lobes of disk-flowers equal, triangular, about twice as long as wide, shorter than the broad upper part of the tube. **Coreopsis**
15b. Lobes of disk-flowers unequal, oblong or linear-lanceolate, more than twice as long as wide, equalling or longer than upper part of the tube. **Thelesperma**

16a. [10] Phyllaries in 1 series, the margins curved to enclose the disk-achenes; rays very short, inconspicuous; weedy glandular annual. **Madia**, TARWEED
16b. Phyllaries not as above . . . . (17)

17a. [16] Receptacle distinctly conical or elongate . . . . (18)
17b. Receptacle flat or only slightly convex . . . . (19)

18a. [17] Receptacle elongate-cylindric; rays often partly maroon; leaves strigose, with narrow divisions. **Ratibida**, PRAIRIE CONEFLOWER
18b. Receptacle merely conic; rays always pure yellow; leaves either simple or with relatively broad divisions. **Rudbeckia**, BLACK-EYED SUSAN

19a. [17] Rays with well-developed styles, producing seeds . . . . (20)
19b. Rays lacking functional styles, not producing seeds . . . . (21)

20a. [19] Leaves mostly opposite, green, and scabrous; ray-flowers persistent, becoming papery in age. **Heliopsis,** OX-EYE
20b. Leaves mostly alternate, silvery-white pubescent beneath, coarsely toothed; annual weed. **Ximenesia.** CROWNBEARD; COWPEN DAISY

21a. [19] Pappus lacking; rays up to 1.5 cm long. **Heliomeris**
21b. Pappus present, although sometimes falling away when the achene is ripe; rays longer . . . . (22)

22a. [21] Pappus persistent; disk-achenes strongly flattened, thin-edged. **Helianthella,** LITTLE SUNFLOWER
22b. Pappus deciduous; fruits only slightly compressed, plump. **Helianthus,** SUNFLOWER

23a. [6] Some leaves pinnatifid or ternately divided . . . . (24)
23b. Leaves simple and undivided . . . . (28)

24a. [23] Plants without basal rosettes of leaves . . . . (25)
24b. Plants with basal rosettes . . . . (26)

25a. [24] Perennials. **Picradeniopsis**
25b. Annuals with slender taproot; phyllaries with large yellow or brown glandular spots. **Dyssodia,** FETID MARIGOLD

26a. [23] Basal rosette leaves with many divisions; ultimate lobes with rounded tips. **Bahia**
26b. Basal rosette leaves with relatively few divisions; ultimate lobes linear with pointed tips . . . . (27)

27a. [26] Phyllaries in 2 distinct series, the outer ones shorter, united at their bases to form a shallow cup; heads less than 2 cm diameter; middle altitudes. **Picradenia**
27b. Phyllaries not in 2 series, the outer ones not at all united; heads solitary, over 3 cm diameter; tundra. **Rydbergia,** OLD-MAN-OF-THE-MOUNTAIN

28a. [23] Annual; leaves opposite . . . . (29)
28b. Perennial with alternate or basal leaves . . . . (30)

29a. [28] Leaves linear, entire, with a few long basal cilia; ray-flowers several; involucre turbinate. **Pectis**
29b. Leaves lanceolate, with shallow, distant teeth; ray-flowers solitary; involucre cylindric. **Flaveria**

30a. [28] Leaves linear, basal. **Tetraneuris**
30b. Leaves not linear nor all basal . . . . (31)

31a. [30] Leaves decurrent on the stem; top of peduncle not lanate. **Helenium,** SNEEZEWEED
31b. Leaves not decurrent on the stem; top of peduncle lanate. **Dugaldia,** ORANGE SNEEZEWEED

KEY D

1a. Leaves mostly opposite. **Arnica**
1b. Leaves alternate or basal . . . . (2)

2a. Phyllaries narrow, in a single series except for 1 or 2 shorter ones from the base of the head . . . . (3)

2b. Phyllaries in 2 or more series, subequal or imbricate . . . . (7)

3a. Heads turbinate, usually nodding in bud, succulent; leaves succulent, coarsely dentate, often with purplish and clasping petiole bases; roots little-branched, ropy; plants often with a strong lemon scent when crushed or after drying. **Ligularia**

3b. Heads not turbinate or nodding, rarely succulent; leaves not as above; roots fibrous-branched; plants lacking lemon scent . . . . (4)

4a. Leaves progressively reduced in size upward . . . . (5)

4b. Leaves about equally distributed or concentrated upward . . . . (6)

5a. Plants rhizomatous or with an erect caudex, with branching fibrous roots; basal leaves entire to pinnatisect but only rarely with callous denticles along the margin; relatively low, less than 0.5 m tall. **Packera**

5b. Plants either with a short, coarse, lateral or suberect rhizome or with a very short, buttonlike caudex, and with long, unbranched, fleshy, fibrous roots; leaves entire to repand-dentate, often with small callous teeth on the margins. **"Senecio"**: *Lugentes* and *Integerrimi*

6a. Plants with numerous stems from the base, forming bushy clumps; leaves linear or with few linear lobes; plants of open steppe or desert. **"Senecio"**: *Suffruticosi*

6b. Plants with relatively few stems; leaves broader, entire, dentate or pinnatifid. **"Senecio"**: *Triangulares*

7a. Heads usually very small and numerous, in panicles; phyllaries rarely distinctly herbaceous at apex . . . . (8)

7b. Heads usually few and relatively large; phyllaries usually distinctly herbaceous at apex . . . . (10)

8a. Leaves linear throughout the stem. **Euthamia**

8b. Leaves broader, or only uppermost linear . . . . (9)

9a. Phyllaries longitudinally striate (having parallel ribs in addition to the midvein); restricted to the plains. **Oligoneuron**, STIFF GOLDENROD

9b. Phyllaries not longitudinally striate; throughout the area. **Solidago**, GOLDENROD

10a. Leaves pinnatifid; phyllaries graduated. **Machaeranthera**, TANSY ASTER

10b. Leaves entire or merely toothed . . . . (11)

11a. Annual, the stem erect, single, from a taproot; leaves spinulose dentate to serrate; rare plant of sand dunes, eastern plains. **Prionopsis**

11b. Perennial . . . . (12)

12a. Leaves not chiefly basal, the leaves always entire . . . . (13)

12b. Leaves chiefly basal; stem leaves reduced, sometimes toothed . . . . . (15)

13a. Involucre up to 25 mm tall and 35 mm wide; pappus brownish; leaves narrowly or broadly linear, glabrous. **Oönopsis**

13b. Involucre much smaller; pappus white; leaves, if linear, not glabrous. (14)

14a. Pappus double, the inner of capillary bristles, the outer of paleae or short bristles; involucre with narrow imbricate phyllaries. **Heterotheca**, GOLDEN ASTER

14b. Pappus single, of capillary bristles; involucre with broad herbaceous-tipped phyllaries. **Oreochrysum**

15a. Plants low, caespitose, with a woody caudex, stiff, shiny, evergreen linear-lanceolate leaves and solitary scapose heads. **Stenotus**

15b. Plants with wholly herbaceous stem, woody only in the short caudex; leaves not evergreen, neither stiff nor shiny . . . . (16)

16a. Plants with a taproot and basal leaves larger than the cauline; heads solitary or racemose on elongate peduncles; disk-flowers widened upwards. **Pyrrocoma**

16b. Plants with short caudices or rhizomes; heads on short peduncles little exceeding the basal leaves; disk-flowers tubular. **Tonestus**

KEY E

1a. Branched yellowish thorns arising in the leaf axils; leaves bicolored; fruit a small cocklebur covered with hooked spines. **Acanthoxanthium**, SPINY COCKLEBUR

1b. Stems not thorny . . . . (2)

2a. Leaves spiny-margined, thistlelike; involucre with spine-tipped or fringed phyllaries . . . . (2)

2b. Leaves not spiny-margined . . . . (5)

3a. Pappus plumose; receptacle densely bristly. **Cirsium**, THISTLE

3b. Pappus bristles simple, merely barbellate . . . . (4)

4a. Receptacle densely bristly, neither honeycombed nor obviously fleshy. **Carduus**, THISTLE

4b. Receptacle fleshy, conspicuously honeycombed on the surface, not bristly or only sparsely and shortly so. **Onopordum**, SCOTCH THISTLE

5a. Heads spherical, phyllaries slender, with hooked tips; leaves huge, cordate-ovate. **Arctium**, BURDOCK

5b. Heads and leaves not as above . . . . (6)

6a. Heads with the phyllaries fused into a single spine-studded bur . . . . . (7)

6b. Heads with separate phyllaries; spines, if present, along the margins . (8)

7a. Burs very small, less than 1 cm, the spines not hooked. **Ambrosia**, RAGWEED

7b. Burs large, over 1 cm long, the spines hooked. **Xanthium**, COCKLEBUR

8a. Phyllaries very broad and rounded, with a broad, papery, entire margin; rhizomatous perennial with usually simple leaves. **Acroptilon**, RUSSIAN KNAPWEED

8b. Phyllaries either with margin spinose or fringed, or lacerate; annuals or perennials, not rhizomatous . . . . (9)

9a. Phyllaries brown, broad, with papery-lacerate margins. **Jacea**, BROWN KNAPWEED

9b. Phyllaries white, with fringed or spiny margins . . . . (10)

10a. Phyllaries with a soft, white fringe; leaves simple or weakly divided; flowers large, blue, pink, or white. **Leucacantha**, CORNFLOWER

10b. Phyllaries with stiff marginal spines; leaves strongly pinnatifid. **Acosta**, KNAPWEED

KEY F

1a. True shrubs . . . . (2)
1b. Herbs or only woody at the base . . . . (5)

2a. [1] Plants dioecious; staminate and carpellate heads on different plants. **Baccharis**, GROUNDSEL TREE
2b. Plants with perfect flowers in the heads . . . . (3)

3a. [2] Flowers white or greenish; leaves scabrous. **Brickellia**
3b. Flowers yellow; leaves not scabrous . . . . (4)

4a. [3] Phyllaries of the same length, in a single series (a few short ones sometimes at the base). **Tetradymia**, HORSEBRUSH
4b. Phyllaries imbricated, in vertical rows. **Chrysothamnus**, RABBITBRUSH

5a. [1] Plants tending to be woody, at least at the base . . . . (6)
5b. Plants herbaceous . . . . (9)

6a. [5] Flowers yellow . . . . (7)
6b. Flowers white or cream-colored . . . . (8)

7a. Phyllaries in well-marked, vertical files, the tips not sharply cuspidate. **Chrysothamnus**, RABBITBRUSH
7b. Phyllaries not in vertical files, the tips sharply cuspidate. **Oönopsis**

8a. [6] Twigs covered with a white felt; plants woody at the base, forming hemispherical compact clumps. **Macronema**
8b. Twigs naked; leaves scabrous; plants irregularly formed. **Brickellia**

9a. [5] Leaves opposite or whorled . . . . (10)
9b. Leaves alternate . . . . (12)

10a. [9] Flowers yellow. **Arnica**
10b. Flowers white or purplish . . . . (11)

11a. [10] Leaves opposite; flowers white or cream-colored; involucre 2-4 mm long; phyllaries almost nerveless. **Ageratina**
11b. Leaves whorled; flowers purplish; involucre about 1 cm long, phyllaries strongly several-nerved. **Eupatorium**, JOE PYE WEED

12a. [9] Flowers all alike, perfect, and fertile . . . . (13)
12b. Outer flowers of the head carpellate or, in some heads, all carpellate, or plants dioecious . . . . (20)

13a. [11] Flowers yellow or orange . . . . (14)
13b. Flowers lavender, purple, white, or cream-colored . . . . (17)

14a. [13] Phyllaries in 1 series, elongate, equal, with a few outer ones (not in a whorl) near the base of the head . . . . (15)
14b. Phyllaries imbricate in 2 or more series (rayless forms of *Aster* and *Erigeron*) . . . . **Key B**

15a. [14] Annual; leaves pinnatifid; phyllaries black-tipped; garden weed. **Senecio** (True *Senecio*)
15b. Perennial; leaves simple; phyllaries not black-tipped; native plants . . (16)

16a. [15] Heads turbinate, nodding, succulent. **Ligularia**
16b. Heads erect, not succulent. **Packera**

17a. [13] Flowers white or cream-colored to pale pinkish; heads in loose panicles. **Brickellia**
17b. Flowers purple . . . . (18)

18a. [17] Heads in an elongate raceme, rarely solitary. **Liatris,** GAYFEATHER
18b. Heads in open, often flat-topped clusters . . . . (19)

19a. [18] Tall plants 1 m or more high; pappus of simple bristles, and an outer series of short scales or broader bristles; plants of the eastern plains. **Vernonia**, IRONWEED
19b. Low plants a few dm high; pappus plumose; alpine. **Saussurea**

20a. [12] Basal leaves over 10 cm long, triangular-cordate, white beneath. **Petasites**, SWEET COLTSFOOT
20b. Basal leaves not as above . . . . (21)

21a. [20] Leaves and stems ± white-woolly; phyllaries with scarious tips . (22)
21b. Leaves and stems not white-woolly; phyllaries not scarious (rayless forms of *Erigeron* and *Aster*) . . . . **Key B**

22a. [21] Plants with taproot, annual or perennial; heads all with outer carpellate and inner perfect flowers . . . . (23)
22b. Plants fibrous-rooted, perennial, often with rhizomes or stolons, without taproot; dioecious or nearly so, the heads on some plants all staminate or carpellate . . . . (25)

23a. [22] Annual with a single, tight, ball-like rosette of leaves and heads terminating the stem, or with a few stiff branchlets from this to form additional ones; phyllaries with strongly green midrib nearly to the tip; receptacle with a few carpellate flowers borne between series of phyllaries. **Evax,** RABBIT-TOBACCO
23b. Annual or perennial; stems leafy, not modified as above; receptacle naked; phyllaries with ± conspicuous scarious or hyaline tips . . . . (24)

24a. [23] Heads very small, imbedded in wool, the clusters leafy-bracted; low annuals, seldom more than 20 cm high. **Filaginella,** CUDWEED
24b. Heads medium-sized (5 mm or more wide), not leafy-bracted; plant usually 30 cm or more high (resembling pearly everlasting). **Gnaphalium,** CUDWEED

25a. [22] Basal leaves forming a conspicuous, persistent tuft; stem seldom very leafy, often with stolons or rhizomes; strictly dioecious, the staminate and carpellate plants often very different in appearance. **Antennaria,** PUSSYTOES
25b. Basal leaves soon withering, not larger than the numerous stem leaves; plants with rhizomes but never stolons; heads of carpellate plants usually with a few centrally located staminate flowers. **Anaphalis,** PEARLY EVERLASTING

KEY G

1a. Phyllaries extremely sticky-gummy, the tips usually recurved. **Grindelia,** GUMWEED
1b. Phyllaries not sticky-gummy nor with recurved tips . . . . (2)

2a. [1] Heads of two kinds, staminate and carpellate; involucre of the carpellate heads burlike or nutlike, with hooked prickles, spines, or tubercles; staminate involucre unarmed; corollas small and inconspicuous, green . . . . (3)
2b. Heads all alike . . . . (4)

3a. [2] Carpellate involucre with hooked spines. **Xanthium**, COCKLEBUR
3b. Carpellate involucre with tubercles or straight spines. **Ambrosia**, RAGWEED

4a. [2] Leaves opposite . . . . (5)
4b. Leaves alternate or basal . . . . (8)

5a. [4] Leaves triangular, attenuate at the tip; plants forming hemispheric bushes up to 1 m tall. **Pericome**
5b. Leaves not triangular; plants not as above . . . . (6)

6a. [6] Tall weeds with large, cordate leaves resembling those of sunflower. **Cyclachaena**, MARSH-ELDER
6b. Low annuals with linear, dissected leaves . . . . (7)

7a. [5] Phyllaries with prominent glandular spots. **Dyssodia**, FETID MARIGOLD
7b. Phyllaries without glands. **Bahia neomexicana**

8a. [4] Receptacle chaffy or bristly . . . . (9)
8b. Receptacle not as above, sometimes with weak hairs . . . . (11)

9a. [8] Heads large (over 1 cm), cylindric, purple-black. **Rudbeckia**, BLACK-EYED SUSAN
9b. Heads small, flat or rounded, not dark . . . . (10)

10a. [9] Leaves oblong; heads single in the leaf axils, nodding; low plants. **Iva**, POVERTYWEED
10b. Leaves triangular-ovate; heads in a panicle; tall, rank weeds. **Cyclachaena**, MARSH-ELDER

11a. [8] Pappus of scales . . . . (12)
11b. Pappus absent, or a minute crown of teeth . . . . (14)

12a. [11] Leaves entire; pink-flowered annuals of the eastern plains. **Palafoxia**
12b. Leaves pinnatisect . . . . (13)

13a. [12] Phyllaries with broad papery tips. **Hymenopappus**
13b. Phyllaries with narrow green tips. **Chaenactis**, PINCUSHION

14a. [11] Phyllaries in 1 equal series, each enclosing an achene; linear-leaved annuals with glandular heads. **Madia**, TARWEED
14b. Phyllaries in several series, not individually enclosing the achenes; annuals, perennials, or shrubs . . . . (15)

15a. [14] Heads yellow, in flat-topped clusters or solitary . . . . (16)
15b. Heads greenish-yellow, in spikes, panicles, or racemes . . . . (17)

16a. [15] Low herb less than 0.5 m high, with pineapple odor. **Lepidotheca**, PINEAPPLEWEED
16b. Tall herb over 1 meter high, with a "tansy" odor. **Tanacetum**, TANSY

17a. [15] Ray-flowers absent; disk-flowers present and fertile (with functional styles, stigmas, and ovary); shrubs. **Seriphidium**, SAGEBRUSH. (Note: *Artemisia bigelovii* resembles this but has heads with only 2-4 flowers, one or two of these with short rays and lacking stamens.)
17b. Ray-flowers (small) present . . . . (18)

18a. [17] Disk-flowers present and fertile; herbaceous or slightly woody at the base. **Artemisia**, SAGEWORT, WORMWOOD

18b. Disk-flowers present but sterile, their achenes aborting; herbs or shrubs. **Oligosporus**, SAGEWORT, TARRAGON

ACANTHOXANTHIUM Fourreau 1869 [Greek, *acanthos*, spine, + *Xanthium*]. SPINY COCKLEBUR

One species, **A. spinosum** (L.) Fourreau. Adventive in disturbed ground, BA (*Xanthium*).

ACHILLEA L. 1753 [so called because its healing powers were thought to have been discovered by Achilles]. YARROW

One species, **A. lanulosa** Nuttall. Meadows and roadsides from sagebrush to alpine. In the tundra, a local race occurs with the phyllaries strongly margined with dark brown-black (var. *alpicola* Rydberg). Very closely related but effectively isolated from the Eurasian cultivated and introduced *A. millefolium*, a hexaploid (*A. lanulosa* is tetraploid). The two species are virtually identical morphologically.

ACOSTA Adanson 1763 [presumably for José d'Acosta, botanist-missionary in Peru from 1569-1588] (formerly in *Centaurea*). KNAPWEED

1a. Phyllaries with a black spot; heads 1 cm high or more; stems relatively little-branched. **A. maculosa** (L.) Holub, SPOTTED KNAPWEED. With the next, but more common in the foothills, and hybridizing with it. Flowers usually purple.

1b. Phyllaries pale, not spotted; heads smaller; stems much- and widely branched. **A. diffusa** (Lamarck) Sojak, TUMBLE KNAPWEED. An abundant adventive along highway rights-of-way and on disturbed ground. Flowers white or lavender.

ACROPTILON Cassini 1827 [Greek, *akron*, summit, + *ptilon*, feather, alluding to the hairy tip of the inner phyllaries]. RUSSIAN KNAPWEED

One species, **A. repens** (L.) de Candolle. An abundant adventive weed along roadsides, especially in the San Luis Valley, also around towns on the eastern plains (*Centaurea*).

AGERATINA Spach 1841 [diminutive of *Ageratum*]

One species, **A. herbacea** (Gray) King & Robinson. Pine forests, Mesa de Maya, LA (*Eupatorium*). The flowers are white, the leaves triangular ovate and deeply crenate-dentate.

AGOSERIS Rafinesque 1819 [Greek, *aex*, goat, + *seris*, chicory]. FALSE DANDELION

1a. Flowers yellow, often drying pinkish or bluish; fruit beak usually comparatively stout, nerved throughout, much shorter than the body (but see var. *laciniata*!). **A. glauca** (Pursh) Rafinesque. Extremely variable in leaf outline and plant size, it forms apomictic populations, each differing slightly from another. Among the better marked ones are var. **laciniata** (Eaton) Smiley, with a scape less than 2 dm tall, pinnatifid leaves, and a narrow head with usually long-beaked achenes and var. **dasycephala** (Torrey & Gray) Jepson, a tall, coarse plant with large woolly heads.

1b. Flowers burnt-orange, often drying purplish; fruit beak slender, not nerved throughout, elongate. **A. aurantiaca** (Hooker) Greene. Meadows, montane, subalpine. The var. **purpurea** (Gray) Cronquist has shorter, blunter phyllaries mottled with purple. Both types are common.

AMBROSIA L. 1753 [food of the gods, a misnomer!]. RAGWEED

1a. Leaves entire to palmately 3-5-lobed; involucre of staminate heads with black ribs. **A. trifida** L., GIANT RAGWEED. Adventive, ruderal weed. An important hay-fever plant.
1b. Leaves once to thrice pinnatifid; staminate involucres not ribbed . . . . (2)

2a. Fruiting involucre naked or with a few very short knobs . . . . (3)
2b. Fruiting involucre burlike, with long, sharp spines . . . . (4)

3a. Perennial with deep-seated rhizomes (appearing annual if the rhizome is not collected; the stems of such specimens can be seen to have been broken away and do not taper to the taproot). **A. psilostachya** de Candolle var. **coronopifolia** (Torrey & Gray) Farwell. Indigenous, ruderal weed, uncommon on the Western Slope. The leaf segments are always broader in this than in the next.
3b. Annual with a slender taproot. **A. artemisiifolia** L. var. **elatior** (L.) Descourtils. Uncommon, adventive weed.

4a. Carpellate heads regularly 2-flowered . . . . (5)
4b. Carpellate heads 1-flowered (rarely 2-flowered in *A. confertifolia*) . . . . (6)

5a. Leaves finely dissected; blades dark green above and white-pubescent beneath. **A. tomentosa** Nuttall. Common in sandy places on the plains (*Franseria discolor*).
5b. Leaves with only a few broad lobes; blades and stems uniformly silvery-gray pubescent. **A. grayi** (Nelson) Shinners. On the plains, easternmost counties.

6a. Mature carpellate head 6-10 mm long; spines usually elongate and straight, not hooked. **A. acanthicarpa** Hooker, SANDBUR, **35C**. Indigenous, ruderal weed.
6b. Mature carpellate heads 2-5 mm long . . . . (7)

7a. Leaves sessile, hardly over 1 cm long, with few narrow divisions, green above, narrowly revolute, the margins and midrib below contrasting with the white tomentose underside. **A. linearis** (Rydberg) Payne. Endemic, rare on the eastern plains, KW, LN.
7b. Leaves petiolate, bipinnatifid with many narrow divisions, uniformly strigose on both surfaces. **A. confertifolia** DC. [crowded-leaves]. Lower Arkansas River Valley, base of Mesa de Maya.

ANAPHALIS de Candolle 1838 [anagram of *Gnaphalium*]. PEARLY EVERLASTING

One species, **A. margaritacea** (L.) Bentham & Hooker. Meadows and forest openings, montane and subalpine.

ANTENNARIA Gaertner 1791 [from the resemblance of the pappus of staminate flowers to the antennae of some insects]. PUSSYTOES

Note: A very difficult group because the species hybridize and subsequent generations often are apomictic; also, some populations may be equally divided between male plants and female plants, while in others only one sex may occur; it is useful to note this in the field. This key gives only a rough guide to the taxonomy.

1a. Heads solitary; low mat-plants; flowering stems hardly higher than the leaves. **A. rosulata** Rydberg. Sagebrush flats, southwestern counties. Plants forming very large mats.

1b. Heads more than one to a flowering stem (or, if occasionally solitary, flowering stems developed) . . . . (2)

2a. Not mat-forming, never with stolons . . . . (3)
2b. Mat-forming, usually with leafy stolons . . . . (4)

3a. Involucre scarious to the base, glabrous or nearly so; basal leaves linear-oblanceolate, middle cauline leaves linear. **A. luzuloides** Torrey & Gray. Meadows, foothills of Park Range in North Park.
3b. Involucre densely pubescent below, not at all scarious; leaves with prominent parallel venation. **A. pulcherrima** (Hooker) Greene subsp. **anaphaloides** (Rydberg) Weber. Dry meadows, sagebrush, and open forests.

4a. Leaves green above . . . . (5)
4b. Leaves white-tomentose on both sides . . . . (6)

5a. Plants all carpellate. **A. howellii** Greene. Infrequent in pine woods, cool north-facing canyons, and forested outwash mesas of the Front Range (*A. neodioica*). This is an apomictic species (the eastern species, *A. neglecta*, which was erroneously reported here, is a sexual species).
5b. Plants evenly divided into male and female populations. **A. marginata** Greene. East base of San Juan Mountains, RG.

6a. Terminal scarious part of phyllaries discolored or brownish to dirty blackish-green; high altitudes . . . . (7)
6b. Terminal part of phyllaries white, yellowish, or pink . . . . (9)

7a. Plant glandular (easily seen on the phyllaries), with citronella odor when fresh; leaves very short and broad, acute. **A. aromatica** Evert. Limestone tundra, Saguache Range. Both sexes present. R. Bayer suggests that our plants belong to *A. rosea* var. *pulvinata*. Time will tell.
7b. Not glandular, odorless; leaves usually oblanceolate . . . . (8)

8a. Outer phyllaries pointed, distinctly brown but not blackish, paler at the tip; underground caudices well-developed, elongate, and branched; stems often 1 dm tall or more, typically with loose, elongate, underground stems. **A. umbrinella** Rydberg. Subalpine meadows, rarely alpine. Both sexes present.
8b. Outer phyllaries blunt, blackish-green to the apex; underground branching relatively slight; plants usually less than 1 dm tall, often dwarfed, usually lacking extensive underground parts. **A. media** Greene (incorrectly referred to the European *A. alpina*). Both sexes present.

9a. Phyllaries with a conspicuous dark spot at the base of the scarious portion; basal leaves narrowly oblanceolate. **A. corymbosa** Nelson. Common, moist meadows and glades. Both sexes present.
9b. Phyllaries not as above; leaves rounded obovate or fusiform . . . . . . (10)

10a. Phyllaries distinctly yellow-greenish; inflorescence and upper stem leaves glandular; basal leaves small, fusiform. **A. microphylla** Rydberg. Sagebrush, forest openings. Both sexes present.
10b. Phyllaries pink or white; inflorescence and upper stem leaves not glandular; basal leaves usually oblanceolate, rounded at apex . . . . (11)

11a. Heads large, involucre 7-11 mm high, the dry carpellate corollas 5-8 mm long; staminate plants rare. **A. parvifolia** Nuttall. Common in open montane forests.
11b. Heads smaller, involucre 4-6 mm high, the dry carpellate corollas less than 5 mm long; apomictic, all plants carpellate. **A. rosea** Greene. Abundant

everywhere in the forested areas. This species is believed to have arisen as a hybrid between two or more of the sexual species listed above.

ANTHEMIS L. 1753 [the ancient name]. CHAMOMILE

1a. Receptacular chaff stiff and awnlike, restricted to the center (upper part) of the conic involucre; usually branched above the base. **A. cotula** L. Adventive, ruderal weed.

1b. Receptacular chaff flat, lanceolate, subtending most of the disk florets; branched from the base and spreading on the ground. **A. arvensis** L. Adventive, ruderal weed.

ARCTIUM L. 1753 [Greek, *arctos*, bear, alluding to the shaggy involucre]. BURDOCK

1a. Heads 1.5-2.5 cm wide, racemosely arranged, short-pedunculate or sessile. **A. minus** (Hill) Bernhardi, **35I**. Adventive, ruderal weed, low and middle altitudes.

1b. Heads 2.5-4 cm wide, in flat-topped corymbs, long-pedunculate . . . . . (2)

2a. Heads naked; spines long (up to 2 cm). **A. lappa** L. Adventive, ruderal weed, not yet found on the Eastern Slope but to be expected in mountain towns.

2b. Heads densely tomentose; spines short (to 1 cm). **A. tomentosum** Miller. Adventive weed from Middle Asia. Occurrence based on two old collections from Denver (1916).

ARNICA L. 1753 [origin of name unknown]

1a. Heads rayless, nodding in bud. **A. parryi** Gray. Meadows and open forests, middle altitudes.

1b. Heads with rays . . . . (2)

2a. Stem leaves mostly 5-12 pairs, no basal rosettes . . . . (3)

2b. Stems less leafy, the stem leaves mostly 2-4 pairs without the basal rosette (if present), often reduced in size upwards . . . . (4)

3a. Phyllaries obtuse or merely acutish, bearing a tuft of hairs at the tip or just within it; tube of disk-flowers 3-4.5 mm long. **A. chamissonis** Lessing subsp. **foliosa** (Nuttall) Maguire. Common in montane meadows.

3b. Phyllaries sharply acute, the tip not more hairy than the body; tube of disk-flowers 2-3 mm long. **A. longifolia** Eaton. Subalpine talus slopes, east side of Park Range, JA.

4a. Pappus subplumose, brownish. **A. mollis** Hooker. Subalpine spruce-fir forests.

4b. Pappus only barbellate, white . . . . (5)

5a. Leaves ovate, at least those of the sterile rosettes with petioles equalling the blades; rhizomes naked or clothed with overlapping scales and leaf bases only near the tip, typically 3-branched near the apex . . . . (6)

5b. Leaves lanceolate, sessile or with shorter petioles; rhizomes clothed with overlapping scales and leaf bases, unbranched near the apex . . . . (7)

6a. Stem leaves sessile; leaves of basal rosettes narrowly ovate; sparingly hairy, often quite green and glabrous; basal leaves not cordate but ovate-truncate; achenes brown. **A. latifolia** Bongard. Moist subalpine forests. A sexual species.

6b. Stem leaves petiolate; leaves of basal rosettes cordate or broadly ovate; hairy, the involucre usually rather densely so; achenes dark gray. **A. cordifolia** Hooker. Dry forests, widely distributed from foothills to subalpine. A completely apomictic species with no known sexual populations. Its great variability is due to many slightly different apomictic clones.

7a. Old leaf bases at base of stem with tufts of tawny hairs in their axils; lower stem-leaves petioled; heads solitary; plants of montane meadows. **A. fulgens** Pursh. Common on outwash mesas of the eastern foothills and meadows in the mountain parks.
7b. Old leaf bases at base of stem lacking tufts of tawny hairs; lower stem leaves sessile; heads 1-usually 3; subalpine or alpine species. **A. rydbergii** Greene. Common on rocky slopes near and above timberline.

ARTEMISIA L. 1753 [ancient name in memory of Artemisia, wife of Mausolus, buried in 353 B.C. in the first "mausoleum"]. SAGEWORT, WORMWOOD

1a. Very tall annual with finely divided leaves and diffuse inflorescence. **A. annua** L. Adventive weed, known from one record in a Boulder alley, of a plant 7 feet tall.
1b. Perennial . . . . (2)

2a. Plant with finely dissected, silvery-hairy leaves, densely massed along long offshoots that may be slightly woody near the base; flower spikes slender, erect. **A. frigida** Willdenow [cold], SILVER SAGE. Abundant in dry meadows and hillsides. The common name, fringed sage, used by some government agencies, may describe the leaves aptly, but is not a correct translation.
2b. Not as above . . . . (3)

3a. True shrubs, woody not only at the very base, the annual growth not dying back to the ground each year; leaves 3-notched, resembling woody sagebrushes (*Seriphidium*) but with 1-2 short ray-flowers. **A. bigelovii** Gray. Arkansas River Valley between Pueblo and Cañon City. Although this is frequently mistaken for *Seriphidium tridentatum* and its relatives, even a single leaf can always be recognized microscopically by the presence of strigose (long, silky) hairs, the ends of which are easily made out, instead of short, matted ones.
3b. Herbaceous plants . . . . (4)

4a. Dwarf alpines, hardly more than 10 cm high, the leaves pinnatisect, mostly basal; phyllaries conspicuously dark-bordered; receptacle long-hairy between the flowers . . . . (5)
4b. Taller plants, if alpine, the receptacle not hairy between flowers . . . . (6)

5a. Heads 5-25; phyllaries with very broad, dark margin, appearing uniformly dark; leaves mostly twice pinnatifid (pinnatifid with the primary divisions divided again). **A. scopulorum** Gray. Common, alpine and subalpine.
5b. Heads 1-4; phyllaries with a narrow, distinct, dark margin, appearing bicolored; leaves once pinnatifid or cleft. **A. pattersonii** Gray. Tundra, Front Range.

6a. With taproots or short, woody caudices . . . . (7)
6b. With well-developed rhizomes . . . . (10)

7a. Stem leaves not reduced in size upwards; basal rosettes withering by flowering time . . . . (8)
7b. Stem leaves reduced in size upwards; basal rosettes usually still evident at flowering time . . . . (9)

8a. Biennial; leaves green, pinnatisect, the segments with sharp points; rachis with short segments between the principal ones. **A. biennis** Willdenow.

Adventive in disturbed forest sites such as logging roads, check dams, and campgrounds.

8b. Perennial; leaves silvery-hairy, pinnatisect with rounded lobes. **A. absinthium** L., ABSINTHE. Adventive in disturbed or cultivated ground.

9a. Heads in a raceme, large, nodding; phyllaries prominently dark-margined; leaves green and glabrate or gray-hairy. **A. arctica** Lessing subsp. **saxicola** (Rydberg) Hultén. Rocky alpine slopes and meadows.

9b. Heads in spikes or panicles, small, erect; phyllaries not prominently dark-margined; leaves usually very hairy . . . . (10)

10a. Leaf lobes rounded at the apex; inflorescence secund. **A. franserioides** Greene. Talus slopes, cliffs, and openings in spruce-fir forests. Pleasantly fragrant with a sweet, heavy odor.

10b. Leaf lobes, or leaves (if undivided) acute; inflorescence not secund . (11)

11a. Leaves silky-pubescent to glabrous, never woolly or tomentose; plants with distinct basal leaves. **A. laciniata** Willdenow subsp. **parryi** (Gray) Weber. Cobbly creek margins in the Creede area and Sangre de Cristo Mountains. Resembling a very tall *A. arctica* with distinctly pinnately compound leaves with acute leaflets and nodding heads (*A. parryi*). *A. franserioides* has rounded leaflets and leaves tomentose beneath.

11b. Leaves tomentose or woolly, especially beneath; plants lacking differentiated basal leaves . . . . (12)

12a. Leaves green, glandular; main leaves divided into slender elongated or linear-filiform lobes 0.5-1 mm wide. **A. ludoviciana** Nuttall subsp. **incompta** (Nuttall) Keck. Rocky slopes and cliffs, middle altitudes. One of the more well marked races.

12b. Leaves white, at least underneath; main leaves entire, toothed or divided into broader segments . . . . (13)

13a. Involucre 2-3 mm wide and 3-4 mm high, almost glabrous, with very wide hyaline, often purplish-margined phyllaries; corollas also purplish; leaves always deeply incised, with narrow, serrate lobes, strongly bicolored, rarely almost green on both surfaces. **A. michauxiana** Besser [for André Michaux, 1746-1803, author of *Flora Boreali Americanae*]. Scree and talus slopes, montane and subalpine, east side of Park Range, JA.

13b. Involucre 1-2 mm wide and high, densely tomentose, as are the leaves; phyllaries not strongly hyaline-margined; corollas yellow; leaves from simple, entire, to toothed and lobed or deeply dissected . . . . (14)

14a. Stems low, up to 3 dm high, very densely leafy with finely divided leaves; inflorescence dense and spikelike; plants forming large and dense patches of uniform height. **A. carruthii** Wood [for James H. Carruth, 1807-1896, Kansas botanist). Eastern plains and mesas, in short-grass prairie.

14b. Stems taller, not extremely densely leafy; leaves simple to variously divided, variable; inflorescence more open; plants loosely aggregated, with long rhizomes. **A. ludoviciana** Nuttall. Abundant along roadcuts, screes, rockslides, etc., except in alpine and desert-steppe; the races are legion and impossible to place into pigeonholes, and their geography becomes clouded by mass movement of soil and seeds by man.

ASKELLIA Weber 1984 [for Áskell Löve, 1916-, renowned Icelandic botanist and cytogeneticist. ALPINE HAWKSBEARD

One species, **Askellia nana** (Richardson) Weber [dwarfed]. A dwarf, fleshy, glabrous alpine with slender roots, growing on unstable scree slopes; leaves oval, often lacking lobes. Infrequent, high peaks (*Crepis*).

ASTER L. 1753 [Greek, *aster*, star]

The nomenclature of asters is now in a state of flux. If one accepts the divisions that are being made of *Aster*, then there are no members of the genus in America, the type species of *Aster* belonging to an exclusively Eurasian group. Our species may all become *Symphyotrichum*.

1a. Dwarf tundra plant not over 20 cm tall, with the habit of a low *Erigeron*; leaves mostly basal, the stem leaves progressively reduced; ray-flowers characteristically rolling back after flowering. **A. alpinus** L. var. **vierhapperi** (Onno) Cronquist. Very rare, collected a century ago on Berthoud Pass and, more recently, on the Continental Divide in the San Juan La Garita Wild area.

1b. Leaves not mostly basal, or not dwarf tundra plants . . . . (2)

2a. Involucre and ultimate branchlets glandular-pubescent; leaves elongate-linear, glaucous, succulent, 1-nerved. **A. pauciflorus** Nuttall, anomalous even among American asters and recently segregated as a separate genus and species *Almutaster pauciflora* (Nuttall) Löve. Alkaline swales, interior basins.

2b. Involucre and branches not glandular-pubescent . . . . (3)

3a. Leaves linear, 2-5 mm wide; rays white . . . . (4)

3b. Plants not as above; rays white or colored . . . . (5)

4a. Stems simple, unbranched; basal leaves not developed; somewhat pubescent. **A. junciformis** Rydberg [like *Juncus*]. Infrequent or rare in wet swales of the mountain parks.

4b. Stems much-branched from a cluster of basal leaves; completely glabrous. **A. porteri** Gray [for Thomas C. Porter]. Endemic. Abundant in the foothill canyons and the outwash mesas of the Front Range.

5a. Pubescence of stem and branchlets occurring in distinct lines decurrent from the leaf bases. **A. hesperius** Gray. A late summer aster of wet meadows and ditches.

5b. Pubescence of stem and branchlets not in lines . . . . (6)

6a. Involucre strongly graduated, at least the outer ones obtuse, markedly shorter than the inner and never foliaceous; instead, with strongly thickened pale cartilaginous margins and base. **A. adscendens** Lindley. Abundant, weedy species of roadsides and gravelly flats in the mountains.

6b. Involucre not strongly graduated or, if so, then the phyllaries acute (if obtuse, they are enlarged and foliaceous) . . . . (7)

7a. Glabrous except for short lines of hairs in the inflorescence; leaves glaucous, entire or toothed. **A. laevis** L. var. **geyeri** Gray. Common montane species of late summer.

7b. Variously pubescent, not glaucous . . . . (8)

8a. Leaves and bracts relatively small and narrow, the middle cauline leaves mostly less than 1 cm wide and less than 7 times as long as wide; phyllaries oblong, the outer ones never enlarged and foliaceous. **A. occidentalis** (Nuttall) Torrey & Gray. Open, often alkaline meadows.

8b. Leaves and bracts relatively large; middle cauline leaves mostly over 1 cm wide and less than 7 times as long as wide; some of the outer bracts enlarged and leaflike. **A. foliaceus** Lindley. Extremely variable, ranging from dwarf plants with very showy heads, to tall plants with medium-sized ones; abundant, montane and subalpine.

BACCHARIS L. 1753 [ancient name of a shrub dedicated to Bacchus]. GROUNDSEL TREE

1a. Leaves elliptic or oblanceolate, with rounded apex; pappus white. **B. salicina** Torrey & Gray. Tall shrub of floodplains, Arkansas River Valley between Pueblo and Cañon City.

1b. Leaves narrowly linear, short, pointed; pappus reddish-brown. **B. wrightii** Gray. Lower Arkansas River drainage.

BAHIA Lagasca 1816 [for Concepción Bay, Chile, where the first species was collected]

1a. Perennial (or biennial) with alternate leaves with oblanceolate divisions, from a basal rosette. **B. dissecta** (Gray) Britton. Common in bare, gravelly soil, mostly along roadsides in the canyons.

1b. Delicate annual; leaves opposite with linear divisions; basal leaves lacking. **B. neomexicana** Gray. Uncommon and scattered, Black Forest, San Luis Valley, upper Arkansas River Valley.

BALSAMORHIZA Nuttall 1840. [so called from the resinous root and caudices]. BALSAMROOT

One species, **B. sagittata** (Pursh) Nuttall. Leaves cordate, entire, appressed silvery-pubescent; root massive beneath several ascending woody caudices; scapes numerous. Abundant in deep soils, sagebrush, North Park. Very long-lived, not flowering before the fourth or fifth year and continuing for over 50 years.

BERLANDIERA de Candolle 1836 [for J. L. Berlandier, died 1851, Genoese botanist and collector in Texas and Mexico]. GREEN EYES

One species, **B. lyrata** Bentham. Common on the plains in southeast corner counties, one collection from the head of Pinos River near La Manga Pass, CN. Easily recognized by its extremely broad, rounded phyllaries, yellow rays, and pinnately lobed leaves, finely white-pubescent beneath.

BIDENS L. 1753 [Latin, *bidens*, two-toothed, alluding to the pappus]. BEGGAR'S TICK

1a. Leaves simple, crenate to coarsely serrate, sometimes incised near the base of the blade but never pinnatifid . . . . (2)

1b. Leaves pinnately divided or dissected . . . . (3)

2a. Peduncle not recurved below the head; achenes with 3 awns and a flat or concave, noncartilaginous apex. **B. comosa** (Gray) Wiegand [hairy]. Typically a low, spreading plant with almost entire leaves tapering to the bases. Muddy swales and pond margins on the plains and intermountain basins.

2b. Peduncle recurved just below the head; achenes with 4 awns and with a distinct paler cartilaginous apex. **B. cernua** L. [nodding]. Typically this is a tall species with strongly serrate leaves. It is said to have characteristically clasping leaf bases, but in Europe and southern United States the leaves may taper to the base. Similar habitats.

3a. Achenes strongly dimorphic, the 1-4 outer ones 5-7 mm long, linear-cuneate, truncate at the apex; inner achenes 8-12 mm long, narrowly linear and tapering to the apex. **B. bigelovii** Gray [for Jacob Bigelow, 1787-1879, professor of botany, Boston]. Lower Arkansas River Valley, BA.

3b. Achenes uniform or nearly so . . . . (4)

4a. Leaves with narrowly linear or filiform segments. **B. tenuisecta** Gray. Common roadside weed in San Luis Valley and near the mountains, from CC southward.

4b. Leaves with few, broad, toothed segments . . . . (5)

5a. Outer phyllaries 5-8 in number, sparsely ciliate; inner phyllaries equalling the disk in length. **B. frondosa** L. [leafy, alluding to the phyllaries], **35E**. Common in swamps and wet ditches, piedmont valley and plains. The distinctions between this and the next species are seldom satisfactory.

5b. Outer phyllaries 10-20, strongly hispid-ciliate; inner phyllaries shorter than the disk. **B. vulgata** Greene [common]. Similar habitats.

BOLOPHYTA Nuttall 1840 [Greek, *bolus*, lump, clod, + *phyton*, plant]

1a. Outer phyllaries up to 4 mm wide; achene densely hairy, with a papery auriculate wing. **B. tetraneuris** (Barneby) Weber [alluding to a resemblance to *Tetraneuris acaulis*, with which it grows]. Endemic on gypsum ridges, Arkansas River Valley, Pueblo-Cañon City area. Both species are extremely inconspicuous plants forming cushions of rosettes from thick woody caudices, the heads, although pedunculate, hidden among the leaf bases. The Western Slope *P. ligulatum* has hairy but wingless achenes and sessile heads (*Parthenium*).

1b. Outer phyllaries narrower; achene almost glabrous, wingless. **B. alpina** Nuttall [a misnomer, since the plant is not at all alpine]. Rare and local, Pawnee National Grassland.

BRACHYACTIS Ledebour 1845 [Greek, *brachy*, short, + *actis*, ray]

1a. Rays about 2 mm long, purplish, surpassing the short styles; phyllaries obtuse or acutish. **B. frondosa** (Nuttall) Gray. Alkaline swales in the piedmont valleys and San Luis Valley (*Aster*).

1b. Ray-flowers tubular, shorter than the styles, virtually absent; phyllaries distinctly acute. **B. ciliata** Ledebour subsp. **angusta** (Lindley.) A. Jones. Similar sites (*Aster*).

BRICKELLIA Elliott 1823 [for Dr. John Brickell, 1749-1809, American colonial naturalist]

1a. Leaves triangular-ovate, regularly crenate or serrate dentate, the largest over 2 cm long; pappus simple . . . . (2)

1b. Leaves linear, elliptic, oblong or, if ovate, smaller, entire or irregularly toothed; pappus plumose . . . . (3)

2a. Leaves crenate; heads small (not over 1 cm high), erect. **B. californica** (Torrey & Gray) Gray. Dry rocky canyonsides in the foothills.

2b. Leaves coarsely and deeply serrate-dentate; heads over 1 cm high, nodding. **B. grandiflora** (Hooker) Nuttall. Common on canyonsides, but going higher in the mountains than the last.

3a. Stem leaves all narrowly linear and entire, not over 3 mm wide; inflorescence broad and open, the branches slender. **B. rosmarinifolia** (Ventenat) Weber subsp. **chlorolepis** (Wooton & Standley) Weber (*Kuhnia chlorolepis*). Dry meadows in the lowlands (*Kuhnia*).

3b. Leaves of at least the main stem broader, lanceolate to rhombic, with prominent teeth; inflorescence usually dense and the branches stout. **B. eupatorioides** (L.) Shinners. Similar habitats (*Kuhnia*).

CARDUUS L. 1753 [the ancient Latin name]. THISTLE

One species, **C. nutans** L. subsp. **macrolepis** (Peterman) Kazmi, MUSK THISTLE. Adventive, abundant weed in overgrazed or neglected fields and roadsides. Stem stout; involucre over 2 cm wide and high, glabrous; phyllaries broad and stout, the outer conspicuously spreading-reflexed. In *Carduus* and *Onopordum* the entire length of the stem is covered by the decurrent leaf bases.

CHAENACTIS de Candolle 1836 [Greek, *chaino*, gaping, + *aktis*, ray]. PINCUSHION

1a. Biennial with leafy stem terminating in a flat-topped inflorescence of several heads; pappus scales 8-14; plants usually 2 dm high or more. **C. douglasii** (Hooker) Hooker & Arnott. Common in dry, open sagebrush, piñon-juniper and oak woods. Absent from the eastern plains.

1b. Perennial with numerous, slender caudices; stem with 1, rarely up to 3 heads; leaves mostly basal; pappus scales 4-6. **C. alpina** (Gray) Jones. Alpine screes, occasionally lower, on roadcuts in upper subalpine forests.

CHLOROCREPIS Grisebach 1853 [Greek, *chloros*, green, + *Crepis*, a genus] (formerly included in *Hieracium*). HAWKWEED

1a. Leaves glabrous (with many minute stalked glands) and glaucous; inflorescence a loose raceme; involucre glandular-pubescent with black hairs. **C. tristis** (Willdenow) Löve & Löve subsp. **gracilis** (Hooker) Weber. Subalpine spruce-fir forests (*H. gracile*).

1b. Leaves with long stiffish hairs; inflorescence a cyme or panicle of heads; involucre not glandular-pubescent . . . . (2)

2a. Flowers white; heads numerous (over 20); involucre 8-10 mm high; achene 3 mm long excluding pappus; phyllaries with a prominent dark median line. **C. albiflora** (Hooker) Weber. Common in dry, forested montane canyons.

2b. Flowers yellow; heads few (less than 10); involucre 12-15 mm high; achene 6 mm long; phyllaries green, without a dark median line. **C. fendleri** (Schultz-Bipontinus) Weber. Infrequent, montane and subalpine.

CHRYSOTHAMNUS Nuttall 1840 [Greek, *chrysos*, gold, + *thamnos*, bush]. RABBITBRUSH

1a. Twigs covered with a feltlike tomentum (scratch with fingernail will remove it) . . . . (2)

1b. Twigs glabrous or puberulent, not tomentose . . . . (8)

2a. Heads in leafy spikelike or racemose clusters, these sometimes branching to form panicles; outer phyllaries often prolonged into slender, herbaceous tips or appendages. **C. parryi** (Gray) Greene. Three subspecies are recognized, as follows . . . . (3)

2b. Heads cymose at the ends of the branches; inflorescence sometimes compound and elongated; phyllaries obtuse to acute, outer ones shortened and without herbaceous tips. **C. nauseosus** (Pallas) Britton. The most abundant and showy species in the area, represented by several races, as follows . . . . (5)

3a. Flowers 10-20 in a head. subsp. **parryi**. Common in the mountain parks.

3b. Flowers 5-7 in a head . . . . (4)

4a. Inflorescence distinctly surpassing the upper leaves; foliage green. subsp. **affinis** (Nelson) L. C. Anderson. North Park.
4b. Inflorescence surpassed by the upper leaves; foliage gray-tomentulose. subsp. **howardii** (Parry) Hall & Clements. South Park, San Luis Valley, Wet Mountain Valley, and Cuchara River drainage.

5a. Plants low, up to about 6 dm high; outermost phyllaries tomentulose. Subsp. **nauseosus.** Common on the eastern plains, foothill mesas, and in North Park.
5b. Plants taller . . . . (6)

6a. Leaves linear but more than 1 mm wide, some 3-5-nerved. Subsp. **graveolens** (Nuttall) Piper. The most common tall subspecies, a tall, gray-leaved shrub common in deep soils or arroyos on the plains.
6b. Leaves linear-filiform, 1 mm or less wide; pappus brownish . . . . (7)

7a. Achenes pubescent; phyllaries all glabrous. Subsp. **consimilis** (Greene) Hall & Clements. Common in and limited to the San Luis Valley.
7b. Achenes glabrous; outermost phyllaries tomentulose; involucre 10-11 mm high. Subsp. **bigelovii** (Gray) Hall & Clements. Wet Mountain Valley, Cuchara Valley, and southward to New Mexico.

8a. Involucre 10-12 mm tall, phyllaries with a large green spot near the tips; corolla 10-14 mm long. **C. pulchellus** (Gray) Greene subsp. **baileyi** (Wooton & Standley) Hall & Clements [pretty; for L. H. Bailey, 1858-1954, one of the greatest of American botanists]. Sand dunes along the Arkansas River, BA.
8b. Involucre and corolla smaller, not green . . . . (9)

9a. Achene glabrous or nearly so, longitudinally 10-striate, 5 mm long. **C. vaseyi** (Gray) Greene. North Park, San Luis Valley, Arkansas River Valley.
9b. Achene usually densely hairy, never striate, 3-4 mm long . . . . (10)

10a. Phyllaries attenuate or abruptly narrowed to a subulate tip; corollas 4-4.5 mm long; leaves very narrow (1.2 mm). **C. greenei** (Gray) Greene. Known in our area only from the San Luis Valley.
10b. Phyllaries obtuse or acute; corollas 4.5-7 mm long; leaves broader, characteristically twisted. **C. viscidiflorus** (Hooker) Nuttall [sticky-flowered]. Common in dry, open sites throughout the middle altitudes of the mountains. Two subspecies (subsp. **viscidiflorus** and subsp. **lanceolatus**) occur but they are not well differentiated morphologically or geographically.

CICHORIUM L. 1753 [altered from the Arabian name for the plant]. CHICORY
One species, **C. intybus** L. Adventive, locally established as a ruderal weed. The roasted roots are a coffee substitute. The flowers open only in the morning, changing a skeletonlike plant to a handsome one with some of the purest of blue flowers in our flora.

CIRSIUM Miller 1754 [Greek, *cirsos*, swollen vein, for which the thistle was considered a remedy]. THISTLE
1a. Perennial reproducing by underground rhizomes (growing in patches often many meters across); heads usually less than 3 cm high . . . . (2)
1b. Biennials with taproots (stems single or few together); heads usually more than 3 cm high; flowers perfect . . . . (4)

2a. Plants with perfect flowers; heads 2-3 cm high; rhizomatous but never forming large colonies; leaves tomentose beneath, the juvenile leaves entire or only slightly lobed. **C. flodmanii** (Rydberg) Arthur [for J. H. Flodman, 1859-?,

Swedish-American botanist, who collected with Rydberg]. Infrequent in wet swales in the piedmont valleys.

2b. Plants dioecious; heads 1-2 cm tall; aggressive, noxious weed, forming dense, spreading colonies . . . . (3)

3a. Leaves and heads glabrous. **C. arvense** (L.) Scopoli [of cultivated fields], CANADA THISTLE. Adventive, aggressive, noxious weed of cultivated ground, roadsides, and disturbed areas. Many communities have ordinances requiring its elimination. However, as agriculture becomes less important along the urban corridor, this species is becoming a real pest in towns and recreation areas.

3b. Leaves strongly tomentose beneath; heads somewhat larger than in the last. **C. incanum** (Gmelin) Fischer [hoary]. Adventive, piedmont valleys. Introduced from southwest Asia and southeast Europe.

4a. Leaves beset on the upper surface with small, sharp spines; decurrent leaf bases extending as narrow wings from node to node; heads conspicuously cobwebby-pubescent. **C. vulgare** (Savi) Tenore, BULL THISTLE. Adventive pasture weed, generally not abundant enough to become a pest.

4b. Leaves not spiny above, never decurrent from node to node . . . . (5)

5a. Phyllaries and/or their spines reflexed or spreading . . . . (6)

5b. Phyllaries and spines straight . . . . (8)

6a. Cauline leaves not at all decurrent; longest phyllary spines about 5 mm; heads with purple flowers. **C. undulatum** (Nuttall) Sprengel. Very common on roadsides on the plains and piedmont valleys.

6b. Cauline leaves decurrent . . . . (7)

7a. Heads with purple flowers. **C. ochrocentrum** Gray. Common in the piedmont valleys. Similar to the last but with fewer and less tightly imbricated phyllaries.

7b. Heads with white or very pale purplish flowers. **C. canescens** Nuttall. Common on the plains and intermountain parks.

8a. Inner phyllaries with dilated, fringed tips, lacking terminal spine. **C. centaureae** (Rydberg) Schumann. Common in forests in the mountains near the Continental Divide.

8b. Inner phyllaries tipped with a spine, sometimes ciliate-fringed along the sides . . . . (9)

9a. Phyllaries glabrous or with a bit of matted cobweb along the upper margins, the back covered with minute, granular, yellowish glands; spines short and broad, flattened; flowers white; plants either reduced to a massive rosette of basal leaves and a cluster of sessile heads, or tall with the heads sessile in the leaf axils. **C. coloradense** (Rydberg) Cockerell. **Pl. 47**. Abundant in mountain meadows and streamsides.

9b. Phyllaries with long, multicellular hairs often giving the head a cobwebby appearance; spines long and not strongly flattened . . . . (10)

10a. Outer phyllaries with spinulose-ciliate margins as well as stout terminal spines . . . . (11)

10b. Outer phyllaries without spinulose-ciliate margins; flowers yellow or purplish to purple . . . . (12)

11a. Flowers lavender; heads always in a tight terminal cluster; leaves regularly pinnatifid. **C. tweedyi** (Rydberg) Petrak [for Frank Tweedy, 1854-1937, the collector]. Infrequent, upper subalpine, northern counties.
11b. Flowers yellow; heads often in branched inflorescences; leaves very irregularly pinnatifid. Streamsides in the montane zone, southern counties.

12a. Heads congested in massive, heavy, commonly nodding terminal clusters or spikes; flowers either yellow (northern populations) or pale purplish (in the Sangre de Cristo Range); upper subalpine and lower alpine. **C. scopulorum** (Greene) Cockerell, **Pl. 29**. Common on tundra along the Continental Divide.
12b. Heads in narrow, erect spikes; flowers deep purple; subalpine and upper montane. **C. hesperium** (Eastwood) Petrak [for Mount Hesperus]. Common in the San Juan Mountains and Spanish Peaks.

CONYZA Lessing 1832 [Greek, *konops*, flea, hence fleabane]. HORSEWEED

1a. Leaves linear, entire, neither arachnoid-tomentose nor minutely glandular; involucre about 3 mm high; heads very numerous, in diffuse panicles. **C. canadensis** (L.) Cronquist. Adventive, abundant, roadside and field weed.
1b. Leaves oblanceolate, coarsely toothed, with minute golden glandular hairs in addition to the tomentum; upper stems arachnoid-tomentose; heads 3.5-5 mm high, on short axillary shoots or in somewhat pyramidal branched panicles . . . . (2)

2a. Very narrow ray-flowers present, about as long as the pappus; pappus off-white or tawny; heads 4-5 mm high. **C. schiedeana** (Lessing) Cronquist [for C.J.W. Schiede, 1798-1836, German collector in Mexico]. Adventive, scattered along animal trails, Rocky Mountain National Park, Pikes Peak.
2b. Ray-flowers absent; plants tending to be dioecious; pappus white; heads 3-3.5 mm high. **C. coulteri** Gray [for J. M. Coulter]. Infrequent in pine forests in the foothills.

COREOPSIS L. 1753 [Greek, *coris*, bug, + *opsis*, appearance, from the form of the achene]

1a. Leaves entire or rarely with 1-2 small lobes but never divided; stems little-branched; achenes winged; ray-flowers 1-3 cm long. **C. lanceolata** L. Adventive escape from cultivation, Denver and Fort Collins area.
1b. Leaves 1-2-pinnately divided with filiform divisions; much-branched above; achenes wingless; ray-flowers 6-15 mm long, often with a dark spot at base. **C. tinctoria** Nuttall. Mud-flats around drying ponds on the plains and piedmont valleys.

CREPIS L. 1753 [Greek name of some plant, from *crepis*, boot]. HAWKSBEARD

One species, **C. capillaris** (L.) Wallroth. Adventive weed, recently appearing for the first time near Fort Collins. Slender annual, leaves linear-oblanceolate, remotely dentate or pinnatifid, on lower part of stem; heads numerous in an open panicle.

CYCLACHAENA Fresenius 1838 [Greek, *cyclos*, circle, + *achaenia*, achene, alluding to the rounded, obovate achene]. MARSH-ELDER

One species, **C. xanthifolia** (Nuttall) Fresenius [with leaves like *Xanthium*]. Tall weed with triangular-ovate leaves and greenish heads in a terminal panicle. Phyllaries 10, the 5 outer green, the 5 inner more membranous, partly enfolding the achenes (*Iva*). When not in flower, this may be mistaken for the common sunflower.

DUGALDIA Cassini 1828 [for Dugald Stewart, 1753-1828, Scottish philosopher]. ORANGE SNEEZEWEED

One species, **D. hoopesii** (Gray) Rydberg [for a Thomas Hoopes]. Tall, coarse, leafy plant with orange-yellow ray-flowers, common in the aspen zone. Very poisonous to livestock, particularly sheep, causing what is called the "spewing sickness" (*Helenium*).

DYSSODIA Cavanilles 1803 [Greek, *dysodia*, stench]. FETID MARIGOLD

1a. Ray-flowers large, conspicuous, 3-4 mm long; pappus scales truncate and erose, without any bristles; leaf divisions not spinulose-tipped. **D. aurea** (Gray) Nelson. Abundant, lower Arkansas River drainage and Mesa de Maya.

1b. Ray-flowers minute, inconspicuous, up to 1.5 mm long; pappus scales dissected into bristles; leaf divisions spinulose-tipped. **D. papposa** (Ventenat) Hitchcock. Native roadside weed, southern counties. The glandular spots on the phyllaries are distinctive.

ECHINACEA Moench 1794 [Greek, *echinos*, hedgebog]. PURPLE CONEFLOWER

One species, **E. angustifolia** de Candolle. Infrequent in moist, tall-grass prairies on the eastern plains; one record from the Boulder area.

ENGELMANNIA Nuttall 1841 [for George Engelmann]

One species, **E. pinnatifida** Gray. Common on prairies in the southeastern counties in the Arkansas River drainage. An herb with pinnatifid leaves, heads with yellow rays and conspicuously ciliate phyllaries.

ERIGERON L. 1753 [Greek, *eri*, early, + *geron*, old man, ancient name for an early blooming, hairy plant]. FLEABANE, DAISY

1a. At least some of the leaves 3-toothed, ternately lobed or pinnatifid . . (2)

1b. Leaves entire . . . . (4)

2a. Caudex elongate, slender-branched; leaves only 3-lobed. **E. vagus** Payson [wandering]. Limestone ridges, Mosquito and Sawatch ranges.

2b. Caudices short, stout, erect; leaves usually twice-ternate or pinnatisect. (3)

3a. [2] Leaves 3-lobed or repeatedly ternately lobed, hirsute. **E. compositus** Pursh. Gravelly soil, middle elevations; white or violet rays; rayless forms common.

3b. Leaves pinnately lobed, glabrous except for cilia along the petioles. **E. pinnatisectus** (Gray) Nelson. Common on rocky tundra.

4a. [1] Annuals or short-lived perennials with very shallow root systems, if appearing perennial, the basal leaves coarsely toothed . . . . (5)

4b. Perennials . . . . (11)

5a. [4] Carpellate (ray-) flowers very numerous, with very narrow, short, erect ligules, these sometimes not exceeding the disk, or the inner carpellate corollas tubular, without an expanded ligule (two subalpine species) . (6)

5b. Carpellate flowers few to numerous (rarely absent), the ligules, when present, well developed and spreading . . . . (7)

6a. [5] Inner phyllaries usually long-attenuate; inflorescence ± flat-topped; pappus reddish brown. **E. elongatus** Ledebour. Subalpine meadows (*E. acre* var. *debilis*). This and the next are only distantly related to our other western American *Erigeron*.

6b. Inner phyllaries merely acute or acuminate; inflorescence racemose, not flat-topped; pappus usually white. **E. lonchophyllus** Hooker [lance-leaved]. Wet meadows and seepage areas of screes and rocky slopes near timberline.

7a. [5] Pappus simple (of a single row of uniform bristles); stem hairs ascending and incurved; plants with many ascending branches. **E. bellidiastrum** Nuttall [daisy-plant]. Restricted to and completely replacing the next three in sandy soils on the eastern plains.

7b. Pappus double (of 2 rows of bristles of different lengths); stem hairs spreading or appressed; plants with relatively few branches . . . . (8)

8a. [7] Hairs of the stem appressed; plant slender, with stolons arising from the base of the plant and rooting at the tips. **E. flagellaris** Gray. Dry meadows, foothills to montane. A form with the rays short or absent, forma **breviligulatus** Weber, occurs in the vicinity of Rocky Flats.

8b. Stem hairs spreading perpendicularly . . . . (9)

9a. [8] Pappus of ray-flowers in 1 row; pappus of disk-flowers of long inner bristles and a shorter outer row; ray-flowers always white. See **Stenactis**

9b. Pappus of ray- and disk-flowers alike; rays commonly pinkish . . . . . (10)

10a. [9] Heads solitary on elongate, mostly leafless stems from the basal leaf clusters; plants developing long, nonrooting, stolonlike, spreading shoots. **E. colo-mexicanus** Nelson. Dry, gravelly floodplains and meadows, mimicking *E. flagellaris* but with spreading stem hairs.

10b. Heads numerous in leafy branches usually terminating stout erect stems. **E. divergens** Torrey & Gray [spreading]. A weedy species of ruderal sites and gravelly floodplains.

11a. [4] Tall and erect; woodland and meadow plants with well-developed, lanceolate or broader stem leaves . . . . (12)

11b. Low; leaves linear or spatulate . . . . (20)

12a. [11] Involucre woolly villous with multicellular hairs. **E. elatior** (Gray) Greene [taller]. Aspen and spruce-fir forests.

12b. Involucre not woolly villous but often hirsute . . . . (13)

13a. [12] Rays white; involucre hairs with black cross-walls. **E. coulteri** Porter [for John M. Coulter]. Aspen and spruce-fir forests.

13b. Rays lavender, only white in mutant plants; involucre hairs without black cross-walls . . . . (14)

14a. [13] Rays mostly 2-3 mm wide; pappus simple. **E. peregrinus** (Banks) Greene subsp. **callianthemus** (Greene) Cronquist [wandering; beautiful-flowered] Open rocky slopes and subalpine meadows. Commonly mistaken for *Aster*, since the rays are so much wider than they are in most *Erigeron*. The pappus bristles are also stouter. The pubescence of the phyllaries and uppermost stem is very distinctive. The stem just below the phyllaries is covered by a close, white pubescence of multicellular, partly glandular hairs; the phyllaries contrast by being quite dark and covered by short, club-shaped, red-tipped glandular hairs. The basal leaves are largest.

14b. Rays narrower; pappus usually double (long and short bristles) . . . . (15)

15a. [14] Cauline leaves glabrous or slightly glandular, not even ciliate on the margins, comparatively few in number and little if at all longer than the internodes. E. **eximius** Greene [extraordinary]. Aspen and spruce-fir forests (*E. superbus*).

15b. Stem leaves either obviously pubescent or at least ciliate on the margins, sometimes also glandular, relatively numerous and longer than the internodes . . . . (16)

16a. [15] Plants uniformly leafy, middle leaves commonly as large as the lower ones . . . . (17)

16b. Plants with upper leaves abruptly reduced, the middle ones commonly smaller than the lowermost ones . . . . (19)

17a. [16] Upper and middle stem leaves glabrous except for the ciliate margins. **E. speciosus** (Lindley) de Candolle [showy]. Abundant.

17b. Upper and middle stem leaves hairy or glandular . . . . (18)

18a. [17] Leaves glandular or glandular-scabrous; stem pubescent above with stiff spreading hairs. E. **vreelandii** Rydberg [for F. K. Vreeland, radio inventor, who collected with Rydberg]. Montane forests and meadows, Spanish Peaks southward (*E. platyphyllus*).

18b. Leaves not glandular; upper middle and stem leaves pubescent. **E. subtrinervis** Rydberg. Generally distributed, possibly a race of **E. speciosus.**

19a. [16] Stem and involucre glandular or viscid, sometimes also hairy; stem curved at the base. E. **formosissimus** Greene [very handsome]. Forest openings and mountain meadows.

19b. Stem and involucre ± hairy, scarcely glandular or viscid; stem usually erect. **E. glabellus** Nuttall [diminutive of smooth]. Similar sites. Hybridization evidently occurs among most of these leafy species, and identifications are often inconclusive, probably for this reason.

20a. [11] Stems and usually leaves glandular; basal leaves linear-lanceolate; caudex branches very stout. E. **vetensis** Rydberg [for La Veta Pass]. Common dwarf species of gravelly slopes or dry meadows, Black Forest and outwash mesas of Front Range to montane and subalpine.

20b. Stems and leaves not glandular; leaves not linear-lanceolate, often rounded at the apex . . . . (21)

21a. [20] Plants of desert-steppe sites at lower altitudes and intermountain parks . . . . (22)

21b. Plants of higher forested elevations, from foothills to tundra . . . . . . (27)

22a. [21] Leaves in a prominent, spreading rosette from a taproot, broadly linear, broadest in the middle, triple-nerved (sometimes obscurely), the basal ones half as long as the floral stems, spreading in a rosette, the floral stems spreading before ascending (base S-shaped) . . . . (23)

22b. Leaves and inflorescence not as above . . . . (24)

23a. [22] Pubescence of stems and leaves dense and spreading. **E. caespitosus** Nuttall. Gravelly sagebrush plateaus, North Park and LR.

23b. Stem hairs sparse, appressed or ascending. **E. eatoni** Gray [for the collector, D. C. Eaton, 1834-1895]. Rare on the Eastern Slope, one collection from Poncha Pass.

24a. [22] Pubescence of stem and leaves stiffly spreading, or, if not, at least the petioles strongly stiff-ciliate . . . . (25)

24b. Pubescence of stem and leaves closely appressed, often giving the plant a grayish cast . . . . (26)

25a. [24] Stem pubescence appressed, but petioles stiffly ciliate. **E. engelmannii** Nelson. Closely related to the next, but a smaller plant in every way, never with many caudices. Lower San Luis Valley, CN.

25b. Stem and leaf pubescence spreading; coarse plant with many caudices, forming a dense clump. **E. pumilus** Nuttall subsp. **concinnoides** Cronquist [little; like *E. concinnus*]. Abundant, desert-steppe and piñon-juniper zone.

26a. [24] Leaves ranging from almost glabrous to sparsely strigose; heads small (involucre less than 1 cm diameter); plant with many thick caudices. E. **nematophyllus** Rydberg [thread-leaved]. In sagebrush areas, North Park.

26b. Leaves and stems densely strigose (appearing gray); heads over 1 cm diameter; plant with few caudices. **E. canus** Gray [hoary]. Infrequent, southern half of the range. The rays are wider than in most related species.

27a. [21] Involucre woolly villous with multicellular hairs . . . . (28)

27b. Involucre variously pubescent or sometimes glabrous but not woolly villous . . . . (30)

28a. [27] Involucre hairs with black or very dark purple cross-walls. **E. melanocephalus** Nelson [black-headed]. One of the most common dwarf daisies on subalpine slopes and meadows, usually replaced by *E. simplex* on tundra; where they occur together, the soil is more moist under plants of *E. melanocephalus*.

28b. Involucre hairs with clear cross-walls, or only the lowermost cross-walls sometimes bright reddish-purple . . . . (29)

29a. [28] Pappus bristles mostly about a dozen, sometimes as many as 15; outer pappus conspicuous, setose-squamellate; involucre and upper stem with moderately long hairs, never appearing shaggy or obscuring the phyllaries. E. **simplex** Greene. Common dwarf alpine species.

29b. Pappus bristles mostly 15-20; outer pappus obscure; involucre and upper stem with very long shaggy (3-4 mm) hairs, obscuring the phyllaries. **E. grandiflorus** Hooker. Uncommon or rare, on tundra. This seems to have many more ray-flowers than the last, and deeper-colored.

30a. [27] Plant with slender rhizomes, these freely rooting along their length; most leaves elongate and acute at the apex. **E. ursinus** Eaton [of Bear River Canyon, Utah]. Dry meadows at and above timberline. Commonly confused with *E. simplex*, although in the field the rhizomatous character is very evident.

30b. Plant with slender or stoutish elongate caudices, these not rooting freely along their length; most leaves oblanceolate and rounded at the apex. E. **leiomerus** Gray [with smooth parts]. Alpine and subalpine screes and rockslides.

EUCEPHALUS Nuttall 1840 [Greek, *eu*, well developed, + *kephalos*, head] (formerly included in *Aster*)

1a. Outer phyllaries obtuse at apex, ivory-white with a green tip; plants glaucous, up to 5 dm tall, strongly rhizomatous and forming extensive clumps. E. **glaucus** Nuttall. Abundant, base of talus and rimrock, piñon-juniper and oak (*A. glaucodes*).

1b. Outer phyllaries acute at apex, green with reddish border; plants not strongly glaucous, over 5 dm tall, not forming extensive clumps. E. **engelmannii** (Eaton) Greene. Common in spruce-fir and aspen forests.

EUPATORIUM L. 1753 [from Mithridates Eupator, King of Pontus, who found one species to be an antidote against poison]. JOE PYE WEED [after an Indian of that name]

One species, **E. maculatum** L. Frequent along streams and ditches at the base of the Front Range.

EUTHAMIA Nuttall 1818 [Greek, *thameios*, crowded, alluding to the flowers]

1a. Inflorescence elongate or rounded and interrupted, with lateral clusters arising from the axils of leafy bracts; plants often over 1 m tall. **E. occidentalis** Nuttall. Common in swales in the Platte River drainage from the base of the foothills to the Nebraska border (*Solidago*).
1b. Inflorescence broad and flat-topped, lacking supplementary floral branches; plants less than 1 m tall . . . . (2)

2a. Heads with fewer than 20 flowers; foliage conspicuously glutinous. **E. gymnospermoides** Greene [alluding to the genus *Gymnosperma*]. Northeastern plains between Julesburg and Sterling, not collected for many years.
2b. Heads with 20-40 flowers; foliage glandular-punctate but not glutinous. **E. graminifolia** (L.) Nuttall. Common in the San Luis Valley, the upper Arkansas Valley (Buena Vista), and one old record from Denver.

EVAX Gaertner 1791 [derivation not given]. RABBIT-TOBACCO

One species, **E. prolifera** Nuttall. A nondescript little weed of disturbed and overgrazed places on the plains. Low and widely branching, each branch naked except for a cluster of tight tomentose heads at the end. Generally taken for a very small *Gnaphalium*.

FILAGINELLA Opiz 1854 [diminutive of the genus *Filago*] (formerly in *Gnaphalium*). CUDWEED

1a. Subtending leaves linear or narrowly oblanceolate, much exceeding the clusters of heads; phyllaries usually dark. **F. uliginosa** (L.) Opiz [of swamps]. Common in drying pools and muddy ditches in the mountains (*G. exilifolium*).
1b. Subtending leaves oblong or oblanceolate, little exceeding the clusters of heads; phyllaries pale. **F. palustris** (Nuttall) Holub. Similar situations.

FLAVERIA Jussieu 1789 [Latin, *flavus*, yellow, the original species used as a dye plant]

One species, **F. campestris** Johnston. Infrequent in wetlands of the lower Arkansas Valley. The heads are narrow, broadest at the base, few-flowered (with usually only one very pale yellow or white ray); the clusters mimic a single head!

GAILLARDIA Fougeroux 1786 [for Gaillard de Charentonneau, French amateur botanist]. BLANKETFLOWER

1a. Leaves deeply and narrowly pinnatifid. **G. pinnatifida** Torrey. Common in the lower Arkansas River drainage, blooming in early spring.
1b. Leaves entire, or some toothed or broadly pinnatifid . . . . (2)

2a. Ray-flowers yellow, red-purple at the base; pappus awns twice as long as the basal scale; perennial; leaves large, over 5 cm long, more than 1 cm broad, stiff-hairy. **G. aristata** Pursh [awned, referring to the pappus], **35F**. Common, sagebrush and lower montane, midsummer.

2b. Ray-flowers reddish-purple, yellow toward the tip; pappus awns about as long as the basal scale; annual; leaves less than 1 cm broad. **G. pulchella** Fougeroux [pretty]. Sandy places on the southwestern plains, KW-BA.

GALINSOGA Ruiz & Pavon 1794 [for M. M. de Galinsoga, eighteenth-century Spanish botanist]. QUICKWEED

1a. Outer phyllaries 1-2, deciduous, with green margins; inner chaffy scales entire or shallowly lobed; ray-flowers to 2.5 mm long. **G. quadriradiata** Ruiz & Pavon. A weed in garden plantings, hardly surviving on its own.

1b. Outer phyllaries 2-4, persistent, with scarious margins; inner chaffy scales deeply 3-parted; ray-flowers rarely over 1.5 mm long. **G. parviflora** Cavanilles. Similar habitats.

GNAPHALIUM L. 1753 [Greek, *gnaphallon*, a lock of wool]. CUDWEED

1a. Leaves bicolored, glandular above, tomentose below; phyllaries white. **G. viscosum** Humboldt, Bonpland & Kunth. Adventive, common in disturbed soil, montane forest clearings (*G. macounii*).

1b. Leaves tomentose on both sides, not at all glandular . . . . (2)

2a. Phyllaries white or slightly tinged with straw-color. **G. canescens** de Candolle (*G. wrightii*). Roadsides and sandy ground, outer foothills and mesas, Front Range to Mesa de Maya.

2b. Phyllaries yellowish. **G. stramineum** Humboldt, Bonpland & Kunth. Pond shores and wetlands in the piedmont valleys (*G. chilense*).

GRINDELIA Willdenow 1807 [for D. H. Grindel, 1776-1836, Russian botanist]. GUMWEED

1a. Heads with ray-flowers . . . . (2)

1b. Heads rayless . . . . (5)

2a. Annual or biennial; basal leaves withered by flowering time . . . . (3)

2b. Perennial; basal leaves usually present at flowering time . . . . (4)

3a. Cauline leaves mostly oblanceolate and narrowed to a petiolelike base, usually sharply serrate; pappus bristles distinctly barbellate. **G. subalpina** Greene. Endemic, common from the outwash mesas to subalpine, on dry mountain slopes.

3b. Cauline leaves mostly oblong and sessile by a broad, somewhat clasping base, the blades bluntly serrate or serrulate; pappus bristles smooth. **G. squarrosa** (Pursh) Dunal. Abundant weed in the piedmont valleys. Occasional rayless plants occur but should not be confused with rayless species, since this is not perennial.

4a. Involucre and phyllaries abundantly and conspicuously resinous. **G. revoluta** Steyermark. Infrequent on the eastern plains near the mountain front.

4b. Involucre and phyllaries little if at all resinous. **G. decumbens** Greene var. **subincisa** (Greene) Steyermark. The common species in the Rio Grande drainage and San Luis Valley.

5a. Heads not very resinous; leaves narrowed to the base, not strongly clasping, serrulate, acute. **Grindelia aphanactis** Rydberg [invisible rays]. Common in the Huerfano drainage and Wet Mountain Valley, and across the Sangre de Cristos in the Great Sand Dunes National Monument.

5b. Heads very resinous; leaves sessile-clasping, sharply dentate-serrate with rounded apex. **G. inornata** Greene [unadorned, i.e. rayless]. Plains near the mountain front from Denver southward.

GUTIERREZIA Lagasca 1816 [for Pedro Gutierrez, 1816, correspondent of the botanical garden of Madrid]. SNAKEWEED

One species. **G. sarothrae** (Pursh) Britton & Rusby. Weedy, bushy herb flowering in late summer in dry sites at low altitudes.

HELENIUM L. 1753 [Greek name of some plant, said by Linnaeus to commemorate Helen of Troy, wife of King Menelaus of Sparta]. SNEEZEWEED

One species, **H. autumnale** L. var. **montanum** (Nuttall) Fernald. Infrequent, montane meadows and roadsides.

HELIANTHELLA Torrey & Gray 1842 [diminutive of *Helianthus*]. LITTLE SUNFLOWER

1a. Basal leaves usually absent at flowering time and, if present, not longer than the cauline ones; phyllaries narrow, uniformly pubescent, not ciliate; paleae of the receptacle stiff. **H. uniflora** (Nuttall) Torrey & Gray. Locally abundant and dominant on bare south-facing hills of North Park. In the field it seems that all species have heads turned at right angles to the stem, but in this species it is not obvious in pressed specimens.
1b. Basal leaves present at flowering time, larger than the stem leaves . . . (2)

2a. Tall and stout; heads 4-5 cm broad excluding the rays; leaves up to 50 cm long, attenuate at both ends, prominently 5-veined. **H. quinquenervis** (Hooker) Gray. Abundant, aspen zone.
2b. Low and slender; heads 1.5-2 cm broad excluding the rays; leaves less than 10 cm long, acute. **H. parryi** Gray, **35B, Pl. 54**. Montane (ponderosa pine) zone, southern counties.

HELIANTHUS L. 1753 [Greek, *helios*, the sun, + *anthos*, flower]. SUNFLOWER

1a. Taprooted annual . . . . (2)
1b. Perennials with rhizomes or branching caudices . . . . (3)

2a. Phyllaries hispid-ciliate, ovate or obovate, with acuminate tips. **H. annuus** L., COMMON SUNFLOWER. Very abundant and variable, native roadside weed.
2b. Phyllaries not ciliate, appressed-short-hairy, lanceolate. **H. petiolaris** Nuttall, PRAIRIE SUNFLOWER. Similar to the preceding and commonly hybridizing with it.

3a. Foliage glaucous blue-green; leaf-margins ciliate; rhizomes long and slender. **H. ciliaris** de Candolle. Adventive, roadsides and fields, San Luis Valley.
3b. Foliage green, not glaucous; otherwise not as above . . . . (4)

4a. Phyllaries clearly imbricate in several series, the tips appressed to the disk; disk flowers usually red-purple but sometimes yellow; leaves mostly opposite, narrowly rhomboidal, reduced in size upwards. **H. rigidus** (Cassini) Desfontaines var. **subrhomboideus** (Rydberg) Heiser. Common on the outwash mesas, Front Range.
4b. Phyllaries with spreading tips or, if appressed, then not in strongly graduated series; disk-flowers yellow; leaves opposite or alternate . . . . (5)

5a. Leaves linear-lanceolate, elongate; plants often over 2 m tall . . . . . . (6)
5b. Leaves broader, narrowed to distinct petioles . . . . (7)

6a. Middle leaves, or at least some of them, folded lengthwise; leaves scabrous above; inflorescence racemiform. **H. maximiliani** Schrader [for its discoverer, Prince Maximilian von Wied-Neu Wied, 1782-1867]. Wet swales, native in the extreme northeast corner counties. Used as a revegetation plant in some seed mixes (probably responsible for Weld County records).

6b. Middle leaves flat; leaves glabrous to pubescent above but not harshly scabrous; inflorescence paniculate. **H. nuttallii** Torrey & Gray. Abundant in wet meadows, irrigation ditches, and around ponds in the piedmont valleys.

7a. Plant low, with many stems from the base, very stiff-hirsute; leaves mostly opposite, ovate. **H. pumilus** Nuttall [low]. Endemic, abundant in the foothill canyons of the Front Range.

7b. Plant tall, simple, merely scabrous, with underground tubers; leaves opposite below, alternate above; narrowly ovate. **H. tuberosus** L., JERUSALEM ARTICHOKE. Adventive, escaped from cultivation, lower Arkansas River Valley.

HELIOMERIS Nuttall 1848 [Greek, *helios*, the sun, + *meris*, part]

One species, **H. multiflora** Nuttall. Common, small-headed sunflower of montane roadsides (*Viguiera*). Leaves opposite, usually narrowly elliptic. Heads numerous, cymosely arranged. Flowering in mid- and late summer.

HELIOPSIS Persoon 1807 [for resemblance to *Helianthus*]. OX-EYE

One species, **H. helianthoides** (L.) Sweet var. **scabra** (Dunal) Fernald. Cuchara Valley, an eastern and midwestern prairie relict also occurring in the Black Hills of South Dakota and in scattered sites in eastern New Mexico.

HERRICKIA Wooton & Standley 1913 [for C. L. Herrick, 1858-1903, geologist, president of University of New Mexico] (formerly included in *Aster*)

One species, **H. horrida** Wooton & Standley. Barely entering Colorado on the south side of Mesa De Maya near Raton. Easily recognized by the hollylike leaves.

HETEROTHECA Cassini 1817 [Greek, *hetero*, different, + *theca*, case, alluding to the unlike achenes]. GOLDEN ASTER (formerly included in *Chrysopsis*)

Note: The species are notoriously variable, with distinct local races, and many specimens cannot be definitely placed. Treatments vary enormously as well; a definitive monograph, fortunately, is in preparation.

1a. Annual herb with a taproot; lower leaves petiolate; upper leaves sessile and clasping. **H. latifolia** Buckley. Barely entering Colorado on sand flats along the Cimarron River, BA.

1b. Perennial herbs; leaves not in two classes . . . . (2)

2a. Heads usually solitary at the apices of the stems; neat, hemispherical plants of subalpine and alpine rockslides; ray-flowers longer than in all other species. **H. pumila** (Greene) Semple.

2b. Heads several; loosely branching species of lower altitude . . . . (3)

3a. Upper stems, leaves, and involucre densely hirsute, nonglandular or only with small inconspicuous sessile glandular dots; upper leaves not markedly coarse or rigid; outer pappus inconspicuous, of narrow setaceous scales . . . . (4)

3b. Herbage less densely pubescent, distinctly greenish, copiously covered with conspicuous, large, sessile and stipitate glands or, if more densely pubescent and less conspicuously glandular, then the upper leaves markedly coarse and stiff, and peduncular leaves broad and closely subtending the heads; outer pappus conspicuous, of lanceolate fringed scales . . . . (5)

4a. Foliage densely appressed-canescent. **H. canescens** (de Candolle) Shinners. Replacing the next on the eastern plains.
4b. Foliage with spreading hairs. **H. villosa** (Pursh) Shinners. Abundant, weedy perennial throughout the lower mountains and canyons.

5a. Heads ± sessile, closely subtended by peduncular leaves not grading into the phyllaries. **H. fulcrata** (Greene) Shinners. Upper montane, subalpine.
5b. Heads appearing pedunculate; peduncular leaves distant from the heads or (if closer) reduced and grading into the phyllaries. **H. horrida** (Rydberg) Harms. Middle altitudes.

HIERACIUM L. 1753 [Greek, *hierax*, hawk; the ancients supposed that hawks used the plant to strengthen their eyesight, according to Pliny]. HAWKWEED

One species, **H. aurantiacum** L. [orange-colored]. Adventive, recently introduced, possibly with flower seeds, and becoming established along the foothills.

HYMENOPAPPUS L'Heritier 1788 [Greek, *hymen*, membrane, + pappus]

1a. Plants with showy, white ray-flowers. **H. newberryi** (Gray) Johnston, **Pl. 52.** Open hillsides, southeastern counties (*Leucampyx*).
1b. Ray-flowers lacking . . . . (2)

2a. Perennial with several to many caudices. **H. filifolius** Hooker, **35G**. Common, piñon-juniper. Several fairly well marked races occur, as follows: . . . . (3)
2b. Biennial with a single crown from a taproot . . . . (5)

3a. Basal leaf-axils without a dense tomentum. Var. **parvulus** (Greene) Turner. South Park and San Luis Valley.
3b. Basal leaf-axils densely tomentose . . . . (4)

4a. Heads 5-60 per stem; stem leaves 3-8; leaf tips of basal rosettes 10-30 mm long; corolla throat 1.3-1.8 mm long. Var. **polycephalus** (Osterhout) Turner. Common on the plains in the northern three tiers of counties.
4b. Heads 1-40 per stem; stem leaves 0-2; leaf tips of basal rosettes 2-50 mm long; corolla throat 1.5-2.5 mm long. Var. **cinereus** (Rydberg) Johnston. Abundant on the eastern plains near the mountain front.

5a. Flowers white; ultimate leaf segments narrowly linear, 0.5-1.5 mm wide. **H. tenuifolius** Pursh. Infrequent but widely distributed on the plains, particularly in sandy soils.
5b. Flowers yellow; ultimate leaf segments short, narrow to broad, 1-6 mm wide. **H. flavescens** Gray [yellowish]. Arkansas River drainage, LA-BA.

HYPOCHAERIS L. 1753 [a name used by Theophrastus]. CAT'S-EAR

One species, **H. radicata** L. [having roots]. An uncommon weed in lawns. The leaves resemble those of dandelion but are rough-pubescent, and there are several heads on a tall scape.

IVA L. 1753 [ancient name of some medicinal plant]. POVERTYWEED

One species, **I. axillaris** Pursh. Abundant, weedy, rhizomatous perennial, alkaline soil around ponds and in swales on the plains.

JACEA Miller 1754 [a pre-Linnaean name for this group]. BROWN KNAPWEED

One species, **J. pratensis** Lamarck. Adventive, locally escaped from cultivation in Boulder and doubtless elsewhere, but evidently not yet established (*Centaurea jacea*).

KRIGIA Schreber 1791 [for David Krig, German physician who collected plants in colonial Maryland]

One species, **K. biflora** (Walter) Blake. Very rare, in meadows of the Black Forest near Colorado Springs.

LACTUCA L. 1753 [Greek, *lac*, milk, alluding to the juice]. LETTUCE

1a. Leaves spiny-margined and often with spines along the midrib and veins. **L. serriola** L., PRICKLY LETTUCE. Adventive, common weed in fields and gardens. Flowers yellow, latex white. Hybridizes in nature with the cultivated lettuce.
1b. Leaves not spiny-margined . . . . (2)

2a. Flowers yellow; latex brownish . . . . (3)
2b. Flowers blue or purplish . . . . (4)

3a. Achene plus beak 5-6 mm long; phyllaries 8-12 mm long; pappus bristles 5-6 mm long. **L. canadensis** L. Infrequent, lower montane gulches.
3b. Achene plus beak 7-9 mm long; phyllaries 7-9 mm long; phyllaries 13-20 mm long; pappus bristles 8-9 mm long. **L. ludoviciana** (Nuttall) Riddle. Frequent, but scattered, especially in sandhills on the plains.

4a. Strongly rhizomatous perennial; leaves simple or narrowly pinnatifid; pappus white. **L. tatarica** (L.) Meyer subsp. **pulchella** (Pursh) Stebbins [of Tartary, in Asia]. Abundant along roadsides in the valleys. An American race of a Siberian species.
4b. Biennial with a basal rosette and taproot; leaves with broad, triangular pinnatifid divisions; pappus brownish. **L. biennis** (Moench) Fernald. Uncommon, in clearings in the foothill canyons.

LAPSANA L. 1873. NIPPLEWORT

One species, **L. communis** L. Adventive weed. From 1916 to 1921 this was collected in JF at "Wadsworth Crossing" of Clear Creek. It has not been seen since that time.

LEPIDOTHECA Nuttall 1841 [Greek, *lepido*, scaly, + *theca*, container, achene]. PINEAPPLE WEED

One species, **L. suaveolens** Nuttall. Common, low herb of disturbed areas, especially on unpaved parking areas in the mountains. The crushed foliage has a pineapple odor (*Matricaria matricarioides*). Native in America and occurring as a weed in Eurasia!

LEUCACANTHA Nieuwland & Lunell 1917 [Greek, *leucos*, white, + *acantha*, thorn]. CORNFLOWER (formerly included in *Centaurea*)

One species, **L. cyanus** (L.) Nieuwland & Lunell. Adventive, commonly escaped from cultivation and spreading to fields.

LEUCANTHEMUM Miller 1754 [Greek, *leucos*, white, + *anthos*, flower]. OX-EYE DAISY

One species, **L. vulgare** Lamarck. Adventive, escaped from gardens and established in meadows, around mines and ghost towns in the mountains. Common in the eastern United States (*Chrysanthemum leucanthemum*).

LEUCELENE Greene 1896 [Greek, *leucos*, white, + *lenis*, soft]. SAND ASTER

One species, **L. ericoides** (Torrey) Greene [like heather, from the leaf shape]. Common on arid gravels or clays, desert-steppe (*Aster arenosus*). Forming small hemispherical clumps, each branch with a single head.

LIATRIS Gaertner 1791 [derivation unknown]. GAYFEATHER

1a. Pappus clearly plumose to the naked eye . . . . (2)
1b. Pappus merely barbellate . . . . (3)

2a. Florets 3-8 per head, the heads crowded, narrow-cylindric; stems several from woody caudices. **L. punctata** Hooker [with translucent dots]. Mesas and roadsides, abundant along the outer foothills, less common on the eastern plains.
2b. Florets 10-60 per head (the heads well separated, broadly cup-shaped; stem solitary from a bulblike base. **L. squarrosa** (L.) Michaux var. **glabrata** (Rydberg) Gaiser. Rare on sandy soils (one record from PL).

3a. Heads large, as broad as long, with 20-70 florets. **L. ligulistylis** (Nelson) Schumann. Wet meadows in the piedmont and Wet Mountain Valley. Threatened by draining of the wetlands.
3b. Heads small, cylindric to turbinate, with 4-18 florets. **L. lancifolia** (Greene) Kittell. Infrequent, plains of the northeastern counties.

LIGULARIA Cassini 1816 [Latin, *ligula*, strap, alluding to the rays] (formerly included in *Senecio*)

1a. Dwarf alpines or, if taller and subalpine, heads with rays . . . . (2)
1b. Tall plants of montane forests and roadsides; rays absent; cauline leaves several . . . . (6)

2a. Plants small, with long slender elastic caudices; leaves cordate-reniform, crenate, usually less than 2 cm diameter. **L. porteri** (Greene) Weber. Endemic. Rare on alpine screes, on the Eastern Slope known only from Mineral Basin, CF.
2b. Plants larger in all respects; caudices stout, short . . . . (3)

3a. Cobwebby-pubescent. **L. taraxacoides** (Gray) Weber, **34B**. Endemic. High, rocky alpine slopes. Leaves usually runcinate-pinnatifid.
3b. Glabrous . . . . (4)

4a. Basal leaves withering by flowering time; cauline leaves elongate, usually sessile and clasping the stem (rarely tapered to a narrow base). **L. amplectens** (Gray) Weber, **34A**. Endemic, subalpine meadows and forest clearings.
4b. Leaves chiefly basal, present at flowering time, all rounded or cordate, with distinct petioles; alpine . . . . (5)

5a. Leaves broadly rounded at apex, abruptly narrowed to the petiole, the teeth remote or almost lacking; rays short and not twice as long as the involucre; plant succulent, strongly reddish-tinged. **L. soldanella** (Gray) Weber, **33B**. Endemic, boulderfields and screes of the higher peaks.
5b. Leaves more tapered to base and apex, usually strongly dentate; rays twice as long as involucre, showy; plants not strongly succulent, green or only reddish-tinged on the petioles. **L. holmii** (Greene) Weber, **33A**. Endemic, frequent on tundra.

6a. Heads large, turbinate, thick and fleshy, on stout peduncles, mostly racemosely arranged. **L. bigelovii** (Gray) Weber var. **hallii** (Gray) Weber, **34D**. Aspen groves, roadsides, montane.

6b. Heads small, cylindric, not fleshy, on slender peduncles, mostly arranged in panicles. **L. pudica** (Greene) Weber, **34C**. Canyons in the foothills and montane.

LYGODESMIA D. Don 1829 [Greek, *lygos*, pliant twig, + *desme*, bundle]. SKELETONWEED

One species, **L. juncea** (Pursh) D. Don. Much-branched, weedy, almost leafless herb, very common on the plains and San Luis Valley. Stems commonly producing spherical pealike galls containing the eggs and larvae of *Aylax pisum*, a Cynipid wasp.

MACHAERANTHERA Nees 1832 [Greek, *machaira*, sword, + *anthera*, anther, alluding to lanceolate processes of the anthers]. TANSY ASTER

1a. Leaves pinnatifid . . . . (2)

1b. Leaves merely toothed . . . . (4)

2a. Rays yellow. **M. pinnatifida** (Hooker) Shinners. A very common and variable weedy perennial in dry, often overgrazed range (*Haplopappus spinulosus*). This and other yellow-flowered species eventually may be transferred to other genera, since they do not fit too well in *Machaeranthera*.

2b. Rays lavender to purple; annual . . . . (3)

3a. Heads very small, involucre about 5 mm high; phyllaries appressed; rays less than 7 mm long. **M. parviflora** Gray. Alkaline flats, San Luis Valley (*Aster parvulus*).

3b. Heads large, involucre about 1 cm high; phyllaries spreading-recurved; rays 8-12 mm long. **M. tanacetifolia** (Humboldt, Bonpland & Kunth) Nees. Common weedy plant in ruderal and overgrazed sites on the plains (*Aster*).

4a. Rays yellow; annual. **M. phyllocephala** (de Candolle) Shinners. Common weed in overgrazed pastures, piedmont and plains.

4b. Rays violet or purple; biennial or perennial . . . . (5)

5a. Low or prostrate mat-plant with woody caudices; heads solitary on short peduncles. **M. coloradoënsis** (Gray) Osterhout, **Pl. 35**. Gravelly places in the higher mountain parks and on dry tundra (*Aster*).

5b. Erect, branching, weedy plant; lower and middle altitudes . . . . (6)

6a. Leaves narrow; heads very numerous, small; phyllaries hardly foliose, canescent or somewhat glandular. **M. canescens** (Pursh) Gray (including *M. linearis*, *M. rubrotinctus*). Abundant, roadside weed with many poorly defined races, subject to being moved around through road construction, possibly hybridizing freely.

6b. Leaves broad; heads relatively few, very large; phyllaries foliose, very glandular . . . . (7)

7a. Plants low, much branched from the base; road cuts and scree slopes in the middle and high mountains. **M. pattersonii** (Gray) Greene [for Harry N. Patterson]. Abundant in the Front Range.

7b. Plants up to 2 m tall, branched only in the inflorescence. **M. bigelovii** (Gray) Greene [for Jacob Bigelow, 1787-1879, professor of botany, Boston]. Foothills of the southern counties.

MACRONEMA Nuttall 1840 [Greek, *macro*, long, + *nema*, thread, alluding to the styles]

One species, **M. discoideum** Nuttall. Frequent on montane slopes, CC-CF. The branches are closely felted as in *Chrysothamnus*, but the heads are rayless and cream-colored (*Haplopappus macronema*).

MADIA Molina 1781 [from *madi*, the Chilean name]. TARWEED

One species, **M. glomerata** Hooker. Adventive, frequent, roadside weed. The foliage and heads are so viscid that they catch dust easily and become very dirty.

MATRICARIA L. 1753 [Greek, *matrix*, womb, for reputed medicinal value]. WILD CHAMOMILE

One species, **M. perforata** Merat. Adventive in disturbed ground, especially of montane roadsides, pastures, and townsites (*M. inodora*).

MELAMPODIUM L. 1753 [Greek, *melampodion*, blackfoot]

One species, **M. leucanthum** Torrey & Gray [white-flowered]. Low, bushy herb, woody at the base, with narrow opposite leaves and white-rayed heads; phyllaries very broad and rounded. Commonly associated with *Zinnia*, Arkansas River drainage.

MICROSERIS Don 1832 [Greek, *micro*, small, + *seris*, a kind of endive]

One species, **M. nutans** (Geyer) Schultz-Bipontinus. Dry, wooded slopes and meadows, foothills to montane and subalpine. Resembles *Agoseris* but with several heads per stalk, nodding at least in bud.

NOTHOCALAIS Greene 1886 [Greek, *nothos*, false, + *Calais*, a genus]. FALSE DANDELION

One species, **N. cuspidata** (Pursh) Greene. A very common, early spring flower of the mesas and plains, superficially resembling a dandelion but easily distinguished by the entire, broadly linear leaves with undulate margins bordered by short white hairs (*Microseris*).

OLIGONEURON J. K. Small 1903 [Greek, *oligo*, few, + *neuron*, nerve]. STIFF GOLDENROD

One species, **O. rigidum** (L.) Small. Common along the outwash mesas of the Front Range, and out onto the plains. The phyllaries, with more than one strong nerve, are distinctive of the genus.

OLIGOSPORUS Cassini 1817 [Greek, *oligo*, few, + *spora*, seed] (formerly included in *Artemisia*). SAGEWORT, TARRAGON

1a. Dwarf plants of desert-steppe, with finely divided pedatifid leaves and with the floral spikes very short and hidden among the leaves. **O. pedatifidus** (Nuttall) Poljakov. Clay soils of desert-steppe. To be expected in North Park and northern LR, since it occurs in adjacent Wyoming.

1b. Not as above . . . . (2)

2a. True shrubs with filiform leaves. Abundant on sandy soil and sandhills on the plains. **O. filifolius** (Torrey) Weber, SAND SAGEBRUSH. Occasionally almost all of the heads may be converted into conical galls caused by the Cecidomyid gall midge, *Rhopalomyia betheliana* [for Ellsworth Bethel, Colorado mycologist].

2b. Herbaceous plants, woody only at the base and dying back almost to the ground . . . . (3)

3a. Perennial from rhizomes; basal leaves absent by flowering time; leaves glabrate and simple at maturity; heads almost sessile, with pedicels 1-2 mm long; leaves commonly 2 mm or more wide. **O. dracunculus** (L.) Poljakov subsp. **glaucus** (Pallas) Löve & Löve, WILD TARRAGON. Frequent throughout the area, often weedy. In the southernmost counties a race occurs with smaller heads, subsp. **dracunculinus** (Watson) Weber.

3b. Biennial, monocarpic, or perennial, with a basal rosette .... (4)

4a. Heads in an open panicle, the bracts inconspicuous; involucre 2-3 mm high, 2-3.5 mm broad; biennial or monocarpic from a taproot. **O. campestris** (L.) Cassini subsp. **caudatus** (Michaux) Weber. Common from the plains to subalpine in dry, open meadows.

4b. Heads in a condensed, spikelike panicle, the bracts conspicuous in the inflorescence; involucre 3-4 mm high, 3.5-5 mm broad; perennial, developing several caudices. **O. groenlandicus** (Hornemann) Löve & Löve. Upper subalpine and alpine (*A. borealis* of manuals).

ONOPORDUM L. 1753 [Greek, *onos*, donkey, + *porde*, flatulence; Pliny stated that it caused this in donkeys]. SCOTCH THISTLE

1a. Foliage tomentose. **O. acanthium** L. [old generic name; prickly]. Both species are huge, aggressive thistle types now becoming established up and down the margin of the Front Range with the building of new highways.

1b. Foliage glabrous. **O. tauricum** L. [from Tauria (Crimea)]. Arkansas River drainage, along roadsides, PE, HF.

OÖNOPSIS Greene 1896 [Greek, *oön*, egg, alluding to the ovate involucre]

1a. Ray-flowers absent; involucre 8-10 mm long and 6-8 mm wide; leaves narrowly linear, less than 3 mm wide. **O. engelmannii** (Gray) Greene. Scattered on the plains except in the northern counties (*Haplopappus*).

1b. Ray-flowers usually present; involucre 12-25 mm long, 20-30 mm wide; leaves linear-oblong, over 4 mm wide. **O. foliosa** (Gray) Greene. Widely distributed in clay soils along the Arkansas River drainage system (*Haplopappus fremontii, O. monocephala*).

OREOCHRYSUM Rydberg 1906 [Greek, *oros*, mountain, + *chrysos*, gold]

One species, **O. parryi** (Gray) Rydberg. Common in spruce-fir and aspen forests (*Haplopappus*).

PACKERA Löve & Löve 1976 [for John Packer, contemporary Canadian botanist] (previously included in *Senecio*). GROUNDSEL

1a. Stem scapose (the stem leaves reduced to linear or bractlike vestiges), less than 2 dm high. **P. werneriifolia** (Gray) Weber & Löve. Rocky alpine and subalpine ridges. Variable in leaf width, tomentum, stature, and ray color, very likely because of hybridization with various other species with which it comes into contact. There seem to be no genetic barriers between the species; they tend to remain uncontaminated when isolated by flowering time, ecological preference, and distance.

1b. Stems with at least a few well-developed leaves .... (2)

2a. Basal leaves entire, ± permanently white-tomentose. **P. cana** (Hooker) Weber & Löve. Widely distributed from the plains to the alpine. A rayless form occurs on Cochetopa Pass.

2b. Basal leaves, at least some of them toothed or pinnatifid, glabrous or becoming so in age .... (3)

3a. Basal leaves and most stem leaves deeply pinnatifid or runcinate-pinnatifid. **P. fendleri** (Gray) Weber & Löve. Abundant in gravelly soil, open forests of the foothills. Producing rosettes from long, slender rhizomes; leaf lobes uniform, shallow; leaves white-tomentose.
3b. Basal leaves oval, rarely pinnatifid except at the very base . . . . (4)

4a. Basal leaves oval or cordate, on long, slender petioles, usually regularly crenate but sometimes almost entire . . . . (5)
4b. Basal leaves narrower, on winged petioles, irregularly toothed or lobed or entire . . . . (9)

5a. Basal leaves relatively thin; stems produced singly or a few together . (6)
5b. Basal leaves thick and leathery, oval, cuneate at the base; strongly rhizomatous plants forming broad mats . . . . (8)

6a. Heads rayless; disk-flowers orange; phyllaries purple; foliage thickish, glaucous, the basal leaves broadly oval, the cauline leaves pinnatifid with broad sinuses and rounded teeth. **P. debilis** Nuttall [weak]. Infrequent in quaking calcareous fens of North and South Park. Very closely related to (and incorrectly reported as) the northern *P. pauciflorus* (Pursh) Löve & Löve, which has narrow leaf sinuses and sharp teeth.
6b. Heads with ray-flowers . . . . (7)

7a. Basal leaves broadly ovate-cordate, subcordate or distinctly truncate at the base, regularly crenate. **P. pseudaurea** (Rydberg) Weber & Löve. Frequent along mountain streamlets and in the parks.
7b. Basal leaves narrow or, if broader, only weakly crenate; cauline leaves prominently pinnatifid with rounded sinuses. **P. paupercula** (Michaux) Löve. Wet meadows of North Park.

8a. Glabrous; cauline leaves sharply serrate, stem leaves usually pinnatisect. **P. streptanthifolia** (Greene) Weber & Löve. Infrequent in dry, open forests, CR and North Park Range.
8b. Floccose-pubescent; leaves crenate, basal ones never pinnatisect. **P. oödes** (Rydberg) Weber. Infrequent in dry forests, upper end of South Park.

9a. Stems clustered, from a taproot with short caudices; upper stem leaves without auriculate or enlarged bases . . . . (10)
9b. Stems solitary or a few together, from a short rhizome; upper stem leaves with enlarged, auriculate-clasping bases . . . . (12)

10a. Leaves narrowly oblanceolate, commonly 3-toothed at the apex but sometimes generally toothed or pinnatifid, usually glabrous. **P. tridenticulata** (Rydberg) Weber & Löve. Open, gravelly flats. Distinct in its characteristic glabrous, 3-toothed form, but completely merging, through hybridization, with the next.
10b. Leaves oval or broadly oblanceolate, variably toothed or lobed, usually distinctly pubescent . . . . (11)

11a. Cauline leaves lyrate to sharply pinnatisect; plants floccose-pubescent, becoming glabrous or nearly so as flowering proceeds. **P. plattensis** (Nuttall) Weber & Löve. Common early spring plant on the piedmont.
11b. Cauline leaves subentire or merely dentate. **P. neomexicana** (Gray) Weber & Löve. Summer-flowering, abundant in relatively dry meadows and open montane forests. Extremely variable, probably due to a tendency to hybridize with other *Packera* species.

12a. Ray-flowers deep orange. **P. crocata** (Rydberg) Weber & Löve. Moist meadows, usually at lower altitudes than the next.

12b. Ray-flowers yellow. **P. dimorphophylla** (Greene) Weber & Löve. Dry gravelly montane and subalpine meadows.

PALAFOXIA Lagasca 1816 [for José de Palafox y Melzi, 1780-1847, a Spanish general]

1a. Heads with disk-flowers only. (Caution: The disk-flowers are deeply 5-lobed and may be taken for ray-flowers.) **P. rosea** (Bush) Cory var. **macrolepis** (Rydberg) Turner. Sandy soil, extreme southeastern corner, BA.

1b. Heads with conspicuous, 3-toothed ray-flowers. **P. sphacelata** (Nuttall) Cory. Generally distributed in sandy soil and sandhills on the plains.

PECTIS L. 1759

One species, **P. angustifolia** Torrey. A low, branched annual with lemon-scented foliage, easily recognized by the conspicuous glandular dots on the foliage and involucre, and especially by the presence of several stiff cilia on the bases of the leaves. On the plains, mostly in the Arkansas River drainage, but also in WL.

PERICOME Gray 1853 [Greek, *peri*, around, + *coma*, hair, alluding to a beard of stiff hairs around the margin of the achene]

One species, **P. caudata** Gray [tailed, from the long attenuate leaf apex]. Common on canyonsides of foothills, from BL southeastward to the Oklahoma border, and along the Conejos River. In the southern part of the range, the plants become strongly glandular, var. *glandulosa* (Goodman) Harrington.

PETASITES Miller 1754 [Greek name for coltsfoot, from *petasos*, broad-brimmed hat]. SWEET COLTSFOOT

One species, **P. sagittatus** (Banks) Gray, **Pl. 60**. Marshy meadows in the intermountain parks and valleys. Leaves triangular-cordate, green above, white-woolly beneath; flowering very early, the fruiting heads very conspicuous because of the copious white pappus.

PICRADENIA Hooker 1833 [Greek, *picros*, bitter, + *aden*, gland, alluding to the very bitter floral glands]. The species are poisonous to sheep.

1a. Low, widely branching annual with a slender taproot. **P. odorata** (de Candolle) Britton. Frequent on the plains in the lower Arkansas River drainage.

1b. Perennial or strong biennial with caudices . . . . (2)

2a. Strong perennial with numerous caudices; leaf segments narrow; heads few or numerous, small (less than 1.5 cm diameter excluding rays). **P. richardsonii** Hooker. Abundant on gravelly flats, intermountain parks (*Hymenoxys*). Several races occur, differing in the size and number of heads, stature, and leaf form. These have never been evaluated. In North Park a very distinctive form occurs, with large and few flower heads.

2b. Biennial with one or only a few caudices; leaf segments broad (2-3 mm wide), many leaves usually simple; heads larger (about 2 cm diameter). **P. helenioides** Rydberg. Known in Colorado from only two localities, one on the Eastern Slope, along Sangre de Cristo Creek, CT (*Hymenoxys*). There is circumstantial evidence that this may be a first-generation hybrid involving *P. richardsonii* and *Dugaldia hoopesii* (J. Anderson, personal communication). While very rare, it always happens to occur with the putative parental species.

PICRADENIOPSIS Rydberg 1901 [alluding to the similarity to *Picradenia*]

1a. Achenes distinctly glandular; pappus scales ovate, with the midrib becoming indistinct halfway up the scale. **P. oppositifolia** (Nuttall) Rydberg. Commonly colonizing roadsides on the plains near the mountain front.

1b. Achenes hairy but not glandular; pappus scales lanceolate, with the midrib prominent, often projecting beyond the apex into a short bristle. **P. woodhousei** (Gray) Rydberg [for S. W. Woodhouse, 1821-1904, physician-naturalist with the Sitgreaves expedition]. Infrequent and scattered, eastern Elbert County and extreme southeastern Colorado.

PODOSPERMUM de Candolle 1805. FALSE SALSIFY

One species, **P. laciniatum** (L.) de Candolle. Adventive. Abundant weed naturalized in and around Boulder and in Larimer County (*Scorzonera*).

PRENANTHES L. 1753 [Greek, *prenes*, drooping, + *anthos*, flower]. WHITE-LETTUCE

One species, **P. racemosa** Michaux. Rare or infrequent in forested areas along streamsides and in willow carrs.

PRIONOPSIS Nuttall 1841

One species, **P. ciliata** (Nuttall) Nuttall. Barely entering Colorado in the southeast corner on sand dunes along the Cimarron River (*Haplopappus*).

PSILOCHENIA Nuttall 1841 [Greek, *psilo*, bare, + *achaenia*, achene] (formerly included in *Crepis*; see also *Askellia*). AMERICAN HAWKSBEARD

1a. Involucre turbinate-campanulate; stem leaves generally all reduced, narrow, inconspicuous or rarely the lowest one similar to the basal leaves. **P. runcinata** (James) Löve & Löve. A very common and variable species of wet montane and subalpine meadows. Easily distinguished from the other species by the broad involucre.

1b. Involucre narrowly or broadly cylindrical, 1-3 stem leaves well developed; plants of dry situations . . . . (2)

2a. Inner phyllaries glabrous. **P. acuminata** (Nuttall) Weber. A Western Slope species to be expected in North Park, since it occurs in adjacent RT.

2b. Inner phyllaries ± tomentose, often glandular or setose as well . . . . . (3)

3a. Involucres thick-cylindric, 5-10 mm wide at the middle, ± glandular-pubescent or glandular setose; plants rarely over 3.5 dm high. **P. occidentalis** Nuttall. Outwash mesas of the Front Range in the Boulder-Denver area. Foliage usually very tomentose.

3b. Involucres narrow-cylindric, 3-5 mm wide at the middle, never glandular; plants commonly taller. **P. atribarba** (Heller) Weber. Foothill canyons, Front Range, Boulder region.

PYRROCOMA Hooker 1833 [Greek, *pyrrhos*, tawny, + *coma*, mane, alluding to the pappus] (formerly included in *Haplopappus*)

1a. Involucre 11-22 mm high; pappus light brown . . . . (2)

1b. Involucre 6-10 mm high; pappus white. **P. lanceolata** (Hooker) Greene. Alkaline flats, North Park and San Luis Valley. Heads racemosely arranged.

2a. Phyllaries very broad and rounded-obtuse; involucre over 15 mm high; achenes glabrous. **P. crocea** (Gray) Greene [saffron colored]. Forest openings and aspen groves, Cumbres Pass; to be expected in western North Park.

Variable in height, sometimes up to 1 m tall, with huge, glaucous basal leaves.

2b. Phyllaries acute; involucre less than 15 mm high; achenes villous. **P. clementis** Rydberg [for F. E. Clements]. Gravelly flats, South Park and upper Rio Grande drainage.

RATIBIDA Rafinesque 1817 [derivation?]. PRAIRIE CONEFLOWER

1a. Receptacle and disk elongate-oblong; rays elongate, yellow or sometimes purple at the base. **R. columnifera** (Nuttall) Wooton & Standley. Common on the outwash mesas and plains. In the pure species the rays are yellow and the receptacle long-cylindric. Plants with shorter-cylindric heads and rays with some red color are introgressants with the southeastern species, *R. tagetes*.

1b. Receptacle short, the disk thimble-shaped; rays very short, deep maroon. **R. tagetes** (James) Barnhart [after *Tagetes*, the marigold]. Plains, Denver southeastward to the state border.

RUDBECKIA L. 1753 [for Professors Olaf Rudbeck, father and son, predecessors of Linnaeus at Uppsala]. BLACK-EYED SUSAN

1a. Leaves entire, harshly pubescent; stem less than 1 m tall. **R. hirta** L. Frequent in dry mountain meadows.

1b. At least the lower leaves lobed or divided . . . . (2)

2a. Stems usually over 1 m tall; all leaves lobed or divided; ray-flowers yellow, 3-6 cm, long; disk yellow or greenish. **R. ampla** Nelson (*R. laciniata* var. *ampla*), GOLDENGLOW. Common along montane streamsides.

2a. Stems lower; upper leaves entire; ray-flowers orange, 1-2 cm long; disk purple. **R. triloba** L. An eastern species, escaped from cultivation in our area and established in marshes around Boulder.

RYDBERGIA Greene 1898 [for Per Axel Rydberg, dean of Rocky Mountain botanists]. OLD-MAN-OF-THE-MOUNTAIN

1a. Some basal leaves entire, others divided at the apex into usually 3 linear segments, almost glabrous; involucre up to 2 cm broad. **R. brandegei** (Porter) Rydberg. Alpine, replacing the next species in the Sangre de Cristo, Culebra, and southern San Juan ranges *(Hymenoxys)*.

1b. Basal leaves with 3-5 or more lobes, sparsely woolly; involucre up to 4 cm broad. **R. grandiflora** (Torrey & Gray) Greene, **Pl. 61**. A stunning, large-headed, dwarf, yellow tundra plant throughout the area except in the south.

SAUSSUREA de Candolle 1810 [for Swiss philosopher H. B. de Saussure, 1740-1799]

One species, **S. weberi** Hultén. Locally common on alpine solifluction lobes, mountains around the north end of South Park. The deep purple stamens and style protruding well out of the corolla, and the beautifully plumose pappus, are distinctive features. *Saussurea* is a large, Asiatic genus with a few species in western North America. *S. weberi* also occurs in northwestern Wyoming and western Montana.

SENECIO L. 1753 [Latin, *senes*, old man, alluding to the white pappus]. GROUNDSEL, BUTTERWEED

Note: *Senecio* is an enormous, very unnatural genus. *Senecio* proper, represented in Colorado by *S. vulgaris*, only occurs as a garden weed. Except for *Packera*, which has a different chromosome base number from the rest of our species, and *Ligularia*, genera have not been proposed for the other Colorado groups of species.

SENECIO: True *Senecio*

One species, **S. vulgaris** L. Adventive, ruderal weed, most common in new garden plantings. The rayless flowers, pinnatifid leaves, and black-tipped phyllaries are diagnostic. Our only annual in the genus in its narrow sense.

"**SENECIO**": *Lugentes* and *Integerrimi*

1a. Plants with a thick rhizome . . . . (2)
1b. Plants with an abruptly shortened, buttonlike caudex . . . . (3)

2a. Tall, up to 1 m high, produced in great masses, tomentose to glabrate; leaves elongate, oblanceolate, margins with dark, cartilaginous denticles. **S. atratus** Greene. Abundant on scree slopes and road embankments, montane.
2b. Low, less than 0.5 m high, growing singly or a few together, glabrous and glaucous; basal leaves broadly oblanceolate; leaf denticles few or lacking. **S. wootonii** Greene. Open, dry montane forests.

3a. Pubescent, losing much of the pubescence in age. **S. integerrimus** Nuttall. Very common in moist meadows from the foothills to subalpine.
3b. Glabrous . . . . (4)

4a. Very tall, glaucous plants, usually over 1 m tall, of swamplands, with numerous, very small heads. **S. hydrophilus** Nuttall. Wet meadows and oxbows, North Park.
4b. Low, glabrous, green plants of mountainsides and meadows . . . . (5)

5a. Rayless; heads numerous (usually over 25), less than 5 mm wide; involucre narrow at base; leaves very coarsely and irregularly dentate. **S. rapifolius** Nuttall. Rare or infrequent, scattered along the canyons of the northern Front Range and in North Park.
5b. Rays present; heads few (usually 3-10), about 10 mm wide; involucre broad-based; leaves usually finely and remotely denticulate, only occasionally coarsely dentate. **S. crassulus** Gray. Common, upper montane and subalpine.

"**SENECIO**": *Suffruticosi*

1a. Foliage irregularly but prominantly woolly tomentose. **S. douglasii** de Candolle subsp. **longilobus** (Bentham) Weber. Lower Arkansas River Valley from Cañon City to the Oklahoma border (*S. longilobus*).
1b. Foliage mostly glabrous, never woolly tomentose . . . . (2)

2a. Leaves simple, linear; heads small, disk 3-6 mm wide; phyllaries about 8. **S. spartioides** Torrey & Gray. Gravelly outwash mesas and open parklands, flowering in late summer and fall.
2b. Leaves regularly pinnatifid with rather short lateral lobes; heads large, the disk 7-12 mm wide; phyllaries about 13. **S. riddellii** Torrey & Gray. Sandhills on the plains.

"**SENECIO**": *Triangulares*

1a. Low, succulent, many-stemmed plants with 1-3 heads per stem; leaves oblong-ovate, sharply dentate. **S. fremontii** Torrey & Gray var. **blitoides** (Greene) Cronquist. Common on scree slopes near timberline.
1b. Tall plants with relatively few stems and thin leaves . . . . (2)

2a. Leaves pinnately lobed or irregularly incised. **S. eremophilus** Rydberg subsp. **kingii** (Rydberg) Douglas & Ruyle-Douglas. Common along roadsides and trails, montane and lower subalpine.
2b. Leaves finely or coarsely dentate but not lobed or incised . . . . (3)

3a. Leaves triangular, truncate at the base, coarsely dentate. **S. triangularis** Hooker. Subalpine forest streamsides.
3b. Leaves lanceolate, finely serrate-dentate. **S. serra** Hooker var. **admirabilis** (Greene) Nelson. Infrequent along streams, montane, Front Range and North Park.

SERIPHIDIUM Poljakov 1961 [Greek, *seriphos*, wormwood] (formerly included in *Artemisia*). SAGEBRUSH

1a. Tall shrubs with simple, broadly linear leaves, occasionally some with terminal lobules. **S. canum** (Pursh) Weber. Typically a plant of the edges of drainage areas, evidently requiring more moisture than the others. This hybridizes with all of the other species where they come in contact.
1b. Low shrubs or, if tall, then most leaves trilobed at the apex . . . . (2)

2a. Heads large (3-5 mm high) in interrupted, little-branched panicles. **S. arbusculum** (Nuttall) Weber subsp. **longilobum** (Osterhout) Weber. Common in North Park. *Artemisia argilosa* and *A. longiloba*, of North Park, may represent crosses involving *S. arbuscula* and *S. canum*.
2b. Heads small (2-3 mm high) in dense, often much-branched panicles . . (3)

3a. Heads very numerous in open panicles; tall shrubs of deep soils, especially along arroyos. **S. tridentatum** (Nuttall) Weber, BIG SAGEBRUSH. Infrequent east of the Continental Divide, along the base of the Front Range, and on the west side of the San Luis Valley.
3b. Heads in narrower panicles; lower shrubs of more rocky and shallow soils. **S. vaseyanum** (Rydberg) Weber, MOUNTAIN SAGEBRUSH. Characteristic of highland sagebrush zones of the intermountain parks.

SHINNERSOSERIS Tomb 1973 [for Lloyd H. Shinners, 1918-1971, iconoclastic Texan botanist who built the Southern Methodist University herbarium and founded the journal of southwestern botany, *Sida*]

One species, **S. rostrata** (Gray) Tomb. Common in sandy soil on the plains (*Lygodesmia*).

SILPHIUM L. 1753 [Greek, *silphion*, ancient name of some resinous plant]

1a. Leaves alternate, deeply pinnately lobed; plants with a taproot. **S. laciniatum** L., COMPASS PLANT. One collection made in 1926 near Palmer Lake, possibly from the last surviving colony of this eastern prairie relict. The plants may be up to 2 m tall.
1b. Leaves opposite, simple, ovate, sessile; plants short-rhizomatous. **S. integrifolium** Michaux. Rare, relictual in prairies of the northeasternmost corner at Wray, probably now extinct.

SOLIDAGO L. 1753 [Latin, *solidus*, whole, for curative powers]. GOLDENROD

1a. Heads in a terminal simple or branched thyrse (an oblong, spikelike panicle), the branches not at all one-sided or scarcely so . . . . (2)
1b. Heads in a terminal, usually large, spreading panicle, its branches arching or recurved and distinctly one-sided (with the heads arranged along the upper side) . . . . (6)

2a. Leaves ± uniformly short-pubescent . . . . (3)
2b. Leaves essentially glabrous . . . . (4)

3a. Low plant (1-3 dm high) of open ground; leaves not particularly scabrous. **S. nana** Nuttall. Frequent on outwash mesas and canyons of the outer foothills. Very similar to *S. mollis*, which may be distinguished by its distinctly 3-nerved leaves that are usually serrate and its 1-sided inflorescence branches. The latter is definitely a plains species.
3b. Tall plant (over 6 dm high), of canyons and oak brush; foliage harshly scabrous-pubescent. **S. wrightii** Gray. Mesa de Maya [for Charles Wright, the collector].

4a. Leaves pale, somewhat glaucous; stems tall (4-8 dm); phyllaries obtuse. **S. speciosa** Nuttall var. **pallida** Porter. Gravelly slopes in the lower foothills. An eastern woodland-prairie relict.
4b. Leaves deep green, not glaucous; stems low (1-4 dm); phyllaries acute. (5)

5a. Lowermost leaves with ciliate-margined petioles; rays mostly about 13 (or more numerous on the terminal head); phyllaries not strongly imbricate. **S. multiradiata** Aiton subsp. **scopulorum** (Gray) Weber. Common in open, sunny, rocky places, subalpine.
5b. None of the leaves with ciliate-margined petioles; rays mostly about 8; phyllaries clearly imbricate. **S. spathulata** de Candolle. Montane and subalpine. Alpine plants belong to var. **nana** (Gray) Cronquist, while taller plants of lower altitudes belong to var. **neomexicana** (Gray) Cronquist.

6a. Leaves, at least the lower ones, oblanceolate, spatulate, or obovate, the upper usually smaller, never regularly sharply serrate . . . . (7)
6b. Stem rather equably leafy, basal leaves not larger than the middle stem leaves, all lanceolate, sharply serrate . . . . (10)

7a. Glabrous or nearly so; leaves somewhat leathery in texture; upper leaves often very narrow. **S. missouriensis** Nuttall. Sagebrush, intermountain basins.
7b. Short-pubescent; leaves thin, at least not leathery in texture . . . . (8)

8a. Stems low, usually less than 3 dm high; leaves short and broadly oblanceolate. **S. mollis** Bartling [soft]. Frequent on the eastern plains.
8b. Stems taller and slender, often over 4 dm high; leaves narrowly lanceolate, the upper usually very small; plants of the foothills and montane . . . (9)

9a. Basal leaf rosette not present at flowering time; leaves characteristically with 3 prominent veins. **S. velutina** de Candolle [velvety]. Piñon-juniper and oak zones (*S. sparsiflora*).
9b. Basal leaf rosette present at flowering time; leaves with 1 prominent vein. **S. nemoralis** Aiton [of woodlands]. Uncommon along the canyons of the outer foothills.

10a. Stem glabrous up to the inflorescence. **S. serotinoides** Löve & Löve. A very tall goldenrod of wet places in the valleys (*S. gigantea* subsp. *serotina*).
10b. Stem ± pubescent . . . . (11)

11a. Involucre 2-3 mm high. **S. canadensis** L., CANADA GOLDENROD. Wet meadows and streamsides in the valleys.
11b. Involucre 3.5-5 mm high. **S. altissima** L., TALL GOLDENROD. Similar habitats. Some regard this as var. *scabra* Torrey & Gray, of the previous species.

SONCHUS L. 1753 [the ancient Greek name]. SOW-THISTLE

1a. Annual; involucre glabrous . . . . (2)
1b. Perennial from deep-seated rhizomes; involucre glandular-pubescent or with glandular dots . . . . (3)

2a. Achenes strongly 3-5-ribbed on each face, thin-margined, not transversely wrinkled; leaf-base auricles rounded. **S. asper** (L.) Hill [harsh], SPINY SOW-THISTLE. Adventive, ruderal weed in cultivated ground.
2b. Achenes striate and also strongly wrinkled transversely, not thin-margined; leaf-base auricles acute. **S. oleraceus** L. [of kitchen gardens], ANNUAL SOW-THISTLE. Adventive. Similar sites.

3a. Involucre glandular-pubescent with spreading yellowish hairs. **S. arvensis** L., PERENNIAL SOW-THISTLE. Adventive tall weed over 1 m tall, in wet meadows and cultivated ground, sometimes on drier sites such as roadcuts.
3b. Involucre glabrous and usually with large glandular spots. **S. uliginosus** Bieberstein, SWAMP SOW-THISTLE. Adventive in similar sites. The species of *Sonchus* resemble prickly lettuce (*Lactuca serriola*), but the involucres are broad at the base instead of narrowly cylindric.

STENACTIS Cassini 1825 [Greek, *stenos*, narrow, + *aktis*, ray]. DAISY FLEABANE

One species, **S. strigosus** (Mühlenberg) de Candolle. Infrequent weed of disturbed ground on the plains, piedmont valleys, and outer foothills *(Erigeron)*.

STENOTUS Nuttall 1841 [Greek, *stenos*, narrow, alluding to the leaves] (formerly included in *Haplopappus*)

One species. **S. armerioides** Nuttall. Rimrock and rocky hillsides, Pawnee National Grassland. In this species the phyllaries are broadly oblong or oval with rounded-obtuse apices. One would have expected the Eastern Slope species to be *S. acaulis*, which is so common in northwestern Colorado, but this paradox of plant geography decrees otherwise.

STEPHANOMERIA Nuttall 1841 [Greek, *stephanos*, crown, + *meris*, part, alluding to the pappus]. WIRELETTUCE

1a. Achenes pitted and tuberculate; plants low, mostly 1-2 dm tall, with the main leaves runcinate-pinnatifid. **S. runcinata** Nuttall. Known on the Eastern Slope from one old collection near the Pawnee Buttes.
1b. Achenes smooth or nearly so, only longitudinally ribbed; plants low or tall; lower leaves usually disappearing by flowering time. **S. pauciflora** (Torrey) Nelson, **35D**. Common along the margin of the Front Range, in the outer foothills and San Luis Valley.

TANACETUM L. 1753 [Greek, *athanatos*, immortal]. TANSY

One species, **T. vulgare** L. Adventive. Common along fencerows in the valleys. Tall, rank-smelling herb with finely pinnatisect leaves and flat-topped inflorescence of yellow, buttonlike heads. A few other species usually placed in *Tanacetum* are cultivated and occasionally escape, but there is no evidence that they persist as this species does.

TARAXACUM G. H. Weber [from Arabic *tharakhchakon*]. DANDELION

The genus has been revised for us by Dr. R. Doll, University of Greifswald, East Germany.

1a. Outer phyllaries recurved-spreading. **T. officinale** G. H. Weber, COMMON DANDELION, **35A**. Adventive. Abundant and ever-present weed in lawns, overgrazed meadows and pastures, responsible, nevertheless, for magnificent early spring floral displays in the mountains. Experimental evidence indicates that *T. laevigatum*, the red-seeded dandelion, is not distinct.

1b. Outer phyllaries appressed, erect; tundra plants . . . . (2)

2a. Brownish hairs present in the axils of the basal leaves; scapes often cobwebby-pubescent. **T. eriophorum** Rydberg. Infrequent and widely scattered, on tundra.

2b. Basal leaves and scapes without hairs . . . . (3)

3a. Outer phyllaries green, with horn-shaped swellings at the tips; plants large (over 5 cm tall); heads large; leaves broad, entire or shallowly sinuate-dentate. **T. ovinum** Rydberg. Common on tundra (*T. ceratophorum* of Colorado reports).

3b. Outer phyllaries dark blackish-green, lacking horns; plants minute (1-5 cm tall); heads very small (about 1 cm); leaves regularly sinuate-lobed. **T. scopulorum** (Gray) Rydberg. Among boulders of fellfields on the higher peaks (*T. lyratum* of Colorado reports).

TETRADYMIA de Candolle 1838 [Greek, *tetradymos*, four-sided, alluding to the involucre]. HORSEBRUSH

One species, **T. canescens** de Candolle. Common in mountain sagebrush habitats from North Park to the San Luis Valley and foothills of the southern counties.

TETRANEURIS Greene 1898 [Greek, *tetra*, four, + *neuron*, nerve] (formerly included in *Hymenoxys*)

1a. Aerial stems arising from numerous, slender, branched caudices. **T. scaposa** (de Candolle) Greene var. **linearis** Parker. Easternmost counties from YM to BA.

1b. Aerial stems arising from very short, thick caudices . . . . (2)

2a. Flowering stems 2-3 dm high. **T. ivesiana** Greene [for the Ives western exploring expedition]. On the Eastern Slope known from a single collection made between Colorado Springs and the Black Forest.

2b. Stems low, foliage pubescent . . . . (3)

3a. Leaves almost glabrous and conspicuously gland-dotted; leaf bases set in a conspicuous tuft of long white hairs. **T. torreyana** (Nuttall) Greene. Rock pavements wet in springtime. To be expected in North Park, since it occurs in adjacent Wyoming.

3b. Leaves strongly pubescent, not conspicuously gland-dotted; leaf bases not set in a tuft of long white hairs . . . . (4)

4a. Leaves appressed-silky. **T. acaulis** (Pursh) Greene. Common on the plains and outwash mesas.

4b. Leaves loosely villous. **T. brevifolia** Greene. Dwarf caespitose alpine tundra plant.

THELESPERMA Lessing 1831 [Greek, *thele*, nipple, + *sperma*, seed]

1a. Heads rayless or the few rays very short and inconspicuous. **T. megapotamicum** (Sprengel) Kuntze [of the Rio Grande]. Generally distributed on the plains and outwash mesas.

1b. Heads with ray-flowers . . . . (2)

2a. Leaves scattered along the stem; leaf segments filiform. **T. filifolium** (Hooker) Gray. Plains and mesas, mostly from Denver southward.

2b. Leaves mostly basal; leaf segments broadly linear. **T. subnudum** Gray. San Luis Valley and lower Arkansas River Valley.

TONESTUS Nelson 1904 [anagram of *Stenotus*] (formerly included in *Haplopappus*)

1a. Phyllaries lanceolate to linear-lanceolate, tapering to an acute apex; stems and leaves glandular; leaves 5-12 mm wide; plants not strongly caespitose. **T. lyallii** (Gray) Nelson. Infrequent on tundra.
1b. Phyllaries broadly oblong, rounded-obtuse or cuspidate at the apex; stems and leaves not glandular; leaves less than 5 mm wide; plants caespitose. **T. pygmaeus** (Torrey & Gray) Nelson. Common on rocky tundra.

TOWNSENDIA Hooker 1834 [for David Townsend, 1787-1858, Philadelphia botanist]. EASTER DAISY

1a. Stems several cm tall; phyllaries acuminate; summer flowering. . . . . . (2)
1b. Stems lacking (the flowers produced in a cluster of linear basal leaves on the surface of the ground); spring flowering, except at high altitudes . . . . (4)

2a. Decumbent; stems much branched, spreading; phyllaries with merely acute apices. **T. fendleri** Gray. Arid hills and benches, upper Arkansas River drainage between Pueblo and Buena Vista; Huerfano Creek.
2b. Erect from basal leaf rosettes; flowering stems unbranched, with a terminal, large head; phyllaries acuminate, stiff . . . . (3)

3a. Pappus of disk-flowers of short scales or bristles and 2-4 (rarely up to 8) longer, coarse bristles. **T. eximia** Gray [extraordinary]. Endemic. Montane to subalpine, Cuchara Valley and southward into New Mexico.
3b. Pappus of disk-flowers of 12 or more plurisetose bristles. **T. grandiflora** Nuttall. Common on dry slopes of the foothills and outwash mesas of the Front Range.

4a. Phyllaries linear to narrowly lanceolate, in 5-7 series; apices acuminate or acute . . . . (5)
4b. Phyllaries broadly lanceolate to ovate or elliptic, in 2-5 series; apices obtuse or acute. **T. rothrockii** Gray [for the collector, J. T. Rothrock]. Late-snow areas above timberline, Hoosier Pass-Boreas Pass.

5a. Phyllaries linear, acuminate, with a tuft of tangled cilia at the apex. **T. hookeri** Beaman [for Sir Joseph Hooker]. Blooming in early spring in open, rocky sagebrush. Widespread on the plains and outwash mesas of the Front Range.
5b. Phyllaries narrowly lanceolate, acute, without a tuft of tangled cilia at the apex . . . . (6)

6a. Disk pappus more than 6.5 mm long; leaf midvein usually conspicuous; leaves ± densely strigose. **T. exscapa** (Richardson) Porter [stemless]. Similar sites and range, also South Park. The distinction is difficult until one gains experience with each.
6b. Disk pappus less than 6.5 mm long (if longer, then the ray pappus less than half the length of the disk pappus); leaf blades glabrous or lightly pubescent. **T. leptotes** (Gray) Osterhout. Local, on volcanic ash beds, Cochetopa Park.

TRAGOPOGON L. 1753 [Greek, *tragos*, goat, + *pogon*, beard]. SALSIFY, OYSTER-PLANT

1a. Flowers violet-purple. **T. porrifolius** L. [with leaves like *Allium porrum*]. Adventive, common, dandelionlike weed with grasslike leaves on a tall stem. Hybridizes with *T. dubius*, producing paler flowers.

1b. Flowers yellow . . . . (2)

2a. Flowers pale lemon yellow, all shorter than the phyllaries; phyllaries about 13 (sometimes as many as 17 on the first head or as few as 8 on the latest heads), long and narrow, not margined with purple, longer than the outer flowers; peduncles strongly inflated in fruit. **T. dubius** Scopoli subsp. **major** (Jacquin) Vollmann. Adventive, ruderal weed in dry, hot valleys.

2b. Flowers chrome yellow, the outer ones about equalling the phyllary length; phyllaries about 8 or 9 on the first head, rarely as many as 13, broad and short, margined with purple, about equalling the outer flowers in length. **T. pratensis** L. [of meadows]. Adventive, replacing *T. dubius* at higher altitudes in more mesic meadow sites.

UNAMIA Greene 1903 [derivation not given]

One species, **U. alba** (Nuttall) Rydberg (*Solidago* or *Aster ptarmicoides*). Infrequent, relictual, eastern and midwestern prairie species, Black Forest to Florissant; also isolated occurrences in LR. The plant looks more like an *Aster* than a goldenrod. *U. subcinerea* Greene evidently is a first generation hybrid with *Oligoneuron rigidum*!

VERNONIA Schreber 1791 [for William Vernon, 16?-1711, English botanist who traveled in North America]. IRONWEED

1a. Leaves and stem short-pubescent; leaves broadly ovate-lanceolate, prominently serrate. **V. baldwinii** Torrey subsp. **interior** (Small) Faust. One collection from meadows on the plains, YM. This is said to differ from the next by having the leaves not pitted beneath, but our material is definitely pitted.

1b. Leaves and stem glabrous; leaves linear or lanceolate, conspicuously pitted beneath, the pits appearing as dark spots under low magnification . . . (2)

2a. Leaves lanceolate; inner phyllaries rounded to weakly acute-tipped. **V. fasciculata** Michaux subsp. **corymbosa** (Schweinitz) Löve & Löve. One collection from the northeast corner, SW.

2b. Leaves broadly linear; inner phyllaries acute to acuminate-tipped. **V. marginata** (Torrey) Rafinesque. Scattered and infrequent, EP, BA.

VIRGULUS Rafinesque 1837 [diminutive of Greek, *virga*, twig, rod] (formerly included in *Aster*). There is ample justification biologically for separating *Virgulus* from *Aster*, but the morphological distinctions are not easily delineated.

1a. Plants up to 1 m tall; leaves over 3 cm long, broadly oblong-lanceolate; rays bright red-purple, with long, narrow, dark phyllaries. **V. novae-angliae** (L.) Reveal & Keener. Boulder-Denver area, either an introduction or a prairie relict, now probably exterminated by development.

1b. Plants low, leaves usually less than 3 cm long, linear to oblong; rays white or purple . . . . (2)

2a. Phyllaries and peduncles glandular-pubescent; rays usually purple . . . . (3)

2b. Phyllaries and peduncles not glandular; rays usually white, pink in the hybrid, **V. x amethystinus** (Nuttall) Reveal & Keener . . . . (5)

3a. Leaves oblong; inflorescence branches with numerous bractlike leaves below the head. **V. oblongifolius** (Nuttall) Reveal & Keener. Mesa de Maya and foothills south of Arkansas River Valley.
3b. Leaves linear; inflorescence without numerous bractlike leaves below individual heads . . . . (4)

4a. Stems usually solitary, branched only in the inflorescence; heads few, phyllaries not strongly graduated. **V. campestris** (Nuttall) Reveal & Keener. Wet meadows in the mountain parks.
4b. Stems widely branched from the base; heads numerous; phyllaries strongly graduated. **V. fendleri** (Gray) Reveal & Keener. Dry hills and outwash mesas along the base of the Front Range.

5a. Involucre 5-7 (-8) mm tall; ray-flowers 20-30 or more; stem hairs spreading. **V. falcatus** (Lindley) Reveal & Keener. Abundant, fall-blooming, weedy aster in fields and roadsides on the plains and piedmont. Pink-flowered plants are *V. x amethystinus*, a putative hybrid with a species having colored ray-flowers.
5b. Involucre less than 5 mm tall; ray-flowers less than 20; stem hairs appressed or ascending. **V. ericoides** (L.) Reveal & Keener. Not as common as the last, in similar habitats.

WYETHIA Nuttall 1834 [for Nathaniel J. Wyeth, early western American explorer]. MULE'S EARS

One species, **W. amplexicaulis** (Nuttall) Nuttall [clasping-leaved]. On the Eastern Slope found only in North Park.

XANTHIUM L. 1753 [Greek, *xanthos*, yellow]. COCKLEBUR.

Nuttall, starting out on a journey to Arkansas in 1818, mentions fighting through masses of "Cuckoldburs" in Ohio. In this instance, the modern word cocklebur may be a later euphemism, since "cuckoldbur" more aptly alludes to the two horns on the fruit!

One species, **X. strumarium** L., **23H**. Adventive, common weed, especially around drying ponds in the valleys.

XIMENESIA Cavanilles 1794 [for José Ximenes, Castilian pharmacist and botanical illustrator]. CROWNBEARD, COWPEN DAISY

One species, **X. encelioides** Cavanilles. Adventive, common weed in disturbed, dry ground in the valleys (*Verbesina*).

ZINNIA L. 1759 [for J. C. Zinn, 1727-1759, professor at Göttingen]

One species, **Z. grandiflora** Nuttall. Low, bushy herb, woody at the base, with broad, bright yellow rays and red disk-flowers. As in other zinnias, the ray-flowers become papery and do not wither in age. Essentially a Mexican genus, only two species reach the United States.

BALSAMINACEAE JEWELWEED FAMILY (BLS)

If the leaves of jewel-weed are held under water they assume a silvery sheen. Possibly this is where the family gets its name. Everything about the plant is fascinating. The orange flowers are shaped like a Persian slipper, and the pods are elastically dehiscent, needing only a slight touch to explode, scattering the round seeds several feet. Jewel-weed has occurred around Boulder for many years and spreads along irrigation ditches. Whether it is indigenous or was introduced deliberately or accidentally by a nurseryman or gardener from the eastern United States probably never will be certain.

IMPATIENS L. 1753 [Latin for impatient, alluding to the explosive capsules]. JEWELWEED

One species, **I. capensis** Meerburgh [from Cape of Good Hope; erroneously thought to have come from there]. Frequent in shade along irrigation ditches and streams, vicinity of Boulder.

BERBERIDACEAE BARBERRY FAMILY (BER)

The barberries are "living fossils" that were common on hillsides of the Florissant region in Tertiary times. They include the true barberries, which have spiny stems and simple leaves, very abundantly represented in Central Asia and South America, and the holly-grapes, represented by a number of species in western North America, the Himalaya, and eastern Asia. The flowers are especially interesting because of the anthers, which open by side-flaps instead of splitting down the sides.

1a. Leaves simple, deciduous, with marginal teeth or weak spines; stems with branched spines at the base of the leaf clusters; sparingly branched, wandlike shrub. **Berberis**, BARBERRY

1b. Leaves compound, evergreen, with stout marginal spines; stems not spiny. **Mahonia**, HOLLY-GRAPE

BERBERIS L. 1753 [from *berberys*, the Arabic name for the fruit]. BARBERRY

1a. Second-year twigs reddish-brown; racemes 6-10-flowered, fruit 4-6 mm long; leaves narrowly oblanceolate, usually less than 2 cm long (rarely larger and broader), entire or spinose-serrate. **B. fendleri** Gray, **36D**. Common in the river valleys, southern counties.

1b. Second-year twigs gray; racemes usually more than 10-flowered, fruit 8-12 mm long; leaves usually over 2 cm long, broadly oblanceolate, always regularly spinose-serrate. **B. vulgaris** L. Adventive, locally established on the Enchanted Mesa near Boulder. The alternate host of black stem rust of wheat, this introduced species has been deliberately exterminated in wheat-growing areas. Even in medieval times, before the connection was scientifically understood, European villages had ordinances prohibiting cultivation of barberry hedges near wheatfields.

MAHONIA Nuttall 1818 [for Bernard MacMahon, a friend of Nuttall who introduced ornamental plants to the United States]. HOLLY-GRAPE, OREGON-GRAPE

1a. Above-ground stem short or almost lacking; leaves green, the leaflets broad, with relatively few weak, spinose teeth; plants of uplands and open coniferous forests, widespread. **M. repens** (Lindley) Don, **36E**. The glaucous-blue berries make a good jelly.

1b. Stems shrubby, well developed; leaves glaucous, the leaflets narrow, with few coarse and strong teeth. **M. haematocarpa** (Wooton) Fedde, YELLOWWOOD. Principal distribution area in New Mexico and Arizona, known in Colorado only from a single old collection (1902) from south of Trinidad (Raton Pass?). This species is a fairly low but erect shrub, unlike the western *M. fremontii*, **36F**, which forms a tree.

BETULACEAE BIRCH FAMILY (BET)

From Goethe's *Erlkönig* to Robert Frost's *Birches*, members of the birche family have always evoked romanticism; they figure in poetry and prose in many languages, especially in the northern world. Birch-bark canoes play a part in our conception of the native American. The bract of the carpellate catkin of birch is distinctive, recalling for some the fleur-de-lis, for others the Tenderfoot pin of the Boy Scouts. These catkins fall apart at maturity, freeing the tiny winged seeds. Birches in springtime yield a sweet sap that, while not collected for sugar-making, has been used to make vinegar. The bark of *B. lenta*, the black birch, has a wintergreen odor.

Our only Colorado stand of paper birch, and the southernmost in the United States, was discovered in 1906 on the back side of Green Mountain by D. M. Andrews, a Boulder nurseryman who specialized in native plants for the garden. Aven Nelson recognized it as very similar to paper birch and planned to name it *B. andrewsii* if it proved different, but he never published this name. My student, Sven G. Froiland, analyzed every birch in the population and published his results in 1952 in the journal *Evolution*. The original tree from which Andrews' specimens came, is almost pure *B. papyrifera* and has the typical white paper-bark, but most of the large trees have bark that peels less readily and have an intermediate color reminiscent of the eastern yellow birch, *B. lutea*. The ravine downstream is mostly populated by the shrubby *B. fontinalis*, which has hybridized with and contaminated the genotype of the paper birch parent, while remaining quite pure itself because backcrosses did not carry paper birch genes into the river birch population. Fortunately, this colony, one of the great rarities of the Colorado flora, is protected in the city of Boulder's mountain parks.

1a. Only the staminate flowers in catkins, catkinlike or conelike structures; carpellate flowers sessile on the twig; fruit a nut enclosed in a green or papery husk; leaves rough-hairy, very irregularly serrate, almost slightly lobed. **Corylus**, HAZELNUT

1b. All flowers in catkins (or the carpellate catkins pine-conelike); leaves smooth or nearly so . . . . (2)

2a. Scales of the carpellate catkins thin, falling separately from the axis at maturity; leaves flat; pith round in cross-section. **Betula**, BIRCH

2b. Scales of the carpellate catkin thick, woody, and persistent, resembling a small pine cone; leaves wrinkled; pith triangular in cross-section. **Alnus**, ALDER

ALNUS Miller 1754 [the classical Latin name]. ALDER

One species, **A. incana** (L.) Moench subsp. **tenuifolia** (Nuttall) Breitung, **36C**. Montane streambanks and pond borders (*A. tenuifolia*).

BETULA L. 1753 [the classical Latin name]. BIRCH

1a. Low shrub of subalpine fens and willow carrs; leaves almost round, thick, crenate-serrate; young twigs dotted thickly with warty resinous glands. **B. glandulosa** Michaux, BOG BIRCH, **36A**. Common around slow streams and beaver ponds, subalpine. Autumn foliage deep red.

1b. Tall shrubs or small trees; leaves ovate or obovate, sharply serrate; young twigs naked or with relatively few glands . . . . (2)

2a. Bark dark, not peeling; shrub with numerous, slender main stems; lenticels elliptical, chalky-white. **B. fontinalis** Sargent, RIVER BIRCH, **36B**. Canyon bottoms, always close to water, outer foothills to montane. Hybridizes with the *B. glandulosa* on Pikes Peak (*B. x utahensis* Britton).

2b. Bark gray, naturally peeling into thin layers, the underneath layers pink or white; trees with a few main stems over 10 cm diameter; lenticels horizontally elongate. **B. papyrifera** Marshall, PAPER or CANOE BIRCH, **Pl. 48**. Extremely rare, in a cool, north-facing ravine in the foothills near Boulder. Most or all of the plants are hybrids (*B. x andrewsii* Nelson) between this and *B. fontinalis* and are prone to trunk rot as the stems reach maximum diameter.

CORYLUS L. 1753 [probably from Greek, *corys*, helmet, from the involucre]. HAZELNUT

One species, **C. cornuta** Marshall. Common in cool ravines in the outer Front Range foothills. In early spring, when the male catkins elongate, look for the single carpellate flower sessile on the twig, enclosed by the embryonic involucre and visible only because of the brilliant red stigmas. Later the involucre enlarges to contain the nut, and its upper end resembles an old-fashioned party "snapper." In this area few nuts grow to maturity or survive the squirrels.

BIGNONIACEAE CATALPA FAMILY (BIG)

Most Bignoniaceae are tropical lianas, but some are trees, including the best-known American one, *Catalpa*, which is widely cultivated on our city streets. The family includes some of the best ornamental climbers and trees in gardens of the warmer parts of the world, and some real oddities, such as *Kigelia*, the sausage tree so much in evidence in Hawaii. The flowers resemble those of scrophs: tubular, showy; sometimes a few stamens are lost or replaced by staminodes. The fruit is often an elongate pod filled with flat, winged seeds.

CAMPSIS Loureiro 1790 ·[Greek, *kampe*, bending, for the curved stamens]. TRUMPET CREEPER

One species, **Campsis radicans** (L.) Seeman. Adventive, commonly cultivated and occasionally escaped and established along fencerows in the warmest areas. The leaves are pinnately compound, coarsely toothed; the flowers are tubular, red-orange; and the pod is linear (*Tecoma*).

BORAGINACEAE BORAGE FAMILY (BOR)

The borages share with the mints and verbenas the unique feature of a gynoecium lobed or divided into four discrete nutlets. When in doubt as to which family you have, remember that the borages alone have a radially symmetrical corolla and alternate leaves. Most borages, with a few exceptions (some *Mertensia* species), characteristically have very stiff and harsh hairs on stems and leaves. The name borage comes from a Middle Latin source, *burra*, meaning rough hair or short wool, just as the modern word, bur; in fact the pronunciation of borage used to rhyme with courage.

1a. Leaves thick, impressed-nerved, appressed-hispid; corolla lobes closed in a cone around the exserted style; nutlets ivory-white, egg-shaped. **Onosmodium**, MARBLESEED

1b. Not as above . . . . (2)

2a. Flowers yellow or greenish-yellow . . . . (3)

2b. Flowers white, blue, or red-purple . . . . (4)

3a. Foliage stiffly hispid; inflorescence a tightly rolled helix. **Amsinckia**
3b. Foliage pubescent but not hispid. **Lithospermum**, PUCCOON

4a. Flowers blue, pink, red, or purple (white mutants may occur) . . . . . . (5)
4b. Flowers white (yellow "eyes" may be present) . . . . (13)

5a. Corolla dull red; nutlets broad and flat, studded with short, hooked bristles. **Cynoglossum**, HOUND'S TONGUE
5b. Not as above . . . . (6)

6a. Dwarf alpine plants forming cushions of small, silky-hairy leaves, and very short to ± elongate peduncles. **Eritrichum**, ALPINE FORGET-ME-NOT
6b. Plants not cushion-forming; taller plants of lower altitudes . . . . (7)

7a. Flowers deep blue, with a well-developed cylindric tube and limb and short corolla lobes; attachment of nutlet surrounded by a swollen, circular rim, strongly convex or pluglike, leaving a pit on the flat or low-convex gynobase . . . . (8)
7b. Flowers otherwise; attachment of the nutlet without a rim, leaving no pit on the gynobase . . . . (9)

8a. Corolla thick-tubular, with campanulate throat, the short lobes erect or recurving at tip; inner corolla appendages lanceolate, acute, with denticulate margins. **Symphytum**, COMFREY
8b. Corolla funnelform or salverform, with poorly defined throat, the elongate lobes spreading; appendages deltoid or oblong, blunt, usually hairy. **Anchusa**, ALKANET

9a. Flowers of the slender raceme mostly without leaflike bracts; adventive plants, often on shaded streamsides. **Myosotis**, FORGET-ME-NOT
9b. At least the lower flowers leafy-bracted . . . . (10)

10a. Corolla with a well-developed tube, limb, and lobes. **Mertensia**, CHIMING BELLS; BLUEBELLS
10b. Corolla rotate, with a very short tube . . . . (11)

11a. Flowers in the axils of the stem leaves; fruiting calyx much larger than the flowers; weak-stemmed annual with retrorsely prickly hispid leaves. **Asperugo**, MADWORT
11b. Flowers in terminal racemes (actually helicoid cymes); in other respects not as above . . . . (12)

12a. Tall perennials over 0.5 m tall; flowers and fruits large, with pedicels recurved or reflexed in fruit; styles shorter than the nutlets. **Hackelia**, STICKSEED
12b. Low annuals rarely 0.5 m tall; flowers and fruits minute; pedicels erect in fruit; styles surpassing the nutlets. **Lappula**, STICKSEED

13a. Corolla limb 15-20 mm diameter, pentangular in outline, obscurely or very broadly if at all lobed. **Euploca**, BINDWEED HELIOTROPE
13b. Corolla limb less than 10 mm diameter, distinctly lobed . . . . (14)

14a. Completely glabrous, succulent, with long, narrow helicoid cymes of small white flowers. **Heliotropium**, HELIOTROPE
14b. Sparsely or densely hirsute, the cymes relatively dense and only elongating somewhat in age . . . . (15)

15a. Annuals without rosettes of basal leaves; flowers minute, less than 5 mm diameter, usually short-tubed with inconspicuous eye . . . . (16)

15b. Biennial or perennial from rosettes of basal leaves; flowers more than 5 mm diameter, often distinctly long-tubular with prominent yellow eye. **Oreocarya**

16a. Delicate weak, sparingly pubescent green annuals of muddy places. **Plagiobothrys**

16b. Strongly hirsute, stiffer annuals of dry sites . . . . (17)

17a. Corolla extremely short, often immersed in the calyx; nutlets less than 3 mm long. Plants of arid desert-steppe and piñon-juniper stands. **Cryptantha**

17b. Corolla distinctly tubular, 4-8 mm long; nutlets about 3 mm long. Infrequent weed of ruderal areas. **Buglossoides**

AMSINCKIA Lehmann 1831 [for William Amsinck, burgomaster of Hamburg and patron of its botanical garden]

1a. Corolla throat closed by a ring of hairs; stamens attached below the middle of the corolla tube. **A. lycopsoides** Lehmann [resembling the genus *Lycopsis*]. Adventive. This and the following are natives of the far West but have weedy tendencies. They have been accidentally introduced in scattered localities in the foothills, where they colonize disturbed ground. At the present time they do not appear to be very aggressive weeds.

1b. Corolla throat open, glabrous inside; stamens attached above the middle of the corolla tube . . . . (2)

2a. Stem with 2 distinct kinds of hairs, the one long, stiff, spreading, the other much more slender, shorter, and bent downwards; pubescence of the leaves tending to be appressed and directed forward. **A. retrorsa** Suksdorf. Adventive.

2b. Stem with coarse, stiff, spreading hairs, basally swollen; hairs of the leaves similar; fine hairs nearly or quite lacking. **A. menziesii** (Lehmann) Nelson & Macbride [for Archibald Menzies, 1754-1842, surgeon-naturalist with the Vancouver expedition]. Adventive.

ANCHUSA L. 1753 [the ancient Greek name]. ALKANET

1a. Corolla 15-20 mm wide; calyx cleft nearly to the base; nutlets longer than wide, erect. **Anchusa azurea** Miller. A handsome ornamental borage commonly escaping from old gardens in and around towns.

1b. Corolla 6-10 mm wide; calyx cleft to about the middle; nutlets wider than long, horizontal. **Anchusa officinalis** L. Similar habitats but probably not as common as the last.

ASPERUGO L. 1753 [Greek, *asper*, rough]. MADWORT

One species, **A. procumbens** L., **37F**. Adventive in MF. The enlarged and flat-open calyx becomes conspicuous after the flowers wither, and it is provided with hooked bristles. An unmistakeable plant.

BUGLOSSOIDES Moench 1794 [for the genus *Buglossa* (=*Lycopsis*)]

One species, **B. arvensis** (L.) I. M. Johnston. Infrequent adventive, occurring in ruderal sites in the Boulder area (*Lithospermum*).

CRYPTANTHA Lehmann 1837 [Greek, *cryptos*, hidden, + *anthos*, flower]

1a. Nutlets all smooth. **C. fendleri** (Gray) Greene. Common weedy species in arid sites on the plains.

1b. Nutlets, or some of them, rough with tubercles or papillae on the dorsal surface . . . . (2)

2a. Odd nutlet (the largest of the four) minutely papillate on the back; flowers (except for a few of the lowest ones) without any bracts. **C. crassisepala** (Torrey & Gray) Greene. Abundant, weedy, desert annual.

2b. Odd nutlet completely smooth; flowers mostly with bracts. **C. minima** Rydberg. Similar sites, often growing together with the last.

CYNOGLOSSUM L. 1753 [Greek, *cyno*, dog, + *glossa*, tongue]. HOUND'S TONGUE

One species, **C. officinale** L., **37A.** Adventive Eurasian weed in forest clearings in the mountains and along fencerows.

ERITRICHUM Schrader 1828 [Greek, *erion*, wool, + *trichos*, hair]. ALPINE FORGET-ME-NOT

One species, **E. aretioides** (Chamisso) de Candolle, **Pl. 38**. On dry stony alpine and upper subalpine mountainsides. Variable in stature. In some areas the plants are virtually stemless, in others the flowering stems are well developed. White-flowered mutants are not uncommon. Plants show flowers of strikingly different sizes: "thrum" plants with large flowers and conspicuous stamens are most common, and "pin" plants with minute flowers and conspicuous stigmas are less. The original spelling is *Eritrichum*, not *Eritrichium*, and must be used. The genus belongs to a distinct Asiatic element in our flora.

EUPLOCA Nuttall 1836 [Greek, *plocamos*, braid, alluding to the inflorescence]. BINDWEED HELIOTROPE

One species, **E. convolvulacea** Nuttall. Sandhills on the plains. The morning-glory shaped corolla is unique in the family (*Heliotropium*).

HACKELIA Opiz 1838 [for Joseph Hackel, 1783-1869, Czech botanist]. STICKSEED

1a. Corolla 1.5-3 mm wide. **H. besseyi** (Rydberg) J. L. Gentry [for Charles E. Bessey, 1845-1915, professor, U. Nebraska, Iowa State]. Endemic, Colorado Springs region.

1b. Corolla 4-12 mm wide. **H. floribunda** (Lehmann) Johnston, **37E**. Common in mountain clearings and along roadsides.

HELIOTROPIUM L. 1753 [Greek, *helios*, sun, + *trope*, turning]. HELIOTROPE

One species, **H. curassavicum** L. subsp. **oculatum** (Heller) Thorne [from Curaçao; with an eye]. Adventive, alkaline flats, San Luis Valley; very old records from Denver and Julesburg.

LAPPULA Moench 1794 [Greek, *lappa*, bur]. STICKSEED, BEGGAR'S TICK

1a. Nutlets with marginal prickles in 2 rows. **L. squarrosa** (Retzius) Dumortier. Adventive, the most robust of the lappulas, North Park (*L. echinata*, *L. myosotis*).

1b. Nutlets with marginal prickles in a single row . . . . (2)

2a. Branched from the base; nutlets with inflated margin (resembling horse-collars); blooming in early spring, common on the plains. **L. marginata** (Bieberstein) Guerke (incorrectly given earlier as *L. diploloma*), **37C**. Probably late-blooming plants hybridize with early-blooming *L. redowskii*, but there are two distinct entities here.

2b. Branched from well above the base, the lateral branchlets typically being almost at the apex of the stem; nutlets rarely with inflated margins; abundant in forested and sagebrush areas; blooming in summer. **L. redowskii** (Hornemann) Greene, **37B**.

LITHOSPERMUM L. 1753 [Greek, *lithos*, stone, + *sperma*, seed]. PUCCOON

The puccoons are biologically interesting. *L. incisum*, late in the season, produces a strange, sprawling, much-branched plant with very narrow leaves and cleistogamous flowers that produce seed without opening. *L. multiflorum* exhibits floral dimorphism or heterostyly, some plants having flowers with long styles ("pin" flowers) and others with short styles and stamens attached high in the corolla tube ("thrum" flowers). This is a device that helps to insure cross-pollination. Read Charles Darwin, *The Different Forms of Flowers on Plants of the Same Species*.

1a. Corolla very pale yellow, almost greenish-white. **L. ruderale** Douglas. Common in the oak belt on the plateaus. A robust species, with many stout leafy stems from a single base. Flowers commonly of 2 distinct sizes on different plants but not heterostyled.

1b. Corolla bright yellow . . . . (2)

2a. Corolla tube 3-4 times as long as the calyx, the lobes fringed, prominent crests in the throat. **L. incisum** Lehmann, **37D**. Common, piñon-juniper and sagebrush. Not heterostyled.

2b. Corolla tube about twice as long as the calyx, the lobes rounded; crests of the corolla throat inconspicuous . . . . (3)

3a. Corolla yellow; inflorescence loose and branched, the floral leaves reduced in size; calyx 4-6 mm long. **L. multiflorum** Torrey. Later-flowering than the preceding (June-July), mesic sites at higher altitudes. Heterostyled.

3b. Corolla orange-yellow; inflorescence condensed in the upper leaves; calyx 6-13 mm long. **L. croceum** Fernald [orange]. Sandhills of the northeastern plains. Heterostyled.

MERTENSIA Roth 1797 [for F. K. Mertens, 1764-1831, German botanist]. CHIMING BELLS, BLUEBELLS

Note: The corolla in *Mertensia* may be divided into three parts: a cylindrical tube, a slightly broader limb, and the lobes. It is important to understand these parts because much depends on interpretation of the relative lengths and of the insertion of the stamens relative to them.

1a. Plants with several pairs of prominent veins in the stem leaves; stems usually 4 dm or more tall; plants of moist sites, flowering in late spring and summer . . . . (2)

1b. Plants without lateral veins in the stem leaves or with only 1 or 2 pairs; stems mostly less than 4 dm high; plants of fairly dry, open habitats, flowering in early spring, or later at much higher altitudes . . . . (3)

2a. Leaves with pustulate-based hairs on the upper surface. **M. franciscana** Heller [for the San Francisco Peaks]. Montane and subalpine streamsides from La Veta Pass south and west.

2b. Leaves glabrous or showing papillae above, but not hairy. **M. ciliata** (James) G. Don. Abundant along mountain streamsides, subalpine and lower alpine.

3a. Hairs of the upper side of the leaf appressed and pointing away from the midvein . . . . (4)

3b. Hairs of the upper side of the leaf not distinctly oriented as above . . (5)

4a. Style short, 1-2.5 mm long; anthers virtually sessile, usually included in the tube, their tips about reaching the level of the fornices. **M. brevistyla** Watson. Common in aspen, lodgepole pine, and sagebrush; to be expected in western North Park.

4b. Style at least 4 mm long; filaments well developed, nearly as long as the anthers, the anther bases elevated above the level of the fornices. **M. fusiformis** Greene. Abundant, aspen and oak brush. The plants arise from a distinctive fusiform, tuberous root. One collection from RG; to be expected in western North Park.

5a. Filaments attached near the top of the corolla tube, the anthers projecting beyond the junction of the tube and limb; limb and lobes not widely spreading. **M. lanceolata** (Pursh) de Candolle. A variable and complex species, separable into alpine and lowland, pubescent and glabrous, broad- and narrow-leaved races, all evidently merging and recombining in puzzling ways. In this sense, I include here *M. bakeri* and *M. viridis*. The alpine *M. viridis*, in the Front Range at least, seems to have received genes from *M. alpina*.

5b. Filaments attached well inside the corolla tube, the anthers not projecting beyond the junction of the tube and the limb; limb and lobes widely spreading . . . . (6)

6a. Leaves glabrous (rarely slightly strigose near the base below). **M. humilis** Rydberg. Sagbrush plains of North Park.

6b. Leaves strigillose above, glabrous below. **M. alpina** (Torrey) G. Don. Endemic, Pikes Peak.

MYOSOTIS L. 1753 [Greek, *myos*, mouse, + *otos*, ear]. FORGET-ME-NOT

One species, **M. scorpioides** L. Adventive. Established as an escape, but growing in wild places where it appears at home. Slenderly rhizomatous, with broadly oblong leaves, basal leaves not developed; delicate plant of streamsides in the mountains.

ONOSMODIUM Michaux 1803 [from a likeness to the Eurasian genus *Onosma*, meaning smell of a donkey]. MARBLESEED

One species, **O. molle** Michaux subsp. **occidentale** (Mackenzie) Cochrane, **Pl. 59**. Common in gulches along the eastern foothills of the Front Range. A unique borage, having strongly impressed-veiny leaves with stiff appressed hairs, and cream-white flowers with the corolla lobes closed to form a cone, with a protruding style.

OREOCARYA Greene 1887 [Greek, *oros*, mountain, + *caryon*, nut] (formerly included in *Cryptantha*)

1a. Mat-forming dwarf plants with many caudices, the floral spikes not over 1 dm tall. **O. cana** Nelson. Rimrock of sandstone buttes in the northeastern counties.

1b. Plants not strongly mat-forming, or taller . . . . (2)

2a. Nutlets completely smooth; stems slender, spreading, the inflorescence laxly branched . . . . (3)

2b. Nutlets rough or tuberculate; stems stout, stiffly erect, the inflorescence a spike or massive, branched panicle . . . . (4)

3a. Stem and foliage gray, densely appressed-pubescent, the pustulate-based hairs not conspicuous. **O. suffruticosa** (Torrey) Greene. Common on the plains (*Cryptantha jamesii*).

3b. Stem and foliage green, almost glabrous except for the very conspicuous pustulate-based hairs. **O. pustulosa** Rydberg. Restricted in Colorado to the Great Sand Dunes, San Luis Valley.

4a. Low plants, usually less than 2 dm high, with a narrow, tight spike, the bracts relatively inconspicuous; pubescence appressed, pustulate hairs inconspicuous.

O. weberi (Johnston) Weber, **Pl. 56**. Endemic, volcanic ash deposits, Cochetopa Pass, and San Luis Hills (CN).

4b. Plants usually over 3 dm high, inflorescence spicate or branched . . . . (5)

5a. Inflorescence bushy-branched, at least when well developed and especially in fruit, inconspicuously bracteate; corolla small (5-8 mm wide); summer-flowering. **O. thyrsiflora** Greene. Common on the plains and in South Park.

5b. Inflorescence spicate and conspicuously bracteate; corolla larger (8-12 mm wide) . . . . (6)

6a. Leaves narrowly linear; inflorescence a tight, narrow spike with bracts exceeding the flower clusters; foliage harshly hispid with pustulose hairs. **O. virgata** (Porter) Greene [wandlike], MINER'S CANDLE, **Pl. 10**. Abundant on gravelly granitic slopes in the outer foothills of the Front Range.

6b. Leaves oblanceolate, rounded at the apex; inflorescence varying in narrowness and length of the flower clusters; foliage hispid but with a strong ground layer of softer hairs. **O. celosioides** Eastwood. Common on the high plains in the northeastern counties.

PLAGIOBOTHRYS Fischer & Meyer 1836 [Greek, *plagio*, oblique, + *bothros*, pit, alluding to the nutlet scar]

One species, **P. scouleri** (Hooker & Arnott) Johnston subsp. **penicillata** (Greene) Löve. Muddy places in meadows, stock pond margins, etc., in the mountains. A very small and inconspicuous weedy plant with small white flowers (*P. scopulorum*).

SYMPHYTUM L. 1753 [Greek, *symphyton*, grown together, alluding to the decurrent leaves]. COMFREY

One species, **S. officinale** L. Adventive, roadside weed, not yet reported from the Eastern Slope, but likely to occur anywhere.

BRASSICACEAE/CRUCIFERAE MUSTARD FAMILY (BRA/CRU)

With very few exceptions, the mustards are a very easy family to learn. There are 4 sepals, 4 separate petals, usually with a narrow base (the claw), 6 stamens, four long and two short (rarely reduced to fewer), and a superior ovary with a unique structure. The fruit is, with few exceptions, dehiscent. There are two enclosing walls, the **valves**, which some believe represent carpels that have lost the capacity to have seeds. Their function now is to protect the seeds produced by the two fertile carpels, which are represented by the **replum**, a thin, papery partition strengthened around the edge by a strong rim. The seeds are attached to this rim and lie against the faces of the partition. The replum is believed to represent a pair of highly modified (solid) carpels. The origin of the partition is open to question. The garden flower called silver dollar plant is a fine example of the situation. There actually are some mustards with 4 fertile carpels.

Crucifers are distinctive because of their cross-shaped flowers, but they can be confused with the Onagraceae, which also have 4 petals in that arrangement, but an inferior ovary. Crucifers typically have the flowers in racemes, and usually there are no subtending bracts. Many crucifers are used in gardens (sweet alyssum, rocket, silver dollar plant) and many are standard table vegetables: *Raphanus* is the radish; *Brassica oleracea* in its many varieties gives us kale, brussels sprouts, cabbage, broccoli, cauliflower and kohlrabi. Other brassicas include rutabaga, turnip, rape, white and black mustard, and many Chinese vegetables. Watercress is

Nasturtium officinale, no relative of the garden *Nasturtium*, which belongs to the Tropaeolaceae. The foliage or seeds of most crucifers have distinctive, tart flavors.

1a. Fruit (the special type of fruit in this family is called a silique) short, hardly more than twice as long as broad . . . . **Key A**
1b. Silique long, at least 3 times as long as broad . . . . **Key B**

KEY A

1a. Silique flattened . . . . (2)
1b. Silique not flattened but spherical and sometimes strongly inflated and papery in texture . . . . (10)

2a. Silique flattened parallel to the papery internal partition (replum), i.e., the shape of the replum is also the shape of the silique in face view (the valves are flat) . . . . (3)
2b. Silique flattened perpendicular to the replum; the replum bisects the silique in face view (the valves are folded) . . . . (6)

3a. Silique round in face view . . . . (4)
3b. Silique oblong, ovate, or elliptical, never round . . . . (5)

4a. Flowers yellow; stellate-pubescent or glabrous. **Alyssum**
4b. Flowers white or purple; upper stem covered by straight hairs, attached by the middle, with pointed ends. **Lobularia**

5a. Silique oval, not more than twice as long as wide; styles 2-3 mm long; petals white, deeply bilobed. **Berteroa**, HOARY ALYSSUM
5b. Silique longer and narrower, or styles shorter; petals white or yellow, not deeply bilobed. **Draba**, WHITLOWWORT

6a. Silique elliptic or oval; seed solitary in each locule . . . . (7)
6b. Silique triangular-obovate or obcordate (if orbicular, then 2 or more seeds in each locule . . . . (8)

7a. Silique flat. **Lepidium**, PEPPERGRASS
7b. Silique concavo-convex, shovel-shaped, with winged margin and apex, minutely whitish pustulate; leaves auriculate at the base. **Neolepia**, FIELDCRESS

8a. Basal leaves pinnatifid; silique triangular-obovate. **Capsella**, SHEPHERD'S PURSE
8b. Basal leaves entire or merely toothed; silique not triangular . . . . (9)

9a. Annual weed; silique large, flat, orbicular, 1 cm long when mature, with broad wings. **Thlaspi**, FANWEED; PENNYCRESS
9b. Native perennial; silique obovate or oblong-cuneate, shovel-shaped, less than 1 cm long. **Noccaea**, WILD CANDYTUFT

10a. Silique inflated and papery-textured, sometimes double . . . . (11)
10b. Silique neither inflated nor papery, never appearing double . . . . . . (12)

11a. Flowers white; silique not constricted down the middle to form twin pods; green, leafy-stemmed. **Cardaria**, WHITETOP
11b. Flowers yellow; silique of twin papery sacks, ovary constricted down the middle; plants low, with rosettes of basal leaves, silvery-pubescent with flat stellate hairs. **Physaria**, DOUBLE BLADDERPOD

12a. Plants of marshy places and moist ditches; leaves often deeply pinnatifid. **Rorippa sphaerocarpa**

12b. Plants of dry sites; leaves never pinnatifid . . . . (13)

13a. Annual adventive weed; stems simple or branched above; silique pear-shaped; leaves green. **Camelina**, FALSE FLAX

13b. Perennial native; floral stems arising from a cluster of stellate-pubescent silvery basal leaves. **Lesquerella**, BLADDERPOD

KEY B

1a. Silique with a long stalk between the point of attachment of the petals and the seed-bearing portion of the ovary; tall, showy plants of adobe hills, selenium indicators. **Stanleya**, PRINCE'S PLUME

1b. Silique sessile on the pedicel or nearly so . . . . (2)

2a. [1] Silique flattened parallel to the replum (if siliques are very slender, try to roll them between the thumb and forefinger, to be sure) . . . . (3)

2b. Silique terete or 4-angled or 4-ribbed . . . . (7)

3a. [2] Valves (silique walls) veinless . . . . (4)

3b. Valves veined . . . . (5)

4a. [3] Leaves either pinnately compound or triangular-cordate; silique always elongate, elastically dehiscent. **Cardamine**, BITTERCRESS

4b. Leaves always simple, usually lanceolate; silique never more than 5-6 times as long as wide, not elastically dehiscent. **Draba**, WHITLOWWORT

5a. [3] Perennial, from several short, woody caudices, basal leaves green at flowering time; silique distinctly flattened, if long and slender, not erect. **Boechera**, FALSE ARABIS

5b. Annual, biennial, or monocarpic; basal leaves withering at flowering time; silique very long and slender, not very distinctly flattened, erect . . . . (6)

6a. [5] Cauline leaves glabrous and glaucous, clasping the stem; basal leaves and stem with simple and forked hairs. **Turritis**, TOWER MUSTARD

6b. Cauline leaves green, not glaucous, usually somewhat hairy, along with the stem. **Arabis**, ROCKCRESS

7a. [4] Leaves round-oval, glaucous, entire, rounded at apex; silique slightly flattened but distinctly 4-angled and -ribbed; flowers pale yellow; annual weed. **Conringia**, HARE'S EAR

7b. Plants not as above . . . . (8)

8a. [7] Without basal leaves, or these very early deciduous . . . . (9)

8b. Usually with well-developed basal leaves or leaves mostly pinnatifid. (14)

9a. [8] Leaves broadly triangular-ovate, cordate, coarsely dentate; foliage with a garlicky scent. **Alliaria**, GARLIC MUSTARD

9b. Leaves not as above; plants not garlic-scented . . . . (10)

10a. [9] Perennial with elongate rhizomes, floral stems slender and reedy; basal leaves lacking, most leaves simple and narrowly lanceolate; flowers purple; siliques very narrow, about 5 cm long. **Schoenocrambe**, SKELETON MUSTARD

10b. Plants with a slender taproot; basal leaves early deciduous . . . . (11)

11a. [10] Flowers large, deep red-purple; leaves broadly lanceolate, serrate. **Hesperis**, ROCKET

11b. Flowers small, pale violet or white; leaves narrowly lanceolate or linear, sometimes pinnatifid . . . . (12)

12a. [11] Delicate, glaucous, winter annual of alkaline flats in South Park; leaves oval or oblong, sessile, auriculate; siliques 1-2 cm long. **Thellungiella**
12b. Not as above . . . . (13)

13a. [12] Silique spreading but not reflexed, very slender and torulose (constricted between the seeds). **Thelypodium**
13b. Silique sharply reflexed, not torulose. **Pennellia**

14a. [8] Leaves all entire, neither pinnatifid, toothed, nor lobed; dwarf alpine perennials, not over 15 cm tall . . . . (15)
14b. Leaves (at least some) dentate, pinnatifid, or lobed . . . . (16)

15a. [14] Totally glabrous; basal leaves long-petioled; silique with 4 strong ribs, plump, not torulose; replum incomplete. **Eutrema**
15b. Pubescent with forked hairs; leaves not petiolate; silique not 4-ribbed, somewhat constricted (torulose) between the seeds; replum complete. **Braya**

16a. [14] Silique with a stout beak extending much beyond the ovule-bearing portion, indehiscent . . . . (17)
16b. Silique without a beak or with a beak not more than 3 mm long, dehiscent . . . . (19)

17a. [16] Flowers white or yellow; silique without transverse partitions between the seeds; lower leaves often pinnatifid . . . . (18)
17b. Flowers pink or purplish; silique with transverse partitions and usually constricted between the seeds; basal leaves merely dentate. **Chorispora**, PURPLE MUSTARD

18a. [17] Silique valves 1-nerved. **Brassica**, MUSTARD
18b. Silique valves with 3 to 7 veins. **Sinapis**, CHARLOCK

19a. [16] Pubescence of forked or stellate hairs (included in this category are the unique hairs of the wallflower, *Erysimum*, which are straight but pointed at each end and attached in the middle) . . . . (20)
19b. Pubescence of simple hairs, or none . . . . (23)

20a. [19] Leaves entire or moderately pinnatifid; glandular hairs absent . . (21)
20b. Leaves pinnately or bipinnately divided or very deeply pinnatifid; pubescence often partly glandular . . . . (22)

21a. [20] Hairs straight, pointed at each end and appressed to the stem and leaves; flowers yellow, rarely clear violet. **Erysimum**, WALLFLOWER
21b. Hairs obviously stellate-branched; flowers never yellow. **Halimolobos**

22a. [20] Weedy annuals with small yellow flowers. **Descurainia**, TANSY MUSTARD
22b. Native alpine perennials with white or pinkish flowers. **Smelowskia**

23a. [19] Silique somewhat 4-angled, elongate. **Barbarea**, WINTERCRESS
23b. Silique terete, elongate or club-shaped . . . . (24)

24a. [22] Silique 3 cm or more long, about 1 mm wide . . . . (25)
24b. Silique not more than 2 cm long, often more than 1 mm wide; aquatic or marsh plants . . . . (26)

25a. [24] Stem leaves deeply and regularly pinnatifid; silique not torulose, stiff, 4-angled; flowers yellow. **Sisymbrium**, JIM HILL MUSTARD
25b. Stem leaves not deeply and regularly pinnatifid, often simple or lyrately lobed; silique torulose; flowers white or purple. **Thelypodium**

26a. [24] Flowers white; leaves succulent, with rounded leaflets. **Nasturtium**, WATERCRESS

26b. Flowers yellow; leaves not especially succulent, with acute lobes or leaflets. **Rorippa**, YELLOWCRESS

ALLIARIA Heister 1759 [name alluding to *Allium*]. GARLIC MUSTARD

One species, **Alliaria petiolata** (Bieberstein) Cavara & Grande. Adventive, collected twice in the 1950s on the grounds of the Broadmoor Hotel, Colorado Springs. The flowers are small and white, and the foliage has the odor of garlic.

ALYSSUM L. 1753 [Greek, *a*, without, + *lyssa*, madness, the plants having been recommended as a cure for rabies]

1a. Sepals persistent and clasping the base of the silique; stellate hairs present on the silique but extremely small and not clearly visible with a lens; petals persistent and turning whitish; plants, when well developed, profusely branching and spreading from the base. **A. alyssoides** (L.) L., **39F**. Adventive, preferring more natural areas than the next, often on wooded slopes.

1b. Sepals deciduous immediately after flowering; mature silique with no trace of the sepals . . . . (2)

2a. Silique completely glabrous. **A. desertorum** Stapf. Adventive, locally abundant Asiatic weed in dry sagebrush areas.

2b. Silique with large hairs, easily visible with a lens . . . . (3)

3a. Annual with a taproot; leaves green both sides; inflorescence the dominant part of the plant. **A. minus** (L.) Rothmaler, **38E**. Adventive, extremely abundant European weed, producing its growth and flowering and dying in very early spring before other plants appear to give it competition. Its dense stands color large areas pale yellow.

3b. Perennial; leaves bicolored, white beneath; inflorescence forming a minor part of the plant. **A. murale** Waldstein & Kitaibel. Adventive, locally established in canyons west of Boulder.

ARABIS L. 1753 [from the country Arabia, according to Linnaeus]. ROCKCRESS

One species, **A. hirsuta** (L.) Scopoli. Adventive, infrequent in disturbed areas and meadows in the forested zone. All other species previously listed under *Arabis* will be found under *Boechera* except *Arabis glabra*, which becomes *Turritis*.

BARBAREA R. Brown 1812 [anciently called the Herb of St. Barbara, the seed of *B. verna* being sown near St. Barbara's day, in mid-December]. WINTERCRESS

1a. Beak of mature silique 2-3 mm long, the silique appearing slender-pointed; petals usually 6-8 mm long; upper leaves shallowly lobed to merely toothed, sessile and clasping. **B. vulgaris** R. Brown. Adventive on wet, irrigated valley floors; difficult to distinguish from the next without mature fruits.

1b. Beak of mature silique to 1 mm long, the silique appearing blunt; petals usually 3-5 mm long; upper leaves pinnatifid or, if not, then narrowed to a winged petiole. **B. orthoceras** Ledebour [straight-beak]. By far the more abundant of the two; similar habitats.

BERTEROA de Candolle 1821 [for Carlo Giuseppe Bertero, 1789-1831, Italian botanist]. HOARY ALYSSUM

One species, **B. incana** (L.) de Candolle [hoary]. Adventive. Abundant in meadows of the Front Range valleys and expected to spread throughout the middle altitudes. It forms dense stands of tall, white-flowered plants in meadows and along roadsides.

BOECHERA Löve & Löve 1976 [for Tyge Böcher, 1909-1983, Danish botanist, specialist in Greenland flora] (formerly included in *Arabis*). FALSE ARABIS

1a. Mature silique strictly erect, mostly appressed to the rachis; plants glabrous, or pubescent only at the base; seeds in 2 rows; stem leaves conspicuously auricled. **B. drummondii** (Gray) Löve & Löve [for Thomas Drummond, 1780-1835, botanist with the Franklin expeditions]. The most common *Boechera* in the montane forests. Most of the others are in sagebrush, piñon-juniper, or alpine.

1b. Mature silique slightly spreading to wide-spreading or reflexed; seeds in 1 row . . . . (2)

2a. Mature silique pedicels ascending, never diverging at right angles to the stem, or silique ascending similarly . . . . (3)

2b. Mature silique pedicels diverging at nearly right angles to the stem, or reflexed . . . . (5)

3a. Basal leaves sparsely and loosely pubescent, or glabrous, not grayish; stems single or few. **B. divaricarpa** (Nelson) Löve & Löve. Open woods, middle altitudes.

3b. Basal leaves densely gray-canescent . . . . (4)

4a. Basal leaves ranging from glabrous to hirsute, often with the marginal hairs longer . . . . (5)

4b. Basal leaves pubescent, never hirsute nor glabrous. **B. fendleri** (Watson) Weber [for August Fendler]. Common, outer foothills of Front Range. In early spring, the new vegetative shoots are affected by a rust fungus, *Puccinia monoica*, which produces an aecial stage of yellow-orange pustules that cover the upper leaves. Every spring someone brings this in to ask what kind of wildflower it might be.

5a. Basal leaves not over 2 cm long; cauline leaves not over 1 cm long; petals 4-6 mm long; stems 6-20 cm tall . . . . (6)

5b. Basal leaves 2-10 cm long; cauline leaves 1-8 cm long; petals 5-14 cm long; stems usually over 20 cm tall. **B. lemmonii** (Watson) Weber [for J. G. Lemmon, 1832-1908, botanist of the Southwest]. Strictly alpine, near melting snowbanks.

6a. Silique pedicels and silique strictly reflexed and appressed to the rachis. **B. retrofracta** (Graham) Löve & Löve [reflexed]. Very common in subalpine meadows and forests (*Arabis holboellii* var. *retrofracta*).

6b. Silique pedicels spreading or descending but not appressed to the rachis. **B. lignifera** (Nelson) Weber [woody]. Sagebrush zone, North Park, Great Sand Dunes. Intermediates connecting this with *A. retrofracta* may reflect hybridization.

BRASSICA L. 1753 [Latin name of the cabbage]. MUSTARD

One species, **B. napus** L. [ancient name for *Bunias*, or nape]. RAPE. Adventive field weed, our single specimen from CC. Other species of *Brassica* are to be expected as weeds in cultivated fields. This one is glaucous and essentially glabrous, the upper cauline leaves with clasping auriculate bases (*B. rapa* subsp. *silvestris* of manuals).

BRAYA Sternberg & Hoppe 1815 [for Fritz Gabriel, Count de Bray, 1765-1832, of Rouen]

1a. Flowering stem leafless; capsules short and thick, not at all curved or torulose. **B. glabella** R. Brown. Alpine, on dolomite, Saguache Range. Recently discovered by Barbara Siems. Widely disjunct from the Canadian Rockies, with a close relative, *B. rosea*, in Altai.

1b. Flowering stem with a few leaves; capsules slender, curved, and slightly torulose. **B. humilis** (C. A. Meyer) Robinson [small]. Infrequent on alpine tundra, confined to the Leadville Limestone, Mosquito Range. Subsp. *ventosa* Rollins is not considered to be of taxonomic significance.

CAMELINA Crantz 1762 [Greek, *chamae*, on the ground, + *linon*, flax, alluding to the presence of *C. sativa* in flax fields]. FALSE FLAX

1a. Petals distinctly yellow, less than 5 mm long; basal leaves usually withering by anthesis; plants little branched, the branches ascending. **C. microcarpa** Andrzejowski, **39G**. Adventive weed, common in early spring along roadsides and in fallow fields. Characterized by the plump, terete, slightly ellipsoid pods topped by a rather long style.

1b. Petals white outside, very pale yellow inside, 6-9 mm long; basal leaves usually present at anthesis; plants with several spreading branches. **C. rumelica** Velenovsky [from Rumelia, in Bulgaria]. Adventive, recently found on the eastern plains.

CAPSELLA Medikus 1792 [Latin, *capsa*, box]. SHEPHERD'S PURSE

One species, **C. bursa-pastoris** (L.) Medikus, **39D**. Adventive, abundant weed in early spring in waste ground, gardens, and roadsides.

CARDAMINE L. 1753 [Greek, *kardamon*, used by Dioscorides for some cress]. BITTERCRESS

1a. Leaves simple, rounded-cordate. **C. cordifolia** Gray. Very common along forest streams. The plant is typically glabrous and only very shallowly sinuate-margined. In the southern counties populations occur with strongly pubescent leaves, and one is known in which they are deeply lobed.

1b. Leaves pinnately compound . . . . (2)

2a. Tall; leaves over 3 cm long; petals 5-6 mm long. **C. breweri** Watson [for W. H. Brewer, 1828-1910, geologist and botanist] Infrequent in meadows, aspen, LR.

2b. Dwarf; leaves less than 2 cm long; petals 2-4 mm long. **C. pensylvanica** Mühlenberg. Infrequent, wet mountain meadows, northern counties.

CARDARIA Desvaux 1815 [for the heart-shaped fruit of *C. draba*]. WHITETOP

1a. Silique densely pubescent. **C. pubescens** (Meyer) Jarmolenko, **39I**. Adventive. All of the whitetops are introduced, noxious weeds abundant in irrigated lowlands. Millions of dollars have been expended in unsuccessful attempts to eradicate them.

1b. Silique glabrous or sparingly pilose . . . . (2)

2a. Tall plants 1-3 m tall; inflorescence much branched, well over 2 dm; flowers purplish; silique triangular-ovate. **C. latifolia** (L.) Spach. Adventive, an abundant and very aggressive weed following watercourses, ditches, and any sites with a high water table. Usually included in *Lepidium* but in all respects this belongs in *Cardaria*.

2b. Low plants less than 1 m tall; inflorescence much branched but seldom over 1 dm; flowers white . . . . (3)

3a. Silique triangular-cordate (broad at the base and coming to a point below the style); main axis of inflorescence pubescent. **C. draba** (L.) Desvaux, **39J**.

3b. Silique rounded top and bottom, broadest at the middle; main axis of inflorescence glabrous. **C. chalepensis** (L.) Handel-Mazzetti [of Aleppo, Syria], **39H**.

CHORISPORA R. Brown 1821 [Greek, *chori*, separated, + *spora*, seed, alluding to the torulose silique]. PURPLE MUSTARD

One species, **C. tenella** (Pallas) de Candolle [slender]. Adventive from southwest Asia, an abundant, early spring weed of fallow fields.

CONRINGIA Heister 1759 [for Hermann Conring, 1606-1661, professor at Helmstadt]. HARE'S EAR

One species, **C. orientalis** (L.) Dumortier. Adventive, locally abundant spring-flowering Eurasian weed. The large rounded entire, clasping-based leaves and pale yellow flowers are diagnostic.

DESCURAINIA Webb & Berthelot 1836 [for Francois Descourain, 1658-1740, French apothecary]. TANSY MUSTARD

1a. Silique very long and narrow, 20-30 mm long; lower leaves 2-3 times pinnate. **D. sophia** (L.) Webb [*Sophia*, a generic name]. Adventive, abundant Eurasian weed of roadsides and cultivated fields. The other species are native.

1b. Silique usually less than 20 mm long, relatively plump; lower leaves 1-2 times pinnate . . . . (2)

2a. Plants with hardly any central stem axis, bushy-branched from the base. **D. ramosissima** Rollins. Endemic, San Luis Valley and Rio Grande drainage, recently found in South Park. The siliques are pointed at each end, as in *D. richardsonii*. Probably best regarded as a variety of that; it would be extremely unusual for an endemic to behave as an abundant roadside weed.

2b. Plants with a well-developed main stem axis, simple or branched above. (3)

3a. Silique plump and blunt at the ends, style almost obsolete; pedicels wide-spreading and silique ascending. **D. pinnata** (Walter) Britton. Early spring weed of the valleys, replacing *D. richardsonii* at lower altitudes.

3b. Silique slenderly pointed, style distinct and up to 0.5 mm long . . . . . (4)

4a. Silique elongate, with parallel sides, more than 4 times as long as wide. **D. richardsonii** (Sweet) Schulz [for Sir John Richardson, botanist on the Franklin expeditions]. The common species of forested areas, but occurring along with *D. pinnata* in lower areas. Many minor races occur.

4b. Silique short, fusiform, less than 4 times as long as wide. **D. californica** (Gray) Schulz. Tall, branched plant, most common in the southwestern counties.

DRABA L. 1753 [Greek, *drabe*, acrid, applied by Dioscorides to some cress]. WHITLOWWORT

1a. Style 0.15 mm or less; annual or perennial; seeds 1 mm or less . . . **Key A**

1b. Style length more than 0.15 mm; perennial; seed length various . . **Key B**

KEY A

1a. Stem leaves absent (rarely 1-2 reduced, near-basal leaves); stems glabrous or sparsely pubescent near the base; leaves prominently ciliate (surfaces glabrous), or pubescent with simple or forked hairs; alpine and subalpine. (2)

1b. Stem leaves present; pubescence various; submontane to low alpine . . (4)

2a. Plants forming cushions with many short caudices, each topped by a cluster of broad and short, incurved glabrous or ciliate leaves, forming minute cabbagelike heads. **D. apiculata** C. L. Hitchcock [apiculate, of the leaves, tipped with a slender point]. Only recently discovered in the Saguache Range west of Leadville. Disjunct from northern Wyoming.

2b. Plants with a taproot and inconspicuous caudices; leaves otherwise . . (3)

3a. Flowers white; caespitose alpine perennial; silique 3-6 x 1.5-2 mm, apiculate; style 0.1-0.3 mm. **D. fladnizensis** Wulfen [of Fladnitz, Austria]. Occasional among rocks on the highest mountains.

3b. Flowers yellow; short-lived subalpine to alpine biennial or perennial; well-developed silique often longer than 6 mm and wider than 2 mm, rarely apiculate; style 0-1.5 mm. **D. crassifolia** Graham [thick-leaved]. Abundant and widely distributed on rocky slopes and meadows (*D. stenoloba* of Harrington, in part).

4a. Submontane (usually below 6,000 ft) flowers white; siliques often crowded in an umbellike raceme . . . . (5)

4b. Low alpine to subalpine; flowers yellow; siliques spread evenly . . . . . (6)

5a. Inflorescence axis and pedicels pubescent; silique often over 2 mm wide; cauline leaves usually dentate. **D. cuneifolia** Nuttall [with wedge-shaped leaves]. Occasional in dry, open places, piñon-juniper.

5b. Inflorescence axis and pedicels glabrous; silique rarely over 2 mm wide; cauline leaves usually entire. **D. reptans** (Lamarck) Fernald [creeping], **39L**. Occasional in similar habitats, flowering in early spring.

6a. Inflorescence markedly pubescent with branched hairs. **D. rectifructa** Hitchcock [upright-fruited]. Simple or branched annual or winter annual, occasional, montane meadows and forest clearings, South Park.

6b. Inflorescence glabrous or becoming so . . . . (7)

7a. Lowest pedicel 1.5 or more times as long as the silique; silique elliptic to elliptic-oblanceolate, often hispidulous (usually glabrous), apex (excluding the style) usually obtuse. **D. nemorosa** L. [of woods]. Adventive, disturbed woodland, submontane to subalpine.

7b. Lowest pedicel less than 1.5 times as long as the mature silique; silique usually linear to linear-oblong, glabrous, apex usually acute. **D. albertina** Greene [of Alberta]. Winter annual or short-lived perennial. Widespread and locally abundant, particularly in moist habitats (*D. stenoloba* and *D. crassifolia* of Harrington).

KEY B

1a. Most flowers bracteate; cauline leaves 0-2, reduced; basal leaves linear to linear-oblanceolate, margins ciliate and surfaces glabrous. **D. graminea** Greene [grasslike]. Yellow-flowered alpine perennial, usually in late snowmelt areas. Endemic, headwaters of Rio Grande, San Juan Mountains.

1b. Few if any flowers bracteate; cauline leaves 0 to many; basal leaves not as above . . . . (2)

2a. Plants scapose, forming extended mats; petals yellow (occasionally whitish in *D. oligosperma*), usually over 3 mm long; silique 2-6 mm wide; leaves stellate-pubescent. **D. oligosperma** Hooker (few-seeded). Alpine, mostly limestone scree slopes, Saguache and Mosquito ranges.

2b. Floral stems bearing 1 to many cauline leaves, or plants small, white-flowered perennials with narrower siliques or shorter petals . . . . (7)

3a. Plants minutely and densely stellate-pubescent, the form of the hairs difficult to make out with a strong lens; plants with numerous, elongate, slender caudices; flowers white; stem leaves several. **D. smithii** Gilg [for the collector, E. C. Smith]. Rock crevices in the southern mountains, from the upper Rio Grande Valley to the Mesa de Maya.

3b. Plants not as above . . . . (4)

4a. White-flowered alpine plants; style usually less than 0.5 mm long . . . (5)

4b. Yellow-flowered, montane or alpine; style usually over 0.5 mm long . . (9)

5a. Cauline leaves 0-2, reduced; plants small, caespitose . . . . (6)

5b. Cauline leaves 2 or more; not caespitose; stems often elongate . . . . . (8)

6a. Stellate hairs absent; stems glabrous; leaves markedly ciliate. **D. fladnizensis** Wulfen [of Fladnitz, Austria]. Occasional among rocks on the highest mountains.

6b. Stellate hairs present on the leaves; stems pubescent or glabrous; leaf margin various . . . . (7)

7a. Leaves bearing fine, multiple-branched stellae (may have simple or forked hairs as well), often cinereous; silique linear to narrowly elliptic (typically 6-12 x 1-2 mm). **D. lonchocarpa** Rydberg [with spear-shaped siliques]. Found sporadically on rocky alpine slopes, sometimes locally abundant (*D. nivalis* of Harrington).

7b. Leaves with a mixture of simple, forked, cruciform, and 5-8-armed stellae, usually not cinereous; silique obovate (typically 4-8 x 2-3 mm). **D. porsildii** Mulligan [for A. E. Porsild, contemporary Danish-Canadian botanist]. Alpine, ST.

8a. Leaves densely canescent with branched stellate hairs on both surfaces; usually some flowers bracteate; petals ca. 4 mm long; seeds ca. 1 mm or more long or less. **D. cana** Rydberg [hoary]. Widespread but sporadic on alpine slopes (*D. lanceolata* of Harrington).

8b. Leaves less densely pubescent with 4-6-rayed stellae; flowers not bracteate; petals ca. 5 mm long; seeds a bit over 1 mm long. **D. borealis** de Candolle [northern]. Local alpine, ST.

9a. Basal leaves semisucculent, oblanceolate to obovate, ciliate with surfaces glabrous; widest basal leaves often over 5 mm wide and 4 cm long; cauline leaves averaging 4(3-8) in number. **D. crassa** Rydberg [thick], **Pl. 37**. Thick-rooted, alpine rosette plant, found sporadically on talus and boulderfields on the highest mountains.

9b. Basal leaves not succulent, bearing hairs on lower surface (may be few in number), dimensions various; cauline leaves 1 to many . . . . (10)

10a. Cauline leaves 4 or more, entire or dentate; longest styles usually over 1 mm long (usually over 1.5 mm except in *D. aurea*, where the range is 0.5-1.5); pollen normal; montane to alpine . . . . (11)
10b. Cauline leaves 1-3(4), entire; alpine only; style usually less than 1 mm long; pollen abortive . . . . (14)

11a. Plants conspicuously hairy with long (often 1-2 mm), stiff, simple or forked hairs; cruciform or stellate hairs absent; leaves usually entire; silique often conspicuously twisted, glabrous except for stiff marginal cilia. **D. streptocarpa** Gray [with twisted fruits]. Open ground, montane to alpine slopes near the Continental Divide.
11b. Simple hairs softer, shorter, or absent; cruciform or stellate hairs predominant on leaves; leaves dentate or entire; silique plane or twisted, lacking stiff marginal cilia . . . . (12)

12a. Lower leaf surface with appressed (usually sessile) cruciform hairs with greatly unequal arm lengths; pubescence usually not dense; cauline leaves dentate or denticulate. **D. spectabilis** Greene [showy]. Locally abundant, montane to alpine, southwestern counties.
12b. Lower leaf surface with stalked, equal-armed cruciform or stellate hairs; pubescence of leaves usually dense; cauline leaves entire or dentate . (13)

13a. Longest styles usually over 1.5 mm (1-3.5) long; cauline leaves usually toothed; seeds averaging 1.3 mm; petals 4-8 mm. long. **D. helleriana** Greene [for A. A. Heller, 1867-1944, California botanist]. Montane to alpine slopes, Rio Grande and Cuchara drainages.
13b. Longest styles less than 1.5 (0.5-1.5) mm long; cauline leaves usually entire; seeds about 1 mm; petals 4-6 mm long. **D. aurea** Vahl [golden]. Widespread and abundant throughout the mountains.

14a. Short-stalked cruciform or stellate hairs present on leaves and inflorescence; silique pubescent or glabrous. **D. streptobrachia** Price [with twisted trichome arms]. Uncommon on alpine scree and fellfields from PA southwestward.
14b. Cruciform or stellate hairs absent; fruit glabrous . . . . (15)

15a. Petals clawless, equalling the sepals, both very tardily deciduous; upper stem glabrous or becoming so; well-formed silique usually 3 or more times as long as wide. **D. exunguiculata** (Schulz) Hitchcock [clawless]. Endemic in northern and central Colorado from the Continental Divide eastward. Occasional in alpine fellfields, GA, ST.
15b. Petals clawed, exceeding the sepals, both early deciduous; stems with dense tangled pubescence; well-formed silique less than 3 times as long as wide. **D. grayana** (Rydberg) Hitchcock [for Gray's Peak, the type locality]. Occasional to locally abundant in alpine fellfields. Endemic in northern and north-central Colorado, often mixed with the last but ranging farther west.

ERYSIMUM L. 1753 [Greek, *eryomai*, help or save, because of medicinal properties]. WALLFLOWER

1a. Petals 12-20 mm long, yellow, orange, or lavender; biennial or perennial; native plants . . . . (2)
1b. Petals usually under 10 mm long; annual or biennial . . . . (3)

2a. Siliques and pedicels densely gray-pubescent, spreading stiffly at a wide angle from the stem. **E. asperum** (Nuttall) de Candolle [rough]. Characteristically a plant of the eastern plains and San Luis Valley, hybridizing with the next along the base of the foothills.

2b. Siliques green and almost glabrous, ascending, usually nearly parallel to the stem, although the pedicels may spread widely. **E. capitatum** (Douglas) Greene. Very common and extremely variable, with perennial alpine races having clear yellow or lavender flowers, and montane races with clear yellow or orange petals, purplish-brown on the back (including *E. nivale*).

3a. Low, widely branching weedy annual plants with sinuate margined leaves and widely spreading siliques; pedicels nearly as thick as the siliques. **E. repandum** L. [sinuate]. Adventive, ruderal weed, open fields in the lower valleys.

3b. Tall, slender, almost unbranched annuals or biennials; siliques ascending; pedicels more slender than the siliques . . . . (4)

4a. Petals 3.5-5 mm long; annual; basal leaves usually gone by fruiting time; silique 1.5-3 cm long. **E. cheiranthoides** L. subsp. **altum** Ahti [resembling *Cheiranthus*; tall]. Adventive along roadsides and in waste places.

4b. Petals 7-11 mm long; biennial; basal leaves present at fruiting time; siliques 2.5-5 cm long. **E. inconspicuum** (Watson) MacMillan. Similar habitats, but evidently native. Except for smaller petals, this resembles *E. capitatum*.

EUTREMA R. Brown 1823 [Greek, *eu*, well developed, + *trema*, hole, alluding to the replum, whose membrane does not extend from side to side, resembling an unstrung tennis racket]

One species, **E. edwardsii** R. Brown subsp. **penlandii** (Rollins) Weber [for John Edwards, surgeon on the *Hecla*; for C.W.T. Penland, 1899-1982, professor at The Colorado College]. Very rare, on solifluction lobes of tundra, Hoosier Pass region. Recognized by the totally glabrous leaves and fruit, the long-petioled ovate basal leaves, and the quadrangular silique with 4 strong ribs (*E. penlandii*).

HALIMOLOBOS Tausch 1836 [Greek, *halimon*, for *Atriplex halimus*? + *lobon*, capsule]

One species, **H. virgata** (Nuttall) Schulz [wandlike]. Local in wet meadows, South Park. The pedicels stand out from the stem at an angle, but the siliques are stiffly erect.

HESPERIS L. 1753 [Greek, *hesperos*, evening, from the evening fragrance of the flowers]. ROCKET

One species, **H. matronalis** L. [from the old name, mother-of-the-evening]. Adventive, escaped from old gardens and well-established around towns at the base of the mountains. A tall plant with serrate lanceolate leaves and red-purple flowers. A white-flowered mutant occasionally occurs.

LEPIDIUM L. 1753 [Greek, *lepidion*, little scale, alluding to the silique]. PEPPERGRASS

1a. Leaves of two strikingly different types, the lower pinnately dissected, the upper simple, orbicular, clasping the stem; flowers yellow. **L. perfoliatum** L., CLASPING PEPPERGRASS, **38C**. Adventive, extremely abundant roadside weed in the warm valleys. The simple "leaves" represent the petiole bases of leaves in which the dissected portion has been suppressed. Transitions are found on most plants.

1b. Leaves uniform; flowers white or greenish . . . . (2)

2a. Style up to 1.3 mm long, exceeding the depth of the sinus; strong perennial. **L. montanum** Nuttall subsp. **alyssoides** (Gray) C. L. Hitchcock. Abundant in the San Luis Valley and elsewhere in the southern counties.

2b. Style not exceeding the depth of the sinus; annuals or perennials . . . (3)

3a. Petals conspicuous, as long as or slightly longer than the sepals. **L. virginicum** L. Adventive, infrequent ruderal weed.

3b. Petals inconspicuous, shorter than the sepals or lacking entirely . . . . (4)

4a. Silique 3-3.5 x 2.5-3 mm, round-obcordate to short oblong-obovate, rounded to abruptly curved into obtuse apical teeth. **L. densiflorum** Schrader, **39M**. Adventive, very common, especially in early spring, lower valleys. Usually erect and symmetrical, each main branch terminating in an erect raceme.

4b. Silique 2.5 x 1.5-2 mm, nearly elliptic, narrowed into acute apical teeth. **L. ramosissimum** Nelson. Flowering in midsummer at higher altitudes than the last, in the intermountain parks and oak-aspen. Often strongly asymmetrical, with the main stems widely spreading and the racemes erect along one side. There is some question as to whether this actually may not be indigenous, but rather the adventive *L. bourgeauanum* Thellung.

LESQUERELLA Watson 1888 [for Leo Lesquereux, 1805-1899, paleobotanist and bryologist]. BLADDERPOD

1a. Siliques glabrous outside . . . . (2)

1b. Siliques pubescent outside . . . . (3)

2a. Trichome rays free and distinct or slightly fused. **L. ovalifolia** Rydberg. Common on limestone and gypsum, Arkansas River drainage.

2b. Trichome rays fused half their lengths or more. **L. fendleri** (Gray) Watson. Similar localities and area.

3a. Pedicels recurved and the siliques pendent . . . . (4)

3b. Pedicels sigmoid or curved, if straight then the siliques more than 3.5 mm long . . . . (5)

4a. Leaves long and narrow; inner basal leaves involute and usually entire; fruiting racemes not secund; valves often pubescent inside. **L. ludoviciana** (Nuttall) Watson [of "Louisiana"], **38A**. Abundant throughout the plains, and in North Park.

4b. Leaves short, the blades rhombic; fruiting racemes usually secund; valves usually glabrous inside. **L. arenosa** (Richardson) Rydberg [sandy]. Northeastern counties.

5a. Dwarf, condensed plants with inflorescence hardly exceeding the linear basal leaves . . . . (6)

5b. Inflorescence well exceeding the oblanceolate or broader leaves . . . . . (7)

6a. Strictly alpine (in our area); leaves uniformly narrow. **L. alpina** (Nuttall) Watson subsp. **parvula** (Greene) Rollins & Shaw. Alpine ridges of the Mosquito Range. On the Western Slope this occurs on desert-steppe in Middle Park!

6b. Plants of the high plains; leaves of varying width, the lowermost ones with a distinct blade and petiole or short and widened toward the apex. **L. alpina** (Nuttall) Watson subsp. **alpina**. Pawnee Grasslands.

7a. Racemes not elongating in fruit, the fruits crowded at the top; leaves oblanceolate to linear. **L. calcicola** Rollins [of limestone]. Arkansas River drainage, on limestone or gypsum.
7b. Racemes elongating in fruit, the fruits well separated; stem leaves with broad blades and obvious petioles, usually secund. **L. montana** (Gray) Watson, **38B**. Abundant on granitic soils in the foothills and montane.

LOBULARIA Desvaux 1815 [a name possibly alluding to the two-pointed hairs]. SWEET ALYSSUM

One species, **L. maritima** Desvaux. Formerly escaped from gardens, but now evidently sown in revegetation mixes.

NASTURTIUM R. Brown 1812 [so called, according to Pliny, *a narribus torquendus*, i.e., a writhing of the nostrils, because of the sharp smell of the seed]. WATERCRESS

One species, **N. officinale** R. Brown [of the shops]. Adventive in slow-flowing ditches and springs in the lower valleys (*Rorippa nasturtium-aquaticum*). While this plant makes a very fine salad ingredient, contamination of the water in which wild plants are growing may be a health hazard. *Giardia* is present in many areas of Colorado.

NEOLEPIA W. A. Weber 1989 [a new name for *Lepia*, an illegitimate one first used for this plant]. FIELDCRESS

One species, **N. campestre** (L.) W. A. Weber. Adventive, ruderal weed. Long included in the genus *Lepidium* but differing fundamentally in several respects.

NOCCAEA Moench 1802 [for Domenico Nocca, eighteenth-century Italian botanist]. WILD CANDYTUFT

One species, **N. montana** (L.) Meyer, **39A**. A ubiquitous species, occurring through the gamut of habitats from piñon-juniper to tundra (*Thlaspi*).

PENNELLIA Nieuwland 1918 [for Francis W. Pennell, 1886-1952, American Scrophulariaceae specialist]

One species, **P. micrantha** (Gray) Nieuwland. Local on cliffs and talus slopes, montane, Pikes Peak and South Platte Canyon.

PHYSARIA Gray 1848 [Greek, *physa*, bellows]. DOUBLE BLADDERPOD

1a. Strictly alpine; flowers large, orange-yellow. **P. alpina** Rollins. Endemic, rocky tundra, Mosquito Range.
1b. Foothills and mesas along the Front Range; flowers lemon yellow . . . (2)

2a. Constriction separating the locules equally deep above and below; locules globose; leaves broadly obovate, obtuse at the apex, rarely toothed or lobed. **P. bellii** Mulligan [for E. F. Bell, Ottawa botanist]. Endemic. Restricted to shales, base of Front Range from Denver northward.
2b. Constriction separating the locules much deeper above than below; locules angular; leaves fiddle-shaped (with a broad blade and small "lobes" on the petiole), rarely oval or obovate. **P. vitulifera** Rydberg [Middle Latin, *vitula*, fiddle]. Endemic. Common on gravelly slopes (siliceous rock) of the outer foothill canyons. Also along the base of the San Juan Mountains.

RORIPPA Scopoli 1760 [Old Saxon name for a cress, *Rorippen*]. YELLOWCRESS

1a. Rhizomatous perennial lacking basal rosettes; petals well exceeding the sepals; leaves regularly pinnatifid . . . . (2)

1b. Annual or biennial with a taproot and with basal rosettes; petals scarcely exceeding the sepals; leaves lyrate-pinnatifid or only toothed . . . . (3)

2a. Petals 2.5-5 mm long, slightly or not at all differentiated into blade and claw; sepals 0.7-4.5 mm long. **R. sinuata** (Nuttall) Hitchcock. Abundant on wet roadside ditches and meadows.

2b. Petals 6-7.5 mm long, strongly differentiated into blade and claw; sepals 3.8-5.0 mm long. **R. coloradensis** Stuckey. Endemic, known only from the type specimen, thought to have been collected in the San Luis Valley near the San Luis Lakes by Brandegee in 1875; probably extinct.

3a. Silique nearly spherical, the replum almost circular as well. **R. sphaerocarpa** (Gray) Britton. Scattered through the region, except on the eastern plains. This may represent merely a form of *R. teres* with very short capsules; it has the characteristic vesicular trichomes of that species.

3b. Silique oblong . . . . (4)

4a. Small, prostrate or decumbent plants . . . . (5)

4b. Taller, erect plants . . . . (6)

5a. Stem leaves unlobed, the margin entire or serrate; siliques smooth. **R. curvipes** Greene var. **alpina** (Watson) Stuckey. Common on muddy shores of drying ponds and streams, montane to subalpine.

5b. Stem leaves lyrate-pinnatifid, the margin entire; siliques minutely papillose. **R. tenerrima** Greene. Floodplain of the South Platte River on the eastern plains.

6a. Siliques very slender, hardly ever producing seed, reproducing by spreading roots and stems; leaves regularly deeply pinnatifid with fairly narrow, lobed segments. **R. sylvestris** (L.) Besser. Adventive, known from the Boulder area.

6b. Siliques short and stout, fertile; leaves varying from merely toothed to deeply lobed . . . . (7)

7a. Upper leaf surface and stem with scattered "vesicular trichomes" (these appear as small round blisters on the leaf surface that often break, leaving holes in the leaf); seeds under 0.5 mm long. **R. teres** (Michaux) Stuckey. This and the next are common in muddy places.

7b. Upper leaf surface and stem lacking vesicular trichomes, but often with ordinary hairs; seeds over 0.5 mm long. **R. palustris** (L.) Besser subsp. **hispida** (Desvaux) Jonsell.

SCHOENOCRAMBE Greene 1896 [Greek, *schoinos*, rush, alluding to the leafless appearance, + *Crambe*, a genus]. SKELETON MUSTARD

One species, **S. linearifolia** (Gray) Rollins. Dry valley floor, Wet Mountain Valley (*Sisymbrium*). Unlike the Western Slope *S. linifolia*, this species has purple flowers.

SINAPIS L. 1753 [ancient name for mustard]. CHARLOCK

One species, **S. arvensis** L. Common, adventive, yellow-flowered mustard invading cultivated fields as a weed (*Brassica kaber*).

SISYMBRIUM L. 1753 [Greek name for some mustard]. JIM HILL MUSTARD

1a. Siliques short, tightly appressed along the inflorescence axis. **S. officinale** (L.) Scopoli. Adventive, known from a few old records in the Denver area.

1b. Siliques elongate, widely spreading . . . . (2)

2a. Flowers pale yellow; pedicels stout, 4-10 mm long, nearly as thick as the fruit; silique widely spreading, rigid, 5-10 cm long. **S. altissimum** L. [very tall]. Abundant ruderal weed at low altitudes, believed to have spread into the West along the railroads (Jim Hill was an early railroad magnate).

2b. Flowers bright yellow; pedicels slender, 7-20 mm long, not as thick as the fruit; silique ascending to erect, 2-3.5 cm long. **S. austriacum** Jacquin. Adventive. Recently found for the first time as a weed in Boulder. This species resembles *S. loeselii*, which occurs on the Western Slope, but the septum of the silique is white and opaque rather than hyaline, and the stem is glabrous.

SMELOWSKIA C. A. Meyer 1830 [for T. Smelovskii, 1770-1815, Russian botanist]

One species, **S. calycina** (Stephan) Meyer [with calyx]. Scree slopes and rocky tundra, Continental Divide and San Juans. A species of our Asiatic element, ranging to Altai and Central Asia.

STANLEYA Nuttall 1818 [for Lord Stanley, 1799-1869, British statesman]. PRINCE'S PLUME

One species, **S. pinnata** (Pursh) Britton, **Pl. 17**. Common on seleniferous soils in the valleys. The presence of *Stanleya* is indicative of the poisonous element selenium in the soil. The plants concentrate the metal in the tissues; selenium indicator plants have a strong, unpleasant odor.

THELLUNGIELLA O. E. Schulz 1924 [for Albert Thellung, 1881-1928, Swiss botanist]

One species, **T. salsuginea** (Pallas) O. E. Schulz. Common on alkaline mud flats, Antero Reservoir, South Park. Known from only a few other localities in North America; otherwise Siberian (*Sisymbrium*).

THELYPODIUM Endlicher 1839 [Greek, *thelys*, woman, + *podium*, foot. Significance?]

1a. Cauline leaves petiolate, at least the lower and middle ones pinnately lobed, sometimes dentate. **T. wrightii** Gray subsp. **oklahomensis** Al-Shehbaz. Clay or sandy soils, Arkansas River Valley from Salida to the Oklahoma border.

1b. Cauline leaves sessile, sagittate, clasping or auriculate at the base; lower and middle stem leaves mostly entire, rarely dentate . . . . (2)

2a. Cauline leaves attenuate at base, neither sagittate nor clasping, auricles absent. **T. integrifolium** (Nuttall) Endlicher. North Park and plains of LR and WL.

2b. Cauline leaves sagittate, clasping . . . . (3)

3a. Siliques 1.5-2.3 mm wide; petals 2.5-5 mm wide. **T. paniculatum** Nelson. Meadows and stream bottoms, reaching its southeastern limit here; collected only once, at Camp Creek, North Park.

3b. Siliques 0.75-1 mm wide; petals 1-3 mm wide. **T. sagittatum** (Nuttall) Endlicher. Meadows and stream bottoms, reaching its southeastern limit here; collected only once, along Nelson Ditch, North Park.

THLASPI L. 1753 [Greek, *thlaein*, to crush, alluding to the flat silique]. FANWEED; PENNYCRESS

One species, **T. arvense** L., **39B**. Adventive, ruderal weed. So called because the large, erect, almost orbicular flat siliques resemble fans or pennies. For other species formerly included, see *Noccaea*.

TURRITIS L. 1753 [ancient name from Latin *turritus*, towered]. TOWER MUSTARD

One species, **T. glabra** L. Disturbed sites, particularly in forested areas, along logging roads and campgrounds, very likely adventive here (*Arabis*).

CACTACEAE CACTUS FAMILY (CAC)

The cacti exhibit a profound compression and condensation of the stem structure resulting in stems that are short and broad and in which the internodes are almost impossible to make out, since all of the branches are reduced to mere clumps of spines (areoles) arranged in ascending spirals. The true leaves, of those cacti that still have them, are little, fleshy, short-lived ones that are not commonly seen except in early spring. The inferior ovary is also imbedded in a condensed branch system. The flowers have numerous floral parts, and the stamens are especially interesting in that they will be activated when touched by a stick, presumably making possible more contact of the pollen with pollinators.

Except for the prickly-pears (*Opuntia* species), we should consider our cacti as threatened or endangered plants and refrain from collecting them in the wild. They are rapidly disappearing because of exploitation for the international rock garden trade. In Arizona the collecting of cacti is prohibited by state law, a precedent that should be followed in Colorado. Generic lines are very difficult to draw in the cacti, and each cactologist seems to have his own notion of them; they change frequently.

1a. Areoles bearing glochids (minute, sharp-pointed, barbed bristles that penetrate the flesh without at first being felt); new pads bearing fleshy leaves, one just below each areole . . . . (2)
1b. Areoles not bearing glochids; stem leafless or with only slight bulges or scales representing them . . . . (3)

2a. Joints of the stem cylindrical, elongate; glochids small and inconsequential; epidermis of the spine separating into a thin, papery sheath; erect or scrambling shrubs. **Cylindropuntia**, CHOLLA
2b. Joints of the stem flat, oval or potatolike; glochids well developed, barbed, and effective; succulent, prostrate or spreading plants. **Opuntia**, PRICKLY-PEAR

3a. Flowers borne clearly below the branch apex, on old growth; stems ribbed. **Echinocereus**, HEDGEHOG CACTUS
3b. Flowers borne at the apex of the branch, on the current growth; stems ribbed or tuberculate . . . . (4)

4a. Plants with tubercles that are not grooved on the upper side. **Pediocactus**, BALL CACTUS
4b. Plants with tubercles that are grooved along the upper side. **Coryphantha**, NIPPLE CACTUS

CORYPHANTHA Lemaire 1868 [Greek, *koryphe*, summit, + *anthos*, flower, alluding to the position of the flowers]. NIPPLE CACTUS

1a. Flowers pink; central spines usually present; fruit green or brown. **C. vivipara** (Nuttall) Britton & Rose var. **vivipara**. Common on the plains and San Luis Valley, very rarely in the outer foothills (Poudre Canyon at 8,000 ft). Our *Coryphantha* species are currently regarded by some as belonging to the genus *Escobaria*.

1b. Flowers green or yellow; central spines usually absent; fruit red, maturing the following year. **C. missouriensis** (Sweet) Britton & Rose, **Pl. 4**. Very inconspicuous and probably infrequent, plains and outwash mesas.

CYLINDROPUNTIA Knuth 1935. CHOLLA

One species, **C. imbricata** (Haworth) Knuth, CANDELABRA CACTUS. Common in the Arkansas River drainage from Colorado Springs to the Oklahoma border. The spines on these treelike cacti are tough and hooked. Falling backward down a hillside into a bush of these is a terrible experience, since each spine must be pulled out individually, at the same time preventing others from taking hold. Fortunately for us, Colorado has no "jumping cholla" species, which have a reputation of reaching out for an unwary passerby.

ECHINOCEREUS Engelmann 1848 [Greek, *echinos*, hedgehog, + *Cereus*, a genus]. HEDGEHOG CACTUS

1a. Spines not over 1 cm long, all or all but the central one appressed to the stem (easily handled) . . . . (2)
1b. Spines usually over 2 cm long, spreading and stout (formidable); flowers scarlet; stems numerous, often forming mounds of over 25 stems. **E. triglochidiatus** Engelmann [with three spines], CLARET CUP. A splendid species common on rimrock of mesas in the southern counties. Unfortunately, it has been eradicated from most accessible sites by the rock garden trade.

2a. Flowers yellow-green; low,rounded plants in grassland. **E. viridiflorus** Engelmann, HEN-AND-CHICKENS. Common on grassland on the plains and mountain parks.
2b. Flowers pink-purple to scarlet; plants narrow-cylindric. **E. reichenbachii** (Terscheck) Haage var. **perbellus** (Britton & Rose) Benson. Limestone outcrops and rimrock in the Arkansas River Valley.

OPUNTIA Miller 1754 [name used by Theophrastus for some plant, not this]. PRICKLY-PEAR

1a. Stem segments terete or only slightly flattened in cross-section; segments brittle, very easily detached. **O. fragilis** (Nuttall) Haworth, BRITTLE CACTUS. Frequent in ponderosa pine forests in the outer foothills. The flowers are yellow, but plants do not bloom every year, many being strictly vegetative.
1b. Stem segments strongly flattened, not brittle nor easily separated . . . . (2)

2a. Joints 15-30 cm long; distance between areoles 3-4 cm; spines brown-tipped. **O. phaeacantha** Engelmann [brown-spined], NEW MEXICAN PRICKLY-PEAR. Usually the pads are very large, glaucous, with wide spaces between areoles, and long brown-tipped spines. Rocky gulches in the outwash mesas from BL to BA. Generally absent from the plains.
2b. Joints 10-15 cm long; distance between areoles 1.5-2.5 cm; spines not brown-tipped . . . . (3)

3a. Joints with rather sparse spines, the flat surface wrinkled transversely; fruits persisting for several months, fleshy, edible. **O. macrorhiza** Engelmann. Common on the plains and mesas. Flowers yellow.
3b. Joints usually very spiny, not wrinkled; fruits dry, withering soon after ripening. **O. polyacantha** Haworth. Abundant on the plains and intermountain parks. Flowers pink, yellow, or copper-colored. A race that forms new pads from elongated horizontal roots is common in the upper Arkansas River Valley and has been proposed recently as a species, *O. heacockii* Arp.

PEDIOCACTUS Britton & Rose 1913 [Greek, *pedion*, flatland]. BALL CACTUS

One species, **P. simpsonii** (Engelmann) Britton & Rose var. **minor** (Engelmann) Cockerell [for J. H. Simpson, army engineer whom Engelmann assisted in the field]. Common in the foothill canyons and in the dry parts of mountain parks. In my experience this has a heavy, rose odor, but evidently some people are unable to detect this.

CALLITRICHACEAE WATER STARWORT FAMILY (CLL)

While the water starworts are easily recognized as a genus by their slender stems, opposite linear or oblong leaves and sessile fruits in the leaf axils, the species are very difficult to identify partly because of their environmental plasticity. Stem length, leaf shape and succulence vary with the degree of submergence. The species are very complex genetically, most of them being partially apomictic. Fortunately, in Colorado there seem to be only two.

CALLITRICHE L. 1753 [Greek, *callos*, beautiful, + *trichos*, hair]. WATER STARWORT

1a. Leaves uniformly linear, all submerged. **C. hermaphroditica** L. Pond margins, slow streams, and ditches.

1b. Leaves both linear and oblong, the submerged ones linear, the upper and emergent or floating leaves broadly oblong. **C. verna** L., **28**. [of springtime]. Common in similar habitats. As wet places dry out, the plants, being weak, become matted on the mud (*C. palustris*).

CALOCHORTACEAE MARIPOSA FAMILY (CCT)

A monotypic family embracing a single genus (formerly placed in Liliaceae) that is restricted to western North and Central America. Its flowers are of remarkable beauty because of their large, often highly colored petals, and especially because each bears an elaborate "gland" near the base, consisting of a depression surrounded by colored hairs. The petals themselves may be hairy inside or marginally ciliate, wine-glass- or bowl-shaped. In California, many species are exceedingly rare and endangered, partly because of their restricted habitats and partly from historical exploitation by plant diggers for the garden trade.

CALOCHORTUS Pursh 1814 [Greek, *callos*, beautiful, + *chortos*, grass]. MARIPOSA, SEGO LILY

One species, **C. gunnisonii** Watson [for Captain J. W. Gunnison of the Pacific Railroad surveys]. Mountain meadows and aspen groves, from the outer foothills to montane. Flowers are white in this species.

CAMPANULACEAE BELLFLOWER FAMILY (CAM)

This family includes some choice rock garden plants, many of them originally native to the meadows and tundra of Eurasia. Most species of *Campanula* are known by the deep bell-shape of the usually blue to purple corolla, and the species differ in the ways the flowers are grouped together as well as by their sizes and shapes. The family also includes the lobelias, a group of plants differing from the bellflowers in having a bilaterally symmetrical corolla, reminding one of *Penstemon* but belonging here by virtue of the 3 stigmas and inferior ovary. Lobelias are commmonly cultivated as flowering border plants.

1a. Flowers tubular, bilaterally symmetrical. **Lobelia**
1b. Flowers radially symmetrical . . . . (2)

2a. Corolla bell-shaped (campanulate); flowers with obvious pedicels. **Campanula**, HAREBELL
2b. Corolla flat open (rotate); flowers sessile in the leaf axils. **Triodanis**

CAMPANULA L. 1753 [diminutive of Latin, *campana*, bell]. HAREBELL

1a. Tall coarse herb with ovate, coarsely serrate basal and stem leaves and purple flowers in a long raceme. **C. rapunculoides** L. [like *C. rapunculus*]. Adventive, formerly cultivated in old-fashioned gardens, but escaped and now a difficult weed to eradicate where it is not wanted. It spreads by deep, underground rhizomes and, although attractive, crowds out other desirable plants.
1b. Tall or low herbs with linear or narrow stem leaves, only the basal ones sometimes ovate . . . . (2)

2a. Stem tall, very leafy; flowers small (about 5 mm diameter), pale purple or white; stems and leaves retrorse-scabrous (like a bedstraw). **C. aparinoides** Pursh [alluding to *Galium aparine*]. Extremely rare, collected in northern South Park in 1861, and once in the Denver region by Eastwood.
2b. Stem tall or low, not very leafy; flowers very variable in size, purple-blue (except for occasional white mutants) . . . . (3)

3a. Corolla narrowly bell-shaped, with deep and narrow lobes; plants usually less than 8 cm tall; anthers 1.5-2.5 mm long. **C. uniflora** L., ALPINE HAREBELL, **41A**. Alpine tundra. The fruit is elongate, club-shaped, in contrast to the short, cup-shaped fruit of the next.
3b. Corolla broadly bell-shaped, shallowly and broadly lobed; plant usually well over 10 cm tall; anthers 4-6.5 mm long . . . . (4)

4a. Corolla lobed halfway, the lobes widely spreading and the bell shallow; capsule erect, opening by pores near the summit; bases of lower leaves ciliate. **C. parryi** Gray, **41C**. Subalpine to near timberline. Flowers usually more purple than in the next.
4b. Corolla lobed only about one-third, the lobes not flaring and the bell deep; capsule nodding, opening by pores near the base; leaf bases not ciliate. **C. rotundifolia** L., COMMON HAREBELL, **41D**. Abundant on dry mountainsides from foothills to the tundra; the alpine race is low, with solitary flowers; these may represent subsp. *groenlandica*.

LOBELIA L. 1753 [for Mathias de L'Obel, 1583-1616, Flemish botanist to James I of England]

1a. Flowers scarlet. **L. cardinalis** L. subsp. **graminea** (Lamarck) McVaugh, CARDINAL FLOWER. Canyon-bottoms in oak woodlands of east base of Mesa de Maya.
1b. Flowers blue-violet, striped with white. **L. siphilitica** L. var. **ludoviciana** de Candolle. Wet meadows in the piedmont and plains.

TRIODANIS Rafinesque 1837 [derivation?]

1a. Leaves broadly ovate, clasping the stem. **T. perfoliata** (L.) Nieuwland, VENUS' LOOKING-GLASS. Infrequent on the outwash mesas of the Front Range. Two collections intermediate between this and the next have been called *T. holzingeri* McVaugh but the likelihood is that these are interspecific hybrid individuals between the two species known to inhabit this area. This produces cleistogamous flowers, especially late in the season even though it still is actively growing.

1b. Leaves lanceolate or linear, not clasping the stem. **T. leptocarpa** (Nuttall) Nieuwland. One record, meadows near Boulder. In fruit the elongate narrow capsule crowned by the stiffly spreading needlelike calyx-lobes is distinctive. The flowers of *Triodanis* are short-lived and often cleistogamous.

CANNABACEAE HOPS FAMILY (CAN)

This is a very small family, formerly placed in the mulberry family (Moraceae) but differing in the herbaceous habit and the 5- rather than 4-parted flowers. Although small, this family contains two of the most important species, where mankind is concerned: *Cannabis*, the marijuana, hashish, or hemp; and *Humulus*, hops. Each plant, in its own unique manner, is used to elevate the spirit or increase perception. The flowers are unisexual; the carpellate flowers are surrounded by persistent bracts, large and conspicuous in *Humulus*.

1a. Erect herb up to several m tall; leaves palmately compound with narrow serrate leaflets. **Cannabis**, MARIJUANA

1b. Trailing vine; leaves palmately lobed with broad, rounded sinuses; leaves and stems very harsh to the touch. **Humulus**, HOPS

CANNABIS L. 1753 [the ancient Greek name, possibly from the Persian, Kanab]. MARIJUANA

One species, **C. sativa** L., **32a**. Adventive, a clandestinely cultivated or encouraged weed.

HUMULUS L. 1753 [Late Latin name of Teutonic origin]. HOPS

One species, **H. lupulus** L. subsp. **americanus** (Nuttall) Löve & Löve [*Lupulus*, an early generic name], WILD HOPS, **32B**. This is a distinctly native race of the species, having been found fossilized in the Oligocene formation at Florissant. Bases of talus slopes in the outer foothills.

CAPPARACEAE CAPER FAMILY (CPP)

A family with close relationships to the mustards, but the fruit lacks a central partition or replum, the stamens are often long-exserted, often more than 6, and the capsule is often stipitate. *Stanleya*, in the Brassicaceae, is sometimes considered a sort of link between the two families.

Capers are the pickled flower buds of *Capparis spinosa* and are essential to the preparation of the German meatball dish called Königsberger Klops. The plant is a usually spiny shrub of the Mediterranean region. The giant spiderflower of gardens, so called because of its slender petals and long-exserted stamens, is *Cleome spinosa*, a giant relative of our common Rocky Mountain bee plant. Many capparids have sticky and unpleasant-smelling foliage and pods. "Cutting capers" has nothing to do with this name but with the Greek word *caper*, meaning billy-goat.

1a. Plants sticky-glandular pubescent; stamens 8 or more; flowers pale pink or white, rarely deeply colored. **Polanisia,** CLAMMYWEED
1b. Plants glabrous; stamens 6; flowers yellow or purple . . . . (2)

2a. Pods several times longer than wide, somewhat contracted between the seeds. **Cleome,** BEEPLANT
2b. Pods short and broad, angular, boxlike. **Cleomella,** STINKWEED

CLEOME L. 1753 [of uncertain derivation, applied early to a mustardlike plant]. BEEPLANT

1a. Leaflets 5-10 mm wide, long-petioled; petals 8-12 mm long; body of capsule 1.5-8.0 cm long. **C. serrulata** Pursh, ROCKY MOUNTAIN BEEPLANT. Abundant, tall weed in midsummer along roadsides. Usually the stamens are longer than the petals, but occasionally a form is found, *forma* **inornata,** with short stamens.
1b. Leaflets narrowly linear, 1-2 mm wide; leaves short-petioled, less than 5 mm; petals 4-5 mm long; capsule 6-15 mm long. **C. multicaulis** Sessé & Moçiño. Restricted to wet meadows and alkaline flats in the San Luis Valley. A species widely distributed in Mexico and probably brought to Colorado by the early Spanish settlers. With the draining of wetlands it has become quite rare in Colorado.

CLEOMELLA de Candolle 1824 [diminutive of *Cleome*]. STINKWEED

One species, **C. angustifolia** Torrey. One record, from Julesburg. A species of the southern Great Plains.

POLANISIA Rafinesque 1819 [Greek, *polys*, + *anisos*, alluding to the numerous unequal stamens]. CLAMMYWEED

1a. Leaflets obovate to lanceolate-elliptic, 6-15 mm wide; fruits 5-10 mm broad; style in fruit withering and deciduous. **P. dodecandra** (L.) de Candolle, **Pl. 27.** [with 12 stamens]. Roadsides and gulches in the valleys. The flowers are cream-white with red stamens.
1b. Leaflets linear to filiform, 1-5 mm wide; fruits 1.5-4 mm broad; style persistent and setaceous in fruit. **P. jamesii** (Torrey & Gray) Iltis. Sandhills on the eastern plains. Flowers white to ochroleucous (*Cristatella*).

CAPRIFOLIACEAE HONEYSUCKLE FAMILY (CPR)

This family comprises mostly trees and shrubs (*Linnaea* an exception) with opposite, usually simple leaves (an exception is our genus *Sambucus*, which may not belong in the family). The flowers are radially or bilaterally symmetrical, with united petals and an inferior ovary. The fruits are mostly berries.

Every gardener is familiar with elderberry, viburnum, honeysuckle, and snowberry. Fewer know the most famous plant of the family–the twinflower, *Linnaea*, which covers forest floors across the Northern Hemisphere. Linnaeus was so proud of this little plant that many of his portraits show him holding a sprig of it. With characteristic modesty he wrote that "*Linnaea* was named by the celebrated Gronovius and is a plant of Lapland, lowly, insignificant, flowering but for a brief space, after Linnaeus who resembles it."

1a. Leaves pinnately compound. **Sambucus**, ELDERBERRY
1b. Leaves simple . . . . (2)

2a. Plant with prostrate-creeping stems, only slightly woody; flowers pink, in nodding pairs on an elongate, erect peduncle. **Linnaea**, TWINFLOWER
2b. Plants definitely shrubby, with erect stems . . . . (3)

3a. Leaves 3-lobed, maplelike. **Viburnum**, BUSH-CRANBERRY
3b. Leaves simple or pinnately lobed, not maplelike . . . . (4)

4a. Flowers numerous in flat-topped inflorescences; style short, 3-lobed or almost lacking. **Viburnum**, BUSH-CRANBERRY
4b. Flowers few, in pairs or terminal axillary clusters . . . . (5)

5a. Flowers seated in a conspicuous, broad, leaflike cup of bracts; flowers yellow; berry purplish-black. **Distegia**, BUSH HONEYSUCKLE
5b. Floral bracts linear, inconspicuous; flowers white (yellowing in age) or pink; berry red or white . . . . (6)

6a. Flowers zygomorphic, with elongated lobes; leaves broadest at the base; berry red; introduced ornamental shrubs sometimes escaped on floodplains. **Lonicera**, HONEYSUCKLE
6b. Flowers with short, triangular lobes; leaves broadly elliptic or oblong; berry snow white; native shrubs. **Symphoricarpos**, SNOWBERRY

DISTEGIA Rafinesque 1838 [Greek, *di*, two, + *stegos*, roof, alluding to the bract subtending the berries]. BUSH HONEYSUCKLE

One species, **D. involucrata** (Banks) Cockerell, **42C**. Common along mountain streams (*Lonicera*). The fruit, a pair of red-juiced, black berries, is extremely bitter and possibly poisonous. The flowers are small, yellow, and cylindric-campanulate, not zygomorphic as in *Lonicera*.

LINNAEA L. 1753 [for derivation, see above]. TWINFLOWER

One species, **L. borealis** L. Subalpine spruce-fir forests. Our mountain race has flowers more the shape of the European type than the far-western American subsp. **longiflora** (Torrey) Hultén.

LONICERA L. 1753 [for Adam Lonitzer, German sixteenth-century herbalist]. HONEYSUCKLE

1a. Peduncles shorter than to about equalling the flowers; leaves pubescent beneath; flowers white, turning yellow in age. **L. morrowii** Gray [for James Morrow, its discoverer, 1820-1865], **42E**. Escaping from cultivation and established in vicinity of towns. Hybridization between this and the next results in an intermediate, *L. x bella*.
1b. Peduncles mostly longer than the flowers; leaves glabrous; flowers pink. **L. tatarica** L. [of Tartary]. Escaped from cultivation.

SAMBUCUS L. 1753 [Greek, *sambuce*, an ancient musical instrument, hence a bark whistle]. ELDERBERRY

1a. Inflorescence broadly pyramidal, with the main axis extended beyond the lowermost floral branches. **S. microbotrys** Rydberg [small cluster], **42D**. The common elderberry of the region (*S. racemosa* of Colorado literature). Berries red, or black in var. **melanocarpa**.
1b. Inflorescence flat-topped . . . . (2)

2a. Leaves green, not glaucous; berries black. **S. canadensis** L. Adventive, escaped from cultivation and occasionally naturalized near towns.

2b. Leaves glaucous; berries covered by a glaucous-blue wax. **S. coerulea** Rafinesque, BLUE ELDERBERRY, **42F**. Native on the Mesa de Maya, but sometimes appearing near farms as if once cultivated or encouraged.

SYMPHORICARPOS Duhamel 1755 [Greek, *symphorein*, to bear together, + *carpos*, fruit]. SNOWBERRY

1a. Flowers tubular-campanulate, the sides more parallel. **S. rotundifolius** Gray, **42A**. Abundant on steep canyonsides, gulches, oak-aspen (including *S. oreophilus*, *S. vaccinioides*, *S. palmeri*). Extremely variable in leaf size, lobation, and stem pubescence.
1b. Corolla bell-shaped, the lobes about as long as or slightly longer than the tube . . . . (2)

2a. Style and stamens shorter than or only equalling the corolla, not exserted; flowers few; leaves 1-1.5 cm long. **S. albus** (L.) Blake. Frequent in cool, forested foothill canyons, a slender shrub never forming large masses.
2b. Style and stamens exserted; flowers in rather dense clusters in the uppermost leaf axils; leaves 2-4 cm long. **S. occidentalis** Hooker. Forming dense colonies in rather moist, open, grassy swales on the mesas and plains.

VIBURNUM L. 1753 [the classical Latin name]

1a. Leaves 3-lobed, palmately veined; fruits red at maturity. **V. edule** (Michaux) Rafinesque [edible], BUSH-CRANBERRY, **42G**. Local along streams in spruce-fir forests. Very similar to the cultivated species, *V. opulus*.
1b. Leaves simple, pinnately veined; fruits black at maturity . . . . (2)

2a. Leaves coarsely serrate-dentate, thick, densely stellate-pubescent, especially beneath. **V. lantana** L. [old name meaning flexible], WAYFARING TREE. Escaped from cultivation and established in foothill gulches near Boulder.
2b. Leaves finely serrate, thin, almost glabrous (with minute reddish sessile glands beneath and branched, reddish hairs scattered on the veins). **V. lentago** L. [same meaning as *lantana*], NANNYBERRY. Escaped from cultivation and established in foothill gulches near Boulder. The acuminate leaves resemble those of *Prunus*.

CARYOPHYLLACEAE PINK FAMILY (CRY)

A very easily recognized family containing some handsome cultivated plants such as carnations, garden pinks, and baby's-breath. In this book I am recognizing those types with a united calyx and generally long-clawed petals as belonging to the Caryophyllaceae, while the forms usually included in the family but differing in having free calyx parts and clawless petals (among other characters) as belonging to the Alsinaceae. A good vegetative character of both families, rarely mentioned in the keys, is the distinctly swollen node at which each pair of leaves arises.

1a. Calyx closely invested at the base by 2 short bracts. **Dianthus**, PINK, CARNATION
1b. Calyx without 2 bracts at the base . . . . (2)

2a. Styles 5; capsule opening by 5 or 10 teeth . . . . (3)
2b. Styles 2 or 3; capsule splitting into 3, 4, or 6 parts . . . . (4)

3a. Flowers unisexual, plants dioecious; petals with blades over 5 mm long; tall, broad-leaved introduced weeds of pastures. **Melandrium**, CAMPION

3b. Flowers perfect; petals smaller; native, narrow-leaved plants of mountains and tundra. **Gastrolychnis**, ALPINE CAMPION

4a. Calyx 10-20-nerved; styles 3; capsule 3- or 6-valved . . . . (5)
4b. Calyx 5-nerved or 5-angled, or terete and only obscurely nerved; styles 2; capsule 4-valved . . . . (6)

5a. Flowers in few-flowered cymes subtended by unreduced leaves; plants functionally dioecious, dichotomously branched, with slender rhizomes; forest plants. **Anotites**
5b. Flowers in cymes with subtended by reduced, bractlike leaves; plants with perfect flowers, not slenderly rhizomatous; annual weeds and native perennials, one an alpine dwarf mat plant. **Silene**, CAMPION

6a. Flowers less than 4 mm long, very numerous, in much-branched cymes. **Gypsophila**, BABY'S-BREATH
6b. Flowers over 5 mm long, relatively few in number . . . . (7)

7a. Calyx 5-angled; flowers deep pink; annual. **Vaccaria**, COW COCKLE
7b. Calyx terete; flowers white or pink; perennial. **Saponaria**, BOUNCING BET; SOAPWORT

ANOTITES Greene 1905 [derivation unexplained, probably from *a*, not, + *notites*, marked, hence unrecognized]

One species, **A. menziesii** (Hooker) Greene [for Alexander Menzies, 1754-1842, Scottish explorer of the Pacific Northwest]. Low, dichotomously branched, glandular-pubescent, somewhat brittle; calyx small, less than 5 mm long. Infrequent in deep shade of montane forests (*Silene*).

DIANTHUS L. 1753 [Greek, *Dios*, Jupiter, + *anthos*, flower]. PINK, CARNATION

1a. Flowers in clusters; bracts lance-linear, as long as the calyx tube; leaves hairy; annual. **D. armeria** L. [for the genus *Armeria*], DEPTFORD PINK. Adventive weed of meadows in the Front Range foothills and piedmont. This species seems to be in a period of active expansion of its range.
1b. Flowers solitary; bracts ovate, half as long as the calyx; perennial. **D. deltoides** L., **40C**. [triangular, alluding to the bracts]. Adventive, naturalized in meadows near Eldora, BL.

GASTROLYCHNIS Reichenbach 1841 [Greek, *gastridos*, pot-bellied, + *Lychnis*, a genus] (formerly included in *Melandrium* or *Silene*). ALPINE CAMPION

1a. Dwarf alpines, usually less than 10 cm tall . . . . (2)
1b. Taller plants of various altitudes. **G. drummondii** (Hooker) Löve & Löve [for Thomas Drummond, ca. 1780-1835, Franklin expeditions botanist]. Dry slopes, foothills to subalpine; very similar in general appearance to *Silene scouleri*. There are more well-developed leaf pairs in *G. drummondii*, and they are not as abruptly reduced above.

2a. Flowers nodding at anthesis; petals included or barely exserted; calyx inflated like a Japanese lantern; seeds 1.5-2 mm, rounded. **G. apetala** (L.) Tolmatchev & Kozhanchikov subsp. **uralensis** Löve & Löve, **27C**. Unstable tundra or scree slopes.
2b. Flowers erect; petals included, barely exserted, or conspicuously exserted; calyx cylindric, only slightly inflated; seeds 0.5-1 mm, angular. **G. kingii** (Watson) Weber [for Clarence R. King, 1842-1901, geologist and western explorer]. On relatively stable tundra. Various Arctic specialists suggest that this is

equivalent to *G. furcatum* or related species, but there has been no serious revision recently and the relationships are still not clear.

GYPSOPHILA L. 1753 [Greek, *gypsos*, gypsum, + *philein*, to love]. BABY'S-BREATH

1a. Low (to 5 dm) green annual; inflorescence relatively few-flowered, the petals about 6 mm long; calyx 3-5 mm long. **G. elegans** Bieberstein. Adventive, commonly sown in "native plant" mixes, MF.
1b. Tall glaucous perennial from stout rhizomes; inflorescence bushy-branched, with many tiny flowers; calyx 1.5-2 mm long . . . . (2)

2a. Inflorescence branches glabrous. **G. paniculata** L., **40A**. Adventive. Established along roadsides and fencerows.
2b. Inflorescence branches glandular-pubescent. **G. scorzonerifolia** Seringe [with leaves like the asteraceous genus *Scorzonera*]. Adventive, first found in Boulder in 1979 and still uncommon. It has recently appeared in the Salt Lake City area.

MELANDRIUM Roehling 1812 [Greek, *melas*, black, + *drys*, oak, used by Homer to denote the dark heartwood of oak, but later used for this plant by Clusius, 1601, in *Rariorus Plantarum Historia*. Why?]. CAMPION

One species, **M. dioicum** (L.) Cosson & Germain [dioecious]. Adventive, common weed of mountain pastures (*Lychnis alba*).

SAPONARIA L. 1753 [Greek, *sapo*, soap]. SOAPWORT, BOUNCING BET

One species, **S. officinalis** L. [of the shops], **40D**. Adventive, escaped from cultivation (old gardens from the mining days) and very well established along roadsides, flowering in midsummer. The leaves make a fair lather when crushed and rubbed under water. Double-flowered sports are frequent.

SILENE L. 1753 [for Silenus, drunken foster-father of Bacchus]. CATCHFLY, CAMPION

1a. Low and densely matted, mosslike; flowers scarcely higher than the short basal leaves. **S. acaulis** L. subsp. **subacaulescens** (Williams) Hitchcock & Maguire, MOSS PINK. Flowers pink, very rarely white. Common on dry tundra. Races occur in the Arctic and most mountain areas of the Northern Hemisphere.
1b. Plants with tall, leafy stems, or at least not matted or mosslike; growing at various altitudes . . . . (2)

2a. Calyx glabrous . . . . (3)
2b. Calyx pilose . . . . (5)

3a. Calyx tight over the capsule; stems usually with localized dark bands of sticky fluid on the upper internodes. **S. antirrhina** L. [with leaves like *Antirrhinum*], SLEEPY CATCHFLY. Occasional plants occur without the sticky bands. Sorry about that!
3b. Calyx ± inflated, becoming ovoid to campanulate or subglobose, the nerves not prominent; stem never glutinous . . . . (4)

4a. Calyx with very prominent reticulations, with translucent areas between veins. **S. vulgaris** (Moench) Garcke. Adventive, established in pastures and roadsides in the mountains (*S. cucubalus*).

4b. Calyx with faint reticulations, the surface ± uniform. **S. czerei** Baumgartner. Adventive, similar sites; very common in the foothills west of Boulder.

5a. Perennial; calyx with 10 dark veins, sticky-glandular; native plant. **S. scouleri** Hooker subsp. **hallii** (Watson) Hitchcock & Maguire. Dry montane and subalpine slopes.
5b. Annual or biennial weed . . . . (6)

6a. Inflorescence an open cymose panicle, viscid-villous; fruiting calyx inflated-ovoid, 1.5-2.5 cm long, with prominent green ribs. **S. noctiflora** L. [flowering at night]. Adventive, established in Boulder Canyon.
6b. Inflorescence of 1-sided racemes . . . . (7)

7a. Inflorescence a simple raceme; flowers ascending; calyx villous or glandular-pilose; limb of petals notched only above the middle. **S. gallica** L. [French]. Adventive, known from a single plant collected in 1930 at Englewood.
7b. Inflorescence dichotomously forking; flowers nodding in anthesis, the fruits appressed ascending; calyx ribs pectinate-hirsute; limb of petals cleft to below the middle. **S. dichotoma** Ehrhardt. Adventive, thus far known from the Western Slope but to be expected in disturbed forest sites.

VACCARIA Wolf 1781 [Sanskrit, *vaca*, cow]. COW COCKLE [cockle being an Anglo-Saxon word meaning tare or weed]

One species, **V. pyramidata** Medikus, **40B**. Adventive weed of cultivated fields (RB). The sharply 5-angled calyx and glaucous leaves are distinctive features.

CELASTRACEAE STAFFTREE FAMILY (CEL)

This small family includes bittersweet, *Celastrus scandens*, a woody vine noted for its seed encased in a brilliant orange aril. The dry capsules dehisce, exposing but not releasing the seed. Sprays of bittersweet are gathered in autumn for dry arrangements. *Euonymus*, the spindle-tree, includes several species, either evergreen or deciduous, with similar arillate dull red seeds. These are desirable ornamentals, often having cork-ridged stems. The fine-grained hard wood was used in making spindles. Possibly the name "staff-tree" is derived, not from a walking stick, but from the spinning distaff. *Forsellesia* has usually been placed in this family, but Thorne has recently shown that it really belongs with the Crossosomataceae.

PAXISTIMA Rafinesque 1838 [Greek, *pachy*, thick, + *stigma*]. MOUNTAINLOVER

One species, **P. myrsinites** (Pursh) Rafinesque, **Pl. 2**. A low evergreen shrub with opposite crenate leaves and inconspicuous reddish 4-merous flowers, common in the forests at middle altitudes. This is one of our Tertiary relicts, with a close relative, *P. canbyi*, found in the southern Appalachians. The original spelling of the name was *Paxistima*; it was not an error and must be followed.

CERATOPHYLLACEAE HORNWORT FAMILY (CTP)

This family consists of a single genus, and, depending on who is speaking, either 1 or 30 species of obligately submerged aquatic plants. Slow streams and ponds are often clogged with dense growths of these plants, which can be easily mistaken for the green alga *Chara*. The repeatedly dichotomous, linear leaf segments are distinctive, but the strange, 1-seeded fruit, with a stiff, spinelike style and often a few spines spreading from the fruit base, is unique.

CERATOPHYLLUM L. 1753 [Greek, *ceras*, horn, + *phyllon*, leaf]. HORNWORT

One species, **C. demersum** L., **43B**. Slow streams, ponds, and irrigation ditches in the piedmont valleys. The whorled leaves are dichotomously branched, with narrow linear divisions, very densely grouped toward the stem apex. The similar *Batrachium* (RAN) has alternate leaves, and the green alga *Chara*, sometimes confused with hornwort, has jointed stems and a characteristic fetid odor.

CHENOPODIACEAE GOOSEFOOT FAMILY (CHN)

Disturbed soils, particularly in urban or ruderal sites, assume a late summer and fall aspect characterized by a welter of unattractive, hairy, white-mealy or spiny plants with inconspicuous greenish flowers, most belonging to the Goosefoot Family. Many ignore them because they are so nondescript and presumably difficult. But chenopods make up such an important part of the landscape, especially in desert-steppe, and mean so much, in terms of interpreting the condition of the land, that everyone should know the common species. Chenopods find their way to the dining table too. *Beta vulgaris* (red beets, swiss chard, and sugar beets) and *Spinacia oleracea* (spinach) belong here. The fruits of spinach have spines or prickles, hence the old name spinage. Chenopods are among the most poorly collected of our plants, with the result that we are unsure of what we really have here. *Atriplex* and *Chenopodium*, particularly, need to be collected with ripe fruit, and small packets of additional fruit should be collected, since they fall away easily.

1a. True shrubs, not merely woody at the base . . . . (2)
1b. Herbaceous or only woody near the base . . . . (3)

2a. Plants with linear, semiterete, green, succulent leaves and spine-tipped branchlets. **Sarcobatus**, GREASEWOOD
2b. Plants without spine-tipped branches or, if so, then the leaves flattened. **Atriplex**, SHADSCALE

3a. Stems jointed and bearing opposite scale leaves, the flowers sunken in depressions in the stem; succulent annuals. **Salicornia**, GLASSWORT
3b. Stems not as above, bearing green leaves, the flowers not sunken in the stem . . . . (4)

4a. Leaves rigid, spine-tipped; plants stiffly branched and forming large tumbleweeds. **Salsola**, RUSSIAN-THISTLE
4b. Leaves otherwise . . . . (5)

5a. Leaves and stem stellate-pubescent . . . . (6)
5b. Leaves and stems not stellate-pubescent . . . . (7)

6a. Leaves and stem densely stellate-tomentose, linear or oblong, with revolute margins; fruiting calyx with tufts of straight hairs; very white plants, becoming rusty in age. **Krascheninnikovia**, WINTERFAT
6b. Leaves green, elliptic-oblong, not revolute. **Axyris**

7a. Foliage with a strong, unpleasant odor; leaves pinnatifid or at least marginally toothed or lobed, glandular. **Teloxys**, WORMSEED
7b. Foliage without a distinctive odor; leaves entire or coarsely lobed, if regularly toothed then with farinose pubescence . . . . (8)

8a. Plants with pilose hairs on the foliage and stems; fruiting calyx with a strong hook or a papery horizontal wing arising from each calyx lobe at maturity. **Bassia**, IRONWEED
8b. Plants with farinose pubescence (small inflated hairs) or glabrous . . . (9)

9a. Monoecious or dioecious, the carpellate flowers enclosed by a pair of bracts of characteristic shape, either separate and forming a sandwich, or fused (like pita bread) around the fruit . . . . (10)
9b. Plants with perfect flowers, without specialized enclosing bracts . . . . (11)

10a. Fruit triangular-conical, the bracts fused and folded sideways, the apex 2-toothed; leaves broadly ovate, coarsely toothed; plants annual, prostrate, extremely variable, in unfavorable sites often reduced to 2 cotyledons and a small cluster of fruits. **Suckleya**
10b. Fruit variously shaped, the bracts separate or fused, not folded, often ornamented on the back and margins with tubercles or teeth; leaves lanceolate to triangular-hastate. **Atriplex**, SHADSCALE, SALTBUSH

11a. Fruiting calyx with a continuous horizontal wing completely surrounding it; tumbleweed with sinuate-dentate leaves. **Cycloloma**, WINGED PIGWEED
11b. Fruiting calyx wingless or at least not as above . . . . (12)

12a. Leaves linear, not farinose . . . . (13)
12b. Leaves wider than linear or, if so, then farinose . . . . (14)

13a. Flowers solitary in the axils of scarious-margined bracts; calyx consisting of a single delicate sepal on the inner side; smooth, widely branching tumbleweeds, never succulent. **Corispermum**, BUGSEED
13b. Flowers in clusters in the axils of the leaves; calyx complete; succulent-leaved plants of salt flats. **Suaeda**, SEABLITE

14a. Calyx a solitary, green, bractlike, fleshy sepal; leaves succulent, not mealy, hastate, passing gradually into leaflike bracts; stem prostrate-spreading. **Monolepis**, POVERTYWEED
14b. Calyx 5-parted, ± enveloping the fruit; leaves often white-farinose; stems ascending to erect. **Chenopodium**, GOOSEFOOT, LAMB'S QUARTERS

ATRIPLEX L. 1753 [the ancient Latin name]. SHADSCALE, SALTBUSH

1a. Perennials or shrubs, erect or rarely prostrate, but definitely woody at the base . . . . (2)
1b. Annual herbs . . . . (4)

2a. [1] Plants with some branches modified to form spines. **A. confertifolia** (Torrey & Fremont) Watson [crowded leaves]. Common on clay hills; aspects vary in plants of different sexes and ages. Low subshrubs with oblong to obovate glaucous leaves, the fruit bracts of the same color and texture.
2b. Plants not at all spiny . . . . (3)

3a. Shrubby throughout; fruit bracts with the margins spreading apart, creating four wings; plant widely and stiffly branched. **A. canescens** (Pursh) Nuttall, FOUR-WINGED SALTBUSH, **44A**. Common, sagebrush zone and greasewood flats on the plains and San Luis Valley.
3b. Woody only at the base; floral stems herbaceous and leafy. **A. gardneri** (Moquin) Standley [for the collector, Alexander Gordon, his name misspelled by Moquin!]. Very common and variable in stature and leaf shape. A number

of species have been proposed in this complex, but they are not clearly distinguishable (*A. nuttallii*).

4a. [1] Leaves green or greenish on both sides, sparsely mealy or scurfy if at all, only when young . . . . (5)
4b. Leaves gray or whitish with a permanent scurf, at least on the lower surface . . . . (7)

5a. [4] Carpellate flowers of two kinds, some with horizontal seeds and a 3-5-lobed perianth, the rest with vertical seeds and 2 bracts, the veins of the latter meeting above the base. **A. hortensis** L., GARDEN ORACHE. Adventive, ruderal weed; plants becoming deep red-purple at maturity.
5b. Carpellate flowers all of one kind, all with vertical seeds and 2 bracts, the veins of the latter meeting near or at the base . . . . (6)

6a. [5] Bracts elliptical or orbicular-cordate, smooth and usually entire; leaves triangular-hastate. **A. heterosperma** Bunge [with variable seeds]. Adventive, ruderal weed.
6b. Bracts rhombic to rhombic-ovate, usually with teeth or appendages on the back; leaves oblong or triangular-hastate. **A. patula** L. Adventive, ruderal weed (including plants that have been called *A. hastata*, which according to *Flora Europaea* is *A. prostrata*).

7a. [4] Fruiting bracts broadest below the middle; leaves coarsely dentate; bracts becoming hard. **A. rosea** L. Adventive, alkaline flats and roadsides.
7b. Fruiting bracts broadest at or above the middle . . . . (8)

8a. [7] Leaves cordate at the base or bracts cuneate at the base and truncate at the apex. **A. truncata** (Torrey) Gray. Alkaline flats.
8b. Leaves neither cordate at the base nor bracts cuneate or truncate . . . (9)

9a. Bracts becoming hard, almost bonelike. **A. rosea** L.
9b. Bracts not becoming especially hard; leaves thick, triangular, pinnately veined. **A. argentea** Nuttall [silver]. Alkaline flats and pond margins.

AXYRIS L. 1753 [Greek, *axyros*, unshorn]

One species, **A. amaranthoides** L. Adventive, established in fields in and around South Park.

BASSIA Allioni 1766 [for Ferdinand Bassi, eighteenth-century Italian botanist]. IRONWEED

1a. Mature calyx provided with a hook protruding from each sepal. **B. hyssopifolia** (Pallas) Kuntze, **45J**. Adventive, common weed of alkaline flats in the valleys.
1b. Mature calyx, at least of flowers produced late in the season, with veiny, triangular-ovate horizontal wings. **B. sieversiana** (Pallas) Weber [for J. Sievers, the collector], **44B, 45H**. Very abundant, especially in towns where it is the dominant tall weed in late autumn (*Kochia*). The wings on the sepals rarely develop on flowers of early season but appear on later flowers of the same plant! The annual species of *Kochia* recently have been merged with *Bassia*, a reasonable realignment.

CHENOPODIUM L. 1753 [Greek, *chen*, a goose, + *podion*, foot, alluding to the leaf shape]. GOOSEFOOT, LAMB'S QUARTERS

1a. Flowers in dense, globose clusters, fleshy or red at maturity, in stout, interrupted spikes; leaves green and glabrous, triangular or triangular-hastate and coarsely dentate . . . . (2)
1b. Flowers in smaller clusters, not becoming markedly fleshy or red; leaves often mealy pubescent (actually with minute inflated hairs) . . . . (3)

2a. Flowers becoming bright red and fleshy at maturity; clusters about 1 cm diameter, not numerous. **C. capitatum** (L.) Ascherson, STRAWBERRY BLITE, **47**. Adventive along trails and in shaded woods in the mountains.
2b. Flowers remaining green, even at maturity when the seeds are shed; clusters less than 5 mm diameter, very numerous in a terminal spike interrupted by leafy bracts. **C. foliosum** (Moench) Ascherson. Adventive. Similar sites (*C. overi*).

3a. Seed usually vertical (the fruit thus laterally flattened), or some of them horizontal in the same cluster . . . . (4)
3b. Seed usually horizontal, the fruit then flattened from the top . . . . . . (5)

4a. Leaves densely mealy beneath. **C. glaucum** L., **46C**. Adventive, common in drying mud of pondshores.
4b. Leaves green, glabrous or only slightly mealy beneath. **C. rubrum** L. Adventive, on muddy pondshores.

5a. Leaves with 1 vein from the base . . . . (6)
5b. Leaves with 3 or more veins from the base . . . . (8)

6a. Pericarp readily separable from the seed. **C. subglabrum** (Watson) Nelson. Infrequent on the plains.
6b. Pericarp closely attached to the seed . . . . (7)

7a. Fruit 0.9-1.2 mm diameter. **C. leptophyllum** (Nuttall) Watson [narrow-leaved]. Sagebrush and piñon-juniper.
7b. Fruit 1.3-1.6 mm diameter; sepals enlarging slightly in fruit, fused for over half their length, with an undulate collar from the sinuses. **C. cycloides** Nelson. Rare or infrequent, southeastern plains.

8a. Pericarp distinctly pitted; fruits appearing honeycombed on the surface. (9)
8b. Pericarp smooth to variously roughened; fruits never appearing honeycombed . . . . (10)

9a. Pericarp white at maturity; fruits about 1 mm diameter. **C. watsonii** Nelson. Infrequently collected on the plains, Platte and Arkansas River valleys.
9b. Pericarp transparent, fruits always dark, 1-2.5 mm diameter. **C. berlandieri** Moquin [for Jean Louis Berlandier, 1805-1851, Swiss botanist collector in Texas]. Abundant, native, ruderal weed.

10a. Lower leaves toothed above the base, never either entire or with only basal lobes or teeth . . . . (11)
10b. Lower leaves nearly always entire above the base, sometimes with 1 or 2 lobes or teeth at the base . . . . (12)

11a. Fruits 1.5-2.5 mm diameter; leaves with 1-4 large, divergent, prominent teeth. **C. simplex** (Torrey) Rafinesque. Infrequent or rare, in rather deeply shaded woods in the outer foothills of the Front Range. The leaves are very large, thin, and triangular (*C. gigantospermum*).

Plate 1. ***Harbouria trachypleura*** Weber
WHISK BROOM PARSLEY

Plate 2. ***Pachystima myrsinites*** Weber
MOUNTAIN-LOVER

Plate 3. ***Shepherdia canadensis*** Weber
BUFFALO BERRY

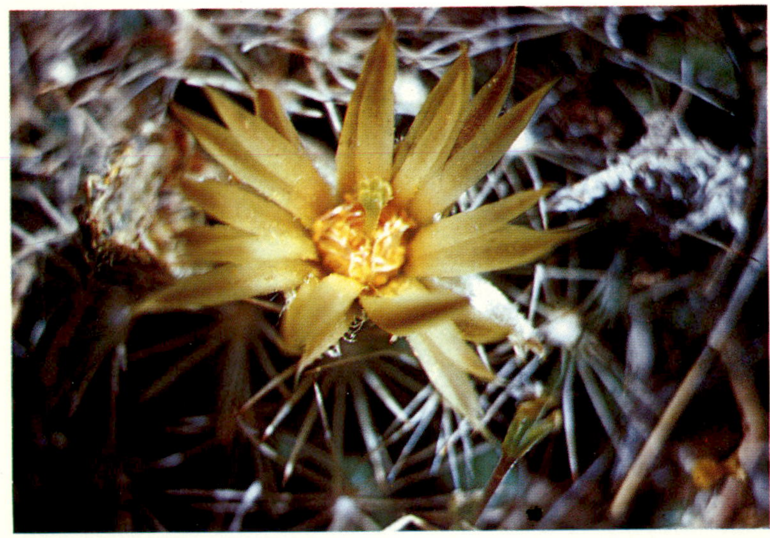

Plate 4. ***Coryphantha missouriensis*** Weber
NIPPLE CACTUS

Plate 5. ***Arceuthobium campylopodum*** Weber
MISTLETOE

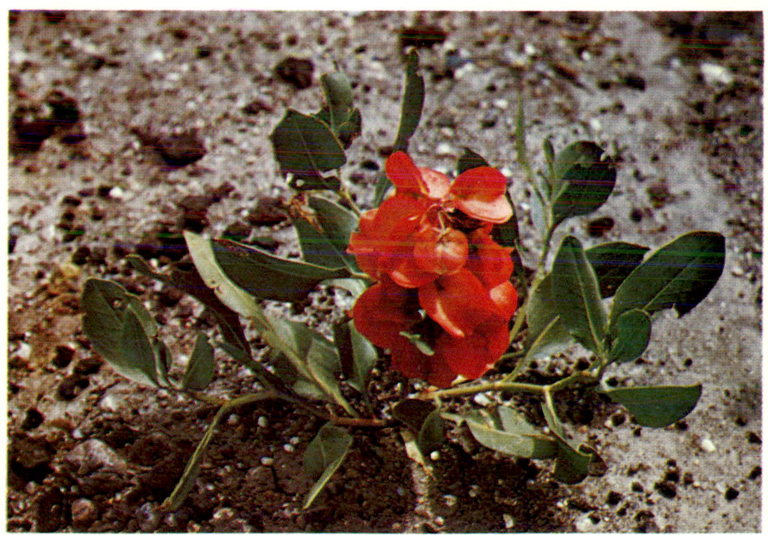

Plate 6. ***Rumex venosus*** Roberts
WILD "BEGONIA"

Plate 7. ***Pulsatilla patens*** Roberts
PASQUE FLOWER

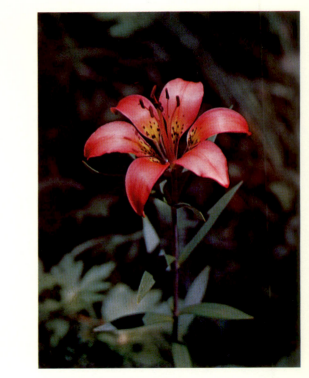

Plate 8. ***Lilium philadelphicum*** Roberts
WOOD LILY

Plate 9. ***Eustoma grandiflorum*** Roberts
TULIP GENTIAN

Plate 10. ***Oreocarya virgata*** Weber
MINERS CANDLE

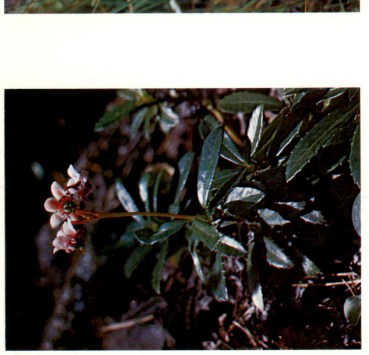

Plate 11. ***Chimaphila umbellata*** Roberts
PIPSISSEWA

Plate 12. ***Gentianopsis thermalis*** Roberts
FRINGED GENTIAN

Plate 13. ***Frasera speciosa*** Roberts
MONUMENT PLANT

Plate 14. ***Mentzelia decapetala*** Roberts
EVENING STAR

Plate 15. ***Leucocrinum montanum*** Weber
SAND LILY

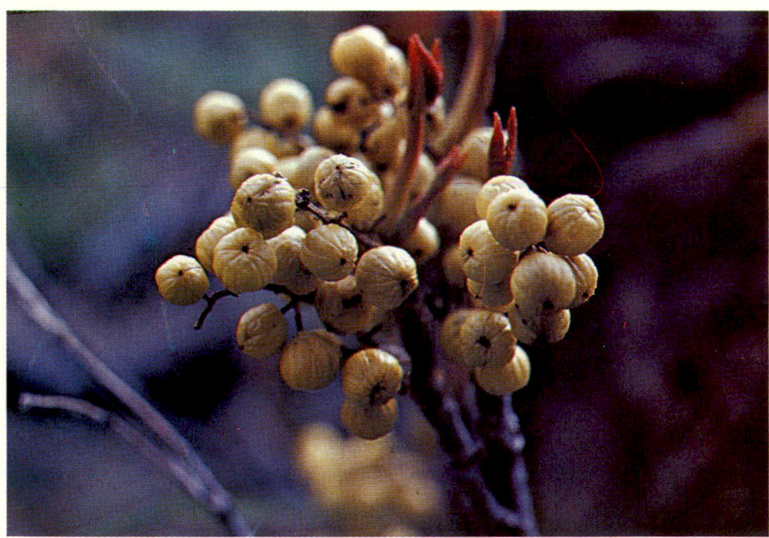

Plate 16. ***Toxicodendron rydbergii*** Weber
POISON IVY, fruit

Plate 17. ***Stanleya pinnata*** Weber
PRINCES PLUME

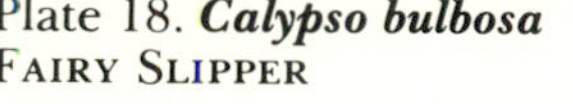

Plate 18. ***Calypso bulbosa*** Roberts
FAIRY SLIPPER

Plate 19. ***Aquilegia caerulea*** f. ***daileyae*** Roberts
SPURLESS COLUMBINE

Plate 20. ***Cypripedium fasciculatum*** Roberts
PURPLE LADY'S SLIPPER

Plate 21. ***Abronia fragrans*** Roberts
SAND-VERBENA

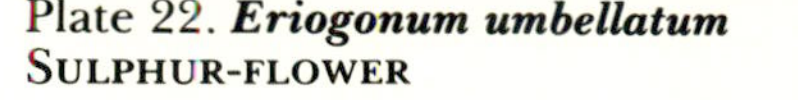

Plate 22. ***Eriogonum umbellatum*** Roberts
SULPHUR-FLOWER

Plate 23. ***Mirabilis multiflora*** Roberts
WILD FOUR-O'CLOCK

Plate 24. ***Drymocallis fissa*** Roberts
CINQUEFOIL

Plate 25. ***Veratrum tenuipetalum*** Weber
CORN HUSK LILY

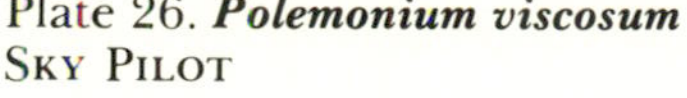
Plate 26. ***Polemonium viscosum*** Weber
SKY PILOT

Plate 27. ***Polanisia dodecandra*** Weber
CLAMMY-WEED

Plate 28. ***Telesonix jamesii*** Roberts
TELESONIX

Plate 29. ***Cirsium scopulorum*** Weber
ALPINE THISTLE

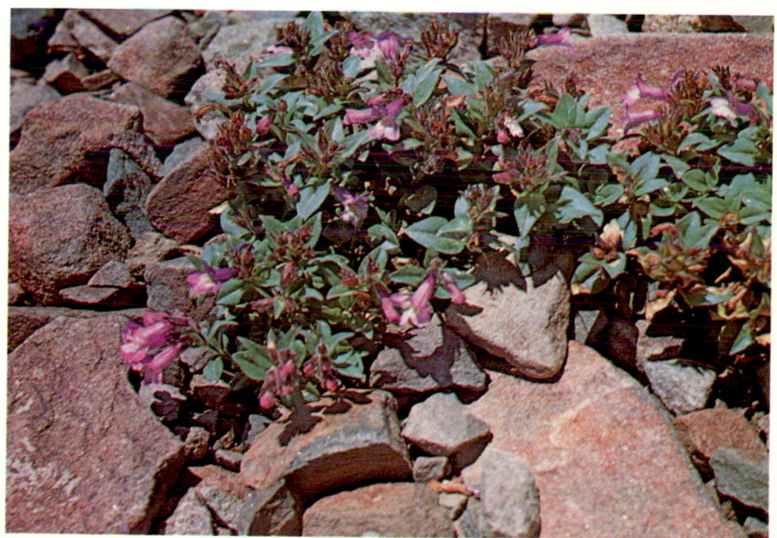

Plate 30. ***Penstemon harbourii*** Weber
SCREE PENSTEMON

Plate 31. ***Argemone polyanthemos*** Roberts
PRICKLY POPPY

Plate 32. ***Clematis columbiana*** Weber
ROCKY MOUNTAIN CLEMATIS

11b. Fruits usually 1.6 mm or less diameter; leaves without prominent, salient teeth. **C. album** L., **46A**. Adventive, in waste ground; resembling *C. berlandieri* but for the smooth fruits (*C. hians*).

12a. Lower leaves triangular to sometimes rhombic, commonly with rounded tips . . . . (13)
12b. Lower leaves ovate or narrower, never triangular . . . . (14)

13a. Fruits 0.9-1.1 mm diameter; sepals covering fruits at maturity. **C. incanum** (Watson) Heller [hoary]. Bare clay flats. This species, unfortunately, shows very many transitions, on the one hand toward *C. fremontii*, and, on the other, toward *C. leptophyllum*.
13b. Fruits 1.2-1.4 mm diameter; sepals exposing the fruits at maturity. **C. fremontii** Watson [for J. C. Frémont], **46B**. Common woodland plant, especially in piñon-juniper and oak.

14a. Lower leaves oval to oblong, entire, thick and succulent, moderately to densely farinose above; stem branched widely from the base. **C. desiccatum** Nelson. Frequent on the plains.
14b. Lower leaves broadly ovate to oblong, lanceolate or rarely nearly linear, entire or with basal lobes or teeth, usually thin, never succulent, sparsely farinose to nearly glabrous above; stem solitary or sparingly ascending-branched . . . . (15)

15a. Lower leaves mostly broadly ovate to oblong, 1.5-3 times as long as wide. **C. atrovirens** Rydberg [dark green]. Frequent along roadsides, up into the middle altitudes.
15b. Lower leaves mostly lanceolate to rarely nearly linear, 3-5 times as long as wide. **C. pratericola** Rydberg. On the plains, southeastern counties.

CORISPERMUM L. 1753 [Greek, *coris*, bedbug, + *sperma*, seed]. BUGSEED
One species, **C. hyssopifolium** L., **45B**. Adventive, sand blowouts on the eastern plains, North Park, and the San Luis Valley.

CYCLOLOMA Moquin 1840 [Greek, *cyclos*, circle, + *loma*, border, from the encircling calyx wing]. WINGED PIGWEED
One species, **C. atriplicifolium** (Sprengel) Coulter, **44C, 45I**. Native weed of sandy ground, dunes, and sandy bottomland on the plains, flowering in late summer and turning red at maturity. A tumbleweed.

KRASCHENINNIKOVIA Guldenstaedt 1772 [for I. M. Krascheninnikov, 1713-1755, Russian botanist]. WINTERFAT
One species, **K. lanata** (Pursh) Meeuse & Smit [woolly], **44D**. Forming large, pure stands on gravelly benches in the lower river valleys (*Eurotia*, *Ceratoides*).

MONOLEPIS Schrader 1831 [Greek, *monos*, single, + *lepis*, scale]. POVERTYWEED
One species, **M. nuttalliana** (Schultes) Greene, **45F**. Muddy ditches and edges of drying ponds. Plants prostrate; leaves hastately lobed at base, over 12 mm long; flowers in axillary clusters. The translucent ovary wall has a beautifully cellular-reticulate pattern!

SALICORNIA L. 1753 [Greek, *sal*, salt, + Latin, *cornu*, horn]. GLASSWORT
One species, **S. europaea** L. subsp. **rubra** (Nelson) Breitung. Frequent on borders of alkaline ponds and river oxbows, North Park. Easily spotted from a distance by its brilliant red autumn color.

SALSOLA L. 1753 [Latin, *salsus*, salty]. RUSSIAN-THISTLE

1a. Bracts broad-based, with stiffly flaring spine tips; plant extremely prickly, difficult to handle, the branches stiffly spreading. **S. australis** R. Brown [southern], **45G, 48B**. Abundant, native (?) tumbleweed (*S. iberica*, *S. pestifer*).
1b. Bracts narrow-based, the tips directed forward; plant easily handled, the branches elongate, gracefully curving. **S. collina** Pallas [of hills], **48A**. Adventive on the plains. A species common in Altai.

SARCOBATUS Nees 1841 [Greek, *sarco*, fleshy, + *batia*, bush]. GREASEWOOD

One species, **S. vermiculatus** (Hooker) Torrey [worm-eaten], **45A**. Abundant on alkaline flats. A poisonous plant containing calcium oxalate, nevertheless a useful forage plant if the diet is mixed and sheep do not graze in pure stands.

SUAEDA Forskål 1777 [an Arabic name]. SEABLITE

1a. A fleshy conical outgrowth on the back of 1 or more tepals, this shriveling in age, giving the flower a contorted appearance. **S. calceoliformis** (Hooker) Moquin [slipper-shaped], **45D**. Locally abundant on drying, alkaline mud flats (*S. depressa*).
1b. Tepals thin, not developing as above. **S. nigra** (Rafinesque) Macbride [black]. Similar habitats.

SUCKLEYA Gray 1876 [for Dr. George Suckley, zoölogist on the Pacific Railroad expedition, 1853-1855]

One species, **S. suckleyana** (Torrey) Rydberg. Locally frequent on drying pond borders and alkaline, often irrigated, soils, from Greeley to Colorado Springs. A prostrate-spreading plant with petiolate, ovate, coarsely toothed leaves. The plants are extremely adaptable to dry conditions and often are reduced to a few leaves and fruits, only 1 cm or so high.

TELOXYS Moquin 1834 [Greek, *telos*, tip, + *oxys*, sharp, referring to the suppressed lateral floral branchlets that become a terminal spine] (formerly included in *Chenopodium*). WORMSEED

1a. Inflorescence of small sessile clusters along straight, elongate spikes; leaves often 10 cm or more long. **T. ambrosioides** (L.) Weber [like *Ambrosia*]. Adventive, a weed in cultivated land.
1b. Inflorescence open, cymosely branched; leaves less than 4 cm long, deeply pinnatifid . . . . (2)

2a. Cymes with central flower developed, the lateral ones abortive and their pedicels becoming naked and almost spinelike; **T. graveolens** (Willdenow) Weber [heavy-odor]. Adventive, upper Arkansas Valley.
2b. Cymes with all flowers equally developed. **T. botrys** (L.) Weber [bunch of grapes], **46D**. Adventive along roadsides, thriving in gravelly soils of the outer foothills.

CISTACEAE ROCKROSE FAMILY (CIS)

Cistus, the rockrose, is a very important genus of evergreen shrubs of the Mediterranean region, with white or pink, characteristically crinkled petals. In America, probably the best known genus is *Hudsonia*, which forms dense shrubby mats on sand dunes along the Atlantic coast.

CROCANTHEMUM Spach 1836 [Latin, *croceus*, saffron-colored, the saffron plant being a *Crocus*]

One species, **C. bicknellii** (Fernald) Janchen, FROSTWEED. A rather nondescript plant, infrequent or rare at the base of the outer foothills of the Front Range and Black Forest (*Helianthemum*). The plant has a cluster of unbranched, wiry stems 2-6 dm high. The flowers are yellow, with 3-10 stamens and canescent elliptic-oval leaves. Only the sterile terminal flowers have petals; many small cleistogamous flowers occur in clusters on short branchlets below them. These produce capsules 2-3 mm in diameter.

COMMELINACEAE SPIDERWORT FAMILY (CMM)

The genus from which the family takes its name contains a homely little weed in city backyards in the eastern United States and northern Europe called the dayflower. The flowers last only through one day, then simply melt into a slimy residue. Linnaeus explained the name he gave the plant: "*Commelina* has flowers with three petals, two of which are showy [blue] while the third [white] is not conspicuous; [named] from the two botanists called Commelin; for the third died before accomplishing anything in botany." The stamen filaments of these flowers have long hairs composed of beadlike strings of enormous cells that can be seen by the naked eye; cell division can be followed with a microscope without special treatment.

1a. Petals all purple; flowers long-pediceled, the bracts not different from foliage leaves. **Tradescantia**, SPIDERWORT

1b. Petals 3, all blue or 2 blue and 1 white; flowers arising on short pedicels from a folded, ovate bract with a long, attenuate apex. **Commelina**, DAYFLOWER

COMMELINA L. 1753 [see above]. DAYFLOWER

1a. Petals 2 blue and 1 white; spathe not drawn out into a narrow tip. **C. erecta** L. var. **angustifolia** (Michaux) Fernald. In gulches, southeasternmost counties (*C. crispa*).

1b. Petals all blue; spathe drawn out into a long, narrow tip. **C. dianthifolia** Delile [with leaves like *Dianthus*, CRY]. One record, from gulches south of Colorado Springs.

TRADESCANTIA L. 1753 [for John Tradescant, gardener to Charles I of England]. SPIDERWORT

One species, **T. occidentalis** (Britton) Smyth. Common in gravelly soil along the bases of roadcuts.

CONVALLARIACEAE MAYFLOWER FAMILY (CVL)

Recently segregated from Liliaceae as a family and characterized by having leafy stems from rhizomes. The flowers are white, with very narrow tepals, and the fruits are red or green berries. Our only genus, *Smilacina*, was recently reunited with *Maianthemum*, which includes the Canada mayflower of the eastern and far western states. *Convallaria majalis* is lily-of-the-valley.

MAIANTHEMUM G. H. Weber 1780 [Greek, *Maia*, May, + *anthos*, flower] (formerly *Smilacina*). FALSE SOLOMON'S SEAL

1a. Flowers few, in a simple raceme; leaves lanceolate. **M. stellatum** (L.) Link. Throughout the lower and middle altitudes in meadows, gulches, streamsides, and forests, and far out on the plains on the sides of gulches and arroyos.

1b. Flowers numerous, in a panicle; leaves broadly oval. **M. amplexicaule** (Nuttall) Weber [clasping-leaved]. Common throughout the forested mountains. The common name comes from the resemblance of the circular leaf scar on the rhizome to a signet. Our species is a diploid, while *M. racemosum*, under which it often has been treated, is tetraploid. Contrary to claims, these do not intergrade.

CONVOLVULACEAE MORNINGGLORY FAMILY (CNV)

Morningglories are favorite ornamental climbers for porches and patios, but several members of the family are used in other important ways. *Dichondra repens* is used as a ground cover in place of grass for lawns in southern California. *Ipomoea batatas* is the true sweet potato (as opposed to the yam, *Dioscorea*, a monocot in the Dioscoreaceae). It is a staple crop in Melanesia, and its introduction, probably from America, is thought to have been effected through Polynesian migrations. *Ipomoea tuberosa* is the curious "wooden-rose" of dry bouquets. The parasitic dodder, once included in this family, now is placed in the Cuscutaceae.

1a. Leaves linear, glabrous. **Ipomoea**, BUSH MORNINGGLORY

1b. Leaves not linear or, if nearly linear, not glabrous . . . . (2)

2a. Erect, not at all climbing or creeping or twining; flowers lavender; leaves elliptic-oblong, gray-pilose. **Evolvulus**

2b. Creeping or twining; flowers white, or pink on the back; leaves triangular-hastate, smooth or nearly so . . . . (3)

3a. Calyx enclosed by large bracts; flowers over 3 cm long; leaves over 5 cm long. **Calystegia**, HEDGE BINDWEED

3b. Calyx not enclosed by large bracts; flowers less than 2 cm long; leaves also small. **Convolvulus**, BINDWEED

CALYSTEGIA R. Brown 1810 [Greek, *calyx* + *stegos*, roof, cover, alluding to the bracts]. HEDGE BINDWEED

1a. Leaf blade basally 2-angled; plants usually glabrous or with a few hairs on the petioles. **C. sepium** (L.) R. Brown subsp. **angulata** Brummitt, **50b**. Infrequent and local, on fences and hedgerows on the plains (*Convolvulus*).

1b. Leaf blade basally rounded; plants normally pubescent on all vegetative parts. **C. macounii** (Greene) Brummitt. Similar distribution (*Convolvulus interior*).

CONVOLVULUS L. 1753 [Latin, *convolvere*, to entwine]. BINDWEED

1a. Leaves almost as broad as long; calyx 3-5 mm long, inconspicuously puberulent or glabrate. **C. arvensis** L. CREEPING JENNY, **50D**. Adventive, common creeping weed on roadsides and in lawns, very difficult to eradicate because of its deep roots and brittle rhizomes.

1b. Leaves usually much longer than broad; calyx 6-12 mm long, densely pubescent. **C. equitans** Benth. Arkansas River Valley. In its extreme expression, this species has leaves with narrow blades and hastate basal lobes with additional teeth or lobes. It is not an aggressive weed and does not form large patches.

EVOLVULUS L. 1753 [Latin, *evolvere*, to unroll, hence, not twining]

One species, **E. nuttallianus** Roemer & Schultes, **50a**. Common in sandy soil on the plains.

IPOMOEA L. 1753 [Greek, *ips*, worm, + *homoios*, resembling; from the twining habit]. MORNINGGLORY

One species, **I. leptophylla** Torrey, BUSH MORNINGGLORY, **Pl. 63**. Frequent on the plains. The massive root almost has the diameter of a fencepost. Flowers are red-purple with a darker throat.

COPTACEAE MEADOWRUE FAMILY (COP)

(formerly in Ranunculaceae)

THALICTRUM L. 1753 [a name of some plant mentioned by Dioscorides]. MEADOWRUE

1a. Plant very tall, deep green; leaflets 3-lobed, the lobes usually entire; inflorescence a showy pyramidal panicle; achenes not flattened. **T. dasycarpum** Fischer & Ave-Lallemant [hairy-fruited]. A tall, handsome plant, abundant in late spring along irrigation ditches in the piedmont valleys. Plants are sometimes over 2 m tall. The only species on the plains.

1b. Plant delicate, slender; leaflets 3-lobed, the lobes usually lobed again; achenes flattened . . . . (2)

2a. Stems very low, less than 20 cm high, leaves chiefly basal; flowers perfect, in a simple raceme; peat fens and tundra, alpine and subalpine. **T. alpinum** L., ALPINE MEADOWRUE, **95B**.

2b. Stem tall and leafy; flowers in panicles, perfect or unisexual (flowers of each sex, however, may be present on the same stem) . . . . (3)

3a. Upper edge of carpel straight or concave, lower edge deeply convex, lateral parallel veins not prominent, but mature carpel with oblique veins. **T. sparsiflorum** Turczaninov [few-flowered], **95A**. Shaded ravines and aspen groves.

3b. Upper and lower edges of carpels convex, lateral parallel veins prominent. **T. fendleri** Engelmann, **95C**. Aspen groves and meadows, montane and subalpine, our most common species.

CORNACEAE DOGWOOD FAMILY (COR)

The name dogwood is given to a great number of unrelated trees, and the origin of the name is unknown. An is said that the wood is so free from scratchy silica that jewelers used small splinters of it to clean out the pivot-holes in watches, and opticians for removing dust from small, deep-seated lenses. Flowering dogwoods (*Cornus*) are found in the ancient relictual Tertiary forests of Eastern and Pacific North America and Japan.

1a. Shrub with red branches; inflorescence not subtended by petallike bracts; leaves opposite. **Swida**, RED OSIER

1b. Herb (10-20 cm tall) from a woody rhizome; inflorescence subtended by 4 to 5 white, petallike bracts (a flowering dogwood in miniature); leaves in a whorl at the top of the stem. **Chamaepericlymenum**, BUNCHBERRY

CHAMAEPERICLYMENUM Hill 1756 [Greek, *chamae*, on the ground, + *Periclymenium*, a honeysuckle]. BUNCHBERRY

One species, **C. canadense** (L.) Ascherson & Graebner, **51B**. Subalpine forests of the Front Range and probably the Park Range (*Cornus*).

SWIDA Opiz 1838 [derivation obscure]. RED OSIER

One species, **S. sericea** (L.) Holub, **51A**. Common in shaded foothill and montane canyons (*Cornus stolonifera*).

CRASSULACEAE STONECROP FAMILY (CRS)

Most sedums are succulents, but not all succulents are sedums. Desert and alpine areas all over the world have evolved the succulent habit in several unrelated families. The Mesembryanthemaceae of South Africa are famous for their succulent leaves that resemble pebbles, North African euphorbias resemble our Saguaro cacti, and many chenopods of saline ground are succulents. In order to make good herbarium specimens of members of this family the stems must be briefly boiled or subjected to a heat lamp to destroy the protective function of the epidermis. Otherwise, plants will survive long periods and actually keep growing in a plant press.

1a. Plants minute, the stems not over 1 cm long, with linear opposite leaves and 4-merous flowers; semiaquatic, rooted in mud. **Tillaea**, PYGMYWEED

1b. Plants well developed; leaves alternate; terrestrial . . . . (2)

2a. Flowers yellow; leaves fleshy, plump to almost round in cross-section; flowering shoots up to 1 dm high. **Amerosedum**, YELLOW STONECROP

2b. Flowers purple, pink, or white; leaves thin; flowering shoots up to several dm tall . . . . (3)

3a. Petals pink or white; flowers perfect, clustered in the axils of the upper leaves; midrib prominent on leaf underside. **Clementsia**, ROSE CROWN

3b. Petals deep red-purple; flowers usually unisexual (and plants dioecious), in a flat-topped terminal cluster; midrib imbedded, not easily visible. **Rhodiola**, KING'S CROWN

AMEROSEDUM Löve & Löve 1985. [American + *Sedum*]. YELLOW STONECROP

One species, **A. lanceolatum** (Torrey) Löve & Löve, **51E**. Common on stony ground from the plains up to the tundra (*Sedum*).

CLEMENTSIA Rose 1903 [for F. E. Clements]. ROSE CROWN

One species, **C. rhodantha** (Gray) Rose, **51F**. Common along subalpine rivulets and in peat fens (*Sedum*). Endemic in the southern Rockies, but a close relative, *C. semenovii*, almost identical to it, grows in the mountains of central Asia.

RHODIOLA L. 1753 [Greek, *rhodon*, rose-colored]. KING'S CROWN

One species, **R. integrifolia** Rafinesque, **51D**. Moist slopes and tundra, usually at higher altitudes than the preceding but often growing with it (*Sedum*). *Rhodiola* is essentially a genus of the central Asiatic mountains. Because of its peculiar sexuality, this species has been placed in the new genus *Tolmatchevia* by Löve & Löve.

TILLAEA L. 1753 [for Michaelangelo Tilli, 1655-1740, Italian botanist]. PYGMYWEED

One species, **T. aquatica** L. Reported by Rydberg in 1906 from Twin Lakes. Probably the site has been destroyed. The plant is exceedingly minute, the spreading stems no more than 1 cm long, with tiny, opposite, linear, fleshy leaves united by a sheathing base, and solitary flowers in the leaf axils. The flowers have 4 sepals, 4 petals, and 4 stamens. In vegetative condition one might confuse this with *Callitriche*, but in the submersed forms of *Callitriche* the leaves are very flaccid, and not at all fleshy. The habitat is muddy pondshores. Perhaps the plant still persists in the wet habitats feeding Twin Lakes.

CROSSOSOMATACEAE CROSSOSOMA FAMILY (CRO)

A very small family, until recently thought to include only the two genera, *Apacheria* and *Crossosoma* of the desert Southwest. Recently our only genus was reassigned to this family from the Celastraceae.

FORSELLESIA Greene 1893 [for Jacob H. af Forselles, 1785-1855, Swedish mining engineer]

One species, **F. planitierum** Ensign, **51C**. A low, densely branched, spiny shrub with small oblanceolate or elliptic leaves and small, white, axillary flowers. Timpas limestone outcrops in the Arkansas River drainage.

CUCURBITACEAE GOURD FAMILY (CUC)

Cultivated cucurbits are a legacy to us from aboriginal man, who used them not only for food but for all sorts of kitchen utensils, musical rattles, floats for fish nets, and drinking cups. To emphasize their importance in our culture, one only has to list a few: squash, pumpkin, calabash or gourd, watermelon, canteloupe, cucumber. Besides these, there are dozens of cucurbits used throughout the tropical regions that are quite unknown to northerners. The inner, spongy pulp of the genus *Luffa* is the original "chore-boy," called dishcloth gourd. Flowers of cucurbits are usually unisexual. Food crops depend on pollination by honeybees and solitary bees.

1a. Vine trailing over the ground and over low plants; leaves rough-pubescent, ovate to triangular, denticulate; flowers yellow, solitary, about 10 cm long; fruit a woody, dry, striped, baseball-shaped gourd. **Cucurbita**, GOURD, CALABAZILLA

1b. Vine climbing over fences and on tall shrubs; leaves palmately 5-lobed, glabrous; flowers small, white, in racemes or panicles; fruit prickly, papery, balloonlike with a spongy center . . . . (2)

2a. Leaves palmately lobed not more than halfway to the base; anthers more or less united but clearly more than one, opening longitudinally. **Echinocystis**, BALSAM-APPLE, MOCK CUCUMBER

2b. Leaves palmately compound (some may be only deeply parted); anthers fused and with the appearance of a ring, opening all around. **Cyclanthera**

CUCURBITA L. 1753 [the classical name]. GOURD

One species, **C. foetidissima** Humboldt, Bonpland & Kunth [stinking], CALABAZILLA, **49B**. Common along roadsides in the southern counties. Native here, but distributed widely as a useful plant among the ancient peoples.

CYCLANTHERA Schrader 1831 [Greek, *cyclos*, circle, + *anthera*, anther]

One species, **C. dissecta** (Torrey & Gray) Arnott. Easternmost counties, blooming in late summer.

ECHINOCYSTIS Torrey & Gray 1840 [Greek, *echinos*, hedgehog, + *cystis*, bladder]. BALSAM-APPLE, MOCK CUCUMBER

One species, **E. lobata** (Michaux) Torrey & Gray, **49A**. Common across the eastern plains and San Luis Valley.

CUSCUTACEAE DODDER FAMILY (CUS)

The dodders are parasitic plants lacking green leaves and consisting only of long, slender, intertangled orange threads climbing over various kinds of plants and attaching themselves to the stems by suckers (haustoria) that penetrate the tissues of the host. The flowers are globular and white. Identification is difficult at best, and impossible without the presence of well-developed flowers and mature fruit. Until recently, most texts included this family with the Convolvulaceae. The seeds evidently have enough food supply to permit them to germinate on the ground, but they must very soon attach their stems to the proper host. Some dodders are very injurious to crops, at least in Eurasia. The name dodder seems to have its origin in old northwestern European languages, describing "yellowness." In all of our species, the capsule is circumscissile. The species are still too little known here to enable us to give much information about their distribution. They are too often collected in immature stages.

1a. Stigmas elongated. **Cuscuta**
1b. Stigmas capitate. **Grammica**

CUSCUTA L. 1753 [derivation uncertain, thought to be from Arabic]. DODDER

One species, **C. approximata** Babington. Apparently localized in the Boulder area, BL, JF.

GRAMMICA Loureiro 1790 [Greek, *grammicos*, linear, alluding to the stringy stems]. DODDER, **50C**

1a. Flowers subtended by large bracts that resemble the sepals. **G. cuspidata** (Engelmann) Hadaç & Chrtek. Mesa de Maya area, LA.
1b. Flowers with scalelike bracts not resembling the sepals . . . . (2)

2a. Corolla tube not enclosed within the short calyx. **G. indecora** (Choisy) Weber. The most common species throughout the plains.
2b. Corolla tube about as long as the calyx and more or less enclosed by it; corolla lobes reflexed. **G. umbellata** Humboldt, Bonpland & Kunth. One collection from the lower Arkansas River Valley.

CYPERACEAE SEDGE FAMILY (CYP)

The word sedge is derived as far back as Middle English *segge* and Teutonic *seg*, and is related to the modern German *Säge,* meaning saw. Many sedges have sharp cutting edges on the leaves, and some of them are actually minutely saw-toothed. Relatively few sedges are of major economic importance, but *Cyperus papyrus* was famous from antiquity as a paper source, and the Incas of Peru used (and still do) the giant reeds (*Scirpus totora*) of Lake Titicaca for making rafts to create land surfaces in the shallow water and for building their houses. Thor Heyerdal proved that such papyrus rafts are seaworthy. And, of course, the most famous cradle of Biblical history was fashioned from papyrus.

1a. Flower cluster resembling a powderpuff or tassel, the perianth consisting of many long, white, silky hairs. **Eriophorum**, COTTONSEDGE, BOGWOOL

1b. Flower cluster not as above . . . . (2)

2a. Floral bracts (scales) in two distinct rows, the spike flattened . . . . . . (3)
2b. Floral bracts arranged in ascending spirals, the spikes not distinctly flattened . . . . (4)

3a. Rachilla of the spike continuous, the scales gradually deciduous from the base of the rachilla to the apex, or articulated, the rachilla breaking at the base of each scale. **Cyperus**
3b. Rachilla of the spike articulated at the base, neither persistent as a unit nor breaking up into segments. **Mariscus**

4a. Flowers unisexual, the plants and spikes either entirely staminate or entirely carpellate, or with both staminate and carpellate flowers in the same spike; gynoecium enclosed in a saclike structure (perigynium) . . . . (5)
4b. Flowers perfect (all alike and never grouped into different types of spikes on the same plant); gynoecium merely subtended by a scalelike bract . . . (6)

5a. Perigynium split down the middle throughout its length with overlapping margins (like the open sheath of a grass). **Kobresia**
5b. Perigynium completely closed except at the apex where the style protrudes (like the closed sheath of a grass). **Carex**

6a. Spike solitary, terminal . . . . (7)
6b. Spikes more than 1, or if solitary, not terminal but protruding from the side of the stem . . . . (8)

7a. Achene red-brown to black, with a differentiated conical or flattened cap (stylopodium); leaves lacking blades. **Eleocharis**, SPIKERUSH
7b. Achene black, lacking a differentiated stylopodium; leaves with short but definite blades. **Trichophorum**

8a. Spikes protruding sideways from the side of the stem or, if appearing terminal, a single erect bract appearing to continue the stem upward . (9)
8b. Spikes terminal, subtended by several leaflike bracts . . . . (11)

9a. Plants hardly over 10 cm tall; leaves and stems very slender, hairlike; spike solitary, rarely 2-3, the tips of the scales slightly spreading. **Hemicarpha**
9b. Plants taller; leaves and stems broader; spikes more than one . . . . . (10)

10a. Spikes numerous, oval, pedunculate, and culms terete, or spikes few, sessile and lateral, and stems trigonous. **Schoenoplectus**, TULE; BULRUSH
10b. Spikes few, cylindric, sessile at the tip of the stem; culms terete. **Amphiscirpus**

11a. Spikes large, over 1 cm long, almost sessile. **Bolboschoenus**
11b. Spikes small, less than 5 mm long, panicled . . . . (12)

12a. Leaves narrowly linear, about 1 mm wide; base of style swollen, but not persisting on the achene. **Fimbristylis**
12b. Leaves broader; base of style swollen and forming a small cone at the top of the achene. **Scirpus**, BULRUSH

AMPHISCIRPUS Oteng-Yeboah 1974 [Greek, *amphi*, around, + *Scirpus*]

One species, **A. nevadensis** (Watson) Yeboah. Alkaline flats, South Park, San Luis Valley. The achenes in this genus are distinctly cellular-reticulate under a lens (*Scirpus*).

BOLBOSCHOENUS Palla 1907 [Greek, *bolbos*, swelling, + *schoinos*, rush, alluding to the stylopodium]

One species, **B. maritimus** (L.) Palla subsp. **paludosus** (Nelson) Löve & Löve, **55A**. Sloughs and ditches in the lower valleys. The large, football-shaped spikelets, leafy subtending bracts and triangular stem are diagnostic (*Scirpus paludosus*).

CAREX L. 1753 [Greek, *keirein*, to cut, alluding to the sharp-edged leaves of many species]. (Key modified from an earlier one contributed by Miriam Colson Fritts.)

1a. Spikes 1 to a culm (careful observation needed here; several species may appear to have 1 spike but on close examination show more than 1 rachis) . . . . **Key A**

1b. Spikes more than 1 to a culm, although sometimes crowded so as to appear single (careful examination will reveal separate rachises or branches of the inflorescence) . . . . (2)

2a. Spikes in a ball-like cluster, the individual ones not easily detected by manipulation, only by dissection; scales brown, never black . . . . . . **Key B**

2b. Spikes either separate or clustered but always distinguishable without dissection . . . . (3)

3a. Spikes sessile, never black unless perigynia wing-margined or very sharp-edged, usually with staminate and carpellate flowers in the same spike, the terminal spike never markedly different from the rest . . . . **Key C**

3b. Spikes pedunculate (at least the lowermost one), or black, or with markedly different staminate terminal spikes . . . . **Key D**

KEY A. (Solitary spikes)

1a. Plants in dense clumps, not obviously rhizomatous; leaf blades always narrow and filiform . . . . (2)

1b. Plants with obvious rhizomes, the culms solitary or a few together; leaf blades up to 3 mm wide . . . . (8)

2a. Perigynium rounded and beakless at the apex, many-nerved. **C. leptalea** Wahlenberg [delicate]. Moist foothill canyons, known from near Colorado Springs and the Tarryall Range.

2b. Perigynium pointed, often beaked, at the apex . . . . (3)

3a. Spike short and broad, shiny brown or black, the terminal staminate portion inconspicuous or spike broadly triangular with conspicuous staminate flowers at the apex . . . . (4)

3b. Spike elongate, narrow, often pale, with a distinct elongate narrow staminate portion, only a few carpellate flowers at the base, bulging when mature. (6)

4a. Spike globose or triangular; stigmas 2; perigynium not stipitate. **C. capitata** L. subsp. **arctogena** (Smith) Böcher [in a head; of the Arctic]. Rare or local in upper subalpine and alpine peat fens.

4b. Spike not globose; stigmas 2 or 3; perigynium stipitate . . . . (5)

5a. Leaves 0.25 mm wide; perigynium barely stipitate, serrulate above; scales not early deciduous. **C. nardina** Fries subsp. **hepburnii** (Boott) Löve et al. [resembling the grass, *Nardus*; for James Hepburn]. On the highest tundra ridges, often on very dry sites with sedimentary rock.

5b. Leaves 0.5-1.5 mm wide; perigynium long-stipitate, smooth above; scales early deciduous. **C. crandallii** Gandoger [for C. S. Crandall]. Snowmelt areas, alpine, subalpine (*C. pyrenaica* of Colorado literature).

6a. Leaf blades 1.5-2 mm wide; culms stout, often rough above; lowest scale awned. **C. oreocharis** Holm [mountain-loving]. Dry grasslands, outwash mesas to montane and subalpine. The spike is thick and very smooth, owing to the broadly overlapping and clasping scales.
6b. Leaf blades 0.25-0.5 mm wide; culms filiform, smooth or nearly so above; lowest scale usually not awned . . . . (7)

7a. Perigynium rounded on the angles, truncately short-beaked, puberulent above; carpellate scales with broad hyaline margins; basal sheaths usually shredded and filamentose; style exserted. **C. filifolia** Nuttall [threadlike leaves]. Dry grasslands, plains to montane.
7b. Perigynium more sharply triangular, slender-beaked, the body slightly puberulent or glabrous at base of beak; margin of scales not as strongly hyaline; basal sheaths not shredded, the old culms and leaves broken (or grazed off by animals) forming dense fascicles. **C. elynoides** Holm [for *Elyna*, another name for *Kobresia*]. Very abundant, subalpine and alpine, and often confused with *Kobresia*.

8a. Spikes unisexual, the plants dioecious . . . . (9)
8b. Staminate and carpellate flowers in the same spike . . . . (12)

9a. Perigynium faces pubescent . . . . (10)
9b. Perigynium faces glabrous . . . . (11)

10a. Culms aphyllopodic, strongly purplish-red-tinged at the base; scales slightly shorter than the perigynium. **C. scirpoidea** Michaux [resembling *Scirpus* (actually *Eleocharis*, which Michaux included in it)]. Rare or local, most well developed in and around calcareous fens in South Park, but also occurring in subalpine and alpine snowmelt areas of the surrounding limestone mountains. Usually a much taller plant than the next, up to 2-3 dm.
10b. Culms phyllopodic, brownish, reddish-brown, or slightly reddish-tinged at the base; scales longer than the perigynium. **Carex pseudoscirpoidea** Rydberg. Occasional in mesic sites, rocky meadow slopes, subalpine, alpine, especially in limestone mountains.

11a. Perigynium broadly obovate to suborbicular, nerveless or nearly so except for marginal nerves; stigmas 3. **C. parryana** Dewey subsp. **hallii** Murray [for C. C. Parry, Elihu Hall]. Open, gravelly meadows, subalpine. This species may have 1-3 minute carpellate spikes (see also Key D).
11b. Perigynium slenderly ovate, finely many-nerved dorsally, obscurely so ventrally; stigmas 2. **C. dioica** L. subsp. **gynocrates** (Wormskiold) Hultén [dioecious, female-dominant]. Infrequent in swampy meadows, subalpine. The solitary spike may be carpellate below and staminate above.

12a. Perigynia few, yellowish, narrow, and pointed, sharply reflexed, a well-developed hooked rachilla protruding from the beak orifice. **C. microglochin** Wahlenberg [small hooks], **52A**. Subalpine willow carrs, often with *Sphagnum*.
12b. Perigynia not as above . . . . (13)

13a. Spikes broad and densely flowered, with numerous perigynia; scales dark brown or black . . . . (14)

13b. Spikes few-flowered, with only a few perigynia; scales pale or reddish-brown . . . . (15)

14a. Perigynia reflexed at maturity, narrow and long-stipitate; leaves 1.5-2 mm wide. **C. nigricans** Meyer [blackish]. Common on wet streamsides, subalpine and alpine.

14b. Perigynia erect to spreading at maturity, broadly obovate and barely stipitate; leaves 0.3-0.5 mm wide. **C. engelmannii** Bailey. Infrequent and local on tundra, CC.

15a. Leaves straight, up to 1.5 mm wide . . . . (16)

15b. Leaves drying and curling at the tip, up to 3 mm wide . . . . (17)

16a. Perigynium beak smooth, with 2 broad, flaring hyaline tips; leaves 1-1.5 mm wide. **C. obtusata** Liljeblad [obtuse, probably the perigynium beak]. Dry montane to subalpine slopes.

16b. Perigynium beak sparingly serrulate without the 2 flaring hyaline tips; leaves 0.5 mm wide. **C. dioica** L. subsp. **gynocrates** (Wormskiold) Hultén [dioecious; female-dominant]. Swampy meadows, often dioecious.

17a. Spikes closely flowered, with 6-15 perigynia; staminate and carpellate flowers close together with no exposed rachis. **C. rupestris** Allioni subsp. **drummondiana** (Dewey) Holub [of rocks; for Thomas Drummond, 1780-1835, botanist on the Franklin expeditions]. Dry alpine and upper subalpine slopes. Even when not in flower, this is an easy species to recognize, with its relatively broad, short, curled leaves with a withered tip.

17b. Spikes loosely flowered with 1-3 perigynia; staminate and carpellate flowers separated, exposing the rachis between them. **C. geyeri** Boott [for Carl Andreas Geyer, 1809-1853, collector on the Oregon Trail], ELK SEDGE, **52E**. Dominant understory in open spruce-fir and Douglas-fir, foothills to subalpine.

KEY B. (Globose spikes)

1a. Culms exceeding the leaves; leaves about 2-4 mm wide, mostly stiffly erect, not withering nor curled at the tips; perigynium ovate-lanceolate, not inflated. **C. vernacula** Bailey [indigenous, as opposed to a European species from which he was distinguishing it]. Infrequent, alpine tundra.

1b. Flowering culms hardly exceeding the leaves; leaves 15 mm or less wide, with a strong tendency to wither and curl at the tips . . . . (2)

2a. Spikes forming a broadly conical cluster, the basal scales preventing the inflorescence from becoming spherical; perigynium oblong-lanceolate, scarcely inflated. **C. maritima** Gunnerus [of seashores]. Frost scars and wet gravels, alpine (*C. incurviformis*).

2b. Spikes forming a shaggy, globose cluster, the lower spikes spreading downward; perigynium broad, almost orbicular, inflated. **C. perglobosa** Mackenzie [very globose], **52H**. Alpine scree slopes.

KEY C. (Sessile bisexual spikes)

1a. Spikes few-flowered, green, scattered along the culm or in a terminal cluster of two; perigynia conspicuous, usually spreading . . . . (2)

1b. Spikes many-flowered in definite spikes rather than short, few-flowered clusters (in the very rare *C. tenuiflora* the spikes are very short, 3-10 flowered, and grouped into a terminal cluster of 2 or 3) . . . . (7)

2a. [1] Culms slender and weak, commonly nodding or reclining . . . . (3)
2b. Flowering culms ± stiffly erect . . . . (5)

3a. [2] Perigynium with slender beak half as long as the body, nerveless ventrally; leaves 2-5 mm wide. **C. deweyana** Schweinitz [for Chester Dewey, 1784-1867, *Carex* specialist]. Infrequent in moist, foothill-montane ravines, an eastern woodland relict.
3b. Perigynium with short beak, at least lightly nerved on both sides; leaves not more than 2 mm wide . . . . (4)

4a. [3] Terminal spike gynaecandrous; beak 1/4-1/3 the length of the body. **C. laeviculmis** Meinshausen [smooth-culmed]. Uncommon on swampy stream-banks or moist woods, montane. Credited to Colorado by Hermann, but we have seen no specimens.
4b. Terminal spike androgynous; beak minute. **C. disperma** Dewey [with 2 perigynia]. Moist forests, willow carrs, and thickets, montane and subalpine.

5a. [2] Perigynia ascending, the inner faces not exposed, broadest near the middle; terminal spike with inconspicuous apical staminate portion (androgynous). **C. occidentalis** Bailey [western]. Foothills to subalpine.
5b. Perigynia widely spreading, exposing their very flat inner sides, broadest just above the base; terminal spike with several staminate scales sheathing the base of the peduncle (gynaecandrous) . . . . (6)

6a. [5] Perigynium 1.5-2 mm wide, the beak 1/4-1/3 the length of the body, shallowly bidentate with short, broad teeth. **C. interior** Bailey [of the midlands]. Moist meadows and forest openings, foothills to subalpine.
6b. Perigynium 1-1.4 mm wide, the beak from more than half to about the length of the body, deeply and sharply bidentate. **C. angustior** Mackenzie [narrower]. Similar habitats.

7a. [1] Culms arising singly or a few together from long-creeping rhizomes. (8)
7b. Culms caespitose or the rhizomes short, with short internodes, never long-creeping . . . . (16)

8a. [7] Perigynium narrowly wing-margined, the beak deeply bidentate; most spikes gynaecandrous, but the lowest usually carpellate and the middle often staminate. **C. foenea** Willdenow [haylike]. Dry gravels, foothills to subalpine.
8b. Perigynium not wing-margined or winged only at the junction of the beak and body, the beak obliquely cut dorsally, becoming only slightly bidentate. (9)

9a. [8] Plants dioecious or very nearly so . . . . (10)
9b. Plants not dioecious, at least the terminal spike androgynous . . . . . (12)

10a. [9] Carpellate scales clasping the perigynia, usually completely concealing them; leaf sheaths dark brown or black. **C. praegracilis** Boott [very slender]. Wet meadows and roadside ditches, valleys, foothills.
10b. Carpellate scales not clasping the perigynia; leaf sheaths light brown. (11)

11a. [10] Perigynium winged at the junction of the beak and body, very small, not longer than 3 mm; beak very short; scales dark brown. **C. simulata** Mackenzie [imitative]. Wet meadows and swamps, foothills to subalpine.
11b. Perigynium not at all winged, 3.5-4 mm long, the beak as long as the body; scales straw-colored. **C. douglasii** Boott [for David Douglas]. Roadside ditches and alkaline flats.

12a. [9] Inflorescence broad, 1-2.5 cm wide; perigynium beak as long as the body. **C. douglasii** Boott.

12b. Inflorescence linear-oblong, 5-10 mm wide . . . . (13)

13a. [12] Upper leaf sheaths green-striate ventrally except near the mouth; staminate flowers unusually conspicuous, most of the middle, and often the upper, spikes entirely staminate. **C. sartwellii** Dewey [for H. P. Sartwell, 1792-1867, New England botanist]. Infrequent, montane marshes and fens.

13b. Upper leaf sheaths hyaline ventrally . . . . (14)

14a. [13] Lower leaf sheaths dark brown or black; carpellate scales clasping the perigynia at the base. **C. praegracilis** Boott [very slender].

14b. Lower leaf sheaths light brown; carpellate scales not as above . . . . . (15)

15a. [14] Scales dark brown; perigynium winged at the junction of beak and body, abruptly narrowed to a very short beak. **C. simulata** Mackenzie.

15b. Scales chestnut to light brown; perigynium not at all winged, contracted to a beak 1/4-1/3 the length of the body. **C. stenophylla** Wahlenberg subsp. **eleocharis** (Bailey) Hultén [narrow-leaved, allusion to genus *Eleocharis*]. Grassy slopes, foothills to subalpine.

16a. [7] Terminal spike androgynous . . . . (17)

16b. Terminal spike gynaecandrous . . . . (25)

17a. [16] Perigynium tapering into a beak almost from the base . . . . (18)

17b. Perigynium abruptly contracted into a beak; inflorescence slender, 5-10 mm wide, the spikes ascending . . . . (20)

18a. [17] Perigynium 4-5 mm long, the beak as long as the body; inflorescence a conspicuously compound spike up to 2 cm wide, the spikes stiffly spreading, like a pincushion. **C. stipata** Mühlenberg [crowded], **53C**. Swamps, frequent in the piedmont valleys.

18b. Perigynium 3-4 mm long, the beak shorter than the body; scales dark brown; heads capitate and single . . . . (19)

19a. [18] Leaf sheaths transversely wrinkled ventrally; culm stout (3.5 mm thick). **C. neurophora** Mackenzie [with nerves, on the perigynium]. Wet meadows, montane to subalpine.

19b. Leaf sheaths not cross-rugulose ventrally; culm slender (2 mm thick at base). **C. jonesii** Bailey [for Marcus E. Jones]. Meadows, montane to subalpine, Park Range, JA.

20a. [17] Leaves 3-8 mm wide, firm or stiff . . . . (21)

20b. Leaves 1-3 mm wide, weak and lax . . . . (22)

21a. [20] Sheaths cross-wrinkled on the ventral side; perigynium 2-2.7 mm long; carpellate scales conspicuously awned. **C. vulpinoidea** Michaux [foxtail]. Open wet meadows in the piedmont valleys.

21b. Sheaths not cross-wrinkled; perigynium 3-5 mm long; carpellate scales pointed but not awned. **C. gravida** Bailey var. **lunelliana** (Mackenzie) Hermann [swollen, alluding to the plump perigynium; for Joel Lunell, 1851-1920, South Dakota botanist]. Sloughs and roadside ditches, easternmost tier of counties.

22a. [20] Perigynium deeply plano-convex, the marginal nerves pulled to the flat ventral face by the expanding dorsal face; leaves 1-1.5 mm wide. **C. vallicola** Dewey [of valleys]. Dry, open slopes and forest clearings.

22b. Perigynium not as above, slightly plano-convex, biconvex, or flat-concave with sharp green margins; leaves 1.5-3.5 mm wide . . . . (23)

23a. [22] Sheaths brown-spotted ventrally, especially near the mouth; spikes often over 10 to an inflorescence; perigynium ovate, biconvex, widest near the base, 2-2.75 mm long. C. **diandra** Schrank [2-stamened]. Infrequent or rare, subalpine willow carrs.

23b. Sheaths not brown-spotted ventrally; spikes 4-10 to an inflorescence; perigynium ovate-elliptical, oblong elliptical to oval, widest near the middle, 2.5-5 mm long . . . . (24)

24a. [23] Perigynium ovate, dark glossy-brown, broadly margined, the vivid green margins conspicuously serrulate above the middle, rather abruptly long-beaked, the beak conspicuously bidentate; scales lustrous, dark chestnut brown; inflorescence stiff. C. **hoodii** Boott [for Sir Samuel Hood, 1724-1816, British admiral]. Montane and subalpine meadows, northern counties.

24b. Perigynium elliptic, greenish-straw-colored to brown-centered, the green margins narrow, usually less serrulate, the beak shorter, shallowly bidentate; scales greenish-brown; inflorescence lax. C. **occidentalis** Bailey.

25a. [16] Perigynium not wing-margined but plano-convex and thin-edged. (26)

25b. Perigynium wing-margined to the base, thin or plano-convex . . . . . . (31)

26a. [25] Scales hyaline with green center (or brownish-tinged at maturity). (27)

26b. Scales medium to dark brown or black . . . . (29)

27a. [26] Spikes in a tight terminal cluster; culms capillary, exceeding the very narrow (0.5-2 mm) leaves. C. **tenuiflora** Wahlenberg. Known from a single population in a quaking fen in Lost Park, Tarryall Range.

27b. Spikes scattered along the culm . . . . (28)

28a. [27] Perigynium apiculate to very short-beaked (beak usually 0.25 mm long or less), appressed-ascending; spikes rather stout, many-flowered (9-20 perigynia); leaves glaucous, 2-4 mm wide. C. **canescens** L. Marshes, lake-shores, montane and subalpine.

28b. Perigynium distinctly beaked (beak 0.5 mm long or more), serrulate, loosely spreading; spikes very slender, few-flowered (5-10 perigynia); leaves green, 1-2.5 mm wide. C. **brunnescens** (Persoon) Poiret [brownish]. Marshes and lake-shores, montane, subalpine; uncommon.

29a. [26] Scales black; perigynium partly black; inflorescence broadly triangular-conic, the spikes very closely aggregated. C. **illota** Bailey [dirty]. Wet subalpine and alpine meadows.

29b. Scales medium to dark brown; perigynium yellow-brown; inflorescence not triangular-conic, the spikes distinct . . . . (30)

30a. [29] Spikes 2-4; perigynium obovate, 2-3.5 mm long, beak smooth, 0.5-1 mm long. C. **lachenalii** Schkuhr [for Werner de Lachenal, 1736-1800, Swiss botanist]. Alpine and upper subalpine.

30b. Spikes 4-5; perigynium oval-ovate, 1.5-2.5 mm long, beak often slightly serrulate, 0.25-0.33 mm long. C. **praeceptorum** Mackenzie [for "the teachers," Professors Morton E. Peck and J. C. Nelson]. Tundra and grassy slopes, upper subalpine and alpine.

31a. [25] Bract of the lowest spike 1-6 cm long, often exceeding the inflorescence (not present on all culms, however!) . . . . (32)

31b. Bract of the lowest spike shorter than the inflorescence, or the inflorescence bractless (occasionally *C. microptera* will have a setaceous bract) . . . (33)

32a. [31] Lower 2 or 4 bracts longer than the inflorescence; scales greenish-white; perigynium subulate-lanceolate. **C. sychnocephala** Carey [many-headed]. Adventive? One record, from a pondshore, subalpine, BL.

32b. Only the lowest bract longer than the inflorescence; scales brown, perigynium ovate. **C. athrostachya** Olney [swollen spike], **52I**. Wet meadows, montane and subalpine.

33a. [31] Beak flat and serrulate to the tip . . . . (34)

33b. Beak terete (at least at the tip), not flat and serrulate . . . . (39)

34a. [33] Scales shorter than the perigynia, noticeably narrower above and largely exposing them . . . . (35)

34b. Scales about the same length as the perigynia, nearly the same width above and nearly concealing them . . . . (38)

35a. [34] Perigynium suborbicular to orbicular, 3-3.5 mm long, 2.5-3.5 mm wide . . . . (36)

35b. Perigynium lanceolate to ovate, 4-8 mm long . . . . (37)

36a. [35] Scales acuminate, reaching to the middle or tip of the beak; spikes more tapered to the base, scattered along the culm. **C. brevior** (Dewey) Mackenzie [shorter], **52G**. Common on rocky grasslands near the base of the Front Range.

36b. Scales blunt, reaching only to the base of the beak; spikes rounded at the base, more or less congested into a loose head. **C. molesta** Mackenzie [troublesome]. One record, from LA.

37a. [35] Perigynium 3-3.5 mm long, narrowly wing-margined to the base. **C. bebbii** (Bailey) Fernald [for M. S. Bebb, 1833-1895, willow specialist]. Moist meadows and banks of ditches, montane.

37b. Perigynium 6-8 mm long, broadly winged, the margins somewhat crinkled. **C. egglestonii** Mackenzie [for W. W. Eggleston, collector, 1863-1935]. Dry, open meadows, montane to subalpine.

38a. [34] Perigynium broadest above the middle, finely nerved ventrally; spikes usually aggregated into a definite head; spikes subtended by several very pale, hyaline, papery, staminate scales, contrasting with the darker carpellate scales above. **C. arapahoensis** Clokey [for Arapahoe Peak]. Rocky places, alpine and subalpine.

38b. Perigynium usually broadest below the middle, nerveless ventrally; spikes in a somewhat moniliform inflorescence or nearly approximate; staminate scales not markedly different from the carpellate scales above. **C. xerantica** Bailey [of dry places]. Ponderosa pine, mesas and montane.

39a. [33] Perigynium flat and scalelike, only distended over the achene . . (40)

39b. Perigynium plano-convex or concavo-convex, often spongy at the base and/or up the sides . . . . (43)

40a. [39] Spikes predominantly green and brown, the brown scales usually contrasting with the green perigynium . . . . (41)

40b. Spikes predominantly brown to blackish-brown, the perigynia themselves partly brown and contributing to the generally dark appearance of the spikes . . . . (42)

41a. [40] Spikes clearly separate and distinguishable; perigynia appressed, the inflorescence thus tapered to the apex and base; scales dark chestnut to blackish-brown. **C. festivella** Mackenzie [diminutive, compared to *C. festiva*]. Meadows and open slopes, montane and subalpine.

41b. Spikes congested and often scarcely distinguishable; perigynia spreading-ascending, the tips conspicuous in the heads, which are more "bristly" as a result; scales dull brown. **C. microptera** Mackenzie [small-wing], **53B**. More common than the last, in similar habitats, but usually drier sites.

42a. [40] Perigynium lanceolate, 5-7 mm long; scales dark brown, appearing black. **C. ebenea** Rydberg [black], **53A**. The most abundant subalpine meadow and roadside sedge.

42b. Perigynium ovate, 4-6 mm long; scales dark brown. **C. haydeniana** Olney [for F. V. Hayden]. Alpine tundra.

43a. [39] Scales shorter and narrower than the perigynia (except sometimes in *C. pachystachya*) . . . . (44)

43b. Scales about the same width and length as the perignia (beaks may protrude slightly) . . . . (47)

44a. [43] Perigynium 2.5-4.3 mm long, usually with 1 or 2 conspicuous transverse folds (tucks) ventrally across the center of the body, not spongy at the base or along the sides . . . . (45)

44b. Perigynium 3.5-5 mm long, without transverse folds ventrally, spongy at the base, sometimes along the sides . . . . (46)

45a. [44] Perigynium ovate-lanceolate to narrowly lanceolate, 2.5-3.5 mm long, 1-1.3 mm wide. **C. limnophila** Hermann [pond-loving]. Wet meadows, foothills to subalpine.

45b. Perigynium ovate, 3.5-4.3 mm long, 1.5-1.9 mm wide; scales with conspicuous white-hyaline margins. **C. macloviana** Urville [of the Falkland Islands, Islas Malvinas]. Meadows, montane and subalpine.

46a. [44] Perigynium oblong-lanceolate to narrowly ovate-lanceolate, 4.5-5 mm long, 1-1.5 mm wide, ascending in the spike; scales oblong-lanceolate, pale to chestnut-brown, not concealing the perigynia, midrib pale yellowish-brown. **C. stenoptila** Hermann [slender-wand]. Dry montane forest openings.

46b. Perigynium ovate, 3.5-5 mm long, 1.5-2.5 mm wide; scales spreading in the spike, brown or blackish, about as wide as perigynia and nearly as long, midrib green. **C. pachystachya** Chamisso [thick-spiked]. Meadows, open woods, montane to subalpine.

47a. [43] Spikes separated along the culm so as to barely overlap the base of one with the apex of the next, the spikes thus forming a slender, nodding, graceful group (moniliform, like a string of beads). **C. praticola** Rydberg [of prairies]. Montane and subalpine meadows.

47b. Spikes more densely aggregated; culm stiff . . . . (48)

48a. [47] Perigynium lanceolate, 5-8 mm long. **C. petasata** Dewey [with a traveling cap on, that is, ready for a journey]. Occasional, foothills, montane.

48b. Perigynium concavo-convex, ovate, 4-6 mm long. **C. phaeocephala** Piper [brown-headed]. Common, subalpine and alpine.

KEY D. (Peduncled or black or with staminate spikes)

1a. Perigynium pubescent on the faces, not merely ciliate-margined . . . . . (2)
1b. Perigynium faces glabrous . . . . (10)

2a. [1] Tall plants of marshes, wet meadows and ditches; staminate spikes 1 or 2, clearly different from the 2-4 elongate carpellate spikes distributed along the culm . . . . (3)
2b. Low, spreading, matted plants of dry, forested areas or otherwise not as above . . . . (4)

3a. [2] Leaf blades flat, 2-5 mm wide, the tips not prolonged-filiform; culms sharply triangular; achenes straight-apiculate. **C. lanuginosa** Michaux [woolly], **53F**. Wet places from lowest altitudes to subalpine.
3b. Leaf blades involute-filiform, 2 mm wide or less, the filiform tips greatly elongated, much exceeding the inflorescence; culms obtusely triangular; achenes bent-apiculate. **C. lasiocarpa** Ehrhart [hairy-fruited]. Recently discovered in subalpine fens on east side of Park Range.

4a. [2] Fertile culms with all spikes approximate, sessile or short-peduncled. (5)
4b. Fertile culms with staminate and upper carpellate spikes approximate, the other carpellate spikes widely separated, nearly basal, long-peduncled, appearing as separate culms . . . . (7)

5a. [4] Bracts reduced to bladeless sheaths. **C. concinna** R. Brown [elegant]. Rare or overlooked in moist subalpine forests.
5b. Bracts with well-developed blades . . . . (6)

6a. [5] Perigynium body (excluding the stipitate base and the beak) oval-obovoid, much longer than wide; scales about half the length of the mature perigynium body. **C. peckii** E. C. Howe [for C. H. Peck, 1833-1917, State Botanist of New York]. Rare, in cool shaded gulches in the eastern outer foothills of the Front Range. An eastern woodland-prairie relict.
6b. Perigynium body suborbicular, or suborbicular-obovoid, or very short-oval, about as long as wide; scales longer than the mature perigynium body. **C. pensylvanica** Lamarck subsp. **heliophila** (Mackenzie) Weber [of Pennsylvania; sun-loving]. The most abundant early flowering *Carex* in the foothills.

7a. [4] Bract of lowest non-basal carpellate spike squamiform, somewhat sheathing, usually shorter than the culm, the spike sometimes bractless. **C. geophila** Mackenzie [ground-loving]. Dry, wooded slopes in the foothills.
7b. Bract of lowest non-basal carpellate spike leaflike, not sheathing, normally exceeding the culm . . . . (8)

8a. [7] Upper carpellate spikes with 1-3 flowers; perigynium beak obliquely cut, in age shallowly bidentate, the margins little if at all ciliate-serrulate. **C. pityophila** Mackenzie [pine-loving]. Occasional in dry pinelands and in sagebrush-grass parks, foothills and montane.
8b. Upper carpellate spikes normally with 3-20 flowers; perigynium beak shallowly to deeply bidentate, the margins ciliate-serrulate . . . . (9)

9a. [8] Perigynium 2.5-3.25 mm long, the beak 0.25-0.75 mm long, shallowly bidentate. **C. brevipes** Boott [short-stem]. Subalpine up to timberline.
9b. Perigynium 3.5-4.5 mm long, the beak more than 1 mm long, deeply bidentate. **C. rossii** Boott [for Captain J. C. Ross, 1800-1862, Arctic and

Antarctic explorer]. Ponderosa pine forests on the mesas and foothills up to dry subalpine forests.

10a. [1] Lower scales leaflike, partly enveloping and much longer than the perigynium; terminal spike androgynous; leaves as long as or longer than the culms . . . . (11)
10b. Lower scales not leaflike; terminal spike not androgynous; leaves shorter than the culm . . . . (12)

11a. [10] Perigynium 5-6 mm long, the upper third of the body empty, the beaks stout, 2-3 mm long, smooth-margined. **C. backii** Boott [for Sir George Back, 1796-1878, Arctic explorer]. Rare, dry woods of the outer foothills and montane, east side of Front Range.
11b. Perigynium 4-5 mm long, the upper part of the body filled by the achene, the beaks 0.5-1 mm long, more or less serrulate on the margins. **C. saximontana** Mackenzie [of the Rocky Mountains]. Rare or infrequent, pine forests and thickets, outer foothills of the Front Range.

12a. [10] Fertile culm with a single staminate spike and 1-3 small, 1- or few-flowered carpellate spikes immediately below it, often so close as to appear to be part of the same spike; some culms entirely staminate or carpellate or with a single unisexual spike (see Key A, 7a). **C. parryana** Dewey subsp. **hallii** (Olney) Murray. Open, gravelly subalpine meadows.
12b. Fertile culm with several staminate or carpellate spikes, the carpellate usually many-flowered . . . . (13)

13a. [12] Scales green, pale brown, or pale reddish-brown, never purple-black; inflorescence never appearing very dark . . . . (14)
13b. Scales dark reddish-brown or purple-black, sometimes with a green or lighter midrib, the inflorescence appearing very dark . . . . (28)

14a. [13] Perigynium beakless, very rounded at apex . . . . (15)
14b. Perigynium strongly beaked and/or tapered to the apex . . . . (17)

15a. [14] Styles 3; achenes trigonous. **C. crawei** Dewey [for its discoverer, I. B. Crawe, 1792-1847]. Known from a single collection on the south side of the Black Forest, EP. An eastern prairie relict.
15b. Styles 2; achenes lenticular . . . . (16)

16a. [15] Mature perigynium whitish-papillose, elliptic-obovoid, not fleshy or translucent, rather obscurely ribbed; scales appressed. **C. hassei** Bailey [for H. E. Hasse, 1836-1915, California lichenologist]. Moist canyons in the piñon-juniper belt. Doubtfully distinct from the next and distinguished mostly by the perigynium color and taller stature.
16b. Mature perigynium golden-yellow or orange when fully mature or brownish, orbicular-obovoid, fleshy, translucent, coarsely ribbed; carpellate scales widely spreading at maturity. **C. aurea** Nuttall [golden], **52C**. Wet mountain meadows.

17a. [14] Carpellate spikes dangling on slender peduncles . . . . (18)
17b. Carpellate spikes on erect peduncles (lower spikes may droop when over-mature . . . . (22)

18a. [17] Tall, robust plants of montane and foothills regions; perigynium beaks long and conspicuous; scales with long filiform tips . . . . (19)

18b. Slender short plants of subalpine and alpine regions; perigynium beaks short; scales not as above . . . . (20)

19a. [18] Perigynium very strongly many-ribbed. **C. hystericina** Mühlenberg [porcupine]. Streambanks and sloughs in the piedmont valleys.
19b. Perigynium nerveless except for 2 prominent ribs. **C. sprengelii** Dewey [for Kurt Sprengel, 1766-1833, German botanist]. Rare, on streamsides in cool ravines in the outer foothills. An eastern woodland-prairie relict.

20a. [18] Lowest bract long-sheathing, that is, with a portion sheathing the stem between the blade and the node of attachment; perigynium nerveless except for the 2 marginal nerves. **C. capillaris** L. [finely threadlike], **52B**. Subalpine and alpine streamsides and willow carrs.
20b. Lowest bract not sheathing . . . . (21)

21a. [20] Staminate spikes 4-12 mm long; carpellate scales much narrower and longer than the perigynium, early deciduous. **C. magellanica** Lamarck subsp. **irrigua** (Wahlenberg) Hultén [from Straits of Magellan; inundated]. Lake shores and willow carrs, subalpine.
21b. Staminate spikes 15-27 mm long; carpellate scales as broad as or broader than the perigynium and barely exceeding them in length, persistent. **C. limosa** L. [of bogs]. *Sphagnum* fens and wet meadows, subalpine, especially abundant in quaking fens of South (Lost) Park.

22a. [17] Lowest bract long-sheathing . . . . (23)
22b. Lowest bract not sheathing . . . . (24)

23a. [22] Carpellate spikes 3-11 mm long, oblong or globose-oblong; terminal staminate spike 1; perigynium with slightly bidentate beak; leaf sheaths glabrous. **C. viridula** Michaux [greenish]. Rare, borders of streams and ponds, east side of Park Range, JA, and calcareous fens in South Park.
23b. Carpellate spikes 5-12 cm long, narrowly cylindric; terminal staminate spikes 2-6; leaf sheaths with long, soft hairs. **C. atherodes** Sprengel [swollen, referring to the perigynium body]. Marshy roadsides and edges of lakes and streams, North Park.

24a. [22] Perigynium plump, virtually beakless, filled by the achene; plants of dry woodland. **C. torreyi** Tuckerman. Very rare, in gulches in the outer foothills near Boulder.
24b. Perigynium tapering to a beak; plants of wetlands . . . . (25)

25a. [24] Perigynia reflexed or horizontally spreading; lowest bract several times exceeding the inflorescence; leaf sheaths loose, forming a prolonged, truncate ventral apex. **C. hystericina** Mühlenberg [like a porcupine]. In swales at low altitudes; local in the piedmont valleys, Boulder area.
25b. Perigynia ascending (sometimes spreading in *C. utriculata*); lowest bracts only moderately exceeding the inflorescence; leaf sheaths tight and concave at the mouth . . . . (26)

26a. [25] Long, slender, horizontal rhizomes formed; lower leaf sheaths not shredding and becoming filamentose; culms thick and spongy at the base, bluntly triangular below the spikes. **C. utriculata** Boott [like a small skin bag], **53D**. Abundant, forming zones on shores of ponds, montane, subalpine (*C. rostrata* of manuals, incorrectly).

26b. Rhizomes short-creeping; lower leaf-sheaths shredding, becoming filamentose; culms rarely spongy-based, sharply triangular below the spikes . . . . . (27)

27a. [26] Perigynium ovoid to globose-ovoid, 3.5-8 mm long, 3 mm wide, abruptly narrowed into the beak. **C. vesicaria** L. [bladderlike]. Very wet habitats, montane and subalpine. Sometimes forms a sterile hybrid (achenes are undeveloped) with the last.

27b. Perigynium lanceolate, 7-10 mm long, 2-3 mm wide, tapering from near the base into the beak. **C. exsiccata** Bailey [dried up]. Rare, wet habitats, montane and subalpine.

28a. [13] Bract at base of the lowest spike long-sheathing . . . . (29)

28b. Bract at base of the lowest spike not sheathing . . . . (30)

29a. [28] Perigynium broadly oval to oblong-oval, rounded at the apex; beak short, 0.3 mm; bract blades exceeding the inflorescence; all spikes gynaecandrous. **C. bella** Bailey [pretty]. Aspen groves and open hillsides, subalpine.

29b. Perigynium narrowly lanceolate with long, ill-defined beak; bract blades short or lacking; terminal spike gynaecandrous. **C. misandra** R. Brown (man-hater, because of the few staminate flowers), **52F**. Tundra slopes and basins.

30a. [28] Terminal spike staminate; stigmas 2 or 3 . . . . (31)

30b. Terminal spike gynaecandrous; stigmas 3 . . . . (40)

31a. [30] Carpellate spikes nodding . . . . (32)

31b. Carpellate spikes erect . . . . (34)

32a. [31] Perigynium shining, with a short, slender beak 0.5 mm long; spikes usually widely spaced; stigmas 2 or 3. **C. saxatilis** L. subsp. **laxa** (Trautvetter) Kalela [of rocks, not stiff]. Pondshores and willow fens, subalpine.

32b. Perigynium dull, somewhat glaucous, not shining, beak minute; spikes approximate; stigmas 3 . . . . (33)

33a. [32] Staminate spikes 4-12 mm long; carpellate scales much narrower and longer than the perigynium, early deciduous; culms a few together; rhizomes rather short and stout. **C. magellanica** Lamarck subsp. **irrigua** (Wahlenberg) Hultén [of Straits of Magellan; inundated]. Lakeshores and willow carrs, subalpine.

33b. Staminate spikes 15-27 mm long; carpellate scales as broad as or broader than the perigynia and barely exceeding them in length, persistent; culms usually solitary, from very long slender rhizomes. **C. limosa** L. [of bogs]. *Sphagnum* fens and wet meadows, subalpine, Rocky Mountain National Park.

34a. [31] Plant strongly glaucous; perigynium beakless; rhizomatous plants of quaking fens, very rare. **C. livida** (Wahlenberg) Willdenow [pale lead-colored]. Local, in *Eriophorum gracile* fen, Lost Park.

34b. Not as above . . . . (35)

35a. [34] Stigmas 3. **C. raynoldsii** Dewey [for W. F. Raynolds, 1820-1894, topographical engineer on Yellowstone expedition]. Infrequent, mountain meadows and alpine slopes. In *Colorado Flora: Western Slope*, immature plants were thought to be *C. paysonis* Clokey, which does not come into Colorado. The latter has flattened perigynia at maturity, the black scales covering them. In our species the perigynia are very plump and green at maturity, forcing the black scales wide apart.

35b. Stigmas 2 . . . . (36)

36a. [35] Carpellate spikes appearing very dark, the scales entirely purple-black; perigynia strongly purple-tinged, irregular-inflated. **C. scopulorum** Holm [of the Rockies], **52D**. Abundant in wet basins, subalpine and alpine.
36b. Carpellate spikes green-and-black, perigynia mostly green, contrasting with the darker scales . . . . (37)

37a. [36] Perigynia nerveless on the faces; spikes slender and elongate. **C. aquatilis** Wahlenberg [of wet places], **53H**. Lakeshores, subalpine. Subsp. **stans** (Drejer) Hultén is a dwarf form occurring around snowbeds in the alpine tundra.
37b. Perigynia slenderly nerved or strongly ribbed . . . . (38)

38a. [37] Perigynia persistent, strongly ribbed; leaves short, broad, spreading, conspicuously glaucous; spikes plump. **C. nebrascensis** Dewey [from Nebraska]. Streamsides, springs and often alkaline meadows, plains to subalpine, readily grazed by stock. Ranges from 1-17 dm tall. The glaucous leaves are conspicuous in early spring.
38b. Perigynia early deciduous, slenderly nerved . . . . (39)

39a. [38] All culms aphyllopodic. **C. emoryi** Dewey [for Major William H. Emory, 1811-1877, Mexican Boundary Survey]. Swampy meadows or springy places, often along irrigation ditches in the valleys and on the plains. One of the most early flowering species, often already dropping the perigynia by mid-June, before most *Carex* hunters are abroad!
39b. Fertile culms phyllopodic. **C. lenticularis** Michaux var. **lipocarpa** (Holm) Standley [lens-shaped; early deciduous, as to the perigynium]. Lake margins and marshy meadows, subalpine, northern counties (*C. kelloggii*). In the Park Range (RT) and to be expected on the North Park side.

40a. [30] Spikes slender, not more than 5 mm wide, scattered along the culm, never forming a dense cluster . . . . (41)
40b. Spikes up to 1 cm wide or more, in a rather dense terminal cluster . (42)

41a. [40] Perigynium finely many-nerved, the beak minute, 0.2 mm long; fertile culms aphyllopodic. **C. buxbaumii** Wahlenberg [for J. C. Buxbaum, 1693-1730, German botanist]. Aspen groves, upper montane, subalpine.
41b. Perigynium not nerved, the beak short, 0.5 mm long; fertile culms phyllopodic. **C. norvegica** Retzius subsp. **stevenii** (Holm) Murray [of Norway; Stevens' Mine on Gray's Peak]. Aspen forests and upper mountain forest openings. **C. norvegica** subsp. **norvegica**, a stouter plant with a more compact inflorescence, occurs on wet tundra.

42a. [40] Spikes short and plump, in a ± dense terminal cluster; all spikes sessile . . . . (43)
42b. Spikes either slightly spaced apart or conspicuously nodding or at least twice as long as broad . . . . (45)

43a. [42] Plants usually less than 2 dm tall, the spikes pointed; perigynium with narrow, sloping shoulders and much purple pigmentation on the faces. **C. nelsonii** Mackenzie [for Aven Nelson]. Alpine snowmelt areas.
43b. Plants usually more than 2 dm tall, the spikes almost globose . . . . . (44)

44a. [43] Perigynium scabrous-margined (the cells high-papillose), the base substipitate; scales blunt, the midrib obsolete; culms erect. **C. nova** Bailey [new]. Subalpine and alpine wet spring-slopes.
44b. Perigynium smooth-margined, the base rounded, not stipitate; scales acuminate with ± prominent midrib; culms slender, generally flexuous. **C.**

pelocarpa Hermann [dark-fruited]. Frequent, subalpine and alpine slopes and meadows.

45a. [42] Spikes nodding . . . . (46)
45b. Spikes erect . . . . (47)

46a. [45] Upper carpellate scales exceeding the perigynia (usually conspicuously so), dark copper-brown; lowest peduncle less than half the length of the spike; apex of perigynium body acute. **C. chalciolepis** Holm [bronze-scaled], **53G**. Abundant, alpine and subalpine slopes.
46b. Upper carpellate scales usually exceeded by the perigynia, dark red-brown to blackish-brown, fading with age; lowest peduncle 1-2 times the length of the spike; apex of perigynium body obtuse. **C. atrata** L. [blackened]. Infrequent, subalpine meadows and rocky alpine slopes. There is no agreement among botanists that true *C. atrata* occurs in America; however, our plants, which Hermann called *C. heteroneura* W. Boott var. *brevisquama* Hermann, compares favorably with the European *C. atrata*.

47a. [45] Scales conspicuously white-hyaline along the sides and at the apex, nearly equalling or wider than the perigynia. **C. albonigra** Mackenzie [white-and-black]. Alpine tundra, fairly common.
47b. Scales not white-hyaline or only slightly so, shorter and narrower than the perigynia . . . . (48)

48a. [47] Perigynium slightly and irregularly inflated, narrowly elliptic, the upper margins forming 2 sides of a triangle. **C. atrosquama** Mackenzie [black-scaled]. Infrequent, open meadows, subalpine and lower alpine.
48b. Perigynium flat, not inflated, broadly ovate to orbicular, the upper margins forming an arc of a circle. **C. epapillosa** Mackenzie [not papillose]. Meadows and margins of lakes, subalpine and alpine.

CYPERUS L. 1753 [*kypeiros*, the ancient Greek name]

1a. Styles 2, achenes lenticular; scales reddish brown, often quite dark. **C. rivularis** Kunth [of streams]. Rare on gravel bars on streams on the piedmont valleys and plains.
1b. Styles 3, achenes trigonous, plump; scales usually yellowish-brown, never dark purple brown . . . . (2)

2a. Small annual less than 10 cm tall; floral spikes less than 1 cm long . . (3)
2b. Taller plants; floral spikes more than 1 cm long . . . . (4)

3a. Scales strongly ribbed, with acuminate or awned, strongly recurved tips. **C. aristatus** Rottboell. Common on drying pond borders, developing late in the season (*C. inflexus*).
3b. Scales not at all ribbed, neither acuminate nor awned, the tips pointing forward. **C. acuminatus** Torrey & Hooker. Infrequent in similar habitats.

4a. Spikelet axis breaking up into units consisting of a scale, the next lowest internode and the attached wings and clasped achene; internodes becoming thickened and cartilaginous. **C. odoratus** L. Adventive, local, around ponds on the plains.
4b. Spikelet axis persistent as a unit after the achenes and scales fall away from it . . . . (5)

5a. Scales 1.4-4 mm long; achenes 1-2 mm long. **C. esculentus** L. [edible]. Probably adventive, one old record from WL, but to be expected anywhere on the plains.

5b. Scales 1.2-1.6 mm long; achenes 0.6-1.2 mm long. **C. erythrorhizos** Mühlenberg [red-rooted], **54D**. Sandy or muddy pond margins in the piedmont valleys.

ELEOCHARIS R. Brown 1810 [Greek, *helos*, marsh, + *charis*, grace]. SPIKERUSH

1a. Achenes with about 6 longitudinal ridges and fine horizontal crossbars between them . . . . (2)

1b. Achenes lacking ridges and crossbars . . . . (3)

2a. Culms strongly flattened, often c-shaped in section. **E. wolfii** Gray. Known in Colorado from a single collection from the Black Forest.

2b. Culms not flattened. **E. acicularis** (L.) Roemer & Schultes [needlelike], **54B**. Very common in wet places from the plains to subalpine.

3a. Culms tiny (1-5 cm tall), in dense mats; achene with pitted surface. **E. parvula** (Roemer & Schultes) Link var. **anachaeta** (Torrey) Svenson [without bristles]. On drying mudflats, piedmont valleys and out along the plains in northeastern counties (*E. coloradoënsis*).

3b. Culms taller, not in dense mats . . . . (4)

4a. Annual, growing in a tuft or clump, easily uprooted . . . . (5)

4b. Perennials with rhizomes . . . . (6)

5a. Achenes shining black. **E. atropurpurea** (Retzius) C. Presl [black-purple]. Rare on the piedmont valleys and plains. Found once at Greeley.

5b. Achenes shining brown or greenish. **E. obtusa** (Willdenow) Schultes var. **detonsa** Gray) Drapalik & Mohlenbrock. Frequent around drying ponds in the piedmont valleys (*E. engelmannii*).

6a. Styles 2; achenes lenticular or biconvex. **E. palustris** (L.) Roemer & Schultes [of swamps], **54A**. The most common, and extremely variable, species in wet places throughout the area (*E. macrostachya*). It rarely is collected in good fruiting condition, since it evidently takes more time to reach maturity than any other species.

6b. Styles 3; achenes trigonous . . . . (7)

7a. Stems flattened. **E. elliptica** Kunth var. **compressa** (Sull.) Drapalik & Mohlenbrock. Frequent in the piedmont valleys.

7b. Stems not flattened . . . . (8)

8a. Tubercle (the swollen base of the style) not well differentiated from the body of the achene, but appearing confluent with it . . . . (9)

8b. Tubercle obviously differentiated from the body of the achene, forming an apical cap . . . . (10)

9a. Plants stoloniferous, the stolons rooting at the tips; culms flattened, 2 mm wide or more. **E. rostellata** (Torrey) Torrey, **54C**. To be expected in wetlands on the plains, although our few records are from the Western Slope.

9b. Plants not stoloniferous; culms not compressed, not over 1 mm wide. E. **quinqueflora** (Hartman) Schwartz. Subalpine wet meadows and fens (*E. pauciflora*).

10a. Spikes few-flowered, ovate, the scales purple-black; achene pale yellow; tubercle broader than high; plants in clumps, not strongly rhizomatous; culms green. **E. bolanderi** Gray [for H. N. Bolander, 1831-1897, State Botanist of California]. To be expected in the montane and subalpine, along spring brooks, although our only collections are from the Western Slope.

10b. Spikes many-flowered, cylindric, the scales brown, with hyaline sides and light midrib; achene golden yellow; tubercle as high as wide; plants with stout black rhizomes; culms glaucous. **E. montevidensis** Kunth [of Montevideo]. Known from a single old record from Fort Collins, this species should be present in alkaline flats on the plains.

ERIOPHORUM L. 1753 [Greek, *erion*, wool, + *phoros*, bearing]. COTTONSEDGE, BOGWOOL

1a. Culms lacking well-developed leaf blades; head solitary at the stem apex. **E. altaicum** Meinshausen var. **neogaeum** Raymond [from Altai; New World race], **55F**. Local, in fens in the Mosquito Range.

1b. Leaf blades well developed; heads several, on distinct peduncles . . . . (2)

2a. Leaves narrow, less than 4 mm wide, channeled throughout, dark brownish-green, the tips reddish; usually only one bract present; bristles not over 2.5 cm long. **E. gracile** Koch. Locally abundant in quaking fens, north end of South Park. Unlike the next, this species forms large uniform stands that are recognizable at a distance because of the reddish color of the tips of the leaves. Also known from a single collection near Stonewall, HF; the locality has been destroyed by draining.

2b. Leaves over 4 mm wide, flat at least below the middle, bright green; 2 or more bracts present; bristles at maturity over 2.5 cm long. **E. angustifolium** Honckeny, **55E**. Subalpine pond margins and sedge meadows (*E. polystachion*), usually not forming uniform stands of any extent.

FIMBRISTYLIS M. Vahl 1805 [Latin, *fimbria*, fringe, + *stylus*, style, the latter being fringed with hairs in the original species]

One species, **F. puberula** (Michaux) Vahl. Wetlands, northeasternmost counties.

HEMICARPHA Nees 1834 [Greek, *hemi*, half, + *carphos*, chaff, alluding to the minute scale between the flower and the axis of inflorescence]

One species, **H. micrantha** (M. Vahl) Pax var. **aristulata** Coville. Wetlands of the piedmont valleys, Fort Collins to Denver.

KOBRESIA Willdenow 1805 [for J. P. von Cobres, 1747-1823, naturalist of Augsburg]

Note: In *Kobresia* the perigynium is an open sheath with margins overlapping abaxially and never has a bidentate beak. It often encloses a staminate and a carpellate floret; these flower pairs are called spikelets. Groups of spikelets on distinct major axes are called spikes.

1a. Spikelets unisexual, 1-flowered, the upper ones staminate, the lower carpellate; spikes several, the lower distinct. **K. simpliciuscula** (Wahlenberg) Mackenzie. Moist gravelly tundra, near the Continental Divide of the Front Range. Strongly rhizomatous, usually not forming dense clumps.

1b. Spikelets consisting of 1 staminate and 1 carpellate floret; spikes simple (2)

2a. Spike 1-3 cm x 2-3 mm; scales 2-3 mm long; perigynium 3-3.5 x 1.25 mm; very densely caespitose, forming hummocks; flowering culms very slender. **K. myosuroides** (Villars) Fiori & Paoli. The climax dominant on mature soils of relatively dry but peaty alpine tundra (*K. bellardii*). In autumn the tundra slopes are colored a rich bronze-yellow by the drying foliage of this species. Very similar to *Carex elynoides*, and distinguished certainly only by the closed perigynium of the latter.

2b. Spike 1-2 cm x 4-5 mm; scales 4-5 mm long; perigynium 5.5 x 1.25 mm; flowering culms stout. **K. sibirica** Turczaninow. Forming dense hummocks in moist tundra, solifluction slopes, and gravelly alpine lakeshores, Continental Divide in the Hoosier Pass region.

MARISCUS M. Vahl 1806 [name used by Pliny for a kind of rush]

1a. Spikes forming a single, dense, sessile, spherical cluster at the top of the culm; scales hardly mucronate. **M. filiculmis** (M. Vahl) Koyama. Infrequent in wetlands along the mountain front (*Cyperus houghtonii*).

1b. Spikes either with well-developed peduncles of different lengths or, if aggregated into a terminal cluster, then the inflorescence consisting of a few recognizable subsidiary sessile spikes . . . . (2)

2a. Scales 2-2.5 mm long, with a prominent spreading or recurved tip; spikes in a sessile cluster. **M. fendlerianus** (Böckeler) Koyama, a perennial with bulbous stem bases; floral axes clustered to form a condensed greenish head. Dry, rocky hillsides of the outer foothills (*Cyperus*).

2b. Scales 3 mm long or more, the tip inconspicuous, often incurved; several spikes exserted on peduncles of varying lengths, suggesting an umbel. **M. schweinitzii** (Torrey) Koyama [for L. D. von Schweinitz, 1780-1834, Pennsylvania botanist]. Dry slopes on the mesas and hogbacks, and in sandy places on the plains.

SCHOENOPLECTUS Palla 1888 [Greek, *schoinos*, rush, + *plectos*, braided, probably alluding to use in making baskets and cradles]. TULE, BULRUSH

1a. Slender caespitose annual. **S. saximontanus** (Fernald) Raynal. Rare, in drying mudflats on the plains and piedmont valleys (*Scirpus hallii*).

1b. Perennials with rhizomes . . . . (2)

2a. Culms triangular; inflorescence of a few sessile, obviously lateral, spikes. **S. pungens** (Vahl) Palla, **55B**. Abundant in very wet portions of stream valleys, occupying a zone somewhat comparable to that of the dark green *Juncus arcticus* and, like that species, visible from a distance because of its color (*Scirpus americanus* of Colorado literature).

2b. Culms terete; inflorescence of oval pedunculate subterminal spikes . . (3)

3a. Spikelets appearing dull gray-brown, the individual scales with prominent red-brown striae on a paler background. **S. lacustris** (L.) Palla subsp. **acutus** (Mühlenberg) Löve & Löve, **55C**. Very common on muddy shores of the lower river valleys (*Scirpus acutus*).

3b. Spikelets more reddish-brown, the scales with a darker ground cover so that the red-brown striae are less distinct. **S. lacustris** subsp. **creber** (Fernald) Löve & Löve [of lakes; thick]. Same habitats, evidently not as common as the last (*Scirpus validus* of Colorado literature).

SCIRPUS L. 1753 [the classical Latin name]. BULRUSH

1a. Spikes not aggregated into heads, each spike on its individual peduncle. **S. lineatus** Michaux. Adventive, known only from the Boulder Valley, where it may have escaped from a nursery. The original colony was destroyed by development, but a large stand has been found on Boulder Open Space wetlands.

1b. Spikes aggregated into dense heads . . . . (2)

2a. Leaf sheaths reddish; midrib of the scales exserted as a short, stiff awn; styles 3. **S. pallidus** (Britton) Fernald. Wet pondshores and ditches at low altitudes.

2b. Leaf sheaths green; midrib of the scales not exserted or very minutely so; styles 2. **S. microcarpus** Presl, **55D**. Same habitats.

TRICHOPHORUM Persoon 1805 [Greek, *trichos*, hair, + *phoron*, stalk]

Recently it has been shown that the name *Baeothryon*, which has been used for this genus, was actually based on a species of *Eleocharis*.

One species, **T. pumilum** (Vahl) Schinz & Thellung. Known only from South Park, but extremely inconspicuous and inhabiting wet moss in rills in calcareous willow fens. The plants are slenderly rhizomatous, with a few slender stems up to 10 cm tall, each with a small few-flowered spike. As each (awnless) scale falls away, the tiny black shiny achene remains attached for a time. Recently rediscovered in Colorado after having not been seen for over a century (*Scirpus pumilus*). The closely related *T. caespitosum* (L.) Hartman, a densely caespitose plant, was reported in 1862 also. However, the specimen, in the Geneva herbarium, proves to be *T. pumilum*. However, it occurs in the Uintah Mountains of Utah, where *T. pumilum* is absent!

CYPRIPEDIACEAE LADY'S SLIPPER FAMILY (CPD)

Traditionally, the lady's slippers have been placed in the orchid family, but recent studies have shown that there is little relationship between these and the true orchids. Not only are the fundamental features of the embryo sac development different, but in the Cypripediaceae there are two functional stamens, and neither of these corresponds to the single stamen of the true orchids. Curiously enough, the family was proposed by John Lindley back in 1833! All species of *Cypripedium* are rare and potentially endangered and should not be disturbed.

CYPRIPEDIUM L. 1753 [Greek, *Kypris*, Venus, + *pes*, foot]. LADY'S SLIPPER

1a. Flowers yellow. **C. calceolus** L. subsp. **parviflorum** (Salisbury) Hultén. Aspen groves and lodgepole pine forests. Rare and local, and very vulnerable to extermination by collectors, a plant of special concern. Many colonies are on private land and protected by conservation-minded landowners.

1b. Flowers purple or dull brown-purple. **C. fasciculatum** Kellogg, **Pl. 20**. Local and vulnerable, openings in subalpine forests, usually under overhanging lower branches of *Abies*.

DIPSACACEAE TEASEL FAMILY (DPS)

The teasel head is a perfect device for raising the nap on woolen fabrics. The process, called fulling, has been used since ancient Roman times, and the English surname Fuller comes from this operation. Although teasels are still grown for this purpose, modern technology has found metal substitutes. To be a satisfactory teasel, the bristles on the head need to be hooked and stiff enough to stand up to tension without shattering and getting caught in the wool. *Dipsacus sativus* is the commercial teasel. Our weedy species has straight bristles and is of little use. The family name comes from the Greek *dipsa*, thirst. "Dipsomaniac" comes from the same stem. When one speaks of teasing something apart, or of teasing someone in the sense of annoying, the word comes from the same source as "teasel." The wild teasels are commonly silvered or gilded and make striking additions to winter bouquets.

1a. Stems 4-angled, these and the simple leaves very harshly hooked; inflorescence an elongate-oval head, the flowers commonly blossoming from the center of the head and proceeding upwards and downwards, few blooming at any one time. **Dipsacus**, TEASEL

1b. Stems not 4-angled, not armed; leaves toothed, lobed, the upper usually pinnatifid; inflorescence capitate, like that of most Asteraceae, with purple flowers, the basal bracts forming an involucre. **Knautia**

DIPSACUS L. 1753 [Greek, *dipsa*, thirst, the plant figuring in ancient Dionysian rituals involving drinking]. TEASEL

One species, **D. sylvestris** Hudson, **56**. Adventive, abundantly established along irrigation ditches along the base of the mountain front.

KNAUTIA L. 1753 [for Christian Knaut, 1654-1716, Saxon botanist]

One species, **K. arvensis** (L.) Duby. Adventive, established on roadsides, RT, and probably on the adjacent eastern slope. Of the generic name Linnaeus said: "*Knautia* has a regular flower made up of irregular florets, and seeds enclosed in a hard coat, being called after a man who zealously sought to promote the welfare of Botany by his study of regularity and irregularity in flowers, and whose works were never bare and unadorned."

DROSERACEAE SUNDEW FAMILY (DRS)

The sundews include, in North America, two genera of insectivorous plants: *Drosera*, the sundew, and *Dionaea*, the Venus' flytrap. Unlike *Dionaea's* "bear-trap" mechanism, the trapping of insects by *Drosera* is by sticky glandular hairs on the leaf surface. When an insect is stuck on a hair, the other hairs move to fix themselves on all the parts, and the insect is slowly digested by proteolytic enzymes. *Dionaea* grows only in bogs on the South Atlantic coastal plain, and until very recently *Drosera* was known no closer to Colorado than Yellowstone National Park.

DROSERA L. 1753 [Greek, *droseros*, dewy]. SUNDEW

One species, **D. rotundifolia** L. One Eastern Slope locality known, recently collected by Betsy Neely in a fen in North Park in the vicinity of Big Creek Lakes. Here the plants occur in *Sphagnum* on the margin of small ponds. Under no circumstances should this rare species be collected. It is abundant enough in the sphagnum bogs of northern North America and is available from biological supply houses.

ELAEAGNACEAE OLEASTER FAMILY (ELE)

This family is unique because of the peculiar peltate scales that cover the leaves and fruits, giving the foliage a satiny or a rusty tint. All are trees or shrubs and many are ornamental cultivars of which the best known is the Russian-olive, one of the hardiest introduced trees on the Great Plains and on Western Slope homesteads. Deserted homesteads are often recognizable by the persisting windrows of Russian-olive trees. In Siberia, a relative, *Hippophaë rhamnoides*, is being bred to improve the yield of its orange berries, which are high in vitamin C content, for which there is a great need in that climate.

1a. Leaves and branches opposite; flowers unisexual and plants dioecious; stamens 8. **Shepherdia**, SILVERBERRY, BUFFALOBERRY
1b. Leaves and branches alternate; flowers perfect or some plants polygamo-monoecious; stamens 4. **Elaeagnus**, RUSSIAN-OLIVE, SILVERBERRY

ELAEAGNUS L. 1753 [Greek, *elaia*, the olive, + *agnos*, Greek name of *Vitex*].

1a. Leaves lanceolate, much longer than wide; young branchlets and petioles silvery gray; small branches often forming spines. **E. angustifolia** L., RUSSIAN-OLIVE, **57C**. Adventive. A hardy dryland species, consisting of many cultivars. Extremely variable in shape and vesture of leaves, the young plants or shade branches have leaves often almost green above and broadly elliptic. Such plants have been called *E. orientalis*, but I doubt that these types represent different species.
1b. Leaves broadly elliptic-oblong, up to 3 times as long as wide; branches and petioles covered by brown scales; branches not spiny. **E. commutata** Bernhardi, SILVERBERRY. Scattered in small colonies, South Park, Florissant, Creede area. Adventive, possibly planted for highway beautification or erosion control but evidently naturalized and spreading.

SHEPHERDIA Nuttall 1818 [for John Shepherd, 1764?-1836, curator of Liverpool Botanical Garden]. SILVERBERRY, BUFFALOBERRY

1a. Leaves silvery on both sides, oblong-elliptic; branches often spiny; berries silvered. **S. argentea** (Pursh) Nuttall, SILVERBERRY, **57B**. Uncommon on the Eastern Slope, in riverbottoms and along irrigation ditches, from LR and WL in the Platte drainage.
1b. Leaves green, broadly elliptic with rusty scales; branches never armed; berries orange-red. **S. canadensis** (L.) Nuttall, BUFFALOBERRY, **57A, Pl. 3**. Open lodgepole pine forests and rocky slopes and summits, montane and subalpine. Dioecious, with unisexual flowers, appearing in early spring before the leaves.

ELATINACEAE WATERWORT FAMILY (ELT)

A small family of semiaquatic plants, containing only two small genera, *Elatine* and *Bergia*. The latter occurs only on the eastern plains. *Elatine* is infrequent, small and inconspicuous and of no economic importance whatever. The genus is so rarely collected that we do not know if we have one or more species in Colorado. Anyone collecting *Elatine* should deposit specimens with the Herbarium.

1a. Plants erect or ascending, glandular-pubescent throughout; sepals and petals 5; sepals conspicuously scarious-margined and midrib clearly visible. **Bergia**
1b. Plants creeping, or some branches ascending, glabrous; sepals 2, petals 3 (vegetatively resembling *Callitriche*). **Elatine**, WATERWORT

BERGIA L. 1771 [for Peter Jonas Bergius, 1723-1817, Swedish botanist]

One species, **B. texana** (Hooker) Seubert [of Texas], **58B**. On muddy shores of ponds in the piedmont valleys.

ELATINE L. 1753 [classical name of some low and creeping plant]. WATERWORT

One species, **E. rubella** Rydberg, **58A**. Old reports from the Denver region, where it may be extinct; recent collections from a pond on the Air Force Academy grounds. The plant grows submerged in shallow water and emerges as the pond dries up.

ERICACEAE HEATH FAMILY (ERI)

Heaths or heathers are characteristic plants of almost every mountain region of the world, but they are not well represented in the southern Rocky Mountains and are mostly absent from our tundra because of our arid continental climate and the lack of acidity in the tundra soils. Even the blueberries (incorrectly called huckleberries) rarely set abundant fruit here, possibly because of unseasonal frosts at flowering time. The flowers of ericads are beautiful creations, like porcelain Easter eggs into which one peers to see exotic scenes, and exotic they are, for the stamens have anthers that open by terminal pores and are often adorned with peculiar horns. The family once included plants that are now removed to two families, the Pyrolaceae and Monotropaceae. *Vaccinium* is probably more properly placed in its own family, the Vacciniaceae.

1a. Leaves thick and evergreen . . . . (2)
1b. Leaves thin in texture, usually deciduous . . . . (3)

2a. Leaves green on both sides, the margins not revolute; not wetland plants, the flowers urn-shaped. **Arctostaphylos**, BEARBERRY, MANZANITA
2b. Leaves paler beneath, with revolute margins; wetland plants with pink parasol-shaped flowers. **Kalmia**, SWAMP-LAUREL

3a. Creeping plants of mossy forests. **Gaultheria**, CREEPING WINTERGREEN
3b. Erect shrubs . . . . (4)

4a. Leaves entire, sparsely rusty-hairy, clustered at the ends of the branches; flowers large, white, open-campanulate. **Azaleastrum**, WHITE RHODODENDRON
4b. Leaves crenulate-serrate or serrate, glabrous, not clustered at the ends of the branches; flowers small, urn-shaped. **Vaccinium**, BLUEBERRY, BILBERRY, HUCKLEBERRY

ARCTOSTAPHYLOS Adanson 1763 [Greek, *arctos*, bear, + *staphyle*, bunch of grapes]. BEARBERRY, KINNIKINNICK

One species, **A. uva-ursi** (L.) Sprengel, **59E**. Gravelly or stony forest openings. Most plants have glandular-hairy young twigs [the diploid, *A. uva-ursi* subsp. *adenotricha* (Fernald & Macbride) Calder & Taylor]. *A. uva-ursi* subsp. *coactilis* (Fernald & Macbride) Löve & Kapoor [thickened], a tetraploid, is frequent on the Eastern Slope and lacks glandular hairs. Recent research tends to deny the validity of these taxa, so one is perfectly justified in simply calling our plants *A. uva-ursi*. *A. adenotricha* is, by far, the most abundant type.

AZALEASTRUM Rydberg 1900 [resembling *Azalea*, a *Rhododendron* segregate]. WHITE RHODODENDRON

One species, **A. albiflorum** (Hooker) Rydberg. Lakeshores and moist forests, Park Range on west edge of North Park (*Rhododendron*).

GAULTHERIA L. 1753 [for Jean-François Gaultier, 1708?-1756, Quebec naturalist and court physician]. CREEPING WINTERGREEN

One species, **G. humifusa** (Graham) Rydberg, **59F**. Cool, mossy subalpine forests. Leaves thin, almost round, the lateral veins prominent. Flowers inconspicuous, greenish-white; berries red.

KALMIA L. 1753 [for Pehr Kalm, 1716-1779, who collected in America for Linnaeus]. PALE- or SWAMP-LAUREL

One species, **K. microphylla** (Hooker) Heller, **59G**. Infrequent but locally abundant, borders of ponds and streams, subalpine (*K. polifolia* var. *microphylla*).

VACCINIUM L. 1753 [Latin, *vaccinus*, of cows, as reflected in the germanic folk-name, *Kuhteke*]. BLUEBERRY, BILBERRY, HUCKLEBERRY

1a. Leaves broadest above the middle, crenulate-serrate above the middle; branchlets not angled and twigs usually brown rather than green. **V. cespitosum** Michaux, DWARF BILBERRY, **59B**. Mossy forest floors, shores of ponds, and moist subalpine slopes.

1b. Leaves broadest at or below the middle, serrate or serrulate from base to apex; branchlets angled, green . . . . (2)

2a. Leaves more than 10 mm long; berry blue-black; branches spreading, not crowded . . . . (3)

2b. Leaves less than 10 mm long; berry red; branches erect, often crowded as broomstraws. **V. scoparium** Leiberg, BROOM HUCKLEBERRY, **59A**. Usually found at higher altitudes than the preceding, often above timberline.

3a. Leaves over 3 cm long, usually very broadly elliptic and obtuse at the apex; plants usually 0.5 m or more tall. **V. globulare** Rydberg (?). What seems to be this species occurs in the Park Range, but it has not been collected in flower or fruit. It looks like a gigantic form of the next, but needs further study in the field. The flowers appear during the leafing-out period and are short and squat (globular), unlike the longer ones of *V. myrtillus*.

3b. Leaves about 2 cm long, usually narrowly elliptic and acute at the apex; plants usually less than 0.5 m tall. **V. myrtillus** L. subsp. **oreophilum** (Rydberg) Löve et al., BLUEBERRY, **59C**. Common understory, montane and subalpine forests under spruces. Sometimes almost impossible to distinguish from *V. scoparium*. Both species are diploid and conceivably could cross, producing hybrids, which, whether sterile or fertile, could reproduce vegetatively.

EUPHORBIACEAE SPURGE FAMILY (EUP)

In this family a curious evolutionary trend is demonstrated in fantastic variety. Whole flower clusters are reduced to one essential part (one stamen or one gynoecium). Bracts take the place of the sepals, and colored glands the place of the petals. Yet each flower cluster assumes the aspect of a single flower. Look closely at the stamen or the gynoecium and you will see that it has its own stalk, marked by a joint, so each is a separate flower and not a floral part. Next Christmas, examine the *Poinsettia* and learn that the beautiful red "petals" are not petals at all but colored leaves surrounding a number of these strange flower clusters, or cyathia. In a number of families, reduction in size of flowers, which might make the flower-insect relationship difficult, is compensated for by grouping the reduced flowers together in such a way as to simulate one large flower.

1a. Leaves silvery, covered by stellate hairs. **Croton**

1b. Leaves glabrous or with simple hairs . . . . (2)

2a. Upper leaves and bracts broadly white-margined. **Agaloma**, SNOW-ON-THE-MOUNTAIN

2b. Upper leaves and bracts not white-margined . . . . (3)

3a. Flowers with a true calyx; cyathium, or involucre, absent . . . . (4)
3b. Flowers without a perianth; cyathium present . . . . (6)

4a. Styles divided. **Argythamnia,** WILD MERCURY
4b. Styles simple . . . . (5)

5a. Leaves bristly with irritating hairs (Sorry!), sharply serrate; low, spreading herb. **Tragia**
5b. Leaves glabrous, regularly crenate; tall plants with many main stems. **Stillingia**

6a. Glands of cyathia with petallike appendages . . . . (7)
6b. Glands of cyathia lacking petallike appendages, lobes crescent-shaped or entire . . . . (8)

7a. Leaves with asymmetrical bases; stipules well developed. **Chamaesyce**
7b. Leaves with symmetrical bases; stipules absent or glandlike. **Zygophyllidium**

8a. Leaves coarsely dentate; petioles up to half the length of the blades; leaves opposite, often with a dark central spot. **Poinsettia**
8b. Leaves entire or serrulate, sessile or narrowed to the base; leaves alternate (except in the inflorescence). **Tithymalus**

AGALOMA Rafinesque 1838 [Greek, *agalma*, delight]. SNOW-ON-THE-MOUNTAIN

One species, **A. marginata** (Pursh) Löve & Löve, **61D**. Common on the outwash mesas and plains. Very ornamental. I have seen this cultivated in a garden in Japan (*Euphorbia*).

ARGYTHAMNIA P. Browne 1756 [Greek, *argyros*, silver, + *thamnos*, bush]. WILD MERCURY

1a. Inflorescence shorter than the leaves; seeds 2.5 mm long, 4 mm wide. **A. humilis** (Engelmann & Gray) Müller-Argoviensis. Known in Colorado from a single old record from Granada, PW.
1b. Inflorescence equalling or longer than the leaves; seeds about 5 mm long and wide. **A. mercurialina** (Nuttall) Müller-Argoviensis. Known in Colorado from two records, LA and BA.

CHAMAESYCE Rafinesque 1817 [Greek, *chamae*, on the ground, + *sykon*, fig]

1a. Perennial with deep-seated, woody root system, with a cluster of slender, contorted, woody stems below ground level . . . . (2)
1b. Annual with a taproot . . . . (3)

2a. Foliage and fruit glabrous. **C. fendleri** (Torrey & Gray) Small, **61B**. Common in sandy places on the plains, usually on or near rock outcrops. The plants are often reddish-brown.
2b. Foliage and fruit pubescent. **C. lata** (Engelmann) Small. Rocky outcrops, lower Arkansas Valley, BA, LA.

3a. The two stipules on each side of the stem at each node united to form a whitish membranous entire or lacerate scale. **C. serpens** (Humboldt, Bonpland & Kunth) Small. Adventive, known from one old collection from New Windsor, WL.
3b. Stipules otherwise or, if appearing united into a scale, then only on one side of the stem, deeply lobed or dissected . . . . (4)

4a. Leaves linear, more than 6 times as long as wide, not serrulate . . . . . (5)
4b. Leaves not linear, or, if narrow, then less than 6 times longer than wide, and serrulate . . . . (6)

5a. Staminate flowers over 20 per cyathium; petaloid appendages up to 4 times longer than the gland is wide; styles bifid half their length. **C. missurica** (Rafinesque) Shinners. Generally distributed on the plains.
5b. Staminate flowers less than 10 per cyathium; appendages about as long as the gland is wide; styles entire or only notched. **C. revoluta** (Engelmann) Small. Lower Arkansas Valley, LA, BA.

6a. Seeds completely smooth . . . . (7)
6b. Seeds minutely pitted, or with obvious transverse ridges . . . . (8)

7a. Leaves entire as viewed with a lens. **C. geyeri** (Engelmann) Small, **52E**. In sandy ground on the plains.
7b. Leaves serrulate. **C. serpyllifolia** (Persoon) Small. Common, adventive weed, often growing in cracks in sidewalks.

8a. Ovary and capsule glabrous; seeds transversely ridged. **C. glyptosperma** (Engelmann) Small, **60A, 61C**. A native, weedy species, widely distributed in disturbed sites.
8b. Ovary and capsule pubescent; seeds minutely pitted and mottled. **C. stictospora** (Engelmann) Small. Frequent in the lower Arkansas Valley.

CROTON L. 1753 [Greek, *croton*, tick, from the seed shape]
One species, **C. texensis** (Klotsch) Müller-Argoviensis, **60B**. Common on the plains.

POINSETTIA Graham 1836 [for J. R. Poinsett, 1799-1851, U. S. minister to Mexico] (commonly included in *Euphorbia*)
One species, **P. dentata** (Michx.) Klotsch & Garcke. Adventive, ruderal weed.

STILLINGIA Garden 1767 [for Dr. B. Stillingfleet, 1702-1771, English naturalist]
One species, **S. sylvatica** L. Only one occurrence known, the plant being abundant on sand dunes of the Cimarron River, BA.

TITHYMALUS Gaertner 1790 [ancient Greek name for a plant with milky sap] (usually placed in the wastebasket genus *Euphorbia)*. SPURGE

1a. Perennials with rhizomes or woody bases; leaves entire . . . . (2)
1b. Annuals with taproots; leaves crenulate near the apex . . . . (6)

2a. Leaves oblong or oblanceolate, succulent or thick and leathery, with numerous stems clustered on a woody base . . . . (3)
2b. Leaves linear, thin-textured; plants rhizomatous . . . . (4)

3a Leaves oblanceolate, mucronate at the apex, very thick and succulent. **T. myrsinites** (L.) Hill. Common in cultivation and established as an adventive on a large tract along South Boulder Creek.
3b. Leaves oblong or ovate, rounded at the apex, only moderately succulent. T. **montanus** (Engelmann) Small, **60B**. Dry sites throughout the lower elevations (including *T. robustus*).

4a. Leaves narrowly linear, 1-2 cm long and less than 0.5 cm wide; floral leaves 4-6 mm long. **T. cyparissias** (L.) Lamarck, CYPRESS SPURGE. Adventive, occasionally escaped from gardens and established on roadsides.
4b. Leaves broadly linear to ribbonlike; larger floral leaves 1-2 cm long . . (5)

5a. Stem leaves oblanceolate or narrowly oblanceolate-oblong, rounded at the apex, broadest above the middle, cuneate, attenuate at the base. **T. esula** (L.) Scopoli [*Esula*, a pre-Linnaean genus name], LEAFY SPURGE. Adventive weed, not as common as the next.

5b. Stem leaves narrowly linear, broadest at or below the middle or of uniform breadth, sharply acute; usually with numerous sterile branches in the upper axils. **T. uralensis** (Fischer) Prokhanov, LEAFY SPURGE, **61A**. Adventive, noxious weed, locally abundant, in the piedmont valleys and in mountain meadows.

6a. Glands of the cyathium elliptical and symmetrical, without the development of slender lateral "horns." **T. spathulatus** (Lamarck) Weber. Infrequent on river benches (*Euphorbia dictyosperma*).

6b. Glands of cyathium crescent-shaped or 2-horned. **T. peplus** (L.) Hill. Adventive weed, established in and around Golden and Fort Collins.

TRAGIA L. 1753 [for the early herbalist, Hieronymus Bock, 1498-1554, Latinized *Tragus*, "Bock" and "Tragus" meaning goat]

One species, **T. ramosa** Torrey, **60C**. Rocky or grassy hillsides, piñon-juniper, and sagebrush. The foliage, applied to the back of the hand, can give one a nettlesome experience.

ZYGOPHYLLIDIUM Small 1903 [the name alluding to the genus *Zygophyllum*]

One species, **Z. hexagonum** (Nuttall) Small. On the plains, northeasternmost counties.

FABACEAE/LEGUMINOSAE PEA FAMILY (FAB/LEG)

Eric Partridge suggests that the word legume probably is derived from the Latin verb *legere* (stem, *leg*, + suffix, *-umen*), "what one gathers or picks, thus a vegetable." In French, the word *legume* still refers to any vegetable, not only those we call legumes: peas, beans, soy beans, lima beans, and pinto beans. A curious extension occurs in the French phrase "*les grosses legumes*," which means "the bigwigs." Aside from their food value, many legumes are poisonous. Species of *Astragalus* absorb large amounts of poisonous selenium salts and, when grazed, cause the ailments of cattle known as "blind staggers" or "alkali disease." Another disease, "loco," evidently is not caused by selenium although the toxic principle is not definitely known. Some *Astragalus* and most *Oxytropis* species are "loco weeds." The ability of plants to absorb minerals differentially from the soil opened up a new field–geobotanical prospecting, now used to search for uranium and heavy metals, and to analyze the extent of heavy-metal pollution in the environment.

1a. Woody plants (shrubs or trees) . . . . (2)
1b. Herbs . . . . (8)

2a. [1] Leaves even-pinnate (lacking a terminal leaflet) . . . . (3)
2b. Leaves odd-pinnate (with a terminal leaflet) . . . . (5)

3a. [2] Leaves bipinnately compound with minute leaflets; branches with flattened, recurved thorns; flowers in globose clusters, pink-purple, with conspicuous exserted stamens. **Mimosa**

3b. Leaves pinnately compound; thorns not flattened or recurved; flowers yellow . . . . (4)

4a. [3] Leaves pinnately compound with over 10 pairs of linear leaflets; thorns over 3 cm long; flowers mimosalike, in axillary spikes. **Prosopis**, MESQUITE
4b. Leaves with fewer than 10 pairs of leaflets; thorns shorter; flowers sweet-pealike, yellow. **Caragana**, PEATREE

5a. [2] Leaves and stems with thorns at the petiole base (modified stipules); leaflets broadly oval; flowers white or purple. **Robinia**, LOCUST
5b. Not thorny; never trees . . . . (6)

6a. [5] Leaflets minute, narrow, 2-3 mm long; low, spreading shrub. **Dalea formosa**
6b. Leaflets larger, oblong or oval, over 5 mm long . . . . (7)

7a. [6] Flowers yellow; petals sweet-pealike; pods balloonlike, papery-inflated. **Colutea**, BLADDER SENNA
7b. Flowers purple; petal solitary; pods not inflated. **Amorpha**, LEADPLANT

8a. [1] Leaves even-pinnately compound, the terminal leaflet missing and replaced by a coiled tendril or a bristle . . . . (9)
8b. Leaves not as above . . . . (10)

9a. [8] Style terete, with a tuft of hairs at the apex. **Vicia**, VETCH
9b. Style flat, hairy along one side. **Lathyrus**, PEAVINE

10a. [8] Trailing vines . . . . (11)
10b. Not trailing vines . . . . (12)

11a. [10] Leaves odd-pinnately compound; flowers purplish brown. **Apios**, GROUNDNUT
11b. Leaves palmately compound; flowers rose-purple, drying yellowish-green. **Strophostyles**

12a. [10] Flowers sweet-pealike, with banner, keel, and wings (papilionaceous); leaves not bipinnately compound . . . . (13)
12b. Flowers not sweet-pealike; leaves bipinnately compound . . . . (31)

13a. [12] Filaments all separate to the base or very nearly so . . . . (14)
13b. Stamens united by their filaments (10 together, or 9 united and 1 separate, sometimes 5 (in *Dalea*) . . . . (15)

14a. [13] Flowers yellow; leaves trifoliate. **Thermopsis**, GOLDEN BANNER
14b. Flowers white; leaves pinnately compound. **Vexibia**. Note: This genus was incorrectly keyed in *Colorado Flora: Western Slope* as having united stamens!

15a. [13] Leaves digitately compound with more than 3 leaflets . . . . (16)
15b. Leaves simple, or pinnately or digitately compound, if digitate then with not more than 3 leaflets . . . . (17)

16a. [15] Annual or perennial, never with deep tuberous roots; anthers of 2 forms, large and small; leaflets commonly more than 5. **Lupinus**, BLUEBONNET
16b. Perennial with deep tuberous root; low, sprawling plants of desert sites; anthers not of 2 forms. **Pediomelum**, INDIAN POTATO

17a. [15] Leaves gland-dotted . . . . (18)
17b. Leaves not gland-dotted . . . . (21)

18a. [17] Pod with hooked prickles (like a small cuckoldbur). **Glycyrrhiza**, WILD LICORICE

18b. Pod unarmed . . . . (19)

19a. [18] Leaves pinnately compound. **Dalea**
19b. Leaves with 3 leaflets (main stem leaves may be 5-foliolate) . . . . . . (20)

20a. [19] Leaflets with the petiolule of the middle leaflet longer than that of the lateral ones. **Dalea**
20b. Leaflets with all petiolules of the same length. **Psoralidium**

21a. [17] Leaflet margins denticulate to serrate; leaves 3-foliolate . . . . . . (22)
21b. Leaflet margins entire; leaves various . . . . (24)

22a. [21] Flowers in elongate, loose racemes; corolla yellow or white. **Melilotus**, SWEETCLOVER
22b. Flowers in heads or short, dense spikes; corolla yellow, white, pink, or purple (sometimes with green cast) . . . . (23)

23a. [22] Leaves pinnately trifoliolate (terminal leaflet with a short petiole jointed to the top of the elongated rachis). **Medicago**, ALFALFA, MEDIC
23b. Leaves palmately trifoliolate, terminal leaflet not as above. **Trifolium**, CLOVER

24a. [21] Flowers in umbels or capitate clusters that do not elongate at all in fruit . . . . (25)
24b. Flowers in racemes, spikes, or solitary (if in capitate clusters, these elongating after flowering) . . . . (27)

25a. [24] Flowers variegated pink, purple, and white; leaves pinnately compound. **Coronilla**, CROWN VETCH
25b. Flowers yellow, white, or dull red; leaves trifoliolate . . . . (26)

26a. [25] Leaflets entire, with only a midvein; pods elongate. **Lotus**
26b. Leaflets with lateral veins; pods short, hidden in the calyx. **Trifolium**

27a. [24] Flowers solitary in the leaf axils, yellow with brown tones; pod elongate, terete, narrow, reflexed. **Lotus**
27b. Flowers not as above, if solitary in the leaf axils then not yellow; pod various . . . . (28)

28a. [27] Keel petals with an abruptly narrowed tip or beak. **Oxytropis**, LOCO-WEED
28b. Keel petals not beaked but rounded or gradually acute; plants usually, but not always, with leafy stems . . . . (29)

29a. [28] Tall, leafy-stemmed, with axillary racemes of orange-red flowers and inflated, stipitate papery pods; introduced weed of irrigated ground. **Sphaerophysa**, BUYAN
29b. Not as above . . . . (30)

30a. [29] Keel longer than the banner and wings, the end squared, apex blunt; pods flat, jointed, forming reticulate, 1-seeded, indehiscent segments. **Hedysarum**, CHAINPOD
30b. Keel usually not conspicuously longer than the banner and wings or, if so then canoe-shaped (curved to the apex); pods not jointed between the seeds. **Astragalus**, MILK VETCH

31a. [12] Stems armed with recurved prickles; leaves sensitive, folding the leaflets at a touch; flowers in heads, pink; petals united in a funnelform, 5-lobed corolla. **Schrankia**. SENSITIVE BRIER

31b. Stems unarmed; petals not united . . . . (32)

32a. [31] Foliage and stems with black dots; flowers in spikes, white or purple. **Dalea**

32b. Foliage and stems not black-dotted . . . . (33)

33a. [32]) Flowers minute, white, in axillary heads. **Desmanthus**

33b. Petals 5, clawed, the upper 2 unlike the others; stamens 10, separate; flowers yellow . . . . (34)

34a. [33] Lower leaf surface with conspicuous orange glands, these becoming black on dried specimens. **Caesalpinia**

34b. Lower leaf surface without orange glands; dried specimens not black-dotted. **Hoffmanseggia**

AMORPHA L. 1753 [Greek, *amorphos*, deformed, from the absence of four of the petals]. LEADPLANT

1a. Plants 1-4 m tall; petioles 2-5 cm long; leaflets 2-5 cm, long. **A. fruticosa** L. var. **angustifolia** Pursh. Common along streamcourses at and near the base of the mountains.

1b. Plants usually less than 1 m tall; petioles 0.5-5 mm long; leaflets 0.5-1.5 cm long . . . . (2)

2a. Foliage and calyces conspicuously pubescent; racemes usually several from the upper leaf axils. **A. canescens** Pursh. Frequent on high plains in easternmost counties.

2b. Foliage and calyces glabrous or nearly so; racemes usually solitary at tips of branchlets. **A. nana** Nuttall [dwarf]. Scattered from Boulder, where it is locally common on the mesas, to the Black Forest and LA.

APIOS Fabricius 1759 [Greek, *apios*, pear, alluding to the swollen tuberous enlargements of the roots]. GROUNDNUT

One species, **A. americana** Medicus. A very rare woodland-prairie relict, known from two collections, YM and BL. It is given protection at the White Rocks locality. No other legume in our flora combines the trifoliolate leaves, creeping habit, and purplish-brown flowers.

ASTRAGALUS L. 1753 [ancient Greek name for a plant]. MILK VETCH, **62E**

Note: *Astragalus* poses a very big problem to a key-writer. Some of the couplets dealing with robustness and height may seem to be a bit vague, but perhaps with some practice the key will become more workable than at first. It is almost impossible to write a simple key without requiring close examination of some difficult features.

1a. Leaves with distinctly spine-tipped leaflets; stems short, prostrate, matted, not rigid, the internodes very short. **A. kentrophyta** Gray subsp. **implexus** (Canby) Weber [matted], **62A**. Sagebrush of intermountain parks, and bare ground up to near timberline.

1b. Leaves with rounded, pointed or emarginate, never spine-tipped leaflets (2)

2a. [1] Pods papery-inflated, thin-textured . . . . (3)

2b. Pods not papery-inflated or, if inflated, thicker-textured . . . . (5)

3a. [2] Plants perennial, with very slender underground caudices and with slender or thick rhizomes . . . . (4)

3b. Plants with a taproot, annual or biennial. **A. wootonii** Sheldon [for E. O. Wooton, 1865-1945, New Mexico botanist]. Recently discovered in the lower San Luis Valley, possibly introduced from farther south.

4a. [3] Pods glabrous, mottled. **A. ceramicus** Sheldon var. **filifolius** (Gray) Hermann [like pottery]. Leaflets narrowly oblong or linear; plants with very slender stems and elongate buried caudices, easily breaking away from the root-crown, which is rarely collected. Sand dunes and blowouts.

4b. Pods gray-strigose, not mottled. **A. cerussatus** Sheldon [white-lead-colored]. Plants in clumps, strongly perennial, with several short, leafy stems from a stout taproot; leaves narrowly oblong; pods sessile. Upper Arkansas Valley, CF-FN.

5a. [2] Scapose or appearing so, leaves usually basal, the stems often in dense clusters from stout or slender underground caudices; if leafy-stemmed, the aerial stems foreshortened . . . . (6)

5b. Plants leafy-stemmed, often tall, the leaves never mostly basal . . . . . (16)

6a. [5] Leaves simple, or with 3 leaflets . . . . (7)

6b. Leaves pinnately compound, with more than 3 leaflets (plants may have occasional leaves with 3 or fewer leaflets) . . . . (11)

7a. [6] Leaves simple; dwarf mat plants with linear, silvery appressed-pubescent basal leaves; flowers small, purple or ochroleucous, in short racemes. **A. spatulatus** Sheldon. Common on stony ground, LR and WL to North Park.

7b. Leaves with three leaflets . . . . (8)

8a. [7] Flowers white, long and narrow; pod beakless, much shorter than the cylindric calyx tube; leathery-textured . . . . (9)

8b. Flowers purple, short; pod beaked, slightly longer than the calyx tube, papery-textured . . . . (10)

9a. [8] Petals glabrous dorsally; flowering in late April-May. **A. gilviflorus** Sheldon [pale yellow-flowered]. Rarely collected, KC.

9b. Petals villous dorsally; flowering in midsummer. **A. hyalinus** Jones [transparent]. Rarely collected, easternmost edge of Colorado, YM.

10a. [8] Flowers very small, the banner 5.2-8 mm long. **A. sericoleucus** Gray. Common on sandstone outcrops, eastern tiers of plains counties. This and the next form extensive, low mats.

10b. Flowers larger, the banner 8-16 mm long. **A. tridactylicus** Gray [3-fingered]. Common in early spring, on shale outcrops against the outer foothills of the Front Range.

11a. [6] Plants appearing scapose but often with visible lower internodes, with long leaves with many leaflets, and tall, many-flowered scapes (resembling and likely to be mistaken for a purple-flowered *Oxytropis*). **A. mollissimus** Torrey var. **mollissimus** [very soft]. In the eastern Colorado race the pods are glabrous, in contrast to the tomentose ones of the Western Slope var. *thompsoniae*.

11b. Plants low, with very short, if any, above-ground internodes . . . . . . (12)

12a. [11] Pod densely shaggy-villous. **A. purshii** Douglas [for Frederick Pursh, 1774-1820, author of *Flora Americae Septentrionalis*]. Dry grasslands, North Park. Flowers ochroleucous with a purple spot on the keel.

12b. Pod appressed-pubescent or glabrous . . . . (13)

13a. [12] Stem and leaves spreading-pilose; flowers ochroleucous, with a purple-tipped keel. **A. parryi** Gray. Endemic. Common in the foothill canyons.
13b. Stem and leaves appressed-pubescent or silky-hairy; stems purple or ochroleucous . . . . (14)

14a. [13] Flowers ochroleucous; plant perennial but with few caudices, often flowering the first year and thus appearing annual. **A. lotiflorus** Hooker [with flowers like *Lotus*]. Sandy soil, uncommon but widely scattered on the plains.
14b. Flowers purple or pink; plants distinctly perennial . . . . (15)

15a. [14] Plants in dense tufts; flowering stems numerous, erect; leaves not silky-pubescent; pods not inflated but small (2-3 cm long) and woody at maturity. **A. missouriensis** Nuttall [of "Missouri" in the old sense, including Wyoming and Colorado]. Common on the plains, flowering in early spring. Largely replaced, on the foothill mesas, by the next.
15b. Plants with few caudices; flowering stems usually solitary or a few together, spreading; pods inflated but firm-textured at maturity, over 3 cm long. **A. shortianus** Nuttall [for Charles Wilkins Short, friend of Nuttall and Gray]. Common in early spring on the mesas. Flowers deep pink, larger than in the previous species.

16a. [5] Pods plum-shaped, fleshy, and juicy, woody only when over-mature; plants prostrate; flowers white with blue- or purple-tipped keel . . . . (17)
16b. Pods not as above . . . . (18)

17a. [16] Pods glabrous. **A. crassicarpus** Nuttall [with thick pod], GROUND-PLUM. Common on the plains and foothill mesas.
17b. Pods pubescent. **A. plattensis** Nuttall [of the Platte River]. Infrequently collected, known from a few specimens from the easternmost tier of counties.

18a. [16] Pods globose, crowded together, pilose. **A. cicer** L. [for the genus *Cicer*, another legume]. Adventive, introduced for revegetation of disturbed forest land.
18b. Pods not globose . . . . (19)

19a. [18] Leaves and stem densely pubescent with soft, spreading hairs . . (20)
19b. Leaves glabrous or sparsely appressed-pubescent, not woolly . . . . . . (22)

20a. [19] Plant low, caespitose; leaves mostly near the base of the flowering stem (see also 13a). **A. parryi** Gray.
20b. Plant tall, erect, leafy-stemmed . . . . (21)

21a. [20] Flowers white; pods stipitate, reflexed, deeply grooved. **A. drummondii** Douglas [for Thomas Drummond, 1780-1835, Scottish collector in Canada with the Franklin expeditions]. Very common along the eastern base of the Front Range.
21b. Flowers purple; pods ascending or erect, not grooved (see also 11a). **A. mollissimus** Torrey.

22a. [19] Pods stiffly erect (the lower flowers usually can be used to indicate the position the pods will assume) . . . . (23)
22b. Pods loosely spreading to reflexed . . . . (25)

23a. [22] Stems 4 dm or more high, solitary or few, stiffly erect; leaflets broadly elliptic. **A. canadensis** L. Rare or infrequent, wooded gulches in the foothills.

23b. Stems rarely over 3 dm high, clustered, and not stiffly erect; leaflets narrowly elliptic . . . . (24)

24a. [23] Flower clusters almost globose; calyx densely black-hairy; flowers lavender; rhizomatous, forming low, spreading patches. **A. agrestis** Douglas. Frequent in grasslands on the plains and mesas [*A. dasyglottis* of Colorado literature].

24b. Flower clusters longer than broad; calyx sparsely black-hairy; flowers either purple or white; rhizomes absent. **A. adsurgens** Pallas var. **robustior** Hooker [cf. *assurgens*, erect; more robust]. Very common in the foothills; whole populations may consist of plants with one or the other flower color. An abundant species also in the Altai!

25a. [22] Tall, rather stout, erect plants . . . . (26)

25b. Low or weak plants with spreading stems . . . . (33)

26a. [25] Stipules at the lower, leafless nodes united on the side corresponding with the suppressed petiole to form an obtuse, entire blade; plant stoloniferous, perennial with 7-15 broad leaflets and pendulous, stipitate, papery, inflated pods. **A. americanus** (Hooker) Jones. South Park, collected in 1862 by Hall & Harbour and not found since then.

26b. Stipules free or connate, but if connate, then united on the side opposite the petiole, the sheath thus formed emarginate or bidentate . . . . (27)

27a. [26] Pods flattened laterally (as in snow peas), 5 mm or more wide, abruptly stipitate . . . . (28)

27b. Pods terete, or triangular in section . . . . (30)

28a. [27] Pods with a deep groove along the upper side. **A. scopulorum** Porter. South Park and San Luis Valley.

28b. Pods not grooved . . . . (29)

29a. [28] Pods broadest near the base, not curved, the sides equal; tall, rank plants of open roadsides and meadows. **A. ripleyi** Barneby [for Barneby's field companion, Dwight Ripley]. Endemic. Southern end of the San Luis Valley, CN. First described from adjacent New Mexico.

29b. Pods broadest near the middle, curved, the sides unequal. **A. aboriginum** Richardson. Infrequent plants of ponderosa pine forests in the foothills.

30a. [27] Pods triangular in section, elongate, stipitate. **A. racemosus** Pursh. Common on the plains.

30b. Pods terete or with 2 grooves along one side . . . . (31)

31a. [30] Pods with 2 parallel grooves along the upper side. **A. bisulcatus** (Hooker) Gray. Common on selenium soils in the mountain parks and on the plains. Two color forms occur, white or variegated purple-and-white. Poisonous to livestock.

31b. Pods lacking grooves . . . . (32)

32a. Flowers cream-colored to white; leaflets linear, widely divergent, lacking any narrowed petiolule separating them from the rachis; pods short and plump, over 1 cm long, firm, glabrous, with a prominent longitudinal ridge. **A. pectinatus** Douglas [comblike, alluding to the leaves]. Common on barren shale-clay areas of the plains.

32b. Flowers purplish-red; leaflets elliptic, not widely divergent, most of them petioled; pods 1.5-2.5 cm long, appressed-pubescent. **A. puniceus** Osterhout [purplish-red]. Mesa de Maya, south of the Arkansas River Valley.

33a. [25] Pods short and plump, up to twice as long as wide . . . . (34)
33b. Pods longer, cylindric or somewhat flattened . . . . (36)

34a. [33] Stems prostrate; pods sparsely covered with short black hairs. **A. bodinii** Sheldon [for the collector, J. E. Bodin]. South Park; flowers pink-purple.
34b. Stems erect; pods densely covered with appressed, white hairs . . . . . (35)

35a. [34] Flowers pale lilac; plants of the plains. **A. gracilis** Nuttall. Common throughout the high plains.
35b. Flowers deep purple; plants of the mountains. **A. eucosmus** Robinson [elegant]. Subalpine and upper montane streamsides.

36a. [33] Annual or short-lived perennial with a slender taproot . . . . . . (37)
36b. Perennial with variously developed root systems . . . . (38)

37a. [36] Annual; pods oblong, strongly curved; flowers purple, in short racemes. **A. nuttallianus** de Candolle var. **micranthiformis** Barneby. Rare on the Eastern Slope, one collection known from the plains, CW.
37b. Perennial, sometimes blooming the first year; pods obovoid; flowers white, scattered along delicate, flagelliform racemes. **A. brandegei** T. C. Porter. Infrequent on gravelly river benches, San Luis Valley. Extremely inconspicuous.

38a. [36] Plants restricted to alpine tundra . . . . (39)
38b. Plants of foothills, montane and subalpine . . . . (41)

39a. [38] Plants tiny, with very slender, elongated caudices and lax stems only a few cm long, gray-pubescent leaves and violet-purple flowers; pods not stipitate. **A. molybdenus** Barneby. Common but very inconspicuous, Mosquito and Saguache ranges.
39b. Plants larger, forming clumps of ascending stems from a thick root; pods stipitate . . . . (40)

40a. [39] Leaves densely gray-strigose beneath; flowers white with purple spot on the keel; pods glabrous. **A. aboriginum** Richardson var. **major** Gray. Mosquito Range. It is difficult to reconcile this distinctive alpine plant with the tall foothills woodland var. **glabriusculus**, although Barneby finds that the species as a whole is interconnected by numerous intergrading races. In my experience the Colorado races are perfectly distinct morphologically and ecologically.
40b. Leaves sparsely appressed-pubescent beneath; flowers purple; pods black-hairy. **A. robbinsii** (Oakes) Gray var. **minor** (Hooker) Barneby [for J. W. Robbins, M.D., 1801-1879]. Rare, on the Eastern Slope only in the Mosquito Range.

41a. [38] Flowers 1-2 cm long, red-purple, in rather dense clusters; pod inflated, somewhat dorsiventrally compressed. **A. hallii** Gray [for the collector, Elihu Hall, 1822-1882]. Common on rocky slopes of the mountain parks, North Park to San Luis Valley.
41b. Flowers less than 1 cm long, in loose racemes; pods not inflated . . . (42)

42a. [41] Leaves with many of the leaflets reduced or absent, leaving an almost naked rachis. **A. convallarius** Greene var. **scopulorum** Barneby [valley-dweller].

Uncommon on the Eastern Slope, near Salida and in the south end of South Park (*A. diversifolius*).

42b. Leaves with normal complements of leaflets . . . . (43)

43a. [42] Pods black-hairy. **A. alpinus** L. Common in moist forests, streamsides, and mountain meadows, upper montane and subalpine; flowers pink-purple.

43b. Pods smooth or, if pubescent, the hairs light-colored . . . . (44)

44a. [43] Pod flattened laterally . . . . (45)

44b. Pod terete, plump . . . . (46)

45a. [44] Pods 15-20 mm long, sessile, somewhat rounded in section, the valves convex; flower clusters usually well-exserted beyond the foliage. **A. miser** Douglas var. **oblongifolius** (Rydberg) Cronquist [wretched, alluding to the condition of the first specimen]. Common in mountain meadows and forest openings.

45b. Pods 8-15 mm long, with at least a short stipe, the valves flat; flower clusters little if at all exceeding the leaves. **A. tenellus** Pursh [delicate]. Common in dry montane and subalpine forests. Plants commonly blackening after drying in the plant press. Eastern Slope plants are white-flowered.

46a. [44] Leaflets usually broad and almost circular. **A. sparsiflorus** Gray [few-flowered]. Rocky slopes in and near the South Platte Valley. There are two races based on the size of the pod. Var. *majusculus* has a pod up to 2.5 cm long, but it grows intermixed with the species proper, which has a pod less than 1 cm long!

46b. Leaflets narrow . . . . (47)

47a. [46] Flowers white; racemes about 3-flowered; stems weak and delicate. **A. leptaleus** Gray. Moist swales and meadows, Middle Park to Wet Mountain Valley.

47b. Flowers purple; racemes with more than 6 flowers; stems wiry, not delicate. **A. flexuosus** (Hooker) G. Don. Common in dry fields and roadsides, lower altitudes.

CAESALPINIA L. [for Andrea Cesalpino, 1519-1603, Italian botanist, "the first orthodox systematist"]

One species, **C. jamesii** (Torrey & Gray) Fisher. A low, perennial herb with bipinnate leaves and yellow flowers. The conspicuous orange glands (turning black when dried) on the lower leaf-surface are diagnostic (*Hoffmanseggia*). Scattered on the plains, WL to BA. Most frequent in the Arkansas Valley from PE southwestward.

CARAGANA Fabricius 1763 [from *Caragan*, a Mongolian name for *C. arborescens*]. PEATREE

1a. Tall shrubs; leaves distinctly pinnate, with 6-18 oval or oblong, mucronate leaflets; spines in pairs, stipular; flowers clear yellow; pods over 2 cm long. **C. arborescens** Lamarck. Commonly cultivated and recently escaping, becoming naturalized particularly near Colorado Springs. A common shrub of the Altai steppe. In this genus the leaves are even-pinnate, lacking the terminal leaflet.

1b. Low, spreading shrubs; leaves with 3-4 crowded, narrow, sharp-pointed leaflets; spines single, formed of modified branchlets; flowers orange-yellow; pods less than 2 cm long. **C. aurantiaca** Koehne. Evidently once planted by the Forest Service, and persisting in foothill canyons near Grant and at the site of the old Monument Nursery. Native to Central Asia.

COLUTEA L. 1753 [the ancient Greek name]. BLADDER SENNA

One species, **C. arborescens** L. Introduced about 1913 around houses in Sunshine Canyon northwest of Boulder, now spreading and becoming established in the foothill canyons. Easily recognized by the large, papery-inflated pods. The leaves are odd-pinnate and flowers are yellow.

CORONILLA L. 1753 [diminutive of Latin, *corona*, crown]. CROWN VETCH

One species, **C. varia** L. Adventive, pasture plant used extensively for revegetation. The pinkish flowers have a slender, purple-tipped keel. The plants thrive in shade and quickly form a dense cover up to several feet high.

DALEA Lucanus [an anonymous citizen of Lucca] 1758 [for Samuel Dale, 1659-1739, British botanist] (including *Petalostemon*)

1a. Low shrub. **D. formosa** Torrey [handsome]. On sandstone "breaks," east end of Mesa de Maya, BA, LA. Flowers purple, calyx lobes long and slender; leaflets minute.

1b. Annuals or herbaceous perennials . . . . (2)

2a. Annual. **D. leporina** (Aiton) Bullock [of rabbits, alluding to the rabbit-foot aspect of the inflorescence]. Flowers white or pale violet; inflorescence a narrow, brownish spike. Rarely collected, San Luis Valley, and a few very old records from the Denver area.

2b. Perennial . . . . (3)

3a. Stems prostrate. **D. lanata** Sprengel [woolly]. Flowers red-violet, in long, slender spikes. Sand dunes of Cimarron Valley, southeast corner of BA.

3b. Stems erect or ascending from a decumbent base . . . . (4)

4a. Leaves essentially with 3 leaflets. **D. jamesii** (Torrey) Torrey & Gray. Flowers yellow, fading purplish-brown. Common on sandstone rimrock and sandy arroyos, Arkansas Valley from Cañon City southeastward.

4b. Leaves with 5 or more leaflets . . . . (5)

5a. Plants variously pubescent below the inflorescence . . . . (6)

5b. Plants essentially glabrous up to the inflorescence . . . . (10)

6a. Flowers yellow; calyx teeth 2-5 mm long, aristate . . . . (7)

6b. Flowers ranging from red to white . . . . (8)

7a. Stems erect, up to 7 dm high, not branched except at the very base; petals not changing color in age. **D. aurea** Nuttall. Flower spike solitary at the top of the stem, thick, like a rabbit foot. Scattered in the easternmost plains counties, and in the Arkansas Valley.

7b. Stems diffuse and branched, less than 4 dm high; petals fading to pink or brown. **D. nana** Torrey [dwarf]. Sand dunes and flats, lower Arkansas Valley, CW, BA.

8a. Leaflets of middle stem leaves 5-8(-12) pairs; foliage villous-pilose throughout; sand dune plants. **D. villosa** (Nuttall) Sprengel. Sandhills on the eastern plains.

8b. Leaflets of middle stem leaves fewer than 5 pairs; not sand-restricted plants . . . . (9)

9a. Spikes relatively loose, especially after flowering, not conelike, the axis visible in pressed specimens; calyx tube and teeth with dense, spreading, usually tawny pubescence. **D. tenuifolia** (Gray) Shinners. A few records from the southeastern edge of Colorado.

9b. Spikes permanently dense and conelike, the axis concealed; calyx teeth and tube with dense, short, white, appressed hairs. **D. purpurea** Ventenat. Common across the plains from the base of the foothills.

10a. Inflorescence remotely flowered, the axis always clearly visible, the floral bracts with a broad, pale margin. **D. enneandra** Nuttall [with 9 stamens]. Common on sandy ground in the easternmost counties.

10b. Spike densely flowered, the axis not visible; floral bracts without a conspicuous pale margin . . . . (11)

11a. Petals rose or purplish . . . . (return to 9)

11b. Petals white or yellowish-white . . . . (12)

12a. Spikes subglobose, up to 15 mm long. **D. multiflora** (Nuttall) Shinners. One record from a roadside near Burlington, KC, thought to have been introduced in a seeding program.

12b. Spikes cylindric, up to 5 cm or more long . . . . (13)

13a. Spikes not over 5 cm long; axis minutely pilose; calyx tube glabrous or with very short hairs. **D. candida** Michaux var. **oligophylla** (Torrey) Shinners [white; few-leaved]. Common across the plains from the base of the foothills.

13b. Spikes 6-16 cm long or more; axis and calyx tube densely pilose. **D. cylindriceps** Barneby. Scattered in sandy areas on the plains from WL to BA (*D. compacta*).

DESMANTHUS Willdenow 1806 [Greek, *desme*, bundle, + *anthos*, flower]

1a. Pods strongly curved, 2-5 times longer than wide; stamens 5; stems erect. **D. illinoensis** (Michaux) MacMillan. Sand dunes along the Cimarron River, BA.

1b. Pods straight, linear, at least 7 times longer than wide; stamens 10. **D. cooleyi** (Eaton) Trelease [for Dennis Cooley, 1787-1860?]. Infrequently collected, Arkansas and Cimarron drainages, HF-BA.

GLYCYRRHIZA L. 1753 [Greek, *glycys*, sweet, + *rhiza*, root]. WILD LICORICE

One species, **G. lepidota** Pursh, **62D**. Abundant along irrigation ditches and on floodplains. Flowers greenish-white. The spiny pods are unique in the family. Extracts of the roots of two southern European species, *G. glabra* L. and *G. echinata* L., are a commercial source of licorice.

HEDYSARUM L. 1753 [Greek name used by Theophrastus for some legume]. CHAINPOD, **62F**

1a. Upper calyx lobes broader but considerably shorter than the lower 3; wing petals with a slender, basal auricular lobe nearly as long as the claw, the 2 petals weakly joined by these lobes above the ovary; pods not noticeably cross-corrugated, the reticulations almost isodiametric. **H. occidentale** Greene. San Luis Valley and eastern base of the San Juans.

1b. Upper calyx lobes slender, subequal to the lower ones and to the calyx tube; basal lobe of the wing petals broad, much shorter than the claws, not joined over the ovary; pods plainly cross-corrugated, the reticulations laterally elongated. **H. boreale** Nuttall, **62C**. Common on soil embankments at low and medium altitudes on the eastern plains.

HOFFMANSEGGIA Cavanilles [for J. C. Hoffmannsegg [sic!], 1766-1849, German botanist, entomologist, and ornithologist]

1a. Stems and inflorescence stipitate-glandular. **H. glauca** (Ortega) Eifert. Rarely collected, lower Arkansas Valley, BN, BA (*H. densiflora*).

1b. Stems and inflorescence not stipitate-glandular. **H. drepanocarpa** Gray [sickle-shaped, alluding to the pod]. Arkansas Valley, FN-BA. Similar to *Caesalpinia jamesii* but lacking the glandular dots on the lower leaf surface.

LATHYRUS L. 1753 [Greek, *la*, very, + *thyros*, passionate, the original species thought to be an aphrodisiac]. PEAVINE

1a. Flowers purple, pink, or red . . . . (2)

1b. Flowers white. **L. leucanthus** Rydberg [white-flowered]. Common in foothills and aspen groves.

2a. Leaflets 2; stem strongly winged; flowers bright pink, rarely white (mutants). **L. latifolius** L., PERENNIAL SWEETPEA. Adventive garden escape commonly colonizing fencerows.

2b. Leaflets more than 2; stem not strongly winged . . . . (3)

3a. Leaves silky-pubescent; flowers variegated pink and white, very fragrant. **L. polymorphus** Nuttall subsp. **incanus** (Smith & Rydberg) C. L. Hitchcock. Gulches and canyonsides, plains and foothills.

3b. Leaves glabrous; flowers blue-purple, not very fragrant. **L. eucosmus** Butters & St. John [elegant]. Open woods, foothills.

LOTUS L. 1753 [ancient Greek plant name, used in many senses]

1a. Flowers bright yellow, in a terminal umbel. **L. tenuis** Waldstein & Kitaibel. Adventive in eastern Colorado around Boulder and Fort Collins, in cultivated and pasture land, evidently not an aggressive weed.

1b. Flowers yellow with brown, solitary in the leaf axils. **L. wrightii** (Gray) Greene [for Charles Wright]. A common plant of the southern counties on the Western Slope, but unknown in our area except in one locality in DA, where it is believed to have been introduced. Possibly to be expected in the San Luis Valley.

LUPINUS L. 1753 [Latin, *lupus*, wolf, because of an old belief that it ruins the soil]

1a. Annual or biennial; cotyledons usually present at flowering time . . . . (2)

1b. Perennials . . . . (3)

2a. Racemes rather loose and usually over 3 cm long; pods 2 cm long or more, constricted somewhat between the seeds; seed faces concave, the sides perpendicular. **L. pusillus** Pursh [very small]. Widely distributed on the eastern plains. In places where this is common, the pinkish, disk-shaped seeds are gathered by ants and used to cover their hills. Local residents call these seeds "ant money."

2b. Racemes short, dense, headlike, usually less than 2 cm long; pods less than 2 cm long, not much constricted between the seeds; seeds convex on both surfaces. **L. kingii** Watson [for Clarence King, geologist on the U. S. Geological Survey, 1867-1868]. Common in the San Luis Valley.

3a. Dwarf, forming low, spreading clumps, the inflorescence shorter than the leaves. **L. caespitosus** Nuttall. Sagebrush, North Park, upper Arkansas Valley, Cochetopa Pass.

3b. Tall, usually erect; inflorescence exceeding the leaves . . . . (4)

4a. Flowers conspicuously bicolored, the banner with a large purple spot near the base; plants rhizomatous. **L. plattensis** Watson [of the Platte River]. Common locally in sandy places on the plains.
4b. Flowers blue or white, not conspicuously bicolored . . . . (5)

5a. Banners reflexing at or near the midpoint, leaving a relatively wide gap above the wings; longest petioles near the base, the upper ones often much reduced . . . . (6)
5b. Banner reflexing above the midpoint, and the ventral groove clasping enough of the wings so that the tip of the banner leaves a small opening between the wing tip and the banner tip; leaves mostly short-petioled, or somewhat longer below . . . . (7)

6a. Leaves with spreading pilose hairs 2-3 mm long; banner glabrous dorsally. **L. prunophilus** Jones [chokecherry-loving]. Sagebrush, upper Rio Grande Valley, possibly in North Park.
6b. Leaflets appressed-silky hairy on both sides; banner pubescent over the central half of the dorsal side. **L. sericeus** Pursh [silky]. Upper Rio Grande Valley.

7a. Keel generally ciliate above and below, as well as ahead of the claw (sometimes cilia below and ahead of the claw are missing); often some lower leaves with longer petioles; leaflets sericeous or sparsely pilose to glabrate above; calyx spur often well developed. **L. caudatus** Kellogg [tailed]. Plains and mountain parks.
7b. Keel glabrous above, below and ahead of the claw; leaves usually all short-petioled; leaflets often glabrous above and conduplicate (folded lengthwise), sometimes thinly pilose to sparsely strigose above . . . . (8)

8a. Tip of keel short and bent back; flowers small and numerous in elongate racemes. **L. parviflorus** Nuttall subsp. **myrianthus** (Greene) Harmon. Common in San Luis Valley, Cochetopa area, and in North Park, but first described from the Platte Canyon.
8b. Tip of keel long and slender, erect or slanting forward; flowers 8-12 mm long, in short or long racemes. **L. argenteus** Pursh. Abundant throughout the mountains. The creamy-white-flowered race in the Front Range foothills is subsp. **ingratus** (Greene) Harmon.

MEDICAGO L. 1753 [Greek name for alfalfa, alluding to the fact that the plant came to Greece from Media]. ALFALFA, MEDIC

1a. Flowers yellow, in very tiny clusters; plants decumbent. **M. lupulina** L. [little hops], BLACK MEDIC. Adventive, common, ruderal weed in gardens and lawns.
1b. Flowers purple to white, sometimes with a greenish-yellow color; heads large; plants erect, branched from the base. **M. sativa** L. [planted], ALFALFA. Adventive, escaped from cultivation, usually established on roadsides.

MELILOTUS Miller 1754 [Greek, *meli*, honey, + *lotos*, some leguminous plant]. SWEETCLOVER

1a. Flowers white. **M. alba** Medikus. Adventive, extensively planted for forage, erosion control, and as a honey plant.
1b. Flowers yellow. **M. officinalis** (L.) Pallas. Adventive, similar sites.

MIMOSA L. 1753 [Greek, *mimos*, mimic, thought by some to allude to the animallike sensitivity of leaves of some species]

One species, **M. borealis** Gray, CATCLAW. Low shrub, branches pale, with flattened, recurved thorns and balls of pink flowers. Rimrock of east end of Mesa de Maya, LA, BA.

OXYTROPIS de Candolle 1802 [Greek, *oxys*, sharp, + *tropis*, keel]. LOCOWEED, **62G**

1a. Pods pendulous, not inflated; stipules only slightly adnate by their bases to the petioles; plants usually with leafy stems . . . . (2)
1b. Pods erect or spreading, never pendulous; stipules adnate to the petiole; plants scapose or nearly so . . . . (4)

2a. Lateral sinuses of the calyx narrow and acute; petals narrow, usually only bluish or purplish-tinged, the banner oblanceolate, about 3 times longer than broad. **O. deflexa** (Pallas) de Candolle var. **sericea** Torrey & Gray. South Park.
2b. Lateral sinuses of the calyx broad and obtuse; petals ample, purple, the banner broadly obcordate, about twice longer than broad . . . . (3)

3a. Copiously and loosely villous-pilose; stems usually developed, with at least one apparent internode at maturity; raceme 10-20-flowered, usually elongating in fruit. **O. deflexa** var. **deflexa**. Alpine, vicinity of South Park. This race is disjunct from Siberia!
3b. Sparingly pilose, the hairs usually appressed; stems usually none, but occasionally with a few developed internodes; raceme 7-10-flowered, nearly always compact in fruit. **O. deflexa** var. **foliolosa** (Hooker) Barneby. Dry lodgepole pine forests, subalpine.

4a. Leaves with some leaflets in whorls or more than one at a node. **O. splendens** Douglas. Stony subalpine meadows. Woolly pubescent; flowers pink.
4b. Leaves strictly pinnate . . . . (5)

5a. Fruiting calyx inflated and completely enclosing the ripe fruit; scapes less than 1.5 cm long, bearing only 1-4 flowers. **O. multiceps** Nuttall [many-headed]. Common on granitic gravels in the middle foothills of the Front Range, LR-EP; Pawnee Buttes.
5b. Fruiting calyx not inflated, not competely enclosing the ripe fruit or, if so, then the scapes much longer and bearing many flowers . . . . (6)

6a. Scapes short, bearing 1-4 flowers; pod papery-inflated; dwarf alpine or subalpine plants . . . . (7)
6b. Scapes tall or bearing many flowers . . . . (8)

7a. Pod papery and inflated. **O. podocarpa** Gray [footlike fruit]. Locally abundant on high mountains, Gray's Peak to Saguache Range.
7b. Pod neither papery nor inflated but leathery or woody at maturity. **O. parryi** Gray. Montane to alpine, evidently rare, BL, CC, PA.

8a. Plants sticky-glandular, at least on the calyx and bracts. **O. viscida** Nuttall. Tundra of central massifs.
8b. Plants not sticky-glandular; lower elevations . . . . (9)

9a. Corolla purplish or red except in rare albino forms. **O. lambertii** Pursh [for A. B. Lambert, 1761-1842, British botanist]. Grasslands of the plains, parks, and foothills. Generally with only a few flowering stems, and spreading leaves. Crosses extensively with *O. sericea* at the upper altitudinal limit of its range.

9b. Corolla white or yellowish, keel often purple-tinged, the whole corolla rarely purplish . . . . (10)

10a. Flowers 18-25 mm long. **O. sericea** Nuttall [silky]. Sagebrush, plains to upper montane, where it hybridizes with *O. lambertii*, forming spectacular variations of color and habit. Typically the flowers of this species are white with a purple spot on the keel, and the clumps have numerous caudices and erect basal leaves. The hybrid populations maintain the robust habit of *O. sericea* while picking up a variety of color shades from *O. lambertii*.

10b. Flowers 12-15 mm long; spikes rather dense; flowers yellowish-white, without the purple spot . . . . (11)

11a. Leaflets 17-33; relatively tall plants (about 3 dm). **O. campestris** (L.) de Candolle var. **gracilis** (Nelson) Barneby. Montane to subalpine (*A. campestris* var. *gracilis*).

11b. Leaflets 7-17; low alpine plants. **O. campestris** (L.) de Candolle var. **cusickii** (Greenman) Barneby [of the fields; for William C. Cusick, 1842-1922, collector in Oregon and Idaho]. Infrequently collected, Saguache Range.

PEDIOMELUM Rydberg 1919 [Greek, *pedion*, flatland, + *mylon*, apple, alluding to the tubers, from the French vernacular name *pomme de prairie*] (formerly included in *Psoralea*). INDIAN POTATO

1a. Pubescence of stem and petioles spreading. **P. esculentum** (Pursh) Rydberg [edible]. Rarely collected, our records from the Pawnee Buttes.

1b. Pubescence appressed . . . . (2)

2a. Stem completely underground; seeds with conspicuous ridges. **P. hypogaeum** (Nuttall) Rydberg [below-ground], **62B**. Infrequent on the high plains. LR and WL south to EP.

2b. Plant with aerial stems 3-8 dm long, procumbent or ascending; seeds smooth. **P. cuspidatum** (Pursh) Rydberg. Rarely collected, one record from sandy soil, YM.

PROSOPIS L. 1767 [an ancient Greek name for a plant]. MESQUITE

One species, **P. glandulosa** Torrey. Extremely rare, only a few plants occurring on the Mesa de Maya near Branson, LA. First reported by E. L. Greene in January 1880 when he discovered this and *Nolina texana* "in the mountains between the Purgatoire and the Apishapa" while traveling on the railroad between Trinidad and La Junta. Greene's locality has not been discovered, but at the Branson locality both *Prosopis* and *Nolina* are present.

PSORALIDIUM Rydberg 1919 [diminutive of *Psoralea*: Greek, *psoraleos*, scabby, from the gland-dotted foliage] (formerly included in *Psoralea*)

1a. Flowers in well-separated whorls, not pedicellate . . . . (2)

1b. Flowers in loose or dense racemes, distinctly pedicelled . . . . (3)

2a. Bracts obovate to spatulate; calyx inflated in fruit. **P. digitatum** (Nuttall) Rydberg. Rarely collected, but reported on the northeastern plains in YM and PL.

2b. Bracts ovate-lanceolate, acuminate; calyx not inflated in fruit; leaves silvery on both sides with appressed-silky pubescence. **P. argophyllum** (Pursh) Rydberg. Scattered but locally abundant from the base of the Front Range foothills across the plains.

3a. Flowers white or cream-colored in dense racemes; pods subglobose. **P. lanceolatum** (Pursh) Rydberg. Sandy soils on the eastern plains and San Luis Valley. In this species the leaves are narrowly linear in contrast to the elliptical ones of *P. tenuiflorum*.
3b. Flowers bluish to purple in loose racemes; pods longer than wide . . . (4)

4a. Leaflets 7-15 times longer than wide; pods gradually tapering to a beak. **P. linearifolium** (Torrey & Gray) Rydberg. Infrequently collected, recorded from YM.
4b. Leaflets 2-6 times as long as wide; pods abruptly short-beaked. **P. tenuiflorum** (Pursh) Rydberg. Very common throughout the eastern plains.

ROBINIA L. 1753 [for Jean Robin, 1550-1629, herbalist to Henry IV of France, and his son Vespasian, 1579-1662, who first cultivated the tree in Europe]. LOCUST
1a. Flowers white, in a hanging raceme; pods smooth; tree. **R. pseudoacacia** L., BLACK LOCUST. Adventive, cultivated as a street tree and persisting around old homesteads.
1b. Flowers purple, the raceme not hanging; pods glandular-hirsute; shrub. **R. neomexicana** Gray. Adventive along streamsides, canyons of the Front Range.

SCHRANKIA Wildenow [for Franz von Schrank, German botanist, 1747-1835]. SENSITIVE BRIER
1a. Mature leaflets with only the midrib visible; herbage puberulent. **S. occidentalis** (Wooton & Standley) Standley. Rarely collected, BA.
1b. Mature leaflets with lateral veins, at least on the distal half; herbage glabrous. **S. uncinata** Willdenow. Rarely collected, BA (*S. nuttallii*).

SPHAEROPHYSA de Candolle 1825 [Greek, *sphaira*, sphere, + *physa*, bellows, alluding to the bloated fruit] (formerly included in *Swainsona*). BUYAN

One species, **S. salsula** (Pallas) de Candolle [alluding to the salt-flat habitat]. Adventive, abundant in the San Luis and lower Arkansas valleys. The plant resembles a gigantic *Astragalus* and is not clearly separated from that genus. However, the strange flower color (red-orange) and the habit and inflated pods mark it sufficiently well. At times the plants may be covered with swarms of blister beetles (Cantharidae); handling them can cause severe skin burns.

STROPHOSTYLES Elliott 1823 [Greek, *strophe*, turning, + *stylos*, style, alluding to the incurved style]

One species, **S. leiosperma** (Torrey & Gray) Piper [smooth-seeded]. Infrequently collected, easternmost plains counties, YM, BA. A slender, vinelike perennial with pinnately trifoliolate leaves with stipels (stipulelike structures) at the base of the leaflets, pale pink to whitish flowers, and a straight pod with very smooth seeds.

THERMOPSIS R. Brown 1811 [Greek, *thermos*, lupine, + *opsis*, like]. GOLDEN BANNER
1a. Pod curled in a circle when mature, glabrous. **T. rhombifolia** (Nuttall) Nuttall. Strictly a plains species, blossoming very early in the spring.
1b. Pod straight or curved, but never strongly so . . . . (2)

2a. Pods stiffly erect, straight, pubescent. **T. montana** Nuttall. Widespread in wet mountain meadows, common in the intermountain parks and San Luis Valley.

2b. Pods widely spreading, curved, glabrous or nearly so. **T. divaricarpa** Nelson [spreading-fruit]. Gravelly meadows and streambottoms, mostly in the foothills.

TRIFOLIUM L. 1753 [Latin, *tres*, three, + *folium*, leaf]. CLOVER

1a. Stems scapose, leaves basal (only in *T. gymnocarpum* a few leaves on the flower stalk) . . . . (2)
1b. Stems leafy, not exclusively basal . . . . (8)

2a. Plants from long, slender rhizomes, not caespitose; flowers pendent, in short racemes and not tight heads. **T. brandegei** Watson. Upper subalpine and alpine, usually on steep, rocky slopes; flowers purple. San Juan Mountains, CN.
2b. Plants not rhizomatous, commonly caespitose; flowers not pendent . . (3)

3a. Very densely caespitose, with many caudices clothed with old dry leaf bases . . . . (4)
3b. Not or loosely caespitose; caudices few, not strongly clothed with old dry leaf bases . . . . (6)

4a. Flowers 1-3 per head. **T. nanum** Torrey [dwarf]. Tundra of the higher peaks. A hard-mat plant, the flowers hardly exceeding the leaves.
4b. Flowers numerous in each head . . . . (5)

5a. Flowers bicolored; banner pale, wings and keel pink- or purple-tipped; usually less than 1 dm tall. **T. dasyphyllum** Torrey & Gray [shaggy-leaved]. Common on tundra in the granitic mountains, evidently absent from the San Juans.
5b. Flowers one color, bright rose-purple; usually forming loose mats over 1 dm tall; rocky ledges at timberline. **T. attenuatum** Greene. Replacing the last in the southern half of the state, often at lower altitudes. Much larger in every way than the last. The extremes are easily separable but from Hoosier Pass to the Sangre de Cristo Range plants become difficult to distinguish. The monographer Zohary wrote: "Though *T. attenuatum* somewhat resembles *T. dasyphyllum* in its habit, it can be easily distinguished by its smaller bracts, deflexed and larger flowers and usually somewhat lanceolate (not oblanceolate) leaflets. Gillett (1965) recorded the two species as growing together without hybridizing."

6a. Spreading, close to the ground; heads less than 1 cm broad, pale purple, no involucre; leaves sharply serrate, gray-green, often with a white mark across the blade. **T. gymnocarpum** Nuttall [naked fruit]. Sagebrush-oak.
6b. Erect; heads over 2 cm broad, deep rose-purple, with an involucre of fused bracts; leaves rarely serrate, grass-green, never marked . . . . (7)

7a. Banner rounded, not much longer than the wings; low, usually less than 1 dm tall. **T. parryi** Gray. Common in subalpine forest openings and moist tundra. Diploid, with 16 chromosomes.
7b. Banner tapered, acute, longer than the wings; tall, larger in every way, usually over 1 dm tall. **T. salictorum** Greene [of willows]. Very wet tundra. A tetraploid with 32 chromosomes. Hybrids are rare and are sterile.

8a. Heads sessile, subtended by a few leaves and a broad, papery, involucrelike bract. **T. pratense** L. [of meadows], RED CLOVER. Adventive. Robust perennial often cultivated for honey and for pasture mixes, naturalized in meadows and along trails. The plants have hairy leaves and large pink-purple heads.

8b. Heads pedunculate . . . . (9)

9a. Involucre present, of fused bracts. **T. wormskioldii** Lehmann [for Morten Wormskiold, Danish botanist, 1783-1845]. Forests and meadows, southern counties (*T. fendleri*).

9b. Involucre absent . . . . (10)

10a. Low, spreading plants forming dense clumps or rooting at the nodes; introduced species . . . . (11)

10b. Erect plants never forming dense clumps nor rooting at the nodes; flowers various; native plants. **T. rusbyi** Greene [for the collector, W. S. Rusby, 1852-?]. Stem and leaves ± pubescent; heads about 1 cm diameter, white or rarely purplish, flowers varying in attitude. Widely distributed, especially in southern counties. Several minor subspecies are recognized.

11a. Flowers rose-pink; calyx papery-inflated in fruit; creeping plants introduced on lawns and golf courses, often escaped and established. **T. fragiferum** L., STRAWBERRY CLOVER.

11b. Flowers white or pinkish-white, turning brownish; calyx not inflated; erect or creeping . . . . (12)

12a. Stems erect or ascending; flowers pinkish-white; calyx pubescent in the sinuses between the teeth. **T. hybridum** L., ALSIKE CLOVER (pronounced ál-si-keh; this was a hamlet near Linnaeus' summer home). Adventive, commonly cultivated and escaped into meadows.

12b. Stem creeping, rooting at the nodes; calyx glabrous or sparsely pubescent at the base. **T. repens** L., WHITE DUTCH CLOVER [creeping]. Adventive, escaped from cultivation and established along trails and in meadows.

VEXIBIA Rafinesque 1825 [derivation?]. WHITE LOCO

One species, **V. nuttalliana** (Turner) Weber. Abundant on the plains. This small genus previously lumped in *Sophora*, a group of dry-tropics trees, is disjunct between western United States and southwest Asia!

VICIA L. 1753 [the classical Latin name]. VETCH

1a. Flowers almost sessile in the leaf axils. **V. angustifolia** (L.) Reichard. Adventive, San Luis Valley.

1b. Flower clusters on distinct peduncles . . . . (2)

2a. Racemes many-flowered; leaves densely villous. **V. villosa** Roth. Adventive, introduced as a nurse crop for freeways, persisting along roadsides.

2b. Racemes few-flowered . . . . (3)

3a. Flowers 12-25 mm long, purple, pink, or blue. **V. americana** Mühlenberg. Common in grasslands and meadows, commonly mistaken for *Lathyrus* because of its large and few flowers.

3b. Flowers 6-9 mm long, white, only purplish-tipped. **V. ludoviciana** Nuttall var. **texana** (Torrey & Gray) Shinners. Infrequent in meadows at the base of the Front Range (*V. exigua*).

FAGACEAE OAK FAMILY (FAG)

Having grown up in the East, I became well acquainted with many species of oaks and had little trouble telling most of them apart. In the West, the story is very different. While in Colorado we have only one widespread, common, and dominant oak, the scrub oak species *Quercus gambelii*, this is so variable that it has been at one time or other divided into *Q. fendleri, gunnisonii, leptophylla, novomexicana, utahensis, venustula*, and *vreelandii*, the differences based on leaf shape and pubescence. We can't pass off these differences as imaginary. They are real and striking, but probably they reflect genetic contamination of the *Q. gambelii* genotype by hybridization with species formerly inhabiting the area along with it. Because this oak reproduces by suckering, very large areas can be populated by clones having a single, distinctive leaf form, and this only magnifies the difference. So one should expect our common scrub oak to vary in the direction of other southwestern species; absolute identifications are often difficult or impossible.

QUERCUS L. 1753 [the classical Latin name]. OAK

1a. Leaves usually over 5 cm long, not rigid, the lobes deep, rounded, with broad open sinuses; tall shrubs or small trees in the foothills. **Q. gambelii** Nuttall [for William Gambel, 1821-1849, Nuttall's assistant in the field], SCRUB OAK, **61E,H**. Abundant from Evergreen and Douglas County southward. Many years ago Ernest Greenman, a Boulder pharmacist and hiker, planted many seedlings in the vicinity of Boulder, on and around Green Mountain, to see if they would survive north of the native normal limit. They still survive, thrive, and are reproducing.

1b. Leaves usually less than 5 cm long, rigid, the lobes shallow or leaves merely very strongly toothed, the lobes or teeth often with sharp points; shrubs less than 2 m tall . . . . (2)

2a. Leaves very small (2-4 cm long), regularly spine-toothed. **Q. turbinella** Greene [diminutive of turbinate], **61F**. Localized in the Arkansas Valley near Cañon City.

2b. Leaves longer, irregularly shallowly lobed or -toothed . . . . (3)

3a. Leaves shallowly lobed. **Q. undulata** Torrey [wavy]. Evidently a variable population representing hybrid derivatives of the cross between *Q. gambelii* and *Q. grisea*. Common on the Mesa de Maya.

3b. Leaves entire to irregularly toothed but not distinctly lobed. **Q. grisea** Liebmann [gray]. Abundant on the Mesa de Maya. The populations here are so terribly mixed and affected by hybridization that it is impossible to name many of the forms to species.

FRANKENIACEAE FRANKENIA FAMILY (FRK)

This is a very ancient family now consisting of four genera of very salt-tolerant, heathlike plants. *Frankenia*, the largest genus, is found widely scattered on seashores and salt deserts in Australia, the Mediterranean region, southern South America, and southwestern North America. The family must have been once much more diversified and widely distributed, but its evolution and dispersal remains a puzzle.

FRANKENIA L. 1753 [for Johannes Franckenius, seventeenth-century Swedish botanist]

One species, **F. jamesii** Torrey, **63A**, restricted to gypsum shales in the Arkansas River Valley near Pueblo. The species is evidently an obligate gypsophile. *Frankenia* is very easy to recognize. It has prominently jointed stems with opposite, linear, tightly revolute leaves. The axils are crowded with short shoots bearing leaves so that they appear to be fascicled. The flowers are very distinctive. The sepals are united into a narrow tube, the petals are conspicuous, white, but are narrowed to claws within the calyx. There are 6 stamens in 2 groups of 3 long and 3 short. The style has 3 terminal branches.

FUMARIACEAE FUMITORY FAMILY (FUM)

Our only native genus of this strange family is a relative of dutchman's breeches and squirrel corn, well-known spring flowers of the eastern and far-western states, and the ornamental species of rose-colored *Dicentra*, the best known of which is the bleedingheart. All species are noted for their unusual spurred flowers and the fruit that resembles a bean pod. *Corydalis* species may be mistaken for legumes. An analysis of the flower might be useful. There are 2 sepals, very tiny and bractlike. Of the 4 petals, the 2 outer ones flare at the top and one of these has a spur at the base. The 2 inner petals are smaller, narrower and united at the top over the stigmas. There are 6 stamens, in 2 sets of 3. The fruit is a 2-valved capsule with parietal placentae.

1a. Flowers yellow or white, over 1 cm long; native species. **Corydalis**
1b. Flowers purplish, minute; introduced annual. **Fumaria**

CORYDALIS Ventenat 1804 [ancient Greek name for the crested lark]

1a. Flowers white; plants erect, up to 2 m tall. **C. caseana** Gray subsp. **brandegei** (Watson) G. Ownbey [for its discoverer, Professor E. L. Case], **63B**. Locally abundant in very wet aspen and spruce-fir forests, near Platoro, CN, and on Monarch Pass. This species also occurs in the Pacific Northwest and represents a distinctly eastern Asiatic section of the genus.
1b. Flowers yellow; plants low and sprawling . . . . (2)

2a. Seeds 1.4-1.6 mm long; plants often bearing racemes of cleistogamous flowers; spurred petal of normal flowers 10-15 mm long. **C. micrantha** (Engelmann) Gray. One record, on sand bars of the Arkansas River, BA.
2b. Seeds 1.8-2.1 mm long; plants seldom producing cleistogamous flowers; spurred petal of normal flowers 14-18 mm long. **C. aurea** Willdenow, GOLDEN SMOKE, **63C**. Common on roadside banks throughout the mountains. Two forms occur: subsp. **aurea**, with the spur about a third the length of the rest of the corolla and the fruits pendent and torulose. This seems to be the plant of the high mountains and intermountain parks; and subsp. **occidentalis** (Engelmann) G. Ownbey has the spur about equalling the body and the fruits erect and hardly torulose. This evidently is the low-altitude plant.

FUMARIA L. 1753. FUMITORY

One species **F. vaillantii** Loiseleur. Recently reported as a weed in moist places in the piedmont valley, JF, LR. Reported incorrectly as *F. officinalis* L., which has much larger flowers.

GENTIANACEAE GENTIAN FAMILY (GEN)

Gentians are characteristic and often among the choicest of alpine wildflowers in the high mountains of the world. In the Rockies we lack the deep blue, low gentians of the Swiss Alps but have some specialties of our own. And we share some of ours with the mountains of the other continents: *Chondrophylla*, most well represented in New Guinea; *Swertia*, *Comastoma*, *Lomatogonium*, and *Gentianodes* are found in the mountains of Eurasia. *Gentiana* proper, tall plants with large, spotted purple or yellow flowers, occur only in Europe. While the tradition in America has been to lump all gentians into a single genus, the genera recognized here are distinct on morphological grounds, chromosome numbers, electron-microscopic characters of the pollen grains, and life histories.

1a. Corolla lobed to near the base, rotate, never distinctly tubular . . . . . (2)
1b. Corolla distinctly tubular . . . . (5)

2a. Flowers large, each corolla lobe 3 cm or more long, blue or purple. **Eustoma,** TULIP GENTIAN
2b. Flowers with corolla lobes less than 2 cm long, blue, white, or greenish (3)

3a. Tall and stout, up to 2 m high; leaves fleshy, in whorls; flowers greenish-white. **Frasera,** MONUMENT PLANT
3b. Plant slender; leaves opposite or basal; flowers blue or white . . . . . . (4)

4a. Annual; flowers white, rarely light blue; several pairs of opposite stem leaves present. **Lomatogonium,** MARSH FELWORT
4b. Perennial; flowers deep blue; leaves chiefly basal, elliptic or oblanceolate. **Swertia,** STAR GENTIAN

5a. Perennial, without a taproot; corolla never with fringed lobes, usually over 2.5 cm long . . . . (6)
5b. Annual or biennial or, if a short-lived perennial, then with a taproot; corolla usually small, but if larger than 2.5 cm, then with fringed lobes . . . . . (7)

6a. Flowers white with dull purple pleats. **Gentianodes,** ARCTIC GENTIAN
6b. Flowers blue or purple. **Pneumonanthe,** BOTTLE GENTIAN

7a. Corolla deep blue, over 2.5 cm long, the principal lobes marginally fringed. **Gentianopsis,** FRINGED GENTIAN
7b. Corolla white, pale, or deep blue, less than 2 cm long, the principal lobes not fringed on the margin . . . . (8)

8a. Sinuses of the corolla plicate, with a smaller toothlike lobe between the principal ones; leaf pairs connate into a tubular base; leaves less than 1 cm long, rounded-oblanceolate or obovate, white-edged. **Chondrophylla,** SIBERIAN GENTIAN
8b. Sinuses of the corolla not plicate, without subsidiary lobes; leaves larger, not connate-based nor white-edged . . . . (9)

9a. Corolla lobes with two fringed scales within; flowers on long, naked peduncles. **Comastoma,** LAPPLAND GENTIAN
9b. Corolla lobes with a single row of hairs forming a fringe inside (occasionally lacking in very late-blooming plants); flowers subtended by bracts, usually in clusters on the stem. **Gentianella,** LITTLE GENTIAN

CHONDROPHYLLA Nelson 1904 [Greek, *chondros*, cartilage, + *phyllon*, leaf]. SIBERIAN GENTIAN

This genus exists widely disjunct in the mountain ranges of the world. I have seen species in the Andes, the mountains of Australia and New Guinea, the Alps, Himalaya, and Siberian Altai. All are tiny gentians, often 4-merous. Annuals are exceedingly rare in our alpine region, but *C. prostrata* seems to be annual or more likely a winter annual (*Ciminalis* of earlier editions).

1a. Capsule broadly obovoid, hardly longer than broad, the 2 valves gaping widely; base of capsule grading into a rather stout stipe, exserted from the corolla.; corolla pale blue. **C. aquatica** (L.) Weber, **65F**. Common in subalpine wet sedge meadows (*Gentiana fremontii*). Apparently not sensitive to light changes.

1b. Capsule narrow cylindrical, at least 5 times as long as broad, the valves spreading only at the top; stipe slender; corolla deep blue (except for white mutants) . . . . (2)

2a. Flowering stems erect; ripe capsule not fully exserted from the corolla; plants usually not over 5 cm tall. **C. prostrata** (Haenke) J. P. Anderson, **65D**. Corolla light sensitive, closing quickly when shaded by a cloud or hand.

2b. Flowering stems arcuate, flowers nodding; ripe capsule fully exserted on a slender stipe up to 3 cm long; plants over 5 cm tall. **C. nutans** (Bunge) Weber. Only recently discovered, a Siberian species new to the Western Hemisphere, on tundra, PT, ST.

COMASTOMA Toyokuni 1961 [Greek, *coma*, mane, + *stoma*, opening, alluding to the fringe inside the corolla]. LAPPLAND GENTIAN

One species, **C. tenellum** (Rottboell) Toyokuni, **64B**. Infrequent on alpine tundra. Easily recognized by the chiefly basal leaves and long-peduncled flowers.

EUSTOMA Salisbury 1806. TULIP GENTIAN

One species, **E. grandiflorum** (Rafinesque) Shinners, **Pl. 9**. Formerly common in wet, usually somewhat alkaline meadows on the plains, but becoming scarce with the disappearance of virgin prairie and wetlands. We consider it an endangered species. It is so beautiful and conspicuous a plant that it falls prey to collectors and casual flower-pickers.

FRASERA Walter 1788 [for John Fraser, colonial American botanist, 1750-1811]. MONUMENT PLANT, GREEN GENTIAN

1a. Tall, unbranched, the floral branches not exceeding the leaves. **F. speciosa** Douglas, **66C, Pl. 13**. Common in pine forests and meadows, montane and subalpine, a very conspicuous plant with its whorls of broad leaves and pale greenish flower clusters. Each petal has a midline of stiff glandular hairs and a fringed basal flap covering the nectary. Once considered biennial but better described as monocarpic, since, like the agaves, they take from 20-60 years of growth before producing a flower stalk, after which the plant dies. The season of 1988 produced enormous blossoming stands of this species.

1b. Low, much branched from the base, the floral branches much exceeding the narrow, white-margined leaves. **F. coloradensis** (Rogers) Post. Endemic. On rocky knolls in the southeastern counties. Much lower in stature than its southwestern counterpart, *F. albomarginata*, and occurring on stable grassland rather than sand dunes.

GENTIANELLA Moench 1794. LITTLE GENTIAN

1a. Calyx lobes distinctly fused into a basal cup, the lobes relatively narrow and not markedly unequal; cilia of internal corolla fringe free to the base or sometimes lacking; plants most commonly with relatively small flowers and stiffly ascending branches, but exceedingly variable in stature. **G. acuta** (Michaux) Hiitonen, **64A**. A very variable and widespread species in moist meadows up to subalpine (*G. amarella* is European). The usual form has pale blue flowers, but white forms occur (often called *G. strictiflora*). In very late-blooming plants the internal fringe of the corolla may be absent.

1b. Calyx lobes free to the base, the lobes variable in width and length, at least one of them broad and bractlike; fringe cilia usually united below; plants averaging much larger than the last, with usually widely spreading branches and very large flowers. **G. heterosepala** (Engelmann) Holub. Similar sites.

GENTIANODES Löve & Löve 1972 [from Gentius, King of Illyria, who, according to Pliny, discovered the medicinal virtues of gentians]. Arctic Gentian

One species, **G. algida** (Pallas) Löve & Löve, **66A**. A very late summer bloomer in the subalpine and alpine along rills, streambanks, and on tundra meadows. Also found in the Alps and Altai.

GENTIANOPSIS Ma 1951. Fringed Gentian

1a. Annual; flowers on long, naked peduncles, not closely bracteate; petals broadened above. **G. thermalis** (Kuntze) Iltis, **65A, Pl. 12**. Locally abundant in wet meadows and subalpine snowmelt basins (considered by some a subspecies of *G. detonsa*). White- or pink-flowered mutants are not uncommon.

1b. Short-lived perennial; flowers short-peduncled in the axils of 2 bractlike leaves; petals narrowly strap-shaped. **G. barbellata** (Engelmann) Iltis, **65B**. Subalpine grassy slopes.

LOMATOGONIUM A. Braun 1830 [Greek, *loma*, hem, + *gone*, gynoecium, alluding to the decumbent stigmatic lines]. Marsh Felwort

One species, **L. rotatum** (L.) Fries subsp. **tenuifolium** (Grisebach) Porsild, **64D**. Willow carrs and marshes, subalpine. Our plants have numerous ascending branches and usually white flowers, while the typical Arctic plants have few branches and purplish flowers.

PNEUMONANTHE Gleditsch 1764 [Greek, *pneumon*, lung, + *anthos*, flower, alluding to the inflated corolla]. Bottle Gentian

1a. Corolla cylindric, the floral bracts narrow, not scarious; plants ascending from a spreading base. **P. affinis** (Grisebach) Greene, **65E**. A common summer-blooming gentian in the intermountain parks and outer foothills.

1b. Corolla barrel-shaped, the floral bracts broad, scarious. **P. parryi** (Engelmann) Greene, **65C**. The common large gentian of montane and subalpine forests and meadows (incorrectly reported as *P. calycosa*, a species of the Pacific Northwest).

SWERTIA L. 1753 [for Emanuel Sweert, Dutch herbalist, born 1552]. Star Gentian

One species, **S. perennis** L., **64C**. Willow carrs and marshes, subalpine. White-flowered mutant individuals occur.

GERANIACEAE GERANIUM FAMILY (GER)

The geraniums have developed a remarkable method of planting their seeds. The gynoecium splits into 5 1-seeded units (mericarps), each attached to a split length of style that coils like a spring. Falling to the ground, the spring coils and uncoils with changes in atmospheric humidity. If the spring lies against a grass stem or other fixed object, it drills the sharp-pointed mericarp containing the seed into the earth. Similar devices have evolved, using different materials, in the grasses (*Stipa*) and in the roses (*Cercocarpus*). Potted geraniums belong to the African genus, *Pelargonium*.

1a. Leaves pinnately compound and dissected. **Erodium**, CRANE'S BILL, ALFILARIA
1b. Leaves palmately lobed. **Geranium**

ERODIUM L'Heritier 1789 [Greek, *erodios*, heron, for the long fruit beak]. CRANE'S BILL, ALFILARIA [Spanish, *alfiler*, pin]

One species, **E. cicutarium** (L.) L'Héritier, **67D**. Flowers tiny, pink, the petals falling early. One of the earliest flowering weeds of early spring in ruderal sites. A winter annual, its leafy rosette is already well developed by October.

GERANIUM L. 1753 [Greek, *geranos*, crane, for the long fruit beak]

1a. Plants erect, with a single or few stems . . . . (2)
1b. Plants with many stems, these often sprawling . . . . (3)

2a. Petals white with purple veins, pilose on the basal half; plants slender; leaves thin in texture. **G. richardsonii** Fischer & Trautvetter, **67A**. Typically found in aspen groves and spruce-fir forests. In the field this species is easier to recognize than from pressed specimens. However, wherever this and the next two species occur adjacent, hybrids are formed that are impossible to assign to either species.
2b. Petals pink to deep purple, pilose only on the basal quarter; plants stout; leaves thick in texture. **G. viscosissimum** Fischer & Meyer subsp. **nervosum** (Rydberg) Weber, **67C**. Wet roadside ditches and meadows.

3a. Plants lacking glandular pubescence; flowers ranging from pale pink to deep purple; stems slender, much-branched. **G. caespitosum** James subsp. **atropurpureum** (Heller) Weber. Common in the southern counties and the dominant race in New Mexico. Ponderosa pine zone.
3b. Plants with glandular petioles, stems, or pedicels; flowers never deep purple. **G. caespitosum** subsp. **caespitosum, 67B**. Abundant in the foothills and very variable in the amount and disposition of glandular hairs. The named varieties, while easily separated on technical characters, occur in mixed and variable populations (*G. fremontii, G. parryi*).

[Note: Several species have been found very rarely as casual introductions, often in garden plots and dooryards, but these evidently do not survive. These are *G. bicknellii* Britton var. *longipes* (Watson) Fernald, *G. columbinum* L., and *G. pusillum* Burmann. These are treated in floras of the eastern United States.]

GROSSULARIACEAE

CURRANT OR GOOSEBERRY FAMILY (GRS)

The word currant is a corruption of Corinth, from whence Zante currant, a small variety of grape, comes (raisins of Corinth). Wild currants are so called because of their resemblance to these. Gooseberries are green, often spiny fruits with an entirely different flavor, and this group is often segregated as the genus *Grossularia*, from which the family gets its name.

RIBES L. 1753 [said to come from Danish colloquial *ribs*, for red currant]. CURRANT, GOOSEBERRY

1a. Spines or prickles absent from the twigs . . . . (2)
1b. Spines or prickles present . . . . (9)

2a. Flowers yellow; petals yellow or red; berry black . . . . (3)
2b. Flowers white or pink . . . . (4)

3a. Hypanthium 12-15 mm long, about twice as long as the sepals; sepals revolute or spreading in the fading flowers; young growth and leaves pilose; leaves with 3 principal lobes but these subdivided. **R. odoratum** Wendlandt. Infrequent on the plains and outer foothill canyons, but probably more widely distributed than records indicate. The flowers of this and the next have a fragrance of cloves.
3b. Hypanthium less than 10 mm long and usually less than twice as long as the sepals; sepals erect and closed in the fading flowers; young growth glabrous or nearly so; leaves with 3 principal lobes. **R. aureum** Pursh, GOLDEN CURRANT, **68C**. Common on streamsides and wet ditches in the lower valleys and on the plains.

4a. Lower leaf surfaces with yellow, resinous dots. **R. americanum** Miller. Rare or local along the base of the Front Range between Colorado Springs and Denver. A protected population occurs in Roxborough State Park. The leaves are large, strongly 3-lobed; the hypanthium is campanulate and the petals cream-white.
4b. Lower leaf surfaces lacking yellow, resinous dots . . . . (5)

5a. Hypanthium very shallowly developed above the ovary, saucer-shaped . (6)
5b. Hypanthium short- or long-tubular . . . . (7)

6a. Flowers pink, arising from buds on last year's growth, not terminal on the branches; leaves with acute lobes, maple-leaf form. **R. coloradense** Coville, **68B**. Common in subalpine forests near the Continental Divide.
6b. Flowers white, in terminal racemes on the current year's growth; leaves with rounded lobes. **R. wolfii** Rothrock, **68A**. Rare on the Eastern Slope, occurring on the east side of the San Juans, CN, ML.

7a. Leaves deeply lobed about halfway to the midrib, not strongly glandular; plant usually with some spines at the nodes. **R. inerme** Rydberg, **68D**. Canyons, from the outer foothills to middle altitudes.
7b. Leaves obscurely lobed, strongly glandular-pubescent . . . . (8)

8a. Flowers pink; hypanthium narrow, 3-4 times as long as wide; leaf blades 1-3 cm diameter; fruit orange-red. **R. cereum** Douglas [waxy], **68F**. Dry gulches, canyonsides, lower altitudes. The berries make a very fine, resinous, home-made wine.
8b. Flowers white; hypanthium about as broad as high; leaf blades larger; fruit black. **R. viscosissimum** Pursh [sticky]. Northern counties near the Continental Divide, GA-RT. Not yet found on the Eastern Slope but to be expected on west side of North Park.

9a. Flowers 2-4 in a sessile cluster; hypanthium tubular . . . . (10)
9b. Flowers several in a raceme, each flower on a slender pedicel; hypanthium saucer- or goblet-shaped . . . . (12)

10a. Petals and sepals narrow-oblong; anthers red; style glabrous, white; sepals not reflexed. **R. leptanthum** Gray [slender-flowered]. Canyonsides in the lower valleys, southern counties.

10b. Petals short and broad, much shorter than the usually reflexed sepals; anthers white; styles densely pilose toward their bases . . . . (11)

11a. Leaves glabrous; spines straight, slender; petals obovate, ochroleucous; filaments to twice as long as petals. **R. inerme** Rydberg, **68E**. Common in canyons, foothills to middle altitudes. The specific epithet *inerme* is a misnomer.

11b. Leaves pilose to villous; spines stout, often somewhat curved; petals flabelliform, brownish-purple; filaments more than twice as long as petals. **R. divaricatum** Douglas. Only recently detected and distribution not well known, BL, LR.

12a. Leaves pubescent and glandular; spines 3 at a node but internodes usually unarmed; hypanthium saucer-shaped, red; low, spreading bushes. **R. montigenum** McClatchie, **68E**. Common in spruce-fir forests, along streams, subalpine.

12b. Leaves glabrous; spines single and internodes also spiny or bristly; hypanthium goblet-shaped, green; tall, little-branched shrubs of streamsides. **R. lacustre** (Persoon) Poiret [of lakes]. Wet meadows and willow fens, montane and subalpine.

HALORAGACEAE WATER MILFOIL FAMILY (HAL)

A small family of mostly Australian species, some of which are shrubs. Aquatic species, although very atypical and unrepresentative of the family, are found across the Northern Hemisphere. The plants will be found submerged in lakes and ponds and may be recognized by their whorled filiform-pinnatisect leaves and interrupted terminal spikes of small greenish flowers. The flowering spikes resemble a cord knotted at intervals, similar to spikes of some of the submerged potamogetons, but in that genus the leaves are never divided.

MYRIOPHYLLUM L. 1753 [Greek, *myrios*, innumerable, + *phyllon*, leaf]. WATER MILFOIL

One species, **M. sibiricum** Komarov, **70B**. Common in lakes and ponds at lower and middle altitudes (*M. exalbescens*).

HELLEBORACEAE HELLEBORE FAMILY (HEL)

The hellebore family encompasses all of the former members of the Ranunculaceae that have follicles rather than achenes. It is named for *Helleborus*, a genus of southern Europe and southwest Asia. The meaning of the word is obscure and was one used by Theophrastus. The type genus, *Helleborus*, is essentially Mediterranean. Its best known species, *Helleborus niger*, the Christmas rose, is a common garden plant blooming in midwinter. Larkspurs and aconites include many species poisonous to livestock. Most species of aconite are Asiatic.

1a. Flowers bilaterally symmetrical . . . . (2)
1b. Flowers radially symmetrical . . . . (3)

2a. Uppermost sepal prolonged into a conspicuous spur. **Delphinium,** LARKSPUR
2b. Uppermost sepal forming a hood that arches over the flower. **Aconitum,** MONKSHOOD

3a. Leaves very large (over 10 dm), compound; carpel solitary, a red (rarely white) several-seeded berry. **Actaea**, BANEBERRY
3b. Leaves smaller, simple, lobed or compound; carpels follicular, dry, dehiscent . . . . (4)

4a. Petals spurred (rarely spurless in occasional mutants); leaves compound. **Aquilegia**, COLUMBINE
4b. Petals spurless; leaves never compound . . . . (5)

5a. Leaves chiefly basal, kidney-shaped or rounded cordate, often with a slight lobulelike auricle at the base; tepals white, bluish on the back. **Psychrophila**, MARSH-MARIGOLD
5b. Leaves basal and cauline, palmately lobed; tepals off-white or cream-colored. **Trollius**, GLOBEFLOWER

ACONITUM L. 1753 [the classical Greek and Latin name]. MONKSHOOD

One species, **A. columbianum** Nuttall, **69A,B**. Forest openings, montane and subalpine. Flowers usually blue-purple. The greenish-white forma *ochroleucum* St. John occurs as a sporadic mutant.

ACTAEA L. 1753 [ancient name for the elderberry]. BANEBERRY

One species, **A. rubra** (Aiton) Willdenow subsp. **arguta** (Nuttall) Hultén, **69C**. Deep shade of moist montane forests. The racemes of red berries are conspicuous in late summer. The occasional white-fruited plant is a genetic variation of the same species and is not, as some assume, the white baneberry, *A. alba*, of the eastern United States. In the latter species the pedicels are much thicker than in *A. rubra*.

AQUILEGIA L. 1753 [Latin, *aqua*, water, + *legere*, to collect, from the nectar at the base of the spur]. COLUMBINE

Note: Spurless mutant individuals occur in populations of most of the species. Also, since there are no genetic barriers between species of *Aquilegia*, hybrids are to be found between any species that come in contact.

1a. Flowers blue-and-white, at high altitudes tending to be mostly white (very rarely all blue) . . . . (2)
1b. Flowers red-and-yellow, sometimes almost all yellow . . . . (3)

2a. Dwarf plants with strongly hooked spurs and small flowers, the spurs and laminae of the petals together not more than 2 cm long. **A. saximontana** Rydberg, DWARF COLUMBINE. Rare or locally abundant, cliffs and rocky slopes, subalpine and alpine, near the Continental Divide, ST. No spurless form is known in this species.
2b. Tall plants with essentially straight spurs and much larger flowers. **A. coerulea** James, COLORADO COLUMBINE. Very common in open forests, meadows, aspen groves, and talus slopes, foothills to alpine. The Colorado state flower. A spurless form is forma **daileyae** (Eastwood) Weber, **Pl. 19**. Occasional populations have the entire perianth blue.

3a. Flowers yellow, with long spurs. **A. chrysantha** Gray var. **rydbergii** Munz. Infrequent in canyons of the foothills, southern counties. Recently, a single plant was discovered in Long Canyon, near Boulder. Most likely this was a casual introduction from a garden in town, or came in a seed mix for revegetation of the canyon.
3b. Flowers bicolored, red-and-yellow. **A. elegantula** Greene, **69E**. Common along mountain streams, spruce-fir forest. This hybridizes with *A. coerulea*, but

because the F_1 generation is most like that species, the backcrosses are with *A. coerulea*, thereby causing some variability in that species and leaving *A. elegantula* pure. [Note: A Californian species, *A. pubescens* Coville, a taller species with red-and-yellow flowers, long spurs, and glandular stems, was collected once in the Front Range subalpine, near Hessie, GL, but it was undoubtedly introduced, possibly in a "wild-flower" packet or "meadow in a can." It has not been found again.]

DELPHINIUM L. 1753 [Latin, *delphinus*, dolphin, in allusion to the shape of the flower bud]. LARKSPUR

1a. Leaves mostly basal or near the base of the stem, forming a rosette, the upper leaves usually few and smaller . . . . (2)

1b. Leaves basal and cauline, the basal ones not forming a rosette, the stem leaves well developed . . . . (4)

2a. Roots fusiform, clustered; flowers deep blue-purple; leaves with many deep narrow lobes. **D. nuttallianum** Pritzel, **69D**. Meadows, sagebrush, open woods, very common in early spring (*D. nelsonii*).

2b. Roots elongate, fibrous; flowers light blue or white . . . . (3)

3a. Stems densely clustered, forming a very bushy clump; flowers bright blue. **D. geyeri** Greene [for C. A. Geyer, 1809-1853, collector along the Oregon Trail in 1844]. Common on the outwash mesas at the base of the Front Range and northeastward in the South Platte drainage. An important range plant, poisonous to livestock.

3b. Stems single or a few together; flowers white or pale bluish. **D. virescens** Nuttall subsp. **penardii** (Huth) Ewan [for Eugene Penard, 1855-1950, Swiss protozoologist, who collected around Boulder in 1891]. Frequent on the outwash mesas and plains (*D. carolinianum* subsp. *penardii*). *D. wootonii* Rydberg is a doubtfully distinct form said to occur in the extreme southwestern corner, BA, said to have a heavier root system and no glandular pubescence.

4a. Flowers narrow, the upper sepal and its spur forming nearly a straight line (even in old flowers); sepals often widest above the middle, not over 12 mm long; stems usually glandular-pubescent; flowers usually pale blue often variegated with white. **D. occidentale** (Watson) Watson. Aspen zone, northern counties.

4b. Flowers not especially narrow, the upper sepal flaring (at least in older flowers); sepals widest at or below the middle; stems either without glandular hairs or, if glandular, then the sepals 14 mm long or more . . . . (4)

5a. Rachis of raceme and pedicels lustrous, glandular-hirsute; sepals dark purple, often acuminate; stems usually 5-20 from a single root; leaf segments broad. **D. barbeyi** Huth [for William Barbey, 1842-1914, Swiss botanist], **Pl. 62**. Common in swampy spruce-fir forests.

5b. Rachis and pedicels nonglandular; sepals dull or bright blue, not acuminate; stems single or few from a single root; leaf segments narrow . . . . . . (6)

6a. Sepals 8-10 mm long; lower petals somewhat exserted; seeds strongly wing-angled; stems seldom over and usually much less than 1 m tall. **D. ramosum** Rydberg. Open sites, middle and high altitudes (including *D. alpestre*, a dwarfed alpine form found in the Hoosier Pass and Culebra Range areas).

6b. Sepals 11-15 mm long; lower petals included; seeds narrowly wing-angled; stems well over 1 m tall. **D. robustum** Rydberg. Local, in broad canyon bottoms, Spanish Peaks, Cuchara Valley, and La Garita Hills, west side of the San Luis Valley.

PSYCHROPHILA Berchtold & Presl 1823 [Greek, *psychros*, frigid, + *philein*, to love]. MARSH-MARIGOLD

One species, **P. leptosepala** (de Candolle) Weber, **95E**. Wet ground, mountain meadows and tundra, flowering right after thaw. This characteristic plant of snowmelt basins belongs to a genus of the mountains of southern South America and Australia-New Zealand, probably representing an ancient Tertiary element in the flora (*Caltha* of Colorado literature).

TROLLIUS L. 1753 [latinization of *Troll*, a globe, from *Trollblume*, the German common name]. GLOBEFLOWER

One species, **T. albiflorus** (Gray) Rydberg [white-flowered], **95D**. Seasonally wet ground around springs, streams, and subalpine meadows (*T. laxus* var. *albiflorus*). *T. laxus*, of New England, is extremely rare and considered to be endangered and has yellow-orange flowers. Easily confused with *Delphinium* when in fruit, but there are more than 3 follicles.

HIPPURIDACEAE MARE'S TAIL FAMILY (HPU)

This family consists of a single genus and species, occurring around the world in the Northern Hemisphere. When emergent, the stems with their whorled leaves stand stiffly out of the water. Submerged forms have very lax leaves that might cause one to mistake the plant for *Elodea*. Flowers in *Hippuris* are extremely reduced and simplified. A single flower occurs in the axil of the leaf. The perianth is reduced to an inconspicuous rim around the top of the gynoecium. There is one large stamen. The ovary is inferior, unicarpellate, with a long slender style, and produces a single seed.

HIPPURIS L. 1753 [Greek, *hippos*, horse, + *oura*, tail]. MARE'S TAIL

One species, **H. vulgaris** L., **70A**. Common in shallow water of slow streams and ponds, montane and subalpine.

HYDRANGEACEAE HYDRANGEA FAMILY (HDR)

This family contains shrubs with opposite, elliptic leaves, fragrant flowers with parts in fours, the petals white, ovary half-inferior, the fruits long-persistent. Some treatments still place this distinctive group in the Saxifragaceae. Our *Jamesia* is a "living fossil" with an interesting distribution including the foothills of the Front Range, a few localities in Utah and Arizona, and the east base of the Sierra Nevada. Belle K. Stewart, working from the University of Colorado Museum, discovered fossil leaf impressions in the volcanic ash formations in the Creede Valley many years ago.

1a. Leaves ovate, regularly crenate, copiously soft-hairy beneath. **Jamesia**, WAXFLOWER

1b. Leaves elliptical or lanceolate, entire. **Philadelphus**, MOCK-ORANGE

JAMESIA Torrey & Gray 1840 [for Edwin James, its discoverer]. WAXFLOWER

One species, **J. americana** Torrey & Gray. Common in canyons of the foothills, up to the subalpine on warm, southern exposures. Some years ago a Scottish geneticist colleague, visiting Boulder, was taken by this species as a potential cultivar and took seed to Glasgow, where he patiently germinated them.

One day in 1957 I visited him and he proudly showed me these plants, which he was to be the first to introduce to Scottish gardens, growing nicely in his lath-houses. Shortly afterward, we walked across the campus to lunch, and, turning a corner, we discovered a beautiful bush, many years old, in full flower! Embarrassing, yes, but a tribute to the fact that very little escaped the Scottish gardeners of the last century.

PHILADELPHUS L. 1753 [said to be named for Ptolemy Philadelphus, King of Egypt, 283-247 B.C.]. MOCK-ORANGE

One species, **P. microphyllus** Gray. Rocky slopes, southernmost counties, from the Wet Mountains to Mesa de Maya. A small-flowered relative of the widely cultivated species. Foliage glabrous or appressed-hairy; outer bark reddish-brown, exfoliating to reveal a pale inner bark; leaves elliptic, 1-1.5 cm long; leaves strongly 3-nerved beneath, appressed-hairy, the hairs without swollen bases; petals entire, not clawed.

HYDROCHARITACEAE FROGBIT FAMILY (HDC)

The floral biology of *Elodea*, our only genus, can only be described as bizarre. The plant is submerged. How does pollination take place? The staminate flowers, formed under water, break away and float to the surface, liberating the pollen on the surface film of water. The carpellate flowers are produced on long, threadlike stalks that remain attached to the main stem but grow to reach the water surface. There the stigmas encounter the floating pollen grains that move to them by surface attraction.

ELODEA Michaux 1803 [Greek, *elodes*, marshy]. WATERWEED

We have too few collections of this genus, but evidently the following three species are present on the Eastern Slope.

1a. Upper and middle leaves opposite. **E. longivaginata** St. John
1b. Upper and middle leaves in whorls of 3 . . . . (2)

2a. Upper and middle leaves mostly 2-3 mm wide, dark green. **E. canadensis** Richardson
2b. Upper and middle leaves up to 1.5 mm wide, pale green, and limp. **E. nuttallii** (Planchon) St. John

HYDROPHYLLACEAE WATERLEAF FAMILY (HYD)

The hydrophylls are probably best recognized by their inflorescences, which are usually tightly coiled into a helix when young, gradually uncoiling as the flowers open. The stamens are usually exserted on long, slender filaments. The family name derives from the succulent, watery stems and leaves of the genus *Hydrophyllum*, but many hydrophylls have rough-hairy foliage like the borages, a family that also has helicoid inflorescences but differs in having the fruit divided into four 1-seeded nutlets.

1a. Flowers solitary on axillary or terminal pedicels; annual; corolla not longer than the sepals . . . . (2)
1b. Flowers in several-many-flowered terminal or axillary clusters; annual or perennial; corollas usually exceeding the sepals . . . . (3)

2a. Leaves with only 2 pairs of lateral lobes; calyx with small reflexed lobules between the sepals. **Nemophila**

2b. Leaves with 4 or more pairs of lateral lobes; calyx without reflexed lobules. **Ellisia**

3a. Flowers in ± dichotomous cymes or ball-like clusters, not strongly helicoid sprays; leaves and stems with copious, watery juice. **Hydrophyllum**, WATERLEAF

3b. Flowers in an elongate, helicoid cymes with a main axis; leaves and stems often harshly pubescent, not watery. **Phacelia**

ELLISIA L. 1753 [for John Ellis, 1710?-1776, naturalist and correspondent of Linnaeus]

One species, **E. nyctelea** (L.) L. [from *Nyctelius*, an epithet of Bacchus, who celebrated his mysteries at night; Linnaeus did not explain; did Mr. Ellis drink?], **71C**. Adventive, riparian sites and disturbed soils of gardens and cultivated ground.

HYDROPHYLLUM L. 1753 [Greek, *hydor*, water, + *phyllon*, leaf, alluding to the succulent, watery petioles]. WATERLEAF

1a. Flowers blue, in a ball-like cluster, hardly exceeding the few obtusely lobed leaves. **H. capitatum** Douglas, **71A**. Common in shaded places in open forests and oak woodlands. Park Range, not definitely reported, but likely present on the west side of North Park.

1b. Flowers ochroleucous, in a more open, dichotomous cyme exceeding the leaves; leaves with sharply serrate lobes. **H. fendleri** (Gray) Heller, **71D**. Common in riparian woodlands, foothills and montane.

NEMOPHILA Nuttall 1822 [Greek, *nemos*, glade, + *philein*, to love]

One species, **N. breviflora** Gray, **71B**. Common in shaded woodlands, Park Range, not definitely reported, but to be expected on west side of North Park.

PHACELIA Jussieu 1789 [Greek, *phakelos*, fascicle, alluding to the clusters of floral branches]

1a. Leaves large, with entire margins, simple or with a few basal lobes or leaflets, the terminal leaflet much larger than the others; coarse, harshly hairy perennials . . . . (2)

1b. Leaves toothed, regularly lobed or pinnatifid . . . . (3)

2a. Leaves green, not silvery-pubescent; flowers white. **P. heterophylla** Pursh, SCORPIONWEED. Common in open ground of the lower mountain areas.

2b. Leaves appressed silvery-hairy; flowers distinctly purplish. **P. hastata** Douglas, SCORPIONWEED. Replacing the last at higher altitudes, up to subalpine.

3a. Corolla white, small (4 mm or less), the lobes erose-dentate. **P. alba** Rydberg. Common in the intermountain basins, from LR to the southern border, especially so in the San Luis Valley.

3b. Corolla purplish, over 4 mm, the lobes smooth-margined . . . . (4)

4a. Perennial; not glandular-hairy but appressed silvery-pubescent; inflorescence condensed to form what appears to be a single spike, not conspicuously helicoid. **P. sericea** (Graham) Gray, PURPLE FRINGE. Abundant on gravelly open slopes, subalpine.

4b. Annual or biennial; usually glandular-hairy; inflorescence of distinctly helicoid units . . . . (5)

5a. Stamens and style included or nearly so; corolla tubular, the lobes denticulate. **P. denticulata** Osterhout. Restricted to the outer foothills from LR to LA, endemic here and in southern Wyoming. Corolla pale blue.

5b. Stamens and style strongly exserted; corolla campanulate, lobes entire or merely crenulate . . . . (6)

6a. Flowers pale lavender; leaf divisions relatively narrow (less than 5 mm wide); plants low, less than 3 dm high. **P. formosula** Osterhout. Narrowly endemic on sandy clay slopes, North Park. A federally endangered species.

6b. Flowers deep blue-purple; leaf divisions larger, broader; plants usually tall and coarse. **P. bakeri** (Brand) Macbride [for C. F. Baker]. Common in the outer foothills, especially in the southern counties. Similar to the Western Slope *P. glandulosa* but differing in not having the seeds excavated on the ventral side. This group has many very closely related taxa, difficult to separate.

HYPERICACEAE ST. JOHNSWORT FAMILY (HYP)

Klamath weed, *Hypericum perforatum*, a European species that is not a nuisance in its homeland, came to us with the westward movement and the livestock industry. Over a span of fifty years it cost Oregon and California millions of dollars in sheep poisoning losses. Two and one-third million acres of California land were infested, and in 1930 this plant was the cause of the worst financial losses on pasture and range lands in California. The plant contains chemicals that sensitize white animals to sunlight, and death usually results from starvation following blindness or refusal to eat.

In Colorado, Klamath weed first appeared on Rocky Flats in Jefferson County, where it may have been introduced with straw during the building of the Moffat Tunnel route. For many years it dominated about 17,000 acres of the mesa but showed no signs of spreading. In the last decade, however, it has evidently selected a strain that is capable of doing well all over Colorado, and it has spread into the foothills to Estes Park and out onto the Arkansas Divide. Recently a stand was found at Glenwood Springs, so Klamath weed is on its way to becoming a first-class pest in Colorado. At Rocky Flats the plant has been controlled, as elsewhere, by the introduction of a beetle, *Chrysolina quadrigemina*, for which *H. perforatum* is its sole food. This is a classic example of the value and possibilities of biological control of pests. While the species has not been eliminated, it is kept in check, at least, by this insect.

Hypericum species may be easily recognized by the translucent dots on the oppositely arranged leaves, seen when held up to the light. In some species the yellow petals have black dots near the margins. The stamens tend to be in five clusters.

HYPERICUM L. 1753 [*hypericon*, the ancient Greek name]. ST. JOHNSWORT

1a. Petals 2-3.5 mm long, not black-dotted; slender annual. **H. majus** (Gray) Britton. Drying pondshores and floodplains in the piedmont valleys; uncommon.

1b. Petals 7-15 mm long, with black dots near the margins; perennials . . (2)

2a. Leaves narrowly oblong; plants profusely branched; flowers very numerous in a broad, flat-topped cluster. **H. perforatum** L., KLAMATH WEED. Adventive, locally abundant on the piedmont valleys and outer foothills.

2b. Leaves broadly elliptic; plants slender, sparingly branched; flowers few, in axillary cymes; inflorescence not flat-topped. **H. formosum** Humboldt, Bonpland & Kunth. Wet meadows and streamsides, upper montane and subalpine.

HYPOXIDACEAE YELLOW STARGRASS FAMILY (HPX)

Inconspicuous, grasslike, herbaceous monocots with 6-merous yellow flowers, the perianth pubescent on the outside, and inferior ovary.

HYPOXIS L. 1753 [Greek, *hypoxys*, somewhat acid]. YELLOW STARGRASS

One species, **H. hirsuta** (L.) Coville. Rare or very infrequent in grasslands on the Arkansas Divide and southern counties.

IRIDACEAE IRIS FAMILY (IRI)

Irises need no introduction. Our wild iris species is so much like some of the cultivated types as to be instantly recognized. Interpretation of the floral parts is not as easy. The perianth consists of 3 outer hanging *falls* and 3 inner erect or over-arching *standards*. The three spreading, flat structures that cover and hide the 3 stamens are the style branches. The folded-triangular grooved leaves of the equitant type are common to Iridaceae and some Juncaceae. Other well-known irids in cultivation are the spring-blooming *Crocus* and the late summer *Gladiolus*.

1a. Flowers more than 5 cm wide; falls spreading or reflexed; standards erect; fruit a cylindrical capsule. **Iris**

1b. Flowers less than 2 cm wide; all perianth segments petaloid and spreading; fruit a round berry or capsule. **Sisyrinchium**, BLUE-EYED-GRASS

IRIS L. 1753 [Greek, rainbow]

One species, **I. missouriensis** Nuttall, WILD IRIS. Wet meadows in the mountain parks and along broad streams, from the plains to the subalpine.

SISYRINCHIUM L. 1753 [name used by Theophrastus for some irislike plant]. BLUE-EYED-GRASS

1a. Spathes sessile and solitary (this does not always hold for individuals, but for the stand as a whole) . . . . (2)

1b. Spathes pedunculate, 1-several, from the axil of a leaflike bract . . . . . (3)

2a. Outer bract of spathe with the base fused to about 4 mm; outer and inner bracts of spathe not greatly dissimilar in length. **S. idahoense** Bicknell var. **occidentale** (Bicknell) D. Henderson. Swales, North Park, piedmont valleys, and sand dunes on the plains.

2b. Outer bract of spathe with the base fused less than 4 mm; outer bract nearly twice the length of the inner. **S. demissum** Greene [weak]. Wet areas, San Luis Valley.

3a. Flowers deep blue. **S. montanum** Greene. Grassy (not necessarily wet) meadows, our most common species. This and the following are distinguished by several more quantitative characters, but the flower color in every instance seen thus far is sufficient.

3b. Flowers pale blue. **S. pallidum** Cholewa & Henderson. Endemic. Most common in slightly alkaline meadows in South Park, but also represented in Rocky Mountain National Park and the upper Laramie River Valley.

JUNCACEAE RUSH FAMILY (JUN)

The rushes form a neat little group whose diversity of small technical characters should appeal to the biometrically inclined. Vegetatively resembling both grasses and sedges, they can always be recognized by their small, brownish or greenish, miniature lily flowers with all floral parts present. As in the sedges, some species display inflorescences on what seems to be the side of the stem, while the lowest bract stands erect and appears to continue the stem to the apex. Since this tendency occurs in several unrelated marsh plants (convergent evolution), one might speculate that this life form may present less resistance to wind than a terminal inflorescence and thus prevent "lodging" of the culms in areas of marshlands swept by strong winds. *Juncus torreyi* and *J. nodosus* often produce galls in which the floral parts are tremendously enlarged, creating a mass of telescoping sheaths. This deformity is caused by a Hemipteran insect, the sedge psyllid, *Livia maculipennis* Fitch.

1a. Plants glabrous; leaf sheaths with the margins overlapping but not fused; ovary usually ± 3-loculed; ovules numerous. **Juncus**, RUSH

1b. Plants with a few long, weak hairs along the leaf blades or sheaths; leaf sheaths with the margins fused; ovary with one locule; ovules 3. **Luzula**, WOODRUSH

JUNCUS L. 1753 [the classical name]. RUSH

Note: I am greatly indebted to my friend, the late Fred J. Hermann, for the essence of this key, which he published in his *Manual of the Rushes of the Rocky Mountains and Colorado Basin*.

1a. Annual; inflorescence making up half the plant or more . . . . (2)

1b. Perennial or, if appearing annual, inflorescence making up less than half the height of the plant . . . . (3)

2a. [1] Capsule oblong, 3-4.5 mm long; perianth 4-6 mm long. **J. bufonius** L. [of toads], **72F**. Muddy pond shores and roadside depressions.

2b. Capsule subglobose, 2-3 mm long; perianth 3-4 mm long. **J. bufonius** L. var. **occidentalis** Hermann. Similar habitats, but rare.

3a. [1] Lowest leaf of the inflorescence erect, terete, and appearing to be a continuation of the stem; inflorescence appearing lateral . . . . (4)

3b. Lowest leaf of the inflorescence divergent, not appearing to be a continuation of the stem or, if so, then the leaf grooved along the inner side; inflorescence appearing terminal . . . . (9)

4a. [3] Rhizomes present; seed with a short white tail at each end . . . . . (5)

4b. Rhizomes absent or plants in dense tussocks; seeds tailed or not . . . . (6)

5a. [4] Flower cluster more than halfway up the stem. **J. arcticus** Willdenow subsp. **ater** (Rydberg) Hultén, **72H**. Streams, lakeshores, and alkaline flats. From a distance this species forms a dark green zone, marking the stream course (*J. balticus*). The correct name for this may, in fact, be *J. ater* Rydberg.

5b. Flower clusters within a few cm of the ground, the portion of stem above them many times as long as that below. **J. filiformis** L. Similar habitats, local but perhaps overlooked, North Park and in Rocky Mountain National Park.

6a. [4] Lowland plant, tall and forming a dense tussock on floodplain marshes; seed not tailed. **J. effusus** L. [loosely spreading]. Adventive, recently discovered near Boulder, probably introduced with seed used in wetland reclamation. Resembling *J. arcticus*, but not rhizomatous and with a more densely bunched flower cluster.

6b. Small plants of montane and alpine areas; seed with a long tail at each end . . . . (7)

7a. [6] Upper leaf sheaths bristle-tipped, the blade lacking; capsule blunt, depressed at the apex. **J. drummondii** Meyer. Very common, tuft-forming, alpine tundra plant.

7b. Upper leaf sheaths bearing blades . . . . (8)

8a. [7] Capsule pointed at the apex. **J. parryi** Engelmann. Wet places, subalpine.

8b. Capsule broad and depressed at the apex. **J. hallii** Engelmann. Uncommon in wet places, subalpine.

9a. [3] Leaves not septate but transversely flattened (inserted with the flat surface facing the stem) or involute or hollow . . . . (10)

9b. Leaves septate inside (with papery cross-partitions visible when the leaf is slit lengthwise), if flattened, with the edge facing the stem, as in *Iris* . . . (23)

10a. [9] Flowers borne singly on the branchlets, each with a pair of bracteoles at the base in addition to the bractlet at the base of the pedicel . . . . . (11)

10b. Flowers in heads, not bracteolate, having only the main bract at the base of the pedicel . . . . (18)

11a. [10] Outer perianth segments obtuse, with incurved or hooded tips, often of 2 colors; leaf sheaths extending halfway up the culm; rhizome horizontal, becoming slender and elongate . . . . (12)

11b. Outer perianth segments acute, uniformly colored, their tips ascending or spreading; leaf sheaths confined to the base or lower third of the plant; rhizomes short, mostly hidden in the tussock of crowded stems . . . . (13)

12a. [11] Anthers scarcely longer than the filaments; capsule globose-obovoid, distinctly exserted. **J. compressus** Jacquin. Adventive, alkaline riverbanks and pondshores, especially common in North Park.

12b. Anthers about three times the length of the filaments; capsule ellipsoid-ovoid, equalling or only slightly exceeding the perianth. **J. gerardii** Loiseleur [for Louis Gérard, 1733-1819, French botanist], BLACKGRASS. A salt-marsh species of the Atlantic coast. Adventive and locally established around ponds in the piedmont valleys (locally introduced by waterfowl?).

13a. [11] Capsule 1-loculed, with the internal septa extending halfway to the center . . . . (14)

13b. Capsule completely 3-loculed, the septa meeting in the center . . . . . (16)

14a. [13] Auricles at the top of the leaf sheath white, thin, and scarious, conspicuously extended beyond the point of origin. **J. tenuis** Willdenow (slender). Adventive, infrequent in the piedmont valleys.

14b. Auricles firm, not conspicuously extended . . . . (15)

15a. [14] Auricles cartilaginous, yellowish, very rigid, and glossy; bracteoles blunt; sheaths of basal leaves straw-colored or brown. **J. dudleyi** Wiegand [for the discoverer, William R. Dudley, California botanist, 1849-1911]. Wet places, mostly in the lower valleys. Some choose to make this a variety of *J. tenuis*, which has papery auricles.

15b. Auricles not rigid, easily broken; bracteoles acuminate or aristate; sheaths of the basal leaves commonly purplish. **J. interior** Wiegand. Common on the mesas and lower foothills.

16a. [13] Seeds long-tailed; leaves terete, with a shallow adaxial groove. **J. vaseyi** Engelmann. Springy slopes and meadows, Rocky Mountain National Park.

16b. Seeds apiculate, not tailed; leaves flat but often involute . . . . (17)

17a. [16] Perianth segments 3.5-4 mm long, broadly scarious-margined, the tips blunt or short-pointed, brownish with a broad greenish midstripe, subequal, little if at all longer than the retuse capsule; flowers few, usually congested; leaves long and very narrow; stem slender. **J. confusus** Coville, **72G**. Around springs and in swampy meadows, plains to subalpine. The flower cluster in this species is characteristically rather compact, without branches of varying lengths, as opposed to the next species, which typically have rather open clusters.

17b. Perianth segments 4.5-5 mm long, the outer series not scarious-margined, the tips acuminate and long-pointed, greenish to straw-colored, conspicuously exceeding the inner series and the capsule; flowers numerous in an open inflorescence; leaves shorter and broader (1-2 mm wide); stem stout. **J. platyphyllus** (Wiegand) Fernald. Probably adventive, on drying pondshores in the piedmont valleys.

18a. [10] Leaves flat; seeds not tailed . . . . (19)

18b. Leaves terete, hollow, or deeply channeled or involute; seeds tailed . (20)

19a. [18] Stamens 3; perianth 2-3.5 mm long. **J. marginatus** Rostkov. Rare, in swampy places on the plains and piedmont valleys.

19b. Stamens 6; perianth 5-6 mm long. **J. longistylis** Torrey, **73A**. Common in swamps and pond margins from the lower valleys to subalpine.

20a. [18] Flowers 5-10 mm long; leaves about 2 mm diameter; stems ± leafy; plants rhizomatous. **J. castaneus** Smith [chestnut]. Subalpine and alpine frost scars and streamlets.

20b. Flowers 3-5 mm long; leaves about 1 mm diameter; stems leafy only at the base; plants caespitose . . . . (21)

21a. [20] Capules retuse; heads 1-2-flowered; perianth dark brown to blackish; involucral bract foliaceous, erect. **J. biglumis** L, **73B**. Infrequent, wet gravels and frost scars on the higher peaks. Bracts and perianth segments are always dark.

21b. Caps obtuse and mucronate; heads 2-5-flowered; perianth light-colored; involucral bract more membranous, divergent . . . . (22)

22a. [21] Bracts and perianth uniformly dark reddish brown. **J. triglumis** L., **73C**. Wet gravel and frost scars, upper subalpine and alpine tundra.

22b. Bracts pale, the perianth very pale or white. **J. albescens** (Lange) Fernald, **Pl. 39**. Subalpine peat fens.

23a. [9] Leaf blades terete, mostly less than 3 mm wide; septa complete . (24)

23b. Leaf blades laterally flattened, equitant (one edge toward the stem, as in *Iris*), mostly 3-6 mm wide; septa incomplete . . . . (33)

24a. [23] Seeds tailed; stamens usually 3 . . . . (25)

24b. Seeds usually apiculate but not tailed . . . . (27)

25a. [24] Heads 4-10, 4-8-flowered; perianth segments 3.5-4 mm long, **J. tweedyi** Rydberg. One record, from Rocky Mountain National Park. Elsewhere usually associated with hot springs.

25b. Heads numerous, small, 2-5-flowered; perianth segments 1.5-2.5 mm long. . . . . (26)

26a. [25] Tails half as long as the body; perianth segments acute, narrowly scarious-margined; inflorescence elongate, strict and generally narrow, the capsules erect-appressed in the head. **J. brevicaudatus** (Engelmann) Fernald. One record, from a swale near Falcon, EP.

26b. Tails no more than 1/3 as long as the body; perianth segments blunt or rounded, soft and broadly scarious-margined; inflorescence open and diffuse, the capsules ± spreading in the head. **J. brachycephalus** (Engelmann) Buchenau. One record, growing with the former. Both species are eastern prairie relicts.

27a. [24] Stamens 3; plant caespitose. **J. acuminatus** Michaux. Infrequent on drying mudflats of ponds in the piedmont valleys.

27b. Stamens 6; plants often stoloniferous or rhizomatous . . . . (28)

28a. [27] Capsules subulate; flowers spreading in all directions . . . . (29)

28b. Capsules oblong to ovoid or obovoid; flowers erect-ascending . . . . . (30)

29a. [28] Plant low, 1-4 dm high; perianth 3-4 mm long, the inner segments equalling or exceeding the outer; heads scarcely 10 mm diameter; leaf blades erect. **J. nodosus** L. [knotted, from the rhizomes, which are thickened at intervals]. Similar habitats, often growing with the last.

29b. Plant taller, 4-10 dm high; perianth 4-5 mm long, the inner segments shorter than the outer; heads 10-15 mm diameter; leaf blades abruptly divergent. **J. torreyi** Coville. Sloughs and ditches in the lower valleys. See discussion of galls in introduction.

30a. [28] Perianth 2-3 mm long; capsule usually exceeding the perianth . . (31)

30b. Perianth 3.5-5 mm long; capsule shorter than the perianth . . . . (32)

31a. [30] Outer perianth segments acuminate, equalling or shorter than the inner; branches of the inflorescence spreading; capsules acute. **J. articulatus** L. Adventive, introduced and established along streams in the piedmont valleys.

31b. Outer perianth segments blunt, longer than the inner; branches of inflorescence stiffly erect; capsules distinctly rounded at apex. **J. alpino-articulatus** Chaix. Widely scattered but infrequent in wetlands, BL, CR, EP, abundant in calcareous fens in South Park (*J. alpinus* of manuals).

32a. [30] Head solitary or rarely 2, more than 12-flowered; perianth deep purple-brown; anthers rarely more than 2/3 as long as filaments. **J. mertensianus** Bongard [for C. H. Mertens, 1796-1830, botanized at Sitka, Alaska], **73D**. Very common in swampy subalpine woodlands, pondshores, and roadsides.

32b. Heads (2)5-many, mostly with fewer than 12 flowers; perianth from light brown to dark purplish-brown; anthers more than 2/3 as long as the filaments. **J. nevadensis** Watson. Infrequent, subalpine (*J. badius, J. mertensianus var. gracilis*).

33a. [23] Stamens 3; involucral bract sword-shaped, usually half the length of the inflorescence or more. **J. ensifolius** Wikström. Very infrequent in Colorado, known from RT, so probably occurring on the west side of North Park.

33b. Stamens 6; involucral bract narrower, usually less than half the length of the inflorescence . . . . (34)

34a. [33] Seeds tailed; style exserted, easily visible in the head. **J. tracyi** Rydberg [for S. M. Tracy, 1847-1920, collector with Baker & Earle in 1898]. Wet places, especially roadside ditches, subalpine and montane.

34b. Seeds not tailed; styles short, hardly visible in the head. **J. saximontanus** Nelson, **72E**. Wet places from the lowlands through the montane. Normally the heads are few, but a form with numerous heads is called forma **brunnescens** (Rydberg) Hermann.

LUZULA de Candolle 1805 [from *Gramen Luzulae* or *Luxulae*, diminutive of *lux*, light; a name given to some species for its leaves appearing to be shining with dew]. WOODRUSH

1a. Flowers on slender pedicels in a loose, drooping panicle; leaves glabrous except for a few long hairs near the throat of the leaf sheath; perianth about 2 mm long, shorter than or barely equalling the capsule. **L. parviflora** (Ehrhart) Desvaux [small-flowered], **73F**. Moist or swampy montane and subalpine forests.

1b. Flowers crowded, subsessile, in a few heads or spikes; leaves sparsely villous with long, loose hairs; perianth longer than the capsule . . . . (2)

2a. Leaves 1-4 mm wide, with subulate (often involute) tips; bracts at bases of flowers ciliate-fimbriate; spikes usually nodding. **L. spicata** (L.) de Candolle, **73E**. Tundra and higher subalpine slopes.

2b. Leaves usually broader, flat, with blunt, callous tips; bracts at base of flowers entire or merely lacerate . . . . (3)

3a. Spikes short-cylindric, short-peduncled, the bracts and tepals pale brownish or straw-colored, capsules darker brown; leaf blades less than 5 mm wide. **L. comosa** E. Meyer [hairy]. Subalpine streamsides (*L. campestris* and *L. multiflora* of Colorado manuals).

3b. Spikes capitate, sessile or a few long-peduncled, the tepals almost as dark as the deep brown capsules; leaf blades 5-8 mm wide. **L. subcapitata** (Rydberg) Harrington. Endemic, subalpine and alpine willow carrs.

JUNCAGINACEAE ARROWGRASS FAMILY (JCG)

This is a very small family with about 16 species worldwide, of which all but one belong to *Triglochin*. The genus is marked by its grasslike habit and slender racemes of greenish, inconspicuous flowers. The carpels, although united, separate when mature into 3 or 6 mericarps, leaving a terete axis standing between them.

TRIGLOCHIN L. 1753 [Greek, *treis*, three, + *glochis*, point, alluding to the fruit of *T. palustris*]. ARROWGRASS

1a. Fertile carpels and stigmas 3; fruits elongate, linear to somewhat clavate, 5-8 mm long; leaf ligules bilobed. **T. palustris** L., **74A**. Mountain meadows and fens, not necessarily strongly alkaline. A very slender plant compared to the others.

1b. Fertile carpels and stigmas 6; fruits oblong or ovoid-prismatic, 4-6 mm long . . . . (2)

2a. Ligules entire or only slightly bilobate, up to 5 mm long; old leaf bases not shredding into many fibers; shoots closely aggregated on the rhizome. **T. maritima** L., **74B**. Alkaline flats, fens, and dry washes from the lower valleys to intermountain basins.

2b. Ligules bilobed or emarginate, up to 1 mm long; rhizome clothed with brown fibrous remains of leaf bases; shoots well spaced along the rhizome. **T. concinna** Davy [beautiful], **74C**. Less frequent, but sometimes growing with the last. Whether *T. concinna* or *T. debilis* is the correct name is moot. Both names were published in 1895.

KRAMERIACEAE RATANY FAMILY (KRM)

A unique family with the single genus, *Krameria*. Its relationships were obscure, and it has been included from time to time with the Fabaceae or with the Polygalaceae. *Krameria* is a low, perennial herb or shrub with linear, silky-hairy leaves, and bilaterally symmetrical flowers with 4-5 sepals, 3 conspicuous upper petals with united claws, and 2 greenish, reduced, glandlike petals. The globose fruit is armed with sharp prickles.

KRAMERIA L. 1758 [for W. H. Kramer, died 1765, early supporter of Linnaeus' system and nomenclature]. RATANY

One species, **K. lanceolata** Torrey. An herbaceous plant, with spreading or prostrate stems from a heavy root system, stipitate-glandular peduncles, and purplish petals. Infrequent, dry grasslands, BA, LA.

LAMIACEAE/LABIATAE MINT FAMILY (LAM/LAB)

What would be left of the good life if we did not have this family? For scent, flavor, and that little something extra in our foods we depend on mints: rosemary, lavender, sage, spearmint, peppermint, basil, thyme, horehound, marjoram, oregano, and savory! *Citronella* was once the only reliable insect repellant. *Coleus* plants used to be in every home, before we learned about African violets. Probably only the Apiaceae come close to supplying as many important culinary herbs.

The family is very easily recognized by the opposite leaves, squared stems, bilaterally symmetrical flowers, and the ovary that is divided into 4 single-seeded units, or nutlets. The foliage is usually, but not always, aromatic. The Verbenaceae are sometimes confused with mints, but they are never aromatic, and the ovary is less obviously divided until it is mature.

1a. Calyx with a prominent transverse ridge across the upper side, this always easily visible because the flowers are never tightly clustered. **Scutellaria**, SKULLCAP

1b. Calyx without a transverse ridge, or flowers too densely clustered to see this . . . . (2)

2a. Calyx radially symmetrical, 10-toothed, 5 long teeth alternating with 5 shorter ones. **Marrubium**, HOREHOUND

2b. Calyx bilaterally symmetrical or, if not, then 4-5-toothed . . . . (3)

3a. Upper lobes of the corolla scarcely discernible, or its lobes appearing laterally on the margins of the lower lip, the corolla then appearing 1-lipped. **Teucrium**, GERMANDER

3b. Upper lobes of the corolla well developed (but the corolla not necessarily 2-lipped) . . . . (4)

4a. Fertile stamens 2 . . . . (5)

4b. Fertile stamens 4 . . . . (8)

5a. Calyx radially symmetrical or nearly so . . . . (6)

5b. Calyx 2-lipped . . . . (7)

6a. Corolla almost equally 4-lobed, very small (less than 6 mm long). **Lycopus**, WATER HOREHOUND, BUGLEWEED

6b. Corolla 2-lipped, more than 10 mm long. **Monarda**, HORSEMINT

7a. Calyx with a well-defined ring of simple hairs within the throat; plants extremely aromatic. **Hedeoma,** PENNYROYAL

7b. Calyx glabrous within; plants not or only moderately aromatic. **Salvia,** SAGE

8a. Inflorescence axillary in general appearance, the flower clusters subtended by unmodified leaves . . . . (9)

8b. Inflorescence terminal in general appearance, the flower clusters solitary, in dense balls or loose, irregular branched units, or numerous in spikes (12)

9a. Flowers and fruits sessile . . . . (10)

9b. Flowers and fruits pedicellate . . . . (11)

10a. Plants erect, stout, with deeply palmately lobed and cleft leaves; flowers whitish to pink or purplish. **Leonurus,** MOTHERWORT

10b. Plants low, creeping, the leaves simple, crenate; flowers purple. **Lamium,** DEAD-NETTLE

11a. Leaves reniform or suborbicular, rounded-crenate; plants creeping. **Glecoma,** GROUND IVY; GILL-OVER-THE-GROUND

11b. Leaves lanceolate or ovate. **Mentha,** MINT

12a. Calyx radially symmetrical . . . . (13)

12b. Calyx bilabiate . . . . (14)

13a. Stamens exserted from the corolla; anther sacs parallel. **Agastache,** GIANT HYSSOP

13b. Stamens included; anther sacs divergent. **Stachys,** HEDGE-NETTLE

14a. Corolla white, the lower lip spotted purple; upper and lower calyx lips similar except in length; plant with characteristic catnip odor. **Nepeta,** CATNIP

14b. Corolla rose, purple, or blue; upper calyx lip with one or more teeth distinctly different from those of the lower . . . . (15)

15a. Perennial; leaves lance-ovate, entire or weakly toothed; upper calyx lip with the lobes fused for at least 3/4 their length. **Prunella,** HEAL-ALL

15b. Annual; leaves regularly sharp-toothed; upper calyx lip distinctly 3-toothed. **Dracocephalum,** DRAGONHEAD

AGASTACHE Clayton 1762 [Greek, *agan*, many, + *stachys*, spike]. GIANT HYSSOP

1a. Leaves whitened by minute, feltlike pubescence beneath; calyx teeth and corolla blue. **A. foeniculum** (Pursh) Kuntze [for its fennellike odor]. Two localities known, Platte Canyon and west end of Mesa de Maya, an eastern woodland relict.

1b. Leaves paler but not white beneath; calyx teeth not blue, corolla white to violet . . . . (2)

2a. Calyx teeth mostly 1.5-2.5 mm long, triangular, similar in texture to the calyx tube; upper corolla lip straight to galeate-curved; stamens held under upper corolla lip, exserted only 1-2(3) mm beyond mouth of corolla; leaves less than 3 cm long, crenate with small, rounded teeth. **A. pallidiflora** (Heller) Rydberg. Rocky places in the middle altitudes, eastern base of the San Juans west of San Luis Valley.

2b. Calyx teeth mostly 3.5-5 mm long, subulate, thinner, and more paleaceous than calyx tube; upper corolla lip spreading or reflexed; stamens spreading, exserted 4-7 mm beyond mouth of corolla; leaves over 3 cm long, with coarse, often sharp serrations. **A. urticifolia** (Bentham) Kuntze. Aspen zone, Park Range on west side of North Park.

DRACOCEPHALUM L. 1753 [Greek, *draco*, dragon, + *kephalos*, head]. DRAGON-HEAD

One species, **D. parviflorum** Nuttall, **75B**. Wide-ranging from clay hills, where it is infrequent, up into mountain meadows and aspen groves and burned forested areas (*Moldavica*).

GLECOMA L. 1753 [Greek, *glechon*, name of a species of *Mentha*]. GROUND IVY, GILL-OVER-THE-GROUND

One species, **G. hederacea** L. Adventive, creeping weed in lawns and orchards.

HEDEOMA Persoon 1896 [Greek, *hedys*, sweet, + *osme*, scent]. PENNYROYAL

1a. Annual; leaves narrowly linear. **H. hispidum** Pursh. Common on mesas and plains.

1b. Perennial; leaves, at least the lower ones, elliptic. **H. drummondii** Bentham [for Thomas Drummond, 1780-1835, naturalist with the Franklin expeditions]. Rimrock, canyons and desert sites. Both species have an extremely strong mint odor.

LAMIUM L. 1753 [old Latin name for a nettlelike plant]. DEAD-NETTLE

1a. Upper stem leaves purple, usually distinctly petioled, not clasping the stem; plant densely pubescent. **L. purpureum** L. Adventive weed in orchards and gardens.

1b. Upper stem leaves green, usually clasping the stem, only the lower leaves with distinct petioles; plant sparingly pubescent. **L. amplexicaule** L., HENBIT. Adventive, similar sites.

LEONURUS L. 1753 [Latin, lion's tail]. MOTHERWORT

One species, **L. cardiaca** L. Adventive, a weed in mostly shaded, often riparian sites near towns. The flowers are pink or purplish-white, densely woolly, and the leaves deeply palmately cleft and lobed.

LYCOPUS L. 1753 [Greek, *lycos*, wolf, + *pous*, foot]. WATER HOREHOUND, BUGLEWEED

1a. Calyx shorter than to barely equalling the nutlets, its lobes acute to obtuse at the apex. **L. uniflorus** Michaux. Local, known only from Boulder Creek floodplain, but probably more widely distributed.

1b. Calyx exceeding the nutlets; lobes acuminate to subulate . . . . (2)

2a. Blades of lower and middle stem leaves tapered to petioles; roots rarely tuberous; nutlets with a smooth, corky ridge. **L. americanus** Mühlenberg. Swamps and streambanks, lowlands.

2b. Blades of lower and middle leaves sessile; roots tuberous; nutlet without a corky ridge. **L. asper** Greene. Similar habitats.

MARRUBIUM L. 1753 [from Hebrew, *marrob*, a bitter juice]. HOREHOUND

One species, **M. vulgare** L., **75A**. Adventive, coarse, ruderal weed. The deeply impressed veins on the almost round leaves, the strongly tomentose stems and leaves, and the dense balls of flowers are diagnostic.

MENTHA L. 1753 [Minthe, a nymph fabled to have been changed by Proserpine into mint]. MINT

1a. Flower clusters in the axils of unmodified leaves. **M. arvensis** L., FIELDMINT, **75D**. Along irrigation ditches, sloughs, and streambanks in the lowlands.
1b. Flower clusters in the axils of short bracts . . . . (2)

2a. Leaves mostly cuneate at the base; calyx over 1.5 mm long. **M. piperita** L., PEPPERMINT. Adventive, escaped from cultivation. The odors of this and the following are commonly understood and distinctive.
2b. Leaves mostly rounded at the base; calyx 1.5 mm long or less. **M. spicata** L., SPEARMINT. Adventive, escaped from cultivation.

MONARDA L. 1753 [for Nicolas Monardes, sixteenth-century botanical writer]. HORSEMINT, BEE BALM
1a. Flowers large, rose-pink. **M. fistulosa** L. var. **menthifolia** (Graham) Fernald, **75C**. [hollow]. Streamsides, canyonsides, and meadows in the foothills.
1b. Flowers small, pinkish to white. **M. pectinata** Nuttall. Common on the plains, outer foothills, and in the San Luis Valley near the Great Sand Dunes.

NEPETA L. 1753 [believed to be derived from Nepete, an Etruscan city]. CATNIP
One species, **N. cataria** L. Adventive, ruderal weed in gardens and shaded pastures on floodplains.

PRUNELLA L. 1753 [of uncertain derivation]. SELF-HEAL; HEAL-ALL
One species, **P. vulgaris** L. Adventive? Common in moist forests and aspen stands.

SALVIA L. 1753 [the old Latin name]. SAGE

1a. Flowers white, in a huge, branched, pyramidal inflorescence; leaves broadly ovate, densely tomentose. **S. aethiopis** L. Adventive weed in the Boulder area, known from a small colony stable for many years but now spreading rapidly along the highways near the mountain front.
1b. Flowers blue or purple . . . . (2)

2a. Leaves cordate-ovate; spikes dense; flowers purple. **S. sylvestris** L., WOODLAND SAGE. Adventive, locally established in northern LR.
2b. Leaves linear to oblong or lanceolate; flowers blue . . . . (3)

3a. Plants low, slender, and weak; leaves oblong-cuneate, entire or nearly so; spikes or racemes long and the small (less than 10 mm long), pale blue flowers in a slender interrupted spike. **S. reflexa** Hornemann. Adventive, weedy annual on floodplains, uncommon.
3b. Plants tall and stout; leaves linear to lanceolate, usually strongly toothed; spikes dense, the flowers large (over 10 mm long), bright blue. **S. azurea** Lamarck var. **grandiflora** Bentham. On the plains, probably adventive from farther east, BL, KW, OT.

SCUTELLARIA L. 1753 [Latin, *scutella*, dish or little shield, alluding to the hump-backed calyx]. SKULLCAP
1a. Flowers in axillary racemes. **S. lateriflora** L. Known only from a single locality, on a mesic floodplain in easternmost YM.
1b. Flowers 2 per node, each arising in the axil of a foliage leaf . . . . (2)

2a. Corolla about 2 cm long; middle stem leaves entire, sessile; plants of dry, gravelly forest openings. **S. brittonii** Porter (for Nathaniel Lord Britton, 1859-1934, American botanist), **75E**. Common in pine forests, middle altitudes.

2b. Corolla shorter; middle stem leaves crenate-serrate, petioled; plants of wet meadows. **S. galericulata** L. var. **epilobiifolia** (Hamilton) Jordal. Wet swales in the piedmont valleys and in the San Luis Valley.

STACHYS L. 1753 [Greek, *stachys*, spike]. HEDGE-NETTLE

One species, **Stachys palustris** L. subsp.. **pilosa** (Nuttall) Epling. Frequent in wet meadows and ditches, lower elevations.

TEUCRIUM L. 1753 [for Teucer, king of Troy, according to Linnaeus]. GERMANDER

1a. Leaves merely serrate or crenate; flowers pink-purple. **T. canadense** L. subsp. **occidentale** (Gray) McClintock & Epling. Frequent in wet meadows and ditches, lower altitudes.

1b. Leaves pinnatifid; flowers white with purple streaks. **T. laciniatum** Torrey. Common on the plains in the Arkansas River drainage.

LEMNACEAE DUCKWEED FAMILY (LMN)

The Lemnaceae represent the ultimate reduction in form and structure in the flowering plants. The entire plant is reduced to a small, flat, floating or submerged disk, part of which represents a spathe such as one sees in Jack-in-the-pulpit. The spathe forms a pocket between the upper and lower side of the disk, and new disks, as well as flowers, are produced within this pocket. In our single genus, *Lemna*, there is a single, unbranched root. Flowering *Lemna* plants are quite rare collectors' items.

1a. Plant with roots hanging from the thallus . . . . (2)
1b. Thallus lacking roots . . . . (3)

2a. Rootlets several; plant body prominently several-nerved, usually purple underneath. **Spirodela**, GREATER DUCKWEED
2b. Rootlet solitary. **Lemna**, DUCKWEED

3a. Thalli minute, spherical to ovoid, sometimes flattened on top, usually floating on the surface. **Wolffia**, WATERMEAL
3b. Thalli to 1 cm long, oblong, stipitate, often strongly colonial, floating under the surface or near the bottom. **Lemna**, DUCKWEED

LEMNA L. 1753 [name of a water plant mentioned by Theophrastus]. DUCKWEED

Note: Duckweeds need much more collecting before we have a clear understanding of the species and their distribution. Two other species, *L. gibba* L. and *L. valdiviana* Philippi, have been reported for eastern Colorado, but the records are doubtful.

1a. Thalli submerged, narrowed to a green stalk at the base; margin of thalli distally denticulate; 3 or more thalli cohering together, forming long and branched chains. **L. trisulca** L. [3-furrowed]. Known from ponds in North Park, but probably widely distributed.
1b. Thalli floating on the surface, not narrowed at the base; when submerged only a few thalli cohering . . . . (2)

2a. Thalli broadly rounded, with 3-5 veins . . . . (3)
2b. Thalli 1-1.7 times as long as wide, with one vein. **L. minuscula** Herter.

3a. Thalli with several papules (minute papillae) of ± equal size above the midline on the upper side; very often reddish beneath. Under unfavorable conditions, small obovate to circular, rootless, dark green to brown turions (resistant budlike thalli) are formed that sink to the bottom. **L. turionifera** Landolt. Common in still water, evidently the most abundant species.

3b. Papules either lacking or the one above the node and at apex bigger than the ones between; never red beneath; thalli rarely forming turions; if turionlike thalli are formed they have short roots and are slowly reproducing daughter fronds. **L. minor** L.

SPIRODELA Schleiden 1839 [Greek, *speira*, cord, + *delos*, evident]. GREATER DUCKWEED

One species, **S. polyrhiza** (L.) Schleiden. Known in Colorado from a very old collection from Denver, and a recent one from YM.

WOLFFIA Horkel 1844 [for Johann Friedrich Wolff, 1788-1806, who wrote on *Wolffia* in 1801]. WATERMEAL

1a. Upper surface of thallus rounded, smooth or minutely papillose; thallus not brown-punctate. **W. columbiana** Karstens. Only recently discovered in Colorado, on the eastern plains, YM.

1b. Upper surface of thallus flattened; thallus often brown-punctate. **W. borealis** (Engelmann) Landolt. *Wolffia* is the world's smallest flowering plant, and probably occurs more often with *Lemna* but easily overlooked. Our collection from YM.

LENTIBULARIACEAE BLADDERWORT FAMILY (LNT)

A small family of mostly aquatic, often carnivorous, plants. The bladderworts have flowers resembling the spurred ones of butter-and-eggs and the submerged, finely divided leaves have some of the leaf segments inflated to form a sac, open at one end, that acts as a trap for small aquatic animals such as *Paramecium*.

UTRICULARIA L. 1753 [Latin, *utriculus*, little bladder]. BLADDERWORT

Note: The genus is poorly collected in Colorado, and most specimens lack flowers, which may be needed for identification. Collectors should note the flower size and shape in the field and be sure to collect some stems that are not slimy and encrusted with diatoms. There are hairs with distinctive branch-types inside the insect traps that may be used for identification. These hairs have four cells, attached by their bases, that spread in characteristic directions. Two of the cells are short and usually form a v; the shorter cells spread horizontally or slightly downward below the v.

1a. Leaf margin and winter buds setose (minute hyaline teeth near the lobe tips, the lobe tips themselves setalike, hyaline) . . . . (2)

1b. Leaf margins and winter buds smooth, not at all setose; plants with very small leaves, the stem and leaves rarely up to 1 cm wide. **U. minor** L., **76B.** Plants are differentiated into aquatic stolons with leaves and subterranean stolons with fewer leaves and more bladders. Subalpine ponds, Boulder watershed, but very likely elsewhere. It is very inconspicuous. Bladder hair cells forming 2 Vs, one inside the other.

2a. Leaves pinnately divided, with a main rachis and more than 20 terete ultimate segments, the segments usually well over 3 mm long; corolla 10-12 mm broad, the spur conspicuous, 10 mm long, hooklike, slightly shorter than the lower lip. **U. vulgaris** L., GREAT BLADDERWORT, **76A.** Common in ponds in the montane and subalpine. Bladder hair cells with the short cells pointing slightly downward.

2b. Leaves dichotomously divided, with fewer than 20 flat ultimate segments, usually without bladders, these usually on leafless stolons; spur pyramidal, 3-5.5 mm long, positioned at a right angle to the lower lip. **U. ochroleuca** Hartman. Until now only known from the upper Arkansas drainage and South Park. Bladder hair cells with the short cells forming a straight line.

LILIACEAE LILY FAMILY (LIL)

(See also Alliaceae, Asparagaceae, Agavaceae, Convallariaceae, Calochortaceae, Melanthiaceae, Nolinaceae, Trilliaceae, Uvulariaceae)

The lily flower is the model of the monocots, perfect in its symmetry, with the parts all alternating in threes. It probably has received more study from beginning botany students than any other single flower and is a good place to learn the basic structure. Unfortunately, the superficial similarity of the flowers in a number of distantly related families tended to result in their placement in this family. Detailed study by Dahlgren & Clifford (1982, 1985) shows that the traditional Liliaceae must be divided into 2 orders and over 20 families, of which our flora contains several.

1a. Leaves appearing basal, the cauline ones, when opposite, much reduced; leaves narrowly linear or grasslike or, if broader, then definitely basal (2)
1b. Leaves arising at nodes on the main stem, not reduced . . . . (4)

2a. Leaves elliptic, not grasslike; flowers yellow, with recurved tepals. **Erythronium**, AVALANCHE LILY
2b. Leaves linear, grasslike; flowers white; tepals erect or at most spreading (3)

3a. Tepals united to form a long tube, the base buried among the basal leaves; lowland plants of early spring. **Leucocrinum**, SAND LILY
3b. Tepals separate; stems bearing a few reduced leaves; plants of alpine tundra. **Lloydia**, ALP LILY

4a. Flowers 1-2 cm long, nodding, purple-brown, speckled; leaves linear, alternate or somewhat whorled. **Fritillaria**, FRITILLARY
4b. Tepals over 5 cm long, erect or spreading, bright red-orange, spotted; leaves whorled. **Lilium**, LILY

ERYTHRONIUM L. 1753 [Greek, *erythro*, red, alluding to the flower color in some species]. AVALANCHE LILY

One species, **E. grandiflorum** Pursh. Abundant in early spring close to melting snowbanks, especially in aspen. Normally the anthers are yellow, but in some populations red-anthered plants are common.

FRITILLARIA L. 1753 [Latin, *fritillus*, dice box, because of the shape of the capsule]. FRITILLARY

One species, **F. atropurpurea** Nuttall, **77D**. Infrequent, rarely occurring more than a few plants in a stand, in aspen groves and montane sagebrush meadows, Rawah Range, LR, but probably on the east base of the Park Range in North Park also. The cubical capsules are very distinctive.

LEUCOCRINUM Nuttall 1837 [Greek, *leucos*, white, + *krinon*, lily]. SAND LILY

One species, **L. montanum** Nuttall, **Pl. 15**. A very common plant of grasslands on the eastern plains, blooming in very early spring. The base of the floral tube, and the ovary, are deep underground. Evidently, the ovary elongates at maturity, placing the seeds just below ground level. The flower buds of the following season push the ovary of the previous year's flower up to ground level, making possible the scattering of the seeds. *Leucocrinum* is out of place in the Liliaceae and has been placed by Dahlgren et al. in the Funkiaceae or the Amaryllidaceae, with the further suggestion that its relationships may really be with the Hemerocallidaceae.

LILIUM L. 1753 [Latin form of *leirion*, the classical Greek name]. LILY

One species, **L. philadelphicum** L., WOOD LILY, **Pl. 8**. Rare or in small isolated stands, aspen groves, very vulnerable to collecting. Although not on a federal endangered list, this is one of the most beautiful of Colorado plants and should never be picked or dug for transplanting into gardens, because it has poor powers of recovery.

LLOYDIA Reichenbach 1830 [for the discoverer, Edward Lloyd, 1660-1709, curator of the museum of Oxford University]. ALP LILY

One species **L. serotina** Reichenbach. Perennial from short, underground rhizomes, although the base of plant parts usually collected resembles a slender bulb. Common on the alpine tundra. A remarkable species, scattered over the high mountains of the Northern Hemisphere, but very rare in the Arctic, where one might expect it.

LIMNANTHACEAE MEADOWFOAM FAMILY (LIM)

A very small family of two genera, exclusively western North American. *Limnanthes*, with about a dozen species, mostly Californian, contains wet meadow plants with often large white or yellow flowers. One species, *L. douglasii*, has yellow petals with white tips and has been called the poached egg flower.

FLOERKEA Willdenow [for G. H. Floerke, eighteenth-century German lichenologist]. FALSE MERMAID

One species, **F. proserpinacoides** Willdenow [for Proserpine, wife of Pluto], a delicate, inconspicuous plant of wet montane meadows, Park Range, RT, but probably also in North Park. The leaves are alternate, pinnately divided into 3-5 oblong or linear leaflets. Floral parts are in 3s, the sepals about 2-3 mm long and the petals white, only half as long. There are 6 minute stamens. The gynoecium consists of about 3 carpels, apparently separate but sharing a common style from the gynobase; thus they are schizocarps as in *Geranium*. The ripe segments are 1-seeded tuberculate nutlets. A very strange little plant in an equally strange family!

LIMONIACEAE THRIFT FAMILY (LMO)

This small family contains several genera familiar in cultivation: the sea lavender, *Limonium*, and statice, *Armeria*. Most species occur along seacoasts and on saline desert-steppes. In our genus, *Armeria*, the plants are perennial from tufts of linear basal leaves. The inflorescence is a ball of pale purple flowers subtended by an involucre of papery bracts. Its structure is peculiar and complicated. The outermost bracts of the head are prolonged downward and form a brown sheath around the top of the stem. The conspicuous part of the flower is the calyx; this is tubular and hairy, with 5 lobes and pleats, each lobe with a stout red vein. The petals are short, oblong, united into a tube, and cucullate at the apex, with the stamens attached on and in front of the cucullate apex. The filaments are dilated, and the 2-locular anthers curve in over the 5 styles of the gynoecium; the ovary is superior. Without careful dissection none of this detail is to be made out in a head of what most will see as simply a pink ball of paper flowers.

ARMERIA Willdenow 1809 [name said to be of Celtic origin]. STATICE, THRIFT

One species, **A. scabra** Pallas subsp. **sibirica** (Turczaninow) Hylander. Very rare, found in America only in the vicinity of Hoosier Pass. Otherwise it occurs in Mongolia. It grows on wet solifluction lobes or even on relatively dry tundra, but it is so extremely restricted in range that it should never be collected unless to document a new locality.

LINACEAE FLAX FAMILY (LIN)

The word linen comes from Greek, *linon*, flax, cultivated from ancient times as a source of fiber that is obtained by the process of retting (curing the stems in water). *Linum* is also the source of linseed oil, a drying oil of a thousand uses. The seeds of flax are used medicinally. Flax blossoms open early in the morning and usually fall by midday. They come in yellow, copper, and one of the truest blues found in nature. Critical differences in the union of the styles, along with different chromosome base numbers, indicate that the genus *Linum* is heterogeneous and that several segregate genera, some proposed over a century ago, are justified.

1a. Flowers blue . . . . (2)
1b. Flowers yellow or coppery. **Mesynium**, YELLOW FLAX

2a. Stigma capitate. **Adenolinum**, WILD BLUE FLAX
2b. Stigma considerably longer than wide. **Linum**, CULTIVATED FLAX

ADENOLINUM Reichenbach 1837 [Greek, *aden*, gland, + *linon*, flax]. WILD BLUE FLAX

1a. Annual; low, infrequently branched. **A. pratense** (Norton) Weber. Rare, very infrequently collected on the southeastern plains. A red-flowered species, *A. grandiflorum* (Desvaux) Weber has been introduced with wildflower seed mixes but evidently does not survive the winter.
1b. Perennial; tall plant producing many branches from the base. **A. lewisii** (Pursh) Löve & Löve. Plains to upper montane. Petals blue, falling in late morning (*Linum lewisii*). Formerly lumped with the Eurasian *L. perenne*, but H. G. Baker showed that the two species have distinctly different reproductive strategies.

LINUM L. 1753 [Greek, *linon*, classical name of flax]. CULTIVATED FLAX

One species, **L. usitatissimum** L. [most utilized], Adventive. Occurring sporadically in the piedmont valleys.

MESYNIUM Rafinesque 1837 [Greek, *meso*, middle, + *syn*, united, alluding to the united styles]. YELLOW FLAX

1a. Plants grayish-puberulent throughout; plants usually less than 1 dm high, densely branched. **M. puberulum** (Engelmann) Weber. Frequent on the plains. The flowers of this species are more copper-colored than yellow.
1b. Plants glabrous or essentially so; stems tall, sparingly branched; petals yellow . . . . (2)

2a. Styles more than 6 mm long; petals more than 10 mm long. **M. rigidum** (Pursh) Löve & Löve. Widely distributed on the plains and San Luis Valley, but never abundant.

2b. Styles less than 6 mm long; petals less than 10 mm long. **M. australe** (Heller) Weber. Upper Arkansas drainage.

LOASACEAE LOASA FAMILY (LOA)

The sandpaper surface of the leaves of Loasaceae is caused by some of the strangest plant hairs known. These multicellular hairs are broad-based, shaped like a pagoda, each cell capped by a ring of stiff, curved hooks, which, unlike the corners of pagoda roofs, curve down, not up. There is hardly an article of clothing that will not carry away the leaves or fruits. The flowers of the larger species are inconspicuous until they open wide at eventide, like the flowers of the night-blooming cereus, which they resemble. Our plants traditionally have been treated in the genus *Mentzelia*.

1a. Flowers deep orange; leaves ovate, irregularly serrate or somewhat lobed. **Mentzelia**
1a. Flowers yellow or white . . . . (2)

2a. Annual; petals 5, only 2-5 mm long; capsule linear-cylindric, widest at the top, less than 5 mm diameter; placentae without horizontal lamellae between the seeds; seeds prismatic, irregularly angular. **Acrolasia**
2b. Biennial or perennial; petals more than 5, usually over 1 cm long; capsule broadly cylindric, over 5 mm diameter; placentae with horizontal lamellae; seeds flat, often winged. **Nuttallia**, BLAZINGSTAR

ACROLASIA K. B. Presl 1831 [Greek, *akron*, summit, + *lasios*, hairy, perhaps referring to hairs at petal tips]
1a. Seeds prismatic, truncate at the ends, grooved along 3 angles, the surface appearing smooth under low magnification. **A. dispersa** (Watson) Davidson [scattered]. Frequent on dry slopes, but usually not in the hot desert-steppe.
1b. Seeds cuboidal, lacking grooves on the angles, the surface generally appearing papillose under low magnification . . . . (2)

2a. Leaves with shallowly and regularly scalloped margins. **A. albicaulis** (Douglas) Rydberg [white-stemmed], **78B**. Common in early spring at low altitudes. This species is hexaploid (chromosome number n=27). The species of this group form a complex series with different chromosome numbers based on x=9.
2b. Leaves irregularly divided. **A. gracilis** Rydberg. Originally described from foothills of LR, but probably widely distributed. This species is an octaploid (chromosome number n=36).

MENTZELIA L. 1753

One species, **M. oligosperma** Nuttall [few-seeded]. Restricted to crevices in sandstone, canyonsides of southeastern corner of Colorado.

NUTTALLIA Rafinesque 1817 [for Thomas Nuttall, British-American botanist and western explorer, 1786-1859]. BLAZINGSTAR
1a. Petals white to cream . . . . (2)
1b. Petals pale yellow to golden . . . . (4)

2a. Petals 10, with numerous narrow staminodia grading to stamens with filaments 1.5 mm wide to very narrow; sepals gradually narrowed from the base, narrowly triangular; petals 3-7 cm long . . . . (3)
2b. Petals 5, plus 5 staminodes, each apiculate; stamens grading from having filaments 2 mm wide to very narrow; sepals narrow almost from the very

base; petals not over 2 cm long. **N. rusbyi** (Wooton) Rydberg [For the collector, Dr. W. S. Rusby, 1852-?]. Intermountain parks from North Park to the San Luis Valley, at higher altitudes and in much more mesic areas than the next.

3a. Petals 1.5-4 cm long, 0.3-1 cm wide, not overlapping in anthesis, white; bracts not fused to ovary wall. **N. nuda** (Pursh) Greene. Abundant in sandy soil on the plains, especially along roadsides and highway medians.
3b. Petals 5-7 cm long, 1-2 cm wide, touching or overlapping in anthesis, cream-colored; bracts partly fused to ovary wall. **N. decapetala** (Pursh) Greene, **Pl. 14**. On and near sandstone outcrops along the base of the Front Range.

4a. Stems stout, mostly unbranched, with numerous closely massed flowers; all fertile stamens with narrow filaments. **N. reverchonii** (Urban & Gilg) Weber
4b. Stems slender, usually branched, the flowers well separated; some fertile stamens with broad filaments . . . . (5)

5a. Petals pale straw-colored, 2n=18. **N. multiflora** (Nuttall) Greene, **78C**. Common in foothill canyonsides, especially Platte and Clear Creek.
5b. Petals golden-yellow . . . . (6)

6a. Leaves, especially the upper, very narrow, linear to linear-lanceolate, coarsely dentate or almost pinnatifid, the teeth or segments ± acute. **N. speciosa** (Osterhout) Greene. Front Range foothills.
6b. Leaves broader, linear-lanceolate to oblong-lanceolate, occasionally oblanceolate, pinnately lobulate, segments rounded or obtuse, often irregular. 2n=18. **N. sinuata** (Rydberg) Daniels. Endemic. Front Range foothills.

The following taxa, for which there is no modern treatment, have been omitted from the key: *N. densa* (Greene) Greene, the type from the canyon of the Arkansas River, and *N. chrysantha* (Brandegee) Greene, the type from Cañon City.

LYTHRACEAE LOOSESTRIFE FAMILY (LYT)

A family with an ambiguous common name, because loosestrifes also occur in the Primulaceae. Three genera and only four species occur on the Eastern Slope, all of them wetland species. Two exotic genera are worth mentioning. *Lagerstroemia indica*, the crepe-myrtle, is a striking cultivar of the Gulf Coast and southern California, a small tree with pink, yellow, or white fringed and puckered petals with narrow claws; and *Lawsonia indica*, the henna, was called by Mohammed "chief of the flowers of this world and the next." However, no one has returned to report the existence of this remarkable plant in the next world, and we do not know whether hair dye or nail coloring is useful there. *Lawsonia* was named for a surveyor-general of North Carolina who was burned by Indians in 1712.

1a. Erect plants with pink-purple flowers; hypanthium elongated, cylindrical or tubular. **Lythrum**, PURPLE LOOSESTRIFE
1b. Low, sprawling plants with inconspicuous axillary flowers and stiffly spreading branches; hypanthium short, hemispheric or globose . . . . (2)

2a. Flowers 2 or more in the leaf axils; capsules bursting irregularly. **Ammannia**
2b. Flowers solitary in the leaf axils; capsule septicidally dehiscent. **Rotala**, TOOTHCUP

AMMANNIA L. 1753 [for Paul Ammann, 1634-1691, German botanist]

One species, **A. robusta** Heer & Regel. Adventive in low, marshy areas of floodplains in the piedmont valleys and plains.

LYTHRUM L. 1753 [Greek, *lytron*, a name used by Dioscorides for *L. salicaria*]. PURPLE LOOSESTRIFE

1a. Flowers solitary or in pairs in the leaf axils; stamens 6. **L. alatum** Pursh. Common in wet swales in the piedmont valleys near Boulder.
1b. Flowers numerous in showy terminal spikes; stamens 12. **L. salicaria** L. Adventive, escaped from old gardens, well established locally along irrigation ditches in the valleys.

ROTALA L. 1753 [name an incorrect diminutive of Latin, *rota*, wheel, from the whorled leaves of the original species]. TOOTHCUP

One species, **R. ramosior** (L.) Koehne. This occurs with, closely resembles, and has been mistaken for *Ammannia*.

MALVACEAE MALLOW FAMILY (MLV)

Everyone knows hollyhocks. Most old folks remember making dolls with long dresses out of the flowers. Most mallow flowers are smaller copies of the hollyhock. The main distinguishing feature of mallow flowers is the column of united stamen filaments forming a sheath around the gynoecium and standing in the midst of the flower like a fountain spraying out hundreds of colored droplets–the anthers. Also, the leaves and stems are usually clothed with stellately branched hairs. Although some species have a capsular fruit, most have a gynoecium resembling a wheel of cheese, with the carpels sloughing away at maturity as 1-seeded disks (mericarps). The confection, marshmallow, used to be based on the mucilaginous contents of the root of the marsh mallow, *Althaea officinalis*, which grows in marshes of western Europe and New England. Now there are synthetic sources. One of the important crops of man, cotton (*Gossypium*), is a mallow, as are the okra or gumbo, *Hibiscus esculentus*, and an ornamental shrub, rose-of-Sharon, *H. syriacus*.

1a. Fruit a loculicidal capsule (opening on the abaxial face into the locule, not separating the locules, which would be septicidal); stamen column bearing anthers along the side, the summit 5-toothed. **Hibiscus**
1b. Fruit a schizocarp (the individual carpels separating as units); carpels 5-many; stamen column bearing anthers at the summit and sometimes along the sides . . . . (2)

2a. Style branches filiform or clavate, the stigmas decurrent along the inner side; carpels with a single ovule . . . . (3)
2b. Style branches terminating in capitate, truncate, or discoid stigmas; carpels 1-9-ovulate . . . . (6)

3a. Calyx with an involucel of 6-9 bracts united basally. **Althaea**, HOLLYHOCK
3b. Involucel of 3 free bracts or none . . . . (4)

4a. Petals obcordate, white with purple lines; ruderal weeds. **Malva**
4b. Petals rose-purple, over 1 cm long, truncate . . . . (5)

5a. Basal leaves shallowly lobed or merely crenate, upper stem leaves deeply and narrowly lobed; slender, erect wetland plants. **Sidalcea**, CHECKERMALLOW
5b. All leaves deeply lobed; sprawling dryland plants. **Callirhoë**, POPPYMALLOW

6a. Leaves over 5 cm long, palmately lobed, maplelike; mountain meadow and streamside plants. **Iliamna**

6b. Leaves smaller, not maplelike; dryland plants . . . . (7)

7a. Carpels sharply differentiated into 2 parts, the upper part seedless, smooth, dehiscent, the lower part with seeds, reticulate, indehiscent. **Sphaeralcea**, GLOBEMALLOW

7b. Carpels not differentiated into upper and lower parts . . . . (8)

8a. Ovules 2 or more in each carpel; petals orange, yellow, rarely pink or red; entire plant covered by a very dense and fine stellate pubescence. **Abutilon**, INDIANMALLOW

8b. Ovules 1 in each carpel; petals never orange or yellow . . . . (9)

9a. Leaves deeply lobed; silvery hairs never present. **Anoda**

9b. Leaves very shallowly lobed; silvery peltate or stellate hairs often present. **Malvella**

ABUTILON Miller 1754 [name *aubutilum* given by Avicenna (Ibn Sina), Persian "prince of physicians," 980-1037]. VELVETLEAF

1a. Tall mostly unbranched annual; carpels 10-15, 10-18 mm long, their beaks divergent. **A. theophrasti** Medikus, INDIANMALLOW. Infrequent, adventive, ruderal weed in the piedmont valleys.

1b. Low branched perennials; carpels fewer than 10, shorter; carpels not divergent . . . . (2)

2a. Stems erect or nearly so; petals orange or yellow; leaves thickish. **A. incanum** (Link) Sweet. A single collection known, from BA.

2b. Stems slender and spreading or trailing; flowers pink or red. **A. parvulum** Gray. All collections are from the Cañon City area.

ALTHAEA L. 1753 [Greek, *althaino*, healing]. HOLLYHOCK

One species, **A. rosea** L. Escaped from gardens, occasionally naturalized along roadsides and in vacant ground.

ANODA Cavanilles 1785

One species, **A. cristata** (L.) Schlechtendal [crested]. Adventive, casually occurring as a weed in the truck garden area of the Arkansas Valley. The leaves are usually 3-lobed, the corolla pale lavender.

CALLIRHOË Nuttall 1821 [a Greek name from mythology]. POPPYMALLOW

One species, **C. involucrata** (Torrey & Gray) Gray. Frequent on the plains. A sprawling perennial from a deep-seated, thick taproot. The flowers are large, rose-purple, and the leaves variously palmately dissected.

HIBISCUS L. 1753 [ancient name for some large mallow]

One species, **H. trionum** L., FLOWER-OF-AN-HOUR. Frequent, adventive weed in tilled land in the valleys. Petals yellowish or whitish with the base and one edge purple.

ILIAMNA Greene 1906 [name not explained, but probably not of Greek origin as usually supposed. In Alaska there are a Mount Iliaminsk and a Lake Iliamna, possibly named by Russian explorers. Perhaps Greene saw this name and found it pretty, like the genus, but kept his readers guessing. Another suggested explanation from Paul Fryxell, MLV specialist, is Greek, *ilyos*, mud,

+ Latin, *amnis*, river, but Greene would never stoop to mixing two classical languages!]. WILD HOLLYHOCK

1a. Sepals narrowly lanceolate, long-acuminate; pedicels slender, 2-3 cm long; seeds glabrous. **I. crandallii** (Rydberg) Wiggins. Endemic, vicinity of Steamboat Springs, probably also on east side of Park Range in North Park.

1b. Sepals broadly triangular-ovate, obtuse or acute; pedicels stout, less than 2 cm long; seeds sparsely puberulent with very short simple or stellate hairs; plants simple or sparingly branched. **I. rivularis** (Douglas) Greene, **Pl. 45**. Infrequent along shaded mountain streamsides, generally distributed in the mountains.

MALVA L. 1753 [Greek, *malache* or *moloche*, for the emollient leaves]. MALLOW, CHEESEWEED

1a. Petals 4-5 mm long, scarcely exceeding the calyx; mericarps prominently rugose dorsally and winged at the angle between the dorsal and lateral walls. **M. parviflora** L. Adventive weed, evidently only collected once. This species evidently requires a more mesic climate than the next.

1b. Petals 6-11 mm long, exceeding the calyx; mericarps smooth or slightly ridged dorsally, not winged . . . . (2)

2a. Pedicels shorter than the calyx; staminal column glabrous; plants erect; calyx accrescent (flexed over the fruit); mericarps 8-11. **M. crispa** (L.) L. Adventive weed, rarely collected in the piedmont valleys, DN-LR.

2b. Pedicels longer than the calyx; staminal column pubescent; plants procumbent; calyx not accrescent; mericarps 12-15. **M. neglecta** Wallroth. An extremely common and tenacious weed of lawns and gardens. The fruits resemble wheels of cheese.

MALVELLA Jaubert & Spach 1855 [diminutive of *Malva*]

1a. Leaf blades narrowly triangular or lanceolate to almost linear; surface with silvery peltate hairs; involucel absent; calyx lobes cordate. **M. sagittifolia** (Gray) Fryxell (*Sida lepidota* var. *sagittifolia*). One record, from near La Junta.

1b. Leaf blades reniform or suborbicular to triangular-ovate; pubescence stellate; involucel usually present; calyx lobes ovate. **M. leprosa** (Ortega) Krapovickas. One record from the Arkansas River Valley, OT (*Sida hederacea*).

SIDALCEA Gray 1849 [combination of two generic names, *Sida* and *Alcea*]. CHECKERMALLOW

1a. Flowers white. **S. candida** Gray. Common in wet montane meadows.

1b. Flowers purple. **S. neomexicana** Gray. Common in swampy, often alkaline meadows, middle altitudes, more rarely in the piedmont valleys. Occasional white mutants are found in normal stands.

SPHAERALCEA St. Hilaire 1825 [Greek, *sphaera*, sphere, + *alcea*, mallow]. GLOBEMALLOW

1a. Lower leaves very deeply palmately divided; leaves silvery from tightly packed stellate hairs; plants with low, bushy form. **S. coccinea** (Nuttall) Rydberg, COPPERMALLOW. Roadsides and ruderal, often disturbed sites in the valleys.

1b. Lower leaves shallowly lobed; leaves green. **S. angustifolia** (Cavanilles) D. Don var. **cuspidata** Gray. Common in the lower Arkansas River drainage.

MARTYNIACEAE UNICORN PLANT FAMILY (MAR)

A small family of herbs confined to the Western Hemisphere. In Colorado we have the single genus *Proboscidea*, which earns its generic name by having a woody pod that resembles an elephant's head with 2 long curved tusks. The plant is sticky all over, with a flower resembling that of catalpa, bilaterally symmetrical with four fertile stamens of 2 different lengths and a sterile staminode. The ovary is superior and unilocular with 2 parietal placentae. Some authors place this genus in the family Pedaliaceae.

PROBOSCIDEA Schmidel 1763 [for the fancied shape of the pod to a proboscis]. DEVIL'S CLAW

One species, **P. louisianica** (Miller) Thellung. Adventive, frequent as a weed, mostly in the southeastern counties, often as solitary plants and never abundant. The flowers are large in relation to the whole plant. The leaves are broadly ovate, somewhat lobed, and sticky-glandular. The fruit is large and becomes black, woody, and springy-textured. Very often the fruit is the only part found.

MELANTHIACEAE FALSE HELLEBORE FAMILY (MLN)

Recently segregated from the Liliaceae, this family includes the false hellebore and death camas groups. It is interesting to note that, even without any knowledge of the modern evidence for segregation of this and other lilylike families, Rydberg presented essentially the same arrangement in his book on the Rocky Mountain flora, but the taxonomic establishment did not follow him.

1a. Tall, rank herbs up to 2-3 m tall, arising from fibrous roots; leaves strongly pleated; inflorescence a pyramidal panicle of greenish-white flowers. **Veratrum**, FALSE HELLEBORE, CORNHUSK LILY

1b. Low herbs usually not over 5 dm tall; leaves not pleated; arising from bulbs; inflorescence a raceme sometimes with short branches at its base . . . (2)

2a. Tepals 7-11 mm long; stamens not distinctly longer than the perianth; tepal gland notched above. **Anticlea**, DEATH CAMAS

2b. Tepals about 4 mm long; stamens distinctly longer than the tepals; tepal gland obovate or almost orbicular, not notched. **Toxicoscordion**, DEATH CAMAS

ANTICLEA Kunth 1843 [from Anticlea, mother of Ulysses]. DEATH CAMAS

One species, **A. elegans** (Pursh) Rydberg. Subalpine meadows and lower, moist tundra. The bulbs are very toxic (*Zygadenus*). Other species occur in Siberia and in Mexico. True *Zygadenus* is a genus of the southern Appalachians.

TOXICOSCORDION Rydberg 1903 [Greek, *toxicon*, poison for arrows, + *scorodon*, garlic]. DEATH CAMAS

One species, **T. venenosum** (Watson) Rydberg. Common in meadows at lower elevations along the Front Range, not venturing very far out on the plains (*Zygadenus*).

VERATRUM L. 1753 [Latin, *vere*, true, + *atre*, black, alluding to the black rhizomes of some species]. CORNHUSK LILY, FALSE HELLEBORE

One species, **V. tenuipetalum** Heller, **Pl. 25**. Forming very dense stands of tall, rank plants, on open slopes along subalpine streams, often associated with overgrazing or the bottoms of avalanche tracks.

MENYANTHACEAE BUCKBEAN FAMILY (MNY)

A small family of 5 genera, 3 in the Northern Hemisphere and 2 in the Southern, and 40 species. All are aquatic or semiaquatic herbs. Most species are tropical, but our single species is widespread in mountains of the Northern Hemisphere. Where abundant, as in northern Eurasia, the leaves are used as a substitute for tea or added to beer, or eaten as an emergency food. Here the plant is uncommon.

MENYANTHES L. 1753 [Greek, *menyanthos*, name of some other plant in this family]. WATERCLOVER

One species, **M. trifoliata** L. Upper montane and subalpine ponds. The leaves and flower stalks rise above water level, and the very spongy stalks and rhizomes are rooted in the mud. The flowers are unusually attractive, with recurved white petals covered with a dense brush of crinkly, white or pinkish hairs. As with the pond lilies, it is a mystery why these plants occur in some ponds and not in others.

MOLLUGINACEAE CARPETWEED FAMILY (MOL)

A small family often placed with the Alsinaceae, Aizoaceae, or Caryophyllaceae, containing only a handful of genera, of which we have a single one. It does resemble a chickweed, but the leaves are whorled and the ovary has 3-5 locules instead of 1, and it dehisces loculicidally.

MOLLUGO L. 1753. CARPETWEED

One species, **M. verticillata** L., **23C**. A prostrate annual with spreading branches with whorls of oblanceolate leaves and several pedicellate flowers at the nodes. Adventive weed of floodplain sand bars, border plantings, mostly in the Boulder area, but there are records from North Park and Twin Lakes.

MONOTROPACEAE PINESAP FAMILY (MNT)

A small family of somewhat fleshy plants with reduced scale-leaves lacking chlorophyll, parasitic on the roots of conifers. This family has traditionally been placed in the Ericaceae.

1a. Corolla of united petals; stem tall (over 20 cm), stout, red-brown, with numerous reddish flowers in a long raceme. **Pterospora**, PINEDROPS

1b. Corolla of separate petals; stem shorter, the entire plant pale yellowish or pinkish, the flowers in a nodding terminal cluster, becoming erect in fruit. **Hypopitys**, PINESAP

HYPOPITYS Hill 1756 [Greek, *hypo*, under, + *pitys*, pine]. PINESAP

One species, **H. monotropa** Crantz, **93B**. Infrequent in dry lodgepole pine forests as well as moist spruce forests (*Monotropa hypopitys*).

PTEROSPORA Nuttall 1818 [Greek, *pteros*, wing, + *spora*, seed]. PINEDROPS

One species, **P. andromedea** Nuttall, **93A**. Common in pine-needle duff in dry pine forests. The seeds of this plant are unique. They are minute (less than 0.2 mm diameter) and are provided with a fragile, lacy, transparent cellular wing many times the size of the seed, attached at one end, providing buoyancy for dispersal.

MORACEAE MULBERRY FAMILY (MOR)

A family of many economic plants mostly of the tropical and subtropical world. All are trees or shrubs with 4-merous unisexual flowers arranged in heads, catkins, or hollowed out receptacles (as in figs). *Artocarpus*, breadfruit, was the plant that Captain Bligh was assigned to bring back to England, sparking the mutiny of the H.M.S. *Bounty*. *Ficus* is a large genus that includes sources of latex, delicious fruit, and several extremely sacred trees with a vast mythology. *Morus*, the mulberry, provides leafy food for the commercial silkworm.

1a. Leaves entire; branches with stout thorns; fruit a baseball-sized mass of individual fruits. **Maclura**, OSAGE-ORANGE
1b. Leaves deeply lobed; branches not thorny; fruit small, blackberrylike. **Morus**, MULBERRY

MACLURA Nuttall 1818 [for William Maclure, 1763-1840, American geologist]. OSAGE-ORANGE

One species, **M. pomifera** (Rafinesque) Schneider. A species of the midwest, escaped and established along fencerows, to be expected in the Arkansas Valley.

MORUS L. 1753 [the classical Latin name]. MULBERRY

One species, **Morus alba** L., WHITE MULBERRY. Adventive, escaped and established along fencerows in the Colorado River Valley and to be expected in the Arkansas Valley.

NAJADACEAE WATERNYMPH FAMILY (NAJ)

An obscure little family of submerged aquatics consisting of the single genus, *Najas*. The leaves are linear, opposite but often clustered at the nodes, and tend to be slightly toothed. The flowers are very reduced; male flowers have a single sessile anther, and the female flower consists of a single carpel with 2-4 linear stigmas. Because *Najas* is a common aquarium plant it gets introduced into ponds with the emptying of the fishbowl.

NAJAS L. 1753 [Greek, Naias, the water nymph]

One species, **N. guadalupensis** (Sprengel) Magnus, **43C**. Adventive, in ponds of the piedmont valleys, LR, BL. This has very narrow, only slightly toothed leaves.

NOLINACEAE SOTOL FAMILY (NLN)

The Sotol family is a small one recently separated from the Lily and Agave families, mostly on anatomical grounds. The two genera commonly represented in the deserts of the American Southwest are of considerable human importance. The young shoots of *Dasylirion*, sotol, were a source of food, and its sugar contributed to the beverage of the same name. The tough leaves of sotol and *Nolina* are used in basketry, thatching, mats, and hats.

NOLINA Michaux 1803 [for P. C. Nolin (dates?), early American horticulturist]. BEARGRASS

One species, **N. texana** Watson (*N. greenei*). One small colony known on the Mesa de Maya, BA. Beargrass was first discovered by E. L. Greene on a winter parish journey from New Mexico to Colorado in January 1880. In great excitement, he sent a sprig of it to Asa Gray, saying that he had found it "in the mountains between the Purgatory and Apishapa rivers north of Trinidad."

Beargrass remained a mystery until Willard Louden rediscovered it on his ranch near Branson, LA, where it is abundant over several hundred acres of rimrock. This is the northernmost locality for the plant, which is dioecious and produces an abundance of large panicles of flowers and fruits. The area is well protected by the owners and by its occurrence in very difficult terrain. Greene's trip also yielded the only collections, until a few years ago, of mesquite, *Prosopis*, which eventually was also found on the Louden ranch.

NYCTAGINACEAE FOUR-O'CLOCK FAMILY (NYC)

A small family characterized by the often tubular perianth, which doubles as petals and calyx, the inferior ovary forming a 1-seeded, often winged, nutlet, opposite fleshy leaves and umbellate flower clusters subtended by conspicuous, often papery bracts. The cultivated garden four-o'clock, *Mirabilis jalapa*, is a native of South America. The flamboyant *Bougainvillea* vines of the tropics are nyctages. The species are most attractive when they are in flower, but the critical characters for identification are in the fruits.

1a. Flowers in umbels surrounded by 4-6 separate bracts; stigmas linear or fusiform; anthers not exserted . . . . (2)
1b. Flowers in few-flowered clusters surrounded by united bracts or subtended by 3 bracts united at the base; stigmas capitate or hemispheric; anthers exserted . . . . (3)

2a. Fruit over 1 cm long and wide, in a loose cluster, the wings broad, papery, strongly veined, transparent (like a cicada's wing); annual. **Tripterocalyx**, SAND-VERBENA
2b. Fruit smaller, in a tight head, the wings not transparent; perennial. **Abronia**, SAND-VERBENA

3a. Leaves 1-2 cm long, elliptic-ovate, densely sticky-glandular; flowers small, purplish; branches spreading out on the ground from a cluster of basal leaves. **Allionia**
3b. Leaves larger or otherwise different . . . . (4)

4a. Leaves perfectly cordate; plants procumbent; involucre less than 1 cm long. **Mirabilis**, FOUR-O'CLOCK
4b. Leaves otherwise (may be broadly triangular-ovate but not cordate); erect or ascending plants with rotate or campanulate involucre over 1 cm long or broad . . . . (5)

5a. Involucre green, leaflike in texture, not enlarging or becoming membranous in fruit; fruit smooth, not constricted at the base, slightly 5-ribbed. **Mirabilis**, FOUR-O'CLOCK
5b. Involucre enlarging and becoming membranous in fruit; fruit strongly 5-angled, constricted at the base, usually pubescent. **Oxybaphus**, UMBRELLAWORT

ABRONIA Jussieu 1789 [Greek, *abros*, delicate, referring to the involucre]. SAND-VERBENA

1a. Bracts 10-20 mm long; fruit 5-10 mm long; perianth 10-30 mm long, the limb white or purplish and 7-10 mm long; leaves deltoid to oblong or lanceolate. **A. fragrans** Nuttall, **Pl. 21**. Common on the plains.
1b. Bracts 5-8 mm long; fruit less than 7 mm long; perianth 13-15 mm long, the limb white, 6-7 mm long; leaves elliptic to lanceolate. **A. carletonii** Coulter

& Fisher. Rare, BA. Plants from Bonny Reservoir may belong here also. This species is the Eastern Slope counterpart of *A. elliptica*.

ALLIONIA L. 1753 [for Carlo Allioni, 1705-1804, Italian botanist, author of *Flora Piedmontana*]

1a. Perennial; margins of fruits with about 3 broadly triangular, nonglandular teeth on each side, usually incurved and covering nearly the entire surface. **A. incarnata** L. One record, from near Cañon City. The small flowers are in clusters of 3, each invested by a bract forming an involucre on a short axillary peduncle.

1b. Annual; margins of fruits with several relatively slender gland-tipped teeth, these spreading or moderately incurved. **A. choisyi** Standley. One record, from Rocky Ford.

MIRABILIS L. 1753 [Latin, *mirabilis*, wonderful]. FOUR-O'CLOCK

1a. Leaves perfectly cordate, not thick and fleshy; involucre less than 1 cm long. **M. oxybaphoides** Gray. Infrequent, piñon-juniper. The perianth is less than 1 cm long, the involucre subrotate, 3-flowered; stamens 3, the filaments free.

1b. Leaves otherwise; erect or ascending plants with rotate or campanulate involucre over 1 cm broad and/or long. **M. multiflora** (Torrey) Gray **Pl. 23.** Abundant along roadsides and on open canyonsides, blooming all summer and fall, widely distributed.

OXYBAPHUS L'Heritier 1797 [Greek, *oxybaphon*, saucer, alluding to the broad, flat involucre]. UMBRELLAWORT

Note: the taxonomy of this genus is very unsatisfactory. Many species have been described on very scanty evidence; they tend to be collected without fruit, and notes are needed concerning their appearance in the field, and whether two or more species grow together. Evidently the widely distributed species tend to form hybrids where they meet the more restricted ones, yielding offspring which are intermediate. Nevertheless, for the most part the species treated here seem to be well defined but a really reliable key will depend on our making better collections and observations.

1a. Principal leaves triangular-ovate, with petioles over 1 cm long; totally glabrous. **O. nyctagineus** (Michaux) Porter & Coulter. A very common ruderal weed, originally native?

1b. Principal leaves sessile or with short petioles; variously pubescent or glabrous . . . . (2)

2a. Flowers axillary. **O. decumbens** (Nuttll) Sweet. Arkansas Valley. The plants may have narrowly linear or oblong leaves, and usually form low, hemispheric clumps branched at the base (*O. bodinii*).

2b. Flowers in terminal cymes . . . . (3)

3a. Anthocarp (fruiting calyx with the enclosed achene) glabrous . . . . . . (4)

3b. Anthocarp pubescent . . . . (6)

4a. Stem and leaves densely glandular-pilose; leaves triangular-ovate. **O. carletonii** (Standley) Weatherby. Southeasternmost counties.

4b. Stem and leaves glabrous and glaucous; leaves linear or oblong . . . . . (5)

5a. Leaves less than 10 mm wide; flowers 1 per involucre. **O. glaber** Watson. Sandhills on the plains.

5b. Leaves 10-25 mm wide; flowers 3 per involucre. **O. exaltatus** (Standley) Weatherby. Entering Colorado in the extreme southeastern corner.

6a. Leaves linear; stems glabrous. **O. linearis** (Pursh) B. L. Robinson. Very common throughout the plains and piedmont valleys. Evidently hybridizes with *O. hirsutus*.
6b. Leaves oblong or broader . . . . (7)

7a. Stem erect, ± unbranched; leaves oblong-ovate. **O. hirsutus** (Pursh) Sweet. Generally distributed along the base of the Front Range, not venturing far out on the plains.
7b. Stem branching at the base, low and spreading; leaves ovate-orbicular, often very glaucous, the stem hairs white and very long and stiff. **O. rotundifolius** (Greene) Standley. Restricted to gypsum soils in the Pueblo-Cañon City area (*O. polytrichus*).

TRIPTEROCALYX Hooker 1909 [Greek, *tri*, three, + *pteron*, wing, + *calyx*]. SAND-VERBENA

One species, **T. micranthus** (Torrey) Hooker, **Pl. 41**. Infrequent, in loose sand.

NYMPHAEACEAE WATERLILY FAMILY (NYM)

The white or pink waterlilies belong to the genus *Nymphaea*. The sacred lotus of the East is *Nelumbo*, cultivated in India for its edible rhizomes and fruit, and of extreme importance in the Buddhist religion. A South American species, *Victoria amazonica*, has floating leaves up to two meters in diameter, strongly reinforced against buffeting of wave action and having an upturned rim. These leaves are claimed to support the weight of a child. In Scandinavian folklore there is a troll called *näck* who sits at the bottom of lakes and fishes for people, using the stem and flower of the waterlily (the *näck*-rose) as a lure.

NUPHAR J. E. Smith 1809 [name said to be of Arabic origin]. YELLOW PONDLILY, SPATTERDOCK

One species, **N. luteum** (L.) Sibthorp & Smith subsp. **polysepalum** (Engelmann) Beal. Subalpine ponds. Someone ought to investigate the occurrence of pond lilies, to determine what factors are responsible for restricting them to particular ponds, while other apparently suitable ones are scattered throughout the region.

OLEACEAE OLIVE FAMILY (OLE)

The ash tree has been famous in mythology; the world ash tree figured prominently in the *Nibelungen Lied*, from which Wagner built his operatic quadrilogy. Ash, to most of us, signifies a tree with pinnately compound leaves and oar-shaped samaras. But in the American Southwest and Mexico several species with simple or trifoliolate leaves occur. They take a bit of getting used to. Privet, *Ligustrum vulgare*, belongs to this family, and our native *Forestiera*, of the Western Slope, bears a close resemblance to it.

1a. Trees; leaves pinnately compound; fruit a 1-seeded samara. **Fraxinus**, ASH
1b. Suffruticose herbs; leaves simple, linear-oblong; fruit a bilobed, circumscissile capsule. **Menodora**

FRAXINUS L. 1753 [the classical Latin name]. ASH

One species, **F. pensylvanica** H. Marshall var. **lanceolata** (Borkhausen) Sargent. Adventive, commonly cultivated and persisting as an escape in the outer Front Range gulches.

MENODORA Humboldt & Bonpland 1809 [Greek, *menos*, force or courage, + *doron*, gift, alluding to the force or strength the plant gives to animals]

One species, **M. scabra** (Engelmann) Gray. Restricted to gypsum soils, desert-steppe sites in the Arkansas River drainage near Pueblo and Cañon City. *Menodora* has an extraordinary distribution involving western North America, southern South America, and southern Africa, and its existence as a genus dates back before the separation of the southern continents. Its distribution constitutes part of the botanical evidence that forced geologists to search for a mechanism of continental movement that now is the science of plate tectonics.

Menodora is a unique genus. Unlike other members of the family, it is herbaceous with only a woody base. The calyx has about 10 slender teeth at the top of a cup that encloses loosely a two-carpellate ovary, which is lobed, each carpel having 2 seeds. Each carpel dehisces circumscissilely. The lid falls off, releasing the seeds, and leaves a smooth-rimmed, persistent cup lying in the cradle of the calyx.

ONAGRACEAE EVENING-PRIMROSE FAMILY (ONA)

Evening-primroses are unrelated to true primroses. Many are attractive, morning- and evening-flowering plants pollinated by night-flying, long-tongued moths. The floral formula for most of them (4 sepals, 4 petals, 8 stamens, 4 united carpels in an inferior ovary) is unique, but because of their 4-merous pattern they sometimes (especially those with small flowers) are mistaken for mustards. Hugo de Vries propounded the mutation theory in 1901 from studies on an evening-primrose, *Oenothera*. The mutation theory stands today, despite the fact that the phenomena de Vries thought were mutations in *Oenothera* turned out to be the result of another genetic mechanism. It remained for others to demonstrate true mutations in other plants and animals. Horticulturally, the family is best known for *Fuchsia*, an Andean genus.

1a. Flowers with parts in twos; ovary spherical; leaves broadly ovate, long-petioled. **Circaea**, ENCHANTRESS' NIGHTSHADE
1b. Flowers with parts in fours; ovary ± elongate; leaves narrower, short-petioled or sessile . . . . (2)

2a. Seeds with a tuft of hairs (coma) at one end; flowers pink or white, never yellow . . . . (3)
2b. Seeds without coma; flowers pink, white, or yellow . . . . (4)

3a. Flowers large, the petals 1-2 cm long, entire, spreading; hypanthium not prolonged beyond the ovary. **Chamerion**, FIREWEED
3b. Flowers smaller, petals usually notched, ascending; hypanthium prolonged beyond the ovary. **Epilobium**, WILLOWHERB

4a. Fruit nutlike, indehiscent; flowers always becoming pink. **Gaura**
4b. Fruit a dehiscent, usually elongate capsule; flowers white, pink, or yellow . . . . (5)

5a. Flowers minute; plants very delicate, slender, with slender branches; ovary with 2 locules; hypanthium not prolonged beyond the ovary; flowers always white or pink. **Gayophytum**

5b. Flowers minute to usually showy; ovary with 4 locules; hypanthium prolonged beyond the ovary as a slender tube . . . . (6)

6a. Stigma with 4 linear lobes; flowers mostly opening in the evening. **Oenothera**, EVENING-PRIMROSE

6b. Stigma capitate, discoid or slightly 4-lobed or -toothed; flowers mostly opening in the daytime . . . . (7)

7a. Hypanthium tube 25-50 mm long; stamens almost equal in length. **Calylophus**

7b. Hypanthium 1-15 mm long; stamens of 2 lengths. **Camissonia**

CALYLOPHUS Spach 1835 [Greek, *calyx*, + *lophos*, crest, alluding to the dorsal appendages of the sepals]

1a. Sepals plane, lacking a keeled midrib; stamens subequal . . . . (2)

1b. Sepals with conspicuously keeled midrib; stamens biseriate, the filaments opposite the sepals about twice as long as the epipetalous ones . . . . (3)

2a. Plants low, frequently caespitose, mostly 0.4-2 dm high; densely gray-strigulose; sepal tips short. 0.3-3 mm long. **C. lavandulifolius** (Torrey & Gray) Raven (*Oenothera*). Common on the plains and into the upper Arkansas Valley.

2b. Plants not caespitose, mostly taller and more openly branched, 0.4-4 dm, high, variously pubescent or glabrous; if strigulose, the sepal tips 2-6 mm long. **C. hartwegii** (Bentham) Raven subsp. **pubescens** (Gray) Towner (*Oenothera*). Barely entering Colorado in southeastern BA.

3a. Flowers small, the petals 5-12 mm long; stigma positioned near the apex of the floral tube or slightly beyond, within the circle of anthers. **C. serrulatus** (Nuttall) Raven (*Oenothera*). Common throughout the eastern plains.

3b. Flowers larger, the petals 9-25 mm long; stigma well exserted, usually to the end of the episepalous anthers or beyond. **C. berlandieri** Spach. A southern, especially Texan species, known in Colorado from a single collection south of Trinidad.

CAMISSONIA Link 1818 [for Adelbert von Chamisso 1781-1838, poet, explorer, and naturalist, creator of Peter Schlemihl]

1a. Leaves pinnatifid; plants ± densely pilose or appressed pubescent. **C. breviflora** (Torrey & Gray) Raven. In Colorado known only from North Park.

1b. Leaves not pinnatifid; plants almost glabrous. **C. subacaulis** (Pursh) Raven. Meadows, upper Yampa River, RT, but possibly occurring in western North Park (*Oenothera*).

CHAMERION Rafinesque 1833 [Greek, *chamae*, lowly, + *Nerium*, the oleander, from the leaf shape] (formerly included in *Epilobium*). FIREWEED

1a. Racemes elongate, many-flowered, not leafy; styles hairy at the base, exceeding the stamens; leaves 5-20 cm long, veiny. **C. danielsii** (Daniels) D. Löve. Abundant along roadsides and in burned areas, middle altitudes (an octoploid related to *C. [Epilobium] angustifolium*).

1b. Racemes few-flowered, leafy; style glabrous, shorter than the stamens; leaves 2-6 cm long, glaucous, not veiny. **C. subdentatum** (Rydberg) Löve & Löve. Talus slopes and along snowmelt streamsides, upper subalpine (a tetraploid related to *C. latifolium*). This group has been called *Epilobium* in America but belongs to a distinct Eurasiatic genus, usually called *Chamaenerion*. The original spelling was *Chamerion*.

CIRCAEA L. 1753 [for Greek goddess Circe]. ENCHANTRESS' NIGHTSHADE

One species, **C. alpina** L. Cool ravines, spruce-fir forests. Delicate, with opposite, ovate, denticulate leaves; flowers tiny, in a raceme; fruit covered with tiny hooked bristles.

EPILOBIUM L. 1753 [Greek, *epi*, upon, + *lobon*, capsule, alluding to the hypanthium tube]. WILLOWHERB

1a. Annual; stems with peeling epidermis; leaves usually alternate. **E. brachycarpum** Presl. Common, weedy herb, disturbed roadsides in the mountains (*E. paniculatum*). Often mistaken for a crucifer or for a very large *Gayophytum*.

1b. Perennial; epidermis not peeling; leaves mostly opposite . . . . (2)

2a. Low and spreading, often in dense clumps, hardly over 20 cm tall, usually shorter; stems often S-shaped; leaves 8-20 mm long. (3)

2b. Erect, solitary or a few together, up to 4 dm or more tall, stems straight; leaves up to 5 cm long . . . . (4)

3a. Inflorescence nodding in bud; leaves oblong to narrowly ovate, thin, nearly entire; seeds smooth, 1 mm long. **E. anagallidifolium** Lamarck [with leaves like *Anagallis*, the pimpernel]. Snowmelt streamlets, subalpine and alpine. The threadlike rootlets, if carefully collected and washed, are seen to bear numbers of spherical, white winter buds or turions.

3b. Inflorescence erect in bud; leaves broadly ovate, thickish, ± serrulate; seeds papillose, 1.5-2 mm long. **E. clavatum** Trelease. Alpine boulderfields, Park and Saguache ranges.

4a. Leaves mostly not more than 3 mm broad, the lateral veins scarcely or not evident. **E. leptophyllum** Rafinesque. Infrequent, wet mountain meadows.

4b. Leaves broader, with distinct lateral veins . . . . (5)

5a. Seeds with parallel ridges; stems mostly 3-10 dm tall and freely branched especially above, if shorter the upper leaves alternate and more numerous; seeds with longitudinal ridges. **E. ciliatum** Rafinesque. Common, weedy species of roadside ditches (including *E. adenocaulon*, *E. brevistylum*, and *E. glandulosum*).

5b. Seeds smooth or papillose; stems mostly 1-3 dm tall, simple above, with few pairs of opposite leaves; nonweedy species . . . . (6)

6a. Turions (globose or ovoid fleshy winter buds) formed at the base of the stem or on the rhizomes and persisting as scales at the base of the stem of the year (the stem of the current year has at the base the remains of the withered scales of these turions) . . . . (7)

6b. Turions not present . . . . (8)

7a. Leaves lance-oblong, not crowded, margins often irregularly dentate; petals white. **E. halleanum** Haussknecht [for Elihu Hall, collector in South Park, 1861-2]. Openings in spruce-fir forests.

7b. Leaves ovate with rounded bases, usually longer than the internodes, margins usually entire. **E. saximontanum** Haussknecht. Moist mountain meadows and forest streamsides.

8a. Vegetative reproduction by filiform stolons with remote pairs of small hyaline scales; leaves narrow, linear, entire or merely undulate, the margins often revolute . . . . (9)
8b. Vegetative reproduction not by filiform stolons; leaves broader . . . . (10)

9a. Upper surface of leaves densely and evenly strigulose; tips of stems not strongly nodding. **E. leptophyllum** Rafinesque [narrow leaves]. In wet meadows in the piedmont valleys and plains, also in South Park.
9b. Upper surface of leaves practically glabrous; stem tips strongly nodding before anthesis. **E. palustre** L. var. **grammadophyllum** Haussknecht. Infrequent, montane meadows.

10a. Petals white or with pink tips, 3-4 mm long; seeds smooth; base of stem with several broad, withered leaves at flowering time. **E. lactiflorum** Haussknecht [milky-flowered]. Common along forest rills, subalpine.
10b. Petals pink-purple, 5-7 mm long; seeds ± papillose; base of stem with small and inconspicuous or no withered leaves. **E. hornemannii** Reichenbach [for Jens W. Hornemann, 1770-1841, Danish botanist]. Similar sites.

GAURA L. 1753 [Greek, *gauros*, superb, not very apt for our species]

1a. Tall plants well over 1 m tall, with spreading branches at the top; anthers oval, 0.5-1 mm long; sepals 1.5-3 mm long; petals 1.5-2 mm long. **G. parviflora** Douglas. Late summer, weedy, roadside plant, lower valleys.
1b. Plants under 1 m tall, the branches not noticeably spreading; anthers linear, 2-5 mm long; sepals 5-11 mm long; petals 3-10 mm long . . . . (2)

2a. Stem erect, 40-70 cm tall; stem leaves 5-10 cm long; hypanthium 7-12 mm, sepals 9-11 mm; petals 8-10 mm long. **G. neomexicana** Wooton subsp. **coloradensis** (Rydberg) Raven & Gregory, **Pl. 58**. Local and infrequent in scattered sites on the plains and piedmont valleys, BL, LR, and WL.
2b. Stem ascending, rarely erect, seldom over 30 cm tall; stem leaves up to 3.5 cm long; hypanthium 5-8 mm, sepals 5-8 mm, petals 3-6 mm long . . . (3)

3a. Fruit abruptly constricted to a thick, cylindric stipe. **G. coccinea** Nuttall [scarlet]. Dry grasslands, roadsides, sagebrush, lower altitudes. Very variable in pubescence.
3b. Fruit with a slender stipe 2-8 mm long; plants densely villous with hairs 2-3 mm long. **G. villosa** Torrey. Barely entering Colorado on sand dunes along the Cimarron River, BA.

GAYOPHYTUM Jussieu 1832 [for Claude Gay, 1800-1873, French botanist]

1a. Pedicels of mature capsules less than 3 mm long; petals less than 2 mm long . . . . (2)
1b. Pedicels 3 mm long or longer; petals 0.5-3 mm long . . . . (3)

2a. Branched only in the lower half; secondary branches few or none, the branching not dichotomous. **G. racemosum** Torrey & Gray. Gravelly soils and roadsides, mountains. *G. decipiens* Lewis & Szweykowski is related to this and reported from Colorado, but it seems to be very difficult to separate from this and the next, not having any distinctive characteristics of its own.
2b. Branched throughout or at least in the upper half; secondary branches evident. **G. diffusum** Torrey & Gray subsp. **parviflorum** Lewis & Szweykowski. Similar habitats.

3a. Seeds crowded, usually 2 rows in each locule; capsules terete . . . . . . (4)
3b. Seeds not crowded, in 1 row in each locule; capsules somewhat flattened or conspicuously constricted at intervals . . . . (return to 2)

4a. Petals less than 1.5 mm long; pedicels equalling or longer than the capsules. **G. ramosissimum** Torrey & Gray. Similar habitats.
4b. Petals 1.5-3 mm long; pedicels equalling or shorter than the capsules. **G. diffusum** Torrey & Gray subsp. **parviflorum** Lewis & Szweykowski. Similar habitats.

OENOTHERA L. 1753 [name used by Theophrastus for a species of *Epilobium*]. EVENING-PRIMROSE

1a. Plants stemless or stem very short, hidden among the basal leaves, or, if with a stem, the leaves very crowded along its length; flowers from amid a cluster of basal leaves or the top of the leaf mass . . . . (2)
1b. Plants with branched or tall, leafy stems . . . . (6)

2a. Flowers white, turning pink; capsule not strongly winged, but usually warty on the surface. **O. caespitosa** Nuttall. Abundant on clay hills and sandy roadcuts in the valleys and canyons . . . . (3)
2b. Flowers yellow, aging orange or brown; fruit sharply winged, not warty. (5)

3a. Annual, stout, erect, simple or few-branched; leaves many, crowded, entire or slightly dentate; petals 2-3 cm long. **O. harringtonii** Wagner et al. [for H. D. Harrington]. Endemic. Arkansas River drainage. Its relationship is with the perennial *O. caespitosa.*
3b. Perennial; essentially stemless; petals larger . . . . (4)

4a. Plants with short appressed to somewhat spreading hairs and no minute glandular hairs. **O. caespitosa** subsp. **caespitosa**. On the plains and intermountain parks north of the Arkansas Divide.
4b. Plants hirsute or villous or sometimes only glandular. **O. caespitosa** subsp. **macroglottis** (Rydberg) W. L. Wagner. Widespread from north to south on the plains and intermountain parks, but not extending far out eastward.

5a. Petals 4-6 cm long; leaves usually broad and very shallowly pinnatifid or almost entire. **O. howardii** (Nelson) W. L. Wagner [for A. M. Howard, its discoverer] (*O. brachycarpa* of Colorado literature). Common on outwash mesas of the Front Range from LR to JF.
5b. Petals 1.5-2.5 cm long; leaves oblanceolate to linear-oblong, irregularly pinnatifid, the lobes variable in shape, rarely the leaves almost entire. **O. flava** (Nelson) Garrett [yellow]. Moist mountain meadows with sagebrush.

6a. Flowers yellow, wilting orange . . . . (7)
6b. Flowers white, wilting pink . . . . (8)

7a. Petals and sepals 25-40 mm long. **O. elata** Humboldt, Bonpland & Kunth subsp. **hirsutissima** (Gray) Dietrich & Wagner [tall; very hirsute]. Common in wet meadows and roadside ditches, San Luis Valley and Arkansas River drainage (*O. hookeri*).
7b. Petals and sepals not over 20 mm long. **O. villosa** Thunberg. Very common on the plains (*O. strigosa*).

8a. Capsule as broad as long, sharply 4-angled, sessile; leaves about 1 cm long, narrowly oblong; low, bushy-branched plants. **O. canescens** Torrey & Frémont. Frequent on the eastern plains, especially on dried-up ponds.

8b. Capsule elongate; plants otherwise not as above . . . . (9)

9a. Capsule oblong-fusiform to somewhat clavate, thin-walled; seeds biseriate in each locule, subcylindric to narrowly obovoid . . . . (10)

9b. Capsule cylindric, gradually narrowed toward the apex; seeds uniseriate in each locule, obovoid . . . . (12)

10a. Perennial, rhizomatous, forming patches of short, erect stems connected underground; hypanthium with a conspicuous tuft of hairs in the throat; petals 7-15 mm long; capsule 8-20 mm long. **O. coronopifolia** Torrey & Gray [with leaves like the crucifer, *Coronopus*]. Gravelly, open, mountain meadows and roadsides.

10b. Annual or winter annual; plants not in patches; hypanthium not long-hairy in the throat; petals mostly 15-40 mm long; capsule 20-40 mm long . (11)

11a. Stem strigulose to sparsely villous; petals 1.5-4 cm long; seeds in 2 rows in each locule. **O. albicaulis** Pursh [white-stemmed]. Common in early spring on bare, sandy or clay flats. A field full of blooming plants looks, from a distance, as if a box of white Kleenex tissues had been blown there by the wind.

11b. Stem densely and uniformly villous with an understory of appressed hairs; petals 1-2.5 cm long; seeds in 1 row in each locule. **O. engelmannii** (Small) Munz. One record for Colorado, from sand dunes on the Cimarron River, BA.

12a. Essentially glabrous; leaves pinnatifid; capsules lacking tubercles; petals shorter. **O. pallida** Lindley subsp. **runcinata** (Engelmann) Munz & Klein. Abundant in sand dunes in the San Luis Valley. Forming hemispherical bushes.

12b. Hoary pubescent; leaves entire or shallowly dentate, ovate to oblong-lanceolate. **O. latifolia** (Rydberg) Munz. Common on sandhills on the plains (*O. pallida* subsp. *latifolia*).

ORCHIDACEAE ORCHID FAMILY (ORC)

(See also Cypripediaceae)

Paradoxically, the orchid family is the second largest family in numbers of species, and it probably contains more rare and endangered species than any other family. They often have exceedingly delicately tuned pollination mechanisms. The extinction of a unique insect pollinator means the extinction of the orchid species. Their germination depends on the presence of symbiotic fungus species. They have very narrow ecological amplitudes and extremely specialized floral structures. For example, the pollen, instead of being dustlike and easily spread, is aggregated into two sticky bags (pollinia) that must be transmitted whole by an insect from one flower to another, the process often involving elaborate tricks of luring the insect to the proper site, causing a trigger mechanism to force the pollinium onto the insect's head, and holding the insect in place until the pollinium's glue dries. Tropical orchids usually occur in very small numbers. In Colorado the species that grow in very wet places seem to be in little danger of extinction except through loss of the habitat, but those that grow on dry or only seasonally moist forest floors are often very rare and endangered. I am greatly indebted to Bill Jennings, engineer and premier Colorado orchidologist, for much help with this group.

1a. Plants without green leaves, saprophytic or parasitic. **Corallorhiza**, CORAL-ROOT
1b. Plants with green leaves . . . . (2)

2a. Lip of corolla a pointed, slipper-shaped, inflated sac. **Calypso**, FAIRY SLIPPER
2b. Lip of corolla not as above . . . . (3)

3a. Flowers with definite spurs (long and narrow or short and saclike) . . (4)
3b. Flowers without spurs . . . . (7)

4a. Corolla lip broad, 2-3-lobed at the apex; spur short, scrotiform; bracts usually longer than the flowers. **Coeloglossum**, GREEN BOG ORCHID
4b. Corolla lip entire; spur short or elongate; bracts usually not much longer than the flowers . . . . (5)

5a. Leaf solitary, basal. **Lysiella**
5b. Leaves several, usually cauline but sometimes most of them basal . . . (6)

6a. Leaves grouped near the base of the stem; inflorescence very slender, up to 30 cm long; floral bracts ovate, shorter than the ovary; flowers small. **Piperia**
6b. Leaves distributed the length of the stem; inflorescence usually stouter, shorter; floral bracts linear or lanceolate, equalling or exceeding the ovary. **Limnorchis**, BOG ORCHID

7a. Blade-bearing leaf solitary, near the base of the stem. **Malaxis**, WHITE ADDER'S-MOUTH
7b. Blade-bearing leaves more than 1 . . . . (8)

8a. Leaves two, opposite, near middle of the stem. **Listera**, TWAYBLADE
8b. Leaves not as above . . . . (9)

9a. Stem leaves absent, or the leaves at least appearing to be basal, usually white along midrib and veins. **Goodyera**, RATTLESNAKE-PLANTAIN
9b. Stem leaves present, green . . . . (10)

10a. Plants of marshes and wet meadows; flowers white, spirally arranged in a tight spike. **Spiranthes**, LADY'S TRESSES
10b. Plants of moist alcoves and ledges of sandstone cliffs; flowers few, greenish-brownish-purple, in a few-flowered raceme. **Epipactis**, HELLEBORINE

CALYPSO Salisbury 1807 [for the Greek sea nymph of Homer's *Odyssey*]. FAIRY SLIPPER

One species, **C. bulbosa** (L.) Oakes. Deep, moist forests; this should never be collected, since its survival is precarious.

COELOGLOSSUM Hartman 1820 [Greek, *koilos*, hollow, + *glossa*, tongue]. GREEN BOG ORCHID

One species, **C. viride** (L.) Hartman subsp. **bracteatum** (Mühlenberg) Hultén (*Habenaria*). Wet spruce-fir forests near streams.

CORALLORHIZA Gagnebin 1755 [Greek, *corallion*, coral, + *rhiza*, root]. CORAL-ROOT

1a. Lip striped with purple. **C. striata** Lindley. Dry pine forests.
1b. Lip plain or spotted with purple . . . . (2)

2a. Lip white, not spotted; sepals and petals 1-nerved; plants usually yellowish, but smaller and more slender than albinos of the next. **C. trifida** Chatelain. Subalpine forests.

2b. Lip spotted with purple, sometimes almost white; sepals and petals 3-nerved; stems purple-brown or bronze . . . . (3)

3a. Lip unequally 3-lobed, the 2 side lobes near the base of the lip; stem purplish or yellowish. **C. maculata** Rafinesque [spotted]. Dry pine forests throughout the area. The plants are usually reddish-brown, but occasional ones are albinos, totally yellow. Blossoming in late spring and summer.

3b. Lip narrowed at the base but not lobed; stem bronze. **C. wisteriana** Conrad (for C. J. Wister, 1782-1865, its discoverer). Smaller and more slender than the last, and with a more purple-brown stem; flowering earlier in the spring, foothills and montane.

EPIPACTIS Zinn 1757 [ancient Greek name for hellebore]. HELLEBORINE

One species, **E. gigantea** Douglas. Local, known on the Eastern Slope only from Poncha Hot Springs.

GOODYERA R. Brown 1813 [for John Goodyer, 1592-1664, British botanist]. RATTLESNAKE-PLANTAIN

1a. Leaves 1-3 cm long, not conspicuously white-veined; lip saccate, with a flaring or recurved margin. **G. repens** (L.) R. Brown subsp. **ophioides** (Fernald) Löve & Simon [creeping; snakelike]. Local, in moist montane forests.

1b. Leaves 5-10 cm long, conspicuously white along the midrib; lip scarcely saccate, the margin involute. **G. oblongifolia** Rafinesque. Infrequent, in duff on fairly dry forest floors.

LIMNORCHIS Rydberg 1900 [Greek, *limnaios*, of a bog] (formerly included in *Habenaria*). BOG ORCHID

1a. Flowers white; lip rhombic-lanceolate, dilated at the base. **L. dilatata** (Pursh) Rydberg subsp. **albiflora** (Chamisso) Löve & Simon. Wet meadows, shores of subalpine ponds.

1b. Flowers greenish; lip lanceolate to linear, not dilated at the base . . . (2)

2a. Inflorescence slender, the flowers remote from each other; lip linear-elliptic; spur always long and narrow; plants of relatively dry woods. **L. ensifolia** Rydberg. Known on the Eastern Slope from a single collection from near Minnehaha, EP. Very infrequent in relatively dry forests, never forming stands (*L. sparsifolia* of Colorado reports).

2b. Inflorescence dense, the flowers often overlapping; lip lanceolate . . . . (3)

3a. Spur saccate to clavate, about half as long as the lip. **L. saccata** (Greene) Löve & Simon. Swampy forests and meadows.

3b. Spur not saccate, subequal to the lip. **L. hyperborea** (L.) Rydberg. Similar habitats. There is disagreement as to whether both of these species occur in Colorado.

LISTERA R. Brown 1813 [for Dr. Martin Lister, 1638-1711, British naturalist]. TWAYBLADE

1a. Corolla lip oblong or linear, 2-cleft for half its length. **L. cordata** (L.) R. Brown subsp. **nephrophylla** (Rydberg) Löve & Löve. Cool, moist ravines and forests, our most common species. When ripe, the capsules split lengthwise, remaining attached top and bottom, to form a delicate cage.

1b. Corolla lip broader, not 2-cleft for half its length . . . . (2)

2a. Lip oblong, sagittate, and broadest at the base, without lateral teeth and with a fleshy ridge in the center near the base. **L. borealis** Morong. Very local, in deep spruce forests, CC, CF.

2b. Lip cuneate to obovate, not auriculate, broadest at the apex, with lateral teeth, without a fleshy ridge. **L. convallarioides** (Swartz) Nuttall [with leaves like *Convallaria*, lily-of-the-valley]. Cool ravines, subalpine forests.

LYSIELLA Rydberg 1900 [diminutive of *Lysias*, another genus]

One species, **L. obtusata** (Banks) Britton & Rydberg. Mossy streamsides in deep spruce forests (*Habenaria*).

MALAXIS Solander 1788 [Greek, *malacos*, delicate]. WHITE ADDER'S-MOUTH

One species, **M. monophyllos** (L.) Solander subsp. **brachypoda** (Gray) Löve & Löve. Extremely rare, foothills near Boulder. Even in the small site where it is locally abundant, it may not appear for several years on end, depending on the season.

PIPERIA Rydberg 1901 [for Charles V. Piper, 1867-1926, botanist of Washington state]

One species, **P. unalascensis** (Sprengel) Rydberg. Very local and infrequent, aspen stands, foothills of Front Range, and best represented on the east side of the Park Range. Inconspicuous and easily overlooked.

SPIRANTHES L. Richard 1817 [Greek, *speira*, coil, + *anthos*, flower]. LADY'S TRESSES

1a. Corolla lip distinctly constricted in the middle, the tip erose; plants usually less than 2 dm tall. **S. romanzoffiana** Chamisso [for Count Romanzoff]. Common in subalpine meadows and willow fens.

1b. Corolla lip not distinctly constricted in the middle, the margins undulate; plants usually more than 2 dm tall. **S. diluvialis** Sheviak [of floodplains]. Wet meadows and floodplains near the base of the Front Range in the Boulder-Denver area. Known also from Utah and Nevada. An amphidiploid species that evidently arose as a hybrid between *S. romanzoffiana* and *S. magnicamporum*, a midwestern species no longer present in the area.

OROBANCHACEAE BROOM-RAPE FAMILY (ORO)

By carefully digging around an *Orobanche*, the holdfast connecting this parasite to the host plant can usually be located. Our species of *Orobanche* are commonly parasitic on species of Asteraceae, including *Artemisia* and *Ambrosia*. The flowers remind one of Scrophulariaceae such as *Penstemon*. Orobanches and their relatives are found in the deserts of the temperate parts of all the continents. One species, *O. crenata*, is parasitic on cultivated legumes and is responsible for crop losses when infestations are high.

1a. Calyx very irregular, spathelike, deeply cleft on the lower side, several-toothed on the upper side; upper lip of the corolla deeply concave. **Conopholis**, SQUAWROOT

1b. Calyx nearly regular, the lobes or teeth nearly equal; upper corolla lip not deeply concave . . . . (2)

2a. Flowers on long pedicels 3-25 cm long, without additional bractlets between the flower and the subtending bract. **Aphyllon**, BROOMRAPE

2b. Flowers sessile or on short pedicels less than 3 cm long, with 1-2 narrow bractlets in addition to the broader, subtending bract. **Orobanche**, BROOM-RAPE

APHYLLON Mitchell 1769 [Greek, leafless]. BROOMRAPE

1a. Stem and axis of inflorescence 0.5-2 cm long; flowers 1-3; calyx lobes longer than the tube. **A. uniflorum** (L.) Torrey & Gray (*Orobanche*). Rare or very infrequent in montane and subalpine meadows.
1b. Stem and axis of inflorescence 5-17 cm long; flowers 4 or more; calyx lobes as long as or shorter than the tube. **A. fasciculatum** (Nutt.) Torrey & Gray (*Orobanche*). Common, parasitic on sagebrush, plains to montane.

CONOPHOLIS Wallroth 1825 [Greek, *conos*, cone, + *pholis*, scale]. SQUAWROOT
One species, **C. alpina** Liebmann var. **mexicana** (Gray) Haynes. Rare, known in Colorado from a single collection in the Raton Pass area. Parasitic on oaks.

OROBANCHE L. 1753 [Greek, *orobos*, vetch, + *anchein*, to strangle]. BROOMRAPE [from the leafless, strawlike stems + an allusion to *Brassica*, rape]
1a. Corolla lobes obtusely rounded, yellow to purple; style persistent in fruit; calyx 10-19 mm long, exceeding the fruit. **O. multiflora** Nuttall. Locally abundant in sand dune areas on the plains, parasitic on *Ambrosia* and *Oligosporus*.
1b. Corolla lobes triangularly acute, light to deep purple; style deciduous; calyx 8-12 mm long, shorter than or equalling the fruit. **O. ludoviciana** Nuttall. Dry grasslands on the plains, not characterictically in sand dune areas.

OXALIDACEAE WOODSORREL FAMILY (OXL)

Oxalis plants, with their 3-parted leaves with heart-shaped leaflets, are commonly sold as Irish shamrocks, but whether the original shamrock used by St. Patrick to symbolize the doctrine of the trinity was an *Oxalis* or a *Trifolium* is debatable. The leaves of *Oxalis* contain oxalic acid and are pleasantly tart when chewed. Tubers of *Oxalis crenata* (the "oca" of crossword puzzles) have been an important foodstuff in Peru since ancient Inca times. The capsules of *Oxalis* are elastically dehiscent; the valves split open explosively and describe arcs, shooting the seeds off some distance from the parent plant.

OXALIS L. 1753 [Greek, *oxys*, sour]. WOODSORREL

1a. Plants with basal leaves from a subterranean tuber; flowers purple. **O. violacea** L. Moist forests, foothills, Florissant and Cuchara Valley. Our plants typically have many small bulblets at the base of the main bulb, a feature that they do not seem to share with the species elsewhere.
1b. Plants with aerial stems; flowers yellow . . . . (2)

2a. Stems tall, usually unbranched, from an underground rhizome; stem and petioles with some septate, multicellular hairs that become crinkled and show prominent reddish cross-walls; leaves green or sometimes deep red. **O. stricta** L. Adventive. Garden weed.
2b. Stems low, branched from the base, without underground, horizontal rhizomes; stem and petioles with straight or curved, simple hairs only, usually appressed to the stem; leaves distinctly glaucous. **O. dillenii** Jacquin [for Jacob Dillenius, British botanist, 1684-1747]. The native species, frequent in rocky prairie at the base of the mountains.

PAPAVERACEAE POPPY FAMILY (PAP)

In poppy flowers the calyx is united from top to bottom. It does not open, but breaks away by a dehiscence line at its base when forced by the pressure of the expanding corolla, which is crumpled in the bud like a handkerchief. Open flowers, therefore, have no calyx. The unopened flower might be misinterpreted to be a fruit since the calyx may be crowned by stylelike horns.

1a. Petals white or scarlet, large (over 4 cm long) . . . . (2)
1b. Petals pale yellow or bright orange, smaller; leaves not spiny . . . . . . (3)

2a. Flowers white; leaves and stems with spines or prickles. **Argemone**, PRICKLY POPPY
2b. Flowers scarlet. **Papaver**, POPPY

3a. Pods short and broad, goblet-shaped; leaves with few, short, hirsute divisions; alpine tundra plants with pale yellow, often almost white flowers. **Papaver**, POPPY
3b. Pods elongate, linear, curved; introduced weeds along roadsides and in vacant lots . . . . (4)

4a. Plant low; leaves with many linear divisions; pod less than 10 cm long; petals orange. **Eschscholzia**, CALIFORNIA POPPY
4b. Plant tall, the leaves with broad, pinnate divisions; pod 15-20 cm long; petals yellow. **Glaucium**, HORNED POPPY

ARGEMONE L. 1753 [an herb mentioned by Pliny]. PRICKLY POPPY

1a. Leaf surfaces prickly only on the primary and secondary veins; stem with widely spaced prickles or almost smooth. **A. polyanthemos** (Fedde) G. B. Ownbey [many-flowered], **Pl. 31**. Common on the plains and outer foothills.
1b. Leaf surfaces prickly on the primary and secondary veins above and below and also minutely hispid or prickly between the veins; stems usually densely prickly . . . . (2)

2a. Largest capsular spines simple, usually 5-8 mm long. **A. hispida** Gray. Common on the plains but more infrequent than the next.
2b. Largest capsular spines compound, i.e., with few to many smaller prickles arising from their bases, usually over 8 mm long. **A. squarrosa** Greene. Southeasternmost counties.

ESCHSCHOLZIA Chamisso 1820 [for J. F. Eschscholz, 1793-1831, physician who accompanied Kotzebue's world voyage]. CALIFORNIA POPPY

One species, **E. californica** Chamisso. Adventive roadside weed probably sown in wildflower packets. Native in the Pacific Coast and southwestern states.

GLAUCIUM Miller 1754 [Greek, *glaucion*, from the glaucous foliage]. HORNED POPPY

One species, **G. flavum** Crantz. Adventive weed, once found in a vacant lot in Boulder.

PAPAVER L. 1753 [the ancient name]. POPPY

1a. Petals scarlet with a purplish-black basal spot; tall, bushy herb. **P. orientale** L., ORIENTAL POPPY. Adventive, a common cultivar escaping from gardens.
1b. Petals not scarlet . . . . (2)

2a. Petals bright orange. **P. croceum** Ledebour [orange], ICELAND POPPY. Adventive, an attractive cultivar persisting around old, alpine, mining townsites.
2b. Petals pale yellow or white. **P. kluanense** D. Löve, ALPINE POPPY. Infrequent, occurring in very small stands on the high peaks.

PARNASSIACEAE GRASS-OF-PARNASSUS FAMILY (PAR)

Usually included in the Saxifragaceae, *Parnassia* shows as little affinity with that family as do the Hydrangeaceae and Grossulariaceae. *Parnassia* is easily recognized. The leaves are basal except for one smaller leaf on the flowering stem (absent in one species). The flowers are white; the row of 5 normal stamens alternates with 5 peculiar staminodia which bear a fringe of shining yellow stalked glands. The ovary is quite superior and has 4 carpels.

PARNASSIA L. 1753 [for Mount Parnassus, Greece]. GRASS-OF-PARNASSUS

1a. Flowering stem with a bractlike leaf, usually above the level of the basal leaves; petals large, 5-13-veined . . . . (2)
1b. Flowering stem bractless; petals small (about equalling the sepals), 1-3-veined. **P. kotzebuei** Chamisso [for Otto von Kotzebue, 1787-1846, Russian navigator, commander of northern Pacific exploring expeditions]. Local, on rocky ledges and rills, subalpine, alpine.

2a. Leaves ovate, lanceolate, or elliptic; petals not marginally fimbriate. **P. parviflora** de Candolle [small-flowered]. Subalpine marshes.
2b. Leaves cordate or reniform; petals marginally fimbriate. **P. fimbriata** Banks [fringed]. Subalpine marshes and streamsides.

PLANTAGINACEAE PLANTAIN FAMILY (PTG)

The word plantain comes from Latin *planta*, the sole of the foot, and alludes to the usually broad, spreading leaf. "Plantar" warts come from the same stem and have nothing to do with gardening. The tropical plantains, related to the banana, bear no relation to our plantains but are monocots in the Musaceae. Some of our plantains are common dooryard weeds, and all are recognized by the cluster of basal leaves and spikes of flowers with papery corollas, and a peculiar ovary that dehisces by a horizontal rift (circumscissilely).

PLANTAGO L. 1753 [Latin, *planta*, sole of the foot]. PLANTAIN

1a. Leaves linear to filiform, rarely over 1 cm wide; annuals . . . . (2)
1b. Leaves lanceolate to ovate, over 1 cm wide; perennials . . . . (3)

2a. Densely woolly pubescent; lower floral bracts commonly exceeding the flowers. **P. patagonica** Jacquin [from Patagonia], WOOLLY PLANTAIN. Abundant on barren soils and overgrazed range at low altitudes.
2b. Almost glabrous, none of the bracts exceeding the flowers. **P. elongata** Pursh. Locally abundant, alkaline flats in the piedmont valleys near Boulder.

3a. Leaf blades broadly obovate, abruptly narrowed to the petiole; seeds 6-20 in each capsule. **P. major** L., COMMON PLANTAIN. Adventive, abundant weed in lawns and grazed meadows.

3b. Leaf-blades lanceolate, or if broader, then tapering to the petiole; seeds few (2-4) . . . . (4)

4a. Petals broad, 2 mm long, spreading and persistent, hiding the fruits; spikes short and broad at anthesis, the stamens with long filaments, forming a ring around the spike. **P. lanceolata** L., ENGLISH PLANTAIN. Adventive lawn weed. There are probably several races present, including one that is almost glabrous and another that is strongly pilose.

4b. Petals narrow, 1 mm long, never hiding the fruits; spikes usually elongate, at least in age, the stamens not as above . . . . (5)

5a. Leaf bases covered with reddish-brown wool; spikes over 5 cm long; leaves thick or succulent. **P. eriopoda** Torrey [woolly foot], REDWOOL PLANTAIN. Wet places and alkaline flats, mountain parks.

5b. Leaf bases not woolly or only slightly so; spikes usually shorter; leaves not thick nor succulent. **P. tweedyi** Gray [for the collector Frank Tweedy]. Mountain meadows, northern counties.

POACEAE/GRAMINEAE GRASS FAMILY (POA/GRM)

(Parts contributed by Janet L. Wingate)

The grass family is usually considered a difficult group, and the terminology used for its floral parts is unique. Once one understands the fundamental structure of the grass spikelet, which actually is very simple, the grasses become a fascinating and not-too-difficult subject. One must be ready to make measurements of very small things, such as anthers, glumes, and lemmas. Every citizen should know the dominant grasses, because these tell a great deal, by their presence, absence, or abundance, about the condition of the range. At the present time, because of new evidence from genetics, comparative anatomy, and scanning electron microscopy, great changes are occurring in the classification of the grasses, resulting in new tribal organization and in the delimitation of genera. The grasses being extremely streamlined plants, their small parts with relatively minute differences have to be more carefully analyzed than those of most other plant families.

1a. Plants dioecious (spikelets entirely staminate or carpellate, on different plants and usually conspicuously different in appearance) . . . . **Key A**

1b. Plants not dioecious (most grasses belong in this category) . . . . (2)

2a. Plants prostrate on the ground and radially spreading, with long, naked internodes and dense fascicles of short, stiff leaves with pale, thickened margins; spikelets hidden in the leaf clusters. **Monroa**, FALSE BUFFALOGRASS

2b. Plants not as above . . . . (3)

3a. Spikelets consisting of hard burs with sharp, hooked spines. **Cenchrus**, SANDBUR

3b. Spikelets not burlike . . . . (4)

4a. Florets converted to bulblets with shiny purple bases and long green tips. **Poa bulbosa**

4b. Florets not as above . . . . (5)

5a. Spikelets sessile, alternating on either side of a flattened rachis . . . . . (6)

5b. Spikelets not alternating on either side of a flattened rachis . . . . (7)

6a. Each spikelet cluster nested in a group of long white hairs. **Hilaria**, GALLETA GRASS
6b. Spikelet clusters not subtended by hairs . . . . **Key B**

7a. Foliage and stem harshly retrorse-scabrous (saw-grass); glumes lacking, the spikelet with a single lemma and palea. **Leersia**, RICE CUTGRASS
7b. Foliage not as above; spikelets with glumes . . . . (8)

8a. Spikelets sessile, subsessile, or very short-pedicelled on 1 side of the rachis, forming 1-sided spikes or spikelike racemes; spikes often resembling little flags . . . . **Key C**
8b. Spikelets not as above . . . . (9)

9a. Spikelets disarticulating below the glumes (falling in 1 piece); glumes and lemmas flat or curved, never folded (the spikelet tends to be terete, without a right and left side) . . . . (10)
9b. Spikelets usually disarticulating above the glumes and between the florets (shattering at maturity and leaving the glumes attached to the rachis); glumes and lemmas strongly rounded or folded (spikelet tends to lie flat, with a right and left side) . . . . (11)

10a. Spikelets in pairs, one sessile and bisexual, the other pediceled and staminate, rudimentary or reduced to a mere pedicel . . . . **Key D**
10b. Spikelets not in pairs . . . . **Key E**

11a. Spikelets with a single floret . . . . **Key F**
11b. Spikelets with at least 2 florets . . . . (12)

12a. Glumes (at least 1) as long as or longer than the lowest floret, usually as long as the whole spikelet, the awn, if present, attached on the back of the lemma or appearing so . . . . **Key G**
12b. Both glumes shorter than the lowermost floret; awn, if present, attached to the tip of the lemma or arising from between the teeth of a bifid lemma apex . . . . **Key H**

KEY A. (Dioecious grasses)

1a. Staminate and carpellate spikelets fundamentally different in structure; plants over 15 cm tall . . . . (2)
1b. Staminate and carpellate spikelets essentially alike; plants very dwarf . (3)

2a. Carpellate spikelets with extremely long-awned lemmas; staminate spikelets with numerous awnless lemmas. **Scleropogon**, BURROGRASS
2b. Carpellate spikelets awnless, the glumes indurate, forming a nutlike structure. **Buchloë**, BUFFALOGRASS

3a. Florets numerous in the spikelet (8-15); lemma 5-11-nerved; plants of low alkaline areas in the valleys. **Distichlis**, SALTGRASS
3b. Florets relatively few in the spikelet (3-7); lemma 3-5-nerved; plants of well-drained mountain soils . . . . (4)

4a. Leaf tip boat-shaped; plants forming dense clumps, not over 5 dm tall. **Poa fendleriana**
4b. Leaf tip not boat-shaped; tall, rhizomatous plants not forming dense clumps, often 1 m tall. **Leucopoa**, SPIKE FESCUE

KEY B. (Alternating spikelets)

1a. Spikelets arranged so as to form a solid cylinder, the rachis bent to accommodate them; spikelets rough and long-awned, the rachis shattering at maturity. **Cylindropyrum**, GOATGRASS
1b. Spikelets loose, not forming a solid cylinder . . . . (2)

2a. Annuals . . . . (3)
2b. Perennials, either rhizomatous or bunch-formers . . . . (6)

3a. Tall, cultivated for grain and escaping to roadsides or volunteering in fallow fields; stems with large diameter straw . . . . (4)
3b. Low annual weeds; stems with slender straw. **Critesion**, FOXTAIL BARLEY

4a. Glumes subulate, 1-nerved . . . . (5)
4b. Glumes broad, 3-nerved. **Triticum**, WHEAT

5a. Spikelets usually 3 at a node (one rare exception). **Hordeum**, BARLEY
5b. Spikelets single at each node. **Secale**, RYE

6a. Spikelets placed edgewise to the rachis; first glume lacking, its function taken over by the rachis. **Lolium**, DARNEL
6b. Spikelets with the flat side next to the rachis; both glumes present . . (7)

7a. Glumes and lemmas truncate at the apex, never awned . . . . (8)
7b. Glumes and lemmas acute at the apex or awned . . . . (9)

8a. Glumes squarely truncate, lacking a mucro; bunch grass. **Lophopyrum**, TALL WHEATGRASS
8b. Glumes blunt but with a small slightly off-center mucro; rhizomatous. **Elytrigia intermedia**, INTERMEDIATE WHEATGRASS

9a. Spikelets with stiffly and widely spreading florets. **Agropyron**, CRESTED WHEATGRASS
9b. Spikelets with erect or strongly ascending florets . . . . (10)

10a. Spikelets 3 or more at a node . . . . (11)
10b. Spikelets 1 or 2 at a node . . . . (14)

11a. Three spikelets per node, 1 central and fertile, 2 lateral, reduced, sterile, and pedicelled. **Critesion**, FOXTAIL BARLEY
11b. Spikelets not as above . . . . (12)

12a. Lemma with awns 10-30 mm long, divergent at maturity. **Elymus canadensis**
12b. Lemma awnless or short-awned . . . . (13)

13a. Lemmas soft-pubescent; spikelets less than 1 cm long; plants robust but not forming bunches over 1 m tall. **Psathyrostachys**, RUSSIAN WILD RYE
13b. Lemmas glabrous; spikelets over 1 cm long; plants forming enormous bunches over 1 m tall. **Leymus**, WILD RYE

14a. Rhizomatous . . . . (15)
14b. Not rhizomatous, forming dense bunches (make careful field observations!). **Elymus**, WHEATGRASS

15a. Glumes tapering from near the base, not widest at the middle. **Pascopyrum**, WESTERN WHEATGRASS
15b. Glumes widest at the middle. **Elytrigia**

KEY C. (Flagged grasses)

1a. Inflorescence forming a digitate cluster of spikes or spikelike racemes, like spokes of an umbrella, sometimes with isolated branches below . . . . . (2)
1b. Inflorescence not digitate . . . . (5)

2a. Plants creeping, with above-ground, scaly stolons. **Cynodon**, BERMUDA GRASS
2b. Plants lacking stolons, although sometimes tending to root at the decumbent lower nodes . . . . (3)

3a. Lemmas distinctly awned. **Chloris**, WINDMILL GRASS
3b. Lemmas not awned . . . . (4)

4a. Spikelets less than 4 mm long with 1 well-developed floret. **Digitaria**, CRABGRASS
4b. Spikelets usually over 4 mm long with 3-8 well-developed florets. **Eleusine**, GOOSEGRASS

5a. Spikelets or groups of them pendent. **Bouteloua**, SIDEOATS GRAMA
5b. Spikelets or groups of them erect or spreading but not pendent . . . . (6)

6a. Inflorescence distinctly brushlike, with the spikelets standing out at a wide angle from the rachis . . . . (7)
6b. Inflorescence not brushlike . . . . (8)

7a. Spikes standing out from the culm at nearly right angles; low plants of dry grassland. **Chondrosum**, GRAMA
7b. Spikes ± appressed to somewhat spreading; coarse tall grasses of wet ditches or seasonally wet alkaline flats. **Spartina**, CORDGRASS

8a. Inflorescence very long and slender, forming recurved arcs, the spikelets minute. **Scheddonardus**, TUMBLEGRASS
8b. Inflorescence not as above, the spikelets fairly large . . . . (9)

9a. Spikelets very broad, almost circular . . . . (10)
9b. Spikelets narrow, pointed . . . . (11)

10a. Spikelets with the glumes folded, the spikelet lying flat, with an open slit where the glumes meet. **Beckmannia**, SLOUGHGRASS
10b. Spikelets with the glumes flat, the spikelet in face view not bisected. **Paspalum**

11a. Spikelets in 2 or 3 very dense clusters at the ends of a few main panicle branches; pastures and lawns. **Dactylis**, ORCHARDGRASS
11b. Spikelets in slender, straight, erect racemes or the inflorescence so condensed as to appear so. **Leptochloa**, SPRANGLETOP

KEY D. (Sorghum group)

1a. Racemes of several to many joints (pairs of spikelets), solitary, digitate, or aggregated in panicles . . . . (2)
1b. Racemes reduced to one or a few joints, these mostly peduncled in a branching panicle . . . . (4)

2a. Inflorescence branches stout, in digitate or densely clustered terminal groups . . . . (3)
2b. Inflorescence branches slender, delicate, not in close groups but spaced along the slender culm. **Schizachyrium**, LITTLE BLUESTEM

3a. Pedicels of sterile spikelets not strongly flattened and grooved on both sides, the central portion not thin and membranous. **Andropogon**, BIG BLUESTEM, TURKEYFOOT
3b. Pedicels of sterile spikelets strongly flattened and grooved on both sides, the central portion thin and membranous. **Bothriochloa.**

4a. Spikelets plump, almost glabrous, lacking awns; pedicellate spikes staminate. **Sorghum**
4b. Spikelets narrow, long-silky-hairy, awned but the awn early deciduous; pedicellate spikelet reduced to a pilose pedicel (no floret present). **Sorghastrum**, INDIANGRASS

KEY E. (Panicum group)

1a. Spikelets subtended by slender bristles that represent the pedicels of suppressed spikelets, the entire spike resembling a bottlebrush. **Setaria**, FOXTAIL, BRISTLEGRASS
1b. Spikelets not subtended by bristles although the lemmas may be slender-tipped . . . . (2)

2a. Spikelets long-pedicelled, in open panicles, the glumes and lemmas never awned . . . . (3)
2b. Spikelets short-pedicelled or sessile on the panicle branches, the glumes or lemmas usually awned; coarse, weedy grasses with broad leaves and narrowly pyramidal inflorescence. **Echinochloa**, BARNYARDGRASS

3a. Basal leaves on short shoots, often distinctly different from those of the flowering culm, forming overwintering rosettes. **Dichanthelium**
3b. Basal leaves similar to the culm leaves, not overwintering as rosettes. **Panicum**, PANICGRASS

KEY F. (One-flowered spikelets)

1a. Panicle very dense and spikelike, forming a cylindric head, the panicle branches suppressed or absent . . . . (2)
1b. Panicle loose or dense, occasionally spikelike but the branches always well developed although sometimes appressed to the rachis . . . . (6)

2a. [1] Annual . . . . (3)
2b. Tall, erect perennial . . . . (4)

3a. [2] Small prostrate-spreading annual. **Crypsis**
3b. Erect plant (close inspection of the floret will show a very inconspicuous sterile lemma on each side of the fertile one). **Phalaris**, CANARYGRASS

4a. [2] Glumes awnless, the keels densely hairy; lemma with a dorsal awn. **Alopecurus**, FOXTAIL
4b. Glumes awned . . . . (5)

5a. [4] Both glumes with a single awn, the keels ciliate; lemma awnless or only mucronate. **Phleum**, TIMOTHY
5b. First glume with 2 awns, the second with 1; lemma awned. **Lycurus**, WOLFTAIL

6a. [1] Lemma with 3 awns. **Aristida**, THREE-AWN
6b. Lemma with a single awn or none . . . . (7)

7a. [6] Lemma with an awn from the back . . . . (8)
7b. Lemma with a terminal awn or none . . . . (10)

8a. [7] Lemma with the awn subterminal; weedy annual with a very narrow panicle; awn several times as long as the lemma; lemma firm. **Apera**
8b. Lemma awned farther down the back; mostly native perennials; awns, if longer than the lemma, bent . . . . (9)

9a. [8] Lemma with a tuft of hairs at the base; palea about as long as the lemma. **Calamagrostis**, REEDGRASS
9b. Lemma naked at the base; palea up to 2/3 as long as the lemma, or entirely lacking. **Agrostis**, BENTGRASS

10a. [7] Lemma indurate, terete; callus well developed, often sharp-pointed. (11)
10b. Lemma membranous or firm, not terete; callus not differentiated . . (13)

11a. [10] Awn plumose, less than 2 cm long; lemma prolonged beyond the base of the awn into a rounded, bifid tip; glumes rounded at apex, often purplish; plants of peat hummocks in subalpine willow carrs. **Ptilagrostis**, FEATHER-GRASS
11b. Awn usually naked, but if plumose, then more than 4 cm long; lemma not prolonged beyond the base of the awn; glumes pointed, straw-colored; plants of dry sites and forest floors . . . . (12)

12a. [11] Awn persistent, bent and twisted; callus sharp-pointed. **Stipa**, NEEDLE-GRASS
12b. Awn deciduous, only slightly twisted and bent; callus blunt. **Oryzopsis**, RICEGRASS

13a. [10] Floret with a tuft of hairs at the base at least 1 mm long . . . . (14)
13b. Floret without a tuft of hairs at the base, or the hairs very short . . (15)

14a. [13] Tall, robust, reedlike grasses often over 1 m tall, of sand dunes and wet ditches on the plains. **Calamovilfa**, SANDREED
14b. Low, delicate mountain grasses. **Muhlenbergia andina**

15a. [13] Articulation below the glumes, the spikelets falling as units . . . (16)
15b. Articulation above the glumes, the florets falling out of the spikelets, leaving the glumes attached to the rachis . . . . (17)

16a. [15] Glumes with awns 4 mm long or more, rarely awnless in one rare species; panicle very dense and compact. **Polypogon**, RABBITFOOTGRASS
16b. Glumes awnless; panicle loose and open. **Cinna**, WOODREED

17a. [15] Lemma awned from the apex, the awn over 1 mm long . . . . . . (18)
17b. Lemma awned from the back or awnless, or with an awn tip less than 1 mm long . . . . (19)

18a. [17] Awn bent and twisted, plumose. **Ptilagrostis**, FEATHERGRASS
18b. Awn straight, never plumose. **Muhlenbergia**, MUHLY

19a. [17] Nerves of the lemma densely silky-hairy. **Blepharoneuron**, PINE DROPSEED
19b. Nerves of the lemma not silky-hairy and, if pubescent, not especially so on the nerves . . . . (20)

20a. [19] Tall reed-grass over 1 m high, in wet ditches in the valleys, with dense, spikelike, pale inflorescence; lemma smooth and shining, hard, with a minute, hairy scale on each side of the lemma base. **Phalaroides**, REED CANARY-GRASS

20b. Not as above . . . . (21)

21a. [20] Glumes as long as the lemma. **Agrostis,** BENTGRASS

21b. Glumes one or both shorter than the lemma . . . . (22)

22a. [21] Grain falling free from the lemma and palea at maturity (Sorry, this is a hard one!); seed loose in the seed coat when wetted; ligule mostly of hairs. **Sporobolus**, DROPSEED [see also *Muhlenbergia asperifolia*]

22b. Grain remaining enclosed within the lemma and palea at maturity; seed fused to the seed coat; ligule membranous . . . . (23)

23a. [22] Panicle small and inconspicuous, hardly exceeding the enclosing culm leaves; leaves with a boat-shaped tip as in *Poa*; very rare alpine grass of permanently saturated gravels. **Phippsia**

23b. Panicle conspicuous, spikelike or open, exserted; leaves not boat-tipped. **Muhlenbergia**, MUHLY

KEY G. (Oats group)

1a. Foliage soft velvety-pilose; spikelets papery-white. **Holcus**, VELVETGRASS

1b. Foliage not velvety-pilose; spikelets not white . . . . (2)

2a. Florets of the spikelet unlike, one bisexual and the other(s) staminate (3)

2b. Florets all essentially alike (the uppermost may be progressively smaller and less developed) . . . . (4)

3a. Spikelets with 2 staminate florets alongside the single bisexual one, all 3 falling attached to each other; foliage fragrant especially when dry. **Hierochloë**, SWEETGRASS

3b. Spikelets with 2 florets, the upper bisexual, the lower staminate, with a bent and twisted awn; tall, oatlike grass. **Arrhenatherum**, TALL OATGRASS

4a. Annual; spikelets very large, the glumes over 2 cm long; awns large and conspicuous except in some cultivated varieties. **Avena**, OATS

4b. Perennial; spikelets smaller, the glumes usually less than 2 cm long; awn, when present, less than 1.5 cm long . . . . (5)

5a. Lemma awnless; plant less than 1 m tall . . . . (6)

5b. Lemma awned (minute or rarely absent in *Trisetum wolfii*, a tall wet meadow plant usually over 1 m tall) . . . . (7)

6a. Articulation above the glumes; glumes unlike, the first narrow, the second wider, broadest above the middle. **Sphenopholis**, WEDGEGRASS

6b. Articulation above the glumes, the glumes essentially similar. **Koeleria**, JUNEGRASS

7a. Lemma with a flattened, twisted awn arising from between the split apex. **Danthonia**, OATGRASS

7b. Lemma with the awn arising from the back, the apex not split . . . . . (8)

8a. Spikelets with glumes over 8 mm long; awns large and conspicuous . . (9)

8b. Spikelets smaller, the glumes less than 8 mm long; awn, if present, less than 10 mm long . . . . (10)

9a. Leaf blades flat or folded; spikelets with 3-6 florets; terminal florets exserted slightly beyond the glumes; culms usually well over 20 cm tall; inflorescence well exserted, golden-brown. **Avenula**, MOUNTAIN OATS

9b. Leaf blades involute; spikelets usually with 2 florets, these included between the glumes; culm less than 20 cm tall; inflorescence not much overtopping the leaves, pale straw-colored. **Helictotrichon**, ALPINE OATS

10a. Lemma folded, awned from well above the middle. **Trisetum**

10b. Lemma rounded on the back, awned from the middle or below . . . . (11)

11a. Glumes longer than the florets; leaf blades flat; callus hairs over 1 mm long; lemmas awned from near the middle. **Vahlodea**

11b. Glumes not exceeding the upper floret; leaf blades usually folded; callus hairs less than 1 mm long; lemma awned from near the base. **Deschampsia**, TUFTED HAIRGRASS

KEY H. (Poa group)

1a. Rachilla with long silky hairs as long as the lemmas; tall reed-grasses with large, tassellike panicles; plants of wetlands. **Phragmites**, GIANT REED

1b. Not as above . . . . (2)

2a. [1] Spikelets minute (less than 2 mm long); inflorescence of very fine capillary branches. **Muhlenbergia asperifolia**

2b. Spikelets more than 2 mm long; inflorescence not as above . . . . (3)

3a. [2] Spikelets of cleistogamous flowers enclosed within the leaf sheaths; annuals of sand dunes and blowouts on the eastern plains. **Triplasis**, SANDGRASS

3a. Leaf sheaths not enclosing cleistogamous spikelets . . . . (4)

4a. [3] Lemma 3-nerved; ligule composed of hairs (except in *Catabrosa*) . (5)

4b. Lemma 5-many-nerved, the nerves usually not conspicuous; ligule membranous (except in **Distichlis**) . . . . (9)

5a. [4] Spikelets 2-flowered; sheath closed at least half its length; ligule membranous; semiaquatic, usually with lower part of stem in water. **Catabrosa**, BROOKGRASS

5b. Spikelets 3-many-flowered; sheath open; ligule composed of hairs; plants of drier sites . . . . (6)

6a. [5] Lemma glabrous to scaberulous along nerves, awnless; annual or perennial (when overmature, the lemmas fall away, leaving the paleae attached, a unique character). **Eragrostis**, LOVEGRASS

6b. Lemma long-hairy along or at the base of the nerves . . . . (7)

7a. [6] Lemma with a tuft of hairs at the base of each nerve; tall plants of sand dunes and blowouts on the plains. **Redfieldia**, BLOWOUTGRASS

7b. Lemma with the entire nerve long-hairy . . . . (8)

8a. [7] Inflorescence short, less than 5 cm long; lemma margins densely long-ciliate. **Erioneuron**, HAIRY TRIDENS

8b. Inflorescence elongate; lemma margins not long-ciliate. **Tridens**

9a. [4] Sheath completely closed or closed at least half its length . . . . . (10)

9b. Sheath entirely open or open more than half its length . . . . (20)

10a. [9] Spikelets in dense, rather 1-sided clusters on a few main branches. **Dactylis**, ORCHARDGRASS
10b. Not as above . . . . (11)

11a. [10] Lemmas of uppermost florets rolled together to form a club-shaped rudiment; spikelets 7-15 mm long, awnless . . . . (12)
11b. Lemma of uppermost florets not rolled together . . . . (13)

12a. [11] Culms bulbous at base; articulation above the glumes and between the florets; panicle not particularly 1-sided. **Bromelica**, ONIONGRASS
12b. Culms not bulbous-based; articulation below the glumes; panicle 1-sided. **Melica**, ONIONGRASS

13a. [11] Lemma with parallel nerves not converging toward the tip (if projected forward). **Glyceria**, MANNAGRASS
13b. Lemma with nerves converging toward the tip (if projected) . . . . . . (14)

14a. [13] Spikelets less than 10 mm long, awnless . . . . (15)
14b. Spikelets over 10 mm long . . . . (16)

15a. [14] Lemmas very deeply spoon-shaped, overlapping, and resembling a very short snake's rattle. **Briza**, QUAKINGGRASS
15b. Lemmas not as above (a good mark is the boat-tipped leaf blade). **Poa**, BLUEGRASS

16a. [14] Callus with a prominent tuft of straight hairs 1-2 mm long; rare or infrequent forest grass. **Schizachne**, FALSE MELIC
16b. Callus not as above . . . . (17)

17a. [16] Annual . . . . (18)
17b. Perennial . . . . (19)

18a. [17] Lemma long and narrow, tapering to the long awn. **Anisantha**, CHEATGRASS
18b. Lemma broad and rounded at apex, abruptly awned. **Bromus**, BROME

19a. [17] Spikelets flattened, the glumes and lemmas sharply folded. **Ceratochloa**, RESCUEGRASS
19b. Spikelets more ± terete, the lemmas rounded on the back. **Bromopsis**, PERENNIAL BROME

20a. [9] Spikelet with 2 unlike florets, the upper one bisexual with a short, straight awn, the lower staminate with a long, bent awn. **Arrhenatherum**, TALL OATGRASS
20b. Florets all alike . . . . (21)

21a. [20] Lemma with an awn 1 mm or more long . . . . (22)
21b. Lemma awnless or merely awn-pointed, with the point less than 1 mm long . . . . (24)

22a. [21] Lemma awned from the back. **Trisetum**
22b. Lemma terminally awned or rarely awned from a minutely bifid apex (23)

23a. [22] Annual of very short duration; plants yellow-green, in age reddish-brown, flowering in early spring. **Vulpia**, SIX-WEEKS FESCUE
23b. Perennial; plant green, not turning brown nor flowering early. **Festuca**, FESCUE

24a. [21] Lemma tough and leathery; palea serrate; ligule mostly of hairs; dioecious; on alkaline flats. **Distichlis**, SALTGRASS
24b. Lemma membranous; palea not serrate; ligules membranous; bisexual, rarely dioecious . . . . (25)

25a. [24] Articulation below glumes; glumes very unlike, first short and narrow, second longer and broad above middle; spikelets usually 2-flowered. **Sphenopholis**, WEDGEGRASS
25b. Articulation above glumes; glumes not as above . . . . (26)

26a. [25] Lemma with parallel nerves not converging at the tip (if projected forward); lemma apex broadly obtuse or truncate . . . . (27)
26b. Lemma with nerves converging toward the tip (if projected); lemma apex usually acute . . . . (28)

27a. [26] Nerves faint; plants of alkaline flats. **Puccinellia**, ALKALIGRASS
27b. Nerves prominent, raised; plants of freshwater marshes and wet places, generally avoiding alkaline soils. **Torreyochloa**, WEAK MANNAGRASS

28a. [26] Lemmas and glumes folded (keeled) . . . . (29)
28b. Lemmas rounded on the back (glumes may be keeled and lemmas may be slightly keeled at the apex) . . . . (30)

29a. [28] Rachis and panicle branches minutely pubescent; panicle dense and spikelike (spreading during anthesis); spikelets usually 2-flowered; lemmas slightly scabrous. **Koeleria**, JUNEGRASS
29b. Rachis and panicle branches glabrous to scabrous; panicle contracted to open; spikelets 2-several-flowered; lemmas often with a tuft of cobwebby hairs at base and/or pubescent nerves. **Poa**, BLUEGRASS

30a. [28] Dioecious; stigmas hispidulous all around; tall, broad-leaved, glaucous plants of dry pine forests. **Leucopoa**, SPIKE FESCUE
30b. Bisexual; stigmas softly plumose; otherwise not as above . . . . (31)

31a. [30] Leaf tip boat-shaped, splitting apart when opened out; lemmas never awned. **Poa**, BLUEGRASS
31b. Leaf tip not boat-shaped; lemmas awnless or awn-pointed. **Festuca**, FESCUE

AGROPYRON Gaertner 1770 [Greek, *agros*, field, + *pyros*, wheat]. CRESTED WHEATGRASS

Note: Realignments in the wheatgrasses, based on genome analysis, have moved our species into several genera, namely *Elymus*, *Elytrigia*, *Eremopyrum*, *Leymus*, *Lophopyrum*, *Pascopyrum*, *Psathyrostachys*, and *Trichopyrum*.

1a. Glumes straight, the hyaline margin broad and conspicuous; spikelets spreading at a narrow angle. **A. cristatum** (L.) Gaertner subsp. **desertorum** (Fischer) Löve. Adventive. These are all Asiatic introductions, planted extensively for soil stabilization.
1b. Glumes twisted, margins very narrow; spikelets spreading at almost right angles to the rachis . . . . (2)

2a. Spikes broad, the lemmas prominently awned. **A. cristatum** (L.) Gaertner subsp. **cristatum**.
2b. Spikes narrow, the spikelets hardly spreading at all, very short-awned. **A. cristatum** subsp. **fragile** (Roth) Löve. Because of extensive breeding and selection, these two, being somewhat compatible, are not always clear-cut.

AGROSTIS L. 1753 [Greek, *agros*, field]. BENTGRASS

1a. Anthers 1-1.6 mm long; palea at least half as long as lemma; rhizomatous and often stoloniferous; ligules of upper stem leaves 3-6 mm long; introduced species . . . . (2)

1b. Anthers not more than 0.7 mm long; plants otherwise not as above; mostly native species . . . . (3)

2a. Rhizomatous; stems erect from the base; panicle narrow before but open after flowering. **A. gigantea** Roth, REDTOP. Adventive. Cultivated in pastures and established in hay meadows and ditches (*A. alba*).

2b. Without rhizomes but sometimes stoloniferous; stems decumbent at the base; panicle narrow at maturity. **A. stolonifera** L., REDTOP. Adventive. Less common, usually along streams (*A. palustris*).

3a. Palea at least half as long as lemma; glumes mostly 1.3-2.3 mm long, blunt to acute at apex . . . . (4)

3b. Palea absent or less than half as long as lemma; glumes 1.5-3 mm long, acute or tapered to a fine tip . . . . (5)

4a. Panicle narrow or open, 3-7 cm long; leaf blades ca. 2 mm wide; rachilla prolonged beyond the palea as a minute prong. **A. thurberiana** Hitchcock. Subalpine carrs and meadows (*Podagrostis*).

4b. Panicle very narrow, spikelike, 1-4 cm long; leaf blades 1 mm wide or less; rachilla not prolonged. **A. humilis** Vasey. Alpine meadows and tundra (*Podagrostis*).

5a. Leaves 2-10 mm wide; ligule 2-6 mm long; panicle narrow, some branches bearing spikelets to the base. **A. exarata** Trinius [plowed out, alluding to the weedy character]. Moist mountain meadows and roadsides, apparently introduced.

5b. Leaves 1-3 mm wide and ligule shorter; panicle open or narrow . . . . (6)

6a. Lemma with a prominent, bent awn exceeding the lemma tip; panicle narrow; dwarf alpine plant. **A. mertensii** Trinius. Common on tundra (*A. borealis* of Colorado literature). Eurasian plants have distinctly open panicles. Possibly the Colorado ones constitute a well-marked subspecies.

6b. Lemma awnless or with a short, very inconspicuous, straight awn no longer than the lemma . . . . (7)

7a. Panicle narrow, at least some of the lower branches spikelet-bearing near the base; leaves short, involute; lemma rarely awned. **A. variabilis** Rydberg. Subalpine and alpine.

7b. Panicle open or or at least with loosely ascending branches, when narrow the lemmas sometimes awned; leaves flat . . . . (8)

8a. Panicle very delicate, with very slender branches forking beyond the middle; relatively tall and slender. **A. scabra** Willdenow. Roadsides and mountain trails; panicles up to 30 cm long.

8b. Panicle with relatively stouter, not capillary branches; usually awnless, but occasionally with a very inconspicuous, straight awn no longer than the lemma; subalpine and low alpine. **A. idahoensis** Nash. The awned form has been called *A. bakeri* Rydberg.

ALOPECURUS L. 1753 [Greek, *alopex*, fox, + *oura*, tail]. FOXTAIL

1a. Spikelets 5-6 mm long; basal leaves curled; introduced species of dry sites. **A. pratensis** L., MEADOW FOXTAIL. Adventive. Used for erosion control and reseeding along highways.
1b. Spikelets 2-4 mm long; native or adventive species of wet places . . . . (2)

2a. Panicle 1-4 cm long, about 1 cm broad; glumes densely covered with long hairs. **A. alpinus** Smith. Subalpine meadows and gravelly stream courses.
2b. Panicle 3-7 cm long, 3-5 mm broad; glumes hairy on keel and nerves only. . . . . (3)

3a. Awn included or exserted less than 1.5 mm beyond the glumes. **A. aequalis** Sobol. Widespread native perennial in muddy places, ditches and ponds.
3b. Awn exserted 2 mm or more beyond the glumes; introduced . . . . (4)

4a. Perennial; anthers usually over 0.75 mm long; often growing in water. **A. geniculatus** L. Two doubtful reports from BL and JA need to be verified.
4b. Annual; anthers shorter; in moist ground, usually not in water. **A. carolinianus** Walter. One old record exists, from WN, in 1909.

ANDROPOGON L. 1753 [Greek, *andros*, man, + *pogon*, beard]. BIG BLUESTEM, TURKEYFOOT

1a. Awns 5 mm long or less; plants with elongate rhizomes; foliage glaucous. **A. hallii** Hackel [for Elihu Hall], SAND BLUESTEM. Sand dunes on the plains.
1b. Awns 1-2 cm long; rhizomes short or lacking; foliage not strongly glaucous. **A. gerardii** Vitman. Common in the piedmont valleys as one of the dominant tall-grass prairie plants.

ANISANTHA K. Koch [Greek, *anisos*, unequal, + *anthos*, flower, alluding to differential sexuality among the florets] (formerly included in *Bromus*). CHEATGRASS

1a. Awns less than 2 cm long; second glume less than 1 cm long. **A. tectorum** (L.) Nevski [of roofs], **86C**. Adventive. Abundant in disturbed ground everywhere. The dry plants are fire hazards and the awned spikelets are a danger to animals.
1b. Awns over 2 cm long; second glume over 1 cm long . . . . (2)

2a. Awns 3-6 cm long. **A. diandra** (Roth) Tutin [with 2 stamens], RIPGUTGRASS. Adventive. Infrequent weed (*B. rigidus*).
2b. Awns not over 3 cm long. **A. sterilis** (L.) Nevski. Adventive. Infrequent weed usually in towns, but common in the foothills, LR.

APERA Adanson 1763 [Greek, *a*, not, + *peros*, maimed, possibly alluding to some feature of the spikelet]

One species, **A. interrupta** (L.) P. Beauvois. Adventive. Recently discovered as a weed in disturbed places on the plains, YM. At first glance one might think this is an annual *Muhlenbergia*, but on closer examination, the awn will be seen to be inserted slightly below the lemma tip.

ARISTIDA L. 1753 [Latin, *arista*, awn]. THREE-AWN

1a. Central awn spirally coiled at base at maturity; annuals. **A. basiramea** Engelmann [branched at the base]. Rare, limited to a few sites on sandstone outcrops of the outer hogbacks, BL, JF (including *A. curtissii*).
1b. Central awn not spirally coiled; perennials (1 annual) . . . . (2)

2a. Annual, much branched just above the base; first glume 2/3-3/4 as long as the second; awns 1-1.5 cm long; callus not sharp-pointed. **A. adscensionis** L. [for the original locality, Ascension Island in the South Atlantic Ocean]. Fairly common, southeast counties, probably an adventive of long standing, possibly brought in by the early Spanish with horses.

2b. Perennial, hardly branched above the base; first glume about equal to the second or only half as long; awns 1-8 cm long; callus sharp-pointed . . (3)

3a. Glumes unequal, the first half as long as the second; lemma without a beak or with a very short one. **A. purpurea** Nuttall. Very common on the plains and valleys, extremely variable (including *A. longiseta, A. fendleriana, A. wrightii*, and probably *A. havardii*).

3b. Glumes equal or nearly so in length; lemma narrowed to a twisted "beak" 2-5 mm long . . . . (4)

4a. Panicle with widely spreading branches. **A. divaricata** Humboldt & Bonpland. Frequent in the lower Arkansas drainage.

4b. Panicle with short and appressed branches. **A. arizonica** Vasey. Infrequently collected and widely scattered along the southern river systems, on sandstone ledges, JF, LA, RN.

ARRHENATHERUM P. Beauvois 1812 [Greek, *arrhen*, masculine, + *ather*, awn, alluding to the awned staminate floret]. TALL OATGRASS

One species, **A. elatius** (L.) P. Beauvois. Adventive, introduced as a nurse crop for new highway rights-of-way.

AVENA L. 1753 [the classical Latin name]. OATS

1a. Lemma with stiff, usually reddish-brown hairs; awn bent and twisted. **A. fatua** L. [useless], WILD OATS. Adventive weed in grain fields and along roadsides.

1b. Lemma glabrous; awn straight or absent. **A. fatua** var. **sativa** (L.) Haussknecht, CULTIVATED OATS. Adventive. Widely cultivated and volunteering on roadsides and horse trails.

AVENULA Dumortier 1868 [diminutive of *Avena*]. MOUNTAIN OATS

One species, **A. hookeri** (Scribner) Holub. Upper subalpine and lower tundra, Front Range, Continental Divide, and South Park. According to Soviet specialists, the Central Asiatic *A. asiatica* is identical to this species (*Avenochloa*, *Avena*).

BECKMANNIA Host 1805 [for Johann Beckmann, 1739-1811, German botanist]. SLOUGHGRASS

One species, **B. syzigachne** (Steudel) Fernald subsp. **baicalensis** (Kuznetsow) Koyama & Kuwano [with scissorslike glumes; from Lake Baikal], **87A**. Irrigation ditches and swamps. The unusual spikelets are arranged like stacks of poker chips.

BLEPHARONEURON Nash 1898 [Greek, *blepharos*, eyelash, + *neuron*, nerve, alluding to the silky-hairy nerves of the lemma]. PINE DROPSEED

One species, **B. tricholepis** (Torrey) Nash. Rocky meadows and gravelly, open spruce or pine forests.

BOTHRIOCHLOA Kuntze 1891 [Greek, *bothros*, pit, + *chloë*, grass, alluding to a glandular depression on the first glume]. SILVER BEARDGRASS

1a. Pedicelled spikelets neuter, smaller and narrower than the sessile ones; inflorescence very silvery-white. **B. laguroides** (de Candolle) Herter subsp. **torreyana** (Steudel) Allred & Gould. Common in southeastern Colorado on the plains and persisting where introduced along highways as far north as Boulder (*Andropogon*).

1b. Pedicelled spikelets neuter or staminate, about as large and broad as the sessile ones . . . . (2)

2a. Panicle axis usually longer than the branches. **B. bladhii** (Retzius) (S. T. Blake [for Peter John Bladh, eighteenth-century collector in China], AUSTRALIAN BLUESTEM. Adventive, introduced along highways in the easternmost counties.

2b. Panicle axis shorter than the branches. **B. ischaemum** (L.) Keng var. **songarica** (Ruprecht) Celarier & Harlan [styptic; Dzungaria, a plateau region in northwestern China], KING RANCH BLUESTEM. Adventive, similar sites.

BOUTELOUA Lagasca 1805 [for Claudio and Esteban Boutelou, eighteenth-century Spanish botanists] (originally spelled *Botelua).* GRAMA

One species, **B. curtipendula** (Michaux) Torrey [short-hanging], SIDEOATS GRAMA, **86E**. Common on the plains and outwash mesas of the Front Range. For other species commonly included in *Bouteloua*, see *Chondrosum*.

BRIZA L. 1753 [ancient Greek name for a cereal grass]. QUAKINGGRASS

One species, **B. media** L. Adventive, one record from Boulder Open Space grasslands. The spikelets recall those of *Bromus briziformis* but are very small, about 5 mm long, and the lemmas spread at right angles to the rachis.

BROMELICA Farwell 1919 [*Bromus* + *Melica*]. ONIONGRASS

One species, **B. spectabilis** (Scribner) Weber. Aspen woodlands, northern counties (*Melica*). In this species the basal swelling of the culm is small, globose, "tailed" at base, i.e., not attached directly to the rhizome; first glume 4-5 mm long, less than half as long as the spikelet. **B. bulbosa** of the Western Slope has a stout basal swelling attached directly to the rhizome.

BROMOPSIS Fourreau 1869 [*Bromus*, + Greek, *opsis*, like] (formerly included in *Bromus*). PERENNIAL BROME

1a. Rhizomes present; floral branches erect or slightly spreading; awn of lemma not over 3 mm long . . . . (2)

1b. Rhizomes absent (bunchgrasses); floral branches nodding; awn of lemma often over 3 mm long . . . . (3)

2a. Lemma scabrous to glabrous; nodes and leaves usually glabrous. **B. inermis** (Leysser) Holub, SMOOTH BROME. Adventive. A Eurasian species widely introduced along roadsides and fields for soil stabilization and pasture forage.

2b. Lemma pubescent; nodes hairy; leaves usually pubescent. **B. pumpelliana** (Scribner) Holub. The native American counterpart of Smooth Brome, montane and subalpine.

3a. Plants well over 1 m tall; leaves 1 cm or more wide; culms with 6-8 leaves. **B. pubescens** (Mühlenberg) Holub. Very rare, along wet streamsides in cool, mesic canyons of the foothills. A very handsome plant with its large nodding heads and broad, drooping leaves.

3b. Plants less than 1 m tall; leaves narrower; culms with fewer leaves; plants preferring drier sites . . . . (4)

4a. First glume (the lower and shorter one; the base of the first glume enfolds that of the second) 3-nerved (best examined from inside). **B. porteri** (Coulter) Holub. Common along roadsides and trails in the mountains.

4b. First glume 1-nerved . . . . (5)

5a. Lower culm sheaths with spreading hairs. **B. lanatipes** (Shear) Holub. Similar habitats.

5b. Lower culm sheaths glabrous. **B. canadensis** (Michaux) Holub. Similar habitats (*B. ciliata*, *B. richardsonii*).

BROMUS L. 1753 [ancient Greek name for oats]. BROME

1a. Awns absent or very short; lemmas broad and inflated, papery, the spikelets rattling when shaken together. **B. briziformis** Fischer & Meyer [like the genus *Briza*], RATTLESNAKEGRASS. Common on the mesas at the base of the foothills. All species are adventive, introduced weeds of ruderal sites.

1b. Lemmas awned; otherwise not as above . . . . (2)

2a. Lower leaf sheaths with slender, soft hairs, these ± reflexed, velvety to ascending shaggy-hairy or loosely hairy to almost glabrous . . . . (3)

2b. Lower leaf sheaths with stout, stiff hairs, ± spreading but never velvety (5)

3a. Lemma thickish, parchmentlike, the veins not very prominent; mature pedicels spreading or pendulous . . . . (4)

3b. Lemma thinner, membranous, with ± prominent veins; pedicels mostly stiffly erect. **B. hordeaceus** L.

4a. Palea margins narrow (0.5 mm), bluntly infolded above the middle; longest pedicels with 2-4 linear-lanceolate spikelets. **B. japonicus** Thunberg, **86A**.

4b. Palea margins 1 mm broad, acutely infolded above the middle; pedicels with 1 or 2 ovate-lanceolate spikelets. **B. squarrosus** L.

5a. Sides of the palea hairy or rough with short spikelike cells (compound microscope!); caryopsis of lowest floret usually shorter than the others; panicle large and loose . . . . (6)

5b. Sides of the palea smooth, lacking hairs of any kind; caryopsis of lowest floret almost as long as the others; panicle ± narrow, not large and loose. **B. racemosus** L.

6a. Margin of palea rounded; caryopsis either ± shriveled or well developed; ripe spikelets with firm axis and thickish florets; lower leaf sheaths glabrous or sparingly hairy. **B. secalinus** L.

6b. Margin of the palea angular-folded; caryopsis always well developed; ripe spikelets with fragile axis and thinner or more slender florets; lower leaf sheaths densely hairy. **B. commutatus** Schrader.

BUCHLOË Engelmann 1859 [abbreviation of Latin, *bubalus*, buffalo, + Greek, *chloë*, grass]. BUFFALOGRASS

One species, **B. dactyloides** Engelmann. A dominant plant of the short-grass prairie, common on the plains and outwash mesas. Engelmann at first thought this to represent two genera, but his brother happened to collect an unusual specimen that had both sexes of spikelets on the same plant.

CALAMAGROSTIS Adanson 1763 [Greek, *calamos*, reed, + *agrostis*, a grass]. REEDGRASS

1a. Awn straight, not over 3 mm long; callus hairs from half to nearly as long as the lemma; rhizomatous marsh grasses . . . . (2)

1b. Awn bent, up to 8 mm long; callus hairs less than half the length of the lemma; robust, stiff bunchgrass (very shortly if at all rhizomatous). **C.**

purpurascens R. Brown. Open talus slopes, gravelly low tundra, forested zone to alpine.

2a. Panicle loose and open; leaves soft-textured, lax. **C. canadensis** (Michaux) P. Beauvois. Very common on borders of montane and subalpine ponds.
2b. Panicle contracted; leaves rather stiff; glumes 2.5-4 mm long; lemma 2.2-3.2 mm long. **C. stricta** (Timm) Koeler. Subalpine willow carrs (*C. inexpansa*, *C. neglecta*).

CALAMOVILFA Hackel 1890 [Greek, *calamos* + *Vilfa*, a genus name]. SANDREED

1a. Lemma glabrous on the back (in addition to the basal callus hairs); spikelets 5-7 mm long; panicle usually narrow. **C. longifolia** (Hooker) Scribner. Common in sandy areas on the plains and piedmont valleys.
1b. Lemma pubescent on the back near the base; spikelets 7-9 mm long; panicle open at maturity. **C. gigantea** (Nuttall) Scribner & Merrill. Sand dunes, lower Arkansas and Cimarron River drainages, CH, BA.

CATABROSA P. Beauvois 1812 [Greek, *catabrosis*, devouring, alluding to the chewed appearance of the glumes and lemmas]. BROOKGRASS

One species, **C. aquatica** (L.) P. Beauvois. Quiet oxbows of mountain streams, and sparingly on the plains (Platte River), LG, WL; usually half-submerged.

CENCHRUS L. 1753 [Greek, *cenchros*, a kind of millet]. SANDBUR

One species, **C. longispinus** (Hackel) Fernald, **87C**. Sandy soil in the lower valleys.

CERATOCHLOA de Candolle & Beauvois 1812 [Greek, *ceratos*, horn, + *chloë*, grass]. RESCUEGRASS

One species, **C. carinata** (Hooker & Arnott) Tutin. Adventive. A species consisting of a number of interfertile races, introduced for range revegetation (*Bromus marginatus*, *B. breviaristatus*).

CHLORIS Swartz 1788 [Greek goddess of flowers]. WINDMILLGRASS

1a. Panicle branches slender, in several whorls along an axis 20 mm or more long; lemma awned but not hairy. **C. verticillata** Nuttall. Adventive weed of urban areas and roadsides on the plains.
1b. Panicle branches stout, in a single whorl or at least the branches crowded; lemma awned and copiously hairy. **C. virgata** Swartz. Adventive. Similar habitats.

CHONDROSUM Desvaux 1810 [Greek, *chondros*, grain]. GRAMA

1a. Annual . . . . (2)
1b. Perennial . . . . (3)

2a. Spikes one to a culm; spikelets 4-6 mm long. **C. prostratum** (Lagasca) Sweet. Adventive, established on the eastern plains from Denver southeastward, and in the San Luis Valley (*Bouteloua simplex*).
2b. Spikes usually 4 or more to a culm; spikelets 3-4 mm long including the awns. **C. barbatum** (Lagasca) Clayton. Infrequent, lower Arkansas Valley (*Bouteloua*).

3a. Culms felty-pubescent; spikes slender, not brushlike. **C. eriopodum** Torrey [hairy-footed]. Rocky slopes, Mesa de Maya (*Bouteloua*).
3b. Culms glabrous; spikes brushlike . . . . (4)

4a. Rachis prolonged beyond the spike as a naked point; glumes with dark tubercles on the surface. **C. hirsutum** (Lagasca) Sweet. Grasslands on the plains (*Bouteloua*).

4b. Rachis not prolonged beyond the spike; glumes without tubercles. **C. gracile** Humboldt, Bonpland & Kunth, BLUE GRAMA, **86F**. Grasslands on the plains, foothills, and intermountain parks (*Bouteloua*).

CINNA L. 1753 [Greek, *kinni*, a name used by Theophrastus for some grass]. WOODREED

One species, **C. latifolia** (Treviranus) Grisebach. Swampy woodlands, montane and subalpine. A tall, somewhat nondescript grass with broad leaves, a 1-flowered spikelet, glumes as long as the lemma, lemma tipped with a very short awn point. The large ligules are membranous and lacerate.

CRITESION Rafinesque 1819 [Greek, *crithe*, barley] (formerly included in *Hordeum*). FOXTAIL BARLEY

1a. Perennial; awns slender; leaves lacking auricles . . . . (2)

1b. Annual, branching at the base; awns mostly stouter; leaves sometimes with auricles . . . . (3)

2a. Spike, including awns, as broad as long or nearly so when mature; awns 2-5 cm long. **C. jubatum** (L.) Nevski. Wet ditches and meadows, a very beautiful plant with nodding yellowish or (at high altitudes) reddish spikes. First generation hybrids, *X Agrohordeum macounii* (Vasey) Lepage are occasionally found involving this and species of *Elymus*.

2b. Spike, including awns, much longer than broad, the awns not more than 1 cm long. Culms stiffly erect. **C. brachyantherum** (Nevski) Weber. Adventive ruderal weed in the valleys and mountain parks (*Hordeum brachyantherum*; *C. jubatum* subsp. *breviaristatum*).

3a. Leaf blades with prominent auricles. **C. glaucum** (Steudel) Löve. Adventive ruderal weed in the piedmont valleys.

3b. Leaf blades lacking auricles. **C. pusillum** (Nuttall) Löve. Ruderal weed in the valleys and plains.

CRYPSIS Aiton 1789 [Greek, *crypsis*, concealment, because of the somewhat hidden inflorescence]

One species, **C. alopecuroides** (Piller & Mitterp) Schrader. Adventive in the Denver area. A low, spreading plant looking like a miniature *Phleum*.

CYLINDROPYRUM Löve 1984 [Greek, cylindric-wheat]. GOATGRASS

One species, **C. cylindricum** (Host) Löve. Adventive weed on the plains and piedmont valleys (*Aegilops*).

CYNODON Richard 1805 [Greek, *cyno*, dog, + *odos*, tooth]. BERMUDAGRASS

One species, **C. dactylon** (L.) Persoon. Adventive. Commonly used for lawns in the southern states, occasionally escaping and becoming established in our area, especially in warm places, such as over underground heating tunnels. Easily known from the digitate inflorescence and stoloniferous habit.

DACTYLIS L. 1753 [Greek, *daktylos*, a finger]. ORCHARDGRASS

One species, **D. glomerata** L. Adventive weed in lawns and fields, sometimes grown in pasture mixes. The clumps of succulent, bluish-green, folded leaves form unsightly spreading clumps, overspreading bluegrass in lawns and not removed easily by mowing. The pollen is a major cause of hay fever.

DANTHONIA de Candolle 1805 [for Etienne Danthoine, nineteenth-century French botanist]. OATGRASS

1a. Panicle open, the slender branches spreading or reflexed; spikelets about 3; lemma pilose on margins, glabrous on the back. **D. californica** Bolander. Infrequent or rare, North Park; TL.

1b. Panicle with erect or ascending branches; spikelets more numerous . . (2)

2a. Lemma glabrous on the back, pilose on the margins only. **D. intermedia** Vasey, TIMBER OATGRASS. Subalpine and alpine grasslands.

2b. Lemma pilose on the back, sometimes sparsely so . . . . (3)

3a. Glumes over 15 mm long; lemma over 9 mm long; culms robust, over 1 mm wide. **D. parryi** Scribner, **86B**. Dry, gravelly hillsides, upper montane and subalpine.

3b. Glumes and lemmas shorter; culms slender; old leaf sheaths not conspicuous. **D. spicata** (L.) Beauvois, POVERTY OATGRASS, **87D**. Locally abundant on the outwash mesas and open pine forests in the foothills.

DESCHAMPSIA P. Beauvois 1812 [for Jean Loiseleur Deslongchamps, 1774-1849, French botanist]. TUFTED HAIRGRASS

One species, **D. cespitosa** (L.) P. Beauvois. Wet meadows and pond margins, subalpine, one of the most valuable native forage grasses in the mountains. It is very tenacious, often being the last survivor when upland wetlands are overgrazed or drained. The leaves are stiff and have sharp points (use palm of the hand), a good identification mark. In alpine situations a race with larger spikelets and denser inflorescence, subsp. *alpicola* (Rydberg) Löve et al., occurs and is often easily separable from the usual type.

DICHANTHELIUM Gould 1974 [Greek, *dicha*, in two, + *anthele*, tuft or plume of a reed, alluding to the branching in the type species, *D. dichotomum*] (formerly in *Panicum*)

1a. Main culm leaves rather prominently basally distributed, long and narrow, not more than 4 mm wide; plants not producing a winter rosette of broader leaves. **D. linearifolium** (Scribner) Gould. Rocky slopes of outer foothill hogbacks (*P. perlongum*).

1b. Main culm leaves distributed up the culm, variable, but either some of them more than 4 mm wide or the plant possessing dried remnants of a winter rosette of broader, shorter leaves . . . . (2)

2a. Spikelets 2.5 mm long or more . . . . (3)

2b. Spikelets less than 2.5 mm long . . . . (4)

3a. Leaf blades long-pubescent on both surfaces, less than 5 mm wide; spikelets 2.5-3.3 mm long. **D. wilcoxianum** (Vasey) Freckmann. Rocky areas along base of Front Range. Very similar to *D. linearifolium* but with winter rosettes.

3b. Leaf blades less strongly pubescent, many of the main culm leaves more than 5 mm wide; spikelets 2.8-5.8 mm long. **D. oligosanthes** (Schultes) Gould var. **scribnerianum** (Nash) Gould. Fairly common on rocky ground along the base of the mountains.

4a. Ligules up to 1.6 mm long; spikelets 2.4-3.2 mm long. **D. wilcoxianum**.

4b. Ligules very conspicuous, more than 1.6 mm long at least on some leaves or, if shorter, then the spikelets well under 2.4 mm long. **D. acuminatum** (Swartz) Gould & Clark. Rocky sites, especially in seeps along base of rimrock cliffs along the Front Range and occasionally in similar sites on the plains (*D. lanuginosum, Panicum tennesseense, P. huachucae*).

DIGITARIA Heister 1759 [Latin, *digitus*, finger]. CRABGRASS

1a. Spikelets silky-pubescent with long white hairs; inflorescence contracted, the branches appressed, closely flowered. **D. californica** (Bentham) Henrard. One record, Mesa de Maya (*Trichachne*). This species does not look like the weedy ones. It is perennial with a knotty base covered with pubescent scale leaves.
1b. Spikelets not silky-pubescent; inflorescence open . . . . (2)

2a. Spikelets 2.2-2.5 mm long; lemma of upper floret light brown or grayish. **D. sanguinalis** (L.) Scopoli [stanching blood, named for its supposed styptic properties]. CRABGRASS. A common and pernicious weed in lawns.
2b. Spikelets 2 mm long; lemma of upper floret dark brown at maturity. **D. ischaemum** (Schreber) Schreber [from Greek, *ischaemos*, styptic]. Not as common as the last, frequent in the Boulder-Denver area.

DISTICHLIS Rafinesque 1819 [Greek, *distichos*, 2-ranked]. SALTGRASS

One species, **D. spicata** (L.) Greene subsp. **stricta** (Torrey) Thorne. Alkaline swales and borrow pits, lower valleys. The grass named *D. stricta* was thought for a long time to be a different species, but it was found that these were only the carpellate plants, which have more rigid spikelets!

ECHINOCHLOA P. Beauvois 1812 [Greek, *echinos*, hedgehog, + *chloë*, grass]. BARNYARD GRASS

One species, **E. crus-galli** (L.) P. Beauvois [cockspur]. Adventive coarse weed in gardens, irrigation ditches, and farmyards in the lower valleys. Very variable as to awn length.

ELEUSINE Gaertner 1788 [from Eleusis, the town where Ceres, goddess of harvests, was worshipped]. GOOSEGRASS

One species, **E. indica** (L.) Gaertner [of India]. Adventive, ruderal weed in cities and towns, from Denver southeastward.

ELYMUS L. 1753 [Greek, *elymos*, name for a kind of millet]. WILD RYE

1a. Spikelets solitary at each node of the rachis . . . . (2)
1b. Spikelets 2 or more at some or all of the nodes (count the glumes; there are 2 for each spikelet) . . . . (3)

2a. Awn of lemma straight or absent. **E. trachycaulus** (Link) Gould [rough-stem]. Meadows and roadsides; an alpine race (subsp. **andinus** [Scribner & Smith] Löve & Löve) has very broad glumes and lemmas.
2b. Glumes and lemmas with long, curved awns; culms decumbent, spreading. **E. scribneri** (Vasey) Jones [for F. Lamson-Scribner]. Very common on dry tundra.

3a. Glumes subulate, extending into long spreading awns; rachis of inflorescence brittle and shattering at maturity . . . . (4)
3b. Glumes broad or narrow but not subulate or extended into long awns; rachis usually remaining intact, or, if shattering, then the awns less than 2 cm long . . . . (5)

4a. Lowermost floret of each spikelet fertile, not modified. **E. longifolius** (Smith) Gould, SQUIRRELTAIL. This and the next are very common, weedy grasses on roadsides and disturbed areas. When ripe the awns spread stiffly and the axis soon breaks apart. Because of minute barbs along the awns, the segments will "walk" if not glued to herbarium sheets (*Sitanion*).

4b. Lowermost floret of one or both spikelets at each node sterile and reduced to a subulate or lanceolate awn, giving the appearance of extra glume segments; glumes entire or bifid. **E. elymoides** (Rafinesque) Swezey (*Sitanion hystrix*).

5a. Glumes linear to linear-lanceolate, usually 1-2 mm wide, the margins hyaline. **E. glaucus** Buckley, BLUE WILD RYE. Aspen glades in the mountains, evidently requiring shade.

5b. Glumes setaceous and less than 1 mm wide or, if wider, the margins never hyaline . . . . (6)

6a. Lemma with long, divergent awns; spike nodding; auricles prominent, 1.5-4 mm long. **E. canadensis** L., CANADA WILD RYE. Fencerows in the valleys, the spikes persisting long into autumn.

6b. Lemma with short, straight awns; spike strictly erect; auricles minute or lacking. **E. virginicus** L. Infrequent in the outer foothills of the Front Range.

ELYTRIGIA Desvaux 1810 [Greek, *elytron*, sheath or husk] (formerly in *Agropyron*)

1a. Glumes blunt, rounded or truncate at the tip and only slightly mucronate. E. **intermedia** (Host) Nevski, INTERMEDIATE WHEATGRASS. Adventive, commonly planted to revegetate depleted range. A race with villous lemmas is subsp. **barbulata** (Schur) Löve (*A. trichophorum*). Löve recently proposed the genus *Trichopyrum* for this species. Easily confused with *Lophopyrum elongatum*, which has truncate glumes without a mucro and lacks rhizomes.

1b. Glumes pointed . . . . (2)

2a. Lemmas with long outcurved awns. **Elytrigia albicans** (Scribner & Smith) Weber. Usually among rocks on slopes, but commonly in moist borrow pits (*Agropyron albicans, A. griffithsii*). Without the rhizomes, this is often misidentified as the Western Slope *Pseudoroegneria*, blue-bunch wheatgrass.

2b. Lemmas with straight awns or none . . . . (3)

3a. Lemmas scabrous or villous. **E. dasystachya** (Hooker) Löve & Löve. Common roadside grass.

3b. Lemmas glabrous. **E. repens** (L.) Nevski, QUACKGRASS. Adventive weed of cultivated ground with deep-seated brittle rhizomes.

ERAGROSTIS Wolf 1781 [Greek, Eros, god of love, + *agrostis*, grass]. LOVEGRASS

1a. Culms creeping and rooting at the nodes. **E. hypnoides** (Lamarck) Britton et al. Adventive, an occasional weed in lawns.

1b. Culms erect or spreading but not rooting at the nodes . . . . (2)

2a. Perennial . . . . (3)

2b. Annual . . . . (7)

3a. Spikelets and their pedicels appressed to stiff, spreading branches. E. **curtipedicellata** Buckley. One record, from sandy ground in southeast corner of BA.

3b. Spikelets either on spreading pedicels or the panicles densely flowered and lacking spreading branches . . . . (4)

4a. Spikelets densely clustered, mostly more than 2.5 mm wide, tightly many-flowered (14-20 lemmas), strongly red-tinged; branches not spreading. E. **secundiflora** Presl subsp. **oxylepis** (Torrey) S. D. Koch. Barely entering

Colorado in southeast BA; one record from an accidental and short-lived introduction near Long's Peak (*E. beyrichii, E. oxylepis*).

4b. Spikelets loosely arranged or remote along the branches; spikelets less than 2.5 mm wide with fewer lemmas, usually not red-tinged (except in *E. spectabilis*) . . . . (5)

5a. Anthers less than 0.5 mm long; grains (caryopses) 0.6-0.8 mm long, not grooved on side opposite the embryo. **E. spectabilis** (Pursh) Steudel, PURPLE LOVEGRASS. Barely entering Colorado in southeastern BA. The branches of the inflorescence are stiffly wide-spreading.

5b. Anthers over 0.8 mm long; grains 0.8-1.6 mm long . . . . (6)

6a. Glumes unequal, the first 1-2 mm long, the second 2-3 mm long; grains not grooved on the side opposite the embryo, pale at maturity. **E. curvula** (Schrader) Nees. Adventive, scattered on the plains.

6b. Glumes equal or nearly so, 2-4 mm long; grain clearly grooved, dark brown at maturity. **E. trichodes** (Nuttall) Wood. Frequent along roadsides on the plains, very likely adventive.

7a. Tall, erect, 6-10 dm tall, with open panicles. **E. mexicana** (Hornemann) Link subsp. **virescens** Presl. Infrequent, adventive weed, our only collections from Bonny Reservoir, YM.

7b. Low, spreading plants . . . . (8)

8a. Plant with a glandular ring near the summits of some internodes or with depressed glands on the panicle branches and sometimes on the keels and faces of lemmas . . . . (9)

8b. Plants not glandular on the internodes, panicle branches, or lemmas. **E. pilosa** (L.) Beauvois [comblike]. Adventive, very common, ruderal weed, late summer. A variable species with evident connecting forms to others (I tentatively include *E. pectinacea* here).

9a. Culms with a glandular ring or band on the summit of the internode just below the base of the next sheath above. **E. barrelieri** Daveau [for Jacques Barrelier, 1606-1673, French botanist]. Adventive weed, scattered on the eastern plains.

9b. Glandular ring absent from the culm, but depressed glands present on panicle branches and/or lemma keels . . . . (10)

10a. Largest spikelets 2.5-3.5 mm wide; glandular depressions prominent on keels of lemmas. **E. cilianensis** (Allioni) Hubbard [of Ciliani, an Italian estate]. Adventive, ruderal weed.

10b. Largest spikelets not more than 2 mm wide, mostly less; glandular depressions mostly on the panicle branches and leaves . . . . (11)

11a. Panicle open, at least one-fourth as wide as long. **E. minor** Host (*E. perplexans, E. poaeoides*). Adventive, ruderal weed, southern counties.

11b. Panicle narrow, rather dense. **E. lutescens** Scribner. One record, from a drying pond in the piedmont valley near Boulder.

ERIONEURON Nash 1903 [Greek, *erion*, wool, + *neuron*, nerve]. HAIRY TRIDENS

One species, **E. pilosum** (Buckley) Nash. Mostly on limestone and gypsum hills and rimrock, lower Arkansas Valley from PE to BA.

FESTUCA L. 1753 [ancient name for a grass]. FESCUE

1a. Leaf blades flat, averaging over 3 mm wide . . . . (2)
1b. Leaf blades involute or, if flat, less than 3 mm wide . . . . (5)

2a. Panicle spikelike; plants dioecious; stigmas bearing branches on all sides; leaves without auricles; native in ponderosa pine forests (see *Leucopoa*)
2b. Panicle narrow but not spikelike; plants not dioecious; stigmas with branches on two sides only; auricles sometimes present . . . . (3)

3a. Spikelets 2-4-flowered, 8-11 mm long; auricles lacking. **F. sororia** Piper. Little known, from spruce-fir forest openings, San Juan Mountains, ML.
3b. Spikelets 5-9-flowered, 10-17 mm long; auricles present . . . . (4)

4a. Margin of auricle ciliate; lemmas 7-10 mm long; first glume 4-6 mm long, the second 5-7 mm long. **F. arundinacea** Schreber [reedlike], ALTA FESCUE. Adventive, introduced in pastures and roadsides in the valleys.
4b. Margin of auricle naked; lemmas 4-7 mm long; first glume 2.5-4 mm long, the second 3.5-5 mm long. **F. pratensis** Hudson, MEADOW FESCUE. Adventive, similar habitats.

5a. Ligule 2-4 mm or more long; lemmas awnless or cuspidate. **F. thurberi** Vasey [for George Thurber, botanist for the Mexican Boundary Survey]. A tall and handsome bunchgrass, relatively infrequent on the Eastern Slope while a dominant grass on mountainsides of the Western Slope. Distinguished from the habitally similar *F. arizonica* by the broader, not glaucous leaves.
5b. Ligule shorter; lemma awnless or distinctly awned . . . . (6)

6a. Culm curved at the base, the new shoots breaking out through the old leaf sheath; basal leaf sheaths reddish, the vascular strands persisting as fibers; culms in loose tufts. **F. rubra** L. Mountain meadows; anthers 2-3 mm long. Besides its native occurrences, the species is widely used as a lawn grass and in revegetation mixes.
6b. Culms erect from the base, the new shoots not breaking out but coming up between a leaf sheath and the culm; basal leaf sheaths not reddish nor fibrillose . . . . (7)

7a. Rhizomatous, always growing in *Kobresia* stands in the tundra. **F. hallii** (Vasey) Piper [for Elihu Hall]. Known in recent time only from Cameron Pass, but originally collected somewhere in or around the north end of South Park.
7b. Plant caespitose, without rhizomes . . . . (8)

8a. Tall, robust plants with large spikelets; lemmas 7-10 mm long, scabrous; lemmas acute, rarely short-awned. **F. campestris** Rydberg. Rare, known from Apishapa Pass (*F. scabrella* in part).
8b. Smaller plants or, if tall, with smaller spikelets and lemmas . . . . (9)

9a. Anthers up to 1.5 mm long; lemmas up to 4 mm long exclusive of the awn . . . . (10)
9b. Anthers 2.5-4 mm long; lemma up to 5-7 mm long excluding the awn, often inrolled, exposing the rachilla . . . . (13)

10a. Anthers 1-1.5 mm long; leaves glaucous; culms tall, about 2-3 times the height of the basal leaves; ligule 3 mm long; lemma 6-7.5 mm long including the awn. **F. saximontana** Rydberg. Dry mountain meadows and forest openings.

10b. Anthers 0.7-0.8 mm long; leaves green; culms usually less than twice the height of the basal leaves; ligule minute or obsolete; lemma 3-4 mm including awn . . . . (11)

11a. Culm minutely and densely pubescent just below the head; spikelets tending to be reddish-brown. **F. baffinensis** Polunin [from Baffin Island]. Infrequent on dry tundra on the Continental Divide, northern counties.

11b. Culm not pubescent below the head; spikelets dark gray-green . . . . (12)

12a. Leaves very slender and lax, the tuft usually less than 10 cm high and tending to spread; culms hardly exceeding the leaves; caryopsis hairy at the apex. **F. minutiflora** Rydberg. Frequent on tundra but not as common as the next.

12b. Leaves stiff, erect, the tuft usually over 10 cm high; culms usually well exceeding the leaves; caryopsis glabrous. **F. brachyphylla** Schultes subsp. **coloradensis** Frederiksen. Very abundant and characteristic of dry tundra (often incorrectly called *F. ovina*; that is a European species with long anthers, only cultivated in America). However, under the misapprehension that our native species is *F. ovina*, the true *F. ovina* has been introduced for revegetation in Rocky Mountain National Park and doubtless other places, the seed source being Turkish!

13a. Awn 2-4 mm long; persistent, papery, basal leaf sheaths less than 4 cm long; leaves seldom up to 30 cm high. **F. idahoensis** Elmer. Infrequent, subalpine. The typical plant of the Pacific Northwest has widely spreading panicle branches, not always the case with our plants.

13b. Awn up to 2 mm long; persistent, papery leaf sheaths 5-10 cm long; leaves filiform, usually over 30 cm long. **F. arizonica** Vasey. Common in dry pine forests, southern counties.

GLYCERIA R. Brown 1810 [Greek, *glycos*, sweet]. MANNAGRASS

1a. Spikelets linear, over 7 mm long; panicle narrow. **G. borealis** (Nash) Batchelder. Margins of ponds, upper montane and subalpine, uncommon.

1b. Spikelets ovate to oblong, less than 7 mm long; panicle open . . . . . . (2)

2a. Leaf blades narrow, 2-6 mm wide; first glume 0.5-0.9 mm long; culm mostly less than 1 m tall. **G. striata** (Lamarck) Hitchcock. Common on swampy streamsides throughout. The ripe florets shatter very easily from the spikelets.

2b. Leaf blades wider; first glume 1 mm or more long; culm mostly over 1 m tall . . . . (3)

3a. First glume 1.5 mm or more long; spikelets 5-7 mm or more long; panicle very compound and open. **G. grandis** Watson. A very tall species of swamps and irrigation ditches in the lower valleys (*G. maxima* subsp. *grandis*).

3b. First glume 1 mm long or less; panicle only moderately compound. **G. elata** (Nash) Jones [tall]. Aspen thickets and pond borders, subalpine.

HELICTOTRICHON Besser 1827 [Greek, *helicos*, twisted, + *trichos*, hair]. ALPINE OATS

One species, **H. mortonianum** (Scribner) Henrard [for J. Sterling Morton, secretary of agriculture]. Dry, alpine tundra. Our only representative of a fairly large Asiatic mountain genus.

HIEROCHLOË R. Brown 1810 [Greek, *hieros*, sacred, + *chloë*, grass]. SWEETGRASS

One species, **H. hirta** (Schrank) Borbas subsp. **arctica** (Presl) Weimarck. Frequent in swampy meadows and lower alpine slopes. Spikelets rich golden brown. The foliage has a sweet odor, and in Poland the plant is used for flavoring vodka.

HILARIA Humboldt, Bonpland & Kunth 1816 [for Auguste St.-Hilaire, 1779-1853, French naturalist]. GALLETAGRASS

One species, **H. jamesii** (Torrey) Bentham, **87B**. Common on river benches and sagebrush stands, lower Arkansas River drainage from PE to BA. The spikelet anatomy in this genus is extremely complex, but it has a unique appearance.

HOLCUS L. 1753 [a name used by Pliny for some kind of grass]. VELVETGRASS

One species, **H. lanatus** L. Adventive, locally naturalized on shady slopes of Boulder Creek, piedmont valleys. No other grass has the very soft hairness of *Holcus*.

HORDEUM L. 1753 [the classical name for barley]. BARLEY

One species, **H. vulgare** L. Adventive. Widely cultivated and occasionally volunteering along roadsides and in fallow fields. Two forms are commonly cultivated: bearded barley, with long-awned lemmas, and hooded barley, with awnless lemmas having a blunt, often 3-lobed apical appendage or hood. A third rarely cultivated type with a single spikelet (var. *distichum*) might be confused with wheat, but in barley the florets taper to the awn and in wheat they are truncate.

KOELERIA Persoon 1805 [for Georg L. Koeler, 1765-1807, German botanist]. JUNEGRASS

One species, **K. macrantha** (Ledebour) Schultes. Very common in meadows. In blossom the panicle is open, glossy, and very different in appearance from its fruiting aspect, a dense, contracted, spikelike panicle (*K. gracilis*).

LEERSIA Swartz 1788 [for Johann Leers, 1727-1774, German botanist]. RICE CUTGRASS

One species, **L. oryzoides** (L.) Swartz. Adventive. Frequent in irrigation ditches in the piedmont valleys. The spikelet, of one floret without glumes, and the saw-edged stems are diagnostic.

LEPTOCHLOA P. Beauvois 1812 [Greek, *leptos*, delicate, + *chloë*, grass]. SPRANGLETOP

One species, **D. fascicularis** (Lamarck) Gray. Muddy shores of ponds and oxbows in the lower valleys (*Diplachne*).

LEUCOPOA Grisebach 1852 [Greek, *leucos*, white, + *Poa*]. SPIKE FESCUE

One species, **L. kingii** (Watson) Weber. A common grass of dry ponderosa pine woods in the foothills (*Hesperochloa*). It is a tall, glaucous grass forming unisexual stands. The only American species of a small Asiatic genus.

LEYMUS Hochstetter 1848 [anagram of *Elymus*] (formerly in *Elymus*). WILD RYE

1a. Strongly rhizomatous, definitely not bunchgrasses. **L. triticoides** (Buckley) Pilger. Frequent on benches and clay flats in the lower valleys.
1b. Bunchgrasses with no rhizomes or very short ones . . . . (2)

2a. Plants gigantic, forming dense clumps up to over 2 m high; leaves yellow-green; leaf blades up to 15 mm broad; spikelets 3-5 at a node. **L. cinereus** (Scribner & Merrill) Löve, GIANT WILD RYE. Common on talus slopes and roadsides in the canyon bottoms.

2b. Plants smaller; leaves dark- or grayish-green; leaf blades narrower; leaves flat, yellow-green; spikelets commonly 2 at a node. **L. ambiguus** (Vasey & Scribner) Dewey. Frequent on rocky mountainsides in the outer foothills.

LOLIUM L. 1753 [the ancient Latin name]. RYEGRASS

One species, **L. perenne** L. Adventive. Common admixture in lawns and becoming a troublesome weed because it lodges and resists mowing (*L. multiflorum*).

LOPHOPYRUM Löve 1980 [Greek, *lophos*, crest, mane, + *pyros*, wheat]. SLENDER WHEATGRASS

One species, **L. elongatum** (Host) Löve. Adventive. Extensively planted to retard erosion and stabilize grasslands. Similar to *Elytrigia intermedia*, but rhizomes are absent and the glumes are exactly truncate, without a mucro extension of a vein (*Agropyron*).

LYCURUS Humboldt, Bonpland & Kunth 1816. WOLFTAIL

One species, **L. phleoides** Humboldt, Bonpland & Kunth [resembling *Phleum*]. Frequent along the base of the Front Range on the mesas and outer foothill hogbacks and canyonsides.

MELICA L. 1753 [Greek, *meli*, honey]. ONIONGRASS

One species, **M. porteri** Scribner [for T. C. Porter]. Rare or only locally abundant on rocky cliffsides in the canyons of the outer foothills, notably lower Clear Creek. A beautiful grass growing in massive clumps with many culms, each with pendent, racemose spikelets (see also *Bromelica*).

MONROA Torrey 1857 [for William Munro, British grass specialist, 1818-1880]. FALSE BUFFALOGRASS

One species, **M. squarrosa** (Nuttall) Torrey. Sandy depressions on rimrock areas, and along roadsides on the plains. Easily recognized by its matted form and very rigid, prickle-pointed, white-edged leaves. In some places a plant louse infests the foliage, resulting in the whole plant being covered by a loose, cobwebby material. [The original name, *Monroa*, must be used although the spelling does not agree with the person being honored.]

MUHLENBERGIA Schreber 1789 [for Gotthilf Mühlenberg, 1753-1815, Pennsylvania botanist]. MUHLY

1a. Annual, mostly weak-rooted . . . . (2)
1b. Perennial . . . . (5)

2a. [1] Pedicels capillary, elongate; panicle open . . . . (3)
2b. Pedicels short, appressed; panicle narrow, contracted . . . . (4)

3a. [2] Pedicels filiform or capillary, much longer than the spikelets; glumes sparingly pubescent; panicles over 5 cm long. **M. minutissima** (Steudel) Swallen. Infrequent and very inconspicuous, on sandy flats, roadsides, borrow pits, without much competing vegetation. A delicate and pretty little species.
3b. Pedicels relatively stout and short, at least the lateral ones shorter than the spikelets; glumes glabrous; panicles less than 5 cm long. **M. wolfii** (Vasey) Rydberg [for John Wolf, 1820-1897, collector for the Wheeler expedition]. Rare or more likely overlooked by reason of its small size, known from one specimen from TL.

4a. [2] Lemma awnless; first glume entire. **M. filiformis** (Thurber) Rydberg. Swampy woodlands, meadows, and marshy streamsides, subalpine.

4b. Lemma long-awned; first glume bifid. **M. brevis** C. O. Goodding [short]. Rocky hills, reported by Harrington from CN, in the San Luis Valley.

5a. [1] Panicles open and diffuse, the branches spreading . . . . (6)
5b. Panicles condensed to very slender, the branches appressed . . . . (11)

6a. [5] Plants not rhizomatous, arising from a cluster of swollen, cormlike bases; stems elongate, zig-zag, the leaf blades soon breaking away from the sheaths. **M. porteri** Scribner. Rare or infrequent, lower Arkansas River Valley.
6b. Plants rhizomatous, forming spreading mats; leaves mostly in basal tufts; leaf blades not deciduous . . . . (7)

7a. [6] Ligules prominently fringed with hairs, these as long or longer than the membranous basal portion. **M. pungens** Thurber [sharp, for the leaf tips]. Sandy blowouts, eastern plains and San Luis Valley.
7b. Ligules membranous, sometimes torn but never with a conspicuous mass of hairs . . . . (8)

8a. [7] Lemma less than 2 mm long, usually awnless or at most only mucronate . . . . (9)
8b. Lemma more than 2 mm long, awned; ligule usually more than 2 mm long . . . . (10)

9a. [8] Leaf margins and midnerve white-cartilaginous; ligule splitting to form 2 auriclelike structures; leaf blades less than 3 mm long; plants of drylands. **M. arenacea** (Buckley) A. S. Hitchcock. Infrequent on the southeastern plains, PE, OT. This resembles *M. torreyi* but lacks awned lemmas.
9b. Leaf margins, midnerve, and ligules not as above; leaf blades longer; plants of wet, alkaline depressions. **M. asperifolia** (Nees & Meyen) Parodi. Abundant in roadside ditches and alkaline flats, the fine panicle branches having a gossamer appearance. A very easy plant to recognize once understood, but one might as easily place it in *Sporobolus* or even *Agrostis*.

10a. [8] Blades short, the longest ones less than 10 cm long, curved, mostly crowded at the base of the culm, few or none of the internodes visible. **M. torreyi** (Kunth) A. S. Hitchcock. RING MUHLY. Sandy soil on the eastern plains, Arkansas Valley, and San Luis Valley. The plants characteristically grow centrifugally, dying in the center and eventually forming a distinct ring.
10b. Blades more than 5 cm long, straight, distributed up the culm, some internodes visible. **M. arenicola** Buckley. Plains, extreme southeast corner.

11a. [5] Lemmas tapering to a definite awn, usually 2 mm long or more . (12)
11b. Lemmas acute, mucronate, or awn-pointed, the point not over 1 mm long (glumes may be awned) . . . . (14)

12a. [11] Hairs near base of lemma long, often as long as the lemma; second glume not toothed; strong, scaly rhizomes present. **M. andina** (Nuttall) A. S. Hitchcock. In seepage at bases of cliffs and rock outcrops, foothills and middle altitudes.
12b. Hairs near base of lemma short or absent; second glume 3-nerved, each nerve ending in a tooth; rhizomes lacking . . . . (13)

13a. [12] Awn of lemma 6-20 mm long; ligule 7 mm or more long; culms usually over 30 cm tall; panicle 5-15 cm long; leaf blades 5-15 cm long. **M. montana** (Nuttall) Hitchcock. Common in the foothills and middle mountains, usually in or adjacent to forested areas. In addition to the relatively poor characters used in the key, I find that this species seems to consistently differ from the next in having broad, loose leaf sheaths that are conspicuous in both live and pressed specimens.

13b. Awn of lemma 2-5 mm long; ligules 3-5 mm long; culms usually less than 30 cm tall; leaf blades usually less than 5 cm long. **M. filiculmis** Vasey. Most common in open, dry, grassy, intermountain parks in the southern counties, mostly absent from forested areas.

14a. [11] Plants rhizomatous . . . . (15)
14b. Plants caespitose . . . . (18)

15a. [14] Slender plants with slender rhizomes and narrow, often involute leaves; panicle narrow. **M. richardsonis** (Trinius) Rydberg [for Sir John Richardson, of the Franklin expeditions]. Common on rocky ledges and gravelly soils, particularly in the intermountain parks.
15b. Robust plants with stout, scaly rhizomes and broader, often flat leaves; panicle usually dense . . . . (16)

16a. [15] Glumes bearing stiff awn tips, exceeding the awnless lemmas . . (17)
16b. Glumes without protracted awn tips, usually shorter than or equalling the body of the floret; lemma awnless or awned. **M. mexicana** (L.) Trinius. Reported by Harrington from CH, LR, and WL.

17a. [16] Internodes dull, puberulent; lemma pilose at the base and along the margins; ligule up to 0.6 mm long; anthers 0.8-1.5 mm long. **M. glomerata** (Willdenow) Trinius. One record, from BA. This usually grows in wetter places than the next, and the culms are seldom branched.
17b. Internodes smooth and polished except near the apex; lemma pilose at the base only; ligule 0.6-1 mm long; anthers 0.5-0.8 mm long. **M. racemosa** (Michaux) Britton et al. Frequent on rocky slopes, usually at the base of cliffs and in gulches, foothills and in similar sites on the plains.

18a. [14] Panicle dense, usually over 5 mm wide; glumes awn-pointed, the awn often up to 1 mm long; ligules 1-3 mm long. **M. wrightii** Vasey [for the collector, Charles Wright, 1811-1885]. Frequent on rocky slopes along the base of the Front Range.
18b. Panicle rather loosely flowered, narrower; glumes not awn-pointed; ligules 0.5 mm long. **M. cuspidata** (Torrey) Rydberg. On the eastern plains, our collections from the lower Arkansas Valley.

ORYZOPSIS Michaux 1803 [Greek, *oryza*, rice, + *opsis*, like]. RICEGRASS
Note: Indian ricegrass is now a *Stipa*.

1a. Spikelets 5-8 mm long, not including the awn; callus densely hairy; leaf blades flat, 5-9 mm wide. **O. asperifolia** Michaux [rough-leaved]. Shaded woods, lower montane.
1b. Spikelets 3-4 mm long, not including the awn; callus not densely hairy; leaves narrower . . . . (2)

2a. Panicle branches spreading or reflexed at maturity. **O. micrantha** (Trinius & Ruprecht) Thurber. Usually in deep shade, rocky slopes. A delicate plant with very slender, weak culms and minute spikelets.
2b. Panicle branches erect or appressed at maturity . . . . (3)

3a. Awn less than 2 mm long or almost lacking. **O. pungens** (Torrey) Hitchcock [sharp]. Infrequent, our records from pine forests, Arkansas Divide, Black Forest area.

3b. Awn 5 mm or more long. **O. exigua** Thurber [short]. Frequent on rocky canyon slopes in the northern Park Range.

PANICUM L. 1753 [Latin, *panus*, an ear of millet]. PANICGRASS

1a. Annual . . . . (2)
1b. Perennial . . . . (5)

2a. Spikelets mostly more than 4 mm long; stems erect. **P. miliaceum** L., PROSO MILLET. A cultivated cereal grass occasionally volunteering as a roadside grass seed contaminant, and now a spreading weed near Greeley, WL.
2b. Spikelets less than 4 mm long . . . . (3)

3a. First glume short, blunt; sheaths glabrous. **P. dichotomiflorum** Michaux. Adventive as a weed in the Denver Botanic Gardens and likely to spread in the general region.
3b. First glume acute or acuminate; sheaths pubescent . . . . (4)

4a. Upper floret with a crescent-shaped mark at the base; palea of lower floret present. **P. hillmanii** Chase [for F. H. Hillman, 1863-1954, American agriculturist]. Lower Arkansas Valley, BA, PR.
4b. Upper floret lacking a crescent-shaped mark; palea of lower floret lacking. **P. capillare** L., WITCHGRASS. Very common weed in disturbed ground, roadsides, and gardens.

5a. Bunchgrasses lacking rhizomes or stolons. **P. hallii** Vasey
5b. Plants with rhizomes or stolons . . . . (6)

6a. Plants strongly stoloniferous; panicle narrow; plants not forming tall, dense stands. **P. obtusum** Humboldt, Bonpland & Kunth, VINE-MESQUITE. Rocky slopes of Mesa de Maya, LA-BA.
6b. Plants rhizomatous, not stoloniferous; panicles open; plants forming tall dense stands. **P. virgatum** L., SWITCHGRASS. Common moist prairie soils on the plains, one of the dominant grasses of the relictual tall-grass prairie.

PASCOPYRUM Löve 1980 [Latin, *pascuum*, pasture, + Greek, *pyros*, wheat] (formerly *Agropyron*). WESTERN WHEATGRASS

One species, **P. smithii** (Rydberg) Löve [for J. G. Smith, USDA botanist]. Abundant, glaucous, rhizomatous plant of dry flats and grasslands. Two races occur, var. **smithii** with glabrous spikelets, and var. **molle** with hairy spikelets. Very easily recognized once one masters the subtlety of the glume shape, in this species tapering from base of apex.

PASPALUM L. 1753 [Greek, *paspale*, meal]

1a. Spikelets suborbicular, 1.8-2.4 mm long. **P. setaceum** Michaux var. **stramineum** (Nash) D. Banks. Sandy soil in the easternmost plains counties.
1b. Spikelets either larger or not suborbicular. **P. pubiflorum** Ruprecht var. **glabrum** Vasey. An infrequent lawn weed in the Boulder area.

PHALARIS L. 1753 [the ancient Greek name]. CANARYGRASS

1a. Glumes wingless or nearly so. **P. caroliniana** Walter. Adventive? A few old records from the lower Arkansas Valley.
1b. Glumes distinctly winged . . . . (2)

2a. Wing of glume raggedly toothed. **P. minor** Retzius. Adventive, one record from LR.

2b. Wing of glume entire. **P. canariensis** L. Adventive, volunteering from "canary" seed dropped around feeders, etc.

PHALAROIDES Wolf 1781 [diminutive of ancient Greek name for some grass]. REED CANARYGRASS

One species, **P. arundinacea** (L.) Rauschert [reedlike]. Adventive, abundant along irrigation ditches and wet meadows, lower valleys (*Phalaris*). The seed was a common ingredient of birdseed mixes, but has been replaced now mostly by species of *Panicum*.

PHIPPSIA R. Brown 1823 [for Constantine John Phipps, second Baron Mulgrave, eighteenth-century Arctic voyager]

One species, **P. algida** (Phipps) R. Brown [cold]. Restricted to cold gravels of snowmelt streamlets fed by snowfields of glacial cirques, usually over 12,000 feet. The culms are very low and spreading, 1-3 cm high, and the foliage somewhat succulent. The leaf blades are very short and have a boat-tip as in *Poa*.

PHLEUM L. 1753 [Greek, *phleos*, name for some marsh reed]. TIMOTHY

1a. Panicle oblong to ovoid, less than 5 times as long as wide; base of culm not bulbous; upper sheaths inflated (loose). **P. commutatum** Gaudin [altered], ALPINE TIMOTHY, **86D**. Common in subalpine meadows (*P. alpinum* is an exclusively European species).

1b. Panicle cylindrical, over 6 times as long as wide; culm base swollen or bulbous; sheaths tight. **P. pratense** L. [of meadows]. Adventive along roadsides and trails, meadows and pastures.

PHRAGMITES Adanson 1763 [ancient Greek name meaning growing in hedges]. COMMON REED

One species, **P. australis** (Cavanilles) Trinius. Locally abundant and forming great stands along rivers and in irrigation ditches in the lower valleys. The stout culms were used to make arrowshafts. Occasional populations have spikelets that are without floral parts within the glumes and lemmas; in such plants, reproduction must be purely vegetative (*P. communis*).

POA L. 1753 [ancient Greek name for grass or fodder]. BLUEGRASS

Note: A difficult genus of variable and often hybridizing species, many forming partly or wholly apomictic populations. The following key will not always work, but should be useful most of the time.

1a. Annual (**Key A, Annuae**)

1b. Perennial . . . . (2)

2a. Rhizomes present and well developed; plants not forming tight clumps (**Key B, Pratenses**)

2b. Rhizomes lacking; plants forming tight clumps (although occasionally the culms are decumbent, rooting at the lower nodes) . . . . (3)

3a. Lemma with a weft of wavy hairs at the base (sometimes scanty in *P. nemoralis*) (**Key C, Palustres**)

3b. Lemma lacking a weft of wavy hairs at the base (sometimes sparsely so in *P. abbreviata*) . . . . (4)

4a. Spikelets flattened; glumes and lemmas keeled (**Key D, Alpinae**)

4b. Spikelets rounded, the glumes not keeled, or only obscurely so at the tip (**Key E, Scabrellae**)

KEY A. (Annuae)

1a. Culms erect, bulbous at the base; flowers proliferated into asexual bulblets with short leafy shoots. **P. bulbosa** L., BULBOUS BLUEGRASS. Adventive. Commonly cultivated and spreading in dry land.
1b. Culms low, spreading, succulent, not bulbous; culms not proliferous . . (2)

2a. Panicle branches, at least the lowermost, spreading; sheaths glabrous. **P. annua** L. Adventive, weedy species in poorly drained lawns, meadows, along wet trails and clearings.
2b. Panicle branches erect, the inflorescence narrow; sheaths scabrous. **P. bigelovii** Vasey & Scribner. One record, from Colorado Springs.

KEY B. (Pratenses)

1a. Culm flattened and 2-edged; exposed nodes marked by a prominent black line; sheaths often paler than the culm. **P. compressa** L., CANADA BLUEGRASS. Common on dry hillsides, a native species, possibly distinct from its Old World counterpart.
1b. Culm not flattened . . . . (2)

2a. Panicle contracted, branches stiffly ascending to erect . . . . (3)
2b. Panicle open, branches spreading or reflexed . . . . (4)

3a. Lemmas rather short and broad, mostly less than 4 mm long, usually more than 1/5 as broad as long viewed from the side. **P. arida** Vasey, PLAINS BLUEGRASS. Alkaline flats on the plains.
3b. Lemmas elongate, slender, mostly over 4 mm long, usually less than 1/5 as broad as long. **P. glaucifolia** Scribner & Williams. (*P. ampla*).

4a. Lemmas with long, crinkly hairs at the base . . . . (5)
4b. Lemmas without long, crinkly basal hairs . . . . (7)

5a. Ligule on culm leaves 2-4 mm long, obtuse or truncate; lemmas 3.5-5.5 mm long. **P. arctica** R. Brown. Common on tundra but sometimes doing well along subalpine roadsides (*P. grayana*, *P. longipila*).
5b. Ligule on culm leaves 1 mm long, truncate; lemmas 2-3 mm long . . . (6)

6a. Basal leaves bright green, 2-3 mm broad, flat or channeled, withering and disintegrating after a season; spikelets mostly 3-flowered; lowest lemma very cobwebby at base. **P. pratensis** L., KENTUCKY BLUEGRASS. Adventive. Widely used for lawns and pasture mixes, always in wet sites in natural habitats.
6b. Basal leaves glaucous, 0.8-2 mm broad, folded and somewhat revolute, remaining intact through the next season; spikelets mostly 2-flowered; lemma only slightly cobwebby. **P. agassizensis** Boivin & Löve. The native counterpart of the last, common in dry, open forests.

7a. Lower sheaths minutely retrorse-hairy and purplish; spikelets commonly purplish. **P. nervosa** (Hooker) Vasey. Common in forests and meadows, montane, subalpine.
7b. Lower sheaths smooth, green. **P. arctica** R. Brown. Upper subalpine and alpine.

KEY C. (Palustres)

1a. Panicle nodding, open, with flexuous capillary branches; blades short, flat, up to 4 mm wide; anthers 0.4-0.9 mm long . . . . (2)

1b. Panicle not nodding nor with flexuous branches . . . . (3)

2a. Glumes very unequal, the lower ones often ± subulate; lemma 3-4 mm long, acuminate, the nerves pilose to glabrate. **P. leptocoma** Trinius. Springs and marshy subalpine forests.

2b. Glumes subequal, the lower similar to the upper; lemma 2-3 mm long, acute, the nerves pilose. **P. reflexa** Vasey & Scribner. Similar habitats, very common.

3a. Culms 5-12 dm high, loosely tufted; ligule 1.5 mm long or more; panicle pyramidal, 15-30 cm long; moist habitats . . . . (4)

3b. Culms 2-5 dm high, densely tufted, stiff; ligule 0.5-1.5 mm long; panicle 5-15 cm long with short, ascending branches; lemma sometimes only scantily cobwebby. **P. nemoralis** L. subsp. **interior** (Rydberg) Butters & Abbe. Common on rocky outcrops and mountain slopes. The short culm blade stands out stiffly at a wide angle from the stem, a good field character.

4a. Ligule 1.5-3 mm long; blades 3-7 mm wide; lemma 3-5 mm long; anthers 1.8-3 mm long. **P. tracyi** Vasey. Forest openings, montane, subalpine. The tall stature and wide blades are distinctive.

4b. Ligule 3-5 mm long; blades 1-3 mm wide; lemma 2.4-3 mm long, the tip bronzed. **P. palustris** L. SWAMP BLUEGRASS. Common in wet meadows and swampy woods.

KEY D. (Alpinae)

1a. Lemma pubescent on keel and marginal nerves . . . . (2)

1b. Lemma glabrous or minutely scabrous . . . . (5)

2a. Basal leaves short and broad, 2-4 mm wide; spikelets broad, rounded or almost cordate at the base; new shoots extravaginal (breaking through the base of the enclosing sheath), these thus spreading horizontally. **P. alpina** L. Abundant on tundra and gravelly upper subalpine.

2b. Basal leaves narrow, elongate; spikelets narrow, not broadly rounded at the base; branching intravaginal, these thus erect . . . . (3)

3a. Culms 25 cm or less tall; spikelets 2-3 mm long; panicles narrow and condensed; alpine and subalpine . . . . (4)

3b. Culms usually over 3 dm tall; spikelets 6-8 mm long in a thick, lax panicle; plants dioecious, mostly carpellate; piñon-juniper to timberline. **P. fendleriana** (Steudel) Vasey, MUTTONGRASS. The basal leaf sheaths are long (4-6 cm), papery, and persistent through the next year. This species is apomictic.

4a. Leaves stiffly erect, the sheaths not elongate or papery; inflorescence slender, stiff, the branches distinct; forming tight clumps. **P. glauca** Vahl. Dry sites, subalpine and alpine (*P. rupicola*).

4b. Leaves gracefully curved, the sheaths elongate and papery, to 4-5 cm long, persistent; inflorescence dense but soft and lax; forming loose, spreading clumps. **P. abbreviata** R. Brown subsp. **pattersonii** (Vasey) Löve et al. Wet, alpine, snowbed gravels and frost scars (*P. pattersonii*).

5a. Dwarf alpine 3-10 cm high; spikelets 3-4 mm long; lemmas 2-3 mm long; leaves all alike. **P. lettermanii** Vasey [for George Letterman]. Boulderfields and screes on the highest peaks, usually above 3,500 m.

5b. Up to 30 cm tall; spikelets 5-7.5 mm long; lemmas 4-4.5 mm long; culm leaves with broad (2-3 mm) blades, new shoot leaves filiform; plants almost or quite dioecious. **P. cusickii** Vasey subsp. **epilis** (Scribner) Weber [for W.

C. Cusick, Oregon collector; hairless], SKYLINE BLUEGRASS. Gravelly alpine ridges (*P. epilis*).

KEY E. (Scabrellae)

1a. Tall, loosely clumped to rhizomatous; leaf blades usually ± flat; lemma mostly scabrous or glabrous, or puberulent on the nerves; ligule truncate or obtuse. **P. juncifolia** Scribner. Wet meadows and gulches, lower and middle altitudes (*P. ampla*).
1b. Low, densely caespitose; leaf blades narrow, involute; lemma puberulent at the base, sometimes scabrous or glabrous; ligules long, acute. **P. secunda** Presl. Very common and variable on dry grassland of mountain parks and desert-steppe (*P. canbyi*, *sandbergii*, *gracillima*, *nevadensis*).

POLYPOGON Desfontaines 1798 [Greek, *polys*, much, + *pogon*, beard]. RABBITFOOTGRASS
1a. Perennial with stolons; glumes lacking awns. **P. viridis** (Gouan) Breistr. Adventive, known in Colorado from two old collections, from BA and MZ (*Agrostis, Polypogon semiverticillatus*). Because of the lack of awns, this would usually key to *Agrostis*. In *Agrostis*, however, the spikelet disarticulates above the glumes, while in *Polypogon* the spikelet falls as a unit.
1b. Annual; glumes with very long, conspicuous awns far exceeding the spikelets. **P. monspeliensis** (L.) Desfontaines, RABBITFOOTGRASS, **87F**. Adventive, abundant in wet, often alkaline swales and ditches.

PSATHYROSTACHYS Nevski 1934 [Greek, *psathyros*, shattering, + *stachys*, spike] (formerly in *Elymus*). RUSSIAN WILD RYE

One species, **P. juncea** (Fischer) Nevski. Adventive. Widely cultivated for range stabilization. The brittleness of the rachis is characteristic.

PTILAGROSTIS Grisebach 1852 [Greek, *ptilon*, feather, + *agrostis*, grass]. FEATHERGRASS

One species, **P. porteri** (Rydberg) Weber [for Thomas C. Porter], **88B, Pl. 51**. Endemic along the edges of South Park, usually in peat of willow carrs. A close relative of the Asiatic *P. mongholica*.

PUCCINELLIA Parlatore 1848 [for Benedetto Puccinelli, Italian botanist, 1808-1850]. ALKALIGRASS
1a. Lower panicle branches becoming reflexed at maturity; lemma 1.5-2 mm long; first glume less than 1.5 mm long; ligule usually less than 1.5 mm long. **P. distans** (L.) Parlatore. Alkaline flats and pond margins. Adventive. Probably impossible to distinguish from the native species.
1b. Lower panicle branches spreading or ascending but rarely reflexed; lemma 2-3 mm long; first glume about 1.5 mm long; ligule usually over 1.5 mm long. **P. airoides** (Nuttall) Watson & Coulter [like the genus *Aira*]. Similar habitats (*P. nuttalliana*).

REDFIELDIA Vasey 1887 [for J. H. Redfield, 1815-1895, American botanist]. BLOWOUTGRASS

One species, **R. flexuosa** (Thurber) Vasey. Common on sandhills and dunes on the plains.

SCHEDONNARDUS Steudel 1854 [Greek, *schedon*, almost, + *Nardus*, a genus]. TUMBLEGRASS

One species, **S. paniculatus** (Nuttall) Trelease. Common on the plains and outwash mesas.

SCHIZACHNE Hackel 1909 [Greek, *schizein*, to split, + *achne*, chaff or lemma]. FALSE MELIC

One species, **S. purpurascens** (Torrey) Swallen. Rare or infrequent on deeply shaded forested slopes.

SCHIZACHYRIUM Nees 1829 [Greek, *schizein*, to split, + *achyron*, chaff]. LITTLE BLUESTEM

One species, **S. scoparium** (Michaux) Nash [broomlike]. Common along the outwash mesas, the piedmont valleys [*Andropogon*] and along the Mesa de Maya.

SCLEROPOGON Philippi 1870 [Greek, *sclero*, tough, + *pogon*, beard]. BURRO-GRASS

One species, **S. brevifolius** Philippi. Grasslands of the lower Arkansas Valley. A sod-forming grass covering large areas as low as a carefully mowed golf green. The staminate plants have *Festuca*like spikelets with numerous awnless lemmas, while the carpellate plants have long-awned lemmas, totally different in appearance. Occasionally plants have perfect flowers. This monotypic genus is an example of a plant that occurs native in the American Southwest, then is found again in Argentina and Chile, a bipolar distribution having as yet no clear explanation.

SECALE L. 1753 [classical Latin name for rye]. RYE

One species, **S. cereale** L. Adventive. Widely used as a roadside revegetation plant, very common in LR and North Park, evidently expanding its range on its own.

SETARIA P. Beauvois 1812 [Latin, *seta*, bristle]. FOXTAIL, BRISTLEGRASS

1a. Perennial. **S. leucopila** (Scribner & Merrill) K. Schumann. Rocky slopes, Mesa de Maya and Arkansas Valley near Cañon City.
1b. Annual weeds . . . . (2)

2a. Bristles downwardly barbed; panicle branches distinct. **S. verticiliata** (L.) P. Beauvois. Adventive weed in cultivated ground and roadsides, lower Colorado River Valley.
2b. Bristles upwardly barbed; panicle branches crowded into a dense spike (3)

3a. Fertile lemmas strongly transversely wrinkled, 5-16 bristles below each spikelet; ripe spikelets yellowish, about 3 mm long. **S. glauca** (L.) P. Beauvois. Adventive, common weed in cultivated ground.
3b. Fertile lemma only faintly wrinkled, 1-3 bristles below each spikelet; second glume about as long as the spikelet; ripe spikelets green. **S. viridis** (L.) P. Beauvois. Adventive, similar sites.

SORGHASTRUM Nash 1901 [*Sorghum*, + *astrum*, resembling]. INDIANGRASS

One species, **S. avenaceum** (Michaux) Nash. A relatively infrequent or at least not dominant plant of the tall-grass prairie remnants, and one of the most beautiful of our grasses, with its ample panicles of silky, golden-brown spikelets.

SORGHUM Moench 1794 [the ancient oriental name]

One species, **S. halepense** (L.) Persoon, JOHNSONGRASS. An infrequent weed of roadsides, escaping from cultivation as a forage grass. This species is perennial, whereas the cultivated *Sorghum vulgare* Persoon (broom-corn, sudan-grass, grain sorghum, kaffir-corn) is annual.

SPARTINA Schreber 1789 [Greek, *spartine*, a cord]. CORDGRASS

1a. Blades usually more than 5 mm wide, flat, at least at the base, when fresh, the tip involute; plants very robust, more than 1 m tall. **S. pectinata** Link [comblike], PRAIRIE CORDGRASS. A tall grass of sloughs and irrigation ditches on the plains, with large, brushlike spikes and long, curved leaves.
1b. Blades less than 5 mm wide, rarely wider, involute or flat; plants slender and less than 1 m tall. **S. gracilis** Trinius, ALKALINE CORDGRASS. Alkaline flats and sloughs on the plains.

SPHENOPHOLIS Scribner 1906 [Greek, *sphen*, wedge, + *pholis*, scale]. WEDGE-SCALE

One species, **S. obtusata** (Michaux) Scribner. Moist woodlands and gulches, scattered through the foothills and montane. Somewhat resembling *Poa* except for the very unequal glumes, one much wider than the other.

SPOROBOLUS R. Brown [Greek, *spora*, seed, + *ballein*, to throw]. DROPSEED

1a. Annual. **S. neglectus** Nash. Infrequent, scattered on the plains, usually in moist depressions, BA, MR, PW.
1b. Perennial . . . . (2)

2a. Panicle with the branches spreading at maturity (the lower portion may be prevented from spreading by the surrounding leaf sheaths) . . . . (3)
2b. Panicle with appressed branches . . . . (6)

3a. Spikelets large, the first glume usually over 2 mm long, the second over 3 mm, lemma over 3 mm long; leaf blades folded in the bud. **S. heterolepis** (Gray) Gray, PRAIRIE DROPSEED. Locally abundant in tall-grass prairie remnants at the base of the Front Range. The leaves are mostly basal, very narrow, but the sheaths are broad and papery.
3b. Spikelets and their parts smaller; leaf blades rolled in the bud . . . . . (4)

4a. Panicle branches seldom more than 3 cm long, with crowded, appressed spikelets; collar of leaf sheaths densely spreading-pilose; much of the panicle often hidden in the upper leaf sheaths. **S. cryptandrus** (Torrey) Gray. Common on roadsides and dry grassland. The plants do not form massive clumps.
4b. Panicle branches longer, the spikelets not densely crowded; collar of leaf sheaths not conspicuously long-hairy; panicles large and very open . . . (5)

5a. Pedicels of the individual spikelets over 5 mm long. **S. texanus** Vasey. A few records from the lower Arkansas Valley. This and the next form massive clumps on alkaline flats.
5b. Pedicels 5 mm long or less. **S. airoides** (Torrey) Torrey, ALKALINE SACATON. Very common on alkaline flats on the plains and San Luis Valley.

6a. Panicles usually less than 10 cm long, mostly included in the subtending sheath; leaf sheaths not conspicuously hairy at corners; spikelets reddish. **S. asper** (Michaux) Kunth [harsh]. Less frequent than the similar *S. cryptandrus*, in the piedmont valleys and outwash mesas.
6b. Panicles elongate, 15-30 cm long; coarse caespitose perennials; sheaths with conspicuous tufts of hair at the corners; spikelets pale green or whitish (7)

7a. Culms robust, 1-2 m tall; lower culms 2-7 mm wide at the base; panicle thick, more than 8 mm wide. **S. giganteus** Nash. Known in Colorado only from the southeast corner, on sand dunes.

7b. Culms slender, less than 1 m tall; culms narrower. **S. contractus** A. S. Hitchcock. Frequent in the San Luis Valley.

STIPA L. 1753 [Greek, *stype*, tow, as unraveled fibers]. NEEDLEGRASS

1a. Lemma densely covered with long hairs; panicle wide-spreading at maturity; awn short, deciduous. **S. hymenoides** Roemer & Schultes [membranous, referring to the thin glumes], INDIAN RICEGRASS, **87E**. An attractive bunchgrass of shale or clay soil in the desert-steppe. The seeds were used extensively by native Americans for food. Occasionally, first generation hybrids are formed by crossing with any of several *Stipa* species, resulting in plants with longer awns and narrower inflorescences; these had been referred to as *X Stiporyzopsis bloomeri*.
1b. Lemma glabrous or covered with short, appressed hairs; awn persistent (2)

2a. Terminal segment of the awn plumose; glumes 3-6 cm long. **S. neomexicana** (Thurber) Scribner. Frequent in rocky places along the base of the Front Range.
2b. Terminal segment of the awn not plumose . . . . (3)

3a. Apex of lemma densely pilose with white hairs 2-5 mm long; awn 11-22 mm long, persistent, bent and twisted. **S. pinetorum** Jones. Pine forests, foothills.
3b. Apex of lemma smooth or, if hairy, the hairs less than 2 mm long . . (4)

4a. Glumes more than 14 mm long; body of the lemma over 7 mm long; awns over 4 cm long . . . . (5)
4b. Glumes, lemmas, and awns shorter . . . . (6)

5a. Lemma 10-15 mm long; most glumes under 3 cm long. **S. comata** Trinius & Ruprecht [maned], NEEDLE-AND-THREAD. Abundant in grasslands; a beautiful grass easily distinguished from a distance because of the very long awns that tend to droop away from the wind.
5b. Body of lemma over 16 mm long; most glumes over 3 cm long. **S. spartea** Trinius [Greek, *spartos*, broom]. Rare and local in relictual tall-grass prairie along the base of the Front Range.

6a. Panicle with divaricately spreading branches, each with a few spikelets near the end. **S. richardsonii** Link [for Sir John Richardson, of the Franklin expeditions]. Open lodgepole forests and gravelly, dry meadows, JA, LK.
6b. Panicle with ascending branches . . . . (7)

7a. Sheaths, at least the lower, velvety-pubescent. **S. williamsii** Scribner [for T. A. Williams, 1865-1900, professor at South Dakota State College]. Rare or overlooked, montane meadows, BL. Some authors feel that this is merely a trivial form of *S. nelsonii*.
7b. Sheaths glabrous or scabrous or sparsely pubescent near the collar . . (8)

8a. Leaf sheath with a tuft of hairs at the throat . . . . (9)
8b. Leaf sheath not villous at the throat, margins not ciliate; lemma usually less than 6 mm long . . . . (11)

9a. Hairs at lemma apex over 2 mm long; awn less than 2 cm long; glumes 10-15 mm long. **S. scribneri** Vasey [for C. Lamson-Scribner, 1851-1938, American grass specialist]. Frequent in the Front Range foothills and Mesa de Maya.

9b. Hairs at lemma apex less than 2 mm long; awns over 2 cm long; glumes 7-11 mm long . . . . (10)

10a. Palea 1.0-2.5 mm long, elliptical (3:1), hyaline, the apex acute, glabrous; panicle relatively narrow. **S. viridula** Trinius. Frequent, tall, roadside grass on the piedmont and plains.

10b. Palea 3.5-5.0 mm long, oblong (5:1), the apex truncate, ciliate; panicle usually very dense and broad. **S. robusta** (Vasey) Scribner, SLEEPYGRASS. More common than the above in the southern counties and the San Luis Valley.

11a. Awn 1-5 cm long; leaves not tightly involute, often flat, 2-5 mm wide. **S. nelsonii** Scribner. Common in dry, montane forests (*S. columbiana*).

11b. Awn 1-2 cm long; leaves tightly involute and filiform. **S. lettermanii** Vasey [for George Letterman]. Similar but usually drier habitats.

TORREYOCHLOA Church 1949 [for John Torrey, 1796-1873, pioneer American botanist]. WEAK MANNAGRASS

One species, **T. pauciflora** (Presl) Church [few-flowered]. Margins of subalpine ponds *(Glyceria)*.

TRIDENS Roemer & Schultes 1817 [Latin, *tres,* three, + *dens*, tooth, alluding to the tip of the lemma]

One species, **T. muticus** (Torrey) Nash var. **elongatus** (Buckley) Shinners. Dry hillsides, lower Arkansas Valley, PE-BA. An occurrence in BL probably came in with range reseeding.

TRIPLASIS P. Beauvois 1812 [Greek, *triplasios*, trifarious, alluding to the lemma tip]. SANDGRASS

One species, **T. purpurea** (Walter) Chapman. Sand dunes and blowouts in the easternmost plains counties.

TRISETUM Persoon 1805 [Latin, *tres*, three, + *seta*, bristle, alluding to the awn and 2 teeth of the lemma]

1a. Awn minute, included within the glumes or sometimes lacking. **T. wolfii** Vasey [for John Wolf]. Infrequent, usually with solitary stems intermixed with other tall marsh grasses, along the borders of swamps and ponds, subalpine. Once learned, this is easily recognized, but being nondescript it is overlooked and commonly misidentified.

1b. Awn large, exserted, divergent . . . . (2)

2a. Panicle dense, thick, often purple; culms densely pilose to nearly tomentose below the panicle. **T. spicatum** (L.) Richter subsp. **congdonii** (Scribner & Merrill) Hultén [for Joseph W. Congdon, 1834-1910, California collector]. Upper subalpine and alpine.

2b. Panicle slender, greenish-straw-colored, rarely with purple tinge; culms almost or quite glabrous below the panicle. **T. spicatum** subsp. **molle** (Michaux) Hultén. At lower altitudes, usually in forested areas. This is a very complicated species, worldwide in distribution, of which the above are two distinguishable races in our area (including subsp. *majus, montanum*). Nevertheless, there are occasional intermediates.

TRITICUM L. 1753 [classical name for wheat]. WHEAT

One species, **T. aestivum** L. [of summer]. Adventive. Many varieties are cultivated, and plants frequently volunteer, surviving for a season along roadsides and trails.

VAHLODEA Fries 1842 [for Martin Vahl, 1749-1804, Danish botanist]

One species, **V. atropurpurea** (Wahlenberg) Fries subsp. **latifolia** (Hooker) Porsild. Subalpine meadows and on soil of ledges in rocky gorges. The spikelets are usually dark purple, but a pale albino phase occurs (*Deschampsia*).

VULPIA Gmelin 1805 [Latin, *vulpes*, fox]. SIXWEEKS FESCUE

One species, **V. octoflora** (Walter) Rydberg. Spikelets with 7 or more florets (some early-flowering, smaller plants may have fewer); leaves short, some less than 5 cm long. Abundant winter annual of early spring in disturbed soil at low altitudes on the plains, turning brown when ripe (*Festuca*).

POLEMONIACEAE PHLOX FAMILY (PLM)

The phlox family provides many of the characteristic wildflowers of the Eastern Slope. They range from extremely dainty and inconspicuous ephemerals (*Gymnosteris*) to showy perennials (*Phlox* and *Ipomopsis*), from desert plants to alpine tundra species. The flowers characteristically have a narrow tube suddenly flaring to 5 wide-spreading lobes and 3 styles. Many species are potential rock garden ornamentals.

1a. Annuals, never with a rosette of basal leaves . . . . (2)
1b. Biennials or perennials, or if winter annual (*Ipomopsis pumila*), then often with rosettes of basal leaves . . . . (6)

2a. Stems leafless except for a few leaflike bracts subtending a flower cluster; plants minute, only 1-2 cm tall, with exceedingly slender stems. **Gymnosteris**
2b. Leaves scattered along the stem . . . . (3)

3a. Leaves divided . . . . (4)
3b. Leaves simple, undivided . . . . (5)

4a. Flowers large, over 5 mm long, tubular; leaves pinnately divided, the leaf divisions linear but not stiff or needlelike. **Ipomopsis**
4b. Flowers minute (a few mm long); leaves palmately divided to the base into needlelike segments . . . . (5)

5a. Leaves stiff, needlelike, sharp-pointed; flowers blue. **Navarretia**
5b. Leaves with linear divisions, but not at all stiff; flowers white. **Linanthus**

6a. Leaves elliptic, obtuse; flowers solitary in the leaf axils. **Microsteris**
6a. Leaves lanceolate or linear . . . . (7)

7a. Leaves narrowly linear; extremely delicate and inconspicuous annual with minute white flowers solitary at the branch tips. **Gilia sinistra**
7b. Leaves lanceolate; fairly stout; flowers in dense clusters surrounded by enlarged bracts. **Collomia**

8a. Leaves simple and entire, opposite. **Phlox**
8b. Leaves variously divided or compound, alternate or opposite . . . . (9)

9a. Leaves pinnately compound with distinct leaflets. **Polemonium**, JACOB'S LADDER, SKY PILOT
9b. Leaves pinnately lobed or dissected, or palmatifid . . . . (10)

10a. Leaves palmatifid, so deeply as to appear simple . . . . (11)
10b. Leaves pinnately lobed or dissected . . . . (13)

11a. Leaves soft-textured, appearing whorled; flowers white, long-tubular, open in daytime. **Linanthastrum**

11b. Leaves needlelike, sharp-pointed, not in whorls; flowers, if white, open only in evening and early morning . . . . (12)

12a. Flowers rotate, deep blue; anthers bright orange. **Giliastrum**, PRICKLY GILIA

12b. Flowers white or cream-color. **Leptodactylon**, PRICKLY GILIA

13a. Flowers with a tube but lacking a differentiated wider limb; upper parts of stem clothed with well-developed leaves; seeds large, usually oblong and slightly curved. **Ipomopsis**, GILIA

13b. Flowers with a tube and a slightly expanded limb; upper part of stem with reduced leaves, the flowering portion essentially leafless; seeds small, spheroidal. **Gilia**

COLLOMIA Nuttall 1818 [Greek, *colla*, gluten, from the mucilaginous seeds]

One species, **C. linearis** Nuttall, **89E**. Common in a variety of habitats, foothills and montane. Flowers pink, inconspicuous, in a dense terminal cluster, surrounded by enlarged, leaflike bracts.

GILIA Ruiz & Pavon 1794 [for Felipe Gil, eighteenth-century Spanish botanist] (Key written with help from Dr. Alva Day.)

1a. Delicate annual lacking a basal rosette, branched from near the base; leaves simple; stems covered with dark glandular hairs; corolla pink. **Gilia sinistra** Jones [on the left hand, the allusion unexplained]. Sagebrush stands, to be expected in western North Park (*G. capillaris*, incorrectly). Disjunct from southern Idaho.

1b. Annual, biennial, or perennial, with a rosette of basal leaves . . . . . . (2)

2a. Anthers distinctly exserted. **G. pinnatifida** Nuttall. Gravelly and sandy soils, usually with little other competing vegetation, very common in the foothills and montane, also on the plains in suitable habitats (*G. calcarea* of Colorado literature).

2b. Anthers not protruding beyond the corolla tube. **G. ophthalmoides** Brand. Gravelly benches and outer foothills of the Front Range and Mesa de Maya.

GILIASTRUM. PRICKLY GILIA

One species, **G. rigidulum** (Bentham) Rydberg subsp. **acerosum** (Gray) Weber. Common on rocky benches along the lower Arkansas River and its tributaries, southeastern counties. The bright blue, rotate corolla and needlelike leaves are unique (*Gilia*).

GYMNOSTERIS Greene 1898 [Greek, *gymnos*, naked, + *sterizo*, support, alluding to the naked stems]

One species, **G. parvula** Heller, **89C**. A very inconspicuous and ephemeral spring flower in sagebrush meadows at middle altitudes, JA, LR. The slender stem is naked, only a few cm tall; the leaves and tiny flowers are clustered at the branch tips.

IPOMOPSIS Michaux 1803 [resembling *Ipomoea*]. GILIA

(Key based on recent published work by Verne Grand and Dieter Wilken.)

1a. Corolla short-tubular . . . . (2)

1b. Corolla with long tube, well over 1 cm long . . . . (8)

2a. Ephemeral annual; flowers in terminal heads; plants usually less than 2 dm tall. **I. pumila** (Nuttall) Grant. Clay soils in the lower Arkansas Valley. Stems ascending, branched from the base, leafy; anthers exserted; corolla 5-9 mm long; styles hairy at the base.

2b. Biennial or perennial . . . . (3)

3a. Flowers cream-colored, crowded in a dense spike; plant sticky-glandular. **I. spicata** (Nuttall) V. Grant, SPIKE GILIA. A common early spring flower on dry slopes in the outer foothills, outwash mesas, and rocky outcrops on the plains.

3b. Flowers white or purplish, in capitate clusters; plant not sticky-glandular; plants of the mountains and intermountain parks . . . . (4)

4a. Inflorescence a terminal capitate, woolly hairy ball over 1 cm diameter; flowers pale purple; strictly alpine. **I. globularis** (Brand) Weber. Endemic in the Hoosier Pass area, one old record allegedly from Mount Elbert. One of the most handsome alpine tundra plants, with a heavy fragrance.

4b. Inflorescence terminal, capitate, less than 1 cm diameter, not particularly villous; flowers white; lower altitudes. **I. congesta** (Hooker) Grant. Several races occur, the most common being var. **congesta** with trifid to pinnatisect arachnoid leaves and strictly herbaceous stems. Plants with woody lower stems and mostly entire leaves belong to subsp. **frutescens** (Rydberg) Day.

5a. Annual; flowers white . . . . (6)

5b. Biennial or perennial; flowers purplish to scarlet, infrequently white or intermediate in color . . . . (7)

6a. Corolla over 3 cm long. **I. longiflora** (Torrey) V. Grant. Common in sandy places on the plains, also common in the San Luis Valley.

6b. Corolla less than 3 cm long. **I. laxiflora** (Coulter) V. Grant. Common in sandy places on the plains and upper Arkansas River near Salida, evidently absent from the San Luis Valley.

7a. Corolla about 1 cm long, purplish; stamens well exserted; leaves simple or trifid. **I. multiflora** (Nuttall) V. Grant. A New Mexican species, known in Colorado from a single collection, CN. Somewhat resembling *Gilia pinnatifida*, but the plant with well-developed, elongate caudices and less-divided leaves.

7b. Corolla several cm long, white, pink, purplish, to scarlet . . . . (8)

8a. Corolla various shades of red, mostly scarlet, but also pink, pinkish-red, magenta, or salmon; corolla trumpet-shaped with a flaring tube; flowers odorless (except subsp. *attenuata*) . . . . (9)

8b. Corolla various colors including red but only rarely the latter; corolla salverform with a nonflaring tube; flowers usually fragrant . . . . (10)

9a. All but one anther included; corolla tube 1.5 mm or more wide at the base, the orifice 3-4 mm diameter; calyx lobes 1-2 mm long. **I. aggregata** (Pursh) V. Grant subsp. **collina** (Greene) Wilken & Allard. Abundant in the Front Range foothills south of the Boulder region.

9b. Most anthers close to the orifice, slightly exserted to slightly included; corolla tube filiform, ca. 1 mm wide at base and flaring gently to a narrow orifice 2-3 mm diameter. **I. aggregata** (Pursh) V. Grant subsp. **attenuata** (Gray) V. & A. Grant. Common in North Park.

10a. Corolla tube filiform, 10-22 mm long; highest anther at the orifice. **I. aggregata** (Pursh) V. Grant subsp. **weberi** Grant & Wilken. Endemic, Rabbit Ears Pass.

10b. Corolla tube narrow but not filiform, 19-45 mm long; highest anther included in the tube. **I. aggregata** (Pursh) V. Grant subsp. **candida** (Rydberg) V. & A. Grant. This is the common white-flowered race in the outer foothills of the northern Front Range. It hybridizes extensively with subsp. *collina*.

LEPTODACTYLON Hooker & Arnott 1839 [Greek, *lepto*, slender, + *daktylos*, finger]. PRICKLY GILIA

1a. Flowers 5-merous; plants forming elongated, loosely asymmetrical stems. **L. pungens** (Torrey) Nuttall, **89F**. Very widely distributed in arid grasslands and sagebrush, from the plains to the intermountain parks.

1b. Flowers usually 4-merous, forming dense, symmetrical clumps with crowded leaves. **L. caespitosum** Nuttall. Uncommon on sandstone outcrops, Pawnee Buttes and Mesa de Maya.

LINANTHASTRUM Ewan 1942 [related to *Linanthus*]

One species, **L. nuttallii** (Gray) Ewan. A stout perennial growing in many-stemmed clumps. The flowers are large, salverform. Open, gravelly slopes, upper montane to subalpine. Locally abundant but scattered, Rabbit Ears, Tennessee, and Fremont passes and western CN (*Linanthus*).

LINANTHUS Bentham 1833 [from the genus *Linum*, + Greek, *anthos*, flower, alluding to the resemblance of the flowers of some species to those of *Linum*]

One species, **L. harknessii** (Curran) Greene var. **septentrionalis** (Mason) Jepson & Bailey [for H. W. Harkness, 1821-1901, California botanist; northern], **89D**. Undoubtedly present in North Park but very easily overlooked. An extremely delicate annual with filiform stems and leaves, and minute flowers, in sagebrush and oak brush. The leaves are so deeply divided that the impression is given of whorls of leaves.

MICROSTERIS Greene 1898 [Greek, *micro*, small, + *sterizo*, stem]

One species, **M. gracilis** (Hooker) Greene, **89A**. Very common but inconspicuous, weedy annual of the northern plains, LR, WL, as well as sagebrush and oak zone, flowering in early spring, and almost always to be found together with *Collinsia*.

NAVARRETIA Ruiz & Pavon 1794 [for Francisco Fernando Navarrete, Spanish botanist-physician]

One species, **N. minima** Nuttall, **89B**. Adventive on the Eastern Slope, known from one collection in a cattle-wallow near Boulder. Flowers lavender; capsules 2-locular, indehiscent or irregularly dehiscent by disintegration of the lower lateral walls.

PHLOX L. 1753 [Greek word for flame; an ancient name for *Lychnis*]

1a. Cushionlike or densely caespitose; leaves crowded . . . . (2)

1b. Loosely branched or matted; leaves not crowded . . . . (5)

2a. Alpine tundra plants; leaves often ciliate but not cobwebby-woolly . . . (3)

2b. Desert-steppe or plains plants; leaves not ciliate but usually somewhat cobwebby-woolly . . . . (4)

3a. Tightly cushioned; leaves short (5 mm), erect; flowers white, tube 7 mm, lobes 3 mm long. **P. condensata** (Gray) Nelson. Common near the Continental Divide, S counties.

3b. Cushions loose; leaves more spreading, over 1 cm long; flowers usually colored, tube 11-12 mm, lobes 5 mm long. **P. pulvinata** Wherry. Near Continental Divide, northern counties (*P. sibirica* subsp. *pulvinata*).

4a. Leaves densely woolly near their bases, less than 5 mm long, scalelike, closely overlapping. **P. bryoides** Nuttall [mosslike]. Common in rocky sites on the plains and outer foothills, LR, WL. Depressed forms of *P. hoodii* may be difficult to separate, but in that the leaves are always somewhat spreading and the tips are more strongly apiculate.

4b. Leaves only slightly cobwebby, usually more than 5 mm long, ascending, not closely appressed. **P. hoodii** Richardson subsp. **canescens** (Torrey & Gray) Wherry [for a companion of Richardson on the voyage to find the Northwest Passage]. Very common throughout, in sagebrush and grasslands.

5a. Stems solitary or a few together, never forming mats; leaves usually over 2.5 cm long; flowers distinctly pedicelled. **P. longifolia** Nuttall. Dry grasslands and sagebrush, lower Arkansas Valley drainage; North Park.

5b. Stems numerous from a stout taproot, forming mats; leaves less than 2 cm long; flowers without obvious pedicels . . . . (6)

6a. Leaves strongly glandular-pubescent; leaves narrow, curved outward, very sharp-pointed. **P. austromontana** Coville. One collection from the eastern foothills of the San Juans, in CN. The identification is tentative.

6b. Leaves not at all glandular . . . . (7)

7a. Leaves very short and broad, imbricate, prominently ciliate along the sides and with a prominent cartilaginous margin. **P. kelseyi** Britton subsp. **salina** (Jones) Wherry, **Pl. 49**. Rare and local, on sedge hummocks in alkaline flats in South Park.

7b. Leaves not especially short or imbricate, nor prominently ciliate; not found in alkaline soils . . . . (8)

8a. Inflorescence, especially calyx, clothed with long crinkly hairs; flowers always white. **P. andicola** Nuttall. Common on sandhills on the plains.

8b. Inflorescence glabrous or ± pubescent, but not as above. **P. multiflora** Nelson. Common in forested areas from the foothills to the montane, also in intermountain parks.

POLEMONIUM L. 1753 [ancient name, possibly commemorating Polemon, Athenian philosopher, or from Greek, *polemos*, war]. JACOB'S LADDER, SKY PILOT

1a. Corolla funnelform; leaflets whorled; leaves chiefly basal . . . . (2)

1b. Corolla bell-shaped; leaflets opposite; leaves mostly cauline . . . . (4)

2a. Corolla narrow, 3 times length of calyx, ochroleucous; rockslides in mountain canyons and alpine screes, never on stable tundra. **P. brandegei** (Gray) Greene. Variable flower color (to pale blue) and corolla tube length is the result of introgressive hybridization with the next.

2b. Corolla broadly funnelform, equalling or up to twice as long as calyx, deep blue or purple . . . . (3)

3a. Corolla tubular, little longer than the calyx, deep purple, not strongly flaring at the mouth; anthers yellowish. **P. viscosum** Nuttall. Common on stable alpine tundra. White mutants occur in normal populations.

3b. Corolla tubular-campanulate, twice as long as calyx, light blue, widely flaring at the mouth; anthers orange. **P. confertum** Gray, **Pl. 26**. Endemic, on unstable alpine talus and scree from Mount Evans southwestward (*P. grayanum*). Like *P. brandegei*, this hybridizes with *P. viscosum* where their habitats make contact.

4a. Stems tall, leafy, stiffly erect, solitary or a few together; plants of open sites . . . . (5)

4b. Stems low (less than 3 dm high), spreading, several to many in tufts; plants of shaded forest floors. **P. pulcherrimum** Hooker subsp. **delicatum** (Rydberg) Brand. Dry, open subalpine forests (*P. delicatum*).

5a. Plants from slender rhizomes; leaflets narrow, almost glabrous; inflorescence longer than broad. **P. caeruleum** L. subsp. **amygdalinum** (Wherry) Munz [blue; with almond odor]. Infrequent in mossy, subalpine, birch-willow carrs.

5b. Plants with stout, woody caudices; leaflets broad, pubescent; inflorescence broad, flat-topped. **P. foliosissimum** Gray. Streamsides and mountain meadows.

POLYGALACEAE MILKWORT FAMILY (PGL)

At first glance the *Polygala* flower reminds one of the legumes or the Fumariaceae. The resemblance is only superficial. The flower has 5 sepals, 3 of which are minute, the other 2 large, resembling the wing petals of legumes. Two of the lower petals are united to form a keel, into which the stamens and style are neatly tucked away. The upper 2 petals of the "banner" are longer and very narrow. The stamens are united to the petals and by their filaments into 2 groups. Their 8 anthers are tiny, 1-locular, and each opens by a terminal pore. The ovary is broadly elliptic, flat, and 2-locular. An amazing flower indeed!

POLYGALA L. 1753 [Greek, *polys*, much, + *gala*, milk, a name applied by Dioscorides to a plant reputed to increase lactation]. MILKWORT

One species, **P. alba** Nuttall. Frequent on the plains in the easternmost tier of counties from SE to BA. The stems are simple, several from the base; each produces a raceme of small white flowers. *P. alba* is kin to a number of herbaceous species most common in eastern North America. Our single Western Slope species, *P. subspinosa* resembles more a number of shrublike and often spiny species of Mexico and Central America.

POLYGONACEAE BUCKWHEAT FAMILY (PLG)

This family contains two important food plants, buckwheat (*Fagopyrum esculentum*) and rhubarb (*Rheum rhaponticum*). Rhubarb is known as an escape around old mountain homesteads. The petioles are edible, but the leaves may cause severe poisoning from oxalic acid. The pleasant flavor of the petioles comes from malic acid. Buckwheat is a photosensitizer like *Hypericum*, and white cattle eating too much of it can develop a lethal sunburn. Like the gentians and the saxifrages, taxonomic treatments have always tended to be very conservative. But as early as 1836 Rafinesque pronounced the genus *Polygonum*, which then included *Bistorta*, *Fallopia*, *Persicaria*, *Reynoutria*, and *Truellum*, a complete absurdity. He seems to have had more sense than he has been given credit for. A good earmark of the family (except for *Eriogonum*!) is the sheathing stipule (called ochrea). This is what one strips off when preparing rhubarb petioles; also diagnostic is the unilocular, 3-sided achene.

1a. Herbaceous vines. **Fallopia**, BLACK BINDWEED
1b. Erect or prostrate, herbaceous or woody, but never vines . . . . (2)

2a. Stems covered with retrorse, hooked prickles; leaves sagittate. **Truellum**, TEARTHUMB
2b. Stems not prickly . . . . (3)

3a. Dwarf annuals of wet gravels in tundra, resembling seedlings, red-tinged, with only a few pairs of small oval leaves and minute axillary flowers. **Koenigia**
3b. Not as above . . . . (4)

4a. Flower clusters subtended by campanulate, turbinate, or cylindric involucres of fused bracts . . . . (5)
4b. Flower clusters not subtended by bracts . . . . (6)

5a. Plant with massive taproot and basal rosette of oblanceolate leaves; flowering stem tall, with panicles of dangling yellow flowers; ripe achenes 3-angled and winged. **Pterogonum**, WINGED BUCKWHEAT
5b. Annual, perennial, or shrubby; basal leaves, if present not as above; inflorescence cymose or racemose; achenes not winged. **Eriogonum**, WILD BUCKWHEAT

6a. Tepals 4 or 6, the outer spreading or reflexed, remaining small, the inner usually erect and enlarged in fruit . . . . (7)
6b. Tepals 5, the outer not smaller, usually petallike, white or pink . . . . (9)

7a. Leaf blades lanceolate to ovate, never basally lobed; stout weedy plants. **Rumex**, DOCK
7b. Leaf blades rounded-reniform or basally lobed; low, relatively delicate plants . . . . (8)

8a. Leaves lanceolate, often with basal hastate lobes; flowers mostly unisexual; weed of fallow fields, roadsides, or burned areas. **Acetosella**, SHEEP SORREL
8b. Leaves rounded reniform; flowers mostly perfect; plants of rocky alpine tundra. **Oxyria**, ALPINE SORREL

9a. Huge, weedy herb forming thickets; stem zig-zag; leaves broadly ovate, truncate at the base; flowers in axillary panicles; escaped from cultivation. **Reynoutria**, JAPANESE KNOTWEED
9b. Not as above . . . . (10)

10a. Leaves with a hingelike joint at point of attachment of blade and sheath; flowers in axillary clusters; bracts of the inflorescence with well-developed blades. **Polygonum**, KNOTWEED
10b. Leaves lacking a joint at point of attachment of blade and sheath; flowers in terminal or axillary spikelike racemes; bracts of inflorescence reduced to sheaths . . . . (11)

11a. Rhizome thickened and tuberlike; basal leaves well developed and stem leaves reduced; alpine and subalpine. **Bistorta**, BISTORT
11b. Rhizome, if any, not tuberlike; basal leaves none; plants of various altitudes, mostly wet places at low altitudes. **Persicaria**, SMARTWEED

ACETOSELLA Fourreau 1869 [diminutive of the genus *Acetosa*]. SHEEP SORREL

1a. Slenderly rhizomatous; leaves less than 5 cm long, most of them hastate. **A. vulgaris** (Koch) Fourreau, **90A**. Abundant in disturbed areas and sites of recent fires. The plants turn red when mature; the leaves, with their small, hastate basal lobes, are unique; the flowers are tiny, reddish, in diffuse panicles (*Rumex acetosella*).
1b. Stoutly taprooted; leaves (many basal) over 10 cm long, never hastate. **A. paucifolia** (Nuttall) Löve [few-leaved]. Common in meadows, upper Yampa drainage and possibly on the east base of the Park Range in North Park (*Rumex*).

BISTORTA Adanson 1763 [Latin, *bis*, twice, + *tortus*, twist, alluding to the knotty rhizomes]. BISTORT
1a. Raceme narrowly cylindric, 4-8 mm wide, bearing reproductive blackish bulblets in place of some of the lower flowers. **B. vivipara** (L.) S. Gray (*Polygonum*). Common, subalpine meadows and tundra. *Bistorta* is a small genus of mountain plants common to western North America and Eurasia.
1b. Raceme broadly cylindric or ovoid, not viviparous, 10-20 mm wide; flowers conspicuous, white or pinkish. **B. bistortoides** (Pursh) Small. Subalpine meadows, the spikes of white flowers often dominating the landscape.

ERIOGONUM Michaux 1803 [Greek, *erion*, wool, + *gonu*, knee, from the woolly leaves and swollen joints of the type species]. WILD BUCKWHEAT
1a. Annual, winter annual, or monocarpic, with slender or stout but easily pulled taproot . . . . (2)
1b. Perennial with well-developed, branched root system . . . . (3)

2a. [1] Stem leafy throughout; basal rosette withering early; leaves lanceolate or oval; peduncles erect. **E. annuum** Nuttall. A tall *Eriogonum* with a broad, flat-topped inflorescence, common in sandy soil, outwash mesas and plains. Appears white at a distance.
2b. Stem leafy only at the base, the rosette present at anthesis; leaves oval; peduncles reflexed. **E. cernuum** Nuttall, NODDING BUCKWHEAT. **90C**. Blossoming in midsummer in the outer foothills and all of the intermountain parks.

3a. [1] Flower clusters arranged in a little-branched, elongate raceme. **E. racemosum** Nuttall. Common in the San Luis Valley. Flowers pink; inflorescence scapose; basal leaves ovate, tomentose beneath.
3b. Flower clusters various but never racemose . . . . (4)

4a. [3] Perianth narrowed at the base to a pedicellike stipe . . . . (5)
4b. Perianth not narrowed at the base . . . . (10)

5a. [4] Perianth externally pubescent . . . . (6)
5b. Perianth externally glabrous . . . . (8)

6a. [5] Umbels solitary; flower stems leafless except for the bracts at the base of the umbel; dwarf plants. **E. jamesii** Bentham var. **xanthum** (Small) Reveal (*E. flavum* of Colorado literature). A race with two distinct areas, common on tundra near the Continental Divide and in rocky areas on the northeastern plains (Pawnee Buttes, Fremont Butte, etc.).
6b. Umbels several, peduncled, with a ring of bracts at the base of the peduncles . . . . (7)

7a. [6] Flowers ochroleucous. **E. jamesii** Bentham var. **jamesii.** Common in the southern counties, especially the San Luis Valley, where it almost completely replaces the next.

7b. Flowers yellow. **E. jamesii** Bentham var. **flavescens** Watson. Open woods in the Front Range foothills of the Boulder region, and the eastern foothills of the San Juans, CN.

8a. [5] Flowers ochroleucous or pinkish. **E. subalpinum** Greene. Subalpine meadows and forest openings. Considered by some to be a variety of the next, but in Colorado at least the two are distinct and grow together without mixing.

8b. Flowers bright yellow. **E. umbellatum** Torrey, **Pl. 22**. Very abundant throughout the forested region and composed of rather distinct races, as follows . . . . (9)

9a. [8] Leaves pubescent at least below. **E. umbellatum** var. **umbellatum**. The common race in the lower forested areas.

9b. Leaves glabrous or nearly so on both sides. **E. umbellatum** var. **aureum** (Gandoger) Reveal (including var. *porteri*). More common in the upper altitudes.

10a. [4] Involucres in capitate or umbellate clusters . . . . (11)

10b. Involucres in compound, open cymes . . . . (13)

11a. [10] Perianth externally glabrous. **E. exilifolium** Reveal. Endemic, sagebrush flats of North Park. The leaves are lance-linear on very short shoots, each bearing a solitary, capitate flower cluster on a long scape.

11b. Perianth externally pubescent . . . . (12)

12a. [11] Leaves all basal, the bases blackening and persistent on the short, thick caudices. **E. lachnogynum** Torrey. Common in the lower Arkansas Valley and on the northwest side of the San Luis Valley.

12b. Leaves on short shoots at the base of the scapes; caudices not short nor very thick; leaves not conspicuously persistent. **E. pauciflorum** Pursh var. **gnaphalodes** (Bentham) Reveal. Rocky buttes of the northeastern plains.

13a. [10] Plants shrubby, woody above the caudices and not dying back at the end of the year; flowers white . . . . (14)

13b. Plants herbaceous, dying back to the caudices at the end of the year; flowers white or yellow . . . . (15)

14a. [13] Inflorescence few-branched, not more than 5 cm long. **E. microthecum** Nuttall var. **simpsonii** (Bentham) Reveal [small-fruit; for J. H. Simpson, 1813-1883, engineer and explorer of the West] (var. *foliosum*). Infrequent, never forming dense colonies. Dry slopes along the rim of the San Luis Valley.

14b. Inflorescence much-branched dichotomously, broomlike, well over 5 cm long. **E. effusum** Nuttall. Very common on the plains, outwash mesas, upper Arkansas Valley and San Luis Valley.

15a. [13] Leaves about 1 cm long, oval, white-tomentose, all basal, densely matted; inflorescence slender-branched, the involucres few-flowered, long-peduncled. **E. tenellum** Torrey [delicate]. Common on rocky benches along the lower Arkansas River Valley.

15b. Leaves over 1 cm long, usually many times longer than wide, distributed at short intervals along the lower flowering shoots, appearing ± basal; involucre not as above . . . . (16)

16a. [15] Inflorescence a single, capitate cluster of involucres . . . . (17)
16b. Inflorescence branched; plants often forming a hemispheric mass of floral branches . . . . (18)

17a. [16] Low, less than 10 cm tall; leaves narrow, less than 1 cm wide, green above, white below, revolute. **E. coloradense** Small. Endemic, north end of South Park.
17b. Over 20 cm tall; leaves over 1 cm wide, densely tomentose on both sides, not revolute. **E. brandegei** Rydberg. Endemic, South Park and upper Arkansas Valley.

18a. [16] Flowers yellow. **E. brevicaule** Nuttall. Common on shales, outer foothills, BL, JA, LR.
18b. Flowers white or cream . . . . (19)

19a. [18] Leaves linear, usually strongly revolute; inflorescence forming more than half the plant height. **E. lonchophyllum** Torrey & Gray. Adventive, a Western Slope species, locally established on roadcuts, mouth of Clear Creek Canyon.
19b. Leaves elliptic, the margins finely undulate; inflorescence generally less than half the plant height. **E. fendlerianum** (Bentham) Small. Selenium clay soils in the Arkansas Valley between Pueblo and Cañon City. Some plants suggest that hybridization occurs between this and *E. effusum*.

FALLOPIA Adanson 1763 [not explained but probably honoring Gabriel Fallopius, 1523-1562, Italian anatomist]. BLACK BINDWEED

1a. Woody, perennial vine forming massive growths over fences and walls; flowers white, in large panicles, the sepals strongly winged; leaves not conspicuously cordate-hastate. **F. aubertii** (Henry) Holub [for A. Aubert du Petit-Thouars, 1793-1864, French admiral, circumnavigator of the globe]. Adventive, escaped from cultivation, and locally established in the Boulder-Denver area.
1b. Herbaceous, annual vine with acuminate, cordate-hastate leaves and simple racemes . . . . (2)

2a. Outer sepals keeled but hardly winged in fruit; achene granular, dull. **F. convolvulus** (L.) A. Löve. Adventive, common weed of disturbed sites in and around towns (*Bilderdykia, Polygonum*).
2b. Outer sepals winged in fruit (the keel projecting outward as a membrane); achene smooth and shining. **F. scandens** (L.) Holub. Known from a few old records from near Denver and Colorado Springs.

KOENIGIA L. 1753 [for J. G. König, 1728-1785, Danish botanist]

One species, **K. islandica** L. [of Iceland], **90B**. Infrequent but locally abundant in frost scars and wet gravel on alpine tundra, our only truly alpine annual, with the possible exception of some *Draba* species. The entire plant is only a few mm high. High mountains near the Continental Divide.

OXYRIA Hill 1765 [Greek, *oxys*, sour, as to the leaves]. ALPINE SORREL

One species, **O. digyna** (L.) Hill [with 2 carpels], **90D**. Rock crevices in tundra, rarely in compensating environments in the subalpine. Resembling a dwarf *Rumex*, easily identified by the kidney-shaped leaves.

PERSICARIA Miller 1754 [from *Persica*, the peach, referring to the leaf shape] (formerly in *Polygonum*). SMARTWEED

1a. Aquatic or subaquatic; spikes all terminal or nearly so; flowers bright pink or red . . . . (2)

1b. Terrestrial although sometimes in very wet places, never floating; inflorescence of axillary and terminal spikes; flowers pink or white . . . . (3)

2a. Leaf blades obtuse or acute, commonly widest near the middle; floral spikes seldom more than 3 cm long, usually over 10 mm wide. **P. amphibia** (L.) S. Gray, WATER SMARTWEED. Floating on ponds or in mud on pond margins. A single plant may exhibit branches with smooth, floating leaves like *Potamogeton* (and often mistaken for that) and erect, terrestrial branches with pubescent, erect leaves.

2b. Leaf blades acuminate, commonly widest near the base; inflorescence 3-10 cm long, seldom more and usually less than 10 mm wide. **P. coccinea** (Mühlenberg) Greene, SCARLET SMARTWEED. Similar sites but not often floating.

3a. Sheaths with marginal bristles . . . . (4)

3b. Sheaths lacking marginal bristles . . . . (6)

4a. Flowers pink, not gland-dotted; racemes dense, thick. **P. maculata** (Rafinesque) S. Gray [spotted], LADY'S THUMB. Adventive on pond margins and irrigation ditches. The leaves commonly have a dark spot in the center, "Our Lady's thumbprint."

4b. Flowers greenish, gland-dotted; racemes very slender . . . . (5)

5a. Sheaths swollen, filled with cleistogamous flowers; achenes minutely granular-papillose, dull. **P. hydropiper** (L.) Opiz, WATERPEPPER. Adventive, pond-shores and irrigation ditches.

5b. Sheaths hugging the stem, not plump from hidden, cleistogamous flowers; achenes smooth and shiny. **P. punctata** (Elliott) Small, DOTTED SMARTWEED. Adventive, similar sites.

6a. Peduncle with granular yellow glands; tepals usually white or cream-colored; inflorescence commonly elongate, drooping. **P. lapathifolia** (L.) S. Gray [with leaves like dock]. Adventive on pond borders and irrigation ditches.

6b. Peduncle with stalked red-purple glands; tepals usually pink; inflorescence usually erect, short . . . . (7)

7a. Spike about twice as long as wide; flowers bright pink; either the style or stamens exserted beyond the tepals at anthesis. **P. bicornis** (Rafinesque) Nieuwland. Common in the easternmost plains counties (*Polygonum bicorne, P. longistylum*).

7b. Spike relatively long and narrow, pale pink, the style and stamens not exserted. **P. pensylvanica** (L.) Gomez, PINKWEED. Common in wetlands and muddy places throughout the plains and piedmont valleys.

POLYGONUM L. 1753 [Greek, *polys*, many, + *gonu*, knee, alluding to the nodes]. KNOTWEED

1a. Prostrate-spreading, if ascending, still low to the ground, densely leafy; coarse, weedy, adventive annual with deep-seated taproot . . . . (2)

1b. Erect or ascending, leaves scattered; native or adventive annuals with slender taproots . . . . (3)

2a. Leaves linear to oblong or elliptic, acute or blunt; fruiting perianth 2-3 mm long, not constricted or beaked; tepals purple to pink; achene dark brown.

P. arenastrum Bourgeau [of sandy places], DEVIL'S SHOESTRINGS (*P. rurivagum*, *P. aviculare* of many authors). Adventive in ruderal sites.

2b. Leaves elliptic to obovate, broadly rounded at apex; fruiting perianth 3.5-4 mm long, strongly constricted below the tip; inner tepals white-margined; achene olive-brown. **P. erectum** L. subsp. **achoreum** (Blake) Löve & Löve. Adventive, recently introduced and now known from the Boulder area, Fort Collins, and North Park towns.

3a. Very delicate plants, creeping or ascending, with elliptic leaves and minute flowers (less than 2 mm). **P. minimum** Watson. Mud or wet sand, seeps or streamsides, near Continental Divide, northern counties.

3b. Erect annuals with narrower, oblong-elliptic to linear leaves . . . . (4)

4a. Tall or at least much-branched from the base; lower leaves usually falling before fruiting time; stem prominently striate, never with regularly reflexed flowers and fruits; introduced ruderal weeds, low altitudes . . . . (5)

4b. Low plants usually less than 2 dm tall; if taller, then without strongly striate stems and with reflexed flowers and fruits . . . . (7)

5a. Leaves all narrowly linear; flowers and fruits less than 2.5 mm long; fruit narrow, slightly longer than the tepals; plants with a hemispheric, bushy-branched form. **P. graminifolium** Wierzbicki (?). Adventive. Evidently recently introduced and nowhere common. Identification uncertain.

5b. Leaves broader or, if not, then flowers and fruits larger; fruit enclosed by the tepals; plants not bushy-branched . . . . (6)

6a. Leaves of main stem distinctly larger than the branch leaves; plants virgate, with a main stem and several elongate branches, all strongly ascending, losing the lower leaves early. **P. ramosissimum** Michaux. Adventive. Late summer-flowering weed.

6b. Leaves of main stem and branches similar; stiffly spreading, horizontal branches at the base and erect main stem; leaves persistent; flowers pink. **P. argyrocoleon** Steudel. Adventive, ruderal weed. There may be other species of Asiatic origin subsumed under this name, but the taxonomy is not clear.

7a. Less than 5 cm tall, the flowers crowded into a dense terminal head with linear bracts longer than the flowers. **P. polygaloides** Meisner subsp. **kelloggii** (Greene) Hickman [resembling *Polygala*; for Albert Kellogg, 1813-1887, California botanist]. Beds of drying ponds, North Park.

7b. Usually 1 dm or more tall; flowers not as above . . . . (8)

8a. Tepals 1.5-2.5 mm long; leaves narrowly linear. **P. engelmannii** Greene. Dry canyonsides.

8b. Perianth 3-5 mm long; leaves variable, from narrowly linear to elliptic. **P. douglasii** Greene, **90E**. Common in a variety of habitats. Extremely variable in leaf form and height. While the flowers are usually reflexed in fruit they need not be (*P. sawatchense*, *P. montanum*).

PTEROGONUM Gross 1913 [Greek, *pter-*, wing, + allusion to *Eriogonum*] (formerly in *Eriogonum*). WINGED BUCKWHEAT

One species, **P. alatum** (Torrey.) Gross. Common on the outwash mesas and intermountain parks, infrequent on the eastern plains. A striking and unusual herb with a rosette of oblanceolate basal leaves from which arises a tall, simple flower stalk crowned with an open, paniculate cyme. The pendent fruits are yellow-green, trigonous, and conspicuously winged. Our plant is monocarpic, that is, the rosettes grow for several seasons and the plant, or at least the flowering stem, dies after it finally blossoms.

REYNOUTRIA Houttuyn 1777 [name unexplained]. JAPANESE BUCKWHEAT

One species, **R. japonica** Houttuyn. Adventive. Occasionally cultivated in gardens but sometimes escaping to form dense thickets of rank growth, lower elevations (*Polygonum cuspidatum*).

RUMEX L. 1753 [the ancient Latin name]. DOCK

1a. Valves (the inner 3 tepals) in fruit 14-20 mm long, no central swellings ("grains") present. **R. venosus** Pursh, WILD-BEGONIA, **Pl. 6.** Abundant along roadsides and sandhills on the eastern plains; Wet Mountain Valley.
1b. Valves in fruit less than 7 mm long; grains present or absent ...... (2)

2a. Valves dentate or denticulate .... (3)
2b. Valves entire or nearly so .... (5)

3a. Plants with broad, ovate leaves, truncate or cordate at the base. **R. obtusifolius** L., BITTER DOCK. Adventive weed, infrequent or rare in the piedmont valleys.
3b. Plants with long, narrow leaves, usually narrowed to the petiole .... (4)

4a. Low, spreading annual; inner tepals almost completely dissected into slender teeth. **R. maritimus** L. subsp. **fueginus** (Philippi) Hultén [of shores; from Tierra del Fuego]. Wet ground of drying pools and streamsides, plains and piedmont valleys, intermountain parks. Plant low and sprawling.
4b. Tall perennial; inner tepals with shallow teeth. **R. stenophyllus** Ledebour. Adventive, pond margins and roadside ditches on the plains.

5a. Stems erect, spreading or ascending with well-developed axillary shoots (6)
5b. Stems erect and lacking axillary shoots .... (8)

6a. No valves with grains (with minor exceptions). **R. utahensis** Rechinger. More frequent westward, but one authentic specimen from BL. Tetraploid. Both species are sometimes lumped into *R. salicifolius* Weinmann, a Californian species.
6b. One or more of the valves with grains .... (7)

7a. Valves, in fruit, about 3 mm long. **R. triangulivalvis** (Danser) Rechinger. Very common in mountain parks (*R. salicifolius* of most manuals). A diploid species.
7b. Valves, in fruit, 4-6 mm long. **R. altissimus** Wood. Wet places on the eastern plains.

8a. Grains present on at least one of the valves; leaf margins ruffled. **R. crispus** L. CURLY DOCK. Adventive weed in wet ditches.
8b. Grains absent .... (9)

9a. Plant with a vertical taproot, often solitary. **R. aquaticus** L. subsp. **occidentalis** (Watson) Hultén. Wet meadows and roadside ditches in the mountains (*R. occidentalis*).
9b. Plant with a stout, horizontal rhizome, forming dense patches. **R. densiflorus** Osterhout. Marshy places, mostly subalpine, usually at higher altitudes than the last (*R. praecox*).

TRUELLUM Houttuyn 1777 [derivation?]. TEARTHUMB

One species, **T. sagittatum** (L.) Sojak. Rare, an eastern North American swamp plant relictual in wet meadows in the Black Forest region (*Polygonum*).

PONTEDERIACEAE PICKERELWEED FAMILY (PON)

This family is best known for the water-hyacinth, *Eichhornia crassipes*, which was introduced as an aquarium plant and escaped to slow streams and now clogs canals and waterways in the south. Its only saving grace is that it is the favorite food of the manatee, an endangered aquatic mammal. In Ecuador I have seen huge rafts of the plants floating down the Guayas River at Guayaquil and eventually out to sea. The Pickerelweed, *Pontederia cordata* is common along estuaries on the Atlantic seaboard, especially abundant around Washington, D.C.

1a. Flowers blue, solitary or several; stamens dissimilar; leaves with or without oval blades. **Heteranthera**, MUD-PLANTAIN
1b. Flowers yellow, solitary; stamens alike; leaves linear, without blades; plant often submerged. **Zosterella**, MUD-PLANTAIN

HETERANTHERA Ruiz & Pavon 1794 [Greek, *hetera*, different, + *anthera*, anther, the original species having anthers of different sizes and colors]. MUD-PLANTAIN

One species, **H. limosa** (Swartz) Willdenow. Infrequently collected in the drainage of the South Platte, DN, LR, WL.

ZOSTERELLA Small 1913 [diminutive of the genus *Zostera*]. MUD-PLANTAIN

One species, **Z. dubia** (Jacquin) Small. One collection known, from Bonny Reservoir, YM.

PORTULACACEAE PURSLANE FAMILY (POR)

This small family makes up for its size in the beauty of its cultivated members. The moss-rose, *Portulaca grandiflora*, is one of the hardiest ever-blooming plants of hot, sunny gardens in our area. Many kinds of *Oreobroma* were at one time nearly exterminated in the Pacific Northwest by root-diggers for the rock garden trade. *Lewisia rediviva*, the bitterroot, is the state flower of Montana.

1a. Delicate annual with long-petiolate, ovate basal leaves and a single disk-shaped, perfoliate leaf subtending the inflorescence. **Montia**
1b. Perennials without a distinctive perfoliate leaf . . . . (2)

2a. Prostrate-spreading, much-branched, matted, with fleshy spatulate leaves and inconspicuous yellow or orange-red flowers. **Portulaca**, PURSLANE
2b. Erect or stemless, without prostrate-spreading branches; flowers pink, red, or white . . . . (3)

3a. Stems stolon-bearing at the base, with several pairs of opposite leaves; plants of wet streamsides. **Crunocallis**, WATER SPRING BEAUTY
3b. Stems low or absent; leaves chiefly basal, or flower stalk with a very few leaves; plants of drier habitats . . . . (4)

4a. Plants with a pair or 3 stem leaves (no basal leaf); flower stalk arising from a deep-seated, round corm . . . . (5)
4b. Plants with a cluster of linear basal leaves from a stout taproot . . . . (6)

5a. Flower stem with a single pair of broadly oval-elliptic stem leaves. **Claytonia**, SPRING BEAUTY

5b. Flower stem with 3 very slender, linear leaves. **Erocallis**

6a. Inflorescence an open cyme on a stalk taller than the succulent, linear basal leaves. **Talinum**

6b. Inflorescence not taller than the leaves . . . . (7)

7a. Leaves broadly spatulate, obtuse, in very dense rosettes; flowers white with pink veins. **Claytonia**, SPRING BEAUTY

7b. Leaves linear, in small tufts, or leaves absent at flowering time; flowers deep solid red or pink, rarely white . . . . (8)

8a. Flowers more than 2 cm diameter, showy, pink, on jointed pedicels, appearing after the leaves wither. **Lewisia**, BITTERROOT

8b. Flowers less than 1 cm diameter, red, pink, or rarely white, not on jointed pedicels, appearing with the leaves. **Oreobroma**, PYGMY BITTERROOT

CLAYTONIA L. 1763 [for John Clayton, Virginia botanist, 1686-1739]. SPRING BEAUTY

1a. Plant with a cluster of succulent, spatulate basal leaves from a stout taproot. **C. megarhiza** (Gray) Parry, ALPINE SPRING BEAUTY, **91G**. Among rocks on tundra of the higher peaks. A very close relative of the similar *C. joanneana* of the Altai.

1b. Plant slender, arising from a deep-seated, round corm . . . . (2)

2a. Basal leaves none; stem with a pair of broadly oval-fusiform leaves. **C. lanceolata** Pursh, **91F**. Infrequent in the subalpine of the Front Range, very common on the Western Slope in the oak and upper sagebrush zone on the plateaus.

2b. One or more basal leaves present; cauline leaves usually narrowly lance-linear. **C. rosea** Rydberg. An extremely early bloomer in pine forests, outer foothills of Front Range.

CRUNOCALLIS Rydberg 1906 [Greek, *crounos*, spring, + *callos*, beautiful]. WATER SPRING BEAUTY

One species, **C. chamissoi** (Ledebour) Cockerell, **91E**. Petals white, with pink streaks. Common by streams, spruce-fir forests (*Montia*, in part).

EROCALLIS Rydberg 1906 [possibly Greek, *erotema*, question, + *callos*, beautiful, Rydberg questioning its former placement]

One species, **E. triphylla** (Watson) Rydberg, **91B**. Locally frequent on moist slopes and screes, RT, and possibly on the east base of the Park Range in North Park (*Lewisia*).

LEWISIA Pursh 1814 [for Meriwether Lewis, of the Lewis and Clark expedition]. BITTERROOT

One species, **L. rediviva** Pursh, **91A**. Locally abundant in early spring on gravelly flats, North Park.

MONTIA L. 1753 [for Giuseppe Monti, 1682-1760, professor of botany at Bologna]. MINER'S LETTUCE

One species, **M. perfoliata** (Donn) Howell. Rare at springs in protected canyons of the Front Range, only two collections known in Colorado, from DG and JF. A plant common in the Pacific Northwest.

OREOBROMA Howell 1893 [Greek, *oros*, mountain, + *broma*, food, alluding to the edible, fleshy root]. PYGMY BITTERROOT

One species, **O. pygmaea** (Gray) Howell, **91C**. Common in open, stony subalpine meadows. White-flowered mutants are common.

PORTULACA L. 1753 [old Latin name, the meaning unknown]. PURSLANE

One species, **P. oleracea** L., **91D**. Adventive. Very common weed in gardens. Plants prostrate, annual, with fleshy, spatulate leaves and inconspicuous yellow flowers.

TALINUM Adanson 1763 [from a tribal name for an African species]

1a. Flowers small, petals not over 7 mm long; stamens 4-8. **T. parviflorum** Nuttall. Rocky, open slopes in the outer foothills of the Front Range, and scattered sites on the eastern plains and Mesa de Maya.
1b. Flowers larger, petals 10-15 mm long; stamens over 12. **T. calycinum** Engelmann. Rocky areas, extreme northeast corner counties, LO, YM.

POTAMOGETONACEAE PONDWEED FAMILY (POT)

The pondweeds are found in midsummer in almost every pond of any size. Their presence is marked by the spikes of dull greenish flowers emerging from the water, and by their floating, lily-pad leaves. Some are completely submerged and may be found by dredging with a rake. The floating leaves of *Potamogeton* are very similar to those of *Persicaria*, but the latter has pinnately veined leaves and spikes of bright pink flowers. Potamogetons are important waterfowl food plants.

POTAMOGETON L. 1753 [Greek, *potamos*, river, + *geiton*, neighbor]. PONDWEED

Note: Our species are not well-enough collected to justify precise comments on habitat or altitude. We are greatly in need of an energetic collector with a rubber raft and a long rake.

1a. Submerged leaves with stipules adnate to the leaf base for 10 mm or more and forming a sheath around the stem, the leaf blade or petiole not directly attached to the node . . . . (2)
1b. Submerged leaves with stipules free from the rest of the leaf, the blade or petiole attached directly at the node . . . . (4)

2a. Sheaths of the main stem inflated 2-5 times the thickness of the stem; floral whorls 6-12 per spike. **P. vaginatus** Turczaninov. In lakes of North Park.
2b. Sheaths of the main stem about as wide as the stem; floral whorls 2-6 per spike . . . . (3)

3a. Stems dichotomously branched from the base, mostly unbranched above; style lacking; fruiting beak wartlike and central; leaves 2-5 mm wide. **P. filiformis** Persoon. Common in the larger lakes in the mountains.
3b. Stems dichotomously branched above; styles short, the stigma on the ventral margin of the achene; leaf blade filiform, up to 1 mm wide. **P. pectinatus** L. Very common in ponds (often alkaline) mostly at lower altitudes.

4a. Submerged leaves linear or nearly so, less than 6 mm wide, mostly 20 or more times their width . . . . (5)
4b. Submerged leaves linear-lanceolate to oblong or ovate, broader in proportion to their length . . . . (9)

5a. Stipules adnate to the leaf blades for mostly 1-4 mm; embryo coil plainly visible through the papery thin walls of the fruit; elliptic floating leaves 5-40 mm long usually present. **P. diversifolius** Rafinesque.

5b. Stipules free of the leaf blades; fruit walls firm, the embryo not visible; floating leaves, if present, mostly larger . . . . (6)

6a. Leaves dimorphic, both floating and submerged leaves present . . . . . (7)

6b. Leaves all alike, submerged . . . . (8)

7a. Submerged leaves reduced to phyllodes (petiolelike) 1-2 mm wide, these often lost in age; floating leaves rounded to cordate at the base. **P. natans** L.

7b. Submerged leaves ribbonlike, mostly 3-6 mm wide, with a cellular-reticulate strip on each side of the midrib; floating leaves tapered to the petiole. **P. epihydrus** Rafinesque.

8a. Fruits with an undulate to dentate dorsal ridge or keel; glands rarely present at the base of the stipules. **P. foliosus** Rafinesque.

8b. Fruits dorsally smooth and rounded; small globose glands usually present at the base of the stipules. **P. pusillus** L. (including *P. berchtoldii*).

9a. Leaves all submerged, sessile, weakly to strongly clasping at the base, often undulate-crisped . . . . (10)

9b. Floating leaves usually present by flowering time, occasionally lacking; leaves sessile or perfoliate, not clasping the stem, not undulate-crisped . . . (12)

10a. Leaf margins finely serrate; fruit beak 2-3 mm long; hardened winter buds commonly produced in the upper leaf axils. **P. crispus** L. Adventive in ponds in the Denver area.

10b. Leaf margins entire; beak 1.5 mm long or less; no winter buds . . . . (11)

11a. Stems whitish; leaves 10-25 cm long; peduncles over 10 cm long; fruits 4-5 mm long. **P. praelongus** Wulfen.

11b. Stems brownish to yellow-green; leaves less than 10 cm long; peduncles 2-10 cm long; fruits 2.5-3.5 mm long. **P. perfoliatus** L. subsp. **richardsonii** (Bennett) Hultén.

12a. Upper submerged leaves folded and falcate, 25-50-nerved; mature fruits 4-5 mm long. **P. amplifolius** Tuckerman. Reported once from LK, and to be expected in North Park because of its occurrence in adjacent mountains of Wyoming.

12b. Upper submerged leaves ± symmetrical and not folded, 3-19-nerved; mature fruits 1.5-4 mm long . . . . (13)

13a. Fruits tawny-olive; floating leaves often lacking, thin and delicate, the blade tapering indistinctly into a short petiole; submerged leaves reddish. **P. alpinus** Balbis var. **tenuifolius** (Rafinesque) Ogden.

13b. Fruits brown, reddish, or greenish; floating leaves leathery, the blades distinct from the petioles; submerged leaves dark green or brownish green . . (14)

14a. Submerged leaves often disintegrating by fruiting time, tapering to petioles 4 cm or longer, acute to blunt-tipped; mature fruits 3-4 mm long. **P. nodosus** Poiret.

14b. Submerged leaves usually persistent, tapering to petioles up to 4 cm long, acute to abruptly acuminate or apiculate; mature fruits green or olive, 1.7-2.8 mm long . . . . (15)

15a. Stems usually freely branched, 0.5-1 mm thick; submerged leaves 3-10 mm wide, 3-7-nerved; floating leafblades 2-9 cm long, 1-3.5 cm wide; fruits 1.7-2.8 mm long, the lateral keels obscure. **P. gramineus** L. Very common in shallow ponds in the mountains.

15b. Stems simple or once branched, 1-5 mm thick; submerged leaves 1.4-4 cm wide, 9-17-nerved; floating leaf blades 4-41 cm long, 2-7 cm wide; fruits 2.7-3.5 mm long, the lateral keels strong. **P. illinoensis** Morong. Our only Colorado record is from the Western Slope, but there is no reason not to expect it in our area.

PRIMULACEAE PRIMROSE FAMILY (PRM)

Primroses, or cowslips, have been cultivated in gardens since Elizabethan times and still are among the choicest of rock garden plants. The showiest come from the mountains of Asia; our red mountain primroses are close cousins of these. *Cyclamen*, known here as a potted plant, grows wild in Europe, and *Soldanella*, a unique genus with deeply fringed, bell-shaped corollas, is a treasure of the Alps. Our own *Dodecatheon*, the shooting-star, used to be called the American *Cyclamen*. The combination of a united corolla with the stamens inserted opposite to, instead of the usual arrangement of alternate with, the petals, makes this family very easy to recognize (but see *Glaux*!).

1a. Plants leafy-stemmed . . . . (2)
1b. Plants bearing leaves at the base of the stem only . . . . (5)

2a. Flowers greenish, inconspicuous, 4-merous, almost sessile in the leaf axils; stems very thin and weak, with small ovate leaves less than 5 mm long. **Anagallis**, PIMPERNEL
2b. Flowers colored; otherwise not as above . . . . (3)

3a. Flowers pink; sepals petaloid, petals absent; leaves oblong; stems low, semiprostrate. **Glaux**, SEA MILKWORT
3b. Flowers with yellow petals; leaves ovate; stems tall . . . . (4)

4a. Flowers 7-merous, in dense axillary racemes. **Naumburgia**
4b. Flowers 5-merous, solitary in the leaf axils or in panicles. **Lysimachia**, LOOSESTRIFE

5a. Corolla lobes reflexed; stamens exserted, the anthers appearing united, forming a beaklike projection. **Dodecatheon**, SHOOTINGSTAR
5b. Corolla lobes erect and spreading; stamens included, separate . . . . . . (6)

6a. Flowers purple-red, only white in rare mutant forms; corolla tube equalling or exceeding the calyx; style filiform, elongate. **Primula**, PRIMROSE
6b. Flowers white (or, in one species, faintly pink and yellow); corolla short, with short tube exceeded by calyx; style very short. **Androsace**, ROCK-JASMINE

ANAGALLIS L. 1753 [probably from Greek, *ana*, again, + *agallein*, to delight in, alluding to the flowers of *A. arvensis*, which close in cloudy weather, reopening with the return of sunshine]. PIMPERNEL

One species, **A. minima** (L.) Krause, CHAFFWEED. In the *Juncus arcticus* zone on floodplains in the piedmont valleys, rare or overlooked. An exceedingly inconspicuous plant consisting of a weak, unbranched stem with small, alternate, ovate leaves and inconspicuous, 4-merous, axillary flowers *(Centunculus)*.

ANDROSACE L. 1753 [name used by Pliny for some unidentified plant; derivation controversial]. ROCK-JASMINE

1a. Perennial; flowers in a dense cluster, almost sessile; capsule few-seeded. **A. chamaejasme** Host subsp. **carinata** (Torrey) Hultén [resembling the genus *Chamaejasme*; keeled], **92D**. Flowers white with yellow center, becoming rose-colored in age. Plants only a few cm tall, locally abundant on alpine tundra.

1b. Annual; flowers on long pedicels; capsule many-seeded . . . . (2)

2a. Bracts at base of umbel broad (lance-ovate to obovate). **A. occidentalis** Pursh, **92C**. Open grassy slopes and ledges, canyonsides at low altitudes, flowering in early spring.

2b. Bracts at base of umbel narrow (lanceolate to subulate) . . . . (3)

3a. Calyx strongly 5-keeled; leaves not distinctly petioled. **A. septentrionalis** L., **92B**. Forested or open sites (except desert), from foothills to alpine tundra, extremely variable in size and length of pedicels and peduncles.

3b. Calyx not keeled; leaves abruptly narrowed to a distinct petiole. **A. filiformis** Retzius, **92A**. Wet places, subalpine.

DODECATHEON L. 1753 [Greek, *dodeca*, twelve, + *theos*, god, name given by Pliny to the primrose, believed to be under the protection of the twelve superior gods]. SHOOTINGSTAR

One species, **D. pulchellum** (Rafinesque) Merrill. Along streams and by springs, from shaded canyons up into spruce-fir forest.

GLAUX L. 1753 [Greek, *glaucos*, sea-green]. SEA MILKWORT

One species, **G. maritima** L., **92E, E'**. Alkaline flats along the rivers and in grazed wet meadows. The stamens are alternate to the petallike sepals, indicating that a whorl of parts, the petals, are missing, for in the primroses a whorl of stamens is missing to start with, causing the remaining whorl of stamens to be opposite the petals. Confusing?

LYSIMACHIA L. 1753 [Greek, *lysis*, release, + *mache*, strife, alluding to a tradition that King Lysimachus of Thrace pacified a mad bull by waving a plant of this before him]. LOOSESTRIFE

Note: A complex genus, each of our representatives belonging to well-marked subgenera, probably meriting, with *Naumburgia*, independent generic status.

1a. Plant prostrate, creeping; leaves round, gland-dotted. **L. nummularia** L., MONEYWORT. Adventive, established as a weed in lawns near Boulder.

1b. Plant tall, erect; leaves ovate . . . . (2)

2a. Flowers in a terminal panicle; corolla divisions entire; staminodia lacking. **L. vulgaris** L., GARDEN LOOSESTRIFE. Adventive along irrigation ditches near Boulder.

2b. Flowers solitary or in pairs, on long pedicels in the leaf axils; corolla divisions erose-denticulate; 5 staminodia alternating with the stamens. **L. ciliata** L. Wetlands in the piedmont valleys, a relictual eastern prairie species (*Steironema*).

NAUMBURGIA Moench 1802 [for J. S. Naumberg (sic), German botanist, 1768-1799]. TUFTED LOOSESTRIFE

One species, **N. thyrsiflora** (L.) Reichenbach. One record, from a willow fen in Rocky Mountain National Park, a relictual eastern prairie plant (*Lysimachia*).

PRIMULA L. 1753 [diminutive of Latin, *primus*, early spring]. PRIMROSE

1a. Flowers small, pink; plants of wet meadows; leaves green on both sides or with white-mealy granules beneath . . . . (2)
1b. Flowers small or large, deeply rose-colored; plants of tundra or snowmelt basins; leaves green both sides . . . . (3)

2a. Leaves green; corolla small, not over 5 mm diameter; pedicels stiffly erect, red-purple. **P. egaliksensis** Wormskiold. Rare, calcareous fens of South Park.
2b. Leaves farinose beneath; corolla larger; pedicels not so strict, green. **P. incana** Jones, BIRDS-EYE PRIMROSE. Wet meadows, intermountain parks, common in South Park before the recent draining, also in Cherokee Park, Upper Poudre Valley, LR.

3a. Plants large (1.5-4 dm high); flowers numerous, very showy, with a skunky odor. **P. parryi** Gray, PARRY'S PRIMROSE, **Pl. 57**. Streambanks, subalpine snowmelt seeps. Superficially very similar to the Altai *P. nivalis*.
3b. Plants small (3-10 cm high); flowers solitary or few. **P. angustifolia** Torrey, ALPINE PRIMROSE. Dry, rocky subalpine meadows and alpine tundra. One collection from a subalpine forest in the Sangre de Cristo Range is unusually tall, up to 1 dm.

PYROLACEAE WINTERGREEN FAMILY (PYR)

A small family of exquisite forest herbs with waxy, sometimes exceedingly fragrant flowers. They are hallmarks of the most mesic montane and subalpine forests, and are most often found in deep shade. This family, traditionally, has been included in the Ericaceae.

1a. Stems bearing several whorls of sharply serrate, oblanceolate, leathery leaves; inflorescence almost umbellate. **Chimaphila**, PIPSISSEWA, PRINCE'S PINE
1b. Stems leafy only at or near the base, leaves not in whorls; leaves ovate or round; inflorescence a raceme, or flower solitary . . . . (2)

2a. Flower solitary, extremely fragrant. **Moneses**, WOODNYMPH
2b. Flowers several on a stem . . . . (3)

3a. Leaves scattered along lower third of stem; inflorescence distinctly 1-sided. **Orthilia**, ONE-SIDED WINTERGREEN
3b. Leaves all basal, rarely absent. **Pyrola**, WINTERGREEN

CHIMAPHILA Pursh 1813 [Greek, *cheima*, winter, + *philein*, to love]. PIPSISSEWA, PRINCE'S PINE

One species, **C. umbellata** (L.) Barton subsp. **occidentalis** (Rydberg) Hultén, **93D, Pl. 11**. Frequent in cool ravines, foothills to subalpine.

MONESES Salisbury 1821 [Greek, *monos*, one, and *hesis*, delight]. WOOD NYMPH; ONE-FLOWERED WINTERGREEN

One species, **M. uniflora** (L.) S. Gray, **93C, Pl. 33**. Cold, mossy forests, usually near streams. Has fragrance of lily-of-the-valley.

ORTHILIA Rafinesque 1840 [Greek, *ortho*, straight, alluding to the straight, elongate style]. ONE-SIDED WINTERGREEN

One species, **O. secunda** (L.) House, **93E**. Mossy forest floors, cool ravines, montane and subalpine (*Pyrola*, *Ramischia*).

PYROLA L. 1753 [diminutive of *Pyrus*, the pear tree, from resemblance in the foliage]. SHINLEAF [corruption of shingle-leaf?]

1a. Style straight. **P. minor** L., LESSER WINTERGREEN, **93F**. Subalpine spruce-fir forests.

1b. Style curved downward and outward . . . . (2)

2a. Leaves pale along the veins. **P. picta** Smith. Deeply shaded ravines, Front Range foothills. This species is a hemiparasite, and sometimes most or all of the green leaves may be absent.

2b. Leaves green, not mottled . . . . (3)

3a. Flowers greenish; petals 4-5 mm long; scape usually less than 20 cm long; leaves 2-3 cm diameter. **P. chlorantha** Swartz [green-flowered]. Upper montane and subalpine forests.

3b. Flowers pink; petals 7-8 mm long; scape tall, up to 40 cm long; leaves commonly over 3 cm diameter. **P. rotundifolia** L. subsp. **asarifolia** (Michaux) Löve, SWAMP WINTERGREEN. Marshy streambanks, subalpine forests (*P. asarifolia*).

RANUNCULACEAE BUTTERCUP FAMILY (RAN)

(Note: the genera with follicular or berrylike fruits are now placed in the Helleboraceae.)

The petals of buttercups have a high, almost mirrorlike gloss. Children test this quality by holding up a flower to another's chin and asking, "Do you like butter?" The basal part of the petal, however, is dull. Lyman Benson explains, in *Plant Taxonomy, Methods and Principles*, that these qualities constitute a device for pollination by rainwater. The stigmas of buttercups are not well situated to be brushed by bees, but bees leave much pollen lying around on the petals. The glossy part of the petal is water repellent, while the dull part is not. If rain or dew falls on the petal, the water will rise only as far as the top of the matte area, draining off between the petals above that point. This water level is usually at about the same level as the stigmas. Pollen thus floats on the water film and is deposited on the stigmas as the water level recedes.

1a. Tiny annual plants with linear basal leaves; fruiting receptacle many times longer than wide; perianth segments spurred. **Myosurus**, MOUSETAIL

1b. Plants not as above; receptacle rarely more than 5 times as long as wide; petals, when present, not spurred . . . . (2)

2a. Petals and sepals distinctly different, the petals usually yellow or white (3)

2b. Petals and sepals similar (tepals), or absent, or only one or the other present, usually white or colored, but rarely yellow . . . . (10)

3a. Submerged aquatics with linear, palmatisect leaves and emergent white flowers; petals not glossy; achenes transversely wrinkled. **Batrachium**, WATER CROWFOOT

3b. Terrestrial plants or, if aquatic, then with glossy yellow petals . . . . . . (4)

4a. Achene with a long straight beak and with 2 pouchlike enlargements at the base; sepals persistent in fruit; small desert annuals with linear-dissected leaves. **Ceratocephala**, HORNHEAD

4b. Achene with a short, often curved beak, or beakless, lacking basal pouches; sepals deciduous . . . . (5)

Plate 33. ***Moneses uniflora*** Weber
WOODNYMPH

Plate 34. ***Salix lanata*** subsp. ***calcicola*** Weber
WOOLLY WILLOW

Plate 35. ***Machaeranthera coloradensis*** Weber

Plate 36. ***Solanum rostratum*** Weber
BUFFALOBUR

Plate 37. ***Draba crassa*** Weber

Plate 38. ***Eritrichum aretioides*** Weber
Alpine Forget-Me-Not

Plate 39. ***Juncus albescens*** Weber

Plate 40. ***Cylactis pubescens*** Weber
CREEPING RASPBERRY

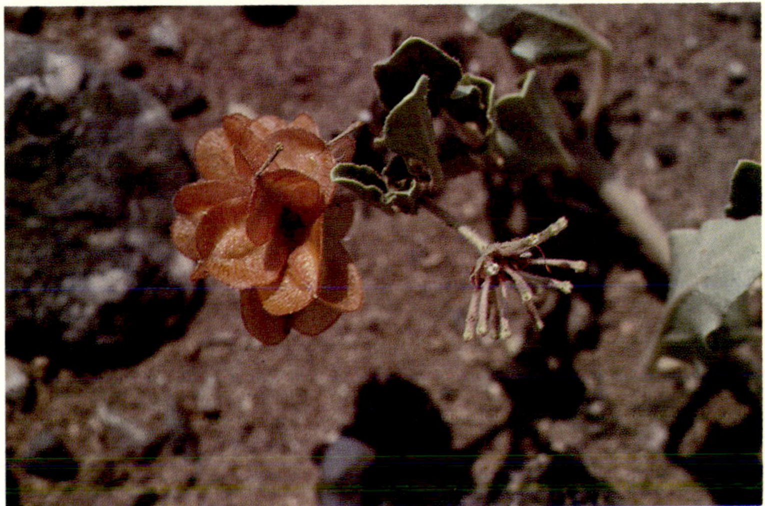

Plate 41. ***Tripterocalyx micranthus*** Weber

Plate 42. ***Aletes acaulis*** Weber

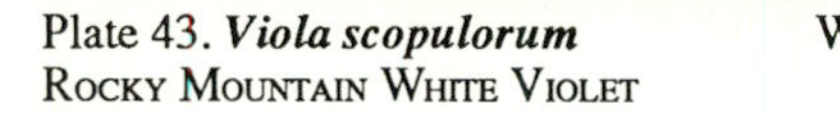

Plate 43. ***Viola scopulorum*** Weber
ROCKY MOUNTAIN WHITE VIOLET

Plate 44. ***Viola rydbergii*** Weber

Plate 45. ***Iliamna rivularis*** Weber

Plate 46. ***Heracleum sphondylium*** Weber
Cow Parsnip

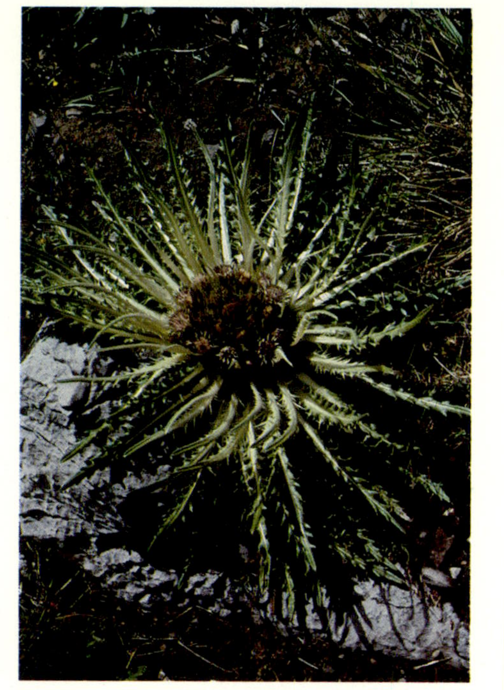

Plate 47. ***Cirsium coloradense*** Weber
THISTLE

Plate 48. ***Betula papyrifera*** Weber
PAPER BIRCH

Plate 49. ***Phlox kelseyi*** Weber
ALKALI PHLOX

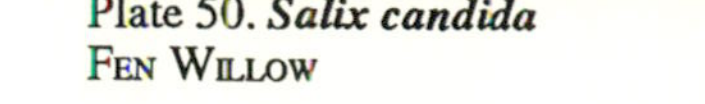

Plate 50. ***Salix candida*** Weber
FEN WILLOW

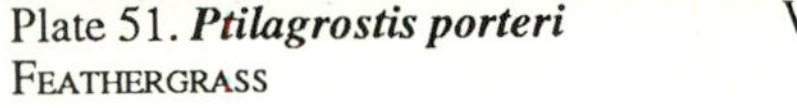

Plate 51. ***Ptilagrostis porteri*** Weber
FEATHERGRASS

Plate 52. ***Hymenopappus newberryi*** Weber

Plate 53. ***Potentilla ambigens*** Weber
CINQUEFOIL

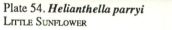

Plate 54. ***Helianthella parryi*** Weber
LITTLE SUNFLOWER

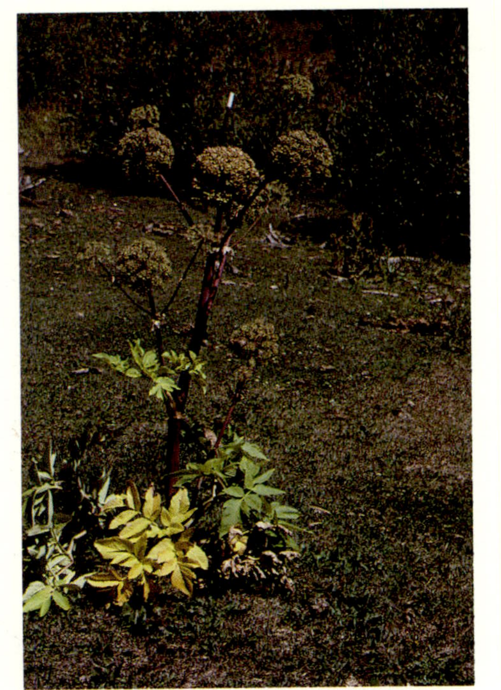

Plate 55. ***Angelica ampla*** Weber
GIANT ANGELICA

Plate 56. ***Oreocarya weberi*** Weber

Plate 57. ***Primula parryi*** Weber
Parry's Primrose

Plate 58. ***Gaura neomexicana*** Weber
subsp. ***coloradensis***
Gaura

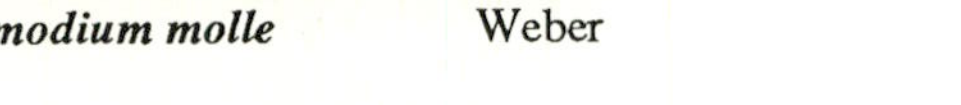

Plate 59. ***Onosmodium molle*** Weber
MARBLESEED

Plate 60. ***Petasites sagittatus*** Weber
SWEET COLTSFOOT

Plate 61. ***Rydbergia grandiflora*** Weber
OLD-MAN-OF-THE-MOUNTAIN

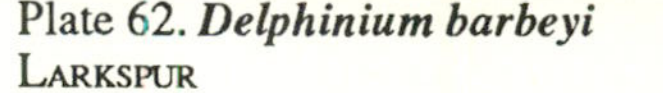

Plate 62. ***Delphinium barbeyi*** Weber
LARKSPUR

Plate 63. ***Ipomoea leptophylla*** Weber
BUSH MORNING GLORY

Plate 64. ***Crataegus macracantha*** Weber
HAWTHORN

5a. Strongly stoloniferous, rooting at the nodes, semiaquatic, rooted in mud or floating in water . . . . (6)
5b. Not stoloniferous, terrestrial . . . . (8)

6a. Leaves linear or narrowly elliptic. **Ranunculus reptans**, SPEARWORT
6b. Leaves not as above . . . . (7)

7a. Leaves round or oval, crenate-toothed, cordate at the base; plants of muddy shores. **Halerpestes**, ALKALI CROWFOOT
7b. Leaves deeply palmately lobed; floating in water or emerging onto muddy banks. **Ranunculus**, BUTTERCUP

8a. Petals narrow, with a clawlike base; flowers perfect, but often almost staminate or carpellate (functionally male or female); achenes longitudinally ribbed. **Cyrtorhyncha**
8b. Petals broad, clawless; flowers with functional stamens and carpels; achenes not ribbed . . . . (9)

9a. Style and beak extremely short; achenes transversely rugose and minutely alveolate; receptacle cylindric, the achenes very numerous. **Hecatonia**, BLISTER BUTTERCUP
9b. Style and beak well developed; otherwise not as above. **Ranunculus**, BUTTERCUP

10a. Tepals small, less conspicuous than the stamens or carpels . . . . (11)
10b. Tepals large and showy, petallike . . . . (12)

11a. Leaves simple, mostly basal, palmately lobed, long-petioled; flowers perfect. **Trautvetteria**, TASSELRUE
11b. Leaves compound, basal, and cauline, with many shallowly lobed leaflets. **Thalictrum**, MEADOWRUE (see Coptaceae)

12a. Tepals commonly 4, not overlapping; leaves not whorled beneath the inflorescence; styles becoming long and feathery at maturity . . . . . . (13)
12b. Tepals 5 or more, overlapping; upper stem leaves in a whorl below the inflorescence, sometimes forming an involucre . . . . (16)

13a. Tepals thick, purple, forming an urn; plants erect or sprawling, not true vines. **Coriflora**, LEATHERFLOWER, SUGARBOWLS
13b. Tepals white or yellow or blue-purple, spreading; plants sprawling or true vines . . . . (14)

14a. Tepals thin, blue-purple. **Atragene**, BLUE CLEMATIS
14b. Tepals white, cream, or yellowish . . . . (15)

15a. Tepals thick, yellow; flowers perfect. **Viticella**, ORIENTAL CLEMATIS
15b. Tepals thin, white, or cream; flowers imperfect, staminate or carpellate (the carpellate flowers with a few sterile stamens). **Clematis**, VIRGIN'S BOWER

16a. Flowers appearing before the leaves; tepals over 2 cm long; styles becoming long and feathery at maturity. **Pulsatilla**, PASQUEFLOWER
16b. Flowers appearing after the leaves; tepals about 1 cm long; styles not greatly elongated in fruit . . . . (17)

17a. Achenes becoming long-woolly at maturity and forming dense, woolly heads at maturity. **Anemone**, WINDFLOWER
17b. Achenes glabrous or pubescent, never woolly . . . . (18)

18a. Flowers several, tepals white or lemon yellow; leaf segments narrow, many; subalpine, alpine. **Anemonastrum**, NARCISSUS ANEMONE

18b. Flowers solitary; tepals white; leaf segments broad, few; foothills. **Anemonidium**

ANEMONASTRUM Holub 1973 [*Anemone* + Latin, *astrum*, resembling]. NARCISSUS ANEMONE

One species, **A. narcissiflorum** (L.) Holub subsp. **zephyrum** (Nelson) Weber, **94A**. The largest-flowered and most showy of our anemones, common in the upper subalpine (*Anemone*). The flowers are so large that some confuse this with *Trollius*, which has follicles rather than achenes and lacks the conspicuous involucre.

ANEMONE L. 1753 [ancient name, corruption of *Na'man*, Semitic name for Adonis, from whose blood the crimson-flowered *Anemone* of the Middle East was said to have sprung. Probably has nothing to do with Greek, *anemos*, wind]. WINDFLOWER

1a. Achenes densely woolly; receptacle cylindrical; tepals white . . . . (2)

1b. Achenes not woolly; receptacle not cylindrical; tepals various . . . . . . (3)

2a. Involucre mostly 5-9 (rarely only 3)-leaved; peduncles mostly naked; plant cinereously silky pubescent; styles crimson. **A. cylindrica** Gray, THIMBLEWEED. Meadows and roadside ditches, medium altitudes along the Front Range.

2b. Involucre 2-3 (rarely 5)-leaved, some of the peduncles bearing involucels; plants greener, loosely pubescent or glabrate; styles pale or merely crimson-tipped. **A. riparia** Fernald. Known in Colorado from a single record, Cuchara Valley, now likely extirpated because of development of the streamside meadows.

3a. Basal leaves 3-parted, with broad, shallowly lobed, glabrous and glossy segments. **A. parviflora** Michaux. Local on cool subalpine rocky slopes.

3b. Basal leaves cleft into 5 or more narrow divisions, pubescent . . . . . . (4)

4a. Tepals usually rose-colored; plants of medium altitudes in forests and meadows. **A. multifida** Poiret subsp. **globosa** (Nuttall) Torrey & Gray, **94C**. Common in dry, open forests.

4b. Tepals white or cream with distinctly bluish dorsal faces; dwarf tundra plants. **A. multifida** Poiret subsp. **saxicola** (Boivin) Weber. Infrequent, Mosquito Range.

ANEMONIDIUM Holub 1974

One species, **A. canadense** (L.) Löve & Löve. Common in low ground, meadows and streamsides, throughout the foothills and venturing onto the eastern plains (*Anemone*).

ATRAGENE L. 1753 [derivation unknown]. BLUE CLEMATIS

1a. Leaves with 3 leaflets, these large, not cleft. **A. occidentalis** Hornemann, **94D**. Climbing on trees, foothills to subalpine, most common north of the Arkansas Divide (*Clematis columbiana* of Colorado literature).

1b. Leaves biternately compound, the leaflets small, deeply cleft and lobed. **A. columbiana** Nuttall, **Pl. 32**. Scrambling and semi-vinelike, hardly climbing, in open forests, most common south of the Arkansas Divide (*C. pseudoalpina*). Very similar to the European *C. alpina*.

BATRACHIUM S. Gray 1821 [Greek, *batrachion*, frog, alluding to the habitat]. WATER CROWFOOT

Note: We need more carefully made collections of the water crowfoots, especially in fruiting condition; they, of course, are conspicuous plants when in blossom, but unfortunately the critical characters are in the fruits. It is almost certain that the three species listed below occur in our region in slow streams and ditches.

1a. Style persistent after flowering; achene beak 0.7-1.1 mm long, body coarsely transversely ridged; dissected leaves once- or sometimes twice-trichotomous, then dichotomous. **B. longirostre** (Godron) Schultz.

1b. Style usually deciduous after flowering; achene beak 0.3 or rarely 0.5 mm long, body obovoid, 1-1.5 mm long, finely transversely wrinkled . . . . . (2)

2a. Pedicels recurved at fruiting time; submersed, dissected leaves usually sessile, the first divisions arising within the usually dilated, stipular leaf bases (the ends of these are often free), usually not collapsing when withdrawn from the water, circinate, much shorter than the internodes; achenes mostly 30-45 or as many as 80; dissected leaves usually once- or twice-trichotomous. **B. circinatum** (Sibthorp) Fries subsp. **subrigidum** (Drew) Löve & Löve, **97B**.

2b. Pedicels not recurved at fruiting time; submersed, dissected leaves usually petioled, the first divisions arising usually but not always well above the non-dilated stipular leaf bases (the ends of these not free), usually collapsing when withdrawn from the water, not circinate, usually about equalling or a little shorter than the internodes; achenes usually about 10 or 20 or as many as 40; dissected leaves usually repeatedly trichotomous. **B. trichophyllum** (Chaix) Bosch.

CERATOCEPHALA Moench 1794 [Greek, *ceratos*, horn, + *cephalos*, head]. HORNHEAD

One species, **C. orthoceras** de Candolle [straight horn], **96B**. Adventive weed of Asia Minor, naturalized widely on the Western Slope but relatively rare as yet on the Eastern Slope, but spreading rapidly, mostly on clay soils of the valleys, BL, LR, blooming in early springtime (*C. testiculata*).

CLEMATIS L. 1753 [Greek, *clema*, sprig]. VIRGIN'S BOWER

One species, **C. ligusticifolia** Nuttall [with leaves like privet]. Common, clambering over fences and trees, valley bottoms. The masses of feathery fruits are conspicuous in late summer.

CORIFLORA Weber 1982 [Greek, *coriarius*, of leather, alluding to the texture of the tepals]. LEATHERFLOWER, SUGARBOWLS

1a. Leaf divisions linear; plants erect, not glaucous; flowers cylindric-turbinate, the margins of the tepals not strongly white-crinkly hairy. **C. hirsutissima** (Pursh) Weber, **94E**. Common on grassy slopes, meadows, and open pine forests (*Clematis*).

1b. Leaf divisions elliptic; plants sprawling, glaucous; flowers conical-turbinate, the margins of the tepals strongly white-crinkly hairy. **C. scottii** (Porter & Coulter) Weber. Common and largely replacing the last in the southern counties.

CYRTORHYNCHA Nuttall 1838 [Greek, *kyrtos*, curved, + *rhynchos*, beak]

One species, **C. ranunculina** Nuttall. Rocky slopes wet in spring from snow runoff, foothills of Front Range (*Ranunculus*).

HALERPESTES Greene 1900 [not explained, but possibly from Greek, *halos*, salt, + Latin, *pestis*, plague]. ALKALI CROWFOOT

One species, **H. cymbalaria** (Pursh) Greene subsp. **saximontana** (Fernald) Moldenke, **96D**. Common on muddy shores and flats. Recognized by the combination of stolons, ovate, crenate leaves, and prominently ribbed achenes. This is a small genus of 4-6 species occurring in Central Asia, western North America, and temperate southern South America (*Ranunculus*).

HECATONIA Loureiro 1790 [Greek, *hecaton*, hundred, from the large number of achenes]. BLISTER BUTTERCUP

One species, **H. scelerata** (L.) Fourreau, **97C**. Adventive weed of muddy places, particularly disturbed sites such as cattle ponds and troughs. Although usually placed in *Ranunculus*, this species is unique, having very different achenes and differing greatly in habit, being a succulent plant with small flowers, producing up to 100 achenes. The leaves are deeply dissected and the stems are stout and hollow.

MYOSURUS L. 1753 [Greek, *myos*, mouse, + *oura*, tail]. MOUSETAIL

1a. Back of the achene scarcely wider on each side than the very prominent keel, prolonged into a beak at least half as long as the body. **M. apetalus** Gay. Drying ponds, sagebrush benches, North Park (*M. aristatus*, *M. minimus* var. *montanus*).

1b. Back of the achene distinctly wider on each side than the relatively low keel, the beak much less than half as long as the body. **M. minimus** L., **96C** Drying pondshores on the piedmont valleys and plains.

PULSATILLA Miller 1754 [possibly diminutive, from Italian, *pulsare*, to throb, alluding to the Passion; first used by Matthioli]. PASQUEFLOWER

One species, **P. patens** (L.) Miller subsp. **hirsutissima** Zamels, **Pl. 7**. One of the first early spring flowers of open forests and sagebrush, but ranging up to timberline. This genus is best developed in the mountain regions of Eurasia (*Anemone*).

RANUNCULUS L. 1753 [diminutive of Latin, *rana*, frog, in allusion to the habitat where buttercups abound]. BUTTERCUP

1a. Leaves all entire or at most denticulate or wavy . . . . (2)

1b. Leaves coarsely toothed or lobed or deeply dissected . . . . (3)

2a. Stoloniferous and rooting at the nodes; leaves only a few mm wide, linear or narrowly oblong. **R. reptans** L. [creeping], SPEARWORT, **96A**. Muddy pondshores and drying catchment basins, montane and subalpine.

2b. Not stoloniferous; leaves broadly lanceolate, over 1 cm wide; petals 7-12 mm long. **R. alismifolius** Geyer var. **montanus** Watson. Wet mountain meadows.

3a. Leaves deeply palmately lobed, floating in water or emerging onto muddy banks . . . . (4)

3b. Leaves not as above, not floating or emergent . . . . (5)

4a. Leaves broadly 3-lobed, the lobes sometimes shallowly notched; submerged leaves not much different from the floating ones. **R. hyperboreus** Rottboel subsp. **intertextus** (Greene) Kapoor & Löve [far-northern; interwoven], FLOATING BUTTERCUP. In small subalpine ponds and peat fens.

4b. Leaves deeply 3-lobed, the lobes again deeply 3-lobed; submerged leaves usually finely dissected. **R. gmelinii** de Candolle var. **hookeri** (D. Don) Benson [for J. G. Gmelin; for J. D. Hooker], WATER CROWFOOT, **97A**. Abundant in meandering streams in the intermountain basins.

5a. Styles and achene beaks lacking or minute, not over 0.2 mm long; basal leaves merely crenate; flowers minute. **R. abortivus** L. subsp. **acrolasius** (Fernald) Kapoor & Löve [runty; hairy top]. Infrequent, slender plants scattered through the eastern foothills, also known from the San Luis Valley.

5b. Styles and achene beaks longer . . . . (6)

6a. Achenes laterally compressed, much wider than thick; sepals not tinged with purple . . . . (7)

6b. Achenes turgid, not more than 2.5 times as broad as thick; sepals tinged with purple . . . . (9)

7a. Stems harshly spreading-pubescent, commonly rooting at the lower nodes. **R. macounii** Britton [for John Macoun, 1831-1920, Canadian botanist]. Common in riparian woodlands.

7b. Stems smooth or pubescent but not as above, not rooting at the lower nodes . . . . (8)

8a. Petals not over 3 mm long; achenes smooth or hispid. **R. uncinatus** Don [hooked]. Moist woodlands, middle altitudes.

8b. Petals 6-18 mm long; achenes glabrous. **R. acriformis** Gray [resembling *R. acris*]. Moist meadows, North Park; also in the Boulder Valley.

9a. Sepals and usually the pedicels covered with blackish or reddish hairs. Basal leaves elliptic to spatulate, toothed at apex. **R. macauleyi** Gray [for the collector, Lieutenant C. H. McCauley], **94B**. Subalpine meadows, Sangre de Cristo and San Juan ranges.

9b. Sepals not covered with dark hairs . . . . (10)

10a. Tiny alpine plants less than 5 cm tall, with small 3-lobed leaves and minute flowers, the petals to 3.5 mm long, only equalling the sepals. **R. pygmaeus** Wahlenberg, **96E**. Local in snowmelt areas, extremely inconspicuous.

10b. Taller plants, if alpine, then with larger flowers and different leaves . (11)

11a. Fruiting receptacle and head of achenes globose. **R. glaberrimus** Hooker var. **ellipticus** Greene. Early spring, foothills of Front Range. Rarely, a population will be composed of plants lacking petals.

11b. Fruiting receptacle and head of achenes ovoid to cylindrical . . . . . . (12)

12a. Flower stems almost scapose, the plant consisting of a cluster of biternately dissected basal leaves on slender petioles from a mass of fibrous roots, most of the plant buried in loose scree. **R. gelidus** Karelin & Kirilow [frigid]. Extremely local, growing on the highest peaks. Found also in Alaska and eastern Siberia. There is disagreement as to whether or not *R. grayi*, described from Gray's Peak, is really synonymous.

12b. Flower stems erect, somewhat leafy, otherwise not as above . . . . . . (13)

13a. Leaves very finely dissected into threadlike divisions; flowers very showy; plants of high tundra. **R. adoneus** Gray [for the god, Adonis], SNOW BUTTERCUP. Along snowbanks, often blossoming through the melting snow.

13b. Leaves with broader divisions; flowers relatively small . . . . (14)

14a. Achenes glabrous; most leaves cleft to the middle or below. **R. eschscholtzii** Schlechtendal [for J. F. Eschscholtz, early nineteenth-century collector with Russian expeditions]. Moist subalpine forests. Some feel that *R. adoneus* is only an alpine race of this, but in Colorado they are distinct.

14b. Achenes pubescent . . . . (15)

15a. Most basal leaves cleft to near the base. **R. pedatifidus** Smith [palmately cleft]. Pond borders, wet meadows, scree slopes, subalpine and alpine.

15b. Blades of the basal leaves, or most of them, merely crenate or shallowly lobed . . . . (16)

16a. Petals large (ca. 1 cm long). **R. cardiophyllus** Hooker [with heart-shaped leaves]. Margins of ponds, wet meadows, upper montane and subalpine. Both flowers and fruits should be available for certain identification.

16b. Petals small (ca. 5 mm or less). **R. inamoenus** Greene [unattractive]. Meadows and pond borders, upper montane, subalpine.

TRAUTVETTERIA Fischer & Meyer 1835 [for E. R. von Trautvetter, 1809-1889, Russian botanist]. TASSELRUE

One species, **T. carolinensis** (Walter) Vail [of the Carolinas], **97D**. Spruce-fir forests and subalpine meadows, San Juan Mountains, CN. The long, white, staminal filaments are the most conspicuous parts of the flowers. The palmately lobed basal leaves recall *Trollius*.

VITICELLA Moench 1794 [diminutive of *Vitis*, the grapevine]. ORIENTAL CLEMATIS

One species, **V. orientalis** (L.) Weber. Adventive. Originally introduced into mining towns in the Clear Creek Valley and still almost confined to it (*Clematis*).

RESEDACEAE MIGNONETTE FAMILY (RES)

A small and unimportant family of the Old World. Its uniqueness comes from the 1-sided flowers. The 12-40 stamens are on one side of the flower, and the other side has a fleshy disk. The petals are 4-7, cleft and unequal. The family is probably related to the mustards and capers.

RESEDA L. 1753 [Latin, *resedare*, to calm, alluding to supposed sedative properties]. MIGNONETTE

1a. Flowers yellow; leaves irregularly pinnately parted or bipinnatifid. **R. lutea** L. Adventive. A colony of this species occurs on the Pierre shales north of Boulder, south of Left Hand Canyon. It has been there for at least 50 years but has never shown any tendency to spread from that site.

1b. Leaves simple, lanceolate. **R. luteola** L. DYER'S ROCKET. Adventive, collected only once, in Denver, in 1888, by Alice Eastwood.

RHAMNACEAE BUCKTHORN FAMILY (RHM)

This family is characterized by a shrubby habit, leaves with 3 principal veins, with the remainder closely parallel and pinnate, and flowers in which the stamens are opposite the petals. Few families have this condition (see Primulaceae and Portulacaceae). *Ceanothus* is most diversified in California with over 40 species including some extremely beautiful and decorative shrubs used horticulturally (California lilac). *Rhamnus purshiana* of the Pacific Coast yielded the bark called *cascara sagrada*, used medicinally as a tonic and laxative. *R. cathartica* is a commonly cultivated ornamental shrub in Colorado.

1a. Leaves with 3 prominent parallel veins; ovary partly inferior; fruit dry, capsular; petals 5, white, long-clawed, 2 mm long or more. **Ceanothus**, BUCKBRUSH

1b. Leaves pinnately veined; ovary essentially superior; fruit a fleshy berry, very bitter . . . . (2)

2a. Leaves less than 5 cm long with 2 main veins on each side; margins regularly fine-toothed, each tooth tipped with a dark gland; flowers appearing with the leaves; calyx lobes, petals, and stamens 4; berry 3-4-seeded; plant polygamo-dioecious. **Rhamnus,** BUCKTHORN
2b. Leaves over 5 cm long with more than 5 main veins on each side; margins entire or nearly so; flowers appearing after the leaves, perfect, 5-merous; berry 2-seeded. **Frangula,** ALDER BUCKTHORN

CEANOTHUS L. 1753 [Greek, *keanothos*, a kind of thistle]. BUCKBRUSH

1a. Plants sprawling, with thornlike branchlets; leaves less than 2 cm long, entire or nearly so. **C. fendleri** Gray, BUCKBRUSH. Common in the foothills and dry montane forests. Occasionally hybridizes, at the zone of contact, with *C. herbaceus*, forming plants with intermediate leaf sizes and thorniness.
1b. Branchlets not thornlike; leaves 3 cm or more long, toothed . . . . (2)

2a. Leaves 4-8 cm long, strongly toothed, thick, inrolled when dry, evergreen, and with a sticky, strong-scented lacquer coating. **C. velutinus** Douglas [velvety], STICKY-LAUREL. Steep canyon slopes and open tors. When very abundant it may be a fire hazard because of the volatile oils in the foliage.
2b. Leaves 3 cm long or less, thin, dull, merely pubescent, not strongly balsam-scented. **C. herbaceus** Rafinesque, REDROOT, NEW JERSEY TEA. A midwest prairie relict occurring on outwash mesas of the Front Range, LR-EP.

FRANGULA Miller 1754 [an ancient generic name]. ALDER BUCKTHORN

One species, **F. alnus** (L.) Miller. Adventive, locally established on slopes above the floodplain of Boulder Creek (*Alnus frangula*).

RHAMNUS L. 1753 [ancient Greek name for this genus]. BUCKTHORN

One species, **R. cathartica** L. Commonly cultivated along the Front Range and escaping to nearby gulches where it establishes itself. The berries are black, very bitter, and cathartic.

ROSACEAE ROSE FAMILY (ROS)

The flowers of most members of the rose family are astonishingly similar, the main differences, besides size and color, being in the number and structure of the carpels. All rosaceous flowers have an hypanthium or fused cup formed by the bases of the calyx, corolla, and stamens. There is often a confusing "extra" set of calyxlike parts alternating with the real sepals. For want of an understanding we give them a name–bracteoles. They also occur in the mallows and mentzelias. In a family that provides so many edible fruits, it is odd to find that the edible parts are formed in many ways from quite different floral parts: hypanthium (apple, Pear), carpel wall (cherry, plum), receptacle (strawberry), the whole carpel group without the receptacle (raspberry), and carpels plus receptacle (blackberry).

1a. Shrubs or small trees . . . . (2)
1b. Herbs, sometimes woody at the very base . . . . (17)

2a. [1] Leaves compound, the leaflets clearly separate from the rachis . . . (3)
2b. Leaves simple or lobed, sometimes very deeply so . . . . (6)

3a. [2] Flowers yellow; leaves pinnately compound but crowded so as to appear to be palmate. **Pentaphylloides,** SHRUBBY CINQUEFOIL

3b. Flowers pink or white; leaves distinctly pinnate . . . . (4)

4a. [3] Leaflets 11-15; small tree with umbellike flower clusters and orange berries; thorns or prickles absent. **Sorbus,** ROWAN TREE, MOUNTAIN-ASH

4b. Leaflets 5-7; shrubs with thorns or prickles . . . . (5)

5a. [4] Leaves strongly glaucous beneath; flowers white; fruit a "raspberry." **Rubus,** RASPBERRY

5b. Leaves green, often pale, but not glaucous; flowers pink; fruit a "hip." **Rosa,** WILD ROSE

6a. [3] Leaves deeply pinnately lobed, with narrow, linear leaflets; flowers white; styles becoming long and feathery at maturity. **Fallugia,** APACHE PLUME

6b. Leaves not lobed or shallowly so; otherwise not as above . . . . (7)

7a. [6] Plants with smooth, shiny thorns along the branches. **Crataegus,** HAWTHORN

7b. Plants not thorny as above, but the main branches may terminate in stiff points . . . . (8)

8a. [7] Leaves and twigs glabrous, leaves finely serrulate, never lobed . . . (9)

8b. Leaves and twigs pubescent or leaves coarsely serrate or lobed . . . . (11)

9a. [8] Flowers in a raceme. **Padus,** CHOKECHERRY

9b. Flowers in clusters on short shoots . . . . (10)

10a. [9] Fruit yellowish, glaucous; stone with 2 lengthwise ridges or furrows; twigs modified to terminate in coarse thorns. **Prunus,** PLUM

10b. Fruit red, not glaucous; stone plump, not ridged as above; twigs not stiff and thornlike. **Cerasus,** CHERRY

11a. [8] Leaves simple or shallowly pinnately lobed . . . . (12)

11b. Leaves palmately lobed, often faintly so . . . . (14)

12a. [11] Flowers white, in terminal, many-flowered, pyramidal clusters. **Holodiscus,** OCEANSPRAY

12b. Flowers white or yellowish, axillary or in few-flowered clusters . . . . (13)

13a. [12] Leaves ovate or oblong, tapering to the base; style becoming long and feathery in fruit; fruit dry, of a single carpel; leaves permanently and densely pubescent beneath. **Cercocarpus,** MOUNTAIN-MAHOGANY

13b. Leaves broadly ovate, abruptly rounded at the base; petiole distinct; style not feathery; fruit several-carpellate; leaves usually losing much of their pubescence at maturity; flowers white, large, in axillary clusters; stamens not conspicuously exserted; tall shrub; fruit a pome. **Amelanchier,** SERVICEBERRY

14a. [11] Leaves oblanceolate, deeply few-lobed at the apex, white-tomentose beneath. **Purshia,** BITTERBRUSH, CLIFF-ROSE

14b. Leaves not oblanceolate nor otherwise as above . . . . (15)

15a. [14] Flowers small, in umbellate cymes; fruit of 1 or a cluster of 2 or more papery carpels. **Physocarpus,** NINEBARK

15b. Flowers large, solitary or in few-flowered cymes; fruit an aggregate of fleshy achenes (raspberry) . . . . (16)

16a. [15] Leaves 3-6 cm wide, the lobes rounded. **Oreobatus,** BOULDER RASPBERRY

16b. Leaves 10-20 cm wide, the lobes acute. **Rubacer,** THIMBLEBERRY

17a. [1] Leaves simple, crenate, white beneath; loosely matted alpine plants; flowers large, white, with usually 8 petals and plumose styles. **Dryas,** MOUNTAIN DRYAD
17b. Leaves compound or variously divided . . . . (18)

18a. [17] Leaves palmately compound, with 3 or more leaflets . . . . (19)
18b. Leaves pinnatifid, ternately subdivided or pinnately compound . . . . (22)

19a. [18] Flowers yellow . . . . (20)
19b. Flowers white or pink . . . . (21)

20a. [19] Petals minute, narrow; leaves few-toothed at the apex; densely matted, snowbed plant with only basal leaves and very short inflorescence. **Sibbaldia**
20b. Not as above. **Potentilla,** CINQUEFOIL, FIVEFINGER

21a. [19] Leaves not basal; stems very slender, rhizomatous; flowers rose-purple; streamsides and willow carrs. **Cylactis,** ARCTIC RASPBERRY
21b. Leaves basal from a stout caudex, stem stoloniferous; flowers white; forest floors. **Fragaria,** STRAWBERRY

22a. [18] Leaves several times ternately divided; flowers minute, white or pinkish. **Chamaerhodos**
22b. Leaves pinnately compound or cleft . . . . (23)

23a. [22] Leaves pinnately compound, with ± uniform leaflets . . . . (24)
23b. Leaves variously pinnatifid, with unequal segments or leaflets . . . . . (30)

24a. [23] Flowers in tight, ball-like heads or short spikes . . . . (25)
24b. Flowers not as above . . . . (26)

25a. [24] Leaflets oval, toothed; flowers greenish, without petals. **Sanguisorba,** BURNET
25b. Leaflets divided to the base into 3 lobes; flowers yellow. **Ivesia**

26a. [24] Petals red-purple; glaucous-leaved rhizomatous plant of wet pondshores. **Comarum,** PURPLE CINQUEFOIL, FIVEFINGER
26b. Petals yellow . . . . (27)

27a. [26] Plant with basal leaves only, with 7-30 leaflets, silvery beneath, spreading by long, usually red stolons. **Argentina,** SILVERWEED
27b. Plant with leafy stems or at least not stoloniferous . . . . (28)

28a. [27] Flowers in a narrow raceme; upper half of mature hypanthium covered with hooked bristles. **Agrimonia,** AGRIMONY
28b. Flowers in a branched inflorescence; hypanthium without hooks . . . (29)

29a. [28] Style attached to near top of ovary; leaves either palmately compound or pinnately compound with narrow leaflets. **Potentilla,** CINQUEFOIL, FIVEFINGER
29b. Style attached near the base of the ovary; leaves pinnately compound with broadly oval leaflets. **Drymocallis**

30a. [23] Style jointed, the lower part persistent and with a terminal hook; leaves pinnately compound with few unequal leaflets, the uppermost one usually larger; flowers erect, yellow, white, or rose. **Geum,** AVENS
30b. Style continuous, not hooked; leaves with many narrow segments . . (31)

31a. [30] Petals pinkish-white; flowers nodding; style plumose at maturity. **Erythrocoma**, PRAIRIE SMOKE
31b. Petals yellow; flowers erect. **Acomastylis**, ALPINE AVENS

ACOMASTYLIS Greene 1906 [Greek, *a*, without, + *coma*, mane, + *stylis*, style]. ALPINE AVENS

One species, **A. rossii** (R. Brown) Greene subsp. **turbinata** (Rydberg) Weber [for Captain James C. Ross, Arctic explorer; turbinate, as to the hypanthium]. Very abundant on rocky tundra, forming a dense, tight turf in areas with relatively little winter snow cover. *Acomastylis* is responsible for the deep red autumn color of the tundra, contrasting with the golden bronze of *Kobresia*. *Acomastylis* is essentially an Asiatic genus (*Geum*).

AGRIMONIA L. 1753 [corruption of *Argemone*, a plant mentioned by Pliny]. AGRIMONY

One species, **A. striata** Michaux. Brushy areas in the bottoms of gulches, outer foothills of Front Range.

AMELANCHIER Medikus 1789 [Provençal name for a European species]. SERVICEBERRY

1a. Petals broadly oval, not more than 3 times as long as wide; leaves permanently soft-hairy beneath. **A. utahensis** Koehne. Uncommon on the Eastern Slope, on the unforested fringes of the Front Range, San Luis Valley, and North Park.
1b. Petals narrowly oblong, more than 3 times as long as wide; leaves and young twigs glabrous or glabrate in age. **A. alnifolia** Nuttall [alder-leaved]. Common in the forested parts of the mountains (including *A. pumila*, a glabrous form).

ARGENTINA Hill 1756 [Latin, *argentum*, silver]. SILVERWEED

One species, **A. anserina** (L.) Rydberg. Mountain meadows and poorly drained roadside ditches, montane, subalpine. The bicolored pinnate leaves and long stolons are diagnostic (*Potentilla*). In China this species produces tubers that are much used for food, but I have not found them on our plants.

CERASUS Miller 1754 [Greek, *kerasos*, cherry]. CHERRY

1a. Small tree; fruit red. **C. pensylvanica** (L.*f*.) Loiseleur. PIN CHERRY. Frequent on canyon slopes in the Front Range foothills, a relictual midwestern species (*Prunus*). One station also in western Conejos County.
1b. Low spreading shrub; fruit purple-black. **C. pumila** (L.) Michaux subsp. **besseyi** (Bailey) Weber [dwarf; for C. E. Bessey, Nebraska botanist, 1845-1915]. Outwash mesas of the Front Range and sandstone outcrops on the plains; also on west side of San Luis Valley, blooming very early in the spring (*Prunus*).

CERCOCARPUS Humboldt, Bonpland & Kunth 1824 [Greek, *cerkos*, tail, + *carpos*, fruit]. MOUNTAIN-MAHOGANY

One species, **C. montanus** Rafinesque. Widespread in the Front Range foothills, San Luis Valley and Mesa de Maya, especially on dry, rocky slopes of hogbacks.

CHAMAERHODOS Bunge 1829 [Greek, *chamae*, dwarf, + *rhodon*, rose]

One species, **C. erecta** (L.) Bunge subsp. **nuttallii** (Pickering) Hultén. Abundant, open, gravelly plains of intermountain parks. The typical subspecies occurs in Siberia.

COMARUM L. 1753 [Greek, *comaron*, ancient name for some plant, used by the author of *Apuleius' Herbarium*, fourth century A.D.]. PURPLE CINQUEFOIL, FIVE-FINGER

One species, **C. palustre** L. Recently discovered by Betsy Neely for the first time on the Eastern Slope, on the eastern side of the Park Range in the Mount Zirkel Wilderness, on the marshy borders of subalpine ponds. The plant trails and roots at the lower nodes and the purple petals are shorter than the sepals. While the leaves are pinnately compound, the leaflets may be close together (*Potentilla*).

CRATAEGUS L. 1753 [Greek, *kratos*, strength]. HAWTHORN

1a. Leaves not distinctly lobed although often distinctly serrate. **C. rivularis** Nuttall [riparian]. San Luis Valley and North Park, essentially a Western Slope species.

1b. Leaves distinctly although shallowly lobed in addition to the normal marginal serrations . . . . (2)

2a. Leaves and petioles pubescent at maturity; marginal teeth not strongly gland-tipped; spines over 4 cm long; inflorescence flat-topped, broad; fruits remaining bright red through leaf-fall; plants usually quite close to streams. **C. macracantha** Loddiges var. **occidentalis** (Britton) Eggleston [big-thorned; western], **Pl. 64**. Common in outer foothills, Front Range.

2b. Leaves and petioles glabrous at maturity; marginal teeth with black glandular tips; thorns shorter or sometimes lacking; inflorescence racemose; fruits soon turning dark purplish red; plants usually on dry hillsides rather than near the streambeds. **C. erythropoda** Ashe [red-based].

CYLACTIS Rafinesque 1819 [Greek, *cylix*, cup, + *actis*, ray, from the flower shape]. ARCTIC RASPBERRY

1a. Plant extensively trailing over the ground, the shoots with several leaves, ultimately ending in a slender whip; flowers white, 1-7 per shoot. **C. pubescens** (Rafinesque) Weber, **Pl. 40**. Infrequent but locally abundant in cool north-facing canyons in the outer foothills, BL, DA. A relictual eastern woodland species. Petals usually remaining closed over the stamens. The leaves usually have 3 leaflets, but the lower pair are sometimes lobed and, in extreme instances, divided to make 5 leaflets (*Rubus*). Confusion with *Fragaria*, which has stolons, is avoidable if one sees that the veins of the leaves are simple and unbranched, while those of *Cylactis* are reticulate-veined.

1b. Plant rarely with prolonged vegetative shoots; shoots erect, with about 3 leaves, terminating with a single, large, rose-pink flower. **C. arctica** (L.) Rafinesque subsp. **acaulis** (Michaux) Weber. Infrequent, mossy willow thickets along mountain streams (*Rubus*).

DRYAS L. 1753 [named for the mythological dryads]. MOUNTAIN DRYAD

One species, **D. octopetala** L. subsp. **hookeriana** (Juzepczuk) Hultén. Dry tundra, especially on limestone or where calcium is available as a leachate from the granite.

DRYMOCALLIS Fourreau 1908 [Greek, *drymos*, woodland, + *callis*, trail] (formerly in *Potentilla*)

1a. Flowers cream-colored, scarcely longer than the sepals. **D. arguta** (Pursh) Rydberg, STICKY CINQUEFOIL. Montane meadows and open, rocky flats in sagebrush, generally replacing *G. fissa* at higher altitudes.

1b. Flowers bright yellow, usually longer than the sepals . . . . (2)

2a. Inflorescence an open cyme; stems slender. **D. glandulosa** (Lindley) Rydberg. A peripheral northern Rocky Mountain species, known from the Rawah Range, and probably also to be found in the Park Range, bordering North Park.

2b. Inflorescence a dense, congested cyme; stems stout. **D. fissa** (Nuttall) Rydberg, **Pl. 24**. Abundant in the foothills of the Front Range; also North Park.

ERYTHROCOMA Greene 1906 [Greek, *erythro*, red, + *coma*, mane]. PRAIRIE SMOKE

One species, **E. triflora** (Pursh) Greene. Mountain meadows and forest openings. The pink nodding flowers, beautifully plumose styles, and pinnatifid basal leaves are diagnostic (*Geum*).

FALLUGIA Endlicher 1840 [for Virgilio Fallugi, seventeenth-century botanical writer]. APACHE PLUME

One species, **F. paradoxa** (D. Don) Endlicher. Abundant and attractive shrub in the San Luis Valley; also in Arkansas Valley near Pueblo. The flowers are white and the feathery styles a delicate pink.

FRAGARIA L. 1753 [Latin, *fraga*, strawberry, implying its fragrance]. STRAWBERRY

1a. Leaves pure green, not glaucous on the upper surface, relatively thin and with impressed veins above; upper surface silky-pilose; terminal tooth of the leaflets ± well developed, usually projecting beyond the uppermost lateral teeth; inflorescence commonly equalling or surpassing the leaves. **F. vesca** L. subsp. **bracteata** (Heller) Staudt. In more mesic sites than the next.

1b. Leaflets glaucous and somewhat bluish-green above, rather thick and not prominently veiny and usually glabrous, the veins on the upper surface not impressed; terminal tooth of the leaflets small, usually surpassed by the adjacent lateral teeth; inflorescence commonly shorter than the leaves. **F. virginiana** Miller subsp. **glauca** (Watson) Staudt. In dry forests.

GEUM L. 1753 [a name used by Pliny]. AVENS

1a. Petals yellow; sepals purplish, reflexed after blossoming . . . . (2)

1b. Petals pale violet; sepals green, not reflexed after blossoming. **G. rivale** L. [of brooksides], PURPLE AVENS. Swamps and wet meadows, subalpine.

2a. Lower section of style glabrous or sparsely pubescent at the base, not glandular; terminal leaf segment not greatly enlarged. **G. aleppicum** Jacquin [of Aleppo, Syria], YELLOW AVENS. Ravines and canyonsides, foothills and montane.

2b. Lower section of style glandular-puberulent; terminal leaf segment usually greatly enlarged. **G. macrophyllum** Willdenow, LARGE-LEAVED AVENS. Moist meadows and streamsides, montane to subalpine. The terminal leaflet is fan-shaped in the typical form, but narrower and incised in subsp. **perincisum** (Rydberg) Hultén.

HOLODISCUS Maximovicz 1879 [Greek, *holo*, entire, + *diskos*, circular plate, describing the flower]. OCEANSPRAY

One species, **H. dumosus** (Hooker) Heller, **98E**. Cliff faces and rocky escarpments, middle altitudes, Front Range from Rocky Mountain National Park southward; margins of San Luis Valley (including *H. microphyllus*).

IVESIA Torrey & Gray 1858 [for Eli Ives, professor of pharmacy, Yale University]

One species, **I. gordonii** (Hooker) Torrey & Gray. Rocky pavements in sagebrush zone up to dry alpine meadows, scattered over the area but rather local, east side of Park Range, JA.

OREOBATUS Rydberg 1903 [Greek, *oros*, mountain, + *batos*, bramble]. BOULDER RASPBERRY

One species, **O. deliciosus** James, **98A.** Common in canyons of the Front Range, upper Arkansas Valley, Mesa de Maya, edges of San Luis Valley (*Rubus*). The original plants were collected by Edwin James at the mouth of Boulder Canyon.

PADUS Miller 1854 [the ancient Greek name]. CHOKECHERRY

One species, **P. virginiana** (L.) Miller subsp. **melanocarpa** (Nelson) Weber. Along streams in the lower valleys, intermountain parks, and in protected gulches on the plains (*Prunus*).

PENTAPHYLLOIDES Duhamel 1755 [Greek, *pente*, five, + *phyllon*, leaf]. SHRUBBY CINQUEFOIL

One species, **P. floribunda** (Pursh) Löve, **98B.** Locally abundant along drainage lines, sagebrush-aspen (*Potentilla*). This is as clear-cut a genus as we have in the Rosaceae, differing from *Potentilla* in morphology and chemistry; it seems to have been kept there purely as a matter of tradition.

PHYSOCARPUS Maximovicz 1879 [Greek, *physa*, bellows, + *carpos*, fruit, from the inflated carpels]. NINEBARK

1a. Leaves mostly wedge-shaped at the base, the blades 3-8 cm long, with 3 main lobes; mature fruits up to 1 cm long. **P. opulifolius** (L.) Maximovicz [with leaves like *Viburnum opulus*]. Relictual in the outer Front Range foothills. This species seems to hybridize with the next wherever they occur together, most plants being intermediate.

1b. Leaves truncate or even somewhat cordate at the base, the blades small (2-3 cm long), with a tendency to be 5-lobed; mature fruits not much more than 5 mm long. **P. monogynus** (Torrey) Coulter [with one ovary; a misnomer], **98D.** This genus is sometimes confused vegetatively with *Ribes*, but *Physocarpus* has stellate hairs on the leaves and calyx. The bark also flakes off in long thin strips. The leaves resemble those of currants but the flowers are in umbellate clusters.

POTENTILLA L. 1753 [diminutive of Latin, *potens*, powerful, originally applied to *Anserina*, for its curative powers]. CINQUEFOIL, FIVE-FINGER

(The key is based, in large part, on unpublished work of Barry C. Johnston)

1a. Plants creeping, with slender-whiplike branches that root at the tips; leaves palmately compound; flowers 4-merous. **P. anglica** Laicharding [of England]. Adventive, established along Boulder Creek below the White Rocks.

1b. Plants not creeping; flowers 5-merous . . . . (2)

2a. [1] Annuals or short-lived perennials, mostly weedy species . . . . (3)

2b. Perennials; native plants . . . . (8)

3a. [2] Leaves white-tomentose beneath, digitately compound with very narrow leaflets. **P. argentea** L., SILVERY CINQUEFOIL. Adventive, infrequent in dry, disturbed ground, BL, LR.

3b. Leaves not white-tomentose beneath . . . . (4)

4a. [3] Leaves digitately compound, very coarsely toothed; flowers pale yellow; achenes rugose-reticulate; pubescence of a short coat of often glandular hairs, and another of long pilose hairs. **P. recta** L. [upright]. Adventive, originally known from old collections in the Boulder Valley, but now an extremely abundant weed at Roxborough State Park, and spreading in the Boulder area.

4b. Leaves pinnately compound or trifoliolate . . . . (5)

5a. [4] Leaves all pinnately compound with 5 or more leaflets; achene with a swelling on the side. **P. supina** L. subsp. **paradoxa** (Nuttall) Sojak [outstretched; strange]. Bottomlands and pondshores, plains and piedmont valleys; San Luis Valley (*P. paradoxa*).

5b. Some or all of the leaves with 3 leaflets (trifoliolate) . . . . (6)

6a. [5] Stems stiffly hirsute below with ± pustular-based, spreading hairs; achenes usually strongly undulate-corrugate longitudinally; stamens about 20; petals mostly at least 3/4 the length of the sepals. **P. norvegica** L., NORWAY CINQUEFOIL. Adventive weed of pastures and grazed meadows.

6b. Stems soft-pubescent below, often with glandular or multicellular pubescence; achenes smooth or very slightly striate; stamens mostly 10-15; petals usually less than 3/4 the length of the sepals . . . . (7)

7a. [6] Basal portion of stems soft-pubescent, often ± lanate; plants without glandular hairs; lower cauline leaves commonly 5-foliolate. **P. rivalis** Nuttall [of brooks]. Floodplains and wet depressions.

7b. Basal portion of stems with multicellular, often glandular hairs; lower cauline leaves trifoliolate; inflorescence glandular. **P. biennis** Greene. Ruderal sites and meadows.

8a. [2] Style 1 mm long or shorter, often conical and thickened at the base and tapered to the stigma, relatively thick just below the stigma . . . . (9)

8b. Style 1.2 mm long or often much longer, usually thin just below the stigma . . . . (13)

9a. [8] Leaves always digitate, ternate, or subdigitate, with 3-5 leaflets, often with flat margins; style often uniformly thickened; lower leaf pubescence usually snow white and formed of long, entangled hairs; stems short, decumbent-ascending; inflorescence openly branched; strictly alpine . . . . (10)

9b. Leaflets 7-15, pinnate, to (less commonly) 5-7, subdigitate, with revolute margins; inflorescence tight-branched, the flowers clustered; plants sometimes alpine but then leaves either clearly pinnate, stems erect-ascending, or with greenish or yellowish pubescence; stems often tall and erect, especially at lower elevations. **P. pensylvanica** L. Moist bottomland with clay soil to rocky montane and alpine ridges. The alpine, subdigitate form is var. **paucijuga** (Rydberg) Welsh & Johnston.

10a. [9] Leaves 5-foliolate, digitate to subdigitate; petioles conspicuously spreading-pilose, rarely also obscurely tomentose. **P. rubricaulis** Lehmann [red-stemmed]. Rocky, exposed alpine ridges. Resembles *P. subjuga*, but *P. rubricaulis* has short styles that often are papillose at the base.

10b. Leaves 3-foliolate; petioles conspicuously tomentose, sometimes also with spreading, straight pubescence . . . . (11)

11a. [10] Flowers (1)2-3 per stem; plants densely matted; petioles usually not visible, hidden in the base of the plant, densely pilose, with or without additional dense tomentum. **P. uniflora** Ledebour. Flowers seem large in comparison to the rest of the plant. Alpine talus slopes and fellfields (*P. ledebouriana*).

11b. Flowers 5-40 per stem, or else petioles plainly visible and plants not matted on talus slopes; petioles sparsely pilose or else densely tomentose . . (12)

12a. [11] Petioles densely tomentose, often with a few straight hairs as well; plants often low, matted. **P. nivea** L. [of snow]. Wind-scarred ridges and edges of exposed alpine ledges; leaflets sometimes broadly and shallowly toothed.

12b. Petioles spreading-pilose, sometimes tomentose as well; plants taller. **P. hookeriana** Lehmann [for W. J. Hooker]. Grassy tundra and protected scree slopes; leaflets usually more deeply and narrowly toothed than in the last.

13a. [8] Plant densely short-glandular, with some long pilose hairs; dwarf, with mostly basal, digitate or subdigitate leaves. **P. subviscosa** Greene. A species of New Mexico and Arizona, known in Colorado from a single locality near Stonewall, LA.

13b. Plant not glandular . . . . (14)

14a. [13] Blossoming in early spring, before leaf maturity; pedicels arched downward in fruit. **P. concinna** Richardson [neat]. Pine woods, rocky ridges, sagebrush to lower alpine. Leaves digitate, white-tomentose below, strigose-pustulose above; calyx broader than long when pressed. Var. **bicrenata** (Rydberg) Welsh & Johnston has only 3 teeth on each leaflet.

14b. Blossoming in summer, after leaf maturity; fruiting pedicels erect to ascending . . . . (15)

15a. [14] Leaves pinnate or, if subdigitate, with 7 or more leaflets . . . . . (16)

15b. Leaves digitate or subdigitate, with 5 leaflets . . . . (23)

16a. [15] Leaves subdigitate with 7 leaflets . . . . (17)

16b. Leaves plainly pinnate, with 9 or more leaflets . . . . (18)

17a. [16] Alpine or high subalpine, above 3,000 m, ridges or upper slopes. **P. subjuga** Rydberg [somewhat paired]. Leaflets narrowly toothed, tomentose below, always with some visible rachis between the terminal 3 leaflets and the lower pairs. A high-alpine form occurs with more finely dissected leaflets.

17b. Montane to submontane meadows and lower slopes, usually below 3,000 m. **P. pulcherrima x P. hippiana.**

18a. [16] Leaves uniformly and sparsely silky or pilose, not tomentose, often green . . . . (19)

18b. Leaves uniformly and densely hirsute, or else densely tomentose, appearing silvery or grayish-green on lower leaf surfaces . . . . (22)

19a. [18] Plant tall and stout, 5-more dm high, with several stems from stout caudices; leaves over 2 dm long, with 6-7 pairs of leaflets, the foliage and stems densely pilose. **P. ambigens** Greene, **Pl. 53**. A gigantic plant, the largest of all Colorado species. Very sporadic, first collected near Morrison, but now known from Wagon Wheel Gap.

19b. Plant smaller in all respects . . . . (20)

20a. [19] Primary pinnae cuneate, broadest toward the apex, toothed but undivided; petioles strongly marcescent, remaining a second year or more. **P. rupincola** Osterhout. Local, on granite cliffs, northern LR.

20b. Primary pinnae deeply lobed; old petioles not strongly marcescent . . (21)

21a. [20] Dry, rocky ridges and slopes, submontane to alpine. **P. ovina** Macoun [of sheep].

21b. Moist to wet bottoms, streamsides, and mountain meadows. **P. plattensis** Nuttall [of the Platte River]. Common in wet meadows and ditches, foothills and mountain parks, sometimes nearly invisible (except for the flowers) in tall sedge-grass stands.

22a. [18] Bracteoles darker than the calyx, bicolored; calyx small, densely white-tomentose; flowers small; leaves usually not bicolored, ± equally tomentose above and below, often toothed only in the upper third. **P. effusa** Douglas [straggling]. Dry hillsides, most abundant in North Park.

22b. Bracteoles the same color as the calyx, which is often green or sparsely tomentose and larger; leaves often bicolored, toothed throughout. **P. hippiana** Lehmann [for Carl Frederick Hippio, a revered colleague of Lehmann]. Dry hillsides, abundant.

23a. [15] All leaves strictly digitate, with no rachis evident between the leaflets even with magnification; leaflets either not tomentose or else not strongly bicolored, ± equally pubescent above and below . . . . (24)

23b. Leaves subdigitate, at least a short rachis visible between leaflets on some leaves; leaves bicolored, tomentose below, less pubescent above . . . . (26)

24a. [23] Leaves slightly subdigitate; plants large, with fine-toothed bicolored leaflets. **P. pulcherrima** Lehmann [very beautiful]. Meadows and rocky slopes, submontane to lower alpine. Often forms hybrid swarms with *P. hippiana*.

24b. Leaves clearly subdigitate, the rachis visible without magnification . . (25)

25a. [24] Alpine and upper subalpine above 3,000 m, ridges or slopes; leaves always with a definite rachis between leaflets; upper leaflets usually 3, the lower 1 or 2 pairs. **P. subjuga** Rydberg. Large for an alpine plant, but smaller in all parts than *P. pulcherrima*.

25b. Montane to submontane, slopes and meadows; leaves highly variable, some pinnate, some subdigitate; upper leaflets usually 5. **P. pulcherrima x hippiana**. A common cross producing many distinctive apomictic clones.

26a. [23] Leaflets finely short-toothed along their whole length (teeth go less than halfway to the midrib), bicolored, densely tomentose below. **P. pulcherrima** Lehmann.

26b. Leaflets either toothed only in upper third, or else more deeply toothed; leaflets not densely tomentose, otherwise pubescent or not bicolored (if strongly bicolored, then narrowly and deeply toothed) . . . . (27)

27a. [26] Plants small, often less than 20 cm tall; leaves green, glaucous, or sparsely silky, never tomentose; leaflets toothed only in upper third. **P. diversifolia** Lehmann. Abundant, alpine and subalpine; closely related to *P. ovina*, which is obviously pinnate.

27b. Leaves grayish green or sparsely tomentose at least below; leaflets deeply toothed throughout into long narrow teeth. Uncommon, montane and lower subalpine. **P. gracilis** Douglas [slender]. The var. **brunnescens** (Rydberg) Hitchcock has strigose lower leaf surfaces, and var. **glabrata** (Lehmann) Hitchcock has sparser, finer pubescence on the lower leaf surfaces.

PRUNUS L 1975 [ancient Latin name of the plum]. PLUM

1a. Teeth of leaves without glands at their tips. **P. americana** Marshall, WILD PLUM. Abundant on the sides of gulches along the outwash mesas, forming dense thickets, the branches modified to form coarse thorns. A very early blooming shrub; the fruits are edible.

1b. Teeth of leaves with glands at their tips . . . . (2)

2a. Leaves ovate, distinctly toothed, strongly reticulate, and hairy on the underside. **P. gracilis** Engelmann & Gray. Entering Colorado only in the southeast corner; it appears to hybridize with the next,

2b. Leaves narrowly oblong, indistinctly toothed except near the apex, weakly if at all reticulate, glabrous or nearly so. **P. angustifolia** Marshall. Entering Colorado only in the southeast corner.

PURSHIA de Candolle [for Frederick Pursh, 1774-1820, describer of the Lewis and Clark collections]. BITTERBRUSH, CLIFF-ROSE

One species, **P. tridentata** (Pursh) de Candolle, **98F**. Abundant in rocky scrublands, Front Range foothills, south to DA; North Park.

ROSA L. 1753 [the ancient Latin name]. WILD ROSE

1a. Floral stems with broad-based thorns and occasionally with intermixed bristles, rarely unarmed; sepals about 2 mm wide at base; woody stems usually purple-black. **R. woodsii** Lindley [for Joseph Woods, English botanist]. Generally distributed from lowlands to subalpine.

1b. Floral stems bristly to apex or nearly so, more rarely with broad-based thorns, very rarely unarmed; sepals about 3 mm wide at base . . . . (2)

2a. Leaflets obovate-cuneate, often pubescent below and above; inflorescence usually 5- or more-flowered; plants dying back each year to near the base. **R. arkansana** Porter [of the Arkansas River]. Common on the plains.

2b. Leaflets ovate, occasionally pubescent below; inflorescence 1-3-flowered; plants not winter-killed. **R. sayi** Schweinitz [for Thomas Say, zoologist with the Long expedition] (*R. acicularis* of manuals). Outer foothills of Front Range, evidently not as common as *R. woodsii*.

RUBACER Rydberg 1903 [from *Rubus* + *Acer*]. THIMBLEBERRY

One species, **R. parviflorum** (Nuttall) Rydberg [small-flowered, a misnomer]. Frequent in moist, shaded forests.

RUBUS L. 1753 [the ancient Latin name, related to *ruber*, red] (see also *Cylactis*, *Oreobatus*, *Rubacer*). RASPBERRY

One species, **R. idaeus** L. subsp. **melanolasius** (Dieck) Focke, RED RASPBERRY [from Mount Ida; black-haired]. Moist forests. The fruits are delicious, but in this region they rarely are produced in any quantity. Two introduced species, *R. laciniatus* Willdenow, an evergreen, Asiatic blackberry, and *R. occidentalis* L., the black-capped raspberry, were each collected only once on Flagstaff Mountain near Boulder, but they have since disappeared.

SANGUISORBA L. 1753 [Latin, *sanguis*, blood, + *sorbere*, to absorb, for reputed styptic properties]. BURNET

One species, **S. minor** Scopoli. Adventive, infrequent in disturbed mountain meadows, La Veta Pass, Cuchara Valley, Poudre Canyon; one very old collection from Denver probably indicates from whence the plant spread.

SIBBALDIA L. 1753 [for Sir Robert Sibbald, 1641-1722, Scottish botanist]

One species, **S. procumbens** L. [prostrate]. Common on tundra, but extending to subalpine forests in snow accumulation areas.

SORBUS L. 1753 [Latin, *sorbum*, ancient name of the fruit of *Sorbus domestica*]. ROWAN TREE, MOUNTAIN-ASH

One species, **S. scopulina** Greene [of rocks]. Shaded moist gulches, montane zone, mostly near the Continental Divide.

RUBIACEAE MADDER FAMILY (RUB)

The madder family gets its name from madder (*Rubia tinctorum*), cultivated since ancient times for a red dye obtained from its roots. It is a large, mostly tropical family. Our little genus *Galium* is a pale shadow of the many useful and handsome ornamental trees and shrubs belonging to the group. Familiar members of the family are coffee (*Coffea arabica*), quinine (*Cinchona* species) and ipecac (*Cephaëlis* species). The name bedstraw derives from the fact that masses of the lightweight stems of *Galium* form a springy "ticking" because the hooked hairs on the corners of the stems and leaves catch on each other and prevent the stack from matting down. *Galium* is unmistakeable with its combination of square stems, retrorse prickles on the stems and leaves of many species, tiny 4-merous flowers and "double," usually hairy or spiny fruits that separate at maturity into 1-seeded ball-like nutlets. For long-haired animals these are as nasty as burdock fruits.

1a. Corolla funnelform, 5-8 mm long; ovary protruding above the calyx; perennials from a stout taproot; leaves opposite, linear. **Hedyotis**, BLUETS

1b. Corolla rotate, minute; calyx above the top of the ovary; annuals or weak perennials with slender roots; leaves usually whorled, if appearing opposite, then elliptic. **Galium**, BEDSTRAW

GALIUM L. 1753 [Greek, *gala*, milk, which is curdled by some species]. BEDSTRAW

1a. Flowers yellow; leaves narrowly linear; leaves 4-6 at a node; plants tall, with very many flowers. **G. verum** L. [true], YELLOW BEDSTRAW, **99G**. Adventive along irrigation ditches in the Boulder area. In Siberia I have traveled with women who collected masses of this to be used for joint ailments.

1b. Flowers white or greenish; leaves usually broader . . . . (2)

2a. Leaves 2 or 4 at a node . . . . (3)

2b. Leaves at least 6 at a node . . . . (5)

3a. Stems tall, erect; leaves 4 at a node, lanceolate, blunt-tipped, broadest at the base; flowers white, in a ± pyramidal inflorescence. **G. septentrionale** Roemer & Schultes, NORTHERN BEDSTRAW, **99C**. This has been lumped with the Eurasian *G. boreale*, which differs in having cream-colored flowers and other measurable differences. *G. boreale* is tetraploid and *G. septentrionale* hexaploid. Common in moist meadows and woodlands, montane, subalpine.

3b. Stems slender and weak, either erect and less than 3 dm tall, or decumbent-creeping . . . . (4)

4a. Leaves usually 2 at a node (or, if 4, one pair smaller than the other); fruits bristly-hairy; plant weak but erect, the stem hardly prickly; flowers solitary at the nodes. **G. bifolium** Watson [2-leaved], **99B**. Shaded woodlands, Rocky Mountain National Park to Rabbit Ears Pass. Essentially a Western Slope species.

4b. Leaves 4 at a node; fruits smooth; plant weak and trailing; flowers often more than 1 at a node. **G. trifidum** L. subsp. **brevipes** (Fernald & Wiegand) Löve & Löve [3-cleft; short-stemmed], **99F**. Wet ground of willow fens and meadows (*G. brandegei*).

5a. Leaves broadly elliptic about 1 cm wide, abruptly mucronate . . . . (6)

5b. Leaves narrowly oblanceolate, not over 5 mm wide, narrowed to a hyaline point . . . . (7)

6a. Ovary with white, spreading hairs (about as long as the width of the fruit), hooked at the tips; flowers white or greenish, mostly in few-flowered axillary cymes. **G. triflorum** Michaux [3-flowered], FRAGRANT BEDSTRAW. Deeply shaded woodlands, foothills to subalpine.

6b. Ovary with very short hairs curving over the fruit, hooked from near the base; flowers purplish, mostly in terminal compound cymes. **G. mexicanum** Humboldt, Bonpland & Kunth subsp. **asperrimum** (Gray) Dempster [Mexican; very harsh]. Rare or infrequent in foothills canyons, LR, EP. Evidently preferring more open sites than the last. The leaves of this species are usually not over 2 cm long, but at times they may be as long as in the last species, up to 3 cm.

7a. Flowers greenish-yellow, up to 1.5 mm diameter; fruits 1.5-2.8 mm long (top to bottom); nodes glabrous or slightly hairy; leaves about 3 mm broad. **G. spurium** L. [false], CLEAVERS, GOOSEGRASS, **99D**. Adventive, brushy places and talus.

7b. Flowers white, 2 mm diam; fruits 2.8-4 mm long; nodes usually tomentose; leaves about 5 mm broad. **G. aparine** L. [old generic name, meaning to scratch or cling]. Adventive, less common than the last, in more mesic sites.

HEDYOTIS L. 1753 [Greek, *hedys*, sweet, + *otium*, leisure]. BLUETS

One species, **H. nigricans** (Lamarck) Fosberg. A plains species known only from YM.

RUPPIACEAE DITCHGRASS FAMILY (RUP)

A very small family consisting of a single genus, *Ruppia*, and containing either one extremely polymorphic species or about seven poorly delimited ones. The plant resembles a finely linear-leaved pondweed, but the fruiting peduncles are very distinctive, being loosely coiled like springs, at the ends of which are a cluster of small black achenes.

RUPPIA L. 1753 [for H. B. Ruppius, German botanist, 1688-1719]. DITCHGRASS

One species, **R. cirrhosa** (Petagna) Grande subsp. **occidentalis** (Watson) Löve & Löve, **43D**. Occasional in shallow water of ditches in the piedmont valleys, especially in the area north of Denver (*R. maritima*). The drying plants form masses of blackish, wiry stems and leaves in late summer.

RUTACEAE CITRUS FAMILY (RUT)

The family takes its name from *Ruta graveolens*, the rue, a witches' drug in medieval folklore, and associated with sorrow in Shakespeare's plays. Meadow-rue, *Thalictrum*, is so called because of a resemblance of the leaves to those of *Ruta*. All citrus plants belong to this family, which encompasses many genera of tropical or subtropical distribution. The flowers are often waxy textured and strong scented, either pleasantly or not. A good recognition feature for the family is the presence, in the leaves, of translucent spots (internal glands) that concentrate the aromatic oils (see also *Hypericum*).

1a. Herbaceous, woody at the base; leaves linear; ovary inflated, 2-lobed. **Thamnosma**, RUDA DEL MONTE

1b. Small tree; leaves trifoliolate; fruit a samara. **Ptelea**, HOPTREE

PTELEA L. 1753 [Greek name for the elm, which has similar fruit]. HOPTREE

One species, **P. trifoliata** L. Frequent in gulches at bases of cliffs, Cañon City to Mesa de Maya, Arkansas River drainage. An easily recognized shrub or small tree with trifoliolate leaves with translucent internal glands, and disk-shaped one-seeded samaras with a single, broad wing.

THAMNOSMA Torrey & Frémont 1845 [Greek, *thamnos*, bush, + *osme*, odor]. RUDA DEL MONTE

One species, **T. texana** (Gray) Torrey. Known only from the Cañon City area, where it was collected over a hundred years ago. The plant strongly resembles *Menodora scabra*, in the Oleaceae, which grows in the same area, but the leaves are narrower, gland-dotted, and aromatic.

SALICACEAE WILLOW FAMILY (SAL)

Willows are difficult to identify because the important characters are ephemeral. One needs to know young leaves, mature leaves, flowering and fruiting catkins, and stipules. These parts appear, mature, and fall at different times of the year and in order to see them all one must tag a bush or tree and return to it through a season. Twig color and plant height are also important. Most of us do not have enough patience, hence the difficulty of telling which willow is which. Much of the variability of willows is developmental. At least in our region we have hardly any real evidence of interspecific hybridization although this is common in higher latitudes. Anyone living near willow stands and in search of a productive hobby would do well to study them. They actually are easy to know if the species are seen in all seasons.

1a. Buds with several overlapping scales, resinous; bracts lacerate (jagged-edged); stamens numerous in each flower; flowers on broad, cup-shaped disks; aments (catkins) pendulous. **Populus**, POPLAR, ASPEN, COTTONWOOD

1b. Buds enclosed by a single scale, not resinous; bracts entire or denticulate; stamens few, 2-5; flowers not borne on disks; catkins usually erect. **Salix**, WILLOW

POPULUS L. 1753 [classical Latin name]. POPLAR, ASPEN, COTTONWOOD

1a. Petiole flattened perpendicular to the plane of the leaf; leaves little or no longer than broad . . . . (2)

1b. Petiole not flattened as above; leaves longer than broad . . . . (3)

2a. Leaf broadly ovate to suborbicular, 3-8 cm diameter, finely serrate; bark smooth, white or greenish; buds conical; stigmas 2, filiform. **P. tremuloides** Michaux [resembling the Eurasian species, *P. tremula*], QUAKING ASPEN, **100B**. There are no genetic barriers whatsoever between the American and Eurasian species, hence our plants recently have been proposed as a subspecies of *P. tremula*. Eastern Slope trees commonly have a greenish tint to the bark. The much whiter bark of Western Slope trees is sometimes the result of a powdery thallus of a lichen.

2b. Leaf deltoid, 5-10 cm long, coarsely serrate; bark furrowed; buds ovoid; stigmas 3-4, broad. **P. deltoides** Marshall subsp. **monilifera** (Aiton) Eckenwalder [like a string of beads, alluding to the racemes of fruits], **100C**. Lower river valleys, reaching to the lower limit of *P. angustifolia*.

3a. Leaf ovate to ovate-lanceolate, paler below; terminal bud 2-2.5 cm long, very sticky-resinous. **P. balsamifera** L., BALSAM POPLAR, **100A**. Montane, subalpine, uncommon.

3b. Leaf lanceolate to ovate-lanceolate, green on both sides; terminal bud less than 2 cm long, slender (may or may not be sticky) . . . . (4)

4a. Leaf with an abruptly acuminate apex; blade ovate-lanceolate to rhombic-lanceolate, never narrowly lanceolate; petiole at least half the length of the blade; buds 6-7-scaled, nonaromatic, not sticky. **P. x acuminata** Rydberg, **100E**. A first generation hybrid between *P. deltoides* and *P. angustifolia* in the lower canyons where they overlap, and reproducing by suckers and branch rooting.

4b. Leaf with merely an acute apex; blade usually lanceolate, but sometimes quite broad; petiole a third the length of the blade or shorter; bud 5-scaled, aromatic, rather sticky. **P. angustifolia** James, NARROWLEAF COTTONWOOD, **100D**. Floodplains and streamsides in the middle altitudes. Our most abundant wild cottonwood, except for aspen.

SALIX L. 1753 [the classical Latin name]. WILLOW
(Key adapted, in part, from G. W. Argus, *The genus* Salix *in Alaska and the Yukon*. 1973.)

1a. Prostrate-creeping, strictly alpine plants less than 10 cm high ...... (2)
1b. Taller plants, sometimes dwarfed by grazing or alpine conditions, but rarely creeping or less than 10 cm high .... (3)

2a. [1] Aments terminating the terminal shoots of the season; apex of most leaves obtuse, the blades glaucous and reticulate beneath. **S. reticulata** L. subsp. **nivalis** (Hooker) Löve et al. A tiny alpine plant, easily overlooked. Typical *S. reticulata* of the Arctic has leaves about 5 cm long; most of our plants have very tiny leaves, but on Trail Ridge very large leaves occur (*S. nivalis* subsp. *saximontana*).
2b. Aments on short, lateral shoots, not on the terminal shoots of the season; apex of most leaves acute, the blades not reticulate beneath. **S. arctica** Pallas subsp. **petraea** (Andersson) Löve et al. Common tundra species.

3a. [1] Trees .... (4)
3b. Shrubs .... (8)

4a. [3] Branches pendulous or crown neatly spherical .... (5)
4b. Branches not pendulous nor crown neatly spherical .... (6)

5a. [4] Branches pendulous. **S. babylonica** L., WEEPING WILLOW [Psalm 137: "by the waters of Babylon, we sat down and wept"]. Adventive, commonly cultivated and persisting after abandonment.
5b. Crown neatly spherical. **S. matsudana** Koidzumi [for a Japanese botanist, Sadahisa Matsuda, 1857-1921], GLOBE WILLOW. Adventive, widely cultivated in the Arkansas Valley, not naturalized yet, but included here because it is such a striking feature of the landscape.

6a. [4] Leaves with a few raised glands at the base of the blade; branchlets very brittle, easily broken by pressing the base toward the main stem. **S. fragilis** L., CRACK WILLOW. Adventive, cultivated, and becoming established in the lower valleys. Hybridizes with *S. alba vitellina*.
6b. Leaves without glands; branchlets not excessively brittle .... (7)

7a. [6] Branchlets greenish; leaves not very different beneath, abruptly slender-acuminate. **S. amygdaloides** Andersson [like *Amygdalus*, the peach], PEACH-LEAVED WILLOW. Common, native species along streams in the lower valleys.
7b. Branchlets yellow; leaves pale beneath, acute or abruptly acuminate. **S. alba** L. var. **vitellina** (L.) Koch [white; egg-yolk color], GOLDEN OSIER. Adventive, commonly cultivated on ranches in the valleys and in urban areas, the branches strikingly yellow in winter.

8a. [3] Leaves commonly opposite as well as alternate. **S. purpurea** L., BASKET WILLOW. Adventive, a cultivated species that has been established for many years in and around Colorado Springs.

8b. Leaves never opposite . . . . (9)

9a. [8] Flowering precocious (before the appearance of the leaves). The catkins will not be subtended by leaves, and the leafy shoots, arising later, will not bear catkins . . . . (10)

9b. Flowering coetaneous (with the leaves). The catkins will arise from short leafy shoots . . . . (17)

10a. [9] Capsules glabrous . . . . (11)

10b. Capsules pubescent . . . . (14)

11a. [10] Twigs with a glaucous bloom; leaves elliptic-lanceolate. **S. irrorata** Andersson [moist with dew]. Common in the lower canyon bottoms of the outer foothills.

11b. Twigs not glaucous . . . . (12)

12a. [11] Stipules persistent for several years, linear to ovate, the apex attenuate; styles longer than 1.2 mm; nectaries 2-3 times longer than the ovary stalks. **S. lanata** L. subsp. **calcicola** (Wiegand) Hultén, **Pl. 34**. A disjunct species of the Canadian Eastern Arctic, recently discovered on calcareous ground in the Mosquito Range just east of the Continental Divide, but to be expected wherever there are extensive alpine outcrops of the Leadville limestone. The aments are stout, long, and stiffly erect, and the shrub is low and rounded, not over 1 m tall.

12b. Stipules not persistent for more than one year, elliptic to broadly ovate, apex rounded; styles shorter than 1.2 mm; nectaries shorter; aments on floriferous branchlets 0-0.5 cm long; styles 0.8-1.2 mm long; branchlets sparsely pubescent; leaves elliptic or obovate . . . . (13)

13a. Aments usually on a short, leafy branchlet; petioles and midribs rarely both red; stipules often early deciduous. **S. monticola** Bebb. This is the common streambank willow of montane valleys, with twigs bright yellow in winter.

13b. Aments usually sessile, rarely on a leafy branchlet to 7 mm long; some petioles and midribs often bright red; stipules tending to persist. **S. pseudomonticola** Ball. Similar sites.

14a. [10] Branchlets glaucous . . . . (15)

14b. Branchlets not glaucous (rarely thinly so in *S. planifolia*) . . . . (16)

15a. [14] Aments subglobose, numerous, 10 (rarely up to 20) mm long, on pubescent, leafy peduncles 5-10 mm long; leaves silky-pubescent on both sides or glabrate, ± glaucous beneath. **S. geyeriana** Andersson [for Carl A. Geyer, collector on the Oregon Trail]. Montane and subalpine, along streams.

15b. Aments longer, 10-50 mm long, usually sessile or nearly so, bracteate at the base; leaves sparingly pubescent above, glaucescent and silky-hairy below. **S. drummondiana** Barratt [for Thomas Drummond, botanist with the Franklin Expeditions], BLUE WILLOW. Upper montane and subalpine, along streams (*S. subcoerulea*).

16a. [14] Branchlets velvety-pubescent; styles 0.2-0.5 mm long; pedicels 0.8-2 mm long. **S. scouleriana** Barratt [for Dr. John Scouler, companion of David Douglas in 1825]. The only willow in our area growing in forests away from streamsides.

16b. Branchlets glabrous or nearly so, purple-black; styles 0.5-1.8 mm long; pedicels 0.2-0.8 mm long. **S. planifolia** Pursh. Subalpine fens, streamsides, and lower tundra slopes (*S. phylicifolia* subsp. *planifolia*).

17a. [9] Capsules glabrous . . . . (18)
17b. Capsules pubescent . . . . (26)

18a. [17] Leaves green or paler beneath, but not glaucous . . . . (19)
18b. Leaves glaucous beneath . . . . (22)

19a. [18] Leaves linear, 7-18 times as long as wide, the margins distantly denticulate; aments often branched; bracts deciduous after flowering; pedicels pubescent. **S. exigua** Nuttall [small], SANDBAR WILLOW. Very variable in leaf pubescence (*S. interior*).
19b. Leaves not linear, only 2-5 times as long as wide; aments not branched; bracts persistent . . . . (20)

20a. [19] Tall shrubs . . . . (21)
20b. Low, sprawling shrubs hardly more than 1 m tall; petioles lacking raised glands . . . . (25)

21a. [20] Petioles with raised glands; leaves acuminate; leaves and twigs glabrous. **S. lucida** Mühlenberg subsp. **caudata** (Nuttall) Argus [shiny; acuminate]. Streamsides at low and middle altitudes. The staminate plants are extremely handsome, with large, plump aments with many yellow stamens subtended by large, oblong, yellowish bracts.
21b. Petioles lacking raised glands; leaves acute; leaves and twigs somewhat pubescent; aments 2-10 mm long; leaves broadly lanceolate, elliptic, or oblanceolate. **S. boothii** Dorn. Mountain parks to subalpine (*S. pseudocordata* of Colorado literature).

22a. [18] Leaves acuminate; capsules 3-10 mm long; subalpine . . . . (23)
22b. Leaves acute; capsules less than 5 mm long; mostly plains species . . (24)

23a. [22] Aments 2.5-5 cm long; capsules 3-4.8 mm long, becoming pale brown when ripe. **S. lucida** Mühlenberg subsp. **lasiandra** (Bentham) Argus [shiny; hairy anthers]. Streamsides at low and middle altitudes. The staminate plants are extremely handsome, with large, plump aments with many yellow stamens subtended by large, oblong, yellowish bracts. Rare if present on the Eastern Slope. In both of the species in this couplet the petioles bear glands, and the staminate flowers have up to 5 stamens.
23b. Aments 2-3.5 cm long; capsules 7-10 mm long, olive-brown, cartilaginous, conic-subulate, opening in late summer or autumn. **S. serissima** (Bailey) Fernald [very silky, probably alluding to the seed coma]. Very rare, known in Colorado only from the vicinity of the old Long's Peak Inn.

24a. [22] Pedicels 0.5-2 mm long; leaves often entire. **S. ligulifolia** Ball. Streamsides in desert-steppe areas. There is still some doubt whether this is distinct from the next.
24b. Pedicels 2-4.5 mm long; leaves usually toothed. **S. lutea** Nuttall [yellow]. Similar habitats. Dorn mentions that "a distinguishing feature for this species is the silvery gray bark on the older twigs."

25a. [20] Leaves small, entire, silky-pubescent when young; aments very short, about 1 cm long; bracts light brown; capsules 3-4 mm long. **S. wolfii** Bebb [for John Wolf, 1820-1897, collector for the U. S. Geological Survey]. A low shrub hardly over 1 m high, common along subalpine streamlets. In winter and early spring the deep purple twigs make striking splotches in the snowmelt basins, often forming large, continuous stands.

25b. Leaves 3-4 cm long, glandular-serrulate; aments up to 4 cm long; floral bracts black. **S. myrtillifolia** Andersson. Recently discovered in a calcareous fen on the east base of the Mosquito Range in South Park.

26a. [17] Pedicels 2.8-4.8 mm long, about 10 times as long as the nectaries. **S. bebbiana** Sargent [for M. S. Bebb, 1833-1895, Oklahoma botanist]. Streambanks and lakeshores, foothills to subalpine. The leaves tend to be thin-textured, oblanceolate, and rounded at the apex, difficult to describe but easily recognized with experience (*S. depressa* subsp. *rostrata*).

26b. Pedicels 0-2 mm long, 1-2 times as long as the nectaries . . . . (27)

27a. [26] Leaves densely dull white, lanate-floccose beneath, floccose to glabrescent above, revolute, narrowly elliptic, 3.5-7 times as long as wide; styles red; plant erect, single-stemmed up to the top, from which a few short branches radiate. **S. candida** Fluegge [white], **Pl. 50**. Known from localities in the Rawah Range and South Park. It is an inconspicuous willow growing in *Betula glandulosa* fens.

27b. Leaves not pubescent as above, obovate to broadly or narrowly elliptic, flat, 2-5 times as long as wide; styles yellow-green . . . . (28)

28a. [27] Pubescence appressed-silky; capsules with pedicels up to 2 mm long; slenderly branched shrubs of streambanks and meadows. **S. gracilis** Andersson. A northern species disjunct in the Black Hills and found here in the vicinity of Estes Park. The plant has longer and narrower leaves than the last (*S. petiolaris* of authors, not Smith).

28b. Pubescence tomentose, not appressed-silky; capsules sessile or nearly so; plants low, bushy-branched from the base . . . . (29)

29a. [28] Petioles 1-3 mm long, reddish; pedicel 0-0.25(-0.5) mm long. **S. brachycarpa** Nuttall. Very common in subalpine willow thickets along streams. Extremely variable in height and pubescence, and difficult to separate from the next. However, *S. glauca* almost never occurs below timberline.

29b. Petiole 3-10(-15) mm long, usually yellowish; pedicel 0.5-1(-2) mm long. **S. glauca** L. Very abundant, forming very dense thickets at and above timberline. Possibly hybridization between the two species has obliterated the differences between them, in Colorado at least.

SANTALACEAE SANDALWOOD FAMILY (SAN)

Comandra is what we call a hemiparasite. It has pale green leaves but at the same time it is parasitic, attached to the roots of other plants and deriving some nutrition from them. Our little herbaceous species is unlike the majority of the Santalaceae, which are usually shrubs or trees, some parasitic on other trees, others on the roots of grasses! Most of them are, or were, found in Australia and southeast Asia. One of the earliest conservation tragedies was the wholesale extermination, in the eighteenth and nineteenth centuries, of the fragrant wild sandalwoods of Australia and New Caledonia by exploiters for the perfumery, incense, and fine woodcarving trades. Sandalwoods are now cultivated for these purposes in India.

COMANDRA Nuttall 1818 [Greek, *come*, hair, + *andros*, male, alluding to the hairs of the calyx lobes that are attached to the anthers]. BASTARD-TOADFLAX

One species, **C. umbellata** (L.) Nuttall, **101A.** Common on the plains and in desert-steppe and sagebrush areas. The cortex of the root is blue in cross-section, a very unusual color in such organs. Hemiparasite on many different plants. Presumably the leaves were thought to resemble the toadflax, *Linaria*, hence the common name. The flowers have 4 greenish or pinkish-white perianth parts, and the ovary is inferior.

SAPINDACEAE SOAPBERRY FAMILY (SAP)

A large family of about 150 genera and over 2,000 species, mostly of the tropics of the Old and New Worlds. The most commonly cultivated of these in Colorado is the varnish tree, *Koelreuteria paniculata*, a small, attractive tree with compound leaves, panicles of yellow flowers, and fruits resembling the Chinese lanterns produced by *Physalis*. The Chinaberry, *Schinus molle*, so widely cultivated in southern California, also belongs in this family. We have one native genus that barely comes into the southeastern corner of Colorado.

SAPINDUS L. 1753 [Latin, *sapo*, soap]. SOAPBERRY

One species, **S. saponaria** L. var. **drummondii** (Hooker & Arnott) L. Benson. Infrequent, on outwash fans below rimrock in canyons, BA, LA. This is a medium-sized tree with pinnately compound leaves that lack a terminal leaflet. The flowers are white, in large, dense, terminal panicles, and the fruits are spherical, about 1 cm in diameter.

SAURURACEAE LIZARDTAIL FAMILY (SAU)

The Saururaceae is a very small family of virtual living fossils. Its four small genera occur in eastern Asia and in the relictual Tertiary forest areas of the eastern United States and California.

ANEMOPSIS Hooker & Arnott 1840 [resembling *Anemone*]. YERBA MANSA

One species, **A. californica** Hooker. Adventive, occasional in marshes in the piedmont valleys, perhaps introduced with the seed of irrigated crops, completely naturalized in the Boulder-Denver area, but disappearing with the draining of wetlands. The illusion of an *Anemone*like flower is created by a ring of large creamy-white bracts subtending the short dense spike of inconspicuous flowers.

SAXIFRAGACEAE SAXIFRAGE FAMILY (SAX)

Because so many saxifrages are rock garden plants and grow, in nature, in rocky crevices, many assume that the name alludes to the ability of these plants to break up rocks. Gerard, on the contrary, wrote in *The Herbal* (1633): "This name, *Saxifraga* or Saxifrage, hath of late been imposed on sundry plants farre different in the shapes, places of growing, and temperature, but all agreeing in this one facultie of expelling or driving the stone out of the Kidneies, though not all by one meane or manner of operation." Saxifrages are much more important horticulturally than they ever might have been in medicine. The fleshy-leaved *Bergenia* of the Himalaya and Siberia, and the deep red coral bells, *Heuchera sanguinea*, native in our Southwest, are favorite rock garden plants. Note that *Parnassia*, usually included in this family, has been moved to its own family; also, that I take a narrower view of the genus *Saxifraga* than is currently popular and adopt a number of additional genera, a move suggested by Rafinesque as early as 1834!

1a. Leaves deeply palmately lobed or even divided into narrow leaflets . . (2)
1b. Leaves entire, toothed or shallowly lobed, never compound . . . . (3)

2a. Petals entire or merely notched; leaves deeply 3- or 5-lobed. **Muscaria**, MOSS SAXIFRAGE
2b. Petals deeply and irregularly cleft into slender, pointed divisions; leaves very deeply lobed, some of them compound. **Lithophragma**, STAR SAXIFRAGE

3a. Plants creeping, imbedded in moss, the leaves round-kidney-shaped, shallowly lobed; flowers in an involucrate cluster, petals lacking. **Chrysosplenium**, GOLDEN CARPET
3b. Plants not as above . . . . (4)

4a. Petals large (1 cm or more), long-clawed, deep rose-pink; plants forming dense clumps with many stems clothed at the base with the old leaf bases; leaves, reniform, doubly crenate, not all basal. **Telesonix**, BOYKINIA
4b. Petals smaller, rarely rose-pink; leaves not reniform or, if so, then all basal, with sharp serrations . . . . (5)

5a. Leaves broadly ovate, cordate at the base, ± pentagonal, serrate or serrulate, never coarsely dentate . . . . (6)
5b. Leaves variously shaped, otherwise not as above . . . . (8)

6a. Petals trifid or pectinately lobed. **Mitella**, BISHOP'S CAP, MITREWORT
6b. Petals entire . . . . (7)

7a. Flowers paniculate, at least in the lower part of the almost spicate inflorescence. **Heuchera**, ALUMROOT
7b. Flowers racemose. **Conimitella**

8a. Plant scapose; flowers in a terminal cluster, the flower parts replaced by green or reddish vegetative bulblets; leaves cuneate, with a few terminal teeth; extremely rare and local alpine. **Spatularia**
8b. Plant not as above; flower parts, including petals, present . . . . (9)

9a. Flowers yellow. **Hirculus**, GOLDEN SAXIFRAGE
9b. Flowers white or pink . . . . (10)

10a. Leaves evergreen, broadly linear, ciliate, branches forming mats; flowers white with purple or orange spots, in few-flowered bracteate racemes. **Ciliaria**, SPOTTED SAXIFRAGE
10b. Leaves neither evergreen, linear nor ciliate . . . . (11)

11a. Stems with basal leaves only; flowers in loose or compact spikes or panicles. **Micranthes**, SAXIFRAGE
11b. Stems leafy; stem leaves may be considerably reduced . . . . (12)

12a. Leaves oblanceolate, merely toothed at the apex; stems with reduced leaves. **Muscaria adscendens**
12b. Leaves reniform, deeply 3-7-lobed. **Saxifraga**, SAXIFRAGE

CHRYSOSPLENIUM L. 1753 [Greek, *chrysos*, gold, + *splen*, the spleen, probably from reputed medicinal value]. GOLDEN CARPET

One species, **C. tetrandrum** Fries [4 stamens], **102D**. Rare or at least overlooked plant of cold, mossy banks along subalpine and alpine snowmelt streams along the Continental Divide.

CILIARIA Haworth 1821 [Latin, *cilium*, eyelash, alluding to the leaf margins]. SPOTTED SAXIFRAGE

One species, **C. austromontana** (Wiegand) Weber [of southern mountains], **104D**. Dry, rocky, forested canyons from the foothills to subalpine. Plants forming dense mats, the leaves awl-shaped (like a tiny *Juniperus communis*); flowers white with purple or orange spots, in loose, few-flowered, open panicles (*Saxifraga bronchialis* subsp. *austromontana*).

CONIMITELLA Rydberg 1905 [Greek, *conos*, cone, alluding to the turbinate hypanthium differing from the shallow one of *Mitella*]

One species, **C. williamsii** (Eaton) Rydberg [for R. S. Williams, 1859-1945, Montana botanist; Mr. Williams also was my first tutor in bird-watching in New York City. He started out as a miner in Montana, built the first cabin at what is now Great Falls, and was the last rider for the Pony Express]. In Colorado, known only from margins of *Pseudotsuga* "islands" on the slopes between the Blue River Valley and Ute Pass (ST), but very likely present in the Park Range as well. A very distinctive plant, resembling in leaf form either a *Heuchera* or a *Mitella*. The leaves are rounded-reniform, not at all pentagonal, and the margins are strongly ciliate with rather stout, curved hairs that follow the leaf margin. The flowers are in a slender raceme of up to 10-15 blossoms. The pinkish petals are clawed, the hypanthium narrowly campanulate and minutely glandular-pubescent, with small pink sepals. The nearest other populations are in northern Wyoming.

HEUCHERA L. 1753 [for J. H. Heucher, 1677-1747, German botanist]. ALUM-ROOT

1a. Flowers large, about 1 cm long, zygomorphic, and very oblique at the mouth, the base of the hypanthium swollen on one side. **H. richardsonii** R. Brown [for Sir John Richardson]. Flowers greenish; foliage and stem hirsute. Rare, found only in pine forests of the Black Forest region northeast of Colorado Springs. It is threatened by development, which may ultimately extirpate the species in Colorado.

1b. Flowers much smaller, not as above . . . . (2)

2a. Stamens shorter than the sepals; leaves with blunt or rounded teeth . (3)

2b. Stamens equalling or exceeding the sepals; leaves with sharp, coarse dentations . . . . (4)

3a. Flowers rather deeply campanulate, the sepals usually much exceeding the open-campanulate or hemispheric hypanthium; beaks of the ovary prominent. **H. hallii** Gray [for Elihu Hall, Illinois botanist, collected in Colorado in 1860, 1862]. Foothills and montane, from Pikes Peak region southward.

3b. Flowers flat-campanulate, the sepals only slightly exceeding the flat saucer-shaped hypanthium; beaks of the ovary broad and flat, often imbedded in a surrounding disk, becoming somewhat prominent in fruit. **H. parvifolia** Nuttall [small-leaved], **104C**. Common on cliffs and rock outcrops from the piñon-juniper to the alpine tundra, where the normal tall form is replaced by the dwarf var. **nivalis** (Rosendahl) Löve et al.

4a. Inflorescence an open panicle; sepals and upper part of hypanthium pink. **H. versicolor** Greene [varicolored]. Known in Colorado only from rimrock of Fisher's Peak, near Trinidad. Similar to the Western Slope *H. rubescens*, which has the filaments noticeably flattened and widened at the base, the stamens attached at or near rather than below the attachment point of the petals, and the petioles finely glandular rather than villous as in this species.

4b. Inflorescence a dense spike; sepals and upper part of hypanthium yellowish. **H. bracteata** (Torrey) Seringe. Rocky canyon walls of the Front Range foothills.

HIRCULUS Haworth 1821 [Latin, *hirculus*, little goat, perhaps alluding to the spreading, short styles or "horns"]. GOLDEN SAXIFRAGE

1a. Lower leaves not arranged in a basal rosette; plants neither in dense mats nor with flagellalike stolons. **H. prorepens** (Fischer) Löve & Löve [creeping], **103F**. Frequent in subalpine and alpine fens (*Saxifraga hirculus* of Colorado literature).

1b. Lower leaves arranged in a basal rosette; plant in dense mats or with flagellalike stolons . . . . (2)

2a. Slender flagellar stolons present; plant very glandular-pubescent; leaves ciliate-margined. **H. platysepalus** (Trautvetter) Weber subsp. **crandallii** (Gandoger) Weber [broad sepals; for C. S. Crandall], **103A**. Rocky tundra (*S. flagellaris* of Colorado literature).

2b. Stolons absent; plants almost glabrous; leaf margins not ciliate. **H. serpyllifolius** (Pursh) Weber subsp. **chrysanthus** Gray) Weber [thyme-leaved; yellow-flowered], **103B**. Rocky tundra, forming tight mats (*S. chrysantha*).

LITHOPHRAGMA Torrey & Gray 1840 [Greek equivalent of Latin, *Saxifraga*]. STAR SAXIFRAGE

1a. Basal leaves glabrous or very sparsely pubescent; cauline leaves usually bearing red bulblets; petals usually 5-cleft; seeds muricate. **L. glabrum** Nuttall. Montane sagebrush.

1b. Basal leaves moderately to copiously pubescent at least on the lower surface; bulblets not produced; petals often only 3-cleft; seeds smooth, warty or reticulate, but never muricate . . . . (2)

2a. Calyx narrowly campanulate (3)4-6 mm long at anthesis, mostly 6-10 mm long in fruit; ovary at least 2/3 inferior; petals commonly 3-cleft. **L. parviflorum** (Hooker) Nuttall [small-flowered]. Similar habitats, Rocky Mountain National Park and probably North Park.

2b. Calyx broadly campanulate, 2-3 (3.5) mm long at anthesis and 3.5-5 mm long in fruit; ovary about 1/2 inferior; petals mostly 5(-7)-lobed. **L. tenellum** Nuttall [delicate]. Similar habitats, known on the Eastern Slope from the La Veta Pass area.

MICRANTHES Haworth 1812 [Greek, *micro*, small, + *anthos*, flower]. SAXIFRAGE

1a. Leaves circular in outline, cordate at base, coarsely dentate; petioles long and slender; panicle loose and open. **M. odontoloma** (Piper) Weber [toothed margin], **104A**. Along mountain cascades, subalpine (*Saxifraga*).

1b. Leaves lanceolate or broader, toothed or entire, tapering to a short, broad petiole; inflorescence a dense head or spike . . . . (2)

2a. Leaves elongate, narrowly oblanceolate; spikes usually compound; wet meadows and streamsides, subalpine. **M. oregana** (Howell) Small.

2b. Leaves short, rhomboid; flower clusters usually simple, headlike in anthesis, but occasionally several heads produced on distinct branches; plants on rocky slopes moist in spring, open ground, not wet meadows or streamsides. **M. rhomboidea** (Greene) Small, **102C**. Common from the outer foothills to the alpine tundra. Some specimens with branched inflorescences have been annotated by Krause, the monographer, as *M. occidentalis* (Watson) Small, but he annotated others of the same sort as variant forms of *M. rhomboidea. M. rhomboidea* is a plant of the northern Rockies. Perhaps these unusual plants represent a trace of an ancient hybridization.

MITELLA L. 1753 [Latin, *mitella*, turban]. BISHOP'S CAP, MITREWORT

1a. Stamens opposite the greenish, pinnatifid petals; leaves rather distinctly lobed, the lobes coarsely toothed. **M. pentandra** Hooker [5 stamens]. Deep shade in spruce-fir forests.
1b. Stamens alternating with the 3-parted or entire petals; leaves scarcely lobed, the teeth very shallow and blunt. **M. stauropetala** Piper var. **stenopetala** (Piper) Rosendahl [cruciform; slender petals]. Less frequent than the last, in similar habitats.

MUSCARIA Haworth 1812 [from *Saxifraga muscoides*, ultimately from Latin, *muscus*, moss]. MOSS SAXIFRAGE

1a. Basal leaves with slightly 3-toothed blades; stems solitary. **M. adscendens** (L.) Small, **102A**. Infrequent and very inconspicuous, on moist tundra (*Saxifraga*).
1b. Basal leaves with prominently 3-cleft blades; caespitose plants . . . . . . (2)

2a. Hypanthium and sepals ca. 5 mm high; petals ca. 4 mm long; flowering stems stout, usually tall (commonly up to 6 cm). **M. monticola** Small. Stony tundra. All of the following were lumped together under the name *Saxifraga* (=*Muscaria*) *cespitosa*, a European and Arctic species.
2b. Hypanthium and sepals 3-4 mm high; petals 3 mm or less long; flowering stems slender, rarely more than 4 cm high, usually less . . . . (3)

3a. Petals equalling or slightly exceeding the sepals. **M. delicatula** Small, **103D**. Probably the most abundant of this group on the tundra.
3b. Petals minute, much shorter than the sepals. **M. micropetala** Small. Infrequent and overlooked on tundra.

SAXIFRAGA L. 1753 [see introduction for derivation]. SAXIFRAGE

1a. All but the relatively large terminal flower replaced by reddish bulblets. **S. cernua** L., **103E**. Frequent along snow-runoff rivulets.
1b. Bulblets absent; all flowers normal . . . . (2)

2a. Inflorescence strict, the pedicels erect; hypanthium narrowly campanulate; calyx lobes usually shorter than the hypanthium; glandular hairs on the pedicel short, straight. **S. hyperborea** R. Brown subsp. **debilis** (Engelmann) Löve et al. Subalpine and alpine, usually in dry shaded hollows under boulders.
2b. Inflorescence with spreading pedicels; hypanthium broadly campanulate; calyx lobes equalling or exceeding the hypanthium; glandular hairs on pedicels long and crinkly. **S. rivularis** L. Edges of alpine rivulets.

SPATULARIA Haworth 1821

One species, **S. foliolosa** (R. Brown) Small, **102B**. Extremely rare, known only in Colorado from mossy, wet tundra on and close to Mount Evans. Our plants never have flowers, but in the Arctic some plants have a single terminal flower with petals. Elsewhere in the United States outside of Alaska, a collection has been made in Idaho (*Saxifraga*).

TELESONIX Rafinesque 1837 [Greek, *teleos*, perfect, + *onyx*, claws]. BOYKINIA

One species, **T. jamesii** (Torrey) Rafinesque [for Edwin James], **104B, Pl. 28**. Scattered sporadically on granite tors of the Front Range from Gem Lake, Rocky Mountain National Park, to Pikes Peak, where it is particularly well developed and showy near Windy Point along the Cog Railroad. One of Colorado's most handsome wild plants (*Boykinia*, *Saxifraga*).

SCROPHULARIACEAE FIGWORT FAMILY (SCR)

The showy, tubular, bilabiate flowers of many scrophs show diverse adaptations to insect pollination. In *Penstemon* one of the stamens lacks anthers and instead has a tuft of golden hairs possibly attractive to insects, or at least offering a claw-hold. Scarlet penstemons are hummingbird-pollinated. The corolla of *Castilleja* is so dingy that the floral bracts and calyx substitute as attractants, and the corolla is so narrow that the stamens can hardly fit unless staggered, a challenge neatly met by attaching them at different points and elongating the anther-sacs. Some scrophs, such as *Pedicularis*, have developed such complicated flowers that potential pollinators either cannot reach the nectar or become so impatient that they bite a hole through the base of the corolla, bypassing the stamens and style completely and cancelling the whole adaptation.

1a. Corolla lacking; flowers in spikes, the stamens exserted. **Besseya**
1b. Corolla present . . . . (2)

2a. [1] Anther-bearing stamens 5: corolla nearly radially symmetrical, rotate, yellow; tall, coarse, very velvety-pubescent herb. **Verbascum**, MULLEIN
2b. Anther-bearing stamens 4 or 2; corolla usually somewhat or quite zygomorphic; flowers variously colored . . . . (3)

3a. [2] Fleshy-leaved plants rooted in mud and either stoloniferous or prostrate and rooting at the nodes; flowers white, not strongly zygomorphic . . . (4)
3b. Plants not as above in all details . . . . (5)

4a. [3] Leaves orbicular; plants prostrate, rooting at the nodes; flowers solitary in the leaf axils. **Bacopa**, WATER-HYSSOP
4b. Leaves narrowly spatulate or linear; plants erect but spreading by short stolons; flowers in a basal cluster, the pedicels about 1 cm long. **Limosella**, MUDWORT

5a. [3] Corolla distinctly spurred . . . . (6)
5b. Corolla not spurred but sometimes somewhat swollen or saclike at the base . . . . (7)

6a. [5] Flowers over 1 cm long, yellow, with an orange palate or, if smaller, bright blue; spur very obvious; foliage glabrous and glaucous. **Linaria**, TOADFLAX
6b. Flowers 5-8 mm long, lilac; foliage glandular and pubescent. **Chaenarrhinum**, DWARF SNAPDRAGON

7a. [5] Upper lip of the strongly 2-lipped corolla helmet-shaped, keeled, or deeply concave; stamens always either 4 or 2 . . . . (8)
7b. Upper lip of the corolla not helmet-shaped, keeled, nor deeply concave; stamens 5, 4, or 2; staminodia often present . . . . (12)

8a. [7] Anther cells equal, parallel; stamens 4 . . . . (9)
8b. Anther cells unequal, separated; bracts often colored . . . . (10)

9a. [8] Leaves opposite, merely toothed; calyx 4-toothed, becoming bladderlike and veiny, completely enclosing the fruit and not filled by it. **Rhinanthus**, YELLOW RATTLE
9b. Leaves alternate or basal, pinnatifid in all but two species; calyx cleft on 1 or both sides, becoming distended but neither bladderlike nor completely enclosing the fruit. **Pedicularis**, LOUSEWORT

10a. [8] Bracts highly colored or white; upper corolla lip (galea) very much longer than the small, 3-toothed or 3-keeled lower lip; plants perennial with few exceptions. **Castilleja**, PAINTBRUSH

10b. Bracts green or purplish; galea not or little surpassing the inflated, saccate lower lip; always annual . . . . (11)

11a. [10] Calyx with 4 equal or nearly equal lobes; leaves entire or 3-cleft; plants generally unbranched. **Orthocarpus**, OWL-CLOVER

11b. Calyx split down the side, lacking lobes, resembling the opposing bract; leaves linear, 3-5-parted. **Cordylanthus**, CLUBFLOWER

12a. [7] Corolla distinctly hump-backed; dainty annuals with minute blue-and-white flowers; leaves generally purplish at least on the underside; anther-bearing stamens 4. **Collinsia**, BLUE-EYED MARY

12b. Corolla not hump-backed; otherwise not as above . . . . (13)

13a. [12] Stamens 5, 4 of these anther-bearing, the fifth a staminode . . . (14)

13b. Stamens 4 or fewer, without a staminode . . . . (17)

14a. [13] Sterile stamen represented by a scale on the upper inside of the corolla throat; corolla greenish, somewhat urn-shaped, broad and open, with little distinction of tube and throat. **Scrophularia**, FIGWORT

14b. Sterile stamen an elongate, often bearded filament not much shorter than the anther-bearing stamens; corolla colored or white . . . . (15)

15a. [14] Corolla salverform (tubular and abruptly expanded into an open, flat limb); staminode smooth; leaves filiform; plant suffrutescent; restricted to sand dunes. **Leiostemon**

15b. Corolla not salverform; staminode almost always hairy (bearded) . . . (16)

16a. [15] Calyx deeply 5-parted or divided; corolla not strongly flattened; plants of various habitats, not restricted to tundra. **Penstemon**, BEARDTONGUE

16b. Calyx obtusely 5-lobed; corolla strongly dorsiventrally flattened; low plants of tundra; flowers yellowish-white. **Chionophila**, SNOWLOVER

17a. [13] Anther-bearing stamens 4 . . . . (18)

17b. Anther-bearing stamens 2 . . . . (21)

18a. [17] Corolla tubular; corolla white or purplish, hardly bilabiate. **Digitalis** L., FOXGLOVE

18b. Corolla bilabiate; corolla greenish, yellow, pink, or reddish . . . . (19)

19a. [18] Corolla green with maroon or purplish tint, urn-shaped with little differentiation of tube and limb; stems square; leaves triangular-ovate, dentate; staminode present, scalelike (may be overlooked). **Scrophularia**, FIGWORT

19b. Corolla variously colored, usually showy; stems not 4-angled . . . . . . (20)

20a. [19] Flowers large, bright pink. **Agalinis**

20b. Flowers large or small, yellow (reddish only if small), two species purple. **Mimulus**, MONKEYFLOWER

21a. [17] Leaves chiefly basal, cauline leaves reduced in size and alternate; corolla very irregular, cleft nearly to the base, or absent; flowers in a dense spike, with strongly exserted stamens. **Besseya**, KITTENTAIL

21b. Leaves chiefly cauline, opposite; corolla zygomorphic but not as above; flowers axillary or terminal . . . . (22)

22a. [21] Corolla 2-lipped, zygomorphic, and deeply tubular, not blue . . . (23)
22b. Corolla 4-lobed, only slightly zygomorphic, rotate, never deeply tubular, usually blue . . . . (24)

23a. [22] Corolla whitish with a yellow tube; foliage and branchlets glandular-pubescent, sticky. **Gratiola**, HEDGE-HYSSOP
23b. Corolla white to pinkish, lacking any yellow; plant glabrous. **Lindernia**, FALSE PIMPERNEL

24a. [22] Weedy annuals . . . . (25)
24b. Perennials, rooting at the lower nodes or with rhizomes . . . . (26)

25a. [24] Flowers solitary in axils of normal foliage leaves. **Pocilla**
25b. Flowers in a single, slender terminal raceme. **Veronica peregrina**

26a. [24] Flowers in axillary racemes. **Veronica,** SPEEDWELL
26b. Flowers in terminal spikes . . . . (27)

27a. [26] Decumbent and with creeping rhizomes; lower leaves petiolate; capsule orbicular to obcordate. **Veronicastrum,** THYME-LEAVED SPEEDWELL
27b. Erect, rhizomes not obvious; leaves all sessile, blackening in drying; capsule elliptic, emarginate. **Veronica,** SPEEDWELL

AGALINIS Rafinesque 1837 [anagram of *Anagallis*?]
One species, **A. tenuifolia** (Vahl) Rafinesque, **105A**. Infrequent in marshy ground in the piedmont valleys. The plant has linear leaves and disproportionately large, bell-like, pink flowers. The plant tends to turn black on drying (*Gerardia*).

BACOPA Aublet 1775 [an aboriginal South American name]. WATER-HYSSOP
One species, **B. rotundifolia** (Michaux) Wettstein, **105B**. Low, sprawling, succulent herb of muddy shores of small ponds, piedmont valleys.

BESSEYA Rydberg 1903 [for Rydberg's teacher, Dr. Charles E. Bessey]. KITTEN-TAIL

1a. Corolla absent. **B. wyomingensis** (Nelson) Rydberg. Barely entering Colorado in northern LR.
1b. Corolla present, white to purple . . . . (2)

2a. Corolla deep violet-purple; less than 15 cm tall, the flowering stem compact; leafy bracts 6 or fewer; usually alpine. **B. alpina** (Gray) Rydberg, **105D**. Common throughout the high mountains.
2b. Corolla purple-tinged; usually much over 15 cm tall; leafy bracts more than 6; never strictly alpine. **B. plantaginea** (Bentham) Rydberg. Frequent on grassy slopes in the foothills and mountain parks.

CASTILLEJA Mutis 1782 [for Domingo Castillejo, eighteenth-century Spanish botanist]. PAINTBRUSH
Note: The keys will be easier to follow if one examines the flowers when they are fresh, to see the relative lengths of the upper and lower lips, and to determine the relative incisions of the calyx.

1a. Flowers greenish-white; leaves and bracts linear; corolla almost twice as long as the calyx; plants of the outwash mesas and plains. **C. sessiliflora** Pursh. Our only strictly plains paintbrush.
1b. Not as above; foothills and mountain species . . . . (2)

2a. Lower corolla lip prominent, 1/3-2/3 as long as the upper lip or galea; galea short, half as long as the corolla tube or shorter; bracts yellowish, never red.

C. puberula Rydberg. Rocky tundra, high peaks of the Continental Divide, PA to LR.

2b. Lower corolla lip relatively small, usually less than 1/3 the length of the galea, never over 1/2 as long; galea over 1/2 length of tube; bracts variously colored . . . . (3)

3a. Calyx incised much more deeply below than above; bracts divided into linear lobes, often less conspicuous than the calyx . . . . (4)

3b. Calyx about equally incised above and below; bracts divided or entire, broad and conspicuous . . . . (5)

4a. Corolla 1.5-2.5 cm long; bracts yellow, rarely reddish-tipped; calyx yellowish. **C. flava** Watson [yellow]. In sagebrush, North Park.

4b. Corolla 3-5 cm long; bracts red or scarlet; calyx red or scarlet. **C. linariifolia** Bentham [with leaves like *Linaria*]. Tall, branched plant with very narrow leaves, outer foothills to upper sagebrush and aspen.

5a. Leaves and stems ± densely tomentose; seed coats dark and often pubescent . . . . (6)

5b. Glabrous to variously pubescent but never tomentose; seed coats light-colored, never pubescent . . . . (7)

6a. Bracts orange-crimson, entire or shallowly cleft; corolla over 2.5 cm long; inflorescence short and broad. **C. integra** Gray. Grasslands of the South Park and outer foothills, from Rocky Flats southward.

6b. Bracts dull yellowish, deeply lobed; corolla under 2.5 cm long; inflorescence narrow. **C. lineata** Greene. Endemic, west end of Mesa de Maya, LA.

7a. Plants with yellow bracts and flowers . . . . (8)

7b. Plants with red bracts and flowers (note: normally red-flowered populations of *C. chromosa* occasionally sport a yellow-flowered plant; *C. sulphurea* and *C. rhexifolia* form hybrid swarms displaying a variety of colors) . . . . . (9)

8a. Plants low, usually under 2 dm high. **C. occidentalis** Torrey [western]. Common in the tundra, generally at lower altitudes than *C. puberula*, which has much narrower leaves and bracts. Difficult to distinguish from *C. sulphurea* except by size and habitat. However, *C. occidentalis* is tetraploid and *C. sulphurea* diploid. They do not intergrade.

8b. Plants tall, usually more than 2 dm high. **C. sulphurea** Rydberg. Subalpine aspen-spruce zone.

9a. Alpine; bracts with linear lobes. **C. haydenii** (Gray) Cockerell [for F. V. Hayden, geological surveyor of the Rocky mountains]. Tundra, Spanish Peaks.

9b. Plants of forests and lowlands . . . . (10)

10a. Leaves deeply cleft into linear, spreading lobes. **C. chromosa** Nelson [colorful]. In deep, sandy loam, sagebrush, North Park.

10b. Leaves entire or upper shallowly lobed near apex; forests . . . . (11)

11a. Bracts entire or very shallowly lobed, typically rose-colored. **C. rhexifolia** Rydberg [the strongly 3-veined leaves resembling *Rhexia*]. Meadows in subalpine spruce-fir, commonly hybridizing with *C. sulphurea* and forming stands of variable bract colors.

11b. Bracts usually deeply cleft; when in doubt, the bract color is typically bright red. **C. miniata** Douglas [painted with red lead]. Montane forests to lower subalpine.

CHAENARRHINUM Reichenbach 1828 [Greek, *chainein*, to gape, + *rhinon*, snout]. DWARF SNAPDRAGON

One species, **C. minus** (L.) Lange. Adventive, locally established in the piedmont valleys near Boulder.

CHIONOPHILA Bentham 1846 [Greek, *chion*, snow, + *philein*, to love].SNOW-LOVER

One species, **C. jamesii** Bentham [for Edwin James]. Alpine tundra. The yellowish flowers are dorsiventrally flattened, unlike most other scrophs. The leaves turn brown or black on drying. This species is thought to be free of any fungal rust parasite. Since rusts evolve along with their hosts, it would be of great interest to discover a rust on *Chionophila* since its relationships to other scrophs are unknown.

COLLINSIA Nuttall [for Zaccheus Collins, 1764-1831, Philadelphia botanist]. BLUE-EYED MARY

One species, **C. parviflora** Lindley [small-flowered], **105C**. Very common but inconspicuous and delicate annual, blossoming very early at low altitudes and following the season upslope to the oak and aspen zone. Leaves usually strongly purplish-tinged. The hump-backed corolla is distinctive.

CORDYLANTHUS Nuttall 1846 [Greek, *kordyle*, club, + *anthos*, flower]. CLUB-FLOWER

Note: In *Cordylanthus,* what appears to be a calyx is a bract, opposite which the calyx proper also looks to be a bract, split down the inner side, lacking any lobes.

One species, **C. ramosus** Nuttall [branched]. Sandy soil, North Park.

Corolla less than 2 cm long, yellow with purple streaks; bract and calyx rounded, very minutely short-glandular-pubescent; leaves puberulent.

DIGITALIS L. 1753 [Latin, of the finger]. FOXGLOVE

One species, **D. purpurea** L. Adventive in foothill canyon bottoms near Boulder. The name foxglove is a modification of the original one, "folks [=fairies] glove." The plant is poisonous and is the commercial source of the drug of the same name.

GRATIOLA L. 1753 [diminutive of Latin, *gratia*, grace, favor, for supposed medicinal properties]. HEDGE-HYSSOP

One species, **G. neglecta** Torrey [overlooked]. Adventive, infrequent in muddy places at the base of the Front Range. The plant has the aspect of a small yellow *Mimulus* but with a more tubular corolla.

LEIOSTEMON Rafinesque 1825 [Greek, *leio-*, smooth, + *stemon*, stamen]

One species, **L. ambiguum** (Torrey) Greene. Abundant on sandhills on the plains and forming huge displays, each plant producing many branches from the base, the flowers pale lavender, elongate, and strongly dorsiventrally flattened (*Penstemon*). For an excellent discussion of the nomenclatural history of this genus, see Crosswhite & Kawano, *American Midland Naturalist* 83:358-367. 1970.

LIMOSELLA L. 1753 [diminutive of Latin, *limus*, mud]. MUDWORT

One species, **L. aquatica** L., **105E**. Drying borders of ponds and springs, middle altitudes. Plant with a rosette of linear leaves and very small, inconspicuous white flowers.

LINARIA Miller 1754 [from *Linum*, flax, because of similar foliage]. TOADFLAX, BUTTER-AND-EGGS

1a. Flowers blue. **L. texana** Scheele. Infrequent on grassland of the foothill outwash mesas in the Denver-Boulder area.
1b. Flowers yellow and orange . . . . (2)

2a. Leaves linear; much less than 1 m tall. **L. vulgaris** Miller [common]. Adventive, locally abundant around the sites of former homesteads, not a very aggressive colonizer.
2b. Leaves ovate; often 1 m tall. **L. genistifolia** (L.) Miller subsp. **dalmatica** (L.) Maire et al. [like the genus *Genista*; from Dalmatia]. Adventive, a recently established, aggressive weed now rampant in many parts of our semi-arid areas (*L. dalmatica*). Hybrid individuals intermediate between the two species have been found recently.

LINDERNIA Allioni 1766 [for Franz Balthazar von Lindern, 1682-1755]. FALSE PIMPERNEL

One species, **L. anagallidea** (Michaux) Pennell [for *Anagallis*, the pimpernel]. Rare in muddy places at the base of the Front Range foothills, near Boulder.

MIMULUS L. 1753 [diminutive of Latin, *mimus*, buffoon, from the "grinning" corolla]. MONKEYFLOWER

1a. Flowers large, purple. **M. lewisii** Pursh [for Meriwether Lewis]. Peripheral species of the Pacific Northwest, along rushing mountain rills, RT, and possibly on the east side of the Park Range in North Park.
1b. Flowers yellow, or if reddish, then less than 5 mm long . . . . (2)

2a. Low, viscid-pubescent, creeping perennial forming mats; leaves broadly ovate, with very short petioles; anthers hairy; corolla yellow with red stripes. **M. moschatus** Douglas [musky]. Streamsides and springs, east slope of Park Range, JA.
2b. Not conspicuously viscid pubescent or, if somewhat so, then annual . . (3)

3a. Petiole base modified to form a pocket that, when mature, falls away from the leaf and stem as a disk-shaped functional, propagulum containing a dormant embryonic shoot; flowers usually abortive or absent, but if present, the pollen sterile. **M. gemmiparus** Weber [forming gemmae]. Endemic. Restricted to massive, smooth, sloping granite outcrops in Rocky Mountain National Park, provided with surface seepage water; growing with other *Mimulus* species.
3b. Petiole bases not modified; flowers always present . . . . (4)

4a. Calyx teeth decidedly unequal, the uppermost longer than the rest . . . (5)
4b. Calyx teeth equal or nearly so . . . . (7)

5a. Throat of corolla open, the whole corolla less than 2 cm long; some of the calyx teeth reduced or absent; plants usually decumbent. **M. glabratus** Humboldt, Bonpland & Kunth. Muddy ditches and pond borders at low altitudes.
5b. Throat of corolla partly or nearly closed by a prominent palate, the whole corolla usually over 2 cm long; calyx teeth all present and distinct; plants usually erect unless dwarfed and alpine . . . . (6)

6a. Plants with definite, creeping, sod-forming rhizomes, often stoloniferous as well; flowers few (mostly 1-5), large, the corolla mostly 2-4 cm long. **M. tilingii** Regel [for S. H. Tiling, Russian botanist]. Low plants, 2 dm tall or less, upper subalpine and alpine rills.

6b. Plants with stolons but only rarely with distinct, creeping rhizomes; flowers often more than 5, usually less than 2 cm long. **M. guttatus** de Candolle [speckled, referring to the corolla]. Usually over 2 dm tall; springs and streams.

7a. Leaves triangular-ovate, coarsely toothed, with distinct petioles, these often longer than the blades; internodes several, with flowers in the leaf axils; calyx inflating at maturity; flowers always yellow. **M. floribundus** Douglas [many-flowered]. Seepy ledges; extremely variable in size of plant and flowers, depending on availability of water.
7b. Leaves oblong or elliptic, entire, sessile or narrowed to a very short petiole; calyx not inflated at maturity; flowers yellow or purple . . . . (8)

8a. Plant minute, consisting only of the 2 small cotyledons and usually only 1 internode above, with the leaves and inflorescence clustered at the apex; corolla persistent after anthesis. **M. breweri** (Greene) Coville [for W. H. Brewer, 1828-1910, American naturalist]. Infrequent in moss on seepy ledges in the subalpine.
8b. Plant usually well over 5 cm tall, freely branched with several internodes and leaf pairs, with pedicellate flowers in the leaf axils; corolla falling after anthesis. **M. rubellus** Gray [reddish]. A plant of arid flats, known on the Eastern Slope only from an old collection near La Veta.

ORTHOCARPUS Nuttall 1818 [Greek, *orthos*, straight, + *carpos*, fruit]. OWL-CLOVER

1a. Flowers yellow. **O. luteus** Nuttall. Common in mountain meadows throughout.
1b. Flowers purple-and-white. **O. purpureoalbus** Gray. Usually in piñon-juniper, western CN, Sangre de Cristo Range, LA.

PEDICULARIS L. 1753 [Latin, *pediculus*, louse, according to Gerard's *Herbal*, so called because of a belief that lousy clothing could be disinfected by the use of this plant]. LOUSEWORT

1a. Leaves crenulate, not pinnatifid . . . . (2)
1b. Leaves deeply pinnatifid or incised . . . . (3)

2a. Corolla white; leaves glabrous. **P. racemosa** Douglas subsp. **alba** Pennell. Dominant in dry, subalpine, spruce forests.
2b. Corolla pink or rose-colored; leaves or stems pubescent. **P. crenulata** Bentham. Wet meadows, particularly along broad stream valleys, montane and subalpine.

3a. Corolla yellowish or white (*P. procera* has reddish streaks) . . . . (4)
3b. Corolla pink or purplish . . . . (7)

4a. Leaves simple, but shallowly or deeply pinnatifid . . . . (5)
4b. Leaves divided into separate leaflets; plants always over 2 dm tall . . . (6)

5a. Inflorescence glabrous; racemes elongate in anthesis; leaves with a very narrow central axis, only a few mm wide; upper lip of corolla terminating in a prominent, narrow, sickle-shaped beak. **P. parryi** Gray. Dry subalpine and alpine slopes.
5b. Inflorescence loosely tomentose; racemes capitate in anthesis; leaves with a broader central axis (up to 1 cm wide); upper lip of corolla more broadly rounded to the beak. **P. canadensis** L. subsp. **fluviatilis** (Heller) Weber. Moist forest floors in the outer foothills from Sedalia southward.

6a. Up to 1 m tall; flowers streaked with reddish; corolla 3-3.5 cm long; lower lip almost reaching the tip of the galea. **P. procera** Gray [tall]. Tall rank herb of deeply shaded spruce-fir forests; the leaves are commonly mistaken for fern fronds (*P. grayi*).

6b. Much less than 1 m tall; flowers not streaked with reddish; corolla less than 3 cm long; lower lip not reaching the tip of the galea. **P. bracteosa** Bentham subsp. **paysoniana** (Pennell) Weber. Dry spruce-fir forests and aspen stands.

7a. Beak of galea short and straight; inflorescence woolly-pubescent, flowers crowded in a short spike. **P. scopulorum** Gray [of the Rockies]. Swampy meadows and lakeshores, subalpine and alpine. Formerly considered to be a race of *P. sudetica*.

7b. Beak of galea long and curved, the flower resembling an elephant's head; inflorescence glabrous or nearly so, flowers in an elongated spike. **P. groenlandica** Retzius [erroneously thought to come from Greenland], ELEPHANTELLA. Wet mountain meadows.

PENSTEMON Schmidel 1763 [Greek, *pente*, five, + *stemon*, stamen]. BEARD-TONGUE

1a. Corolla scarlet. **P. barbatus** (Cavanilles) Roth var. **torreyi** (Bentham) Keck [bearded, alluding to the inside of the corolla in the species proper], **106C**. Rocky canyonsides and piñon-juniper.

1b. Corolla blue or purple, rarely pink or white . . . . (2)

2a. [1] Flowers white or very pale violet . . . . (3)

2b. Flowers not basically white, but some shade of blue, pink, or purple . (5)

3a. [2] Flowers large, the throat ± inflated; leaves broadly lanceolate or ovate (white or pale forms of **P. whippleanus** Gray)

3b. Flowers small, the throat not at all inflated; leaves relatively or very narrow . . . . (4)

4a. [3] Leaves narrowly linear, mostly basal; foliage and corolla not glandular-pubescent. **P. laricifolius** Hooker & Arnott subsp. **exilifolius** (Nelson) Keck [with leaves like *Larix*; slender-leaved]. Dry grasslands, northwestern LR, North Park. The basal tufts of narrow, linear leaves and the erect flowering stems are unique.

4b. Leaves lanceolate, not mostly basal; stems sticky-glandular above. **P. albidus** Nuttall. Outwash mesas of the Front Range, and on the plains.

5a. [2] Anther sacs pubescent along their sides (away from the line of dehiscence), although often sparsely so . . . . (6)

5b. Anther sacs glabrous . . . . (9)

6a. [5] Anther pubescence sparsely long-villous to lanate, the hairs usually longer than the anther sacs. **P. strictus** Bentham [straight]. Tall plants of sagebrush, piñon-juniper, mountain-mahogany, and relatively mesic mountain meadows; basal leaves usually broadly lanceolate. Common throughout the middle altitudes, variable, the races not well marked (including *P. strictiformis* Rydberg).

6b. Pubescence of anthers short, straight or sometimes flexuous hairs shorter than the length of the anther sacs . . . . (7)

7a. [6] Corolla 15-24 mm long, glabrous in the throat. **P. saxosorum** Pennell [of the Rockies]. North Park and northern Medicine Bow Mountains.

7b. Corolla 22-38 mm long, usually hairy in the throat . . . . (8)

8a. [7] Staminode scarcely or shallowly notched, usually bearded at the apex with yellow hairs; corolla 24-32 mm long; stem glabrous. **P. glaber** Pursh. Gravelly slopes, middle altitudes, near the Continental Divide in the Front Range (*P. alpinus*).

8b. Staminode deeply notched, glabrous or with a few hairs; corolla 30-38 mm; stem puberulent below. **P. brandegei** Porter [for T. S. Brandegee]. Mountain slopes, southern counties. Usually treated as a subspecies of the last.

9a. [5] Plants glabrous and glaucous, the leaves rather succulent; plants erect, often tall . . . . (10)

9b. Plants not as above in all respects, green (look for even sparse pubescence in the inflorescence) . . . . (15)

10a. [9] Flowers in broad-bracted, interrupted spikes. **P. cyathophorus** Rydberg [cupped-base, referring to the subtending bracts]. Sagebrush meadows of North Park.

10b. Flowers not in broad-bracted, interrupted spikes . . . . (11)

11a. [10] Corolla 35 mm or more long. **P. grandiflorus** Nuttall. On the plains, easternmost counties. Our largest-flowered species, becoming very rare or almost extinct in Colorado, persisting only along highway rights-of-way not grazed by cattle.

11b. Corolla smaller . . . . (12)

12a. [11] Dwarf alpine plant with a short, few-flowered inflorescence. **P. hallii** Gray [for Elihu Hall, 1820-1882, collector]. Common on tundra in the inner ranges.

12b. Tall plant of outer foothills and middle altitudes . . . . (13)

13a. [12] Inflorescence not distinctly 1-sided, the flowers more closely massed; flowers blue (rarely individuals occur with magenta flowers); sepals lanceolate. **P. angustifolius** Nuttall. Common on the plains (including *P. buckleyi*).

13b. Inflorescence distinctly 1-sided and elongate; flowers magenta to red-purple; sepals ovate to ovate-lanceolate . . . . (14)

14a. [13] Staminode glabrous or nearly so; flowers very numerous, in 1-sided, wandlike spikes; leaves narrowly lanceolate; flowers lavender-purple. **P. virgatus** Gray subsp. **asa-grayi** Crosswhite. Abundant throughout the foothills and middle altitudes in the Front Range.

14b. Staminode densely bearded with golden hairs; flowers in 1-sided spikes but not numerous; leaves usually ovate; flowers magenta. **P. secundiflorus** Bentham, **106A**. Common along the Front Range foothills; a dwarf form with narrow leaves occurs on volcanic ash of Cochetopa Pass.

15a. [9] Stems very short, decumbent, the roots elongate and elastic; plants of loose scree slopes. **P. harbourii** Gray, **Pl. 30**. Low, with a few flowers from the axils of unmodified leaves at the stem apex. The flowers are a peculiar powder blue.

15b. Stems erect or somewhat spreading, but not as above . . . . (16)

16a. [15] Leaves (at least the basal ones) narrowly linear or narrowly oblanceolate, not over 5 mm wide and mostly under 20 mm long . . . . (17)

16b. Leaves various, but if linear then regularly over 5 mm wide and 20 mm long . . . . (19)

17a. [16] Foliage and flowers glandular-pubescent; staminode exserted, very conspicuous with bright orange hairs. **P. auriberbis** Pennell [golden-beard], Abundant in the lower Arkansas Valley, especially near Pueblo.
17b. Foliage not strongly glandular-pubescent; staminode inconspicuous . (18)

18a. [17] Corolla with two ridges within on the lower side, the throat gradually enlarged above the tube. **P. crandallii** Nelson [for C. S. Crandall]. Common in grasslands and piñon-juniper from South Park southward. Variable in habit from decumbent to erect. The extreme with narrowly linear leaves is var. **glabrescens** (Pennell) Keck.
18b. Corolla rounded, not 2-ridged, on the lower inside (best examined fresh; dried plants must be boiled to determine this), the throat abruptly widened above the tube. **P. linarioides** Gray subsp. **coloradoënsis** (Nelson) Keck [with leaves like *Linaria*]. Piñon-juniper, South Park to San Luis Valley.

19a. [16] Corolla with expanded throat, bell-shaped . . . . (20)
19b. Corolla trumpet-shaped, the throat gradually widened . . . . (23)

20a. [19] Stems totally glabrous below the inflorescence; corolla with 2 grooves on the underside, mostly dull maroon, occasionally off-white (bluish in southern counties). **P. whippleanus** Gray, **106B**. Very common in dry forests of middle altitudes.
20b. Stems and/or leaves pubescent or glandular below the inflorescence; corolla pink or lavender, not grooved . . . . (21)

21a. [20] Leaves and stems densely puberulent and/or villous; staminode strongly exserted and long-bearded; leaves not at all toothed. **P. eriantherus** Pursh [woolly anthered, alluding to the bearded staminode]. Rocky outcrops on the northeastern plains.
21b. Leaves glabrous or minutely puberulent; staminode not exserted; leaves with occasional teeth . . . . (22)

22a. [21] Corolla 25-32 mm long, strongly bilabiate, long-bearded within. **P. jamesii** Bentham. Rare in Colorado, known from a few collections, LA.
22b. Corolla 40-50 mm long, hardly bilabiate, with rounded lobes; glandular-pubescent but not long-bearded within. **P. cobaea** Nuttall [after the genus *Cobaea*]. Known only from BA.

23a. [19] Flowers almost sessile, in very dense clusters forming a terminal head or a few interrupted ones . . . . (24)
23b. Flowers spread out along the stem . . . . (25)

24a. [23] Corolla 6-10 mm long; flowers usually declined; sepals not conspicuously scarious-margined. **P. confertus** Douglas subsp. **procerus** (Douglas) Clark [crowded; tall]. Wet mountain meadows, not as common as the next.
24b. Corolla 10-16 mm long; flowers usually horizontal; sepals scarious-margined. **P. rydbergii** Nelson. Common in wet mountain meadows.

25a. [23] Lower leaves and stem totally glabrous . . . . (26)
25b. Lower leaves and stem minutely pubescent . . . . (27)

26a. [25] Corolla 10-15 mm long, deep blue-violet; leaves very obscurely and weakly toothed or almost entire; stems numerous, forming dense clumps. **P. virens** Pennell [green]. The most abundant small-flowered penstemon of the foothills and montane.

26b. Corolla 15-23 mm long, pale; leaves regularly and finely serrate-denticulate to almost entire; stems slender, few. **P. gracilis** Nuttall. Rather rare, on the outwash mesas of the Front Range.

27a. [25] Basal rosette leaves absent at anthesis. **P. radicosus** Nelson. North Park.
27b. Basal rosette leaves present at anthesis . . . . (28)

28a. [27] Lower side of corolla deeply 2-ridged; mouth and staminode densely covered with golden hairs. **P. griffinii** Nelson. Common from South Park to the San Luis Valley and valleys of the Rio Grande.
28b. Lower side of corolla less strongly ridged; mouth with a few white hairs; staminode orange-bearded. **P. degeneri** Crosswhite [for Otto Degener, Hawaiian botanist]. Endemic, south side of the Royal Gorge.

POCILLA Fourreau 1869 [Latin, *pocillum*, little goblet, alluding to the capsule] (formerly included in *Veronica*)

1a. Erect; corolla 2-4 mm wide. **Pocilla biloba** (L.) Weber, **108B**. Adventive, a newly established weed rapidly spreading along roads, middle altitudes.
1b. Plant decumbent and trailing; corolla 5-11 mm wide. **P. persica** (Poiret) Fourreau. Adventive weed in gardens.

RHINANTHUS L. 1753 [Greek, *rhinon*, snout, + *anthos*, flower, the name applying to plants now excluded from the present genus and thus meaningless in our context]. YELLOW RATTLE

One species, **R. minor** L. subsp. **borealis** (Sterneck) Löve. Mountain meadows and clearings. The calyx is very conspicuous in fruit, being almost circular and flat, with a small aperture.

SCROPHULARIA L. 1753 [from the fleshy knobs on the rhizomes of some species, which, by the medieval Doctrine of Signatures was supposed to cure scrofula and to remove "fig warts"]. FIGWORT

One species, **S. lanceolata** Pursh. Fencerows, ravines, and roadside ditches, middle altitudes. The leaves are triangular-ovate and coarsely dentate.

VERBASCUM L. 1753 [the ancient Latin name used by Pliny]. MULLEIN

1a. Foliage sparingly pubescent or glabrate; leaves coarsely toothed; flowers in loose racemes. **V. blattaria** L. [ancient name for a moth], MOTH MULLEIN, **107C**. Introduced along rights-of-way and spreading to overgrazed range on the outwash mesas and piedmont valleys. A sterile hybrid between this and *V. thapsus* was found once along the Boulder-Denver turnpike. It was twice as tall as either parent and had great numbers of racemes from a stout main stem. It never appeared again, having produced no seeds. The hybrid is called *V. x pterocaulon* Franchet.
1b. Foliage very densely woolly-pubescent; flowers in dense terminal spikes or spikelike racemes . . . . (2)

2a. Leaves decurrent on the stem, entire. **V. thapsus** L. [classical name, from ancient Thapsus, in North Africa near Tunis, where Julius Caesar defeated the Pompeiians and ended the war in Africa], GREAT MULLEIN, **107A**. Adventive, very common and conspicuous roadside weed in disturbed, overgrazed, or burned areas, often growing to a height of 2 m or more. It is said that in colonial times young ladies reddened their cheeks by rubbing them with the tomentose leaves.
2b. Leaves not decurrent but often with clasping bases, crenate. **V. phlomoides** L. [resembling the mint, *Phlomis*], **107B**. A European species recently

discovered as a weed in the outer foothills near Golden and very likely established elsewhere.

VERONICA L. 1753 [from St. Veronica]. BROOKLIME, SPEEDWELL [so named for its alleged curative powers]
(See also *Pocilla*, *Veronicastrum*)

1a. Flowers in racemes arising from the leaf axils . . . . (2)
1b. Flowers in terminal spikes or racemes . . . . (4)

2a. Leaves narrowly linear to narrowly lanceolate; pedicels filiform, reflexing in fruit; capsule much wider than long, deeply 2-lobed. **V. scutellata** L. [with a shield, probably referring to the capsule]. Marshes, RT and GA, probably on the east side of the Park Range also; infrequent or inconspicuous.
2b. Leaves ovate-oblong . . . . (3)

3a. Leaves all short-petioled, serrate. **V. americana** (Rafinesque) Schweinitz, AMERICAN BROOKLIME, **108E**. Muddy places, valleys.
3b. Leaves sessile and clasping the stem, or only the lowermost short-petioled, serrulate or entire. **V. catenata** Pennell [in chains, possibly referring to the fruiting racemes], **108D**. Common in similar habitats (*V. salina*). In this species the pedicels are widely spreading; in the closely related *V. anagallis-aquatica* L. at least the uppermost ones are said to be ascending; this is a very difficult matter to decide; furthermore, the two species hybridize, forming a very robust, sterile hybrid.

4a. Flowers pale pink to white; leaves narrowly elliptic. **V. peregrina** L. subsp. **xalapensis** (Humboldt, Bonpland & Kunth) Pennell [wandering; from Xalapa, Mexico], PURSLANE SPEEDWELL, **108C**. Ruderal weed of disturbed and wet places. Probably merits status as a distinct genus, differing from other species, not only in morphology, but with a unique basic chromosome number.
4b. Flowers deep blue; leaves ovate, blackening in drying. **V. nutans** Bongard [nodding], ALPINE SPEEDWELL, **108A**. Subalpine meadows and tundra; flowers dark blue (*V. wormskioldii* of northeast America is tetraploid; our western plant is diploid, 2n=18).

VERONICASTRUM Heister 1759 [Greek, *-astrum*, diminutive suffix]. THYME-LEAVED SPEEDWELL

One species, **V. serpyllifolium** (L.) Fourreau subsp. **humifusum** (Dickson) Weber [thyme-leaved]. Muddy ground, montane and subalpine. Lower leaves petioled, drying green; plant decumbent, rooting at the nodes (*Veronica*).

SIMAROUBACEAE QUASSIA FAMILY (SMR)

A small tropical family with plants having medicinal and other economic uses. *Kirkia*, the white syringa from South Africa, has swollen roots that store liquid that can be tapped in times of drought. Our representative is a Chinese tree cultivated for its attractive leaves, rapid growth, ornamental fruit, and as a host for the domesticated silkworm. In America it has become a symbol of ultimate urbanization. This is the tree alluded to in the title of the novel *A Tree Grows in Brooklyn*. Its exceptional hardiness under most extreme urban conditions symbolized the stamina of the novel's protagonists.

AILANTHUS Desfontaines 1788 [said to be derived from a Moluccan common name, alluding to the great height it achieves in the wild]. TREE-OF-HEAVEN

One species, **A. altissima** (Miller) Swingle. Adventive, a rapidly growing weed tree in backyards and vacant lots. The leaves have a strong odor (in New York City we called it stinkweed), the branches are weak and contain a disproportionate amount of pith, but in autumn the great masses of oblong, twisted samaras are very attractive with tints of red and brown. The tree is becoming a pest in the Eastern Slope cities.

SMILACACEAE SMILAX FAMILY (SML)

A small, mostly tropical family of four genera, the largest of which is *Smilax*. Most species are woody climbers with prickly branches and tendrils. The plants are dioecious. Commercial sarsaparilla, used medicinally, has been made from *Smilax*. The most widely used species, *S. china*, has been used in China for centuries to aid in treatment of rheumatism, syphilis, and other diseases and is a dye plant. The North American *S. pseudochina* has tuberous rhizomes that have been used to fatten hogs and to make a domestic beer.

SMILAX L. 1753 [ancient Greek name for the yew]

One species, **S. lasioneura** Hooker [hairy-nerved], CARRIONFLOWER. Infrequent in gulches of the outwash mesas, outer foothills of the Front Range. Although related closely to the eastern North American *S. herbacea*, our plant, in my experience at least, does not have the odor of putrefying flesh of that species. Also, while it has strongly developed tendrils, the stem stands erect at least in early stages of development, and the main stem only becomes somewhat woody in age. The plant is dioecious and produces umbels of large blue-black berries.

SOLANACEAE NIGHTSHADE FAMILY (SOL)

More than most families, the Solanaceae have affected, for good or ill, the course of history. Many species are gifts to Western civilization from the American Indian. The white potato, *Solanum tuberosum*, went from Incan Peru to Europe, where it became the major crop of Ireland. A catastrophic fungal blight destroyed potato farming there, and thousands of Irish migrated to Boston and New York. Sir Walter Raleigh introduced tobacco, *Nicotiana*, into British society with well-known results. The tomato, *Lycopersicon esculentum*, was a native American plant, thought to be poisonous not too long ago. Eggplant, *Solanum melongena*, native in southern Asia, is as important in Greek cooking as in Indian. Mexican foods would not be the same without the multitude of races of chile and bell peppers, *Capsicum frutescens*. The drug atropine, used for dilating eyes, comes from *Atropa belladonna*, and in Delibes' grand opera, *Lakme*, the heroine commits suicide by eating the flower of *Brugmansia*. In our gardens, *Petunia violacea* continues to brighten the patio long into autumn. Charles Heiser has written a fascinating account of the family in his book, *Nightshades, the Paradoxical Plants*.

1a. Shrubs or woody vines. **Lycium**, MATRIMONYVINE
1b. Herbs . . . . (2)

2a. Stems and leaves spiny. **Solanum**, NIGHTSHADE
2b. Stems and leaves not spiny . . . . (3)

3a. Flowers white, over 10 cm long. **Datura**, JIMSONWEED

3b. Flowers various, but not enormous . . . . (4)

4a. Flowers pale violet, with a network of purple veins, in a 1-sided spike; fruits in 2 rows; capsule circumscissile, the calyx much enlarged at maturity. **Hyoscyamus**, HENBANE

4b. Flowers and fruits not as above . . . . (5)

5a. Flowers narrowly long-tubular, yellowish-white, very glandular; leaves with pungent taste. **Nicotiana**, TOBACCO

5b. Flowers short-tubular or rotate . . . . (6)

6a. Peduncles arising on the internodes, not in the leaf axils; calyx not enlarged nor inflated and not at all enclosing the fruit (except in one spiny species); anthers opening by terminal pores or slits, not dehiscent throughout. **Solanum**, NIGHTSHADE

6b. Peduncles arising in the leaf axils; calyx inflated and concealing the fruit, or enlarging and enclosing the fruit except at the top; plants never spiny; anthers longitudinally dehiscent throughout their length . . . . (7)

7a. Sepals not united to form a lantern, cordate at the base. **Nicandra**, APPLE-OF-PERU

7b. Sepals united to form a closed lantern, the individual sepals not distinguishable at the base . . . . (8)

8a. Calyx closely fitted to the fruit, thin and obscurely veined, the lobes not closing at apex (hence the top of the fruit exposed). **Chamaesaracha**

8b. Calyx bladdery-inflated and conspicuously veiny, the lobes closing or connivent over the top of the berry . . . . (9)

9a. Corolla yellow; flowers nodding at anthesis; seeds glossy, the surface minutely pitted. **Physalis**, GROUND-CHERRY

9b. Corolla purple; flowers erect at anthesis; seeds dull, the surface alveolate or reticulate. **Quincula**, CHINESE LANTERN

CHAMAESARACHA Bentham 1876 [Greek, *chamae*, on the ground, + *Saracha*, a tropical American genus named for Isadore Saracha, an eighteenth-century Spanish Benedictine]

1a. Plants pubescent with simple and glandular hairs. **C. conioides** (Moricand) Britton [alluding to *Conium*]. Dry plains and disturbed soils, lower Arkansas Valley.

1b. Plants sparsely pubescent with stellate hairs. **C. coronopus** (Dunal) Gray [alluding to resemblance of the leaves to those of the mustard, *Coronopus*]. Shortgrass plains and sandstone rimrock, lower Arkansas Valley from Pueblo eastward. A low, widely branching, weedy herb with small yellow flowers and stellate or branched hairs on leaves and stems; the leaves are oblong-lanceolate to linear and sinuate-dentate.

DATURA L. 1753 [altered from the Arabic name, *tatorah*, or the Hindustani *dhatura*? Linnaeus disagreed, derived it from Latin, *dare*, to give, because "given to those whose sexual powers are weak or enfeebled"]. JIMSONWEED, THORN-APPLE

One species, **D. stramonium** L., **109A**. A coarse, weedy, adventive herb with ovate, dentate leaves and flowers up to 20 cm long, with a broad flaring tube and attenuate lobes. The fruit is spiny, but not nodding as it would be in the southwestern *D. wrightii*.

HYOSCYAMUS L. 1753 [Greek, *hyos*, of a hog, + *kyamos*, bean, because poisonous to swine]. HENBANE

One species, **H. niger** L. [black], **109C**. A huge, adventive weed of disturbed sites, with large, deeply dentate-lobed leaves and bracteate spikes, not widely distributed but locally abundant where it occurs. Contains a very poisonous alkaloid, hyoscyamine.

LYCIUM L. 1753 [Greek, *lycion*, a prickly shrub growing in Lycia]. MATRIMONY-VINE, WOLFBERRY

1a. Corolla purple, the tube 3-7 mm long; leaves narrowly oblong; stems arching and curving down; berry salmon-red, not glaucous. **L. barbarum** L. [from Barbary?]. Adventive, escaped from old gardens and occasionally established on roadsides (*L. halimifolium*).

1b. Corolla greenish or purple-tinged, the tube 15-20 mm long; leaves oblong to elliptic; berry red to reddish-blue, glaucous. **L. pallidum** Miers. Native species, Arkansas River drainage.

NICANDRA Adanson 1763 [for the ancient Greek poet Nicandros of Colophon]. APPLE-OF-PERU

One species, **N. physalodes** (L.) Gaertner. Formerly cultivated for ornament, but locally established as a weed around towns on the plains. A tall weed with large ovate leaves and panicles of hanging fruits.

NICOTIANA L. 1753 [for Jean Nicot, who sent seeds of tobacco to France in 1650]. TOBACCO

One species, **N. attenuata** Torrey, **109B**. One old record from BL, but to be expected as a weed in the southern counties. Glandular annual with ovate to lanceolate leaves; flowers greenish-white, 2-4 cm long, narrowly tubular.

PHYSALIS L. 1753 [Greek, *physa*, bellows, referring to the inflated calyx]. GROUND-CHERRY

1a. Fruiting calyx with 5 sharp folds, the calyx teeth acuminate; annual; corolla 6-7 mm long, bluish-spotted; anthers bluish; foliage with capitate glandular hairs. **P. foetens** Poiret var. **neomexicana** (Rydberg) Waterfall [stinking]. Infrequent, southern counties.

1b. Perennial (rhizomes are deep in the soil!); fruiting calyx inflated and not sharply folded; corolla larger; anthers yellow . . . . (2)

2a. Flowering pedicels usually 3-8 mm long; corolla limb often reflexed when fully open . . . . (3)

2b. Flowering pedicels 10-15 mm long; corolla limb usually not reflexed when fully open . . . . (4)

3a. Plants with long jointed hairs mixed with shorter hairs or with glandular ones; leaves usually broadly ovate, almost entire. **P. hederifolia** Gray var. **comata** (Rydberg) Waterfall [ivy-leaved; shaggy]. Common along the base of the Front Range and on the plains.

3b. Plants with short, not strongly glandular pubescence; leaves commonly narrowly ovate, coarsely toothed. **P. hederifolia** Gray var. **cordifolia** (Gray) Waterfall. Common, lower Arkansas Valley.

4a. Pubescence dense, villous; leaves broadly ovate. **P. heterophylla** Nees. Common along the base of the Front Range in the Boulder-Denver area. Resembling *P. hederifolia* var. *comata* but with longer pedicels and corolla limb not reflexed.

4b. Pubescence not dense, often almost absent; leaves lanceolate or narrowly ovate . . . . (5)

5a. Pubescence of stiff ascending or appressed hairs, especially on the stem. **P. pumila** Nuttall subsp. **hispida** (Waterfall) Hinton. Common in sandy places on the plains (*P. virginiana* var. *hispida*).

5b. Pubescence almost lacking, or extremely minute, and often the hairs retrorse. **P. virginiana** Miller. Common in the piedmont valleys and out onto the plains.

QUINCULA Rafinesque 1832 [diminutive of Latin, *quinque*, five, alluding to the number of petals and calyx lobes]. CHINESE LANTERN

One species, **Q. lobata** (Torrey) Rafinesque. Common and weedy, mostly along roadsides on the plains (*Physalis*).

SOLANUM L. 1753 [the classical Latin name]. NIGHTSHADE

1a. Stems and leaves with prickles . . . . (2)

1b. Stems and leaves lacking prickles . . . . (5)

2a. Anthers dissimilar . . . . (3)

2b. Anthers all alike . . . . (4)

3a. Flowers yellow. **S. rostratum** Dunal [beaked, referring to the odd anther], BUFFALOBUR, **Pl. 36**. Adventive weed of cultivated ground in the valleys. The lowest anther is much larger and longer than the others, with an incurved beak.

3b. Flowers violet. **S. heterodoxum** Dunal [unequal, alluding to the anthers]. Adventive weed, infrequently collected on the eastern plains.

4a. Leaves and stems white with a dense, scurfy, stellate pubescence; leaves lanceolate; corolla purple. **S. elaeagnifolium** Cavanilles [with leaves resembling those of *Elaeagnus*]. Adventive, lower Arkansas Valley, once collected near Boulder along a railroad track, and evidently recently spread to LR.

4b. Leaves and stems green; leaves broadly ovate and very coarsely lobed, with scattered stellate hairs; corolla white. **S. carolinense** L. Once collected as a weed in Boulder, and perhaps established elsewhere.

5a. Leaf blades deeply lobed or pinnatifid . . . . (6)

5b. Leaf blades entire . . . . (8)

6a. Leaf blades deeply pinnatifid with acute, triangular segments. **S. triflorum** Nuttall. Adventive weed of cultivated ground, lower river valleys; flowers white, with yellow anthers.

6b. Leaf blades with broad, rounded lobes . . . . (7)

7a. Flowers purple; plant a somewhat woody vine, climbing over other plants and fences. **S. dulcamara** L. [sweet; bitter], BITTERSWEET NIGHTSHADE. Adventive, semiclimbing, fencerow weed, once collected in the Boulder Valley, and more recently along the lower Poudre River, LR.

7b. Flowers white; low herb with small, round tubers. **S. jamesii** Torrey, WILD POTATO. Adventive in our area, rare in moist, shaded, disturbed sites, piedmont valleys. Probably gathered for food, or encouraged as a weed, by the native Americans.

8a. Leaves thin, translucent; glabrous or nearly so; calyx remaining small, not covering part of the berry at maturity. **S. americanum** Miller, BLACK

NIGHTSHADE. Weed of cultivated ground, lower valleys. In *Solanum* the peduncles, instead of arising from the leaf axils as one would expect, arise from the middle of the internode!

8b. Leaves thick; plants hirsute or glandular-villous; calyx enlarged at maturity, covering the lower half of the berry. **S. physalifolium** Rusby var. **nitidibaccatum** (Bitter) Edmonds [with leaves like *Physalis*; shiny berry]. Adventive, ruderal weed, sandy soil, lower valleys (*S. sarachoides*, incorrectly, of Colorado literature).

SPARGANIACEAE BURREED FAMILY (SPG)

The bur-reeds inhabit the margins of ponds. With their balls of flowers, the lower clusters carpellate and the upper staminate, sessile on a zig-zag rachis, they are unmistakeable. When they get out in deep water, however, they do not flower, their leaves become extremely long and the ribbonlike blades float on the water. Identification of *Sparganium* species requires specimens with mature fruits.

SPARGANIUM L. 1753 [Greek, *sparganion*, swaddling-band, alluding to the strap-shaped leaves]. BURREED

1a. Carpellate heads about 1 cm diameter; staminate heads solitary; plants small, with leaves 1 cm or less wide. **S. minimum** (Hartman) Fries. Infrequent in subalpine marshes and old beaver ponds.

1b. Carpellate heads over 1 cm diameter; staminate heads 2 or more; plants usually robust, with broader leaves . . . . (2)

2a. Stigmas mostly 2; achenes sessile, obovoid or obpyramidal, distinctly flattened on top; sepals nearly as long as the achene. **S. eurycarpum** Engelmann [broad-fruited]. Local in wetlands on the eastern plains.

2b. Stigma one; achenes mostly stalked, tapering at each end; sepals much shorter than the achene . . . . (3)

3a. Stems and leaves usually partly out of water; leaves mostly more than 5 mm wide; fruiting heads 2 cm thick or more; beak of achene (including stigma) over 2 mm long. **S. emersum** Rehmann. Not yet found on the Eastern Slope, but this occurs at Grand Lake and probably in North Park.

3b. Stems and leaves usually submerged or floating; leaves mostly less than 5 mm wide; fruiting head usually less than 2 cm thick; beak of achene (including stigma) scarcely 1 mm long. **S. angustifolium** Michaux. Common in ponds in the mountains and intermountain parks.

TAMARICACEAE TAMARISK FAMILY (TAM)

Tamarix and certain other plants that grow in low, alkaline areas are able, by means of salt-excreting glands, to get rid of surplus salts, sometimes in such quantity that the salt may be gathered by humans. *Tamarix* is a phreatophyte, that is, a plant capable of reaching the water table. Phreatophytes are so successful in using water that they can actually lower the water table and therefore they are a real problem in areas of water impoundment such as the Colorado River Basin. They seem to be impossible to control; burning is ineffective, and the burned trunks are hard enough to quickly ruin chain saws. It is claimed that *Tamarix* was introduced from the Middle East within recent times, but in 1776 the Spanish explorer Padre Escalante mentions in his journals that he crossed floodplains covered by it in the American Southwest, indicating that it had been introduced by the Spanish in the sixteenth century or earlier!

TAMARIX L. 1753 [the classical name]. TAMARISK; SALT-CEDAR

1a. Flowers 4-merous, appearing before the leaves; mostly cultivated and never as abundant as the next. **T. parviflora** de Candolle. Adventive, one collection from BA, along the Cimarron River.

1b. Flowers 5-merous, appearing with and after the leaves. **T. ramosissima** Ledebour, **110A**. Adventive. Widely naturalized in canyon-bottoms and floodplains, lower Arkansas, Poudre, and Platte valleys, a potentially serious weed. The flowers can be pink or white. Some claim that the correct name for this is *T. chinensis* Loureiro.

TRILLIACEAE TRILLIUM FAMILY (TRL)

Trilliums are among the most beautiful of American monocots. Anyone raised in the East, Midwest, or Far West needs no introduction to these striking plants: a stem with three leaves in a whorl, supporting a handsome white, pink, or red flower with parts in threes, the outer ones clearly sepals and the inner ones clearly petals. One curious species appears to be stemless, with the leaves at ground level; but the stem extends vertically deep below the surface, so it really is like all the rest. Our only species is native to the Pacific Northwest; it extends barely into the Park Range of Northern Colorado, giving us a small taste of the northern Rocky Mountain flora.

TRILLIUM L. 1753 [Latin, *trilix*, triple, alluding to the parts in threes]. WAKE-ROBIN

One species, **T. ovatum** Pursh. On the Eastern Slope restricted to subalpine forests of the Park Range, JA. Unfortunately, once the general public learned of the presence of this desirable garden plant in Colorado, the accessible stands of it were all but wiped out, and it should be regarded as a threatened species here.

TYPHACEAE CATTAIL FAMILY (TYP)

The flat leaves of cattails seem to be too weak to stand up to high winds, but note that the cattail leaves are spirally twisted so that the whole leaf surface is never presented to the wind. Cattail marshes are important nesting grounds for sora rails, blackbirds, and marsh wrens and should be preserved and encouraged as miniature wildlife sanctuaries.

TYPHA L. 1753 [*typhe*, the ancient Greek name]. CATTAIL

1a. Staminate and carpellate parts of the spike not separated by a bare portion of the axis; pollen remaining in tetrads; carpellate spikes 1.5-3 cm, thick; leaves broad, up to 20 mm wide. **T. latifolia** L., BROAD-LEAVED CATTAIL. Very common along ditches and ponds in the lower valleys.

1b. Staminate and carpellate parts of the spike separated by a bare portion of the axis; pollen usually separating to single grains; carpellate spikes slender; leaves narrower . . . . (2)

2a. Mature carpellate spike light brown; uppermost leaf sheaths lacking auricles, open at the throat, the margins free, tapering to the blade; brown-punctate mucilage glands (visible when dry or in late season) extending above the sheath onto the inner surface of the blade; carpellate bracteoles lighter brown than stigmas. **T. domingensis** Persoon. Similar habitats.

2b. Mature carpellate spikes dark brown, slender; uppermost leaf sheaths with auricles, usually closed at the throat, margins free but parallel, not tapering at the throat; mucilage glands absent from leaf blade; carpellate bracteoles darker than the stigmas. **T. angustifolia** L. NARROW-LEAVED CATTAIL.

ULMACEAE ELM FAMILY (ULM)

Most members of this family characteristically have leaves with unequal (oblique) bases, and the fruit is a samara with a circular wing. Our species flower early in the spring, before the period of leafing-out.

1a. Leaves sharply serrate, smooth above, cuneate at the base. **Ulmus**, ELM

1b. Leaves sparingly serrate or entire, the contours rounded, often somewhat cordate at the base. **Celtis**, HACKBERRY

CELTIS L. 1753 [Pliny's name for the "lotus with sweet berries" described by Herodotus]. HACKBERRY

One species, **C. reticulata** Torrey, **110B**. Canyons and arroyos along the east base of the mountains. The trees are often stunted and misshapen, with the leaves and twigs infested by insect galls of many kinds. A common one on the leaves, caused by *Pachypsylla pubescens*, is a nipple-shaped gall with long hairs and a craterlike depression at the top; the opposite side of the leaf has a smooth depression. Another insect produces characteristic "witches brooms," clusters of affected twigs.

ULMUS L. 1753 [the classical Latin name]. ELM

One species, **U. pumila** L. CHINESE ELM. Adventive. This Central Asian import was brought here because of its drought-hardiness. It has been extensively planted around homesteads for shade and shelter from wind. As the land was abandoned the elms have survived and now colonize floodplains in the vicinity. It appears to be able to spread vegetatively by breaking and rooting in wet sand.

URTICACEAE NETTLE FAMILY (URT)

Nettles sting by means of epidermal hairs that are filled with an irritant substance, including acetylcholine and histamine. The hairs are silicified at the tip, thus are brittle and break when brushed against. The irritation is brief but severe in humans. Hunting dogs are prone to more serious systemic disorders. This family contains a major fiber plant, ramie (*Boehmeria nivea*), a native of Asia.

1a. Leaves alternate, entire; plants without stinging hairs; flowers axillary, few. **Parietaria**, PELLITORY

1b. Leaves opposite, sharply serrate; plants with stinging hairs; flowers in axillary spikes, numerous. **Urtica**, NETTLE

PARIETARIA L. 1753 [Latin, *paries*, wall, from the habitat of the original species]. PELLITORY

One species, **P. pensylvanica** Mühlenberg, **111A**. Small, weak herb found in shade of trees and rocks in the canyons. The generic name is very apt, since in Europe *Parietaria* commonly grows on walls.

URTICA L. 1753 [Latin, *urere*, to burn]. NETTLE

One species, **U. gracilis** Aiton, **111B**. Along irrigation ditches and streams. Touching this plant causes extreme irritation for most people (*U. dioica* var.).

UVULARIACEAE BELLWORT FAMILY (UVU)

A segregate family, formerly in Liliaceae, characterized by having leafy stems with elliptic-lanceolate leaves and axillary or terminal flowers with narrow, recurved tepals, and a round or angular berry.

1a. Flowers axillary, dangling at the ends of slender pedicels; tepals recurved; berry smooth, round, red. **Streptopus**, TWISTEDSTALK

1b. Flowers terminal at the ends of the branches, on stout pedicels; tepals erect; berry angular, orange. **Disporum**, BELLWORT

DISPORUM Salisbury 1825 [Greek, *dis*, double, + *spora*, seed, alluding to the 2-seeded berries of some species]. BELLWORT

One species, **D. trachycarpum** (Watson) Bentham & Hooker [rough-fruited, from the strongly papillose fruit]. Deep shade in conifer forests.

STREPTOPUS Michaux 1803 [Greek, *streptos*, twisted, + *pous*, foot, alluding to the bent or twisted peduncles]. TWISTEDSTALK

One species, **S. fassettii** Löve & Löve. Moist, deeply shaded forest floors near streams (*S. amplexifolius* var. *chalazatus*). Our plant is diploid and distinct from the tetraploid *S. amplexifolius* on morphological grounds.

VALERIANACEAE VALERIAN FAMILY (VAL)

Although the valerians are a small family, they are very conspicuous in moist forests and meadows in late summer. Because of their compound leaves and umbellike flower clusters they are often mistaken for Apiaceae, but actually they are more closely related to Asteraceae. Two features clearly mark our species: the corolla with a small swelling at the base on one side, and the plumose parachute at the top of the fruit; this unrolls when the fruits are mature and functions just as a dandelion pappus.

VALERIANA L. 1753 [in honor of Publius Aurelius Valerianus, Roman emperor, 253-260]. VALERIAN

1a. Plants with thick, fleshy, vertical taproots; leaves and leaflets thick, narrow; venation almost parallel; inflorescence very open even at flowering time; flowers unisexual. **V. edulis** Nuttall [edible], **112A**. Gravelly hillsides and meadows, montane and subalpine.

1b. Rhizomatous; leaves and leaflets thin, broad; veins distinctly pinnate; inflorescence a dense, compound cyme, becoming more open in fruit; flowers perfect or evidently so . . . . (2)

2a. Corolla narrowly cup-shaped, without a definite cylindric tube and not noticeably swollen at the base. **V. occidentalis** Heller. Wet meadows and streamsides, montane and subalpine. The flowers in this species tend to be more greenish than in the next.

2b. Corolla funnel-shaped or trumpet-shaped, with a definite cylindric tube and usually swollen at the base on one side . . . . (3)

3a. Leaves predominantly cauline and ovate, or basal and mostly spatulate; corolla up to 9 mm long. **V. capitata** Pallas subsp. **acutiloba** (Rydberg) Meyer, **112B**. Similar sites to the last but not so much a forest plant and going higher into the subalpine and lower alpine.

3b. Leaves predominantly basal and ovate; corolla up to 15 mm long. **V. arizonica** Gray. Mountains of the southern counties, from Cripple Creek southeastward.

VERBENACEAE VERVAIN FAMILY (VRB)

Our verbenas might be mistaken for mints, but the foliage lacks any minty odor. The stems are often square, however, and the flowers mintlike. Verbenas are cultivated for their handsome flower clusters. This family includes teak (*Tectona grandis*), one of the finest of timbers for furniture, and, in the days of wooden ships, shipbuilding. Teak was especially sought for armored vessels because, unlike oak, the wood did not corrode iron. Oddly enough, the wood sinks in water unless dried for two years. Trees were girdled and left standing that long before harvesting.

1a. Flowers white or pale pinkish-lavender, in globose or short-cylindric tight heads; plants trailing and rooting at the nodes. **Phyla**, FOGFRUIT

1b. Flowers pink, blue, or purple (rarely white in mutant individuals); flowers in spikes elongating in age; plants erect or prostrate but not rooting at the nodes . . . . (2)

2a. Flowers showy, lavender; corolla tube much exceeding the calyx; leaves very deeply pinnatifid. **Glandularia**, SHOWY VERVAIN

2b. Flowers small, blue or purple; corolla tube scarcely longer than the calyx; leaves merely toothed or very shallowly pinnatifid. **Verbena**, VERVAIN

GLANDULARIA Gmelin 1792 [Latin, *glandula*, acorn, alluding to the shape of the fruit]. SHOWY VERVAIN

One species, **G. bipinnatifida** (Nuttall) Nuttall, **113B**. A low, spreading, roadside plant, common along the base of the mountains but now venturing far out onto the plains (*Verbena ambrosifolia*).

PHYLA Loureiro 1790. FOGFRUIT

1a. Leaves very narrowly oblanceolate, tapering to the base from near the apex, with only a few teeth. **P. cuneifolia** (Torrey) Greene, **113D**. Common in wetlands in the piedmont valleys and where such places occur on the plains.

1b. Leaves oblong-elliptic, tapering to base and apex, with many teeth. **P. lanceolata** (Michaux) Greene. Known in Colorado only from Bonny Reservoir, YM.

VERBENA L. 1753 [Latin name for any sacred herb]. VERVAIN

1a. Floral bracts leaflike, equalling or exceeding the flowers; leaves not especially thick, not rugose-reticulate; plant prostrate or strongly spreading. **V. bracteata** Lagasca & Rodriguez, **113C**. Adventive, ruderal weed.

1b. Floral bracts shorter than the flowers, not leaflike; tall, erect plants . . (2)

2a. Leaf blades thin, not reticulate, sometimes hastately lobed at the base; plants green; fruiting spikes narrow, less than 7 mm wide, subtended at the base only by inconspicuous bracts; spikes usually many. **V. hastata** L., **113A**. Frequent in wetlands in the piedmont valleys.

2b. Leaf blades thick, with raised nerves, not hastate at the base; plants densely gray-pubescent; fruiting spikes thick, over 7 mm wide, subtended at the base by leaflike bracts; spikes relatively few . . . . (3)

3a. Bracts 1-2 mm longer than the calyx; leaves oblong-elliptic to ovate-lanceolate, short-petioled, usually acute. **V. macdougalii** Heller. Fields and roadsides, San Luis Valley.
3b. Bracts about as long as the calyx; leaves ovate or oval, sessile or nearly so, acute or obtuse. **V. stricta** Ventenat. Frequent in dry meadows on the plains.

VIOLACEAE VIOLET FAMILY (VIO)

Many violets produce attractive and fragrant flowers, but these often do not produce seeds. The effective seed-producing flowers are cleistogamous, that is, they never open, lack attractive floral parts, and are subterranean or emerge only after fruit is matured. They are obviously self-pollinated in such instances. Many violets are adapted for dispersal of the seeds by ants and aiding the ant in grasping the seed there may be a small, irregularly shaped growth on the side of the seed (a caruncle). This relationship between ants and plants is called myrmecophily.

1a. Leaves sessile, linear-lanceolate, simple, entire, not basal; lowermost petal not spurred. **Hybanthus**, GREEN VIOLET
1b. Leaves not as above, often chiefly basal; lowermost petal spurred. **Viola**, VIOLET

HYBANTHUS Jacquin 1760 [Greek, *hybo*, hump-backed, + *anthos*, flower]. GREEN VIOLET

One species, **H. verticillatus** (Ortega) Baillon, **114D**. On shale and sandstone outcrops along the base of the Front Range and Mesa de Maya, and on rocky sites on the plains, east to the Kansas border.

VIOLA L. 1753 [the classical name]. VIOLET

1a. Annual; weedy species with tricolored flowers; stipules large, leaflike, palmately divided; petals pale bluish-violet. **V. kitaibeliana** Roemer & Schultes var. **rafinesquei** (Greene) Fernald [for Paul Kitaibel, 1757-1817, Hungarian botanist; for Constantine Rafinesque, 1783-1840, pioneer American naturalist]. JOHNNY-JUMP-UP, **114A**. Frequent weed in gardens and in disturbed meadows on the outwash mesas.
1b. Perennial . . . . (2)

2a. Petals yellow, often brown on the back and with brown pencilling . . . (3)
2b. Petals white or some shade of blue-violet . . . . (6)

3a. Leaves deeply cordate-reniform, regularly crenate, hardly showing a terminal point. **V. biflora** L. Alpine plants in shelter of boulders, also lower altitudes in moss along streams in deep forests.
3b. Leaves lanceolate or elliptic or triangular-ovate, always distinctly pointed, entire, crenate, or dentate . . . . (4)

4a. Leaves triangular-ovate, coarsely few-toothed or -lobed; leaves and petals usually purple on the back. **V. purpurea** Kellogg subsp. **venosa** (Watson) Baker & Clausen. Unstable screes in the higher mountains, Park Range, RT, and likely on the North Park side of the range.
4b. Leaves lance-ovate, or elliptic-lanceolate, entire or crenate . . . . (5)

5a. Leaf blades narrowly lanceolate or lance-elliptic, at least 3 times as long as wide; plants small (usually less than 5 cm). **V. nuttallii** Pursh, **114C**. Blossoming in early spring at lower altitudes, often in protection of rocks.

5b. Leaf blades broader and often much larger, abruptly narrowed to the petiole; plants large, leaves usually more than 5 cm long. **V. praemorsa** Douglas subsp. **major** (Hooker) Baker. Common in relatively mesic sites at higher altitudes and blooming longer into the summer than the last. These taxa comprise a polyploid series, with *V. nuttallii* tetraploid, n=12, and *V. praemorsa* octoploid, n=24.

6a. Leaves palmately dissected into narrow lobes. **V. pedatifida** G. Don, BIRDFOOT VIOLET, **114B**. Infrequent on rocky sites on the outwash mesas, flowering in early spring.

6b. Leaves entire or merely toothed . . . . (7)

7a. Plants with erect, leafy stems bearing flowers in the leaf axils . . . . . . (8)

7b. Plants stemless, sometimes with creeping stolons from which leaves may arise . . . . (10)

8a. Petals white, usually violet on the back; stem well developed; leaves cordate . . . . (9)

8b. Petals blue-violet; stem short, often obscure; leaves seldom distinctly cordate . . . . (10)

9a. Upper stems and petioles glabrous or extremely minutely pubescent, not easily seen without a very strong lens; leaves dark green, small, the blades 3-4 cm long; flower small, less than 1 cm long and wide. **V. scopulorum** (Gray) Greene, **Pl. 43**. Foothill canyons, usually not in deep shade (*V. canadensis* var. *scopulorum*. Our plant differs from the eastern *V. canadensis* in having smaller flowers. The *V. canadensis* group is still far from understood.

9b. Upper stems, petioles, and the veins, of the underside of the leaves with spreading hairs, easily seen with a lens or naked eye; leaves paler green, large, over 5 cm long; flower twice the size of the last, over 1 cm long and wide. **V. rydbergii** Greene, **Pl. 44**. Foothill canyons, usually close to streamsides and in deep shade. These grow very close together, separated by their habitats, and do not intergrade. This plant has been called *V. rugulosa* Greene, which was described from Minnesota. In view of the complex problems in the various races or species in this group, it seems more appropriate, for the time being, to give ours a name based on a Rocky Mountain type.

10a. Leaves pubescent; plants of middle altitudes, usually more than 5 cm tall. **V. adunca** Smith [hooked, alluding to the spur]. The most abundant summer-blooming violet. Tetraploid. Löve claimed that this plant should be called *V. aduncoides* and that the next is the real *V. adunca*, but the question is not settled.

10b. Leaves glabrous; alpine plants, usually less than 5 cm tall. **V. labradorica** Schrank. A diploid species usually treated as a variety of *V. adunca*, but in Colorado at least they are distinct. This small violet occurs from Greenland to Alaska essentially identical to the Rocky Mountain plant and is genetically distinct from the lowland species. They also differ in the structure of the style (*V. bellidifolia*, *V. adunca* var. *minor*).

11a. Leaves with scattered, straight, appressed, glassy hairs on the upper side. **V. selkirkii** Pursh [for Thomas Douglas, Earl of Selkirk]. Flowers blue, long-spurred; rhizomes slender; plant often stoloniferous. Very rare, usually at the bases of aspens, known from a few collections, Rocky Mountain National Park, and DA.

11b. Leaves glabrous or otherwise pubescent . . . . (12)

12a. Style hooked at the top; stoloniferous. **V. odorata** L., English Violet. Adventive. Common in lawns and occasionally escaping to moist gulches in towns. Flowers vary from blue to purple, pink, or white. Plants usually very fragrant.

12b. Style capitate, not hooked . . . . (13)

13a. Flowers blue-violet, usually more than 10 mm long; leaves large, cordate, strongly pointed. **V. sororia** Willdenow subsp. **affinis** (LeConte) McKinney, unpublished. Infrequent on floodplains, piedmont valleys (*V. nephrophylla*, *V. papilionacea*).

13b. Flowers white or faintly purple-tinged, with purple veins, small; leaves small, reniform or obtuse at the apex . . . . (14)

14a. Plants with very wide reniform leaves, not at all stoloniferous; flowers white, never with any violet tinge. **V. renifolia** Gray var. **brainerdii** (Greene) Fernald. Subalpine wet forests and streamsides near the Continental Divide.

14b. Plants with obtusely pointed leaves, with long filiform stolons; flowers white or sometimes with a slight purple tinge. Subalpine wet forests and streamsides. **V. epipsiloides** Löve & Löve?

VISCACEAE MISTLETOE FAMILY (VIS)

The dwarf mistletoes are important parasites of coniferous trees in western North and Central America. Almost every tree species has its own distinctive species or race of *Arceuthobium*. These mistletoes are extremely reduced plants. The flowers, leaves, branches, and root system are so simplified and condensed that to the unitiated the species look almost identical. The seeds are explosively shot from the fruits at high speed (27 m/sec) for distances up to 15 m. They are sticky and adhere to pine needles. When the needles become wet from rain the seeds slide down to a branch, where they germinate by a penetrating holdfast. Many mistletoes produce characteristic "witches brooms" on the branches of trees. This key is based on Frank Hawksworth & Del Wiens, *Biology and Classification of Dwarf Mistletoes (Arceuthobium)*.

ARCEUTHOBIUM Bieberstein 1819 [Greek, *arceuthos*, juniper, + *bios*, life]. Dwarf Mistletoe

1a. Stems with branching always whorled; fruits in whorls; internodes about 10 times longer than wide; on lodgepole and occasionally ponderosa pine, where it grows nearby. **A. americanum** Nuttall.

1b. Stems flabellate; staminate flowers never whorled . . . . (2)

2a. Carpellate plants usually less than 4 cm high; shoots scattered along the host stem near the apex; host forming systemic brooms. **A. douglasii** Engelmann. On *Pseudotsuga*.

2b. Carpellate plants usually more than 4 cm high; shoots in individual clusters; host generally not forming systemic brooms . . . . (3)

3a. Flowering in winter or spring; internodes less than 4 times as long as wide. **A. vaginatum** (Willdenow) Presl subsp. **cryptopodum** (Engelmann) Hawksworth & Wiens. On ponderosa pine.

3b. Flowering in summer and fall; internodes 5 times as long as wide . . . (4)

4a. Shoots olive green to brownish; parasitic on piñon pine. **A. divaricatum** Engelmann.

4b. Shoots generally yellowish-green to light gray or purplish; parasitic on limber and bristlecone pines. **A. cyanocarpum** Coulter & Nelson [blue-fruited] (*A. campylopodum* of Colorado literature), **Pl. 5.**

VITACEAE GRAPE FAMILY (VIT)

The Vitaceae include about twelve genera, mostly tropical and warm-temperate. From a very small number of species of *Vitis* come many important kinds of grapes: muscatels, sultanas, raisins, dried currants (not to be confused with true currants in the Grossulariaceae), and of course all wine grapes. Some curious traits of these plants: The inflorescence is formed on the stem opposite, rather than in the axil, of a leaf. The flowers, which are hardly noticed except by viticulturists, are tiny and mostly unisexual. The tendril was the subject of special studies by Darwin. It begins as a straight shoot reaching out to a place to attach itself. Once attached, it becomes coiled, but not as one might suppose. Since it is attached at each end, it cannot coil in one direction, but reverse coils begin at the middle of the tendril and work in each direction!

1a. Leaves simple, cordate with shallow palmate lobing. **Vitis,** GRAPE

1b. Leaves palmately compound. **Parthenocissus,** VIRGINIA CREEPER

PARTHENOCISSUS Planchon 1887 [Greek, *partheno*, virgin, + *cissus*, ivy]. VIRGIN'S [later corrupted to Virginia] CREEPER

1a. Tendrils ending in adhesive disks; leaves dull above. **P. quinquefolia** (L.) Planchon, **115C**. Adventive, widely cultivated, and covering stone buildings, occasionally established in fencerows in and around towns.

1b. Tendrils lacking adhesive disks or with very few; leaves shiny above. **P. inserta** (Kerner) Fritsch, **115B**. Native in gulches and canyons, but relatively infrequent.

VITIS L. 1753 [the classical Latin name]. GRAPE

One species, **V. riparia** Michaux [of streamsides]. Gulches and canyons of the outer foothills. In the southeastern corner a pubescent race occurs along the Mesa de Maya (usually called *V. longii*).

ZANNICHELLIACEAE HORNED PONDWEED FAMILY (ZAN)

A very small family, in Colorado represented by a single species. Somewhat resembling the linear-leaved potamogetons, *Zannichellia* differs in having opposite linear leaves with a sheathing stipule not joined to the leaf blade. The flowers are extremely simple. They are unisexual, in pairs. The staminate flower consists of a single stamen on a filament.

ZANNICHELLIA L. 1753 [for Gian G. Zannichelli, 1662-1729, Venetian botanist]. HORNED PONDWEED

One species, **Z. palustris** L., **43A**. In slow streams and ditches, lower elevations.

ZYGOPHYLLACEAE CALTROP FAMILY (ZYG)

The few genera and species in our flora give no clue to the extent of this family, which is distributed mostly in the tropics and Southern Hemisphere. *Lignum vitae*, a durable tropical hardwood, comes from *Guaiacum*, and seeds of a Mediterranean genus, *Peganum*, produce the dye turkey red. Australia has many species of *Zygophyllum*, adapted to desert or saline sites. The schizocarpous fruit, a capsule that breaks into indehiscent, 1-seeded units, is characteristic of many genera. Our genera produce schizocarps, but there is at least one old record from the San Luis Valley (possibly a garden plant) of *Zygophyllum fabago* L., a curious plant that has a typical capsule, white flowers, and leaves dichotomously divided into 2 or sometimes 4 oblong, petiolate leaflets. The petals may be from 4-6 in number.

1a. Mericarps 5, spiny, each 3-5-seeded; beak of fruit falling with the mericarps; glands associated with the stamens. **Tribulus**, PUNCTUREVINE

1b. Mericarps 10, tuberculate, 1-seeded; beak of fruit persisting after mericarps fall; no glands associated with the stamens (petals yellow-orange in both genera). **Kallstroemia**

KALLSTROEMIA Scopoli 1777 [name possibly derived from Greek, *callos*, beautiful, + *Stroemia*, a genus of Capparidaceae]

One species, **K. parviflora** Norton. Infrequent in sandy soil, Arkansas River drainage.

TRIBULUS L. 1753 [Greek, *tribulosus*, thorny]. PUNCTUREVINE

One species, **T. terrestris** L., **115A**. Adventive. Prostrate-spreading weed with small, pinnately compound leaves and yellow flowers, common in sandy soil along roadsides and backyards in the valleys. The fruits break up into spiny segments that can puncture bicycle tires.

Figures

The figures used in this volume are a selection of those used in *Rocky Mountain Flora* and *Colorado Flora: Western Slope*. Some species that are limited to the Western Slope have been left in place so as not to incur the cost of reconstructing the plates,. These items are indicated by the abbreviation: W.S. The figures are grouped together as a block so as not to interrupt the flow of the text.

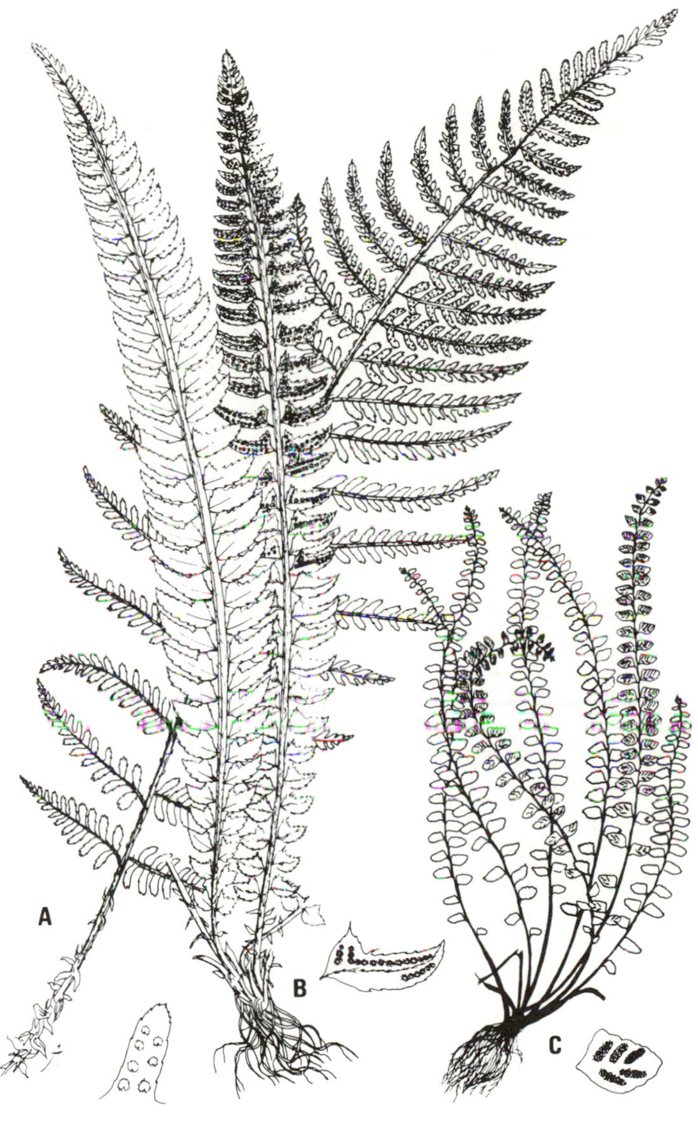

Fig. 13. A. *Dryopteris filix-mas*; **B,** *Polystichum lonchitis*; **C,** *Asplenium trichomanes*

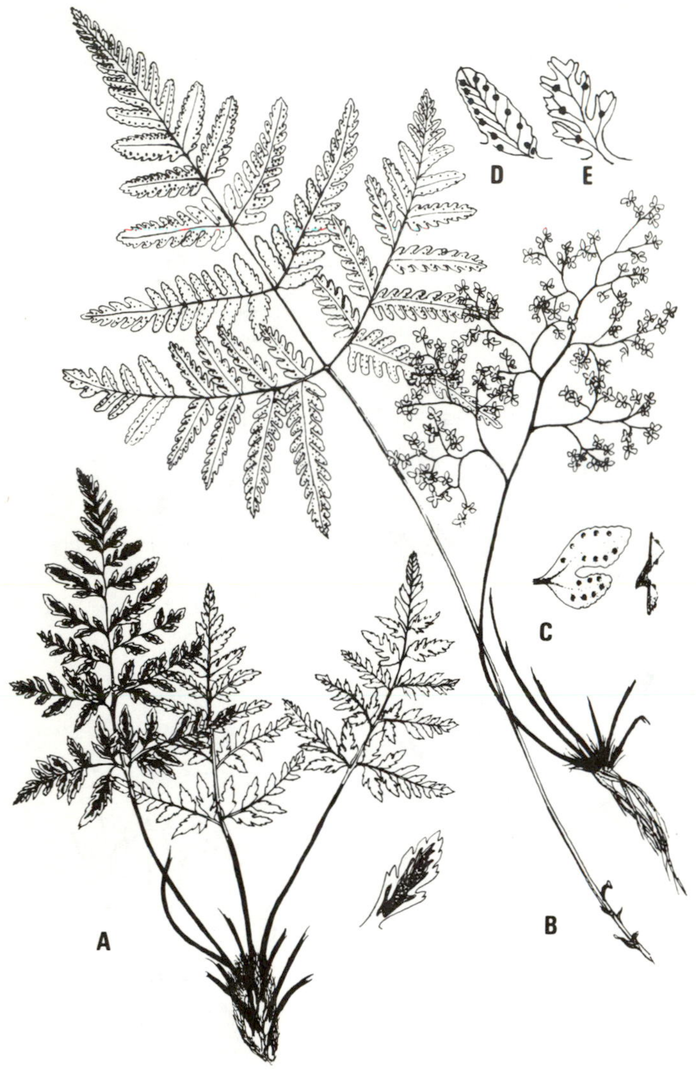

Fig. 14. A, *Asplenium andrewsii*; **B,** *Gymnocarpium*; **C,** *Argyrochosma*; **D, E,** venation of *Cystopteris fragilis* and *C. bulbifera*

Fig. 15. A, *Botrypus virginianus*; **B,** *Botrychium lunaria*; **C,** *B. lanceolatum*; **D,** *B. simplex*; **E,** *B. multifidum*

Fig. 16. A, *Hippochaete laevigata*; **B,** *H. hyemalis*; **C,** *Equisetum arvense*

Fig. 17. A, *Lycopodium annotinum*; **B,** *Huperzia*, habit, sporophyll; **C,** *Marsilea*; **D,** *Isoëtes bolanderi*, habit, megaspore above, microsporangium below

Fig. 18. **A**, *Asplenium septentrionale*; **B**, *Selaginella densa*; **C**, *S. selaginoides*; **D**, *S. underwoodii*; **E**, *S. mutica*

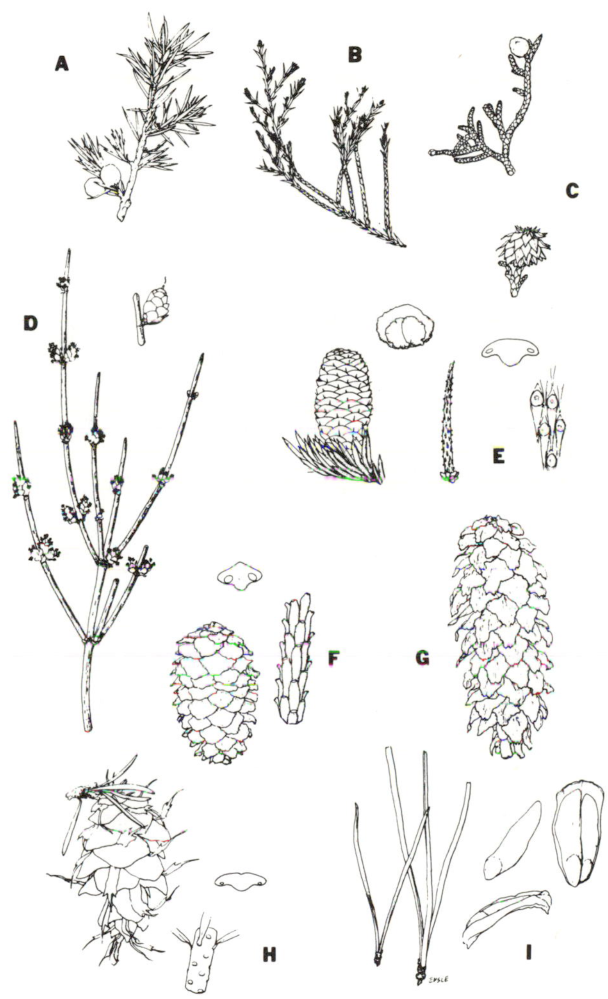

Fig. 19. A, *Juniperus*; **B,** *Sabina scopulorum*, showing some juvenile leaves; **C,** *S. osteosperma* (below, gall), comparable to *S. monosperma*; **D,** *Ephedra* (western slope); **E,** *Abies lasiocarpa*, cone, cone axis, needle section, leaf scars; **F,** *Picea engelmannii*, cone, leaf section, twig; **G,** *P. pungens*, cone; **H,** *Pseudotsuga*, cone, twig, leaf section; **I,** *Pinus species*, needles, seed, face and side view of cone scale

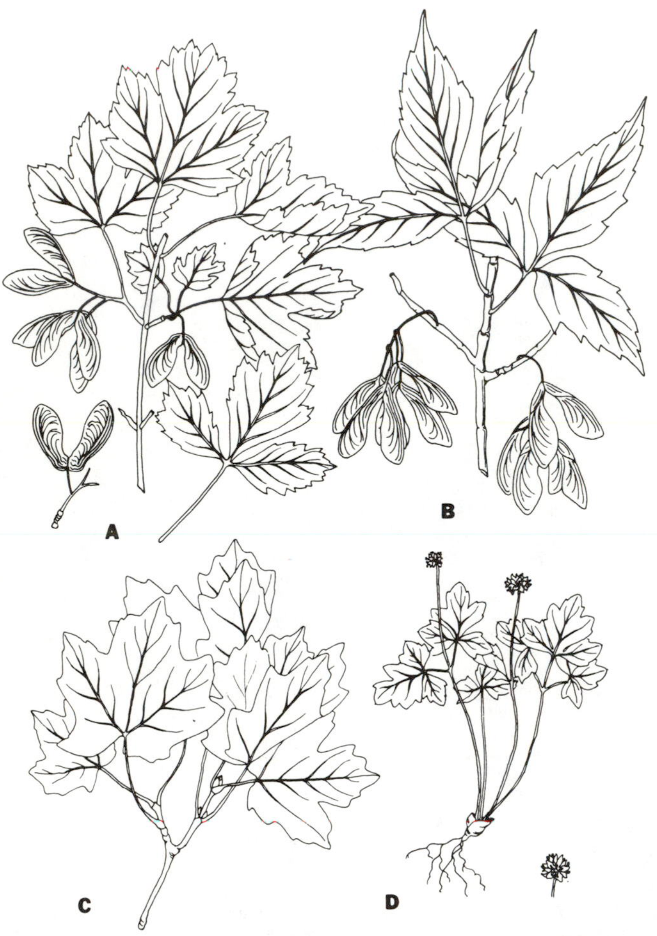

Fig. 20. A, *Acer glabrum*, with leaf of *forma trisectum*; **B,** *Negundo*; **C,** *Acer grandidentatum* (W.S.); **D,** *Adoxa moschatellina*

Fig. 21. A, *Alisma gramineum*; **B,** *Alisma triviale*, plant, carpel; **C,** *Sagittaria cuneata*, carpel; **D,** *S. latifolia*, carpel

Fig. 22. A, *Amaranthus retroflexus*; **B,** *A. albus*; **C,** *A. blitoides*; **D,** *A. arenicola*

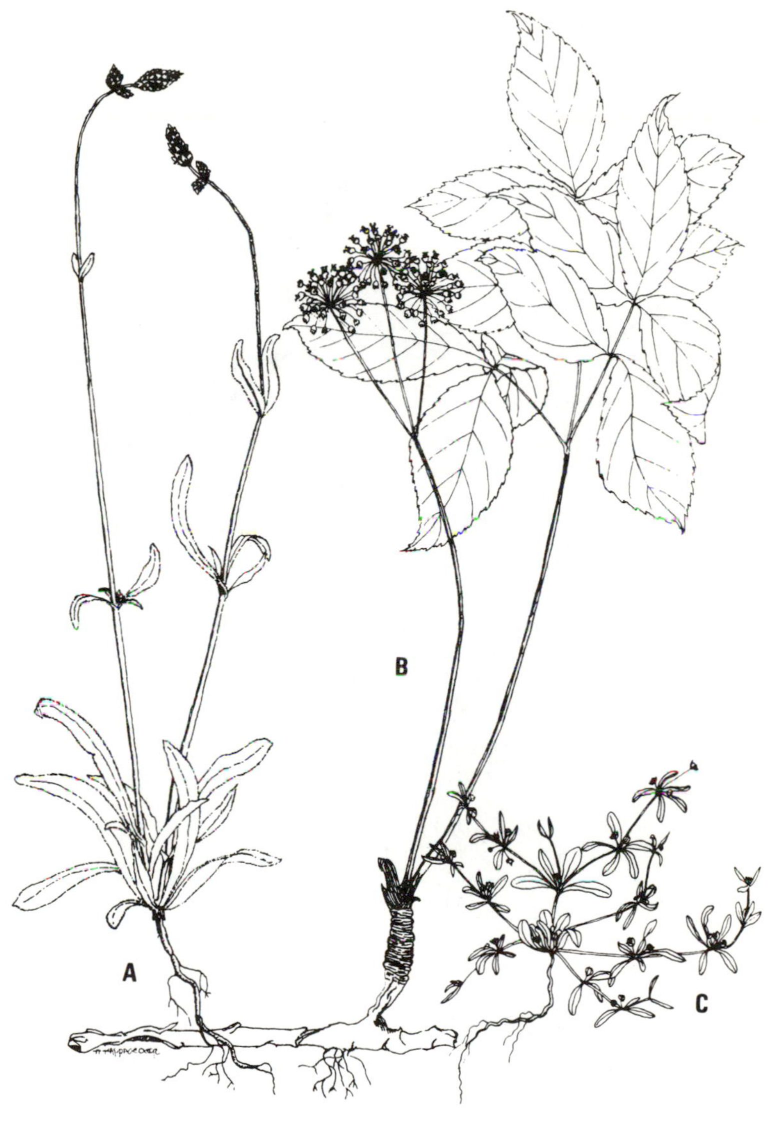

Fig. 23. A, *Froelichia*; **B,** *Aralia nudicaulis*; **C,** *Mollugo*

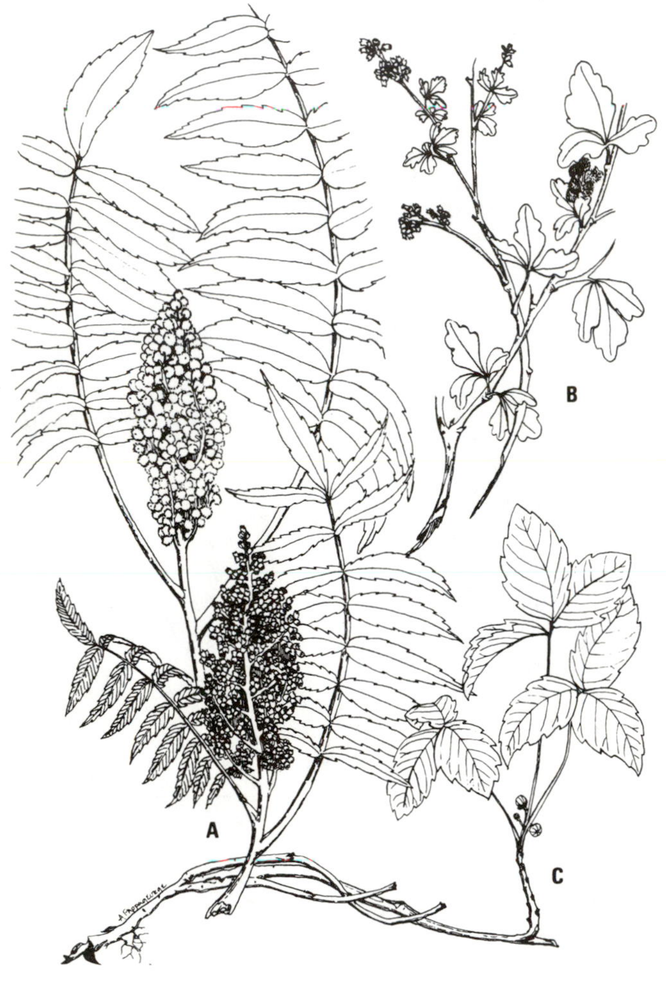

Fig. 24. A, *Rhus glabra*; **B,** *Rhus aromatica*; **C,** *Toxicodendron*

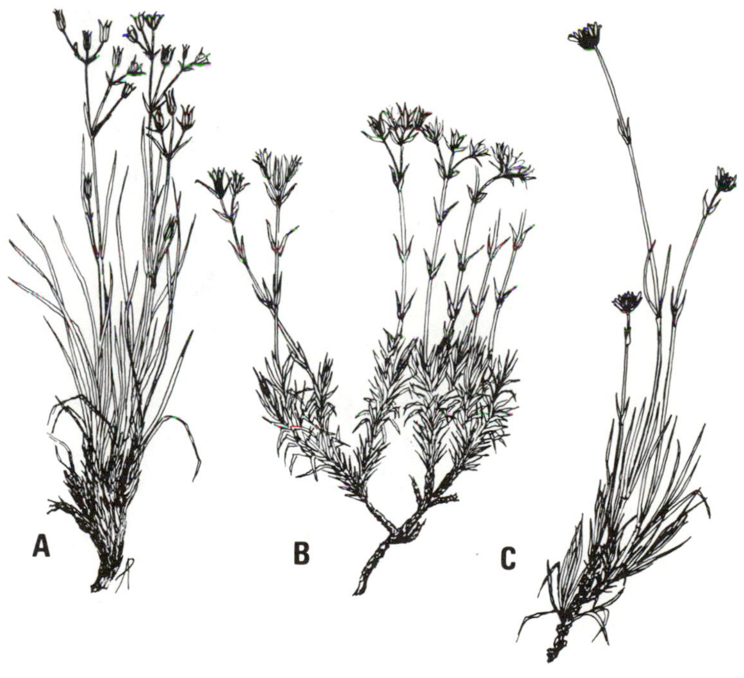

Fig. 25. A, *Eremogone fendleri*; **B,** *E. hookeri*; **C,** *E. congesta*

Fig. 26. A, *Pseudostellaria*; **B,** *Alsine*; **C,** *Stellaria umbellata*; **D,** *Cerastium strictum*; **E,** *C. beeringianum*

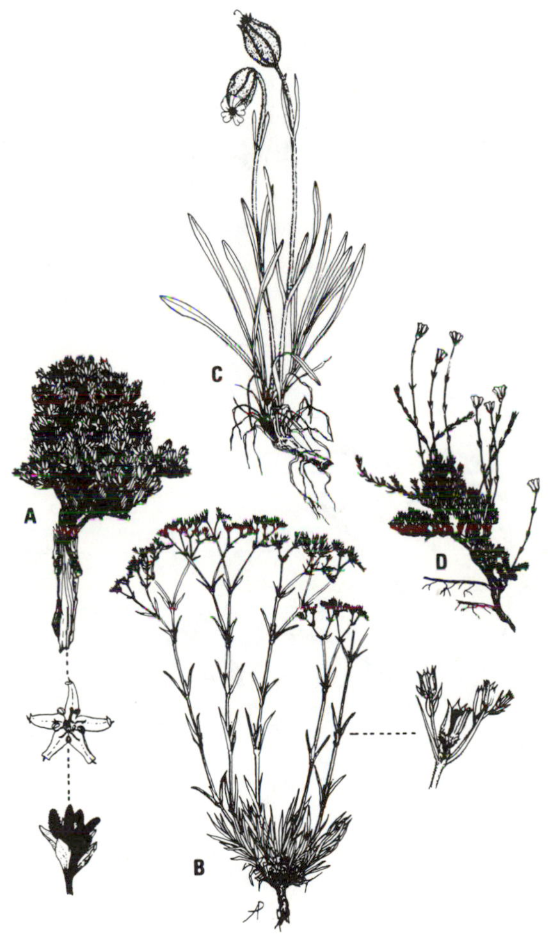

Fig. 27. A, *Paronychia pulvinata*; **B,** *P. jamesii*; **C,** *Gastrolychnis apetala*; **D,** *Lidia*

Fig. 28. *Callitriche verna*

Fig. 29. A, *Asparagus officinalis*; **B,** *Commelina dianthifolia*

Fig. 30. A, *Conium maculatum*; **B,** *Cicuta douglasii*

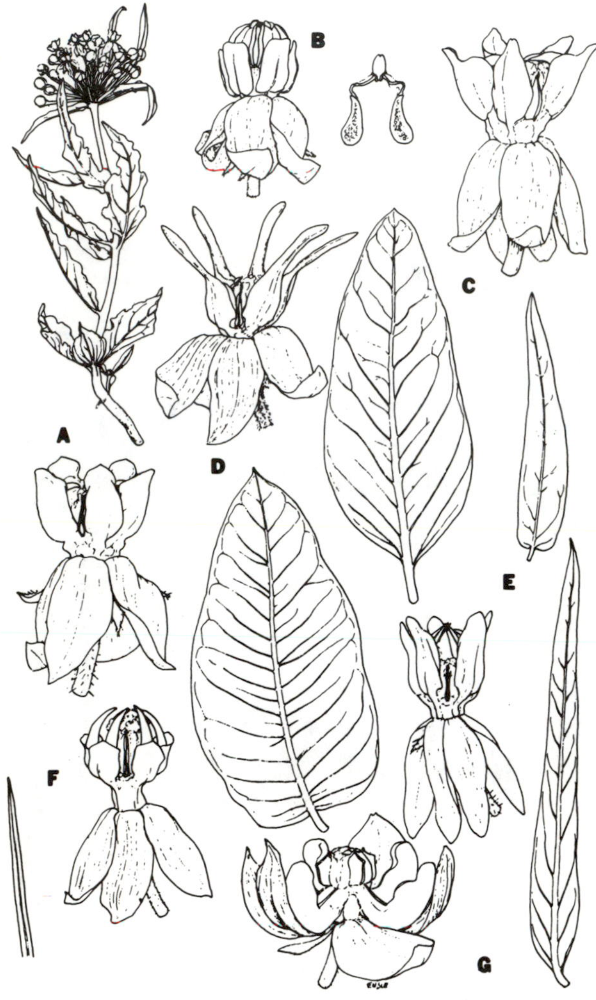

Fig. 31. **A**, *Asclepias macrosperma*, plant, flower below (W.S.); **B**, *A. engelmanniana*, flower, pollinia; **C**, *A. hallii*, flower, leaf below left; **D**, *A. speciosa*, flower, leaf below; **E**, *A. tuberosa*, flower below left, leaf above right; **F**, *A. subverticillata*, flower, leaf; **G**, *A. asperula*, flower left, leaf right

Fig. 32. A, *Cannabis*; **B,** *Humulus*

Fig. 33. A, *Ligularia holmii*; **B,** *L. soldanella*

Fig. 34. A, *Ligularia amplectens*; **B,** *L. taraxacoides*; **C,** *L. pudica*; **D,** *L. bigelovii*

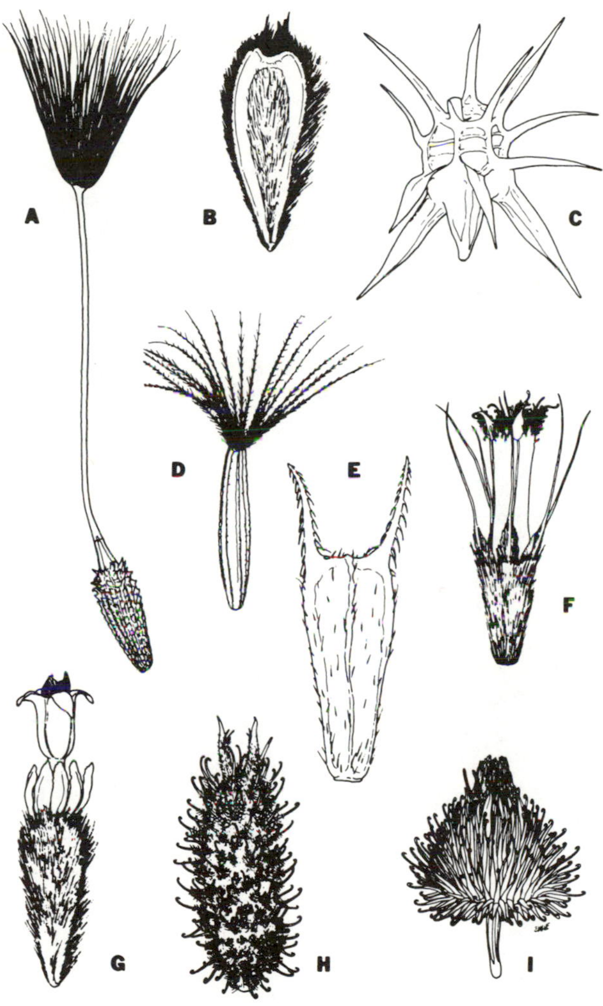

Fig. 35. A. *Taraxacum officinale*; **B,** *Helianthella parryi*; **C,** *Ambrosia acanthicarpa*; **D,** *Stephanomeria pauciflora*; **E,** *Bidens frondosa*; **F,** *Gaillardia aristata*; **G,** *Hymenopappus filifolius*; **H,** *Xanthium*; **I,** *Arctium minus*

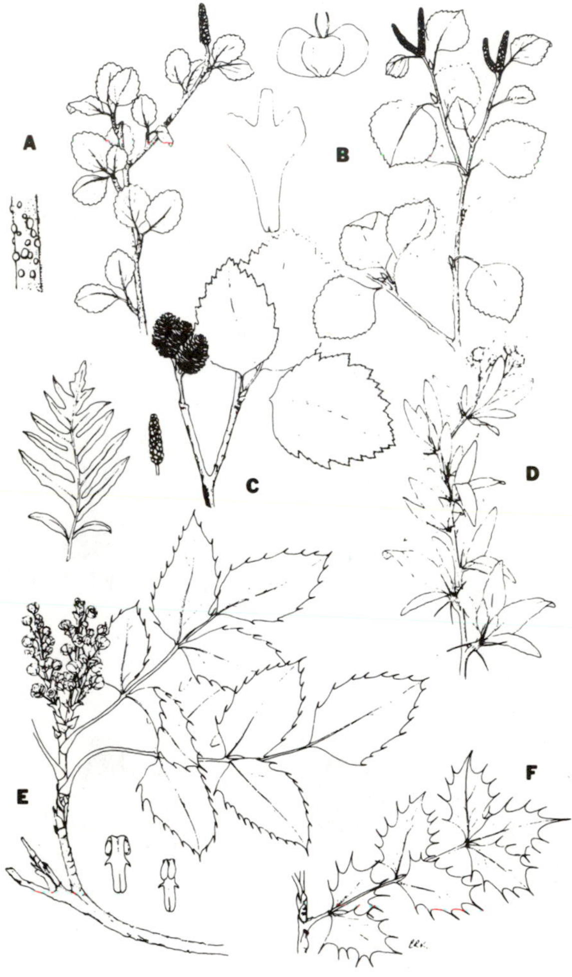

Fig. 36. A, *Betula glandulosa*, twig, branch; **B,** *B. fontinalis*, branch, bract, fruit; **C,** *Alnus incana*, branch, staminate ament, leaf of *forma incisa*; **D,** *Berberis fendleri*; *E, Mahonia repens*; **F,** *M. fremontii* (W.S.), comparable to *M. haematocarpa*

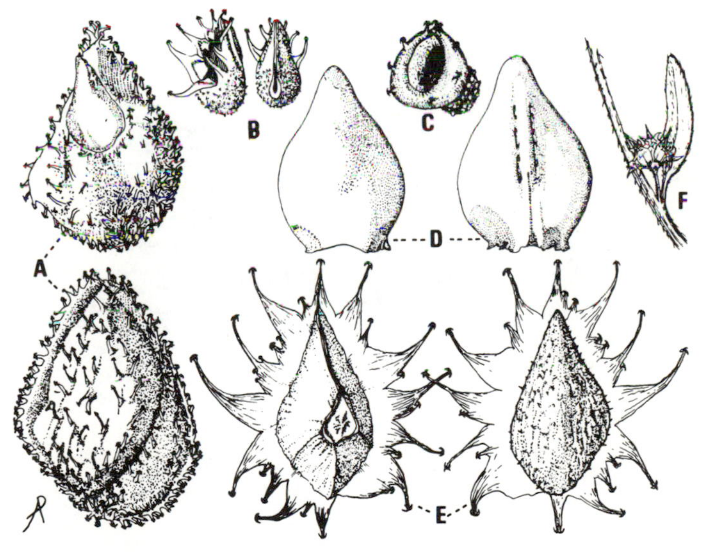

Fig. 37. A, *Cynoglossum*; **B,** *Lappula redowskii*; **C,** *L. marginata*; **D,** *Lithospermum incisum*; **E,** *Hackelia floribunda*; **F,** *Asperugo procumbens*

Fig. 38. A, *Lesquerella ludoviciana*; **B,** *L. montana*; **C,** *Lepidium perfoliatum*

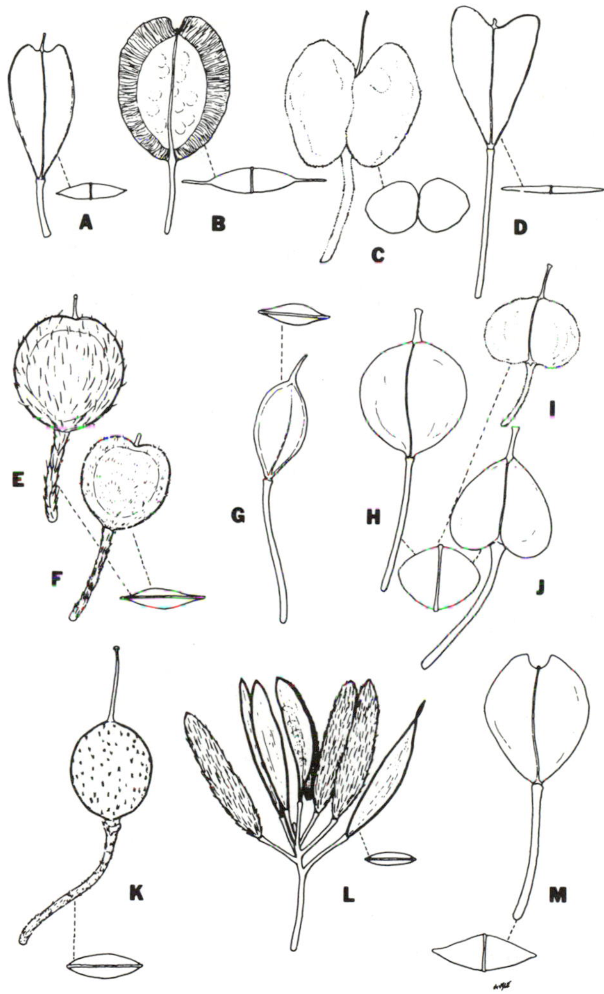

Fig. 39. **A**, *Noccaea*; **B**, *Thlaspi*; **C**, *Physaria acutifolia* (W.S.), comparable to *P. bellii*; **D**, *Capsella*; **E**, *Alyssum minus*; **F**, *A. alyssoides*; **G**, *Camelina microcarpa*; **H**, *Cardaria chalepensis*; **I**, *C. pubescens*; **J**, *C. draba*; **K**, *Lesquerella rectipes* (W.S.); **L**, *Draba reptans*; **M**, *Lepidium densiflorum*

Fig. 40. A, *Gypsophila paniculata*; **B,** *Vaccaria*; **C,** *Dianthus deltoides*; **D,** *Saponaria*

Fig. 41. **A,** *Campanula uniflora*; *B, Heterocodon rariflorum* **(W.S.); C,** *Campanula parryi*; **D,** *C. rotundifolia*

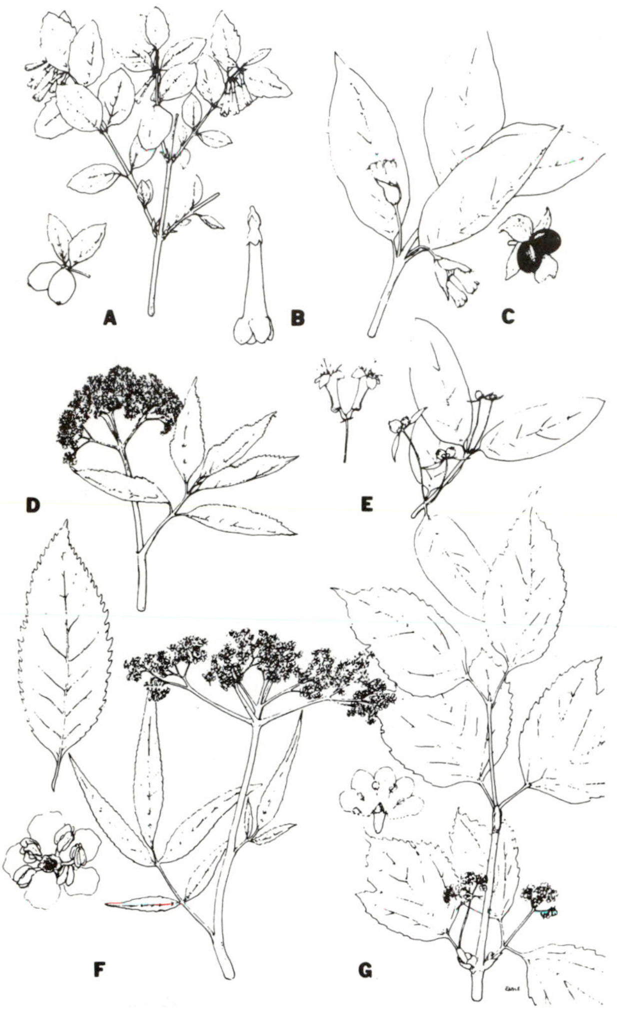

Fig. 42. A, *Symphoricarpos rotundifolius*; **B,** *S. longiflorus*, flower (W.S.); **C,** *Distegia*; **D,** *Sambucus microbotrys*; **E,** *Lonicera morrowii*; **F,** *Sambucus coerulea*; **G,** *Viburnum edule*

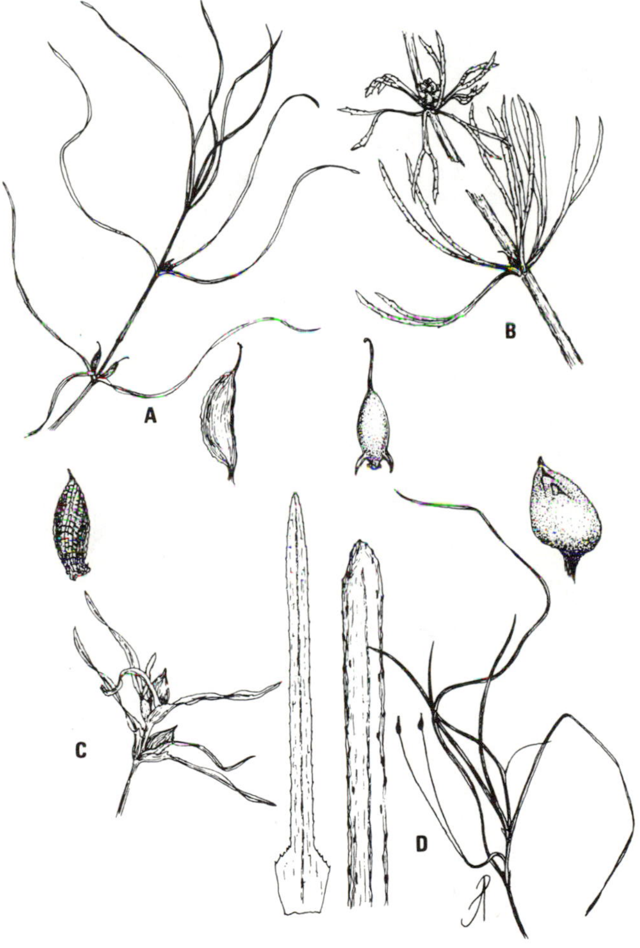

Fig. 43. **A,** *Zannichellia*; **B,** *Ceratophyllum*; **C,** *Najas*; **D,** *Ruppia*

Fig. 44. A, *Atriplex canescens*; **B,** *Bassia sieversiana*; **C,** *Cycloloma*; **D,** *Krascheninnikovia*

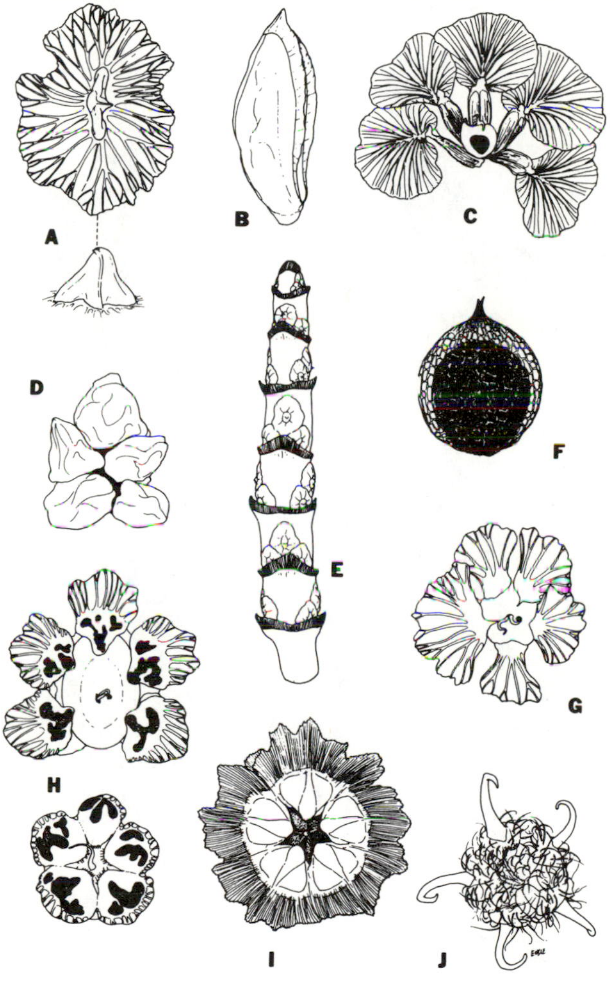

Fig. 45. A, *Sarcobatus*; B, *Corispermum*; C, *Halogeton* (W.S.); D, *Suaeda calceoliformis*; E, *Salicornia*; F, *Monolepis*; G, *Salsola australis*; H, *Bassia sieversiana*; I, *Cycloloma*; J, *Bassia hyssopifolia*

Fig. 46. A, *Chenopodium album*; **B,** *C. fremontii*; **C,** *C. glaucum*; **D,** *Teloxys botrys*

Fig. 47. *Chenopodium capitatum*

Fig. 48. **A,** *Salsola collina*; **B,** *S. australis*

Fig. 49. A, *Echinocystis*; B, *Cucurbita*

Fig. 50. A, *Evolvulus*; **B,** *Calystegia*; **C,** *Grammica*; **D,** *Convolvulus arvensis*

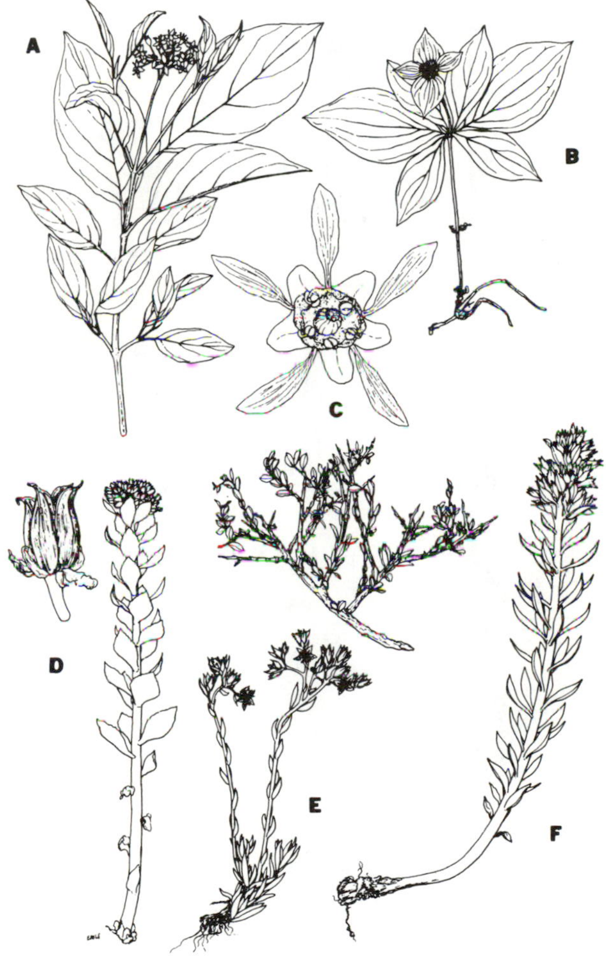

Fig. 51. **A,** *Swida*; **B,** *Chamaepericlymenum*; **C,** *Forsellesia meionandra* (W.S.), comparable to *F. planitierum*; **D,** *Rhodiola*; **E,** *Amerosedum*; **F,** *Clementsia*

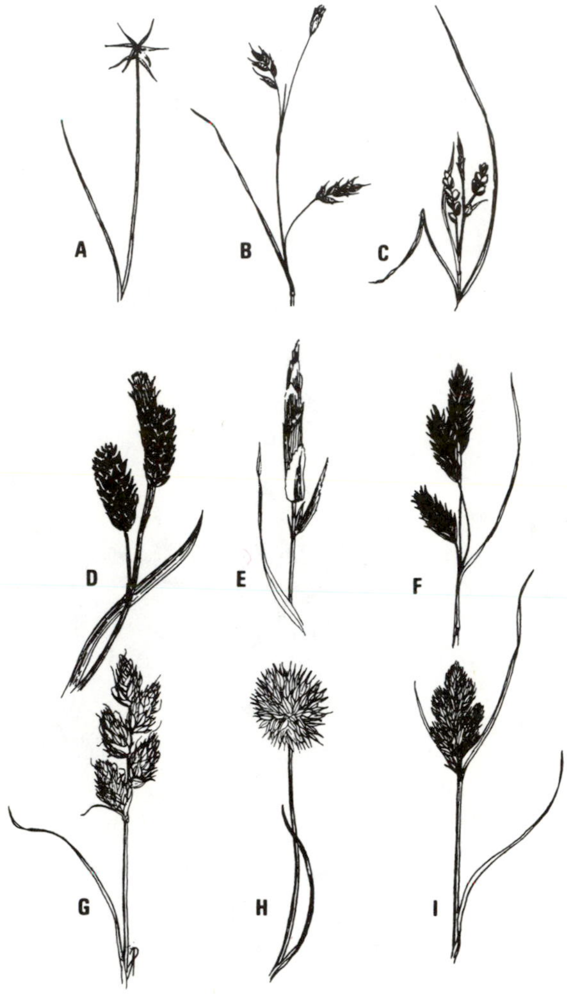

Fig. 52. **A,** *Carex microglochin*; **B,** *C. capillaris*; **C,** *C. aurea*; **D,** *C. scopulorum*; **E,** *C. geyeri*; **F,** *C. misandra*; **G,** *C. brevior*; **H,** *C. perglobosa*; **I,** *C. athrostachya*

Fig. 53. A, *Carex ebenea*; **B,** *C. microptera*; **C,** *C. stipata*; **D,** *C. utriculata*; **E,** *C. hystericina*; **F,** *C. lanuginosa*; **G,** *C. chalciolepis*; **H,** *C. aquatilis*

Fig. 54. A, *Eleocharis palustris*; **B,** *E. acicularis*; **C,** *E. rostellata* (W.S.); **D,** *Cyperus erythrorhizos*

Fig. 55. A, *Bolboschoenus maritimus*; **B,** *Schoenoplectus pungens*; **C,** *S. lacustris*; **D,** *Scirpus microcarpus*; **E,** *Eriophorum angustifolium*; **F,** *E. altaicum*

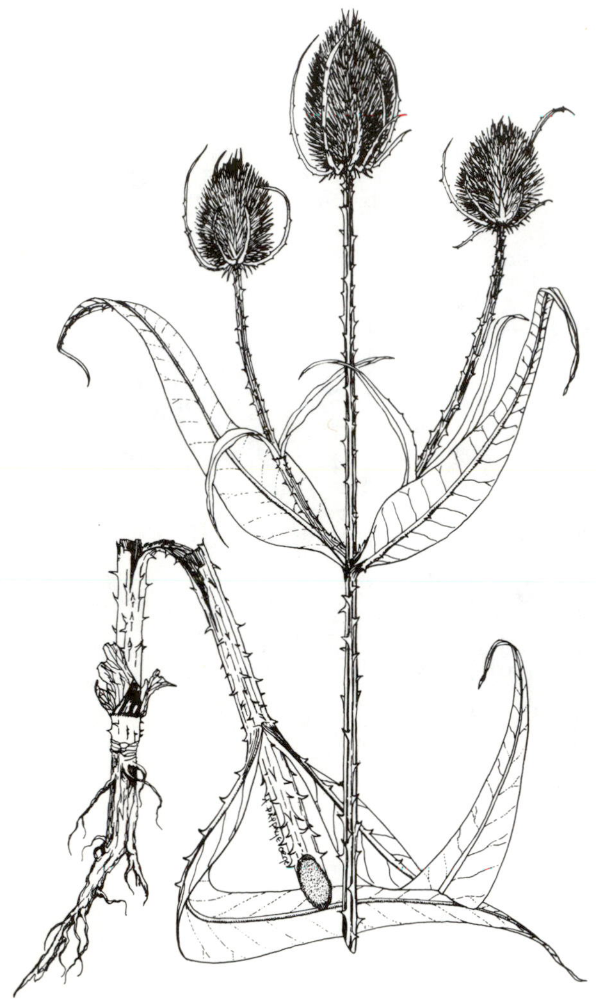

Fig. 56. *Dipsacus*

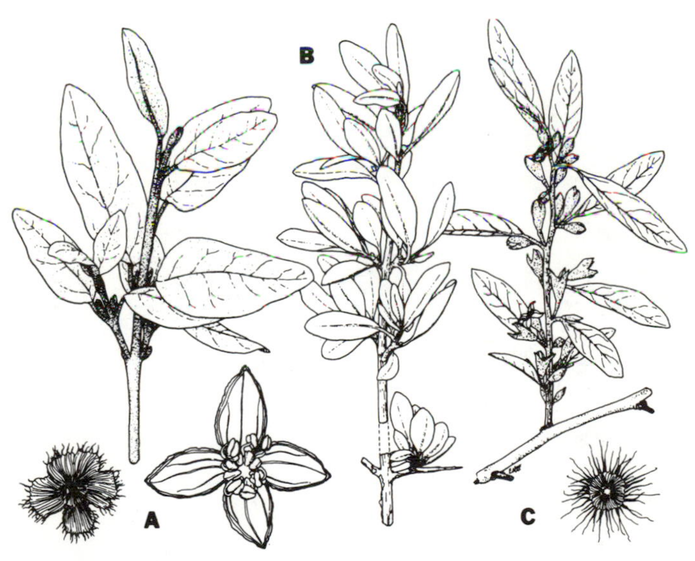

Fig. 57. A, *Shepherdia canadensis*; **B,** *S. argentea*; **C,** *Elaeagnus angustifolia*

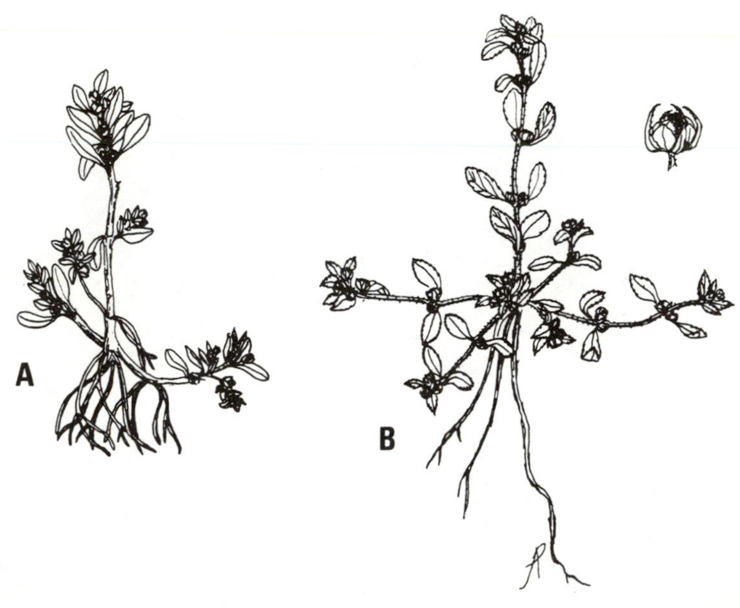

Fig. 58. **A,** *Elatine*; **B,** *Bergia*

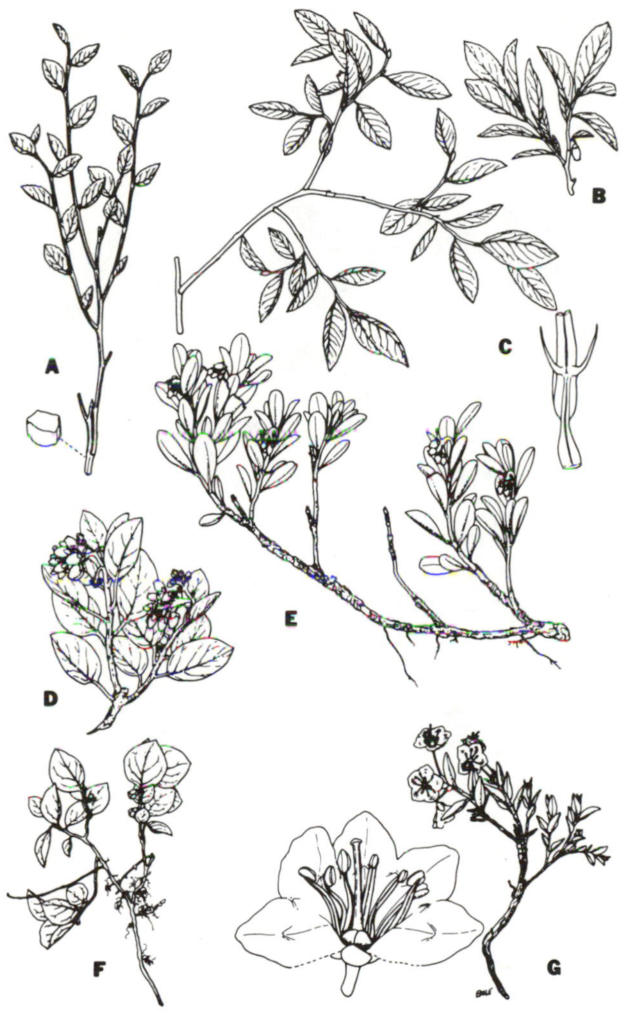

Fig. 59. A, *Vaccinium scoparium*; **B,** *V. cespitosum*; **C,** *V. myrtillus*; **D,** *Arctostaphylos patula* (W.S.); **E,** *E. uva-ursi*; **F,** *Gaultheria humifusa*; **G,** *Kalmia*

Fig. 60. A, *Chamaësyce glyptosperma*; **B,** *Tithymalus montanus*; **C,** *Tragia*; **D,** *Croton*

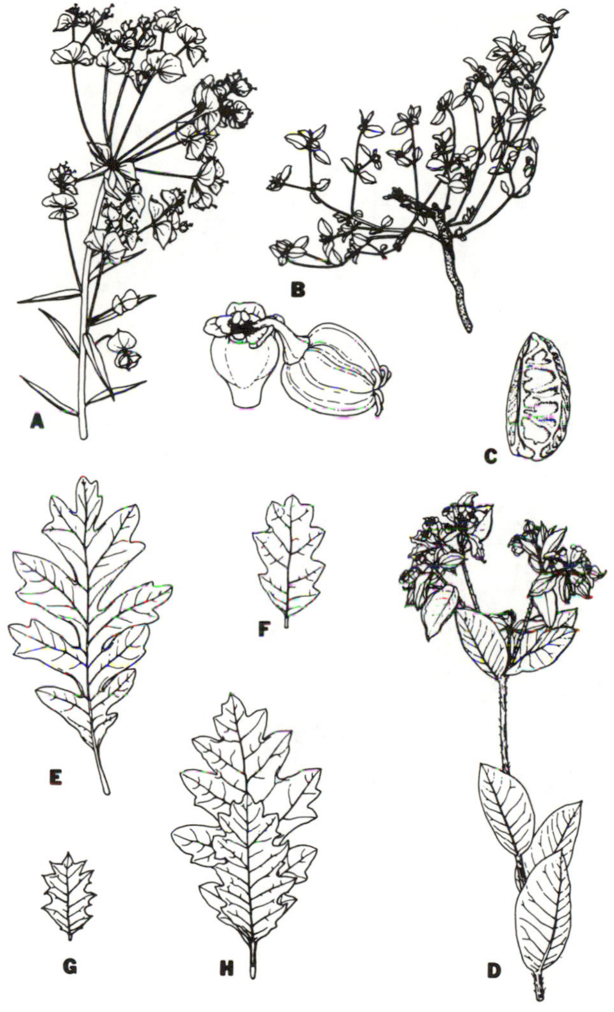

Fig. 61. **A,** *Tithymalus uralensis*; **B,** *Chamaesyce fendleri*; **C,** *C. glyptosperma*, seed; **D,** *Agaloma marginata*; **E,** *Quercus gambelii*; **F,** *Q. turbinella*; **G,** *Q. ajoensis* (W.S.); **H,** *Q. gambelii*, variants

Fig. 62. A, *Astragalus kentrophyta*, leaf; **B,** *Pediomelum megalanthum* (W.S.), comparable with *P. hypogaeum*; **C,** *Hedysarum boreale*; **D,** *Glycyrrhiza*; **E, F, G,** keels of *Astragalus, Hedysarum, Oxytropis*

Fig. 63. A, *Frankenia*, plant, flower; **B,** *Corydalis caseana*, plant, flower; **C,** *C. aurea*

Fig. 64. **A,** *Gentianella acuta*; **B,** *Comastoma*; **C,** *Swertia*; **D,** *Lomatogonium*

Fig. 65. A, *Gentianopsis thermalis*; **B,** *G. barbellata*; **C,** *Pneumonanthe parryi*; **D,** *Chondrophylla prostrata*; **E,** *Pneumonanthe affinis*; **F,** *Chondrophylla aquatica*

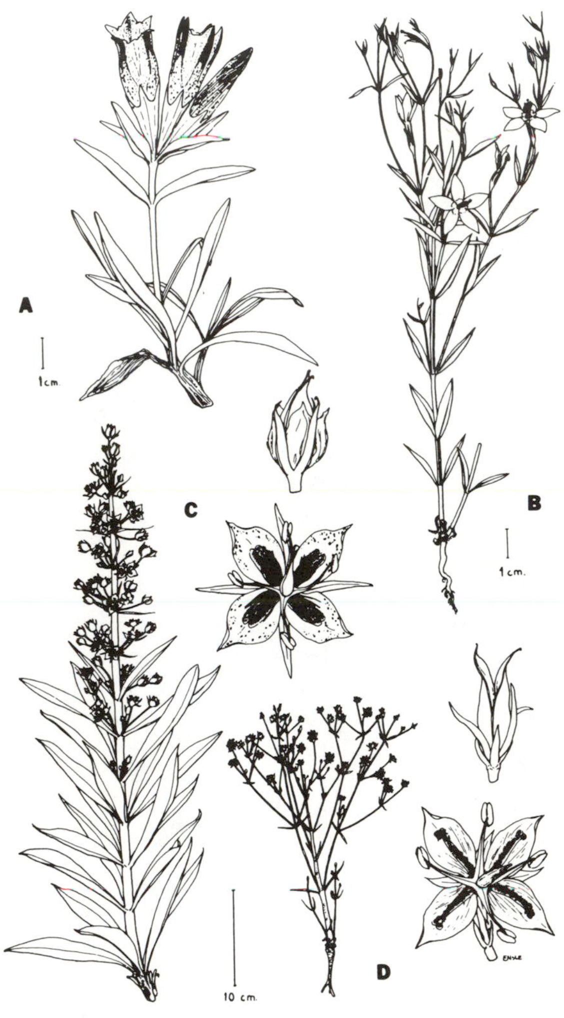

Fig. 66. A, *Gentianodes*; **B,** *Centaurium calycosum* (W.S.); **C,** *Frasera speciosa*, habit, flower, fruit; **D,** *F. albomarginata* (W.S.)

Fig. 67. A, *Geranium richardsonii*, plant, petal; **B,** *G. caespitosum*, branch, fruit, petal; **C,** *G. viscosissimum*, branch, petal; **D,** *Erodium cicutarium*, branch, fruit

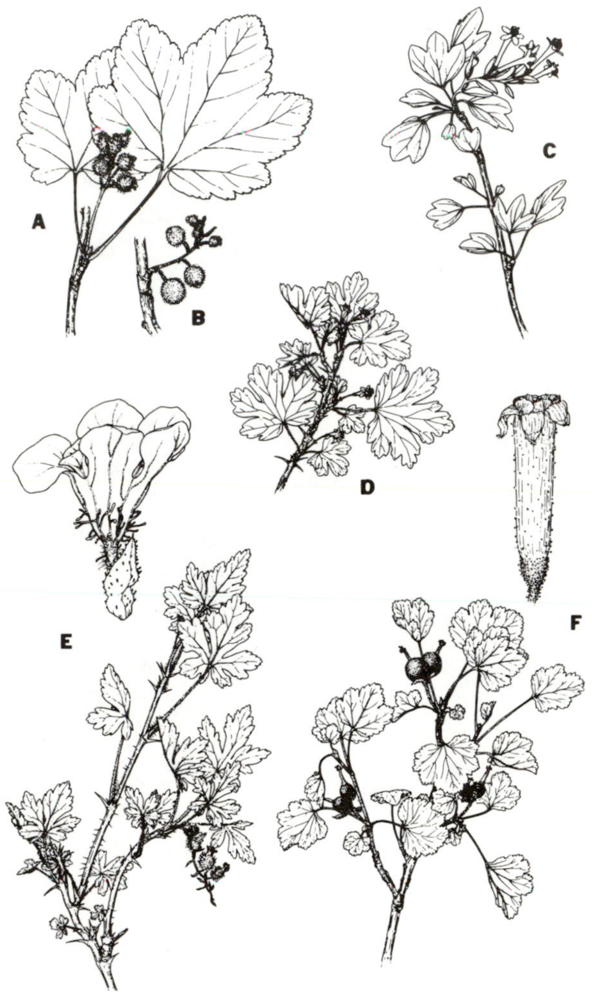

Fig. 68. A, *Ribes wolfii*; **B,** *R. coloradense*; **C,** *R. aureum*; **D,** *R. inerme*; **E,** *R. montigenum*; **F,** *R. cereum*

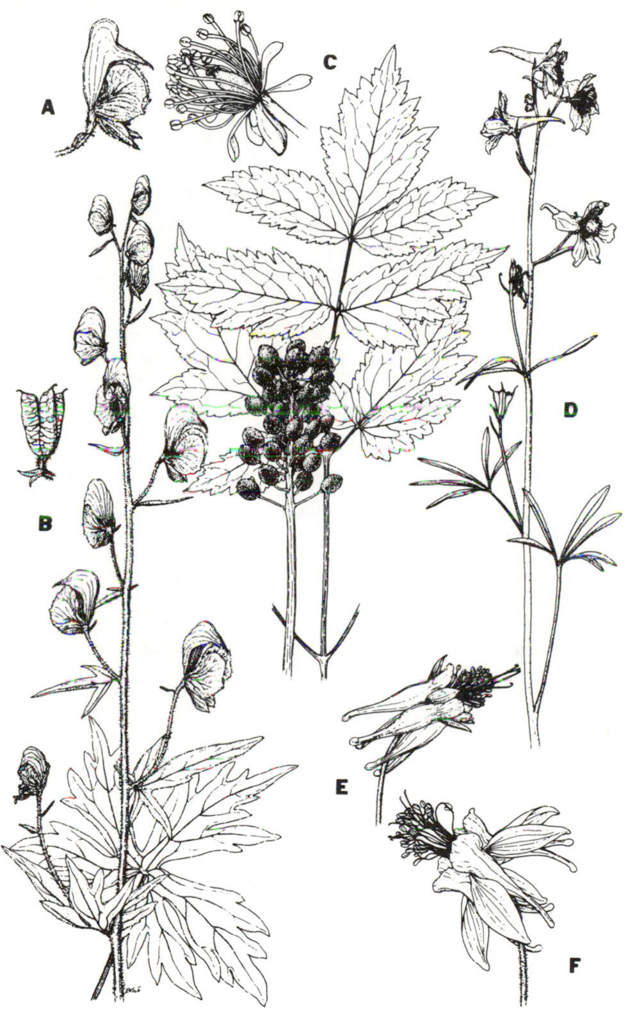

Fig. 69. A, B, *Aconitum*, above, *"bakeri"* form; **C,** *Actaea*; **D,** *Delphinium nuttallianum*; **E,** *Aquilegia elegantula*; **F,** *A. barnebyi* (W.S.)

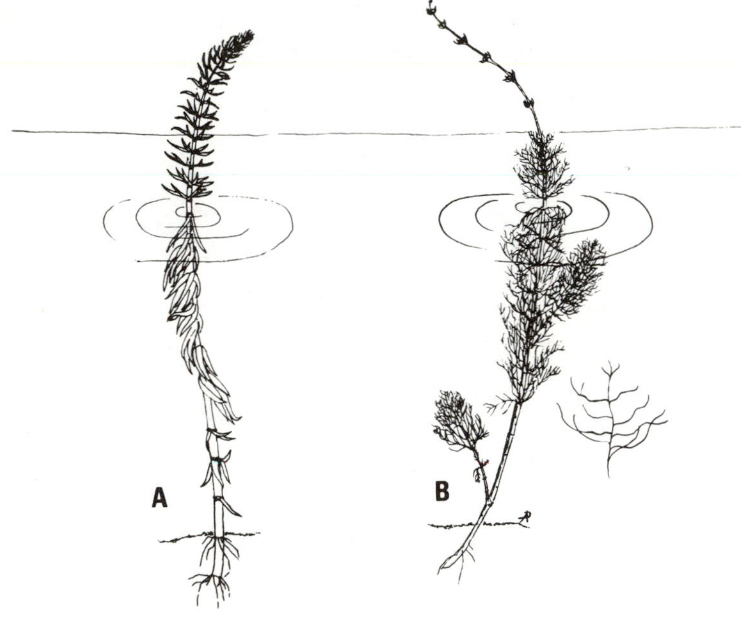

Fig. 70. A, *Hippuris*; **B,** *Myriophyllum*

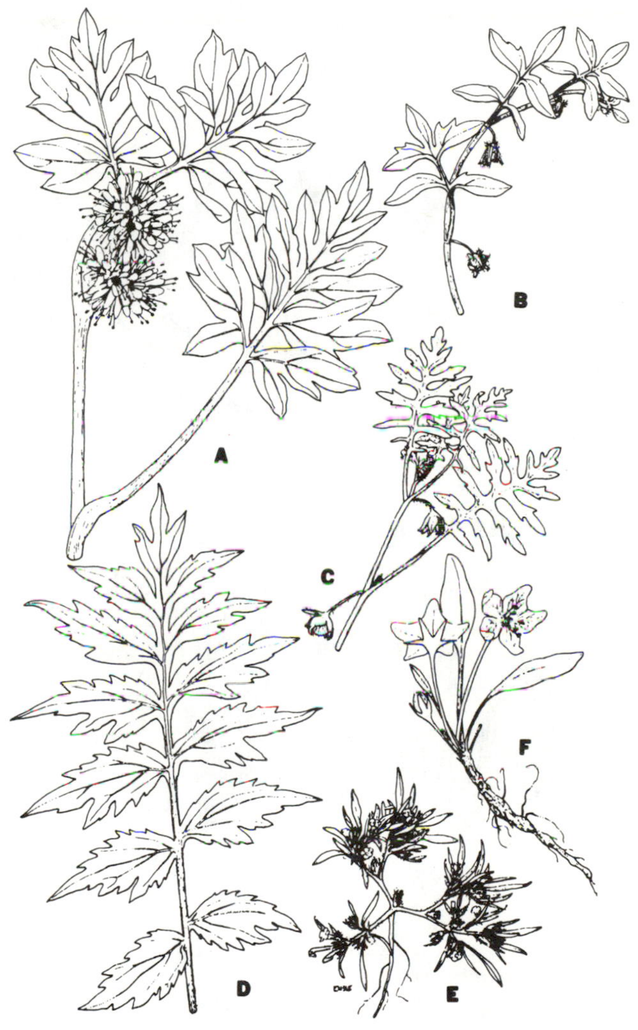

Fig. 71. A, *Hydrophyllum capitatum*; **B,** *Nemophila*; **C,** *Ellisia*; **D,** *Hydrophyllum fendleri*; **E,** *Nama* (W.S.); **F,** *Hesperochiron*(W.S.)

Fig. 72. A–D, Seeds of *Juncus* species; **E,** *J. saximontanus*; **F,** *J. bufonius*, habit, flowers, seed; **G,** *Juncus confusus*, habit, seed; **H,** *J. arcticus*

Fig. 73. **A**, *Juncus longistylis*; **B**, *J. biglumis*; **C**, *J. triglumis*; **D**, *J. mertensianus*; **E**, *Luzula spicata*, habit, fruit; **F**, *Luzula parviflora*

Fig. 74. **A**, *Triglochin palustris*; **B**, *T. maritima*; **C**, *T. concinna*

Fig. 75. **A,** *Marrubium*; **B,** *Dracocephalum*; **C,** *Monarda fistulosa*; **D,** *Mentha arvensis*; **E,** *Scutellaria brittonii*

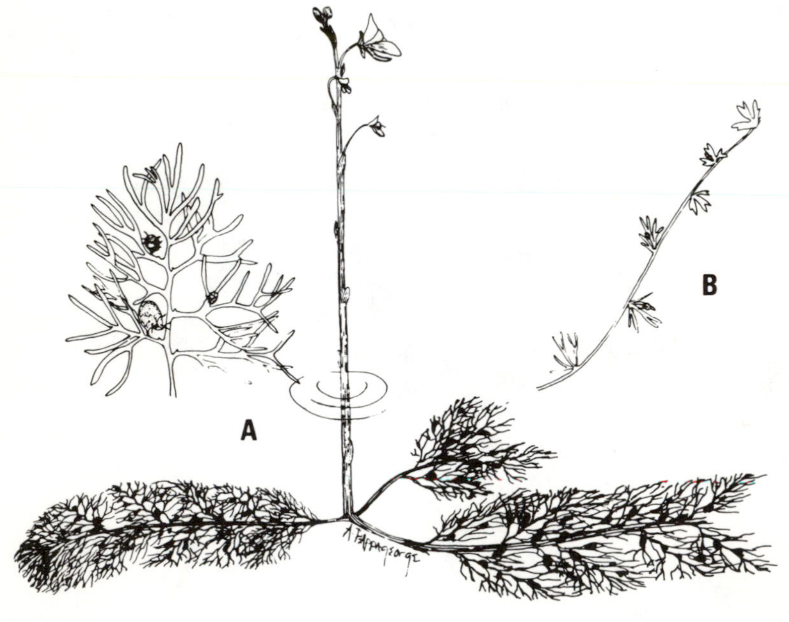

Fig. 76. A, *Utricularia vulgaris*; **B,** *U. minor*

Fig. 77. A, *Disporum*; **B,** *Streptopus*; **C,** *Fritillaria pudica* (W.S.), **D,** *F. atropurpurea*

Fig. 78. A, *Acrolasia humilis* (W.S.); B, *A. albicaulis*, habit, petal upper right; C, *Nuttallia multiflora*, petal-stamen transitions above

Fig. 79. **A,** *Iliamna rivularis*; **B,** *Sidalcea neomexicana*, upper and lower leaves; **C,** *S. candida*; **D,** *Malva neglecta*; **E,** *Sphaeralcea coccinea*; **F,** *S. fendleri* (W.S.), leaf comparable to *S. angustifolia*; **G,** *S. parvifolia* (W.S.); **H,** *S. leptophylla* (W.S.)

Fig. 80. *Menyanthes*

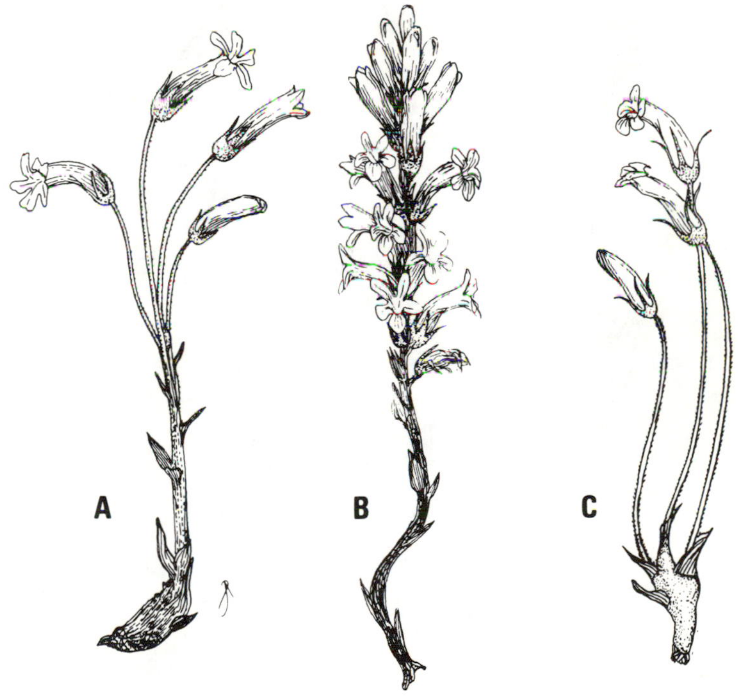

Fig. 81. A, *Aphyllon fasciculatum*; **B,** *Orobanche multiflora*; **C,** *Aphyllon uniflorum*

Fig. 82. A, *Gayophytum*, habit, fruit; **B,** *Camissonia scapoidea* (W.S.); **C,** *Gaura coccinea*; **D,** *Circaea*, habit, flower, fruit; **E,** *Epilobium hornemannii*

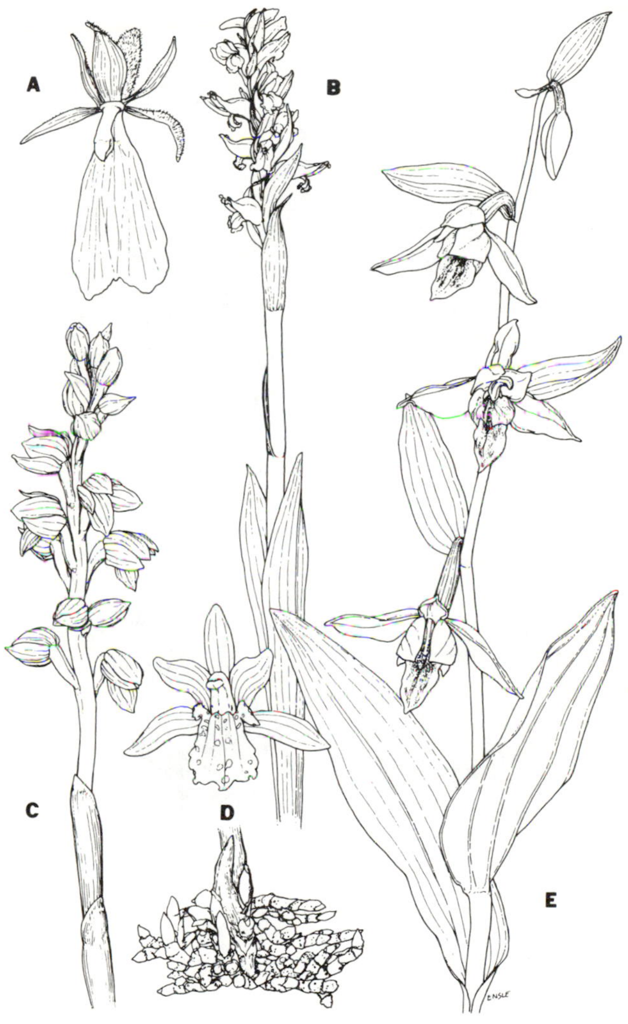

Fig. 83. A, *Listera convallarioides*, flower; **B,** *Spiranthes romanzoffiana*; **C,** *Corallorhiza striata*; **D,** *C. maculata*, flower and root; **E,** *Epipactis*

Fig. 84. **A,** *Parnassia parviflora*; **B,** *P. kotzebuei*; **C,** *P. fimbriata*

Fig. 85. A, *Plantago patagonica*; **B,** *P. elongata*; **C,** *P. major*; **D,** *P. lanceolata*

Fig. 86. A, *Bromus japonicus*; B, *Danthonia parryi*; C, *Anisantha tectorum*; D, *Phleum commutatum*; E, *Bouteloua curtipendula*; F, *Chondrosum gracile*

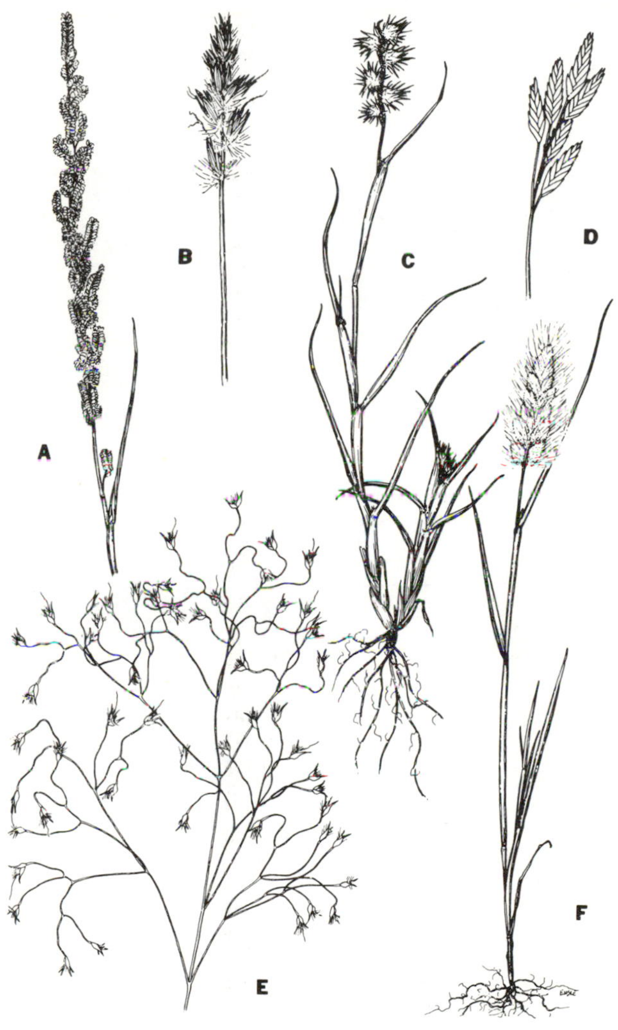

Fig. 87. **A,** *Beckmannia*; **B,** *Hilaria*; **C,** *Cenchrus*; **D,** *Distichlis*; **E,** *Stipa hymenoides*; **F,** *Polypogon monspeliensis*

Fig. 88. **A,** *Ptilagrostis mongholica* (specimen from USSR); **B,** *P. porteri*

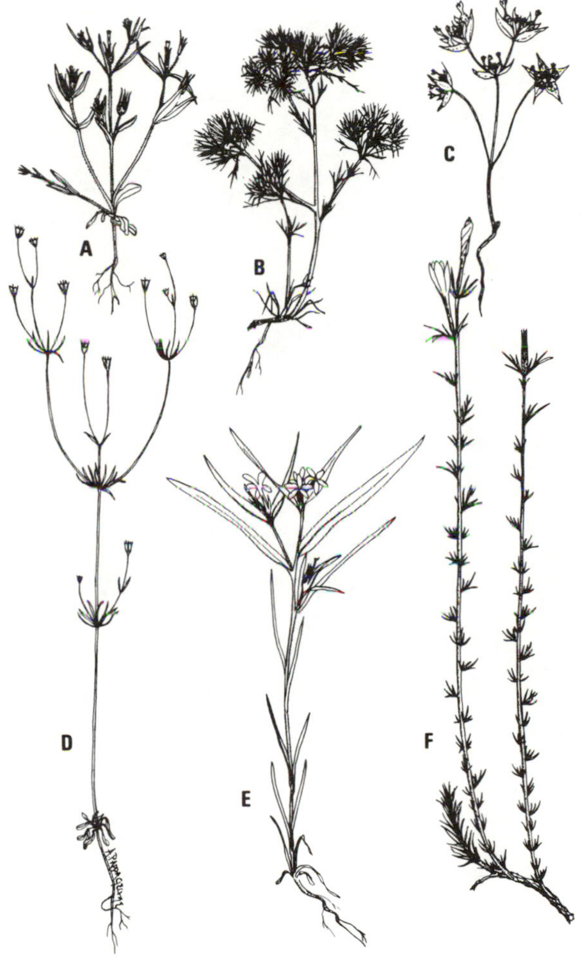

Fig. 89. **A,** *Microsteris*; **B,** *Navarretia*; **C,** *Gymnosteris*; **D,** *Linanthus harknessii*; **E,** *Collomia*; **F,** *Leptodactylon pungens*

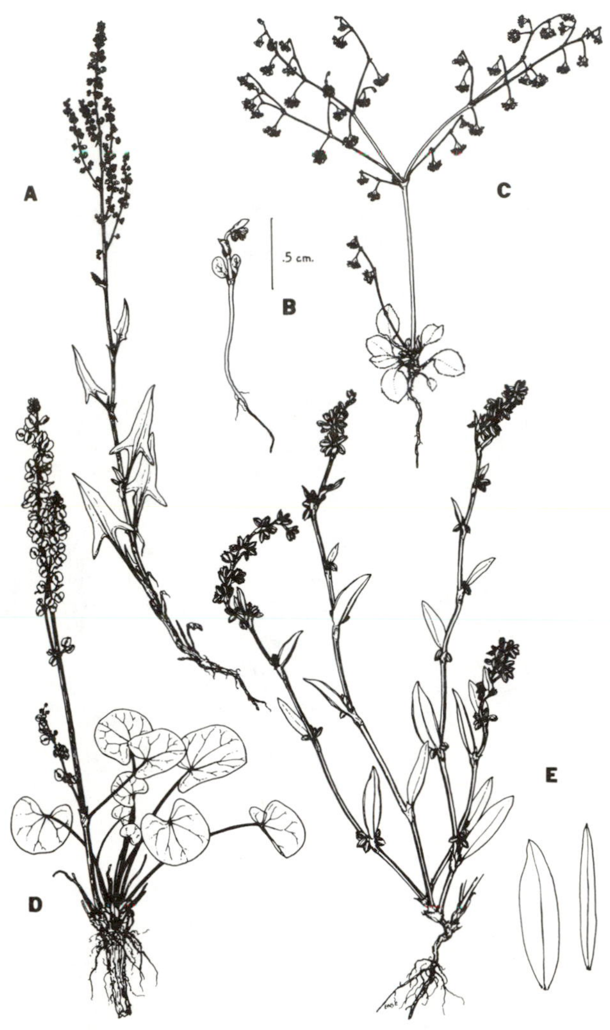

Fig. 90. A, *Acetosella vulgaris*; **B,** *Koenigia*; **C,** *Eriogonum cernuum*; **D,** *Oxyria digyna*; **E,** *Polygonum douglasii*

Fig. 91. A, *Lewisia*; **B,** *Erocallis*; **C,** *Oreobroma*; **D,** *Portulaca*; **E,** *Crunocallis*; **F,** *Claytonia lanceolata*; **G,** *C. megarhiza*

Fig. 92. A, *Androsace filiformis*; **B,** *A. septentrionalis*; **C,** *A. occidentalis*; **D,** *A. chamaejasme*; **E, E',** *Glaux*, growth forms

Fig. 93. **A,** *Pterospora*; **B,** *Hypopitys*; **C,** *Moneses*; **D,** *Chimaphila*; **E,** *Orthilia*; **F,** *Pyrola minor*

Fig. 94. A, *Anemonastrum*; **B,** *Ranunculus macauleyi*; **C,** *Anemone multifida*; **D,** *Atragene occidentalis*; **E,** *Coriflora hirsutissima*

Fig. 95. **A,** *Thalictrum sparsiflorum*; **B,** *T. alpinum*; **C,** *T. fendleri*; **D,** *Trollius*; **E,** *Psychrophila*

Fig. 96. **A,** *Ranunculus reptans*; **B,** *Ceratocephala orthoceras*; **C,** *Myosurus minimus*; **D,** *Halerpestes*; **E,** *Ranunculus pygmaeus*

Fig. 97. A, *Ranunculus gmelinii*; **B,** *Batrachium circinatum*; **C,** *Hecatonia*; **D,** *Trautvetteria*

Fig. 98. A, *Oreobatus*; **B,** *Pentaphylloides*; **C,** *Purshia stansburiana* (W.S.); **D,** *Physocarpus*; **E,** *Holodiscus*; **F,** *Purshia tridentata*

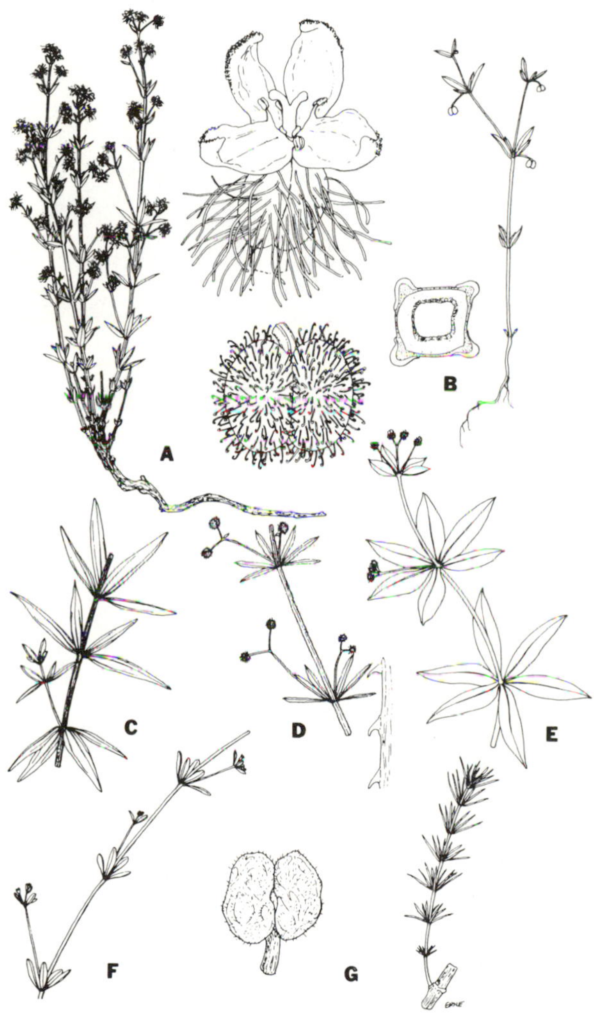

Fig. 99. **A,** *Galium coloradoënse* (W.S.), **B,** *G. bifolium*, habit, stem section, fruit; **C,** *G. septentrionale*; **D,** *G. spurium*; **E,** *G. triflorum*; **F,** *G. trifidum*; **G,** *G. verum*, habit, fruit

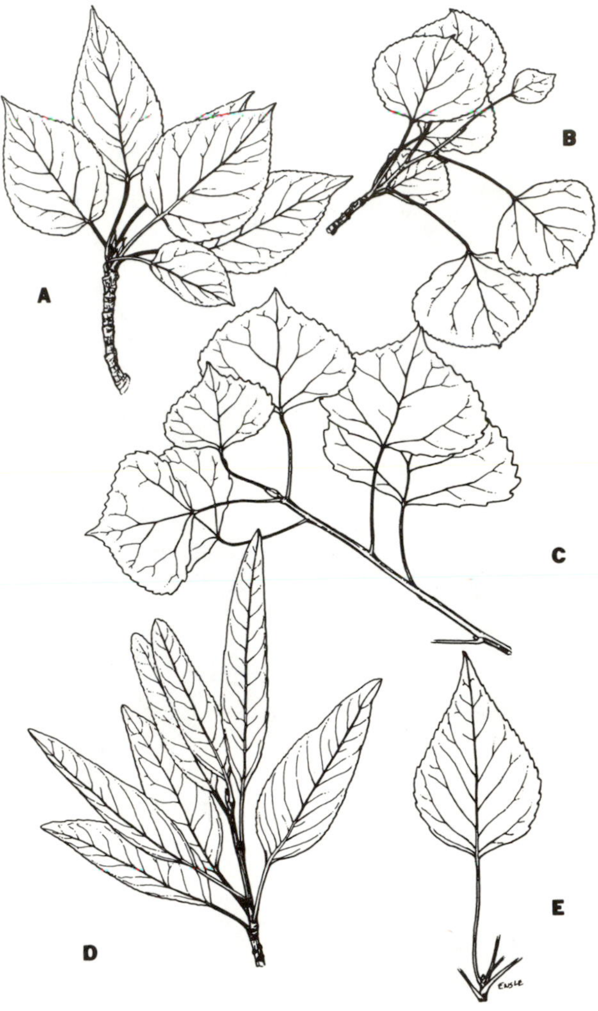

Fig. 100. A, *Populus balsamifera*; **B,** *P. tremuloides*; **C,** *P. deltoides*; **D,** *P. angustifolia*; **E,** *P. x acuminata*

Fig. 101. **A,** *Comandra*; **B,** *Anemopsis*

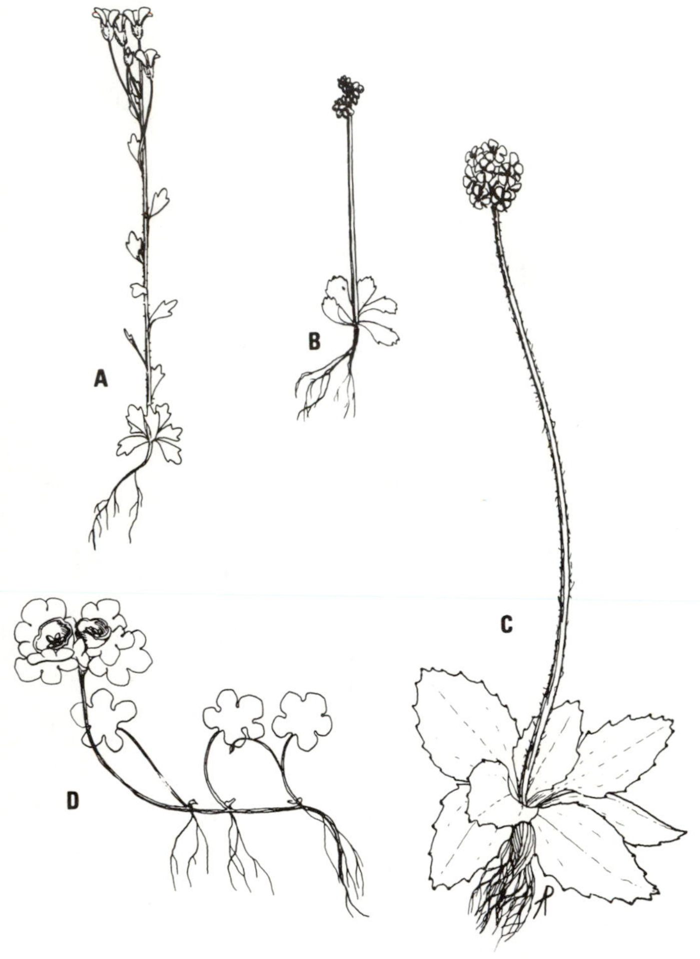

Fig. 102. A, *Muscaria adscendens*; **B,** *Spatularia foliolosa*; **C,** *Micranthes rhomboidea*; **D,** *Chrysosplenium*

Fig. 103. **A,** *Hirculus platysepalus*; **B,** *H. serpyllifolius*; **C,** *Saxifraga hyperborea*; **D,** *Muscaria delicatula*; **E,** *Saxifraga cernua*; **F,** *Hirculus prorepens*

Fig. 104. **A,** *Micranthes odontoloma*; **B,** *Telesonix*; **C,** *Heuchera parvifolia*; **D,** *Ciliaria*

Fig. 105. **A,** *Agalinis*; **B,** *Bacopa*; **C,** *Collinsia*; **D,** *Besseya alpina*; **E,** *Limosella*

Fig. 106. A, *Penstemon secundiflorus*; **B,** *P. whippleanus*; **C,** *P. barbatus*

Fig. 107. A, *Verbascum thapsus*; **B,** *V. phlomoides*; **C,** *V. blattaria*; **D,** *V. x pterocaulon*

Fig. 108. A, *Veronica nutans*; **B,** *Pocilla biloba*; **C,** *Veronica peregrina*; **D,** *V. catenata*; **E,** *V. americana*

Fig. 109. A, *Datura stramonium*; **B,** *Nicotiana*; **C,** *Hyoscyamus*

Fig. 110. A, *Tamarix ramosissima*; **B,** *Celtis*

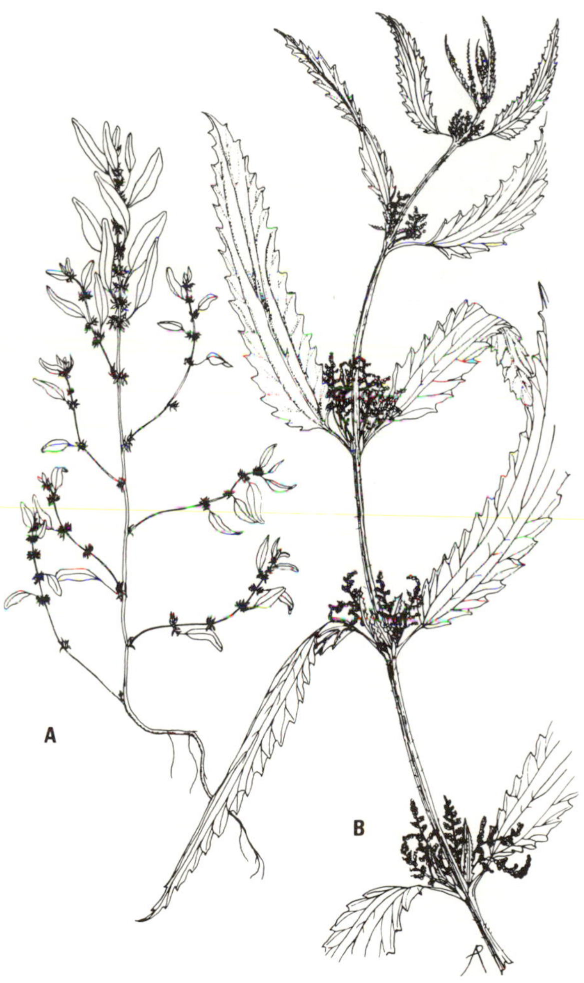

Fig. 111. A, *Parietaria*; **B,** *Urtica*

Fig. 112. A, ***Valeriana edulis*****; B,** ***V. capitata*****, habit, flowers, fruit**

Fig. 113. A, *Verbena hastata*; **B,** *Glandularia bipinnatifida*; **C,** *Verbena bracteata*; **D,** *Phyla cuneifolia*

Fig. 114. A, *Viola kitaibeliana*; **B,** *V. pedatifida*; **C,** *V. nuttallii*; **D,** *Hybanthus*

Fig. 115. **A,** *Tribulus*; **B,** *Parthenocissus inserta*, habit, tendril; **C,** *P. quinquefolia*, tendril

GLOSSARY

Acerose Needle-shaped.

Achene A small, dry indehiscent, one-loculed, one-seeded fruit consisting usually of a single carpel (in Asteraceae it is derived from two carpels).

Acicular Needlelike.

Actinomorphic Having a radial symmetry (same as *regular*).

Acuminate Drawn out at the apex into a gradually tapering point.

Acute Terminating in a sharp or well-defined point.

Adaxial Facing the axis (ventral, in the botanical sense).

Adnate Attached or fused to.

Adventive Not native in the area; introduced by accident or spreading after being deliberately planted for another purpose.

Aecial One of the spore (aeciospore) stages of a rust fungus.

Akene (achene) See *achene*.

Alternate Of leaves, having one leaf arising at each node; (floral parts) having the members of one whorl attached between the members of the next outer or inner whorl.

Alveolate Honeycombed.

Ament Same as *catkin*.

Amphi(di)ploid A fertile population arising from the doubling of chromosome sets from two incompatible parental stocks.

Androecium Collective name for the stamens. The total set of stamens is called the *androecium*.

Androgynous In *Carex*, having the staminate flowers above the carpellate ones, and in the same spike.

Angiosperms Seed plants in which the ovules are enclosed in carpels; flowering plants.

Annual Living through one season only.

Anterior In flowers, the side of the flower facing away from the axis of the inflorescence.

Anthelmintic Used to treat worm infestations.

Anther The pollen-bearing organ of the flower. See *stamen*.

Anthesis Flowering time.

Aphyllopodic In *Carex*, having only bladeless sheaths (originally bud scales) at the base of the flowering culm; this culm matures in one season.

Apiculate Suddenly prolonged to a small point (*apiculus*).

Apogamous In ferns, producing a sporophyte from a gametophyte by asexual means.

Apomictic Producing seeds from unfertilized ovules, by parthenogenesis. The result is progeny genetically identical to the parent. A common phenomenon in several genera (e.g., *Agoseris*, *Taraxacum*).

Appressed Lying close to or flat against.

Arachnoid Cobwebby.

Arcuate Curved.

Areole In cacti, the point at which a cluster of spines arises, equivalent to a node.

Aril A fleshy, usually colored appendage or covering on a seed.

Articulate Jointed.

Articulation In grasses, the point at which organs (glumes or lemmas) break away from the stem. In a grass spikelet, if at maturity the florets fall away from the plant and leave the glumes attached, we say the spikelet disarticulates above the glumes and between the florets. If the spikelet falls completely without leaving the glumes attached to the plant, we say the spikelet disarticulates below the glumes. Manipulating the spikelet with one's fingers or with a tweezers helps to determine the type of disarticulation.

Ascending Growing obliquely upward or curving upward during growth.

Attenuate Drawn out into a long, slender tip (extremely acuminate).

Auricle In milkweeds, an ear or flaplike appendage at the base of the hood; in grasses, a similar appendage at the summit of the leaf sheath.

Auriculate With auricles.

Awn A stiff, bristlelike appendage.

Axil The angle formed by a leaf with the stem to which it is attached. Buds, for example, are found in the axils of leaves, that is, at the place where the leaf joins the stem.

Axile A type of placentation in which the ovules are attached to the adaxial (ventral) suture of the carpel. Peas and beans, for example, show axile placentation involving only one carpel. Tomato, cucumber, and apple show axile placentation involving several united carpels.

Axillary Situated in, or arising from, the axil of a leaf. Usually opposed to terminal.

Axis An imaginary line running lengthwise through the center of an organ such as a flower or stem.

Banner The broad, erect, upper petal of the flower of legumes, as in sweet-peas.

Barbellate Having minute prongs. Commonly refers to the pappus of Asteraceae, in which each bristle has very short barbs, as seen with a lens.

Basal Of leaves, produced at ground level; of placentation, having the ovules attached at the base of the ovary only (as in green peppers). In many instances the ovary contains only one seed, which is attached at the base of the ovary and fills the locule.

Basifixed Attached at the base, as anthers to the filament.

Beak A prominent, firm, slender tip. In *Oxytropis* the keel petals are abruptly narrowed to form a beak; in mustards the tip of the fruit is sometimes abruptly narrowed with the non-ovule-bearing portion forming a beak.

Bearded Having a tuft of long hairs.

Bidentate Two-toothed. In *Carex*, this is an important characteristic in some species in which the tip of the perigynium is bidentate.

Biennial Of two years duration. A biennial plant produces a rosette of basal leaves the first year, sends up a flower stalk the second year, produces seed, and dies. See also *monocarpic*.

Bifid Cleft in two.

Bilabiate Two-lipped, referring especially to the corolla in such groups as mints and scrophs.

Bipinnate Twice pinnately compound.

Bipinnatifid Twice pinnatifid.

Biseriate In two rows.

Bisexual In flowers, having both stamens and carpels in the same flower; same as *perfect*.

Blade The flat, expanded portion of a leaf or petal.

Bloom A whitish waxy or powdery (glaucous) covering on leaves or twigs, easily rubbed off; pruinosity.

Bract A much-reduced leaf, usually subtending a flower.

Bracteole Small bracts on the cup of a calyx, as in mallows.
Bulb A spherical, underground bud or stem with fleshy scales or roots, as in onions. In a bulb the spherical structure consists mostly of scales, whereas in a corm the scales are minute and the round mass consists of the fleshy stem.
Bulblets Asexually reproductive structures derived from flowers or branch primordia, or divisions of a bulb.

Caducous Dropping off early, as the sepals in Papaveraceae.
Caespitose Growing in clumps.
Calcareous Having to do with limestone.
Calciphile Growing on limestone.
Callous (callose) Hard and thick in texture.
Callus Hardened base of the lemma in some grasses, especially *Stipa.*
Calyx The outer set of perianth segments, usually green; collective name for the sepals (see *tepals*).
Campanulate Bell-shaped.
Canescent Having a hoary, grayish pubescence of short hairs.
Capillary Threadlike.
Capitate Headlike; collected into a dense, short cluster.
Capsule A dry, dehiscent fruit composed of more than one carpel (e.g., *Yucca*).
Carpel The basic unit of a gynoecium, a single "inrolled spore-bearing leaf" (stigma, style, and ovary). A good example of a typical carpel is the pod of a pea, or a peanut. See also *gynoecium*, *pistil.*
Carr A wetland willow thicket, incorrectly referred to as a bog.
Caryopsis The grain (fruit) of grasses, a two-carpellate achenelike fruit containing one seed.
Catkin A spike of inconspicuous and usually unisexual flowers, as in willows and birches. Same as *ament.*
Caudate Tailed.
Caudex (plural, **caudices**) The persistent, woody, underground base of an otherwise herbaceous stem; an erect or ascending underground stem (*rootstock* is a less precise term).
Cauline Borne on the stem, above ground. Refers to leaves; opposed to basal.
Centimeter Ten millimeters (2.54 cm = 1 inch).
Chartaceous Papery.
Ciliate Marginally fringed with hairs (cilia).
Cinereous Ashy gray.
Circinate Coiled.
Circumscissile Dehiscent by a transverse, circular line, as the capsules of plantains.
Circumpolar Distributed around the world in the Northern Hemisphere.
Cladode (cladophyll; phylloclad) A branch consisting of a single internode flattened and expanded to function as a leaf.
Clavate Club-shaped.
Claw The narrow stalk of some petals, especially in mustards.
Cleft Deeply cut.
Cleistogamous With fertilization occurring within unopened flowers.
cm Centimeter.
Collar A horizontal line crossing the outside of a grass leaf where the blade joins the sheath. The collar is often thickened or covered with hairs.
Colluvial Of sediments, accumulated through torrential rains.
Coma A tuft of hairs, as on the seeds of *Epilobium.*

Compound Composed of from two to many similar united parts, as carpels in a compound ovary (a tomato fruit is a compound ovary, consisting of four or five united carpels), or divided into a number of similar parts, as the leaflets of compound leaves.

Compressed Flattened. For example, in a laterally compressed grass spikelet the flattening involves the side of the spikelet, so that the individual lemmas are folded in half. In a dorsally compressed spikelet the florets on opposite sides of the axis are pressed toward each other, and the lemmas are flattened out rather than folded.

Concavo-convex With one side concave and the other convex.

Concolorous Without differentiation by color.

Conduplicate Folded, with the halves together.

Confluent Running together.

Connate United, usually by fusion or pressure in the bud.

Connivent Coming into contact or converging.

Cordate Heart-shaped, referring to the outline or the base of a leaf.

Coriaceous Leathery in texture.

Corm Enlarged, fleshy base of a stem, bulblike but solid (gladiolus, spring beauty). See *bulb*.

Corolla Collective name for the petals, the inner whorl of perianth segments.

Corona A crown or collar attached to the inside of the corolla, as in daffodils and milkweeds.

Corymb A flat-topped inflorescence.

Cotyledons The first or seed leaves of a plant; the two halves of a peanut kernel are its cotyledons. The two great groups of flowering plants, monocots and dicots, are so called because of the difference in the number of cotyledons in the seeds.

Crenate With rounded, marginal teeth (diminutive, *crenulate*).

Crescentic Of a crescent shape.

Cruciform Cross-shaped.

Cucullate Hooded.

Culm The "stem" of grasses and sedges, consisting principally of overlapping leaf-sheaths.

Cuneate Wedge-shaped, usually referring to the base of a leaf.

Cuspidate Tipped with a firm, sharp point.

Cyathium In Euphorbiaceae, a unit of the inflorescence consisting of a group of extremely reduced flowers, the whole mimicking a single flower.

Cyme A flower cluster, usually opposite-branched, in its simplest form consisting of three flowers, the central or terminal one blooming first. Same as *dichasium*.

Deciduous Falling off at the end of a growing season; not persistent or evergreen (see also *caducous*).

Decimeter Ten centimeters.

Declined Directed down toward the base (not as sharply as reflexed).

Decumbent Prostrate except for the ascending tips of the branches.

Decurrent Referring to the bases of leaves, which sometimes continue down the stem beyond the point of attachment.

Decussate In pairs alternately at right angles.

Dehiscent Splitting open at maturity.

Deltoid Triangular, shaped like the Greek letter *delta*.

Dentate Toothed, with the teeth directed outward rather than forward (diminutive, *denticulate*).

Denticle An extremely small tooth.

Depauperate Impoverished as if starved, reduced in size or function.

Diadelphous Of stamens, united into two sets. In some legumes, nine of the ten stamens in a flower are united by the filaments, the tenth is separate.

Dichasium A simple inflorescence consisting of a terminal flower plus a pair of flowers produced by the nearest pair of subtending leaves or bracts (a *simple cyme*).

Dichotomous Equal, forked branches, most commonly occurring in ferns.

Digitate Compounded or veined in a way as to suggest fingers of a hand.

Dimorphic Having two different-sized parts or positions of parts. See discussion under borages and pinks.

Dioecious Bearing the staminate flowers on one individual and the carpellate on another of the same species. Note: *Plants* may be dioecious; their *flowers* are then imperfect or unisexual; flowers are never themselves dioecious.

Diploid Having two sets of homologous chromosomes.

Disarticulating Breaking off from the main axis, as spikelets of grasses. See *articulation*.

Disjunct Occurring in two widely separated geographic areas.

Disk-flowers The central, actinomorphic, tubular flowers of Asteraceae. In sunflowers and daisies the central part of the "flower" (head) is composed of a great number of disk-flowers, while the "petals" are really each whole flowers (rays). See introduction to Asteraceae.

Dissected Cut into numerous narrow segments.

Distal Remote from the place of attachment; opposite of *proximal*.

Distinct Separate, not united. (This has nothing to do with visibility!)

Divaricate Extremely divergent, at right angles.

Divergent Spreading apart, curving away from the main axis.

Divided Cut to the base into lobes or segments.

dm Decimeter.

Dolabriform Of trichomes, attached at the middle, with two arms in a straight line.

Dorsal Pertaining to the part of an organ facing away from the axis, as the underside of a leaf (preferably called *abaxial*). This is a usage quite different from that of zoology.

Dorsiventral With an upper and lower side (dorsiventrally compressed: flattened from the back rather than the sides).

Drupe The fruit of cherry or plum, a fleshy, one-seeded fruit in which the seed is enclosed in a hard "stone."

Echinate Spiny.

Elliptical Having the shape of an ellipse.

Emarginate Having a shallow notch at the tip.

Endemic Confined to a given region; *narrowly endemic*, confined to a very small area.

Endosperm Nutritive tissue in the seed, other than the embryo.

Ensiform Swordlike.

Entire Without marginal teeth or lobes.

Epigynous Borne on top of the ovary (flowers are epigynous if they have an inferior ovary).

Equitant Folded over, as if astride, as the leaves of *Iris*.

Erose Ragged-edged.
-escent (-ascent) Becoming.
Even-pinnate Pinnately compound, with the terminal leaflet missing.
Excurrent Going beyond, as a vein exceeding the length of the leaf blade.
Exfoliating Coming off in thin sheets.
Explanate Spread out flat, as opened anthers of some *Penstemon*.
Exserted Projecting beyond the enveloping organs.
Extravaginal Of buds or branches that push through the side of a leaf sheath, thus arise "outside of the sheath," in grasses and sedges.

Facultative Optional.
Falcate Sickle-shaped.
Farinose With a mealy or powdery covering of wax or inflated hairs.
Fascicle Bundle, cluster.
Fen A calcareous (basic), marshy, often quaking expanse, usually subalpine, incorrectly referred to as a bog, which is acidic.
Fertile Having a functional gynoecium; producing seed; in ferns, bearing sporangia.
Fibrillose Shredding into fine fibers, usually the vascular bundles, as in some grass and sedge leaf sheaths.
Filament The stalk supporting an anther.
Filiform Threadlike.
Fimbriate Fringed.
Fistulose Hollow, as the stems of onions.
Flabellate (-iform) Fan-shaped.
Flagelliform Slender, whiplike.
Flexuous Curved, wavy.
Floccose Having loose tufts of soft, cottony hairs.
Floret A small flower, specifically applied to those of grasses, sedges, and composites.
Foliaceous Leaflike, either in texture or shape, or both.
Foliolate Referring to leaflets in a compound leaf (a clover leaf, unless you are lucky, is trifoliolate).
Follicle A single carpel that dehisces along one edge only (*Delphinium*, *Aquilegia*).
Forma The lowest taxonomic category; a sporadic mutant in a population.
Fornix A scale or glandlike protuberance in the flower tube, as in many borages.
Free Not united; separate.
Free-central A type of placentation in which the ovules are attached to a central stalk within the ovary that is not connected to the carpel margins by partitions.
Fruit The part of a plant that bears the seeds; usually an ovary, its contents, and any floral parts that may be associated with it at maturity. The term is also loosely used to refer to cones of gymnosperms and to spore-bearing structures of ferns, mosses, and other lower plants.
Fruticose Shrubby.
Fugacious Quickly withering.
Fusiform Thick but tapering toward each end.

Galea A hood- or helmet-shaped sepal or petal or the upper lip of some zygomorphic corollas.
Geniculate Bent abruptly, like a knee. Most commonly refers to the bent awns of some grasses.
Gibbous Swollen on one side.
Glabrate (-escent) Almost glabrous, becoming glabrous.

Glabrous Completely smooth, without trichomes.

Gladiate Sword-shaped, like the leaves of *Iris*.

Gland An organ of secretion; also commonly used to refer to any minute structure in flowers whose function is unknown.

Glandular Having glands; sticky. Glandular hairs are usually ball-tipped, and stems having these hairs may collect dirt and trash, are sticky to the touch, or stain the pressing-papers.

Glaucous Having a bloom or whitish covering, usually waxy, on the stem or leaf. This may disappear if the plants are dried with heat.

Globose Spherical.

Glochid A barb.

Glochidiate Pubescent with barbed bristles.

Glomerate Crowded into a compact, spherical mass.

Glume One of the two basal, empty bracts forming the enclosing base of the grass spikelet (used to be called *sterile lemmas*).

Glutinous Sticky.

Graduate In Asteraceae, having the inner phyllaries longer than the outer.

Granulate Composed of small grains.

Gynaecandrous In *Carex*, having the carpellate flowers above the staminate ones in the same spike.

Gynobase The often swollen or otherwise differentiated base of the style.

Gynoecium A carpel or an aggregation of carpels, either separate or united; collective name for all the carpels in a single flower.

Gypsophile A plant adapted to soils containing gypsum.

Habitat The kind of locality in which a plant usually grows. If very specific, it is called a *microhabitat*.

Habitus The growth form of a plant.

Hastate Like an arrowhead but with the basal lobes pointing outward.

Head A compact, usually hemispherical flower cluster.

Helicoid Curled in the form of a spring or snail shell.

Herbaceous Not woody.

Herbage The vegetative portion of the plant.

Hirsute Clothed with coarse, straight, spreading hairs (diminutive, *hispidulous*).

Hispid Clothed with stiff, bristlelike hairs.

Hispidulous Diminutive of hispid.

Hyaline Transparent or translucent.

Hypanthium A cup or tube formed by the fused bases of the stamens, petals, and sepals.

Hypogynous Refers to flowers in which the stamens, petals, and sepals are attached below the ovary; flowers with superior ovaries are hypogynous.

Imbricate Overlapping like shingles.

Imperfect Having only stamens or carpels, not both.

Incised Cut sharply, deeply, and irregularly into lobes or segments.

Included Not protruding beyond the enveloping organs (opposite of *exserted*).

Indehiscent Not splitting open at maturity.

Indurate Hardened.

Indusium A membranous flap or "umbrella" covering the sorus of ferns; usually withers and disappears as the sporangia ripen.

Inferior Refers to ovaries that are either imbedded in the receptacle or fused with the surrounding floral parts. The ovary of an apple is inferior, i.e., it is imbedded in the fused floral parts, which form a fleshy covering.

Inflorescence Flower cluster.

Internerves In grasses, the portion of a lemma, palea, or glume situated between the nerves or veins.

Internode The portion of a stem between two nodes.

Interrupted Having parts of the inflorescence not continuous but separated by spaces of stem.

Intravaginal Of buds or branches that arise between the sheath and culm of a grass or sedge.

Introgressant Transferring genes from one population into another through backcrossing following hybridization.

Involucel A bract of the smallest umbel, in Apiaceae.

Involucre A circle or cluster of bracts at the base of a flower cluster, sometimes fused into a cup. In the Asteraceae these bracts are called *phyllaries*.

Involute Having the edges rolled inward (*revolute* leaves are rolled outward).

Irregular Showing inequality in size, shape, or arrangement of the parts, often loosely used as a synonym for *zygomorphic*.

Isodiametric Of equal dimensions.

Keel A prominent dorsal rib, ridge, or crease (or, in the legumes, the name given to the two fused petals enclosing the stamens).

Labiate With a differentiated, usually larger lower lobe, as the corollas of orchids, mints, and scrophs.

Lacerate Ragged, as if torn.

Lamella A thin plate.

Lamina (plural, **laminae**) Blade.

Lanate Woolly.

Lanceolate Long and narrow, but broadest at the base.

Lateral Referring to the side, as opposed to *dorsal* or *ventral*, sometimes used in contrast to *terminal*.

Leaflet A segment of a compound leaf.

Legume The fruit or pod (a single carpel with two sutures), of plants belonging to the Fabaceae; also, any member of the family.

Lemma The outer bract of the grass floret.

Lenticels Wartlike, usually light-colored, spots on the bark of twigs.

Lenticular Disk-shaped, with two convex sides (lens-shaped).

Ligule In grasses, the flap of tissue on the ventral (adaxial) side of a leaf at the place where the blade joins the sheath, i.e., the ligule is between the blade and the culm; in Asteraceae, a ray-flower or strap-shaped corolla is called a ligule or ligulate corolla.

Limb The expanded part of a tubular corolla, between the tube and the throat.

Linear Long and narrow, with parallel margins.

Lobe A partial division or segment of an organ (diminutive, *lobule*).

Locule One of the cavities or chambers in an ovary or anther (commonly called a cell).

Loculicidal Dehiscing by the rupture of the outer wall of the locule (see *septicidal*).

Loment A legume that is constricted and jointed between the seeds, breaking up into several indehiscent, one-seeded segments.

Lunate Shaped like a crescent moon (diminutive, *lunulate*).

Lyrate Pinnatifid with the terminal lobe large and rounded, the lower ones small.

m Meter.

Marcescent Persisting beyond a single season as dried parts.
Marginal Along the edge.
Massif A more or less discrete group of peaks in a mountain range.
Megaspore The large spore, which in *Selaginella*, produces the female gametophyte (see *microspore*).
Mericarp A segment of an ovary that separates intact, as in Apiaceae, Malvaceae and Zygophyllaceae.
-merous Refers to the number of segments in a whorl of floral parts (a flower with three petals, stamens, and carpels is three-merous).
Mesic Having medium conditions as to moisture and light.
Mesophyte A plant adapted to medium conditions as to moisture and light.
Meter ten decimeters; 39.36 inches.
Microhabitat A very special or narrowly restricted environment.
Microspore The minute spore that in *Selaginella*, produces the male gametophyte.
Millimeter One-tenth of a centimeter.
mm Millimeter.
Monad Of pollen grains, dispersed singly (as opposed to *dyad* or *tetrad*).
Monadelphous United into a single group, as the filaments of a group of stamens.
Moniliform Like a string of beads.
Monocarpic Flowering and fruiting but once in its lifetime (as in *Agave* and *Frasera*).
Monoecious Having the stamens and carpels in different flowers on the same plant. A *plant* may be monoecious; its *flowers* are unisexual or imperfect.
Monotypic Having only one species in the genus (or one genus in a family, etc.).
Mucro A minute and abrupt point at the apex.
Mucronate With a mucro (does not have the connotation of stiffness implied in *cuspidate*). .
Muricate Having minute, sharp-pointed outgrowths (usually on fruits or seeds).

Nectary A gland or locus of nectar production.
Nerve Vein.
Nodal spines Thorns situated at the nodes.
Node The point on a stem where leaves, buds, or branches usually arise. Occasionally flowers arise on internodes (*Solanum*) and buds appear above nodes (*superposed buds*).

Ob- A prefix implying "the reverse." For example, an obovate leaf is ovate with the widest part near the apex rather than the base.
Obligate Without exception (opposite of *facultative*).
Oblong Rectangular in general outline but with the corners rounded.
Obsolete Describing a part or organ usually present but in this instance much reduced.
Obtuse Blunt or rounded at the tip.
Ochroleucous Off-white, buff.
Odd-pinnate Pinnately compound, with the terminal leaflet present (having an odd number of leaflets).
Opposite Of leaves, originating in pairs at the nodes; of stamens, attached directly in front of a petal rather than between petals.
Orbicular Round, circular.
Ovary The basal part of the gynoecium or carpel that contains the seeds.
Ovate Egg-shaped and broadest near the base (a two-dimensional concept).
Ovoid Egg-shaped (three-dimensional).

Ovule The seed before fertilization.

Palate An upward-arching part of the lower lip of a zygomorphic corolla, tending to close the throat (as in snapdragon).

Palea The adaxial (inner) of the two bracts of a grass floret; the bract opposite and enfolded by the lemma.

Paleae (receptacular) Bracts subtending the individual flowers in a composite head (often referred to as *chaff*).

Palmate Having veins, lobes, or segments that radiate from a single point, as maple leaves. See also *digitate*.

Palmatifid Partially divided in a palmate way (compare *pinnatifid*).

Panicle A repeatedly branched inflorescence with pedicelled flowers.

Paniculate Arranged in panicles.

Pannose With the appearance of felt or woolen cloth.

Papilla(e) Minute epidermal wart(s).

Papillose (-ate) Minutely warty or pimply.

Pappus Appendages at the apex of the ovary, in Asteraceae.

Papule In *Lemna*, a minute pimple on the surface of the frond, seen best with a strong lens when fresh.

Parasitic Depending on living tissue of other organisms as a source of food.

Parietal A type of placentation in which the ovules are attached to the side of the ovary. This term only applies to ovaries that consist of more than one carpel.

Parthenogenesis Production of fruit without benefit of fertilization.

Pectinate Comblike.

Pedatifid Palmately cleft, with the divisions again cleft (as opposed to *pinnatifid*).

Pedicel The stalk of a single flower (adjective, *pedicellate*).

Pedicellate Having a pedicel.

Peduncle The common stalk of a flower cluster (adjective, *pedunculate*).

Peltate Shield-shaped, attached in the center as by a stem of an umbrella.

Perennial Living year after year.

Perfect Having all the essential organs (stamens and carpels); bisexual.

Perianth Collective name for the sepals and petals. See also *tepals*.

Pericarp The ovary wall.

Perigynium The inflated sac enclosing the ovary of *Carex*, represented in *Kobresia* by an open sheath.

Perigynous Half-inferior, as an ovary with the lower half fused to the surrounding parts, and the upper half free.

Peripheral Marginal, as concerning species that barely enter Colorado from neighboring states.

Persistent Lasting, not deciduous, remaining attached to the stem.

Petal One of the white or colored inner perianth segments (adverb, *petaloid*).

Petiole Leaf stalk (adjective, *petiolate*).

Petiolule The stalk of a leaflet of a compound leaf.

Phyllary A bract of the involucre in Asteraceae.

Phyllopodic In *Carex*, having leaves with blades at the base of the flowering culm (the culm is in its second year of growth).

Pilose Having long soft hairs (more sparsely so than *villous*).

Pinna A primary division of a fern frond (the whole fern "leaf" is called a frond). Fronds are divided into main branches, or *pinnae*; pinnae may be divided further into pinnules.

Pinnate Having veins, lobes, or divisions in the form of a feather, i.e., with one main axis having lateral offshoots.

Pinnatifid Pinnately cleft into segments, but the segments not stalked.

Pinnatisect Pinnately dissected.

Pinnule A secondary division of a fern frond (a division of a *pinna*).

Pistil A vague term applying variously to a carpel or an entire gynoecium (not used in this book).

Placenta The part of the ovary to which the ovules are attached. Not referring to the stalk of an ovule, but merely to the point of attachment.

Placentation The mode of attachment of the ovules to the ovary wall (axile, parietal, basal, or free-central).

Plane Level, flat.

Plano-convex Flat on one surface, convex on the other.

Plicate Pleated.

-ploid Suffix referring to numbers of sets of chromosomes; *-ploid* has no intrinsic meaning, having been cut away from the word diploid (*diplo* + *oid*), then grafted, part from one stem and part from another, to form *tetraploid*, *hexaploid*, etc.

Plumose Feathery (usually applied to a style, bristle, or awn having delicate side-branches).

Polygamo- Bisexual, used as a prefix with *dioecious* or *monoecious*, implying the presence of perfect as well as unisexual flowers on the same plant.

Pome The fruit of apples and their close relatives; a fleshy inferior ovary with several carpels.

Posterior The side of the flower facing the axis of the inflorescence (in *Castilleja*, the upper side).

Processes A term referring to projecting appendages, otherwise difficult to name, that stand out from a plant organ (e.g., knobs on the fruits of *Atriplex*).

Proliferous Producing new plants as offshoots.

Propagulum (plural, **propagula**) A structure (such as a seed) functioning as a means of propagation.

Prostrate Lying flat on the ground.

Proteolytic Capable of destroying proteins.

Proximal Nearest the point of attachment.

Pruinose With a white wax or dusty coating; glaucous.

Pseudoscape In Apiaceae, a slender, erect, usually partly subterranean stem connecting the root and the first leaves.

Puberulent Very minutely pubescent.

Pubescent Hairy, a deliberately vague term often used to refer generally to hairiness.

Pustulose Hirsute, with basally swollen trichomes.

Raceme An elongated inflorescence with a single main axis along which single, stalked flowers are arranged. Compare with *panicle*, *spike*, and *cyme*.

Rachilla In grasses and sedges, the axis within the spikelet; the stalk of the individual floret.

Rachis The axis of the inflorescence or of a compound leaf.

Ray-flowers The strap-shaped marginal flowers of Asteraceae. Although they resemble petals, each ray-flower is complete with corolla and, usually, essential organs.

Receptacle The tip of the floral axis, to which the sepals, petals, stamens, and gynoecium are attached.

Reflexed Bent abruptly downward.

Regular Radially symmetrical.

Regularly Evenly, uniformly.
Relict Rare survivor of past times.
Remote Widely separated, as flowers on a raceme.
Reniform Kidney-shaped, broader than long, usually curved.
Repand Of teeth, tending to be directed backward; with slightly uneven margin.
Replum In mustards, the partition between the two valves of the fruit.
Reticulate Forming a network.
Retrorse Directed backward or downward, like hairs on the nape of the neck.
Retuse With a shallow notch at a rounded apex.
Revolute Having the margins rolled back or under; opposite of *involute*.
Rhizome A prostrate underground stem or branch, rooting at the nodes; differs from a root in possessing nodes and internodes, and usually scale leaves. See also *caudex*.
Rhombic Equilateral, with obtuse lateral angles.
Rib A prominent vein or ridge, particularly on carpel walls.
Riparian Of riversides.
Rootstock A loose or vague term for the underground parts.
Rosette A cluster of closely crowded, radiating leaves at ground level.
Rosulate Forming a small rosette.
Rotate Wheel-shaped, flat and circular in outline; term applied to very open, united corollas.
Ruderal Growing in waste places or among rubbish.
Rugose Wrinkled (diminutive, *rugulose*).
Runcinate Saw-toothed or sharply incised, the teeth retrorse.

Saccate Bag-shaped.
Sagittate Arrow-shaped, with the basal lobes directed downward.
Salient Projecting, protruding.
Salverform Referring to a narrow, tubular corolla that opens out to form a very open, dishlike apex, as in primroses.
Samara An indehiscent winged fruit, such as that of maple.
Saprophytic Depending on dead organic materials for a source of food.
Scaberulous Minutely scabrous.
Scabrous Rough to the touch.
Scape A leafless flower stalk arising from the ground or from a cluster of basal leaves (adjective, *scapose*).
Scarious Dry, thin, scalelike, not green.
Schizocarps Carpels of a united gynoecium that separate as indehiscent units, as in *Geranium*.
Scrotiform Pouch-shaped.
Scurfy Minutely scaly in appearance.
Secund One-sided.
Seed A ripened ovule.
Seleniferous Containing selenium salts; soils with selenium, and the plants growing on them, usually have a distinctive, unpleasant odor. Selenium-loving plants are usually toxic.
Sepal One of the outer perianth segments; a segment of the calyx.
Septate Having obvious cross-partitions, usually referring to hollow leaves.
Septate-nodulose In sedges, having strengthening partitions crossing between the veins. These can usually be seen without splitting the leaf or felt by pressing the fingers along it.

Septicidal Dehiscing by the breaking or separation of the septa dividing the carpels (see *loculicidal*).

Sericeous Silky, clothed with closely appressed, soft, straight trichomes.

Serrate Having sharp teeth pointing forward, like teeth of a rip-saw (diminutive, *serrulate*).

Sessile Lacking a stalk.

Setaceous Bristlelike.

Setose Covered with bristles.

Sheath In grasslike plants, the basal portion of a leaf that wraps around the stem.

Sigmoid S-shaped.

Silicle A short silique.

Silique The fruit of mustards. A silique consists of two carpel walls, called *valves*, separated by a partition, the *replum*. The seeds are attached to the rim of the replum. At maturity, the valves fall away from the fruit, the replum remaining as a very thin, papery plate. If the silique is flattened parallel to the replum, the valves are flattened against the face of the replum, and the replum is roughly the same shape as the valve. If the silique is flattened perpendicular to the replum, the valves are folded, and the replum bisects the face of the silique.

Simple Not branched (stems); not compound (leaves).

Sinuate Wavy-margined.

Sinus The cleft or indentation between lobes.

Solifluction Downslope creep of alpine soils aided by subsoil water, commonly resulting in terraces.

Sorus (plural, **sori**) A cluster of sporangia. The sori are the dark dots on the underside of fruiting fern fronds.

Spatulate Oblong, but narrowed at the base.

Spicate Arranged in or resembling a spike.

Spike An elongated inflorescence bearing sessile flowers.

Spikelet In grasses and sedges, the smallest unbranched flower cluster in an inflorescence, usually forming a distinct and compact, and repetitive unit.

Spinescent Ending in a spine or sharp point.

Spinulose Having minute spines.

Sporangium Structure containing spores.

Spore The asexual reproductive cell in ferns (other meanings, not applicable here, also apply).

Sporocarp In *Marsilea*, a hard nutlike organ containing sporangia.

Sporophyll A structure, often leaflike, bearing sporangia.

Spur A hollow projection of a petal or sepal, as in columbine and violet.

Squamellate Having small scales.

Squamiform Scalelike.

Squarrose Spreading or recurved at the tip.

Stamen The pollen-producing organ of the flower, situated between the petals and the carpels.

Staminate Having stamens but not carpels.

Staminodia Nonfunctional stamens, usually lacking well-developed anthers, or with the filament broadened and petallike; inner petals of double flowers (roses) arise from stamens as staminodia.

Stella(ae) The cluster of rays of a stellate trichome.

Stellate Star-shaped.

Sterile Not producing seed; lacking a gynoecium, or (in stamens) lacking anthers.

Stigma The part of the style that is receptive to pollen, usually recognized by its sticky, pollen-covered surface.

Stipe A stalk, as of a gynoecium (adjective, *stipitate*).

Stipule An appendage, sometimes leaflike, sometimes papery, at the base of the petiole of a leaf. Stipules usually occur in pairs.

Stolon A slender, modified stem running along the ground above the soil surface, as in strawberry.

Stramineous Straw-colored.

Strap-shaped Oblong, as the ray-flowers of Asteraceae.

Striate Marked with fine, longitudinal stripes (striae) or furrows.

Strict Close or narrow and upright, very straight.

Strigillose Diminutive of *strigose*. Also, *strigulose*.

Strigose Beset with sharp-pointed, straight appressed hairs.

Style The slender upper part of the carpel or gynoecium. A style is not necessarily present on a gynoecium.

Stylopodium The enlarged base of the style, as in *Eleocharis* and Apiaceae.

Sub- Prefix meaning *almost*, as in *subequal*.

Submersed Growing under water (same as *submerged*).

Subspecies A subdivision of a species, usually having a distinct geographic range as well as morphological differences. See *variety*, a term sometimes used for the same thing although the category is lower than that of subspecies.

Subtend To occur below, as a bract subtends a flower.

Subulate Awl-shaped.

Suffrutescent Becoming shrubby.

Suffruticose Shrublike, woody at the base.

Superior Referring to the gynoecium, when it is attached only at its base and is not fused to the surrounding parts. The ovary is superior even if surrounded by a floral tube or hypanthium (as in rosehips), so long as its wall is not fused to the surrounding parts. See *hypogynous*.

Suture A junction or seam or union; also, the line of dehiscence. In the pea, the pod splits along the dorsal and ventral sutures. The ovules are attached along the ventral suture.

Syncarpous Having united carpels.

Taproot A primary, often fleshy, vertical root.

Tawny Tan or brownish.

Taxon (plural, **taxa**) Any named taxonomic category, such as a genus, family, or species.

Tendril A slender clasping or twining, threadlike outgrowth of stems or leaves, often a modified leaflet or stipule.

Tepal One of the segments of a perianth when these are not differentiated into sepals and petals.

Terete Cylindrical; circular in cross-section.

Ternate Compounded into divisions or groups of three.

Tessellate Like a mosaic pavement.

Tetrad A group of four, as pollen grains.

Tetraploid Having four sets of homologous chromosomes.

Thallus A relatively undifferentiated plant body, without stems or leaves, as in liverworts.

Thyrse A compact, cylindrical or conical panicle.

Tomentose Densely clothed with woolly or cottony hairs without definite orientation (noun, *tomentum*).

Tor A prominent, isolated rocky outcrop.
Tortuous Bent or twisted in various directions.
Torulose Constricted at intervals.
Travertine Rock formed by the action of hot springs.
Trichome The specific term for any type of plant hair.
Trifarious Arranged in three ranks.
Trifid Split into three parts.
Trifoliolate Having three leaflets.
Trigonous Three-angled, three-sided (generally applied to achenes).
Triquetrous Three-cornered.
Truncate Abruptly cut off at the end.
Tuber A fleshy, underground stem, as in potato, or root, as in *Dahlia*.
Tubercle A small expanded structure, such as the base of the style in some sedges, or very large papillae on fruits.
Tuberculate Having tubercles.
Turbinate Top-shaped; inversely conical.
Turgid Swollen, plump.
Turion A fleshy, scaly winter bud at the base of the stem.
Type In taxonomy, the original specimen to which the name of a taxon is forever attached.
Type locality The place from which the original specimen, from which a species was named, came.

Umbel An inflorescence in which the pedicels radiate from a single point, like the spokes of an umbrella.
Undulate Wavy.
Unisexual Having only stamens or carpels, never both.
Utricle In amaranths, an inflated, dry fruit in which the papery carpel wall loosely invests the single seed).

Valve One of the pieces into which a capsule splits.
Variety A subdivision of a species occupying an area within the range of the species; a minor category lower than *subspecies*.
Ventral On the side facing the axis (the upper side of the leaf is its ventral side); adaxial.
Verrucose Warty.
Vesicle A little bladder (adjective, *vesicular*).
Vesture Clothing, covering.
Villous Clothed with long, soft hairs, often without special orientation (less matted than *tomentose*).
Viscid Sticky.
Vitreous Transparent, hyaline.

Whorl A circle or ring of organs. When three or more leaves occur at a node, they are said to be whorled.
Winter annual A plant that begins growth in the autumn, but flowers, sets seed, and dies the following season, as winter wheat.

Xerophytes Plants adapted to very dry conditions.

Zygomorphic Bilaterally symmetrical. A zygomorphic flower can be divided only one way to produce mirror images (example: snapdragon).

INDEX TO COMMON NAMES

INDEX TO GENERA

Names of accepted genera are italicized. Synonyms are in Roman type.